P9-EDG-114

WASHINGTON
HANDBOOK

SECOND EDITION

WASHINGTON
HANDBOOK

DIANNE J. BOULERICE LYONS

moon
PUBLICATIONS, INC.

WASHINGTON HANDBOOK

Please send all comments, corrections, additions, amendments, and critiques to:

**DIANNE J. B. LYONS
c/o MOON PUBLICATIONS
722 WALL STREET
CHICO, CA 95928 USA**

Published by
Moon Publications
722 Wall Street
Chico, California 95928 USA
tel. (916) 345-5473

Printed by
Colorcraft Ltd., Hong Kong

PRINTING HISTORY

First edition
March 1989
Second edition
June 1990

© Copyright Moon Publications Inc. 1990. All rights reserved.

© Copyright Dianne J. Boulerice Lyons 1990. All rights reserved.

Library of Congress Cataloging in Publication Data

Lyons, Dianne J. Boulerice, 1958-
    Washington Handbook / Dianne J. Boulerice Lyons. —2nd ed.
       p.   cm.
    Includes index.
    Includes bibliographical references: p. 386
     1. Washington (State)—Description and travel—1981—Guide-books. I. Title.
F889.3.L96 1990
917.9704'43—dc20   90-36336
                                               CIP

ISBN 0-918373-58-1

Printed in Hong Kong

Cover photograph by Paul A. Souders

All rights reserved. No part of this book may be translated or reproduced in any form, except brief extracts by a reviewer for the purposes of a review, without written permission of the copyright owners.

Although the publishers have made every effort to ensure that the information was correct at the time of going to press, the publishers do not assume and hereby disclaim any liability to any party for any loss or damage caused by errors, omissions, or any potential travel disruption due to labor or financial difficulty, whether such errors or omissions result from negligence, accident, or any other cause.

To Sarah Ellen Frenette,
as she embraces
the precious first moments of life,
and to Uncle Phil,
in loving memory

CONTENTS

LIST OF MAPS

LIST OF CHARTS

ABBREVIATIONS

a/c—air conditioned
C.—century
d—double occupancy
E—east
I—interstate highway
L—left

N—north
OW—one way
pp—per person
R—right
RR—railroad
RT—roundtrip

s—single occupancy
S—south
t—triple occupancy
W—west

MAP SYMBOLS

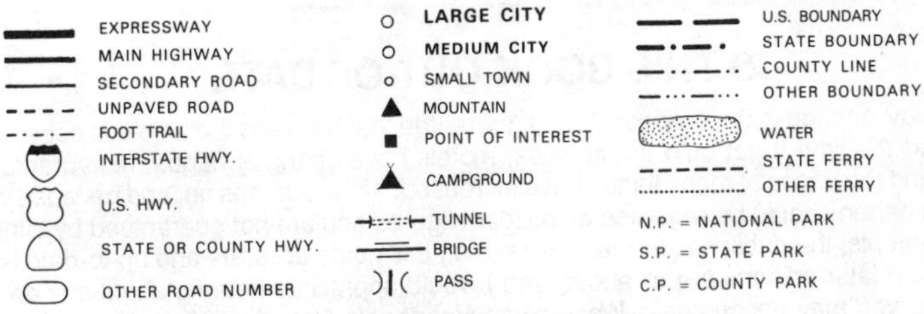

▬▬▬ EXPRESSWAY	○ **LARGE CITY**	▬▬▬ U.S. BOUNDARY
▬▬▬ MAIN HIGHWAY	○ **MEDIUM CITY**	—·—·—· STATE BOUNDARY
—— SECONDARY ROAD	○ SMALL TOWN	—··—··— COUNTY LINE
- - - - UNPAVED ROAD	▲ MOUNTAIN	—···—···— OTHER BOUNDARY
-··-··- FOOT TRAIL	■ POINT OF INTEREST	
INTERSTATE HWY.	▲ CAMPGROUND	WATER
U.S. HWY.		▬▬▬ STATE FERRY
STATE OR COUNTY HWY.	TUNNEL	OTHER FERRY
	BRIDGE	N.P. = NATIONAL PARK
OTHER ROAD NUMBER	)|(PASS	S.P. = STATE PARK
		C.P. = COUNTY PARK

ALL MAPS ARE ORIENTED WITH NORTH AT THE TOP OF THE MAP
UNLESS OTHERWISE NOTED.

ACKNOWLEDGEMENTS

For this second edition, I'd like to say thanks to all the chambers of commerce and visitors bureaus, bed & breakfast owners, and others who helped me update much of this information. Thanks to all the readers who have written with encouraging (and sometimes not-so-encouraging) words—your input helps to make this the best book possible. I'm most grateful to Norm and Diane Perreault for the use of their great photos, book, and other Mt. Baker information. Thanks to Chuck Hindman, Don Downing, and Karen Boulerice for helping with promotion! Thanks, of course, to Asha Johnson, Bob Race, Nancy Kennedy, Beth Rhudy, and all the other Moonies for their help in rushing out this second edition ahead of schedule. Again, a big thank you to Barbara Steele for the most loving daycare possible; to Scott and Kristina, the best kids on earth; and to Bob, who tolerates much, expects little, and still buys me flowers.

PHOTO AND ILLUSTRATION CREDITS

Florence Boulerice—pages 4, 5, 8, 171, 172, 179, 199, 215, 225, 272, 275, 323, 385; **Dianne Boulerice Lyons**—pages 2, 3, 6, 8, 20, 28, 40, 46, 53, 57, 61, 81, 93, 102, 115, 117, 120, 123, 128, 129, 134, 151, 155, 160, 164, 180, 181, 186, 188, 190, 195, 196, 202, 207, 211, 216, 222, 234, 238, 243, 244, 255, 258, 261, 264, 280, 286, 289, 291, 309, 314, 324, 331, 355, 356, 377; **Norm and Diane Perreailt**—pages 2, 176, 177; **State of Washington Tourism Division**—pages 10, 12, 25, 90, 204, 277; **Tacoma Public Library**—pages 11, 14, 17, 18, 21, 47, 74, 88, 91, 94, 96, 103, 194, 219, 249, 332, 361; **Seattle-King County Convention and Visitors Bureau**—pages 16, 22, 33, 36, 37, 41, 42, 43, 146, 167; **East King County Convention Bureau**—pages 65, 66; **Tacoma/Pierce County Visitor and Convention Bureau**—pages 82, 300; **Bob Race**—pages 1, 33, 179, 225, 279, 295; **Louise Foote**—pages 60, 11, 141, 184, 265, 325, 340; **Brian Bardwell**—pages 56, 259, 285; **Barbara Brangel**—page 25; **Paul Boyer**—page 206.

IS THIS BOOK OUT OF DATE?

As they say, change is the only constant. I guarantee that between the time this book went to press and the time it got onto the shelves, motels have changed hands, restaurants have closed, and the prices of many things have increased. Time marches on, and because of this, all prices herein should be regarded as ballpark figures and are not guaranteed by either the establishments, the publisher, or me. But keeping this guide accurate and up-to-date is what second and later editions are all about, and I would appreciate hearing about any errors or omissions you may encounter in *Washington Handbook*. Also, if you have a very good—or very bad—experience with any of the establishments listed in the book, please pass it along. If an attraction is out of place on a map, tell us; if the best restaurant in town is not included, point it out. Artwork is always welcome, and if we use your B&W photos or color slides in the next edition, you'll be listed in the photo credits. All contributions will be acknowledged, though all artwork will become the property of Moon Publications and, in most cases, can not be returned. Address your letters to:

Dianne J. B. Lyons
c/o Moon Publications,
722 Wall St.
Chico, CA 95928

INTRODUCTION

THE LAND

CLIMATE AND GEOGRAPHY

Washington sits in the NW corner of the United States, bounded on the N by British Columbia, on the W by the Pacific Ocean, on the S largely by the Columbia River and Oregon, and on the E by Idaho. The state is neatly divided into eastern and western halves by the Cascade Range (so named for its countless waterfalls), which extends 600 miles from Canada into northern California. Besides creating vastly different climates on either side, this mountain range serves as a physical and psychological barrier between E and W, resulting in virtually 2 distinct states within one. In winter, crossing the passes is an adventure that most Washingtonians prefer to forgo; snow tire and chain requirements, snowpacked and icy roads, and possible pass closures make it far easier to stay close to home. In summer, the Cascades themselves are often the destination for travelers from either side: North Cascades and Mt. Rainier national parks, Mt. St. Helens National Volcanic Monument, Lake Chelan, Mt. Baker, Mt. Adams, and numerous other wilderness areas, national forests, and wildlife refuges comprise the backbone of Washington's recreational areas.

The Cascade Range is about 25 million years old, but the Cascade volcanoes—Rainier, St. Helens, Adams, and 15 others—are less than a million years old. Although none are dead, only 2 have erupted in this century: Lassen, in California, in 1914, and Mt. St. Helens in 1980. Mt. Rainier is the highest, at 14,410 feet; Mt. Baker is the most heavily glaciated, and an 80-foot annual snowfall provides it with the longest ski season; most years it doesn't end until July 4.

The only break in the Cascade Range is the Columbia Gorge, separating Washington from Oregon along the Columbia River and permitting an exchange of air between E and

W that is impossible elsewhere along the range. The resulting winds provide some of the country's best windsurfing conditions. The rest of the range continues uninterrupted, shielding the interior from storms coming off the ocean and resulting in 2 vastly different climates: wet on the W, dry on the east. This weather variation is caused by what is commonly called "the rainshadow effect": incoming storms dump nearly all of their rain and snow on the western side of the ridge as the air is forced up and over the mountain range.

This rainshadow effect can be seen on a smaller scale in western Washington's Olympic Range. The Olympics (the backbone of Olympic National Park) are some of the world's youngest mountains, just one or 2 million years old. Though not exceptionally tall (Mt. Olympus is the highest at 7,965 feet), they produce dramatically varied weather. Storms spawned in the Pacific dump 70-100 inches of annual rainfall on the coastal plains, and 150 inches or more (with a record of 184 inches at Wynoochee Oxbow) in the rain forests on the western and southwestern slopes—the heaviest precipitation in the continental United States. But on the NE slopes of this range, Port Angeles, Sequim, Port Townsend, Whidbey Island, and the San Juans are in the driest area of western Washington, receiving only 12 to 20 inches of annual rainfall.

Western Washington

Aside from the Olympic rain forests, the "wet side of the mountains" isn't all that wet: Seattle's annual rainfall of 32-35 inches is less than that of Chicago or New York. Winter snowfalls are generally light and melt quickly; a real snowstorm paralyzes the city for days due to the lack of snow removal equipment and little snow-driving expertise among natives. Typical western Washington weather is mild and wet in the winter, warm and dry in the summer. Semi-permanent high- and low-pressure systems in the N Pacific create predictable patterns of clouds and light rain beginning in Oct., with daytime temperatures in the 40s throughout winter; Dec. and Jan. are the region's wettest months. In spring, the clouds give way to partly sunny days, and it's not unusual to have 4-6 weeks of cloudless skies in July and August. Summer daytime temperatures are usually in the 70s and 80s, with perhaps half a dozen 90-degree days each year. Thunderstorms are rare, and humidity is low.

Seattle averages about an inch of snow per month in winter, though many winters are snowfree; the record snow depth is 29 inches. Mt. Rainier is the place to go for snow—

Mount Baker from Table Mountain

*Grand Coulee at
Dry Falls*

in the winter of 1955-56, the Paradise ranger station (elev. 5,500 feet) received 1,000 inches! Cascade ski areas usually open up in Nov. and remain open through early spring, beginning and ending with Mt. Baker's 8-month ski season.

Western Washington's skiing may be good, but the swimming is something else again. Water temperatures along the Pacific Coast and in the Strait of Juan de Fuca average 45 degrees in Jan., rising to 53 degrees in July, with some secluded coves and bays getting into the 60s. Puget Sound stays around 55 degrees year-round, though again some protected areas warm up to the mid-60s and become swimmable. Most swimming and waterskiing is done in the region's numerous lakes.

Eastern Washington

Compared to western Washington, the "dry side of the mountains" has hotter summers, colder winters, more snow, and less rain. The Ellensburg Valley and Columbia Basin E to the Palouse River have the hottest, driest weather in eastern Washington, with 7-15 inches of annual rainfall and summer daytime temperatures in the 90s, with many days each year over 100 degrees; the state's record high of 118 degrees occurred at Ice Harbor Dam (near Pasco) in 1961. Hey, at least it's not humid. July and Aug. are the driest

months, often devoid of any precipitation at all; what rain they do receive generally comes packaged in thunderstorms. Winters bring 10-35 inches of snowfall and daytime temperatures in the 20s and 30s.

The Okanogan and Methow valleys, in the North central of the state, are a cross-country skier's paradise. Annual winter snowfalls range from 30-70 inches, beginning in Nov. and staying on the ground through March or April. January maximum temperatures are right around 30 degrees, with some nighttime below-0 temperatures recorded each year. In summer, the Okanogan Valley is another eastern Washington hot spot, with average temperatures from 85-90 and several 100s each season, plus occasional thunder- and hailstorms.

As you travel toward Spokane and the state's eastern boundary, the elevation rises and the weather moderates. The clouds start to rise toward the Rocky Mountains, and drop some of their precipitation here: rainfall averages 10-20 inches per year, with 20-40 inches of snow. Summer temperatures are in the upper 80s, winter averages in the 30s, with a few extremes of 0 and 100 recorded every year. The Blue Mountains in the SE corner get up to 40 inches of precipitation, while Pend Oreille County in the NE corner gets 28 inches of rain and 40-80 inches of snow.

FLORA AND FAUNA

Washington boasts a delightfully varied assortment of flora and fauna due to its rich diversity of climate and geography. The Pacific Ocean and saltwater Puget Sound, the Olympic rain forest, the mountainous regions of the Cascades and Olympics, and the arid land of eastern Washington each support a unique population of birds, animals, and plant life.

MARINE LIFE

Killer Whales

The orca, or killer whale, is the largest member of the family *Delphinidae,* a classification that includes toothed whales and dolphins. The males are significantly larger than the females of the species: up to 32 feet long, weighing 5 to 6 tons, with dorsal fins up to 6½ feet high and 4 feet wide and tail flukes spanning 9 feet. Unencumbered by its size, the orca frequently travels at upwards of 30 mph. Named "killer whale" because they take warm-blooded prey, these cetaceans eat anything from harbor and ringed seals to seabirds, otters, dolphins, fish, and squid, depending on the area food supply. In Puget Sound, they generally eat only fish—mostly salmon, rockfish, and cod—and leave the other species alone. Reports of killer whale attacks on humans and boats have been recorded as far back as 1911. In that year, H.G. Ponting, a photographer for the Scott expedition to the South Pole, was reportedly standing within 6 feet of the water when 8 whales broke through the ice he was standing on and threw him into the sea. Reports such as these are few and far between, however, and the orca is much more famous in this country for kissing women at Sea World.

Orcas are highly social, traveling in packs or "pods" of 2-40 individuals. Families stay together, protecting their young (who, at 8 feet long and 400 pounds at birth would seem to require little protection) and mourning their dead. There are 3 resident pods in Puget Sound and along the Washington Coast, with a total of about 80 members; other transient pods occasionally swim into the area but don't stay long. The most frequent sightings are around the San Juan Islands, from aboard a whale-watching cruise boat, or from the shore at Lime Kiln State Park on the W side of San Juan Island—the only park in the U.S. dedicated exclusively to whale watching.

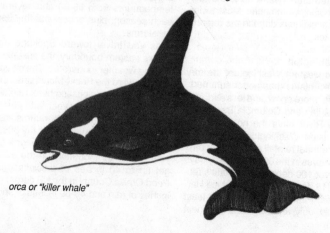

orca or "killer whale"

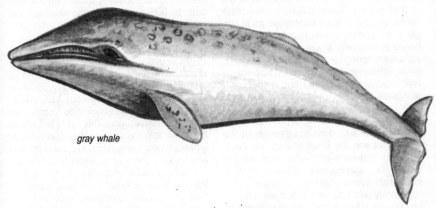

gray whale

Gray Whales

Every spring, tour boats leave the docks at Westport and other coastal towns for a close-up look at the migrating California gray whales. These enormous whales—ranging up to 42 feet in length and upwards of 30 tons—migrate from the Bering and Chukchi seas to the warm breeding lagoons off Baja California in winter, passing the Washington coast southbound in Nov. and Dec. and northbound from April to June. A handful of whales come into Puget Sound, but most follow the outer coastline. The gray is a baleen whale: it feeds by stirring up mud in shallow water, sucking in the water, mud, and organisms, and using its baleen—a fringelike sieve in its mouth—as a filter to trap its prey while forcing the mud and water back out. Gray whales are easily spotted by their gray color, absence of a dorsal fin, and bumpy ridges on their backs; their faces are generally covered with patches of barnacles and orange whale lice. Unconcerned with their appearance, gray whales often lift their faces out of the water up to about eye level in a motion referred to as "spyhopping." Although gray whales aren't aggressive and are often even friendly, whale watchers in small boats should keep a respectful distance, since the whales may "breach," or jump completely out of the water, creating one heck of a wave as 30 solid tons splash back into the water.

Porpoises

Visitors often think that the black-and-white sea creatures riding the bow waves of their ferry or tour boat are baby killer whales, but these playful characters are Dall's porpoises. Commonly seen in the Strait of Juan de Fuca alongside the ferry *Coho* from Port Angeles to Victoria, B.C., the porpoises frequently travel S through the Admiralty Inlet and, on rare occasions, as far S as Tacoma. Dall's porpoises reach lengths of 6½ feet and weights of up to 330 pounds; they feed primarily on squid and small fish.

The harbor porpoise is Puget Sound's smallest cetacean, ranging up to less than 6 feet in length and 150 pounds. Though similar in appearance to the Dall's porpoise, the harbor porpoise is much more shy and rarely spotted in the wild. Accurate counts are impossible, but the population around the San Juan Islands has been estimated at less than 100; none live in Puget Sound, though resident populations were spotted there in the 1940s.

In summer and early fall, schools of up to 100 Pacific white-sided dolphins enter the Strait of Juan de Fuca, traveling as far inshore as Port Angeles but rarely any farther east. Reaching up to 7 feet in length and 200 pounds, these dolphins are common off the shores of Japan, where their numbers are estimated at 30,000-50,000, and along the continental shelf from Baja California to the Gulf of Alaska. These dolphins have black backs, white shoulders and bellies, and hourglass-shaped streaks that run from their foreheads to their tails; the rear half of their dorsal fins are light gray. Like the Dall's porpoise, white-sided dolphins enjoy riding bow waves and often leap full-length out of the water alongside a boat.

Seals And Sea Lions

Harbor seals are numerous throughout Puget Sound and the Strait of Juan de Fuca, with their statewide population estimated at 7,000. They can be seen at low tide in isolated areas sunning themselves on rocks, but will quickly return to the water if approached by humans. Though they appear clumsy on land, these 100- to 200-pound seals are poetry in motion underwater; they flip, turn, and glide with little apparent effort, staying underwater for as long as 20 minutes. (You can see harbor seals up close at the underwater viewing tank at Point Defiance Zoo in Tacoma.) Harbor seals have a bad reputation with area salmon fishermen, although studies of the seals' stomach contents and fecal material indicate that they feed primarily on flounder, herring, pollock, cod, and rockfish, as well as some mollusks and crustaceans.

The California sea lion is a seasonal visitor to the Strait of Juan de Fuca and northern Puget Sound, though on some mornings in winter and early spring their barking can be heard in shoreline communities as far S as Tacoma. These dark brown sea lions breed off the coast of California and Mexico in the early summer, then some adventurous males migrate as far N as British Columbia for the winter. A large group of them collects just offshore from Everett, where a commercial tour boat takes visitors out for a closer look.

The lighter-colored northern sea lions are more numerous in the Puget Sound area, numbering up to several hundred in winter, primarily around Sucia Island in the northern Sound. The males of the species are much larger than the females, growing to almost 10 feet in length and weighing over a ton, while the females are a dainty 6 feet long and 600 pounds. Both are almost white when wet; the male has a yellow mane.

Others

Puget Sound is home to the largest species of octopus in the world. Though it grows to 12 feet across the arms and weighs 25-30 or more pounds, it's not dangerous, and, in fact, often plays with divers. These octopi can make themselves incredibly flat to get where they have to go: according to a local octopus legend, one of these giants slid out of its tank and under a door into its owner's bedroom.

Another peculiar Puget Sound inhabitant is the geoduck (pronounced GOO-ee-duck, from the Indian "gweduck" meaning "dig deep"). These large, obscene-looking clams can dig as deep as 5 feet, weighing in at 4-5 pounds with reports of some clams exceed-

geoduck, the Pacific Northwest's most revolting clam

ing 15 pounds. The fleshy part of the body is so large that neither the entire body nor the siphon can be completely withdrawn into the shell. (Stop by Pike Place Market in Seattle to see what these creatures look like.) Geoducks are generally cut up and used in chowder, but some quality restaurants serve them as regular menu items or specials. The horse clam is the second largest Pacific Northwest clam, weighing up to 5 pounds; they can't completely withdraw their siphons, but at least their bodies fit inside their shells. Horse clams only dig about 2 feet deep, so they're much easier to gather, and can be found in Cultus and Useless bays at the S end of Whidbey Island. Both geoducks and horse clams prefer sandy or sand-gravel beaches.

LAND ANIMALS

Bears

Black bears are fairly widespread in Washington, with large populations on the Olympic Peninsula and in Pend Oreille County. All of the black bears on the Olympic Peninsula are black; in other areas, they may be black, brown, or honey-colored. They'll eat anything, from carpenter ants to berries to dead elk to salmon, plus anything you pack in from Safeway. Black bears are so numerous that 400 of them are "harvested" each year in NE Washington.

Grizzly bears are rare in Washington, but there may be a few in the N Cascades and in the NE corner of the state, spilling over from Idaho's Selkirk Mountains. Grizzlies once roamed throughout the western states, but now fewer than 1,000 bears live in remote areas of Washington, Idaho, Montana, and Wyoming, and they are considered a threatened species. A female grizzly must be 5-8 years old before reproducing, and she cares for her cubs for 2-3 years before having any more offspring, so her reproductive capacity is low. The best way to protect both the grizzly bear population and yourself is to avoid encounters with them.

When hiking in bear country, make noise: sing, talk, or wear bear bells so they'll hear you coming, and don't hike after dark. If you see bear tracks or droppings, don't be a hero; hike somewhere else. Don't let your dog run free—it may sniff out a bear and lead it back to you. When camping in the backcountry, store all food, soaps, garbage, and clothes worn while cooking in a sack hung from a tree branch at least 10 feet up and 4 feet out from the tree trunk. In an established campground, keep those items in your car's trunk. Don't sleep where you cooked dinner, and keep sleeping bags and gear away from cooking odors. Stories are sometimes heard about grizzlies attacking women during their menstrual period; though nobody knows for sure if the scent actually causes an attack, cautious women may choose to hike in grizzly country at another time. If you do encounter a bear, here's how to identify it: a grizzly is generally lighter in color than black bears, though color alone can't be used for identification. Look for the shoulder hump (behind its head) and a "dish face" profile, with a distinct snout (black bears have no hump and a straight profile). While you're looking for identifying marks, slowly detour out of the bear's path and stay upwind so the bear will know you're there; don't make abrupt noises or movements. While retreating, look for a climbable tree—one in which you can get at least 12 feet up. Don't try to outrun the bear—grizzlies can hit 40 mph in short bursts, and you can't beat that, no matter how scared you are. If the bear comes after you, drop your pack or jacket to distract him, get up that tree, or roll up into a ball with your face and stomach protected, and play dead.

Slugs

Western Washington is famous for its slugs. The damp climate is just what slugs need to thrive: not too wet, because slugs aren't waterproof (they will absorb water through their outer membranes until their bodily fluids are too diluted to support them), and not too dry, because insufficient humidity makes them dry up and die. Optimum humidity for

banana slug

slugs is near 100 percent, which is why you'll see them crossing the sidewalk very early in the morning, at dusk, or on misty days. During the dry parts of the day, they'll seek refuge under the pool cover you casually tossed onto the lawn, or under the scrap lumber piled in the back of your lot—giving you a real surprise when you go to clean up.

Slugs look like snails who've lost their shells, or little green or brown squirts of slime about 3 to 5 inches long. Though more than 300 species of slugs exist worldwide, the Northwest is home to little more than a dozen. The native banana slug, light green or yellowish with dark spots, has been rapidly outnumbered by the imported European black slug, which is now far more common in area gardens than the native variety. Slugs can curl up into a ball to protect themselves, or flatten and elongate themselves to squeeze into tight places. They move on one long foot by secreting mucus that gets firm where the foot must grab hold and stays slimy under the part that must slide. They see (probably just patterns of light and dark) with eyes at the ends of a pair of tentacles; they have a mouth, and eat primarily plants and mushrooms. Getting rid of slugs is no easy matter. Traditional home remedies include salt shakers and beer traps, both of which require a strong stomach. Most residents just try to avoid stepping on them.

BIRDS

Bald Eagles

Approximately 300 pairs of bald eagles make their year-round home in Washington, primarily W of the Cascades. In winter that number swells to over 1,600 birds, drawn to rivers throughout the state by the abundant carcasses of spawned-out salmon. Several whitewater rafting companies operating in the North Cascades offer mid-winter Skagit float trips just for the thrill of seeing these majestic birds (see p. 286 for more information).

The bald eagle often gets bad press, being blamed for the deaths of sheep and other domestic animals. Actually, eagles much prefer dead and dying fish to anything running around on hooves; their common fare, aside from dead salmon, is sick or injured waterfowl or rabbits that didn't make it across the road. An aggressive bird, the eagle will often purloin the catch of an osprey or other bird in favor of finding its own. Occasionally a pair of eagles will team up to catch a gull or diving bird, with each eagle taking a turn at striking the bird when it surfaces from its dive and following above it as it attempts to escape underwater. When the prey eventually becomes exhausted from the diving and dodging, it is snatched from the water and carried off to shore.

bald eagle wintering on the Skagit River

The adult bald eagle's distinctive white head and tail make it easy to spot. But it takes 4 years to acquire its distinctive markings, making the immature eagle confusing to identify, as it may show whitish markings anywhere on its body. In contrast, the somewhat similar golden eagle has distinct white patches on its tail and underwings.

Bald eagles are sensitive to disturbances in their environment; the Department of Game recommends that an undisturbed circle 660 feet in diameter surround a nest during the breeding season to preserve the nest site. Their large nests, sometimes measuring over 8 feet wide and 12 feet high, are often found in old-growth spruce and fir; snags are popular for sunning, resting, and watching for their next meal.

The state's heaviest concentration of breeding bald eagles can be seen on the San Juan Islands, enjoying the warm updrafts around Mt. Constitution on Orcas Island and mounts Findlayson and Dallas on San Juan Island, and along the Strait of Juan de Fuca. The annual "salmon festival" brings the resident and migrating birds to the inland reaches of the Skagit, Sauk, Nooksack, and Stillaguamish rivers, with some enterprising pairs seen along southern Puget Sound and the lower Columbia River.

Owls

The bird of the hour in western Washington is the northern spotted owl, which nests in old-growth forests along the Pacific Coast—forests that are more than 150 years old, filled with snags and broken trees that provide ideal nesting spots, and smaller, sheltered trees for young owls who can't yet fly properly and must use their feet to climb from tree to tree. These forests are full of spotted owl food: snowshoe hares, flying squirrels, and woodrats. They are big eaters and quite territorial: 1,000 acres of old-growth forest will support but a single pair of owls. Because suitable forest is being greatly reduced by logging, the spotted owls' numbers are diminishing—only an estimated 2,500 pairs remain in the Pacific Northwest's old-growth forests,

and researchers believe that they'll all be gone in 30 years if logging continues at its present rate.

Everybody wants to save the owl, but the wood in these old-growth forests is worth billions of dollars. An "owl plan" discussed in Oregon would allegedly cost the timber industry 9,000 jobs and $3.6 million in timber sales; according to the U.S. Forest Service, the cost is more like $25,000 in lost revenue for each pair of owls. The issue is, then, how much is a spotted owl worth?

Other Birds

Other noteworthy birds in western Washington include the great blue heron, frequently seen along harbors or suburban lakes. The belted kingfisher is a common year-round resident of Puget Sound and the Strait of Juan de Fuca. Red-tailed hawks are often perched along I-5 and other highways, waiting for a meal. Noisy Stellar's jays, blue with a black head, are common in picnic areas and neighborhoods. The beautiful mountain bluebird is sometimes spotted in snags in open areas around Mt. St. Helens. East of the mountains, striking black and white magpies are frequently seen flitting over the highway.

Birders will find Eugene S. Hunn's *Birding in Seattle and King County* an invaluable guide to birding sites from Seattle to Snoqualmie Pass. Included are maps, charts, bird lists, and additional information on mammals and plant life. The *Pacific Coast Bird Finder*, by Roger J. Lederer, is geared more toward the beginning or backyard birdwatcher; it describes 61 common Pacific Coast birds (with illustrations) and their habitats.

FLORA

The Forests

In 1946, an Oregon newspaper teased Washington, "The Evergreen State," for not having a state tree. Oregon had already chosen the Douglas fir, so Washington State Representative George Adams suggested the western hemlock, which he claimed would become the backbone of the forest industry. Now the state tree, the western hemlock is widely used in the forest industry as a pulpwood species, and it and Douglas fir are 2 of the most abundant low-elevation trees in the state; above 3,000 feet elevation, silver fir and mountain hemlock take over. Big-leaf maples are distinguished by—you got it—their big leaves, often as much as a foot across. The Pacific madrone, or madrona, is characterized by waxy, evergreen leaves and peeling reddish bark that exposes a smooth underskin. Other common trees are the western red cedar, black cottonwood, red alder, and vine maple.

Olympic Rain Forest

At Olympic National Park, the Hoh, Queets, and Quinault valleys comprise the better part of the Olympic rain forest, an area unique in

Hoh River Rain Forest in Olympic National Park

the world. Purists would say that 150 or more inches of annual rainfall don't qualify this region as a rain forest, a term usually reserved for the steamy jungle tropics. Whatever it's called, this area produces some of the world's largest trees. The largest known western hemlock is growing in the Quinault Valley; the largest Douglas fir is in Queets; and the largest red alder is in the Hoh. The 4 major species here—the Sitka spruce, western red cedar, Douglas fir, and western hemlock—all grow very tall: trees average 200 feet, with many topping 300. The height of the trees isn't the only fascinating aspect of the rain forest: the visitor is immediately struck by how green everything is, and how pristine. These areas have never been logged; what you see is nature, pure and simple. Enormous trees spring out of the long-since-decayed "nurse-logs" that gave them life, with clubmoss eerily draping the branches; ferns and mosses cover nearly every inch of available ground in a thick carpet. Though most rainfall occurs from fall to spring, even summer days feel damp from high humidity and ocean fog.

Rhododendron

In 1892, Washington needed a flower to represent the state at the Chicago World's Fair. Many flowers were nominated, but the contest came down to 2: the coast rhododendron and the common clover. While it doesn't seem that clover would offer much competition, it was a close call—the rhody won with just 53% of the vote. The region from British Columbia S to northern California and E to the foothills of the Cascades is prime rhody-growing territory. There are about 500 pure species hardy to the climate, and several hundred more greenhouse varieties, that are combined and cross-pollinated to produce thousands of hybrids. Rhodies are standard equipment in western Washington gardens, relatively easy to grow and beautiful to behold, in colors from yellows to pinks to bright reds and whites. The well-known rhododendron gardens on Whidbey Island and smaller gardens in area parks have impressive displays in spring and early summer.

HISTORY

Pre-history

Although Washington is one of the more recent additions to the United States, archeological evidence suggests that the Pacific Northwest was one of the first populated areas in North America. In recent years, animal and human remains as much as 13,000 years old have been found throughout the state.

One of the most fascinating discoveries occurred in 1977, when Emanuel Manis, retired on a farm outside of Sequim, was digging a pond on a back corner of his acreage and found 2 enormous tusks. A Washington State University archeological team, led by zoologist Carl Gustafson, concluded that these were mastadon tusks, between 12,000 and 14,000 years old. The group discovered other mastadon bones, including a rib that contained the bone point of some prehistoric weapon used to kill the animal. These bones are now on display at the Sequim-Dungeness Museum in Sequim (see p 194 for details).

Throughout the late 1950s and early 1960s, archeologists uncovered numerous artifacts and partial skeletons of 10 people known as "Marmes Man" near the Palouse River. These people lived 10,000 years ago in pithouses: circular pits covered by grass mats.

In the state's northwest corner, archeological work has been underway since 1970 on the Hoko and Ozette sites near Neah Bay, once inhabited by ancestors of the Makah Indians. Thumbnail-sized quartz knife blades have been found at the Hoko River site and radiocarbon dated at 2,500 years old; some artifacts from the Ozette site date back 2,000 years. At Ozette, an entire village was covered by a mudflow apparently set off by an earthquake some 500 years ago. Over 50,000 well-preserved artifacts have been found and catalogued, many of which are now on display at the Makah Museum in Neah Bay.

American Indians

According to one theory, Native Americans originally crossed over to Alaska from Asia at the end of the last ice age, when the sea was 300 or more feet below present levels and the strait was a walkable passage. As these

American Indians spread throughout the Pacific Northwest, they adopted significantly different lifestyles on each side of the Cascades.

West of the mountains, salmon, seafood, shellfish, and whales made up a large part of the Indian diet; western red cedars provided ample wood for canoes, houses, and medicinal teas and ointments. A mild climate and plentiful food allowed these coastal Indians to stay in one place for most of the year. They often built "longhouses," wooden structures up to 100 feet long and 40 feet wide that housed several families. Coastal Indians were skilled canoe carvers, and could travel up the Columbia as far as The Dalles, where rapids prohibited further progress. Inland Indians would meet them here for an annual fair with trading, dancing, gambling, and general hell-raising.

East of the Cascades and particularly near the Columbia River, salmon was still an important part of the Indian diet, though dependence on deer, elk, bear, squirrel, and rabbit led these tribes to live semi-nomadic lives. The introduction of the horse to eastern Washington in the mid 1700s made hunting, especially for large bison, much easier. Indians in eastern Washington lived in caves or rock shelters while hunting, and in well-insulated pithouses that could hold several families.

The Pacific Northwest Indians were introduced to the by-products of white man's culture, such as knives, guns, and the deadly smallpox virus, before ever laying eyes on a white explorer. White man's arrival was met with reactions ranging from tolerant acceptance to swift murder. Relations between the races are still strained today; the interpretation of peace treaties signed in the 1850s are being hotly debated in the 1980s, with many lawsuits concerning property, water, and fishing rights pending. Though they make up only 1.3% of the Pacific Northwest's total population, today's Native Americans are a growing force: there were nearly 100,000 Indians in Washington, Idaho, and Oregon in 1980, representing an 88.5% increase since 1970. Most of them do not live on reservations, though there are 22 reservations scattered throughout the state, the largest being the Yakima and Colville.

Early Explorers

In 1592, a Greek explorer sailing under the Spanish name Juan de Fuca, claimed to have discovered the fabled "Northwest Passage," an inland waterway crossing North America from the Pacific to the Atlantic. Later explorers did find a waterway close to where de Fuca indicated, but it led only to today's Puget Sound, not the Atlantic Ocean.

Spain, hoping to regain some of its diminishing power and wealth, sent an expedition out in the 1700s to explore the Northwest Coast from a base on the western coast of Mexico. In 1774, Juan Perez explored as far N as the Queen Charlotte Islands off Vancouver Island, and was the first European to describe the Pacific Northwest coastline and Olympic mountains before being forced to turn back by sickness and storms.

In 1775, a larger Spanish expedition set out, led by Bruno de Heceta and Juan Francisco de la Bodega y Quadra. Heceta went ashore at Point Grenville, just N of Moclips on the Washington coast, and claimed all the Northwest for Spain. Farther S, Quadra sent 7 men ashore in a small metal craft for wood and water; they were quickly killed and their boat torn apart in white men's first encounter with coastal Indians. The 2 ships sailed away

Totem poles such as this are common throughout Washington.

without further incident; Quadra named the island "Isla de Dolores" ("Isle of Sorrows"), today's Destruction Island. Quadra continued his exploratons as far N as Sitka, Alaska, while Heceta sailed N to Nootka Sound. Heceta failed to note the Strait of Juan de Fuca, but he did come across "the mouth of some great river," presumably the Columbia, though the death or illness of much of his crew prevented further exploration and robbed Spain of an important claim.

Russian exploration of the Pacific Northwest began in the mid-1700s, when Vitus Bering led 2 expeditions to determine whether a land bridge connected Russia with North America. Bering sailed as far S as the Columbia River before turning back. The abundance of sea otters and beavers led Russian fur traders to establish posts from Alaska to northern California, which posed a serious threat to other nations hoping to stake a claim.

Robert Gray sailed out of Boston to explore and trade along the Northwest Coast for the United States in the late 1700s. Stopping first at Nootka Sound, the hot spot to trade on Vancouver Island, Gray worked his way S and spent 3 days anchored in today's Gray's Harbor. Continuing S, Gray discovered the mouth of the Columbia River and traded there with the Chinook Indians before heading home.

England was the force to be reckoned with in the battle for the Northwest. In 1776, Captain James Cook took 2 ships, the *Discovery* and the *Resolution*, and 170 men on an expedition that brought him to the Hawaiian Islands, the Oregon Coast, and Vancouver Island's Nootka Sound. Though he charted the coastline from Oregon to the Bering Sea, he made no mention of the Columbia River or the Strait of Juan de Fuca. Cook was killed by hostile Hawaiians in a dispute over a boat in 1779, and his crew returned to England.

Other English sailors continued in Cook's footsteps. In 1787, Charles Barkley and his wife Frances explored and named the Strait of Juan de Fuca. In 1788, John Meares named Mount Olympus and other features of the Olympic Peninsula. Best known today, however, was the expedition led by George Vancouver in 1792. His goal was to explore the inland waters and make one last attempt at finding the Northwest Passage. Vancouver's lieutenants and crew members read like a list of Washington place names: Baker, Peter Rainier, Joseph Whidbey, Peter Puget. The expedition carefully charted and thoroughly described all navigable waterways and named every prominent feature. When Vancouver heard of Gray's discovery of the Columbia River, he sent William Broughton upriver to a point E of Portland to strengthen England's claim on the land.

The United States' answer to Vancouver was Charles Wilkes, a naval captain who sailed up the Columbia and into Puget Sound as part of a worldwide expedition in 1841. Wilkes added details to Vancouver's charts, naming some of the less prominent features such as Anderson Island, Elliott Bay, and McNeil Island.

Until 1792, only the coastal areas of the Pacific Northwest had been explored. The first explorer to cross North America N of Mexico was a British trader, Alexander Mackenzie. In 1788, he traveled as far as the Arctic in search of the fabled Northwest Passage. In 1792-93, Mackenzie followed the Bella Coola River from the Canadian Rockies to just N of Vancouver Island. His 2 expeditions proved that there was no Northwest Passage, at least N of the 50th parallel.

The best-known overland expedition began in St. Louis in 1804, led by Meriwether Lewis and William Clark. Thomas Jefferson sent these men and their party to study the geology, animal, and plant life of the 827,000 square miles acquired in the Louisiana Purchase, which extended as far W as the Rocky Mountains, and to explore and map the rivers and lands W of the Rockies. The group left St. Louis in canoes, heading N on the Missouri River to present-day North Dakota. After wintering there with the Mandan Indians, the party set out again on the Missouri River, crossed the Rockies on foot, and headed down the Clearwater River in search of the

Columbia. In October, 1805, the party got their first view of the Columbia, and followed it downriver for many a "cloudy, rainey, disagreeable morning" until they reached the Pacific Ocean. They built a winter camp, Fort Clatsop, S of the river and spent a cold, wet winter there, plagued by sickness. In spring they headed for home. The 2 leaders split up, with Lewis returning much the way they had come and Clark exploring the Yellowstone River to the south. They met up again in North Dakota and returned to St. Louis in Sept., 1806.

Wilson Price Hunt, partner in the fur-trading business with John Jacob Astor, led the second American overland expedition in 1811. His party joined others who arrived by ship—first the *Tonquin,* in 1811, and then the *Beaver,* arriving a year later—to establish Astoria, a fort on the S side of the Columbia River. Hunt was instructed to follow Lewis and Clark's route through Montana, but aggressive Blackfeet Indians changed his mind. Instead he traveled through present-day Wyoming, taking to canoes—a poor choice for the wild Snake River. One canoe was smashed and its experienced navigator killed, leading to Hunt's decision to divide the expedition into 3 groups and continue on

overland. Donald McKenzie's team reached Astoria in Jan., 1812; Hunt's group arrived a month later. The last third of the expedition straggled in a year after the first, in Jan., 1813.

British overland exploration was accomplished mainly by David Thompson, a fur trader and chief cartographer for the North West Company in the early 1800s. In 1810, under Thompson's direction, Finan McDonald and Jacques Finlay built Spokane House, the first trading post in the state of Washington. Thompson traveled extensively throughout the Canadian Rockies, S into Kettle Falls and downriver to the mouth of the Columbia in 1811, where he found the Americans had already established a fort at Astoria—Astor's men had arrived 4 months earlier. Though he was disappointed, Thompson's detailed maps and sketches of the Columbia were used for many years by settlers and traders.

The First White Settlers
During the time between the early exploration and the permanent settlement of the Northwest, British and American trading posts emerged to take advantage of the area's abundant supply of beaver and sea otter pelts. Two English companies, the North

Fort Vancouver, one of the Pacific Northwest's most successful settlements

West Company and Hudson's Bay Company, merged in 1821; American fur-trading outfits included many small, independent companies as well as John Astor's Pacific Fur Company and the Rocky Mountain Fur Company. Probably the most influential, Hudson's Bay Company built its temporary headquarters on the N side of the Columbia, 100 miles inland at Fort Vancouver. The settlers planted crops (including the apples and wheat that are so important to Washington's economy today), raised livestock, and made the fort self-sufficient as possible. At its peak, 500 people lived at or near the fort. Fort Vancouver served as a model for other Hudson's Bay Company posts at Spokane, Okanogan, and Nisqually (in Tacoma). When settlers began arriving in droves and the beaver population diminished, Hudson's Bay Company moved its headquarters N to Fort Victoria on Vancouver Island.

Missions were another important method of establishing white settlements in the Northwest. The first missionary, Jason Lee, was sent by the Methodist Church in 1834 to introduce Christianity to the Native Americans, but instead spent much of his time and resources ministering to whites at Fort Vancouver. A second group, led by Dr. Marcus Whitman and his wife Narcissa, was sent out in 1836 by a group made up of various Protestant churches. The Whitmans established a mission among the Cayuse Indians near Walla Walla, and soon thereafter Narcissa gave birth to a daughter, Alice Clarissa. When she was 2 years old, little Alice wandered off and drowned in the Walla Walla River; though the Whitmans had no more children of their own, they adopted the orphaned Sager children and cared for others whose parents were dead or away. When Indians got sick from the laxatives and poisons Marcus Whitman used to keep animals away from his gardens, and when the Indians contracted measles and other heretofore unknown diseases, the Cayuse became convinced that the Whitmans were trying to kill them to make room for white settlers. So, on November 29, 1847, the Indians attacked and murdered the Whit-

mans and 12 others. This attack only added fuel to the increasing hostilities between the Indian and white man. The ensuing Indian Wars, particularly the Yakima Wars between the Plateau Indians and the settlers and the U.S. Army from 1855-58, halted white settlement in eastern Washington until the Indians agreed to accept reservation lands and the army declared the lands safe for settlement.

In the 1840s, "Oregon Country" N of the 42nd parallel was jointly occupied by the U.S. and England. The westward movement gained momentum when a New York editor coined the phrase "Manifest Destiny" to symbolize the idea that all of the land W of the Rockies rightfully belonged to the United States. Between 1840 and 1860, 53,000 settlers moved W to Oregon Country to take advantage of the free land they could acquire through the Organic Act of 1843 and the Donation Land Law of 1850. Under the Organic Act of the Provisional Government, each adult white male could own 640 acres (one square mile) by simply marking its boundaries, filing a claim, and building a cabin on the land. The Donation Land Law put additional restrictions on land claims: 320 acres were awarded to white or half-white males who were American citizens and had arrived prior to 1851; another 320 acres could be claimed by his wife. These and other restrictions effectively eliminated claims by Blacks, Asians, single women, non-U.S. citizens, and Native Americans, thereby giving pioneers the legal right to take Indian land. These land grants were too large for most families to farm and prevented towns and industries from growing as quickly as they might have; people were simply too far apart. By 1855, all the land in the Willamette Valley had been claimed.

The promise of free land fueled the "Great Migration" of 1843, in which 875 settlers traveled to Oregon Country, 6 times the number of the previous year. More pioneers followed: 1,500 in 1844 and 3,000 in 1845. Most settlers came by way of the Oregon Trail, a 40-foot-wide cleared "road" from Missouri along the North Platte River to the Columbia River

Valley. The settlers congregated around 5 fledgling cities: Seattle, Port Townsend, Oysterville (now a historic community on Willapa Bay), Centralia, and Walla Walla, and other smaller communities at Tumwater, Steilacoom, Olympia, and Fort Vancouver.

Growth Of A New State

By 1846, only the United States and England retained claims to Oregon Country; Spain and Russia had sold or lost their North American possessions. Negotiators brought the U.S. and England to agreement on a division at the 49th parallel from the Rockies to the main channel between Vancouver Island and the mainland, running through the center of the Strait of Juan de Fuca to the Pacific Ocean. The unspecified "main channel" was viewed to be either the Rosario Strait or the Haro Strait, leaving the San Juan Islands in the middle of the disputed waterway. Both American and British troops set up posts on San Juan Island, and got along famously until an American settler shot and killed a British pig that had wandered into his garden. The ensuing "Pig War," a 13-year dispute during which no further shots were fired, ended in 1872 when German arbitration awarded the islands to the Americans and pronounced the Haro Strait as the dividing channel.

In 1848, President Polk created Oregon Territory and appointed Joseph Lane as the first territorial governor a year later. In the early 1840s, most Americans lived S of the Columbia River. By 1849, only 304 people lived N of the river, but in the next year that number tripled as more and more settlers ventured northward. As they moved farther away from the territorial government, the settlers felt left out of governmental matters and decided to separate from Oregon. Delegates met at the Monticello Convention in 1852 to list reasons for the proposed separation, and Congress found little opposition to the bill. Washington Territory, which included much of present-day Idaho, was created in 1853. In 1863, Idaho Territory was created, followed by Montana Territory in 1864, giving the territories much the same boundaries that the

Seattle's Space Needle, a legacy from the 1962 World's Fair

states occupy now.

When Washington became a territory, its population was under 4,000 people; by the 1880s, it had grown to over 125,000 and was considered a serious candidate for statehood. Washington was admitted as the 42nd state in 1889, with Olympia as its capital and a growing population of over 173,000.

The Twentieth Century

The 40 years between 1870 and 1910 marked a period of tremendous growth in Washington. In 1870, the territory's population was just shy of 24,000; in 1910, the new state, created with the same boundaries, had 1,142,000 residents. Much of this growth was a direct result of the arrival of the Northern Pacific and Great Northern railways in the late 1880s, bringing industry and settlers to

Puget Sound and creating new towns all along their routes. Spokane saw rapid economic growth during the 1880s outfitting miners for the gold, silver, and lead rush in Idaho. The 1880s also spelled disaster for Spokane, Ellensburg, and Seattle, when major portions of these cities' thriving downtown areas were destroyed by fire. Though the cities were rebuilt quickly in brick, the state was hit hard by a nationwide depression, the Panic of 1893, when growth slowed on both sides of the mountains and businesses failed. A gold rush in the Yukon and the emergence of hydroelectric power helped get the state back on its feet. At the end of this period of growth, the Alaska-Yukon-Pacific Exposition brought nationwide attention and over 3,700,000 visitors to the University of Washington campus in Seattle in 1909, to promote the ties between Washington, the far N, and Pacific Rim countries.

The Great Depression slowed Washington's growth to a population increase of just 11% between 1930 and 1940. Seattleites were the first to call makeshift "towns" of boxes and crates "Hoovervilles"; one of the largest covered 9 acres about where the Kingdome stands today. The first and second World Wars changed Washington's economy from one based largely on mining, farming, logging and fishing to manufacturing, ship and airplane building, highlighted by Boeing's B-17: over 13,000 of the "Flying Fortresses" were built for WW II. Boeing continues to be one of the state's largest employers and most important industries.

Seattle's 1962 World's Fair was the first such exposition to be an economic success, drawing over 9,600,000 people during its 6-month run and creating a permanent addition to the city's culture at Seattle Center. Spokane followed suit 12 years later with Expo '74, emphasizing environmental concerns and cleaning up its own Spokane River in the process. Perhaps all of this self-imposed media attention was a mistake: Washington, especially W of the Cascades, continues to grow at a rate that many residents find alarming. Cities and suburbs alike are beginning to suffer from overcrowding, pollution, traffic, increased crime, and other big-city problems as more and more visitors are opting to stay for good, putting stress on water, refuse, and highway systems that were designed for smaller populations. The challenge of the '90s and beyond will be to preserve the state's unsurpassed natural resources and beauty while allowing controlled growth.

INDUSTRY AND ECONOMY

Washington's earliest industries—fishing, mining, farming, and logging—depended upon the abundant natural resources that the pioneers found here. Even today, lumber remains one of the "Evergreen State's" most important industries (though Weyerhauser's multi-million-dollar operation is a far cry from Yesler's turn-of-the-century waterfront mill), farming remains the basis for much of eastern Washington's economy, and hydroelectric power creates jobs and low electric rates from the state's plentiful resources. Over the years, though, manufacturing, shipping, and other industries have become increasingly important to the state's economy.

Mining

Coal was first discovered E of Bellingham in 1849, and mining began in 1855. Later discoveries of coal in the Cascades in the late 1800s gave rise to a number of small mining towns on both sides of the Cascades such as Black Diamond, Carbonado, Wilkeson, Newcastle, Cle Elum, and Roslyn. Though coal was plentiful—geologists today believe there are from 6 to 65 billion tons in the state—it was soft and therefore limited in its uses;

often found in steep ravines or streams, it was difficult to extract and transport. Underground explosions and other accidents gave Washington more mining fatalities per number of miners than any other state for several years in the late 1800s. By the turn of the century, coal from the Rocky Mountains had become a cheaper and more practical fuel source, and by 1930 coal mining had virtually disappeared. Today, coal mining is seeing a minor revival: for the past several years, over 5 million tons of coal per year have been strip mined near Centralia for use in a thermal electric power plant there.

Other minerals begat industries that met with varying degrees of success. Discoveries of gold and silver in the mountains of Washington's NE corner caused short-lived rushes—and Indian wars, as whites crossed onto reservation lands—but outfitting miners for the gold rushes of Idaho and the Yukon yielded a better return for Seattle and Spokane. Silver, gold, and lead mines in Monte Cristo were to have been the economic basis of John D. Rockefeller's city on Port Gardner Bay, until the depression of 1893 forced him to withdraw his support. A steel mill in Kirkland, an iron refinery in Port Townsend, and a copper mine in Holden either never got started or met with limited success. A successful silver, gold, and lead refinery in Tacoma was started in 1890 by William R. Rust; he later sold the plant to the American Smelting and Refining Company (ASARCO) for processing copper. Recent mining at Wenatchee's Asamera's Cannon gold mine is predicted to yield over a million ounces of gold over the next 10-15 years. However, Washington's most valuable minerals are still the least exotic: 60% of the money made from mineral production is derived from cement, stone, and gravel pits in the western half of the state.

Lumber

The Pacific Northwest states of Washington, Oregon, and Idaho supply about 60% of the total lumber in the United States. Washington is generally the third or fourth largest producer of the 50 states, with Oregon taking the lead since 1938. Douglas fir, western hemlock, and western red cedar are some of the commercially important trees native to the area W of the Cascades.

Wood and wood products have been a vital part of Washington's economy ever since the Coastal Indians first began using cedar for longhouses, totem poles, canoes, and even clothing made from cedar bark. The first white settlers and missionaries used wood for construction of their forts, homes, and blockhouses, and British explorer John Meares was the first to ship lumber to the Orient in 1788. Seattle's founding fathers depended on shipments of lumber to San Francisco for much of their income; Yesler's waterfront sawmill was an important part of the city's early economy. The lumber business boomed with the cheaper transportation provided by the arrival of the railroads in Puget Sound in the late 1880s and '90s. In 1900, Frederick Weyerhauser purchased 900,000 acres of prime forest land from the Northern Pacific Railroad for $6 an acre, later increasing his holdings to over 2 million acres by 1913. With over 6 million acres today, the Weyerhauser Corp. is now the largest lumber company in the country.

Forests cover over 23 million Washington acres, 18 million of which are commercial forests. It's difficult to look at the shaved hillsides of the Cascades and not think it offensive, but the trees are replanted, and the logs and wood products produce $5 to 7 billion annually and employ a large proportion of Washington's workers.

Farming

Washington's Native Americans relied on hunting and food gathering rather than agriculture to supply their families' needs. It wasn't until Fort Vancouver was established in the 1820s that commercial agriculture took hold in Washington, as Hudson's Bay Company acquired a surplus of cattle to sell to the early settlers. Farming took hold slowly west of the Cascades, as the heavily forested land first had to be cleared, and the acidic soils produced minimal yields. As settlers spread E of the Cascades, the wide-open spaces were perfect for cattle ranching, sheep herding, and grain growing. Agriculture grew rapidly through the turn of the century due to the arrival of the railroad, irrigation projects, and the free land provided by the Organic Act of 1843 and the Donation Land Law of 1850. Agriculture flourished during the first and second World Wars, and quickly rebounded after the Depression when refrigeration allowed Washington farmers to compete on a national scale. More recently, the 1952 Columbia Basin Irrigation Project opened up a half million parched acres for farming around Moses Lake. Today, Washington farmers and ranchers produce more than $3 billion annually, over 80% of which is derived from agriculture E of the Cascades. The biggest money crops are wheat, hay, and potatoes, followed by livestock, apples, pears, cherries, grapes, onions, and other fruits and vegetables.

One of the state's fastest growing crops is wine grapes. In 1972, Washington had just 6 wineries; today there are over 60, and visitors come to tour the Columbia and Yakima valleys much as they would California's wine-producing regions. Washington is now recognized as one of the prime wine producers in the country, with many award-winning wines, most notably those produced by Chateau Ste. Michelle, being sold nationwide.

Fishing

Fishing is one of the state's oldest industries, as the original Native Americans on both sides of the Cascades depended on Columbia River salmon and other fish for much of their diet, and Coastal Indians from the Neah Bay area were whalers. Commercial fishing, less important to the early settlers than logging and other industries, wasn't firmly established until the 1860s, when canneries, new salmon fishing techniques, and new markets at home and abroad led to the industry's rapid expansion. The Pacific Northwest salmon industry now harvests over 250,000 pounds of salmon annually, worth about $100-150 million. To ensure adequate numbers of the commercially valuable chinook, coho, sockeye, chum, and pink salmon, Oregon and Washington have developed state fish hatcheries; Washington alone has 26, producing a total of 150 million salmon and half of the commercial catch every year.

Hydroelectric And Nuclear Power

Washington's first hydroelectric power was generated in the late 1880s in Spokane, when Spokane Falls were used to power a saw to cut wood for a local hotel. Uses multiplied to include street lighting, trolley lines, and more, and in 1899 Spokane's Washington Water Power Company was established as one of the first hydroelectric power companies in the country. Tacoma was the first major city to produce its own power when, in 1898, it took over a local utility company and later built dams on the Nisqually and Skokomish rivers.

Franklin D. Roosevelt's "New Deal" paved the way for the construction of the first federally built dam on the mighty Columbia River: the Bonneville Dam, completed in 1938. It was quickly followed by the Grand Coulee Dam and others, until 14 Columbia River dams produced electricity and provided water for irrigation to much of the Pacific Northwest and California. By the 1970s, 96% of the state's power was hydroelectric in origin.

Inexpensive hydroelectric power has been taken for granted since its inception; Tacoma City Light has been boasting for years that it offers the cheapest electric rates in the nation. But the state's recent drought has demonstrated that even in the soggy Pacific Northwest, low electric rates are not guaranteed, and other energy alternatives must be considered. Even with the abundance of

Grand Coulee is one of 14 dams on the Columbia River.

Washington led the country in mining disasters for many years. Here, miners at the Carbonado mining disaster of 1930.

dams, the Pacific Northwest has to import energy from Canada to supply the growing demand.

Public outrage, way-over-budget construction costs, and safety concerns have made nuclear power a poor second choice. In 1968, the Washington Public Power Supply System (WPPSS) began work on 5 nuclear generators, 3 at the Hanford site near Tri-Cities and 2 at Satsop in Grays Harbor County. The $6 billion budget stretched to $24 billion, and public outcry over the inevitable rate hikes to pay for the construction resulted in approval of an initiative limiting such groups' spending and the mothballing of all but one reactor at Hanford, which was completed in 1981 and began producing power in 1984. The other 2 partially constructed reactors at Hanford and Satsop will likely never be completed, though customers are paying for these white elephants through the Bonneville Power Administration's substantial rate hikes.

What's left? Coal-fired plants, such as the Centralia Steam Plant, may become more important if coal reserves can be efficiently and economically mined. Solar energy, geothermal energy, and other alternatives will require years of research and economic support before they can become any more than token energy producers.

Aircraft Manufacturing

Washington's economy is closely tied in with the success of the Boeing Company, the state's largest employer and manufacturer of both commercial and military aircraft. Its founder, William E. Boeing, started his fledgling aircraft business in a shipyard on the Duwamish River in 1916. World War I brought orders for training planes, and the company held on after the war by producing boats, furniture, and other items, plus U.S. Post Office transport planes and Army fighter planes. World War II brought over 13,000 orders for its B-17 bomber, and at the end of the war, B-29 bombers dropped the infamous atomic bombs on Nagasaki and Hiroshima. After the war, William Allen took over as president of Boeing and the company produced its first passenger plane, the 707, in 1958. In the late 1960s, Boeing's 747 plant opened in Everett in the world's largest building, and Boeing was established as the world leader in aircraft manufacturing. The late '60s and early '70s were hard times for Boeing, as government contracts for the SST and other military air-

Seattle and Tacoma economies depend heavily on containerized shipping.

craft fell through; employment fell from 110,000 to 38,000 workers. The company had to diversify to survive, so created subdivisions in commercial aircraft, military aircraft, hydrofoils, helicopters, and more. In the '80s, Boeing's employment has been stabilized at 68,000 to 80,000 workers, and the company is still the world's leader in commercial aircraft production, supplying over 180 airlines worldwide.

Shipping

From the time when Seattle's earliest settlers dropped a horseshoe on a rope to determine the depth of Elliott Bay, shipping has played an important role in the development of Puget Sound communities. Today, Seattle and Tacoma are among the most important seaports in the world, and other sea- and riverports along the Columbia as far inland as Kennewick helped to establish waterborne trade as one of the state's largest industries.

The first goods shipped from Seattle were logs that would be used as dock pilings in San Francisco. Lumber and wood products still account for a good portion of the area's exports, particularly from smaller ports such as Everett, Port Gamble, Port Angeles, Hoquiam, Olympia, and Bellingham. Seattle and Tacoma are important containerized shipping ports, where bulk and manufactured goods from airplanes to wheat are exported to Japan, China, Taiwan, Canada, and Australia. Telecommunications equipment, cars and trucks, clothing, and petroleum products are the primary imports, arriving from Canada, Japan, Taiwan, and Hong Kong. Oil tankers also arrive in Port Angeles from Alaska to supply the oil refineries in Anacortes and Ferndale. As the port of Tacoma plans a major expansion and Seattle continues to be a national trade leader, the future for containerized shipping in Washington looks very bright.

TRANSPORTATION

TOURS

Your travel agent can come up with numerous bus tours of Washington's highlights; or, phone one of the following tour companies for dates and rates. Gray Line offers one-day and longer tours of Seattle, Mt. Rainier and Mt. St. Helens, Olympic National Park, the North Cascades, Washington wine country, and Spokane, often including Vancouver and Victoria, B.C., Lake Coeur D'Alene, Portland, or other western national parks. In Washington, phone (800) 426-7532 or (206) 624-5813 for details. American Sightseeing has one-day tours of Seattle, Mt. Rainier, and Victoria, B.C.; phone (206) 626-5208. Don and Diane FunTours operates one-day and longer tours from Seattle to Spokane, Leavenworth, Mt. Rainier, Olympia, and out to Reno, San Francisco, and beyond; phone (206) 282-3508 or write Box 21007, Seattle, WA 98111, for a brochure. Creative Tours, (206) 771-4721, offers one-day tours to western Washington sights and events from Poulsbo's Midsommer Viking Fest to Port Townsend's Historic Homes Tour; write Box 403, Edmonds, WA 98020, for information. Continental Crown, (509) 456-5104, offers bus tours through eastern Washington and on to Idaho and Montana or N to British Columbia.

BY AIR

Washington's 2 major airports are Seattle-Tacoma International (Sea-Tac), and Spokane International, served by most major carriers and a handful of smaller airlines. United, 627-6561, Eastern, 927-5600, Continental, (800) 525-0280, Delta, 927-6550, and American, 535-8801, among others, provide national and international service. Alaska Airlines, 927-7800, serves the western states; USAir, (800) 435-9772, took over PSA's western states route; America West, (800) 247-5692, flies to California, Las Vegas, and the southwest and midwest states. Horizon Air, (800) 547-9308, is the big "little" airline, connecting many medium-to-large Washington cities, including Seattle, Spokane, Pullman, Yakima, and Pasco, to Portland, Boise, and others. Even smaller carriers, such as San Juan Airlines, (800) 438-3880, offer limited routes and schedules in smaller aircraft.

Try for a S-side window seat (on an E-W route) when flying into or out of Sea-Tac for a spectacular close-up view of Mt. Rainier and, in the distance, Mt. St. Helens.

BY TRAIN

Amtrak serves Washington with 2 major routes. The W coast route, aboard the *Coast Starlight,* has daily service to Seattle, Tacoma, E. Olympia, Centralia, Longview/Kelso, and Vancouver, through Oregon and S to San Francisco and Los Angeles. The *Mount Rainier* runs Thurs. through Sun. from Seattle to Portland, stopping at the Washington cities listed above.

Amtrak's E-W route, aboard The *Pioneer,* operates 3 days a week in winter, daily from spring through late fall; the train departs Seattle, passing through Tacoma, E. Olympia, Centralia, Longview/Kelso, and Vancouver as it continues through Portland and Idaho to Salt Lake City and Chicago. Another daily E-W route to Chicago on The *Empire Builder* stops at Spokane, continuing to Portland with stops at Pasco, Wishram, Bingen/White Salmon, and Vancouver, or to Seattle through Ephrata, Wenatchee, Everett, and Edmonds.

For route, schedule, and fare information, phone Amtrak at (206) 464-1930 in Seattle, (509) 747-1069 in Spokane, or (800) 872-7245 toll-free nationwide.

BY CAR

The national parks and other remote areas of the state are not served by any air, rail, or bus lines, and the public transportation within cities is often limited and difficult for the newcomer to use, so having a car of your own is a vital part of getting the most from your visit. Numerous car rental agencies operate at or near Sea-Tac and Spokane International airports, as well as in all large cities. (It's virtually impossible to rent a car without a major credit card; if this is your situation, call the car rental company ahead of time to have your employment verified or provide whatever other proof of adulthood they require.) Washington's major interstates are I-5, running N to S from the Canadian border through Seattle, Tacoma, and Olympia to Vancouver, and I-90, running W to E from Seattle to Spokane; I-82 heads S from Ellensburg almost to the Tri-Cities. These are all multi-lane freeways with speed limits of 55 mph in metropolitan areas and 65 mph in more desolate regions.

From late fall to early spring, expect snow at I-90's Snoqualmie Pass (between North Bend and Cle Elum in central Washington). Snow tires or chains are frequently required, and the pass is sometimes closed during storms because of hazardous road conditions, blocking accidents, or avalanche danger. Skiers and other winter travelers passing through the Casades would do well to rent a 4-wheel-drive vehicle and/or carry chains. Before you set out, be sure to phone 1-976-7623 for the state patrol's mountain pass report (there's a $.30 toll); they give road and weather conditions for all of the Cascade passes from Nov. through March or April.

Out-of-state visitors may be surprised by the abundance of wide, open spaces, particularly in the mountains and eastern half of the state—and the long distances between gas stations, rest rooms, and other niceties. Worse yet, some little towns close up tight after 5:00 p.m. and on Sundays. Play it safe and fill the tank whenever you pass through a moderately populous area; stock a cooler with drinks and sandwiches; and be sure your destination motel has a room ready and waiting for you.

BY BUS

Greyhound, 624-3456, serves most major cities in Washington, providing nationwide connections. Their main routes are along I-5 from Canada to Vancouver, and along I-90 from Seattle to Spokane, with additional service on the Oregon side of the Columbia Gorge and W to Astoria.

Regional and city bus lines can get you around most western Washington cities and a few large eastern cities as well. Seattle's Metro, (800) 542-7876, has extensive service within the city and regular daily routes throughout most of King County. Pierce Transit, 593-4500, serves Tacoma and Pierce County. Intercity Transit, 786-1881, has daily routes throughout Olympia and Thurston County. Grays Harbor Transit, (800) 562-9730, connects Olympia with Hoquiam, Ocean Shores, Westport, and Lake Quinault in Olympic National Park. Pacific Transit, 875-6541, has service to the Long Beach Peninsula from Raymond with connections to Astoria, Oregon. C-Tran, 695-0123, serves Vancouver and Clark County with connections to Portland. Longview, Kelso, and Cowlitz County are served by Community Urban Bus Service (CUBS), 577- 3399. In Chehalis, take Twin Transit, 748-4873, to Centralia and parts of Lewis County. The bus line coverage in eastern Washington isn't nearly as thorough. In Spokane, take Spokane Transit, 328-7433, throughout Spokane and Cheney. Valley Transit, 525-9140, serves Walla Walla and College Place. Yakima Transit, 575-6175, has 9 routes throughout Yakima and the surrounding area. The Tri-Cities have Ben Franklin Transit, 735-5100, with service to Kennewick, Pasco, Richland, W. Richland, and the Tri-Cities Airport.

BY BOAT

The most scenic way to get around western Washington is by Washington State Ferry; be sure to take a ride, even if it's just "there and back." The best sightseeing is on the Anacortes-San Juan Islands route, which continues once daily to Sidney, B.C. (see "San Juan Islands," p. 141, for details). Ferries also connect Port Townsend with Keystone (Whidbey Island); Clinton (Whidbey Island) with Mukilteo (S of Everett); Edmonds with Kingston (on the Kitsap Peninsula); Seattle with Winslow (Bainbridge Island) and Bremerton; Fauntleroy (S. Seattle) with Southworth (SE of Bremerton) and Vashon Island; and Tacoma (at Point Defiance) with Tahlequah (at the S end of Vashon Island). Fares range from $2.15 RT for a walk-on passenger (Mukilteo to Clinton) to $19 RT for car and driver (Anacortes to Friday Harbor), depending on route and season (some fares are higher in summer). Senior citizens receive a 50% discount with proof of age, applied only to the passenger or driver portion of the fare (not the vehicle). Fares must be paid with cash, traveler's checks, or personal checks (Washington residents only); no credit cards. The larger ferries have food service (including beer) and vending machines; the smaller boats have vending machines only. Pets on leashes are allowed on the car decks or in carrying containers on passenger decks. The ferries operate every day, including holidays. For more information about the ferry system, phone (800) 542-0810, (800) 542-7052, or in Seattle, 464-6400.

Other western Washington ferries include the Anderson Island Ferry, 588-3127, which has daily service between Steilacoom, Anderson Island, and Ketron Island. Ed's Charter, (800) 562-0107, provides passenger-only ferry service between Westport, Aberdeen, and Hoquiam in summer. The Horluck Transportation Co., 876-2300, has a daily route between Bremerton and Port Orchard for foot traffic only.

Take the MV *Coho* from Port Angeles to Victoria, B.C., across the Strait of Juan de Fuca; from Seattle, the *Princess Marguerite* and the quicker *Victoria Clipper* also sail to Victoria daily in summer from the waterfront piers 69 and 63. See "Port Angeles," p. 191, and "Seattle," p. 60, for details. Independent tour and charter boat companies in Seattle, Tacoma, Everett, San Juan Island, Westport, and other coastal cities offer sightseeing, fishing, whale- and sea lion-watching tours throughout the year.

BY BICYCLE

Though parts of the larger cities can be hazardous for cyclists, much of Washington is bicycle-friendly. Puget Sound's numerous islands provide great scenery, some of the state's best weather, and little automobile traffic: Whidbey Island, for instance, gets about a third of Seattle's annual rainfall, and offers spectacular vistas from little-traveled back roads, plus plenty of camping at the state parks. The beauty of the San Juan Islands is best experienced on a bike, and you'll save $10 or more on the ferry toll to Friday

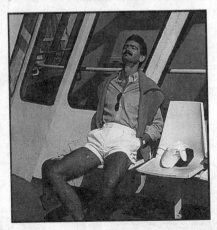

soaking up the sun on a Washington State ferry

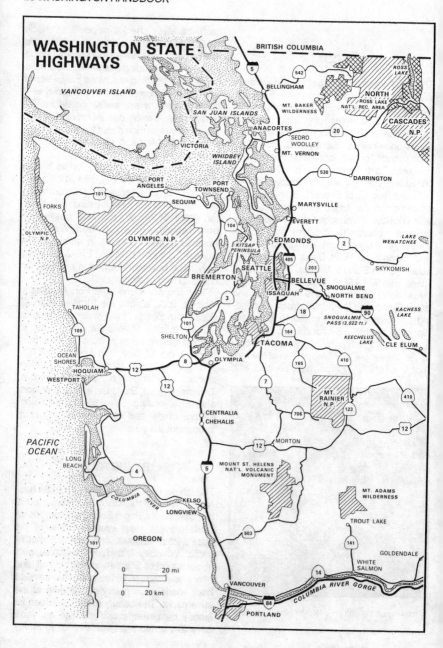

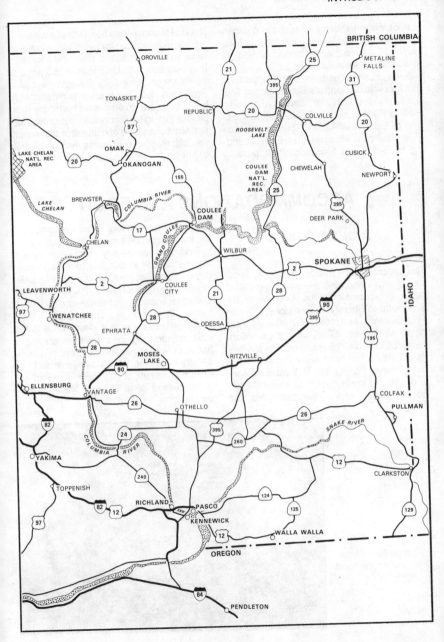

Harbor when traveling without the cumbersome automobile. Vashon, Bainbridge, Mercer, and Camano islands are also easy to get to and have little automobile traffic.

Even urban areas have ample opportunities for cyclists. Seattle's Burke-Gilman Trail is a 12½-mile paved bike path from Gasworks Park to Kenmore's Log Boom Park at the N end of Lake Washington. The Sammamish River Trail runs 9½ miles from Bothell Landing to Redmond's Marymoor Park, passing

just E of Woodinville's Ste. Michelle winery—a great place to stop for lunch with a bottle of wine. In W. Seattle, the road and bike path from Alki Beach to Lincoln Park is a popular 12-mile loop. Five Mile Drive in Tacoma's Point Defiance Park is open to cars as well, but cyclists are given a wide berth; the road passes through an impressive old-growth forest. Most chambers of commerce can supply you with maps of bike routes throughout their city or county for a nominal fee.

ACCOMMODATIONS AND FOOD

ACCOMMODATIONS

Hotels And Motels
The largest cities—Seattle, Spokane, Tacoma, Olympia and others—have the greatest range of accommodations, from Motel 6's $24 rooms to Sheratons, Red Lions, Olympic Four Seasons, and more for $100 and up per night. All of these cities, without exception, have dirt-cheap lodging just outside city limits, so stay a half hour away and spend the extra money having fun. In Seattle or Spokane, stay at the budget chains near the airport; in Tacoma, stay up the road in Fife. Call

ahead for reservations whenever possible; the least-expensive rooms fill up fast.

Finding a room—any room—can be extremely difficult in summer (even on weekdays) at popular resort areas such as Lake Chelan, the national parks, or Ocean Shores. Call as far ahead as possible—don't just drive there with your fingers crossed, or it'll be a long night in the car or a sleepy drive to the next vacancy. Again, sometimes staying a half hour from the action can save you money—try the motels in Wenatchee when Lake Chelan's filled up, or stay in Forks or Port Angeles instead of at Olympic National Park lodges.

Victorian B&Bs abound in Port Townsend.

Bed And Breakfast

Some parts of the state, particularly Port Townsend, are filled with restored turn-of-the-century Victorian homes that have been converted to B&Bs. Other B&Bs are old farmhouses, lodges, or modern homes with private entrances. In most cases, a room at a B&B will cost as much as a moderately priced motel room. You may miss the cable, HBO, pool, and room service, but you'll get breakfast (ranging from coffee and cinnamon rolls to a full eggs-bacon-and-toast feast), often complimentary evening wine or tea, and peace and quiet. Many B&Bs don't allow kids, pets, or smoking; probably half the rooms won't have a private bath. B&Bs are a good choice for people traveling alone, since you'll have opportunities to meet fellow travelers in the library, over tea, or at breakfast.

Camping

Washington's state parks offer excellent camping facilities in clean, scenic parks for next to nothing: $7 for tent sites, up to $9.50 for hookups. (See "Camping in the State Parks," p. 95, for more details.) Some parks accept advance reservations, but most operate on a first-come first-served basis. The national parks and forests also have good camping at generally more primitive sites; some are free, but most campgrounds charge a small fee. Private campgrounds are a last resort; they're usually combination mobile home/RV parks with a minimum of natural surroundings and a maximum number of vehicles per acre.

FOOD

Be sure to taste "Northwest cuisine" before going home. Salmon is big out here, and can be found on virtually every restaurant's menu, from Ivar's Fish Bars to Black Angus steak houses. Red snapper, halibut, and cod are also served fresh almost everywhere in western Washington. Rarer are the local Olympia oysters and geoduck (some question, once you've seen one, as to whether they're fit to eat). As you head E, the seafood is generally frozen, though some restaurants pride themselves on their fresh fish and will mention it in their ads. Steaks are often imported from the midwest and are generally very good.

Eastern Washington is the place to go for fresh produce. Washington apples are mostly of the Red and Golden Delicious, Rome Beauty, and Granny Smith varieties. The Walla Walla sweet onion is reputedly mild enough to bite into, raw, like an apple. Asparagus, pears, and berries of all kinds are also big eastern Washington crops.

Wine grapes are a large part of the Yakima and Columbia river valleys' agriculture. Wineries line the highway between Yakima and the Tri-Cities and into Walla Walla; others are scattered E to Spokane. Washington wines have become world class in just a few years, winning awards and gaining in popularity across the country. Try to visit at least a few wineries (western Washington also has a number of them, though the grapes are often grown in the E); or, stop by the local grocery store for a wide selection of Washington and Northwest wines.

MONEY, MEASUREMENTS, AND COMMUNICATIONS

Money

Prices of all hotels, tours, attractions, and services were current at press time, and will inevitably go up; use them as a basis for comparison, not as absolutes. Most prices are given before sales tax has been added, a whopping 7.8% on most all purchases and 8% on restaurant meals and lodging. Large Seattle banks (and some hotels) will exchange foreign currency, but don't count on passing off your Canadian change as American—stores won't accept it. Canadian coins *are* good for wishing wells, Salvation Army bell ringers, tipping bad waiters, makeshift screwdrivers, and aiding in the decision-making process.

Measurements

The metric system's major contribution to Washington is the 2-liter bottle, although you will see signs in both miles and kilometers as you approach the Canadian border; some banks display the temperature in both centigrade and Fahrenheit (though it hardly matters, since it's almost always wrong). For the most part, though, Washington is sticking stubbornly to the good old English system.

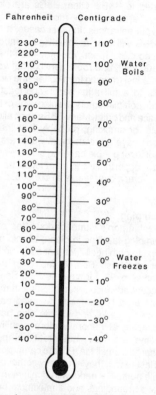

1 inch	= 2.54 centimeters
1 foot	= 0.31 meter
1 mile	= 1.61 kilometers
1 sq. mile	= 2.59 sq. kilometers
1 acre	= 0.40 hectare
1 pound (lb.)	= 0.45 kilogram

Communications

Post offices generally open between 7:00 a.m. and 9:00 a.m. and close between 5:00 p.m. and 6:00 p.m.; few are open on Saturdays. Some drug or card stores also operate a postal substation where you can buy stamps or mail packages within the U.S. (you'll have to go to a real post office for mailing to foreign addresses, Federal Express, or other special services). Many grocery stores also sell books of stamps with no mark-up.

Washington has 2 telephone area codes; generally speaking, 206 is W of the Cascades and 509 is E of the Cascades, but it can get tricky in the middle. For directory assistance, dial 1-555-1212 for local numbers or 1-(area code)-555-1212 for out-of-area numbers.

HEALTH AND HELP

In most of Washington, dial 911 for medical, police, or fire emergencies. More remote areas have separate numbers for all 3, and they're listed under "Services And Information" in each section; as a last resort, dial 0 for the operator. Most hospitals have 24-hour emergency room service; some cities have dial-a-nurse services that offer free medical advice.

OUTDOORS

Dealing with black bears is discussed under "Flora And Fauna," p. 4. But by far the greater danger to the outdoors enthusiast is hypothermia, often referred to in the past as "exposure," in which the victim's core temperature drops to 95 degrees or below. It doesn't have to be below freezing for hypothermia to be a threat; exposure to wind and/or water can cause a serious loss of heat at temperatures well above freezing. Prevention is the best bet: wear wool (the best insulator even when wet), and put on rain gear *before* it starts raining; head back or set up camp when the weather looks threatening; eat candy bars, keep active, or snuggle with a friend in a down bag to generate warmth. If the conditions are right for hypothermia, watch your hiking partner for signs of slurred speech, stumbling, drowsiness, memory lapses, shivering (particularly if shivering stops once it's started), or poor judgment. Once the victim's core temperature falls below 95 degrees, he'll be unable to recover by himself and immediate action must be taken on his behalf, whether or not he thinks he needs help. Get him out of the wind or rain and into dry clothing and a pre-warmed sleeping bag (have another hiker strip to the skin and warm the bag first, or in severe cases, have the victim and warmth donor skin-to-skin in the bag). Be sure the sleeping bag is well insulated from the ground, and build a fire on each side of the bag if possible; warm, wrapped rocks or canteens can also help. If he can eat, feed him candy bars or sweetened snacks; if he's semiconscious, keep him awake.

Frostbite is a less serious but quite painful problem for the cold-weather hiker, caused by direct exposure or by heat loss due to wet socks and boots. Frostbitten areas will look white or gray and feel hard on the surface, softer underneath. The best way to warm the area is with other skin: put your hand under your arm, your feet on your friend's belly. Don't rub it with snow or warm it near a fire. In cases of severe frostbite, in which the skin is white, quite hard, and numb, immerse the frozen area in water warmed to 99-104 degrees until it's thawed. Avoid refreezing the frostbitten area. If you're a long way from medical assistance and the frostbite is extensive, better to keep the area frozen and get out of the woods for help; thawing is very painful and it would be impossible to walk on a thawed foot.

The most important part of enjoying—and surviving—the backcountry is to be prepared. Know where you're going; get maps, camping information, and weather and trail conditions from a ranger before setting out. Don't hike alone. Two are better than one, and 3 are better than 2; if one of you gets hurt, one person can stay with the injured party and one can go for help. Bring more than enough food so hunger won't cause you to carry on when weather conditions say "stop." Tell someone where you're going and when you'll be back. Bring a compass, and know how to use it. Carry a water bottle, first aid kit, flashlight, matches and fire starter, knife, and extra clothing (a full set, in case you fall in a stream), including rain gear. Check your ego at the trailhead; stop for the night when the weather gets bad, even if it's 2:00 p.m., or head back, and don't press on when you're exhausted—tired hikers are sloppy hikers, and even a small injury can be disastrous in the woods.

INFORMATION

Ranger stations at the national parks and forests can supply you with forest and topographical maps, campground and trail information, and other printed material. For a list of books, maps, and pamphlets available by mail, write the Pacific Northwest National Parks and Forests Association, Forest Service/National Park Service, Outdoor Recreation Information, 1018 1st Ave., Seattle, WA 98104, or phone (206) 442-0170. Get more specific information on your destination (trail and campground descriptions, maps, sightseeing, wildlife) by writing or phoning one of these offices:

Colville National Forest
Colville Ranger Station
775 S. Main St.
Colville, WA 99114
(509) 684-4557

Gifford Pinchot National Forest
Mt. Adams Ranger Station
Trout Lake, WA 98650
(509) 395-2501

Gifford Pinchot National Forest
Mt. St. Helens National Volcanic
Monument Headquarters
Rt. 1, Box 369
Amboy, WA 98601
(206) 247-5473

**Mt. Baker/Snoqualmie
National Forest**
Supervisor's Office
1022 1st Ave.
Seattle, WA 98104
(206) 442-5400

Okanogan National Forest
Supervisor's Office
Box 950
Okanogan, WA 98840
(509) 422-2704

Olympic National Forest
Supervisor's Office
Box 2288
Olympia, WA 98507
(206) 753-9535

Wenatchee National Forest
Supervisor's Office
301 Yakima St.
Wenatchee, WA 98801
(509) 662-4335

For national park information, see the"Services And Information" section under the appropriate chapter.

Every city or town has a chamber of commerce. Most have offices that are filled with free brochures, maps, information on lodging and restaurants, and more. Take advantage of the help they offer. See "Services And Information" in each chapter for the chamber's address and phone.

THE PUGET SOUND REGION

SEATTLE

Seattle is consistently ranked as the best U.S. city in which to live, visit, raise kids, or locate a business (by organizations as varied as *Money* magazine, Rand McNally, *USA Today*, and the National Conference of Mayors). The phenomenal growth the Puget Sound region has experienced in recent years attests to the area's increasing popularity—and causes natives to shudder at the "Californication" of their once-pristine state. The obvious charms of Seattle and the Puget Sound region are drawing more tourists each year, many of whom come back to stay.

Throughout its history Seattle has been a gateway: first to Alaska during the Klondike Gold Rush, today to the Orient as planes refuel here for their Asian destinations, and of course to the wonders of the Pacific Northwest: 3 of the country's most spectacular national parks and moody Mt. St. Helens National Monument are within a couple hours' driving time from the city; skiing, hiking, year-round boating, swimming, and fishing are less than an hour away. But Seattle's charm isn't just a function of what it's near, but also what it is—and was. Oddly shaped towers and preserved historical districts stand alongside modern skyscrapers and busy waterfront in a jaunty kind of disharmony. Every major event in the city's short life span, from Yesler's 1850s sawmill to the 1962 World's Fair, has left its legacy; the resulting mishmash of periods gives the city a flavor absent in showpieces of urban renewal.

But history doesn't make a city livable. No one event or attraction here can ever take that credit. Rather, it's a thousand incidents, enjoyed daily: dining at the waterfront, watching the sun set behind the Olympics as sailboats head home; reading the *Seattle P.I.* on your early-morning ferry commute, accompanied by a lively porpoise escort service; listening to an outdoor lunchtime concert at Freeway Park; stopping for fresh vegies at Pike Place Market; cleansing your lungs with fresh, rain-rinsed air as you dodge slugs and puddles on your morning run; holding a summertime office party on a harbor tour boat; being surprised by a clear view of bashful Mt. Rainier from the highway or the Safeway parking lot. All these unique moments, as well as cultural events, shops, and restaurants, make Seattle such a delightful, relaxing place.

Climate

Despite the stories you've heard, it doesn't rain here *all* the time. Seattle actually gets less annual rainfall than New York—it just falls more slowly here. Gray and drizzly is standard fare from October to May; when it does rain, it's usually a who-needs-an-umbrella sprinkle. The winter weather pattern remains nearly constant; storms off the Pacific coast send swirling clouds over Seattle for months, leading you to believe that the TV weather forecaster uses the same satellite photo all season. Nearly all of the precipitation is rain; less than an inch of snow per month is the average, so plows are few . . . and generally in disrepair. When snowstorms dropped 17 inches on Seattle in November of 1985, only 4 of the city's 7 snowplows worked; commuters relied on chains to traverse the I-5 snowfield.

When spring arrives the clouds move more quickly; rain comes in unpredictable spurts. Summer convinces many visitors to move here: low humidity, temperatures in the high 70s to 80s, and cloudless skies. Then, as suddenly as it began, summer ends: clouds return, temperatures go down, and residents stockpile firewood for the soggy season ahead.

HISTORY

The city was named after Suquamish Chief Sealth, or Seattle—Indian names didn't translate well into English, and both spellings are used on his tomb. Seattle claimed to have witnessed Capt. George Vancouver's visit in 1792, and 50 years later befriended early settlers, encouraging a policy of peace between Indians and white newcomers. Most Indians feared the consequences of the utterance of their name after death; historians debate whether the chief was happy that the city was to be named in his honor. Some claim it was against his will; others hold that Seattle was paid handsomely by the city's founders for his name. In any case, the name stuck. Today a bronze sculpture of Chief Seattle stands at the corner of Fifth and Denny Way; his burial site, a peaceful Suquamish cemetery across the Sound, overlooks his namesake's skyscrapers.

David Denny and Lee Terry were the first white men to arrive at Alki Point. Twenty-two pioneers had left Cherry Grove, Illinois, for Portland, Oregon; they then boarded the schooner *Exact* and sailed to Alki Point in 1851. The settlers ambitiously planned to develop "the New York of the Pacific Coast" at their landing site. Lumber was the focus of their early economy, beginning with the arrival of the *Leonesa* from San Francisco in 1852. The ship's captain had been wandering northward when he stumbled across the Alki settlement. The settlers sold the skipper 35,000 board feet of logs. Seeing an economic future in shipping lumber, the pioneers took to the waters in Indian canoes, and with the help of Mrs. Denny's clothesline and Lee Terry's horseshoes, took soundings along the Puget Sound shoreline. Discovering that the deepest waters were in today's Elliott Bay, the group relocated to Pioneer Square. Logs were rolled down the original "Skid Road," now Yesler Way, to Henry Yesler's steam-powered sawmill. Yesler enjoyed such success that by the 1880s Yesler's Wharf was a town unto itself, with saloons, warehouses, shops, homes, and offices built on pilings extending 900 feet over the mudflats.

Women were scarce in Seattle's early years, so in the 1860s, Asa Mercer made 2 trips to New England to find refined, educated, single women willing to endure a little hardship to get a husband. The "Mercer Girls" brought culture and class to this rowdy pioneer town.

Until the 1880s, most transport to and from Seattle was by boat. Hopes for alternative methods were dashed when the Northern Pacific Railroad chose Tacoma as their Northwest terminus. Though they received intermittent service via Tacoma by 1883, Seattleites wanted to be part of a regular, mainline route. As James J. Hill began ex-

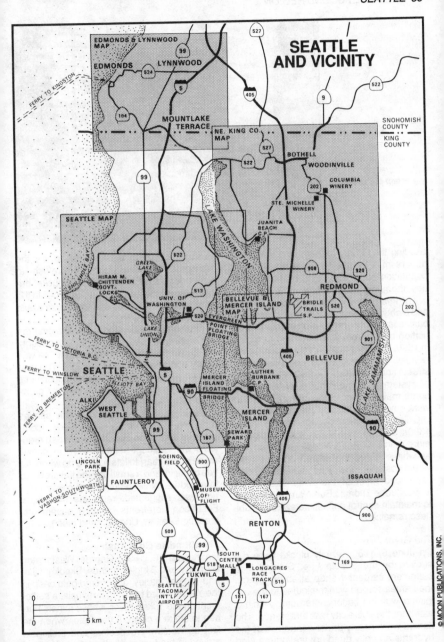

© MOON PUBLICATIONS, INC.

turn-of-the-century
Seattle

panding the Great Northern Line westward, rumors of a Seattle terminus resulted in a population boom and rising real estate values; the rumor became fact in 1893.

The intermittent railroad service of the '80s and highly successful lumber and coal export businesses encouraged a phenomenal population boom: from 3,500 in 1880 to 43,000 in 1890. The city's quality of life also improved rapidly, with the grading and planking of streets and sidewalks, the installation of sewer systems, electric lights, telephones, and home mail delivery. Horse-drawn streetcars were quickly replaced by the electric variety.

Chinese workers began arriving in the 1860s; by the mid-1880s they numbered more than 500. Anti-Chinese sentiment rose as whites feared that cheap Chinese labor would cost them their jobs; the ensuing riots convinced most of the Asian laborers to leave. Judge Thomas Burke and others tried to maintain control and ultimately some Chinese remained.

The Great Fire
On June 6, 1889, 58 city blocks were destroyed by the Seattle Fire. Starting in a basement carpenter shop at about 2 p.m., the flames spread within minutes to the adjoining wooden liquor storeroom. Within a half-hour the entire city was threatened. The flames were nearly under control when the hydrants abruptly dried up; firefighters tried

to stop the blaze by blasting structures in the fire's path, to no avail. Jacob Levy refused to surrender his house; his 70-man bucket brigade repeatedly doused it, while a man in the street laid 10 to 1 odds that the house would burn down. Levy won.

Firemen threw burning sidewalks over the cliff, ripped up roadway planking, and fought the flames with bucket brigades; the fire was finally contained at 8:30 that night. The next morning it was decreed unanimously that wooden structures would be forever prohibited in the burnt district.

Business was conducted under canvas tents until the rebuilding—in brick—was completed a year later. Seattle always had problems with drainage: streets were mudflows much of the year; toilets backed up when the tide came in; and a small boy (no lie) drowned in a puddle. While rebuilding, a clever solution was suggested: raise the sidewalks! First-floor storefronts became basements, creating Seattle's Underground (see p. 40).

The Klondike Gold Rush
On August 16, 1896, George Washington Carmack and 2 Indian friends, Skookum Jim and Tagish Charley, discovered gold deep in the Yukon. Word reached Fortymile, a settlement on the Yukon River, whose miners hurried to stake a claim. A year later, when the first 68 wealthy prospectors and their gold arrived in the Lower 48, the "Klondike Gold

Rush" began. The first ship to return, the *Excelsior*, arrived in San Francisco on July 15, 1897; the *Portland* arrived in Seattle 2 days later. Beriah Brown of the *Seattle Post-Intelligencer* wrote that the ship was laden with "a ton of gold"; actually more than 2 tons left the ship in suitcases, crates, and coffee cans. The rush was on: fathers left their families, mothers left their families, even the city's mayor resigned to seek his fortune in the Klondike.

The Klondike trip wasn't an easy one: a 1,000-mile sea voyage to Skagway, then an arduous hike over the snowy 33-mile Chilkoot Trail to Lake Bennett, where would-be prospectors slapped together all manner of craft for floating down the Yukon to the Klondike. The Northwest Mounted Police required that each prospector carry a year's supply of food plus necessary tools and clothing, leading to the catchphrase, "a ton of gold, a ton of goods."

Erastus Brainerd formed a publicity committee for the chamber of commerce and promoted Seattle as *the* place to get outfitted for the Klondike. Tacoma, Seattle, Vancouver, and Portland competed for the gold-rushers' dollars, but Brainerd ensured that Seattle received 5 times as much advertising as the other cities by writing feature articles and encouraging citizens to write "letters to the editor" for papers worldwide. Brainerd was enormously successful—Seattle emerged as undisputed outfitting leader. The streets became open markets: clothing, condensed milk, evaporated potatoes, and tools were piled high. Anything named "Klondike" was a potential big-seller, giving rise to "Klondike underwear" and "Klondike milk." Shady operators capitalized on their customers' eagerness: the Trans-Atlantic Gopher Company sold gophers allegedly trained to dig for gold. Siberian Huskies and other rugged breeds were enlisted to help pull dogsleds through the Alaskan snowfields. As the supply dwindled, families had to keep a close eye on their pets—dogs of every breed and size were stolen.

Though a handful of prospectors did strike it rich, the best claims had been staked long before most treasure-hunters arrived—leaving thousands of men worse off than when they began. Seattle emerged as the real winner, though: many of those who found gold returned to the city to establish businesses, while Seattle's "gold" was gained from outfitting the prospectors.

Modern Seattle

At the start of WW II the Boeing Airplane Company employed only 4,000 workers, manufacturing planes on a subcontract basis for the Douglas Company of California. Orders for Boeing's B-17 bomber, developed in the mid-'30s, swelled their employment to 30,000 by 1942. Sales peaked in 1944 at $600 million, while employment figures

modern Seattle

topped 50,000. After the war, Boeing's sales figures fell sharply—to $14 million in 1946, when 11,000 workers were laid off. Business picked up again during the Korean conflict and the U.S./Russia cold war with the sale of B-47s and, later, B-52s. William M. Allen, Boeing's post-war president, sought to end this roller-coaster economy by gambling all of the company's reserves on a commercial plane, the 707, that permanently changed civilian air travel. Later successful developments—the short-range 727, 737, and jumbo 747—brought employment figures up to 58,000 in 1959 and established Boeing as a worldwide leader in aviation.

Civic leaders decided to throw a party to celebrate Boeing's—and, synonymously, Seattle's—success. City Councilman Al Rochester was a leading advocate of "Century 21," the 1962 World's Fair. Rochester wanted something very special, "not just another showcase for the state seal done in corn tassels, milk cans, and steers' rears." Senator Warren G. Magnuson weaseled $9 million out of the Pentagon for the event—which became the first world's fair to show a profit. Century 21 drew over 9½ million people, and left the Space Needle, monorail, Pacific Science Center, Opera House, Coliseum, and more as a legacy to "The Emerald City."

SIGHTS

The Waterfront

Generally a sightseer's first stop, Eliott Bay's piers 48-70 comprise the Waterfront: restaurants, gift shops, tourist traps, museums, and harbor-tour departure points, connected by a sidewalk and the Waterfront Streetcar. These three 1927 Australian trolleys run the 1.6 miles between piers 48 and 70 every 20-30 minutes and continue to Pioneer Square. It's a good way to bypass the empty warehouses and ferry terminals between the 2 developed ends of the waterfront. Park your car under the highway and try for a meter; as a last resort pay the exorbitant fees at the Diamond lots. Get a streetcar ticket for $.55 ($.75 peak) at the self-serve ticket machine at any streetcar station.

Pier 59's **Seattle Marine Aquarium** features an underwater dome for viewing life in the Sound. Open daily at 10 a.m., admission $3.25 adults, teens and seniors $1.50, kids $.75; 625-4357. **The Omnidome,** also on Pier 59, 622-1868, lets you experience erupting volcanoes, outer space, foreign countries, and ocean excursions on their 180-degree dome screen with 6-channel sound. The 45-minute-long programs run continuously from 10 a.m.; admission $6.95 adults, $4.50 students/seniors, and $2.95 kids. Public fishing is allowed at Waterfront Park on Pier 57; but have a look at the water before you decide to eat what comes out of it. Worth a stop is **Creative Northwest** at Pier 55; everything they carry has been caught, grown, or handcrafted in the Northwest. Pick up Anacortes smoked salmon, Oregon glass and ceramic goblets, Mt. St. Helens' ash ornaments and oil lamps, and gift packs with teas, jams, and chocolates. **Ye Olde Curiosity Shop,** a combination museum-gift shop on Pier 51, specializes in the bizarre: shrunken heads, mummies, "Skinny Stubbs" human skeleton, a 2-headed calf, plus souvenirs and curios. Pier 70 has more stores

SEATTLE

1. Latitude 47
2. Anthony's
3. Liz's
4. Ray's Boathouse
5. Hiram's at the Docks
6. Hiram M. Chittenden Locks
7. Franco's Hidden Harbor
8. Triple's
9. Ivar's Salmon House
10. Lake Union Cafe
11. University Bookstore
12. Burke Memorial Museum
13. Henry Art Gallery
14. Husky Stadium
15. Seattle Museum of History & Industry
16. Japanese Tea House & Garden
17. Volunteer Park/Seattle Art Museum/Conservatory
18. Seattle Center
19. aquarium

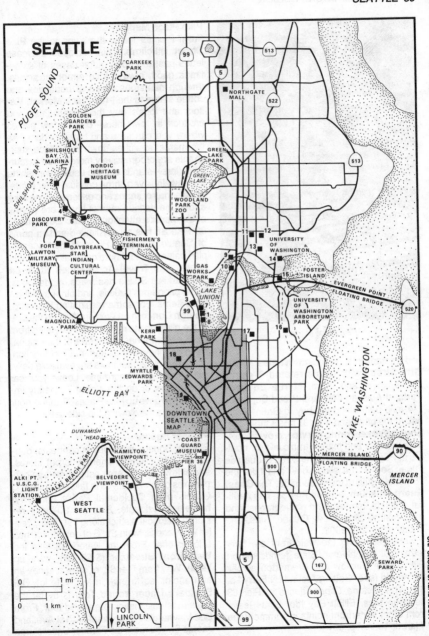

SEATTLE

PUGET SOUND

CARKEEK PARK

GOLDEN GARDENS PARK

SHILSHOLE BAY MARINA

SHILSHOLE BAY

NORDIC HERITAGE MUSEUM

NORTHGATE MALL

GREEN LAKE PARK

GREEN LAKE

WOODLAND PARK ZOO

DISCOVERY PARK

FISHERMEN'S TERMINAL

FORT LAWTON MILITARY MUSEUM

DAYBREAK STAR INDIAN CULTURAL CENTER

UNIVERSITY OF WASHINGTON

GAS WORKS PARK

LAKE UNION

FOSTER ISLAND

EVERGREEN POINT FLOATING BRIDGE

UNIVERSITY OF WASHINGTON ARBORETUM PARK

MAGNOLIA PARK

KERR PARK

LAKE WASHINGTON

MYRTLE EDWARDS PARK

ELLIOTT BAY

DOWNTOWN SEATTLE MAP

DUWAMISH HEAD

HAMILTON VIEWPOINT

COAST GUARD MUSEUM

PIER 36

MERCER ISLAND FLOATING BRIDGE

ALKI PT. U.S.C.G. LIGHT STATION

BELVEDERE VIEWPOINT

MERCER ISLAND

WEST SEATTLE

SEWARD PARK

0   1 mi

0   1 km

TO LINCOLN PARK

© MOON PUBLICATIONS, INC.

Pike Place Market

and restaurants, including **Whales World Gift Shop,** with whale-related T-shirts, books, toys, and more. **Myrtle Edwards Park,** at Alaskan Way and Broad St., has a 1¼-mile path along the bay to Grain Terminal. At the other end, Pier 36 hosts the **Puget Sound Vessel Traffic Service,** providing 24-hour weather and marine traffic info for boaters in Puget Sound and the Strait of Juan de Fuca. See a free slide show and take the 15-minute guided tour; 286-5650. The **Coast Guard Museum,** also on Pier 36, has nautical artifacts, models, and photographs, and a 15-minute slide show. Closed Tues. and Thurs., free; 286-9608.

Scattered along the waterfront are ferry terminals. Washington State ferries depart Pier 52 for Winslow and Bremerton across the sound (see "Getting Around By Ferry," p. 60). The *Victoria Clipper* docks at Pier 63 between trips. Elliott Bay tour boats leave from other waterfront points in summer (see "Harbor Tours," p. 59).

Pike Place Market

From Pier 59 follow the signs to the **Pike Street Hillclimb.** This enclosed staircase leads past the open guitar cases of sometimes good, always loud street musicians, through numerous levels of boutiques and coffee shops to the **Pike Place Market.** Visitors and locals buy the freshest fish and produce in town here—one of few places where you can see, and buy, geoduck. As the market stretches down Pike Place, merchants are progressively more tuned to tourist dollars—stands sell the usual sweatshirts and jewelry, even some unusual laser prints. But a series of shops and galleries along Pike and in the various market levels are worthy of the visitor's attention: **Studio Solstone** at 93 Pike St. has quality limited-edition prints of Seattle and Pike Place Market scenes, plus calendars and note cards at reasonable prices. **The Travel Accessories Store** on the market's S side has maps, guidebooks, bags, car games for kids, and other travel-related items. For some fascinating browsing, **Design Concern** on Western Ave. (to the side of the hillclimb staircase) has everything from watches to phones to cookware; the emphasis is on innovative design, not just function, of the object. Market tours are available daily; call 682-7453 for more info. Leave your car down below or up the street; it's nearly impossible to drive up Pike Place with lunch-hour pedestrians overflowing the sidewalks.

Pioneer Square

Pioneer Square is a study in contrasts: boutiques, art galleries, Oriental carpet stores, and sidewalk cafes are nestled between corner missions; executives in tailored suits and Guccis pass Occidental Park's shadowy, homeless residents. Still, the 20-block restored historical district along 1st Ave., Yesler Way, and S. Main St., S of downtown, has a lot to offer. From the waterfront take the **Waterfront Streetcar** ($.55-.75), walk up Yesler Way from Pier 52, or drive and pay an arm and/or leg to park in a private lot. **Bill Speidel's Underground Tour** is by far the city's most fascinating organized tour. From Doc Maynard's Public House at 1st Ave. and James St. you roam the Pioneer Square area above and below; a guide provides humorous anecdotes along with local history. The 1½-hour tours leave 3-7 times daily; $4 adults, $2 kids, $2.75 seniors, reservations recommended; phone 682-1511 for schedule, 682-4646 for reservations. **Smith Tower,** 42 stories counting the spire, was the tallest building W of the Mississippi when completed in 1914. Now dwarfed by neighboring skyscrapers, you can still view Pioneer Square from its observation deck ($1 fee includes a genteel elevator operator); a museum is scheduled to open soon. The **Klondike Gold Rush National Historic Park,** 117 S. Main St., is Seattle's portion of a 4-part national park commemorating the gold rush (the other 3 parts are in Skagway, Alaska, and Dawson and Whitehorse, Yukon). Housed in the 1901 Union Trust Annex, the park traces Seattle's role in the 1897 gold rush with national park-quality films, exhibits, and gold-panning demos. Open daily from 9 a.m.-5:30 p.m., free; 442-7220. Get a free brochure here with a map pointing out the historical buildings in the square. Some intriguing shops here include **Iris Fine Crafts,** handcrafted jewelry, pottery, glassware, and gifts at 317 1st Ave. S, and **SoundWinds/AirArts,** a colorful windsock showcase at 206 1st Ave. South. Art galleries include **Silver Image Gallery,** 318 Occidental S, devoted to photography by masters and contemporary artists, and **Northwest Gallery of Fine Woodworking,** 202 1st Ave. S, exhibiting wood sculpture and furniture produced by Northwest artists.

Policemen dressed in 19th-century costumes patrol Pioneer Square.

Seattle Center

From Pier 59, walk up Pike and take a L onto 4th Ave. to get to the **Monorail Terminal.** Ride the monorail ($.60) from downtown West lake Center to Seattle Center, between 5th Ave. N, Denny Way, 1st Ave. N, and Mercer Street. The **Space Needle,** 447-3100, is Seattle's trademark, with 2 restaurants, observation deck, banquet facility, and gift shops; the elevator ride costs $3.75 ($2 kids) if you're not having dinner. The **Pacific Science Center** has a science museum with over 120 hands-on exhibits, the IMAX (Image Maximum) Theater, and a Laserium. Admission is $5 adults, $4 seniors, $2 kids, and includes the IMAX Theater and Laserium shows; 443-2001. The **Center House,** a tri-level shopping and eating emporium, caters to the tourist: 50 shops and restaurants feature international cuisine and Northwest gifts, plus free entertainment year-round. Some restaurants are open for breakfast.

Seattle Center has a lot of options for kids. The **Seattle Children's Museum** is now on the lower floor of the Center House; their hands-on exhibits cater to the under-10 crowd but grown-ups will enjoy them too. Admission is $2.50, closed Mon.; 441-1767. **World Mother Goose,** next door, is a non-profit professional theater company with performances geared toward kids 2½-8. Their regular season runs from May to Oct., and special carnivals and performances fill out the off-season; 441-SHOW. **Fun Forest,** the Center's amusement park, is open late spring to early autumn.

Seattle Center also contains the **Coliseum,** home of the NBA's Seattle SuperSon-

The monorail carries passengers from downtown to Seattle Center.

ics; the **Bagley-Wright Theater** where the Seattle Repertory Theatre performs; and the **Opera House,** home of the Seattle Opera, Seattle Symphony, and Pacific Northwest Ballet (see "Entertainment," p. 54).

International District

Once called "Chinatown," now many people of Japanese and Vietnamese ancestry live here as well. Start your exploration of this area with an **International District Tour,** beginning with a 45-minute multi-media show in Nippon Kan Theater, a national historic site at 628 S. Washington Street. The rest of the tour is self-guiding; all roads lead to Hing Hay Park, a Chinese pavilion donated by the city of Taipei. Individuals are fit into scheduled group tours; admission $2; 624-6342. **Vi Mar Travel,** 803 S. King St., offers Chinatown Discovery Tours for $18.75 (daytime) and $26 (evening), which include a narrated tour plus lunch or dinner; reservations required, 236-0657. For a do-it-yourself tour, the **Wing Luke Memorial Museum** at 414 8th St. S is a good starting point; their changing exhibits of Asian folk art are displayed Tues. through Sun. afternoons; admission $1.50 adults, $.50 kids, 623-5124. King St. is the heart of the district; Chinese shops line both sides. The 2nd-largest Japanese supermarket on the West Coast, **Uwajimaya,** at King and 6th streets, sells everything from groceries to furniture.

Shilshole Bay And Marina

Located N of the city along Seaview Ave. NW, Shilshole Bay and nearby Ballard were the Nordic section of Seattle when immigration from Finland, Norway, and Sweden peaked from 1890-1910. By 1900, Nordic immigrants made up one-fourth of Seattle's wood industry work force, and also significantly contributed to mining, farming, fishing, and shipbuilding. Sivert Sagstad established his Ballard Boat Works in Shilshole Bay 4 months after his arrival, and built more than 300 wooden boats there and at his newer (1916) location at 20th Ave. NW. Today Shilshole Bay is home to the Shilshole Marina, Seattle's major pleasure boat moorage.

Along Seaview are quality seafood restaurants (see p. 53) with Sound views and outdoor decks. One, the rebuilt Ray's Boathouse, is the departure point for **Major Marine Tours'** saltwater fishing trips. Their 48-foot *Emerald Star* departs at 6 a.m. for Puget Sound fishing holes. You're "guaranteed" to catch good edible fish, or the next trip is on them. The 5½-hour trip costs $42 pp, 292-0595. At the N end of Seaview, **Golden Gardens** is one of the Sound's best bathing beaches (real sand!). South of Seaview, on N.W. 54th St., the **Hiram M. Chittenden Government Locks,** 783-7001, connect saltwater Puget Sound with freshwater Lake Washington. Watch the tugs and pleasure craft make the transition, and see the salmon return home to spawn via the fish ladder.

Watching sailboats skim by may inspire you to take up the sport. **Wind Works Sailing School,** headquartered at Shilshole Bay Marina, has "Learn to Sail" packages starting at $47.50 for a 4-hour introductory sail, or $95 for 2 4-hour lessons, available daily year-round. For a skippered trip, charter a sailing excursion to Elliott Bay, Poulsbo, or Bainbridge Island; $160 for 4 hours, $300 for 8 hours, 6-person maximum; 784-9386. Or, board the research vessel *Snow Goose* for one of **Anchor Excursions'** 4-hour marine-science cruises on Puget Sound. A scientific expedition, these cruises depart from Fisherman's Terminal, SE of Chittenden Locks, as demand requires; $15 adults, $10 under 12; 282-8368.

West Seattle

Take Spokane St. to W. Seattle where viewpoints, a scenic drive, a beach, parks, and a bike path await. For photography buffs, **Hamilton Viewpoint** at California Way SW provides a panoramic view of Seattle's skyline, the Cascades, and Elliott Bay, as does **Belvedere Viewpoint** at SW Admiral Way and 36th Ave. SW. For a leisurely scenic drive, proceed up Harbor Ave. SW to **Duwamish Head,** then S on Alki Ave. to **Alki Beach Park,** a long, narrow, sandy stretch—as close to a real beach (outside Golden Gardens, above)

as you'll find on this part of Puget Sound. In warm weather a whole beach culture emerges here: illegally parked cars, bonfires, suntan goop, the works—even though the water rarely gets above 55 degrees, so only the hardiest souls actually go in. Keep going on Alki Ave. to the **Alki Point Light Station.** Tours of the station are available Mon. through Fri., day's notice required; 932-5800. Continue S on Beach Dr. SW to **Lincoln Park's** trails and beach. A bike path follows the same scenic route.

Other Parks

Ranked among the world's best, the **Woodland Park Zoo** features a 5-acre "African savanna" where zebra, lions, and giraffes roam freely. Their "Nocturnal House" is home to bats and other creatures of the dark. Also included are a tropical forest and gorilla habitat. The big field in the middle, with convenient hot-dog stand, is a good place for a lunch break. Between Phinney and Aurora, N. 50th and N. 59th, the zoo opens daily at 8:30 a.m.; admission $3 adults, $1.50 teens, seniors, and kids; 789-7919.

A 3-mile paved bicycle, jogging, and skating loop—watch out for errant skateboards—encompasses **Green Lake** at Green Lake Way N, north of Woodland Park Zoo. Sail and swim to your heart's content, or rent a paddleboat. A "children only" fishing pier is at the E end of the lake. Crocodile hunting was popu-

Sailboats are a common sight year-round in Puget Sound.

lar here in 1986 when assorted reports of a lake creature took on the proportions of a Loch Ness Monster. When the little critter was finally caught, the 3-pound, 28-inch **caiman** was shipped to a private breeder in Kansas City and the lake was unofficially declared crocodile-free.

All but hidden from view in a ravine under the 15th Ave. NE bridge, **Ravenna Park** has 52 acres of woodlands and a babbling brook, accessible via a ¾-mile loop trail, plus a children's play area and soccer field, all in a most unlikely location. Douglas fir, Pacific madrone, western red cedar, bigleaf maple, and English and Pacific yew line the nature trail (borrow a pamphlet from the box at the trailhead). Take I-5 exit 170 (Ravenna Blvd.); turn R at the light, then L on 20th Ave. NE; the street ends at the bridge over the park, and the park entrance is on the right.

North of Shilshole Bay is **Carkeek Park,** N.W. 110th St., where you'll find a beautiful picnic area, playground, hiking, and Puget Sound access via a footbridge over the railroad tracks. If the tide's in, chances are the beach will be out.

At 34th Ave. W and W. Government Way, 535-acre **Discovery Park** is the city's largest, featuring a 2.8-mile loop trail through forest and meadow, with access to 2 miles of Puget Sound beaches, plus the half-mile interpretive Wolf Tree Nature Trail. Discovery Park's West Point is reputedly Seattle's best birding spot, with frequent sightings of loons, grebes, cormorants, terns, and other marine birds. Army memorabilia nuts should visit their **Fort Lawton Military Museum,** while a fine collection of American Indian art and an all-Indian dinner theater are part of the park's **Daybreak Star Indian Cultural Education Center.** If you happen to be here for this irregularly scheduled event, don't miss the authentic ethnic experience, which includes Indian fry bread, alder-smoked salmon, and dancers from various Indian clans. Tickets are about $20; call 285-4425 for reservations. Discovery Park's Visitor Center is open Tues. through Sun.; 625-4636.

Magnolia Park, perched upon a high bluff, affords generous views of Puget Sound and the Olympics from its location on Magnolia

DOWNTOWN SEATTLE

1. Le Tastevin
2. Hansen Baking Co.
3. Jake O'Shaughnessy's
4. Bahn Thai
5. Thai Restaurant
6. Monorail Terminal/Westlake Center
7. Space Needle
8. Best Western Executive Inn
9. AAA Auto Club of Washington
10. Tropics Motor Inn
11. Seattle Times Building
12. Myrtle Edwards Park
13. Old Spaghetti Factory
14. Edgewater Inn
15. Two Bells Tavern
16. Best Western Loyal Inn
17. Days Inn Town Center
18. Regency
19. Jazz Alley
20. Sixth Ave. Inn
21. Warwick Hotel
22. Cutters Bay House
23. Kaleenka Russian Cafe
24. Westin Hotel
25. visitor information
26. Vance Downtown Hotel
27. Greyhound Bus Depot
28. Century Square
29. public fishing pier
30. Victoria Clipper to Victoria, B.C.
31. Seattle Aquarium and Omnidome
32. Rainier Square
33. Four Seasons Olympic Hotel
34. YWCA
35. Hotel Seattle
36. Gray Line Water Sightseeing and public fishing pier
37. Seattle Harbor, Alderbrook Sightseeing, and public fishing pier
38. Creative Northwest
39. Major Marine Tours & Ivar's Acres of clams
40. Washington State Ferry Terminal
41. Ye Olde Curiosity Shop
42. Alexis Hotel
43. public library
44. YMCA
45. Metro
46. Comedy Underground
47. Amtrak
48. Frye Art Museum
49. Egyptian Theatre
50. Intiman Theatre Co.
51. House of Hong
52. Nikko
53. F.X. McRory's

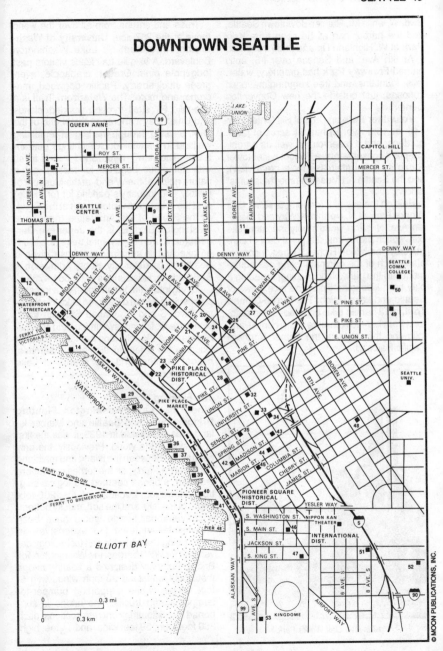

DOWNTOWN SEATTLE

© MOON PUBLICATIONS, INC.

Blvd. W, while Mt. Rainier, downtown Seattle, and the harbor can all be seen from **Kerr Park** at W. Highland Dr. and 2nd Ave. West.

At 6th Ave. and Seneca *over* I-5, aptly named **Freeway Park** has greenery, waterfalls, fountains, and free summertime lunch concerts, just outside the new Convention Center.

Volunteer Park on Capitol Hill (enter from 14th or 15th Ave. E) has 44 acres of lawn, gardens, and a reservoir, as well as a tropical-plant conservatory, a 75-foot water tower (climb its spiral staircase for a great view), and the Seattle Art Museum (see "Museums" below).

Built on the site of a former gas plant, **Gas Works Park** at N. Northlake Way and Meridian Ave. N is the world's only industrial site conversion park. Amidst a great deal of controversy, architect Richard Haag incorporated much of the original rusting gas equipment into the park's landscaping, including a play barn kids love. Enjoy the nice views of Seattle and Lake Union. The **Burke-Gilman Trail,** a 12½-mile bike and pedestrian path, runs from here to Kenmore's Log boom Park, following the route of the former Northern Pacific Railroad.

Kids love Gas Works Park.

Trees and shrubs from all over the world thrive at the 267-acre **University of Washington Arboretum** on Lake Washington Boulevard. A ½-mile trail leads visitors past lodgepole pine, Oregon crabapple, evergreen huckleberry, Pacific dogwood, madrone, and more. The **Waterfront Trail** is a one-mile RT stroll through wooded islands and Union Bay's shores at the N end of the park, passing through the largest remaining wetland in Seattle (duck sightings guaranteed!). The newly refurbished trail is level, with numerous benches for resting; get a nature guide at the W end, at the Museum of History and Industry's parking lot (or inside) or at the Arboretum visitor center at the E end. At the S end of the Arboretum (near Lake Washington Blvd. E) is the **Japanese Garden:** manicured ornamental trees, a secluded lake, and an authentic tea house, given to Seattle by its sister city, Kobe. Admission is $1.50 adults, kids/seniors $.75; 684-4725.

Jutting into Lake Washington on a forested peninsula is **Seward Park,** on Lake Washington Blvd. S and S. Juneau St., with trails, picnic areas, fishing, swimming, and Mt. Rainier views. A 1¾-mile loop trail takes you past Douglas firs 6 feet in diameter, madrones, bigleaf maples, and the shores of Lake Washington.

The Floating Bridges

When the **Lake Washington Floating Bridge,** connecting Seattle and Mercer Island, was completed in 1939, it was the first of its kind in the world. Previously, the only connection between the island and mainland had been via ferry; as the ferries grew more crowded, a bridge seemed the logical solution. However, because of the 200-foot depth of the lake and the soft, mucky bottom, a conventional bridge would have been impossible—at least too expensive!—to build. Using the concrete cell technology developed for WW I barges, the Washington Toll Bridge Authority designed a floating bridge that could withstand 90-mph winds with 6-foot waves, while supporting bumper-to-bumper 20-ton trucks. The bridge is supported by 25 floating concrete sections, each 350 feet long, 59 feet wide, and 14 feet high;

each concrete pontoon contains 96 watertight 14-foot-square compartments, or cells. The pontoons are cabled together and connected to stationary fixtures at either end. When seasonal variations cause the lake level to rise or fall (as much as 3 feet), the pontoons attached to the stationary approaches are flooded or emptied to ensure that the rest of the pontoons maintain their flotation level. The Lake Washington, or Lacey V. Murrow, Floating Bridge, now an everyday part of I- 90 traffic, is just over 1¼ miles long; the **Evergreen Point Floating Bridge,** connecting Seattle with Bellevue and Kirkland on Route 520, is the world's longest at 1.4 miles.

Museums

The **Seattle Art Museum,** Volunteer Park at 14th St. E and Prospect, has an outstanding Oriental art collection, plus photography, sculpture, graphics, and paintings. Open daily till 5 p.m., Thurs. till 9 p.m.; closed Mondays. Admission is $2 adults, $1 students/seniors; 443-4670.

The city's best museum for local history is the **Museum of History and Industry** at 2161 E. Hamlin Street. Exhibits include Boeing's first plane and films and displays of Seattle in the 1880s. Open daily, 324-1125; admission $3 adults, $1.50 kids/seniors. The entire Pacific Northwest, from Petersberg, Alaska, to Eureka, California, has a large Nordic population. Discover the contributions of Seattle's immigrants at rotating exhibits and a small permanent display at the **Nordic Heritage Museum,** 3014 N.W. 67th St., 789-5707. Open daily till 4 p.m., Thurs. till 9 p.m. (closed Mon.); admission $2.50 adults, $1.50 seniors/students, and $1 kids.

The Museum of Flight, 9404 E. Marginal Way S, 764-5720, has displays of the history of aviation in the Pacific Rim. Open daily till 5 p.m., Thurs. till 9 p.m.; admission $4 adults, $3 teens/seniors, $2 kids.

American and European artists of the 19th and 20th centuries are represented in **Frye Museum** at 704 Terry Ave., 622-9250. Open daily till 5 p.m.; free.

the Fine Arts building constructed for the 1909 Alaska-Yukon-Pacific Expo

University Of Washington

The turn-of-the-century "Expo"—the Alaskan-Yukon-Pacific Exposition of 1909—was held on the UW campus. In exchange for use of the grounds, the fair's promoters constructed several permanent buildings and landscaped the grounds, making UW one of the nation's largest and most beautiful single-campus universities. Park your car ($3) and stroll through the grounds: exquisite architecture, fountains, and views of the Evergreen Point Floating Bridge. The Visitor Center is located at 14th Ave. NE and N.E. Campus Parkway. Here also, the **Henry Art Gallery** exhibits 19th- and 20th-century American and European prints, paintings, and ceramics daily except Mon.; $2 admission, 543-2280. Another campus attraction is the **Thomas Burke Memorial Washington State Museum** with North American Indian artifacts and natural history displays, at 17th Ave. NE and N.E. 45th Street. Open daily; phone 543-5590 for hours. Donations requested.

Other Tours

The *Seattle Times,* Fairview Ave. N and John St., 464-2285, offers free one-hour tours of its press room and news departments on Mon., Tues., and Thurs. from Sept. to May. Reservations required; no kids under 9. Take a free tour of **Rainier Brewery** weekdays from 1 p.m.-6 p.m. Kids must be accompanied by an adult. Take Airport Way S (exit from I-5), 622-2600.

ACCOMMODATIONS

See charts on pages 49-51 for inexpensive downtown and airport motels plus moderately priced hotels in the heart of Seattle. The "budget" listings include only those places where you won't be afraid to close your eyes at night, and where a family can feel at ease. If you're on a tight budget, stay near the airport rather than in rundown city center hotels; motels with little more than a bed and shower line Pacific Hwy. S near Sea-Tac and generally display their rates—often $20 or less—on reader boards. From there it's a short $.90 hop on Metro to the city. Some of the B&Bs below also offer clean, friendly accommodations at budget prices. For lodging in neighboring areas, see the cities listed under "Vicinity of Seattle," p. 61. For camping info, see Renton, p. 61, and Federal Way p. 87.

Bed And Breakfasts

B&Bs are popular in the Northwest, and Seattle has its share. In the heart of Pike Place Market at 1923 1st Ave., **Pensione Nichols,** 441-7125, is a new European-style B&B with views of Puget Sound and the Market. Eight antique-furnished guest rooms share 3 baths for a reasonable $45 s, $65 d, including continental breakfast.

The College Inn, 4000 University Way NE, 633-4441, is a budget-priced European-style B&B, with 27 rooms featuring period furnishings, sinks, shared baths, and a deli, pub, and cafe on the 1st floor. Rooms are a steal at $32-39 s, $39-48 d, including continental breakfast; children are welcome.

The Williams House, atop Queen Anne Hill at 1505 4th Ave. N, 285-0810, is a family B&B—the owners have 2 kids of their own to make yours feel welcome! Most of their 5 rooms command city and mountain views (shared and private baths); rates are $60-75 s, $65-85 d. No pets or smoking in the rooms.

Galer Place Bed and Breakfast, 318 W. Galer St., 282-5339, was built as a private south Queen Anne Hill residence in 1906. Today it offers comfortable lodging in antique-furnished rooms, plus all-day tea and lemonade and a bottomless cookie jar. Their 4 rooms, all with private bath, are $65-70 s, $70-80 d. No kids under 12; small pets OK with prior approval; smoking in the lounge or outdoors only.

At 1727 15th Ave., the stately **Gaslight Inn,** 325-3654, has 2 rooms with shared bath at $52-60, 5 rooms with private bath for $64-74, a library, outdoor pool, and continental breakfast. **The Beech Tree Manor,** a turn-of-the-century mansion at 1405 Queen Anne Ave. N, 281-7037, sits atop Queen Anne Hill with convenient access to downtown Seattle via trolley. The 4-bedroom, 3-bath inn features English decor, period fireplace, and wicker rockers on the shady porch. Rooms are $60-70 s, $65-75 d. Smoking outdoors only; kids over 5 are welcome.

Chelsea Station, 4915 Linden Ave. N, 547-6077, is directly across from the rose gardens at the S entrance to Woodland Park Zoo, within walking distance of Green Lake. Enjoy a hot tub, endless supply of cookies, all-day coffee and tea, and a library of books to help with your sightseeing. Three guest rooms, each with private bath, are $69 s or d; 2 spacious suites, also with private bath, offer uncommon comfort for $85. No pets or smoking, kids 12 and over OK.

Chambered Nautilus, 5005 22nd Ave. NE, 522-2536, offers Cascade views on a hill within walking distance of UW and just 10 minutes from downtown. The Georgian colonial home was built in 1915 by Dr. Herbert Gowen, founder of yoo-dub's Department of Oriental Studies. Their 6 rooms go for $60-89 d; 2 have private baths. No indoor smoking or pets; kids under 12 by prior arrangement.

Some of the cities surrounding Seattle have less expensive B&Bs; check them out in "Vicinity of Seattle," p. 61. For a wider selection call **Pacific Bed and Breakfast,** 701 N.W.

SEATTLE BUDGET LODGING

Name	Address	Phone	Rates	Comments
Best Western Continental Plaza	2500 Aurora Ave. N	284-1900	44-64 s 50-66 d	restaurant, pool
Best Western Loyal Inn	2301 8th Ave.	682-0200	44-62 s 48-68 d	jacuzzi, sauna
Days Inn Town Center	2205 7th Ave.	448-3434	49 s or d	coffee shop
Marco Polo Motel	4114 Aurora Ave.	633-4090	28 s 30-34 d	
Rodeside Lodge	12501 Aurora Ave. N	364-7771	36-50 s 39-55 d	exit 174 N/175 S; exercise room, pool
TraveLodge	200 6th Ave. N	441-7878	48-54 s 54-70 d	near Space Needle; pool
TraveLodge	2213 8th Ave.	624-6300	45-54 s 50-66 d	
Tropics Motor Inn	225 Aurora Ave.	728-7666	36-58 s 38-60 d	indoor pool, restaurant
Vance Downtown Hotel	620 Stewart St.	441-4200	41-46 s 47-54 d	restaurant
YMCA	909 4th Ave.	382-5000	25-39 s 31-50 d	men/women; use of facilities
YWCA	1118 5th Ave.	447-4888	21-26 s 32-37 d	women and kids only

60th St., 784-0539, a reservation service for more than 200 B&Bs in the Seattle area.

Luxury Accommodations

The Warwick, Fourth and Lenora, caters to the well-heeled traveler or expense-account utilizer. Their 230 rooms go for $125-145 s, $150-170 d, with suites—living room, panoramic city views, and personal whirlpool—starting at $325. Even the basic rooms include a marble bath with handy bathside telephone, plus a wet bar, refrigerator, balcony, use of the hotel's indoor pool, sauna, whirlpool, and fitness center, and complimentary transportation within downtown Seattle. Their restaurant, the **Liaison,** serves seafood, steak, and chicken accompanied by a relaxing piano concerto. The Warwick's weekend packages start at $100 d and include such goodies as breakfast in bed, gourmet chocolates, and Champagne. For information and reservations (ask about half-off weekend specials) call (800) 426-9280 or 625-6700.

For luxurious accommodations with a European flair, try the **Alexis** at 1st and Madi-

LODGING NEAR SEA-TAC AIRPORT

Name	Address	Phone	Rates	Comments
Airporter Inn Motel	14845 Pac. Hwy. S	248-1061	23 s/29 d	shuttle
Allstar Inn	16500 Pac. Hwy. S	246-4101	25 s/32 d	shuttle
Best Western Airport Executel	20717 Pac. Hwy. S	878-1814	69-80 s 75-86 d	pool, hot tub, exercise room, bar, restaurant, shuttle
Comfort Inn	19333 Pac. Hwy. S	878-1100	52-54 s 58-60 d	shuttle, sauna, jacuzzi
Hilton	17620 Pac. Hwy. S	244-4800	89-113 s 104-128 d	pool, hot tub, shuttle, restaurant, bar
Holiday Inn	17338 Pac. Hwy. S	248-1000	72-88 s 82-98 d	pool, bar, restaurant, shuttle
Imperial Inn	17108 Pac. Hwy. S	244-1230	34 s/37-40 d	shuttle, pool
La Quinta	2824 S. 188th St.	241-5211	56-61 s 64-69 d	shuttle
Mini-Rate	20620 Pac. Hwy. S	248-2442	29 s/35 d	shuttle, car rentals
Motel 6	18900 47th Ave. S	241-1648	25 s/31 d	pool
Nendel's	16838 Pac. Hwy. S	248-0901	42-48 s 48-54 d	shuttle
Nendel's Value Inn	13910 Pac. Hwy. S	244-0810	39-49 s 44-56 d	pool, hot tub, shuttle, exercise room
Quality Inn	3000 S. 176th St.	246-9110	51-55 s 59-65 d	pool, bar, restaurant, shuttle
Ramada	18118 Pac. Hwy. S	244-6666	61-95 s 71-105 d	across from airport, indoor pool, bar, restaurant, exercise room
Red Lion	18740 Pac. Hwy. S	246-8600	100-115 s 100-125 d	2 restaurants, bar, shuttle, pool
Sandstone Inn	19225 Pac. Hwy. S	824-1350	42 s/44-52 d	shuttle, bar, restaurant
Sea-Tac Crest	18845 Pac. Hwy. S	433-0999	32 s/36-48 d	shuttle
Super 8	3100 S. 192nd St.	433-8188	39 s/42-46 d	shuttle, laundry
Tac-Sea	17024 Pac. Hwy. S	241-6511	24 s/30 d	
West Coast Sea-Tac Hotel	18220 Pac. Hwy. S	246-5535	54-64 s 58-65 d	sauna, hot tub, pool, shuttle

son; (800) 426-7033 or 624-4844. Take your choice of 18 styles of guest rooms, all decorated in subdued, classic colors, from fireplace suites ($275) to courtyard rooms ($145 s, $160 d) to the cheapies ($95 s or d). Every guest receives a bottle of sherry upon arrival, nighttime turndown service, a shoeshine, continental breakfast, morning paper, and use of the steam room. Their restaurant (same name) is about the only Seattle hotel restaurant that draws customers from outside its confines, particularly for its expensive (over $60 for 2) seafood.

The **Four Seasons Olympic Hotel** 411 University St., (800) 828-1188 or 621-1700, opened as the posh Olympic Hotel in 1924, had been sorely neglected for years. Prior to its 1982 reopening, Four Seasons Hotels from Toronto invested $60 million in the renovation of the Italian Renaissance-style hotel where senators and presidents stayed during its earlier era of elegance. Today the hotel still hosts political celebrities in its silk-wallcovered, $800-a-night Presidential Suite, as well as the proletariat in its $95-160 singles, $111-235 doubles. All guests receive twice-daily

SEATTLE MODERATE LODGING

Name	Address	Phone	Rates	Comments
Best Western Executive Inn	200 Taylor Ave. N	448-9444	63-94 s 70-100 d	near Space Needle; restaurant, bar, shuttle, some rooms jacuzzi, wet bar
Edgewater Inn	Pier 67 2411 Alaskan Way	624-7000	70-90 s 85-105 d	higher-priced rooms overlook bay
Inn at the Market	Pike Place Market 86 Pine St.	443-3600	75-180 s 85-180 d	French country design; most rooms have view; rooftop deck
Hotel Seattle	315 Seneca St.	623-5110	48-52 s 54-58 d	restaurant
Mayflower Park	405 Olive Way	623-8700	66-77 s 74-85 d	near shopping; bar, restaurant
Meany Tower	4507 Brooklyn NE	634-2000	69-79 s 79-93 d	near UW; all rooms have lake/mountain view; bar, restaurant
Quality Inn City Center	2224 8th Ave.	624-6820	47-57 s 52-62 d	restaurant
Ramada Inn	2140 N. Northgate Ave.	365-0700	75-80 s 85-90 d	exit 173; pool
Sixth Avenue Inn	2000 6th Ave.	441-8300	54-61 s 54-61 d	restaurant
West Coast Camlin	1619 9th Ave.	682-0100	69-72 s or d	luxury for less; restaurant, lounge

maid service, 1-hour pressing, shoeshines, evening turndown service, ribbons on their laundered socks, and chocolates on their pillows. The **Georgian,** the hotel's French restaurant, serves breakfast from $5, lunches from $12, and dinners up to $30 à la carte under the original hotel's crystal chandeliers. For dinner reservations call (800) 828-1188.

The **Westin Hotel,** twin corncobs at 1900 5th Ave., (800) 228-3000 or 728-1000, is another of the city's most luxurious hotels. Standard rates for the 865 rooms start at $110 s, $135 d, escalating to $200 d if you'd like a view. The Westin has all the usual: sauna, pool, exercise center with fitness specialists, piano bar, plus 3 restaurants, including **Trader Vic's** for Polynesian-style food and **The Palm Court,** a *Travel/Holiday* award winner. The good news is you can get 50 percent off on weekends.

The **Holiday Inn Crowne Plaza,** 6th and Seneca, 464-1980, is among the best in town, though perhaps less elaborate in appearance. Weekday room rates are $125-155 s, $125-175 d; enjoy their quality surroundings, including sauna, hydrotherapy pool, and exercise room, in the heart of downtown for as little as $76 s or d on weekends.

FOOD AND DRINK

Entire books have been written on dining in the Emerald City; probably the best restaurant-and-everything-else guide to Seattle is *Seattle Best Places* by David Brewster (see "Booklist"); Brewster's other tome, *Northwest Best Places,* offers restaurant and lodging reviews for Washington, Oregon, and B.C. What follows here is a tiny percentage of what's available.

Dinner With A View
So many cityscapes, plus lakes, mountains, and boats are in and around Seattle that view restaurants are commonplace. **Cutter's Bay House,** at 2001 Western Ave., 448-4884, just up the street from Pike Place Market, has a lively bar with a long list of hors d'oeuvres; their specialties—Mako shark, fresh Northwest fish, and regular pasta and steak dishes—are moderately priced ($10-12 aver-

age), accompanied by an extensive wine-by-the-glass list and imported beers served at their proper temperatures. Sunsets over the Olympics are striking.

Ivar's Captain's Table, perhaps the best of the late Ivar Haglund's 22 restaurants and fish bars, serves fresh seafood amid Elliott Bay and Olympic views at 333 Elliott Ave. W; 284-7040. **Ivar's Acres of Clams,** on the waterfront at Pier 54, was the folksinger's original restaurant, open since 1938; prior to his restaurateur days, Haglund sang a ballad called "Acres of Clams" telling of the Sound's then-lonely beaches resting atop a wealth of clams. **Maximilien's** French restaurant-cafe in Pike Place Market offers bay and mountain views, open from breakfast to dinner with moderate prices; 682-7270.

The **Mirabeau** restaurant atop the black Sea-First Building at 1001 4th Ave., 624-4550, is known more for its spectacular city view, as seen from 46th-floor ceiling-to-floor windows, than for its expensive steak and seafood (not for the acrophobic). When it was completed in 1968, the Sea-First Building was not-so-affectionately called "the big ugly" or "the box the Space Needle came in." Enjoy a sweeping Elliott Bay view along with excellent—and expensive—seafood, steaks, and pasta at **The Other Place,** 96 Union St., 623-7340.

Shilshole Bay And Marina
A number of restaurants on Shilshole Bay are worthy of mention, if not for their seafood then at least for their spectacular sunsets. As you drive from the locks toward the marina and Golden Gardens (see G.G. in Parks Section) restaurants are all on the L, or water, side.

Hiram's at the Locks, 5300 34th NW, 784-1733, undeservedly maligned by some Seattle restaurant critics in the past, serves steak and seafood that is properly prepared and simply delicious ($15-20), plus a popular Sunday brunch. Besides, it's fun to watch the Chittenden Locks in action. Just up the street, **Ray's Boathouse,** 6049 Seaview, 789-3770, came back better than ever after a fire destroyed the restaurant in 1987. A bit expensive, but the seafood is great, and so is the view—reservations are a must. **Anthony's**

view from the Space Needle Restaurant

Homeport, just up the road with moderately priced fresh fish and a saucy cioppino, has Sunday brunch too; 783-0780.

Lake Union

Ivar's Salmon House, on Lake Union at 401 N.E. Northlake Way, 632-0767, is famous for its alder-smoked salmon but also offers prime rib and barbecued chicken in a cedar facsimile of an Indian longhouse. **Franco's Hidden Harbor,** 1500 Westlake Ave. N, 282-0501, has a mellow harbor view, particularly hypnotic over a Champagne Sunday brunch. **Liz's,** across the street from Franco's at 1515 Westlake Ave. N, serves homemade soups, sandwiches, chili, and some of the best burgers in town, for lunch or dinner daily. **Lake Union Cafe** has free live comedy with its seafood and pasta dinners Thurs. through Sun. nights; 323-8855. **Triple's,** 1200 Westlake N, 284-2535, specializes in seafood with a varying menu ranging from Hawaiian *kiawe*-grilled fish to Norwegian salmon to sushi. **Latitude 47,** 1232 Westlake Ave. N, 284-1047, serves fresh salmon and 40 other seafood items on the shores of Lake Union; open for lunch and dinner plus Sunday brunch.

Seattle Center

The Center House is lined on 2 levels with fast-food restaurants serving everything from Mexican food to apple strudel. The **Space Needle Restaurant** is a top-of-the-world dining experience at 600 feet, very popular with tourists, visiting relatives, and teens on prom night. As much as it seems a tired cliché, the food is good and the view is unsurpassed, as the revolving restaurant completes a 360-degree turn by the time you get to dessert. Summer Sunday Champagne brunches, are a moderately priced way to see the daytime views unfold; 443-2100. The **Emerald Suite,** adjacent to the Space Needle restaurant at the top of the tower, is a little dressier (restaurant *and* patrons) and a tad more expensive; 443-2150.

Foreign Flavors

As you might guess, the International District is loaded with Chinese restaurants. Among the best is **House of Hong,** 409 8th S, with seafood, chicken, and Hong Kong barbecue. For Japanese chow, the International District has **Mikado,** home of one of the city's best sushi bars at 514 S. Jackson and well-known for their fresh fish. **Nikko,** 1306 S. King, 322-4905, is best known for their sushi bar, accompanied by a moderately priced Japanese menu. For Thai cuisine try the **Thai Restaurant** at 101 John St. N, 285-9000, or **Bahn Thai,** 409 Roy St., 283-0444; both are inexpensive and popular with the locals.

European taste buds can feel at home in Seattle too. For French cuisine, **Le Tastevin** at 19 W. Harrison St., 283-0991, is considered by many to be the best, though pricey; also noteworthy is **Le Gourmand,** fairly expensive, at 425 N.W. Market St. in Ballard, 784-3463.

Enjoy an Italian feast at Pioneer Square at **Umberto's,** 100 S. King St., 621-0575; it's a little on the expensive side, but worth it. **Paparazzi,** 2202 N. 45th St., 547-7772, has more moderately priced Italian meals. Try **Labuznik** (Czech for "Lover of Good Food") at 1924 1st Ave., 682-1624, for a high-priced Czechoslovakian dinner, or **Kaleenka Russian Cafe,** a homey, lace-curtained change of pace at 1933 1st Ave., 728-1278.

Others
Cafe Sport, 2020 Western Ave. at the N end of Pike Place Market, 443-6000, is one of the most popular spots in town, serving lunch to the exercise nuts next door and dinner to people who love good food, with an emphasis on Northwest specialties; breakfast is a treat of omelets, waffles, and more; moderate prices. At 100 Mercer, **Jake O'Shaughnessy's,** 285-1897, has good steak, fresh seafood, and giant stuffed potatoes big enough to share for moderate prices, plus a noisy Irish bar that warrants a visit. Join the crowds for oysters, steak, or just a beer at **F.X. McRory's** before and after Kingdome events; it's just across the street from the Kingdome's parking lot at 4199 Occidental Ave. S, 623-4800. Open weekdays for lunch, daily for dinner. **Noggins** at Westlake Center brews its own beer and serves big burgers and sandwiches, English pub style; pick up your order at the counter. **Thirteen Coins** is open 24 hours, offering over 100 menu items in 2 locations: 125 Boren Ave. N, 682-2513, in downtown Seattle or 18000 Pacific Hwy. S, 243-9500, near Sea-Tac Airport. For those on tight budgets, **The Dog House,** 2230 7th Ave., has probably the best-value eats in town and a rowdy bunch at the piano bar. **The Old Spaghetti Factory,** across from Pier 70 at 2801 Elliott Ave., is always noisy, good, and inexpensive—a popular family spot—with a pasta-only menu that stays under $8; 441-7724. For a quick burger or sandwich try the **Two Bells Tavern,** a small, artsy bar at 2313 4th Avenue. **Olympia Pizza and Spa-**

ghetti House, 1500 Queen Anne Ave., 285-5550, or 1330 N. 45th St., 633-3655, serves some of the city's best pizza, plus pasta and subs. When the chains lose their charm, try **El Puerco Lloron,** 1501 Western Ave. on the Pike Place Market Hillclimb, 624-0541. "The Crying Pig" is inexpensive, a good place to take the kids, and the food is fresh, genuine Mexican fare. **El Toreador,** 9747 4th Ave. NW, 784-4132, is another popular, inexpensive Mexican spot.

ENTERTAINMENT

Nightlife
The best guide to Seattle's current goings-on is *The Weekly,* a $.75 weekly newsmagazine with concert info, club dates, restaurant reviews, movie, lecture, sports, dance, and theater listings—everything a visitor needs. *The Weekly* is available at stores or in paper boxes throughout the city. The *Seattle Times* and *Seattle Post-Intelligencer* also have weekly entertainment sections in their Fri. editions.

New wave may come and go, but jazz lives on in Seattle, particularly at **Dimitriou's Jazz Alley,** 6th and Lenora, where big-time national acts and up-and-coming talent can be heard. No cover charge—food and drink prices make up the difference. The **New Orleans Restaurant,** 81 Yesler Way, besides having popular Creole food, serves up Dixieland jazz on Mon. nights with varying performances on weekends. Ballard's **Owl Cafe,** 5140 Ballard NW, has been staging "Dixieland Sundays" for the past 5 years with other types of music during the week.

For a taste of salsa music try **La Esquina** at 5000 Rainier South. The **Old Ballard Firehouse,** 5429 Russell Ave., serves up reggae, jazz, blues, and more, often from top-name artists.

Seattle's biggest comedy club is **Comedy Underground,** 222 S. Main St., where local and national talents perform for capacity crowds. **Giggles,** another comedy club at 5220 Roosevelt Way NE, has cheap food and beer with local, smaller-time acts.

For a bar with a view, check out the view restaurants listed above at Shilshole Bay, the waterfront, Lake Union, and of course, the Space Needle (where, if you're not having dinner, you have to pay the $3.75 elevator fee). In addition, the **Cloud Room** atop the Camlin Hotel at 1619 9th Ave. has great cityscape and Lake Union views. The **Adriatica,** 1107 Dexter Ave. N, offers a view of Lake Union and the Cascades. More casual drinking can be enjoyed on **Red Robin's** outdoor deck overlooking Portage Bay at the corner of Eastlake E and Fuhrman E; their extensive list of gourmet hamburgers is a plus. The sunset view draws the crowds to **Ray's Boathouse,** 609 Seaview Ave. NW at Shilshole Bay.

The bars at **Jake O'Shaughnessy's,** 100 Mercer, and **F.X. McRory's,** across from the Kingdome at 4199 Occidental Ave. S, are at least as popular as the restaurants themselves. For 24-hour food (diner price and quality) plus a rowdy piano bar, try **The Dog House** at 2230 7th Avenue.

Pub Tours

Groups of 6 or more can enjoy an escorted tour of 3 or 4 Seattle pubs and alehouses, complete with van transportation, free beer samples and snacks, and souvenirs. Tours average 3½ hours and can be scheduled for the afternoon or evening; $22 pp. Call Towerbridge Marketing, 547-1186, for schedule and information.

Sports

Major league sports are thoroughly represented in Seattle. Baseball's **Mariners,** playing at the Kingdome to generally diminutive crowds, make for lively, if not victorious, entertainment. The money lost on ticket sales is apparently recovered at the concessions: beware the $4 beer. Also, *all* beer purchasers must show ID; even a bald head and false teeth won't get you by. Call 628-3555 for ticket and schedule information. The NFL's **Seahawks,** 827-9766, draw good crowds at the Kingdome, as do the NBA's **Supersonics** at the Seattle Center Coliseum; 281-5850. Seahawks tickets are scarce—most are sold to season-ticket holders—but the Sonics are generally not sold out until the day of the game, if ever. The Seattle **Thunderbirds,**

728-9124, play minor-league hockey at the Seattle Center Arena for the Western Hockey League from Oct. to May; tickets run $4.50-$7.50. College sports are big here too, particularly the **University of Washington's** (pronounced yoo-dub) Husky football (543-2200) and basketball (543-2200) teams. Other big Seattle-area sporting events are nearly year-round auto and motorcycle racing at **Seattle International Raceway,** 31001 144th in Kent, 631-1550, and thoroughbred racing at **Longacres** in nearby Renton (see p. 61) during the summer months.

The Arts

Theatergoers have lots of options. **The Seattle Repertory Theatre** produces 6 plays, from Oct. to May, at the Bagley-Wright Theater at Seattle Center, 443-2222. **ACT** (A Contemporary Theatre), fills out the other half of the year, performing at 100 W. Roy; 285-5110. **Pioneer Square Theater's** Mainstage, a former burlesque joint at 512 2nd Ave., and 2 smaller stages host local and national dramas and comedies, including Seattle's longest-running production, *Angry Housewives,* going strong for over 5 years; phone 622-2016 for tickets. The **Intiman Theatre Company** brings classic theater to Seattle from June through Nov. at Seattle Center's Intiman Playhouse, 626-0782.

Seattle Center Opera House hosts the **Seattle Opera Association,** 443-4711, whose Sept. to May regular season is highlighted by the special July performance of "Ring of the Nibelungen" in German (not scheduled for 1990). The Opera House is also home to the **Seattle Symphony** from Oct. through April, 443-4747; the **Seattle Youth Symphony,** 362-2300, which will make you wish you'd practiced more; and the **Pacific Northwest Ballet** from Oct. to May, which produces the traditional "Nutcracker" for Christmas, 628-0888.

Movies

For rainy-day moviegoing, **Cinerama** at 2100 4th Ave., 443-0808, and **UA Cinema 150** at 6th and Blanchard, 728-1622, offer first-run movies in a standard movie-house atmosphere, as do the cinemas at Northgate and

Southcenter malls. The **Egyptian Theatre** at 801 E. Pine, 323-4978, and **Market Theatre** at 1428 Post Alley, 382-1171, are both part of the annual **Seattle International Film Festival** held in May; they show off-the-beaten-track films the remainder of the year.

Festivals And Events

Chinese New Year is celebrated in late Jan. or early Feb. when the International District comes alive with parades and colorful displays; call 623-8171 for info. **Fat Tuesday** is Seattle's week-long Mardi Gras celebration at Pioneer Square in Feb., with jazz and Cajun music, arts and crafts, and a parade. The **University Street Fair** brings over 400 artists to display their wares on University Way NE on the 3rd weekend in May. Musicians, dancers, and craftspeople display their talents while enormous amounts of food are consumed at the **Northwest Folklife Festival** held at Seattle Center on Memorial Day weekend; 684-7300. Over 1,500 runners participate in July's **Emerald City Marathon**, 285-4847. Seattle's biggest fair of the year, **Seafair,** 623-7100, is a 3-week-long extravaganza of crafts, parades, triathlons, and ethnic festivals, culminating in the unlimited hydroplane races on Lake Washington in early August. New restrictions on alcohol consumption

have made the infamous rowdy, beer-guzzling hydroplane crowds a thing of the past. **Bumbershoot,** Seattle's Labor Day weekend arts festival, brings writers, performing artists, and craftpeople together at Seattle Center, 684-7200. The holiday season brings the **Christmas Ships Parade,** a lighted flotilla that cruises Lake Washington in mid-Dec.; the Visitors and Convention Bureau, 447-7273, has route and viewing information.

SHOPPING

Unlike most other cities around the Sound, Seattle's downtown shopping district has not died out under the pressure of surrounding suburban malls. In fact, downtown shopping is more alive than ever, with the addition of **Westlake Center** at 5th Ave. and Pine St. and **Century Square** at 4th Ave. and Pike Street. Top-shelf jewelry, perfume, art, leather goods, and clothing stores abound; slogging around in torn jeans and a sweatshirt just won't cut it here. The giants still lurk downtown as well: **Nordstrom** and **Frederick and Nelson** at 5th and Pine, **The Bon** at 4th and Pine, **I. Magnin** at 6th and Pine. Another downtown shopping center is **Rainier Square** at 4th Ave. and Union St., with smaller, tastefully refined—and expensive—shops, including the **Lynn McAllister Gallery,** with a fine collection of Northwest paintings, prints, art glass, and sculptures. On 5th near University, **Wild Wings** specializes in wildlife and Western art, with limited edition prints by Bateman, Parker, Maass, and more, plus duck stamp prints and wood carvings. Seattle's **Waterfront** and, up the hillclimb, **Pike Place Market** are loaded with tiny wine shops, boutiques, craft stores, plus the big, obvious produce stands and tourist traps; see pages 38 and 40 for a detailed description of these areas. **Pioneer Square** offers some of the city's finest galleries, antiques, and book and clothing stores; see p. 40. The **Elliott Bay Book Company,** 101 S. Main St., 624-6600, is something of a local legend, with both a good selection and wonderful atmosphere, plus cafe and monthly readings. **University Bookstore,** across from UW at 4326

University Way NE, is reputedly the nation's largest bookstore, carrying an impressive array of books plus office supplies, clothing, cameras, records, and more. **The Hansen Baking Co.** at the foot of Queen Anne Hill, 100 Mercer St., houses shops and restaurants in a block of renovated early 20th-century buildings. Shopping malls abound in the Seattle area, the biggest being the **Northgate Shopping Mall** 7 miles N of Seattle (exit 173 from I-5), the **Southcenter Mall,** down I-5 into Tukwila, and **Bellevue Square** (see "Vicinity of Seattle" below).

Photographers can stock up on supplies or have their film processed at **Cameras West,** 1908 4th Ave., 622-0066. Other services include in-shop camera repairs and quantity film discounts; open daily, free parking.

You'll find one of the widest selections of Northwest wines at, believe it or not, **Safeway** grocery stores. The prices are low and you can pick up your cheese and crackers at the same time. Shop at the one nearest you: 530 Broadway E (closest to downtown), 3020 N.E. 45th in the University district, 516 1st W in the Queen Anne section, and 3920 Stone Way N in the Wallingford area. If your tastes run closer to Europe, try the tiny brick **Esquin Wine Merchants** shop at 1516 1st Ave. S, 682-7374; big on Italian wines, they also carry Northwest varieties and offer tastings, classes, and low prices. **Pike and Western Wine Merchants** at the Pike Place Market has groceries, Northwest wines, a Northwest wine expert, and European selections.

Shoppers are drawn to Pike Place Market and stores along the hillclimb.

SERVICES

For information on Seattle attractions and events, plus maps or other assistance contact the **Seattle-King County Convention and Visitors Bureau,** 666 Stewart St., Seattle, WA 98101, 461-5840. Statewide information is available toll-free by calling (800) 541-WASH (out-of-state) or (800) 562-4570 (statewide). Whether you're a member or not, the **AAA Travel Store** at 330 6th Ave. N is a good source of maps and area information plus travel guidebooks, luggage, and other travel-related accessories. You might find the information you need for free at the main branch of the **Seattle Public Library,** 1000 4th Ave.; 625-4952.

For an automobile emergency, call **AAA** (if you're a member) at 292-5353. For mountain pass conditions, call the State Department of Transportation at 1-976-7623 (for $.35) from Nov. to March.

Exchange foreign currency at **First Interstate Bank,** 1215 4th Ave., 292-3111; **Rainier Bank,** 1301 5th Ave., 621-4111; **Westin Hotel,** 5th and Westlake, 624-7400; **Four Seasons Olympic Hotel,** 411 University St., 621-1700.

TRANSPORTATION

Arriving By Air
Flying in, you arrive at **Sea-Tac Airport,** midway between Seattle and Tacoma. If you've got a touch-tone phone handy, call (800) 544-1965 or 431-4444 for updates on airport park-

ing, weather and traffic conditions, ground transportation schedules and rates, and other airport services. **Gray Line Airport Express** has airport pick-up service to and from 9 downtown hotels about every half-hour; $5.50 OW adults, $4 OW kids, 626-6088. **Shuttle Express,** (800) 942-0711 or 286-4800, has door-to-door limo-van service from Sea-Tac to downtown Seattle ($7-12 OW), Everett, and Tacoma ($12-15 OW). **Metro's** buses #174 and #194 run between Sea-Tac and downtown Seattle about every half-hour; OW fare is $.85 off-peak, $1 peak; 447-4800. **Suburban Airporter,** 455-2353, runs between the east side (Bellevue, Kirkland, Issaquah, etc.) and Sea-Tac for $9-22. To do it the easy way, grab a cab on the airport's second level; they're all required to charge the same rates—$17.50 to $24, depending on destination and number of passengers, OW to Seattle.

Arriving By Train
Amtrak serves Seattle at its King St. station (3rd Ave. S and S. King St.); 464-1930 or (800) USA-RAIL. The *Coast Starlight* has daily service connecting Seattle with Tacoma, Portland, and S to San Francisco and LA; the *Pioneer* connects Seattle with Salt Lake City (also daily); and the *Mount Rainier* connects Seattle and Portland.

Getting Around By Bus
Metro buses run from 6 a.m.-1 a.m. every day, about every 30 minutes on the city routes. The Metro customer assistance office is at 2nd and Marion; get a handy one- or 3-day pass. If you ride outside the "Magic Carpet" area—a free zone extending from the waterfront to 6th Ave. and from S. Jackson to Battery—fares are $.55 off-peak, $.65 peak within the city, $.85 off-peak, or $1 peak outside city limits. Call 447-4800 (24 hours) or (800) 542-7876 for info.

Trailways, 728-5955, provides daily service to Vancouver, B.C., via Everett and Anacortes, and loop service N through Whidbey Island to Anacortes, Everett, and back 3

times a week. **Greyhound,** the bigger carrier, serves Vancouver, B.C. to the N; Portland, San Francisco, Los Angeles, and San Diego to the S; Port Angeles to the W; and eastern Washington from their terminal at 9th and Stewart; 624-3456.

Getting Around By Car
Driving around downtown Seattle is much more difficult than walking, because at some point you've got to park the car. Diamond and U-Park lots are scattered throughout the city; rates rise with the desirability of the area; $4 for up to 2 hours near the waterfront, but they generally have empty spaces. The cheaper metered spaces are taken the moment they're surrendered, but if you're fortunate enough to get one, remember to put money in—the meter readers are fleet of foot. By all means avoid the 4 p.m.-5 p.m. weekday rush hour, when I-5 and the floating bridges in particular are virtual parking lots. One of the more difficult aspects of Seattle city driving isn't getting there, but getting *back:* finding an I-5 entrance ramp can be frustrating, especially after you zig-zag over and under the highway a few times. One sure cure: head for the black glass Park Place building (the city's tallest) via 5th Ave.; signs for both N and S entrances are right across the street from the building.

Air Tours
To see the city from about 1,500 feet, try one of **Chrysler Air's** 20-minute scenic floatplane rides over Seattle; only $22.50 pp, 2-person minimum. Longer flights are available to Mt. St. Helens, Mt. Rainier, or the San Juan Islands for $130 per hour for 1-3 people and $155 per hour for 4-5 people. Flights take off and land at Lake Union 7 days a week, year-round; reservations are recommended but not required, 329-9638.

Bus Tours
Gray Line, 626-5208 or (800) 426-7532, offers a number of Puget Sound tours. Discover Seattle with a 2½-hour tour highlighted

by the Ballard locks, Kingdome, UW, and waterfront for $16 adults, $8 kids 5-12; operates year-round. A 6-hour city tour, offered March through Nov., includes the Space Needle, UW, International District, and Chittenden Locks for $24 adults, $12 kids. A 6- hour land and water excursion runs April through Oct. for $29 adults, $14.50 kids. Gray Line has several other sightseeing trips, including 1-day tours to Victoria, B.C., Blake Island, the San Juans, Mt. Rainier, and Everett's Boeing 747/767 plant, plus 3-day tours combining several Puget Sound attractions (see below for harbor and Blake Island tours).

Don and Diane FunTours offers scheduled 1-day tours throughout western Washington, including a cruise aboard the *Goodtime III* in December's Christmas Ships Parade on Lake Washington for $38. Write them at Box 21007, Seattle, WA 98111, for a current brochure, or call 282-3508.

Harbor Tours

A number of boat tours and ferry services depart from Seattle's waterfront, providing a relaxing, scenic change of pace for the foot-weary traveler. Probably the most popular is offered by **Seattle Harbor Tours;** their 1-hour informative tour of Elliott Bay and the waterfront describes the hows and whys of containerized shipping along with historical background. The tours depart at least 3 times daily from Pier 55 starting in April (weekends only) with daily service from May through Oct.; $6.50 for adults, $3 kids, 623-1445. No reservations necessary.

Gray Line Water Sightseeing operates from April through Oct., taking you to Elliott Bay from Lake Union via the Lake Washington ship canal and Government Locks. Their 3-hour narrated tour costs $16.50 adults, $8.50 kids. Reservations are required: 626-5208.

Departing hourly from Pier 54, **Major Marine Tours** offers 1-hour narrated tours of Elliott Bay, complete with barbecued chicken at no extra charge. Tours run from June to mid-Sept. $7.50 for adults, $5 kids. Leave the kids with a sitter and enjoy a night out aboard

1 of Seattle's premier nightclubs, the *Emerald Sea.* Enjoy a fully licensed bar, appetizers, and dancing on this 2-hour cruise (mid-June to mid-Sept.); fares are $6 (must be over 21). Major Marine Tours also offers a 1½-hour dinner cruise, with live music and a grilled chicken dinner for $16 adults, $10 kids up to 12. Reservations are suggested for all of these tours; phone 292-0595.

Tillicum Village Tour

For a full-day trip including dinner, try Gray Line's **Tillicum Village Excursion** to Blake Island, a state park accessible only by boat. Enjoy a salmon bake, interpretive Indian dances, craft displays, nature trails, and Indian artifacts. Departing from the Seattle waterfront, the 5½-hour tour is available daily from May through mid-Oct.; fares are $34 adults, $17 kids 2-12. Reservations required: 626-5208.

Victoria Cruises

For an all-day excursion, take the *Victoria Clipper* from Pier 63 to Ogden Point in Victoria. Reservations are required for the 2½-hour cruise: 448-5000 or (800) 888-2535. The round-trip cruise can be completed in 1 day (8:30 a.m. departure and 9:30 p.m. return) while allowing a generous stay in Olde English Victoria. Round-trip fares are $69 mid-May to mid-Sept., $55 off season, for adults; $59 for kids/seniors in summer, $44 off season.

BC Stena Line's *Victoria Island Princess* departs Pier 69 for Victoria, B.C., at least once daily, year-round. Getting there is half the fun, with a Scandinavian buffet, gaming rooms, and live entertainment on each cruise. Fares start at $22 OW adults. Vehicles can be brought along (starting at $40 OW for car and driver), but do make reservations; phone (800) 962-5984 or 624-6986 for more information.

Hood Canal Cruise

Another day-long adventure is the **Alderbrook Sightseeing Cruise,** departing from

Pier 56 at 9 a.m. and arriving at the Alderbrook Inn Resort on the Olympic Peninsula at noon. The cruise takes you into Hood Canal, past the Trident nuclear submarine base, and beneath the Hood Canal floating bridge. Have lunch at the Alderbrook and return to Seattle at 6 p.m., or stay on at the resort. The cruises run from May to Oct. on most Sun., Tues., and Thurs. mornings; RT fares are $30 adults, $25 seniors, and $20 kids under 12, 623-1445.

Getting Around By Ferry

Washington State Ferries depart from Pier 52 for Winslow and Bremerton, giving you an inexpensive harbor tour. To either destination, car-and-driver fares are $6.65 OW; passengers and walk-ons pay only $3.30 RT. The Fauntleroy ferry dock in west Seattle serves Southworth on the Kitsap Peninsula every 30-50 minutes for the same rates as the Seattle runs above; also, a 15-minute Fauntleroy-Vashon Island crossing costs $4.50 OW car and driver, and runs about every 30-40 minutes.

VICINITY OF SEATTLE

RENTON/TUKWILA

Thoroughbred horse racing at **Longacres Race Track,** 1621 S.W. 16th St., 226-3131, is this area's premier attraction, as evidenced by the race-night traffic jams squeezing off I-405. From April to early Oct. they run 10 races a day Wed. through Sun. and holidays; kids are welcome (admitted free with parents). Admission is $3 grandstand, $5 clubhouse; parking is $1. To get there, follow the signs from I-5 or I-405.

For slower-paced action, try the **Renton Historical Museum** at 235 Mill Ave. S, 255-2330. Among the displays are pioneer furniture, antique vehicles, and Indian and mining artifacts.

Accommodations

As always, **Motel 6,** 20651 Military Rd. at I-5 exit 51, 824-9902, features the least expensive area lodging: their 124 rooms go for $27 s, $33 d, with pool and jacuzzi. **Traveler's Inn,** just off I-405 at 44th (7710 Lake Washington Blvd.), 228-2858, also offers convenient budget lodging from $28 s, $30-32 d. Near Longacres at 3700 E. Valley Rd., 251-9591, **Nendel's Valu Inn** has 130 rooms from $38-56 s, $43-61 d, with a hot tub,

airport shuttle, and adjacent restaurant and lounge. At 15901 W. Valley Rd., 226-1812 or (800) 547-0106, **Nendel's Inn** has 147 rooms from $76-82 s, $82-88 d, with a heated pool, hot tub, exercise room, airport shuttle, restaurant, and lounge. For about the same money, you can stay at the **Sheraton Renton Inn,** just off I-405 at 800 Rainier Ave. S, 226-7700 or (800) 325-3535. Rooms start at $57-67 s, $65-75 d, and include a heated pool, dining room, lounge with entertainment, and airport shuttle. At the Southcenter Mall, the **Doubletree Inn,** 246-8220, has an indoor pool, playground, shuttle, restaurant, and lounge with entertainment, not to mention 200 rooms starting at $65-79 s, $75-89 d.

Campers and RVers will enjoy the amenities at **Aqua Barn Ranch,** 15227 Renton-Maple Valley Hwy., 255-4618. The 200 RV and tent sites (starting at $13.50) come with an indoor pool, horse rentals, a big-screen TV, and movies. **Riverbend Park,** 17410 Maple Valley, 255-2613, has 42 adults-only tent sites on 12 acres from $12. Both campgrounds are open year-round.

Food, Shopping, And Services

You don't have to kiss off the diet because you're on vacation; **Andy's Tukwila Station** has approved "Diet Center" meals, as well as steaks, seafood, chicken, sandwiches, and salads, served in restored railroad cars at 2408 W. Valley Hwy.; open for 3 meals. Stop by **T.C. Colby's Restaurant and Bar,** 200 S.W. 43rd at E. Valley Rd. near Longacres, for a post-race brew.

Rainier Ave. is the city's commercial strip, lined with fast- and slow-food restaurants, shopping centers, a smattering of motels, and some of the most obnoxious new car salesmen this side of the Cascades. For consistently good steak and seafood, visit **Stuart Anderson's Black Angus Restaurant** just off Rainier near the airport at 95 Airport Way, 226-9600. Mexican food fanciers will appreciate this member of the **Mazatlan** chain at 540 Rainier. The major shopping center here is **Renton Center,** with Sears, J.C. Penney, and other shops; also on Rainier are KMart, Payless Drugstore, and grocery stores.

Southcenter, at the Southcenter exit off I-5, is one of the largest shopping malls in the area with major department stores that include the Bon Marché, Nordstrom, and J.C. Penney. Several smaller shopping plazas and fast-food restaurants surround it, including **The Pavilion,** an off-price mall one mile S of Southcenter.

For medical emergencies, dial 911 or phone **Valley Medical Center,** 400 S. 43rd, 228-3450 for the main switchboard or 251-5185 for 24-hour emergency room service.

Getting There
From Seattle, go S on I-5, then take I-405 N to Renton. The city has daily **Metro** service to Seattle and throughout King County; 447-4800.

MERCER ISLAND

Mercer Island is primarily an upper-middle-class Seattle suburb, connected to the city only at its N end by I-90's floating bridge. **Luther Burbank Park** on 2040 84th Ave. SE is worth a visit; the island's best waterfront park, it has a beach, hiking trails, picnic area and fishing in Lake Washington. Start here for a 15-mile loop bike tour of the island: first go E on N. Mercer Way, then S on E. Mercer Way to the island's southern tip, then back up

N on W. Mercer Way (not a great deal of imagination was shown by the street-naming committee). At S.E. 68th St. and Island Crest Way, **Pioneer Park** has equestrian and hiking trails in a natural, wild setting (no rest rooms), including a ¾-mile interpretive nature trail.

Escape from the frenzied pace of the city to a quiet night at **Mercer Island Hideaway,** 8820 S.E. 63rd, 232-1092, in a wooded area at the at the S end of the island adjacent to Pioneer Park. Facilities include a music room with 2 grand pianos, reed organ, and harpsichord, plus a full breakfast. The rates beat most of Seattle's downtown hotels: $40 s, $55-65 d, with a 2-night minimum; no smoking.

Getting There
To drive to Mercer Island, take I-90 over the Mercer Island (Lacey V. Murrow) Floating Bridge; see "Seattle," p. 46, for insight into the bridge's history and construction. **Metro** has regular if infrequent service to the island; 447-4800.

BELLEVUE

Across Lake Washington, Bellevue has grown from a Seattle suburb to Washington's 4th-largest city and home of expanding high-tech industries. Bellevue attracts folks con-

BELLEVUE & MERCER ISLAND

1. Mercer Island Hideaway
2. Bellevue B&B
3. Fountain Court Off Main
4. Marian's
5. TraveLodge
6. Red Lion
7. Hilton
8. Holiday Inn
9. library
10. Bellevue Chamber of Commerce
11. Best Western Greenwood
12. Overlake Memorial Hospital
13. C.I. Shenanigan's
14. Thai Kitchen
15. Days Inn
16. Petersen B&B
17. Residence Inn

BELLEVUE
AND MERCER ISLAND

© MOON PUBLICATIONS, INC.

cerned about living in the "right" neighborhood; most of the houses here are no nicer than other Seattle suburb clones, but you can add about $40,000 to the price for the pleasure of saying that you live in Bellevue, dahhhling.

Parks

Chism Beach off 100th Ave. SE has swimming, trails, and picnic areas on the shores of Lake Washington. **Bellefields Nature Park,** along the Mercer Slough at 118th Ave. SE, has 48 acres of marshland and trails in the city's center, outlined by a 1-mile loop trail around its perimeter. At 128th Ave. SE is **Kelsey Creek Park,** Bellevue's largest; a Japanese garden, 1-mile loop trail, children's zoo, and 1888 pioneer log cabin add to your picnicking pleasure. Bellevue's newest park, **Lake Hills Greenbelt,** off 156th Ave. SE, offers a 1½-mile paved trail through wetlands and pines in the heart of the city. Open to joggers, cyclists, wheelchairs, and hikers, the first section of trail was developed in 1986; now the greenbelt trail links Larsen and Phantom lakes.

Tours

Paul Thomas Winery, 1717 136th Pl. NE, 747-1008, is open Fri. and Sat. noon-5 p.m. for tours and tastings; open Mon. through Thurs. (for sales only). Stop in and taste his award-winning Chenin Blanc, Chardonnay, or pear and rhubarb wines. **Vernell's Fine Candies,** 11959 Northup Way, 455-8400, offers guided tours of their candy factory for groups of 4 or more.

The Arts

The **Bellevue Art Museum,** 454-3322, in the 3rd-floor atrium of Bellevue Square (see "Shopping" below), has ancient and modern art exhibits, including work by Northwest artists; open daily except Mon., admission $2 adults. See celebrity international artwork and openings at **Universal Fine Art,** 2032 148th St., 454-2484. For your listening pleasure, the city boasts the **Bellevue Philharmonic Orchestra,** with classical and pops

concerts performed at Westminster Chapel, 13646 N.E. 24th, 455-4171. The **Eastside Theater Company** performs at Bellevue Community College, 300 Landerholm Circle, 641-2415.

Accommodations

Bellevue Bed and Breakfast, 830 100th Ave. SE, 453-1048, offers a homey atmosphere, kitchen and laundry privileges, gourmet coffee, and city and mountain views for a reasonable $50 s or d. No pets, smoking, or kids under 10. **Petersen Bed and Breakfast,** 10228 SE 8th, 454-9334, welcomes kids in their modern home 5 minutes from Bellevue Square. A homestyle breakfast and use of the spa on the deck are included in their low rates of $40 s, $45 d (8th night free). No smoking.

Just because it's in Bellevue doesn't mean it has to be expensive: **Days Inn,** 3241 156th Ave. SE, 643-6644, has 108 rooms complete with marble baths, balconies, and queen-size beds for a budget price: $39-44 s, $44-49 d. The **Bellevue TraveLodge** is another inexpensive motel (with a pool) at 11011 N.E. 8th, 454-4967; the 55 rooms start at $41 s, $46-50 d.

Prices jump up from there, as the major chains cater more to business travelers than tourists. The **Holiday Inn,** 11211 Main, 455-5240, has 182 rooms from $71-76 s, $81-86 d, plus a heated pool, restaurant, and some balconies. The **Best Western Greenwood Hotel,** 625 116th NE, 455-9444, has an outdoor pool, 2 restaurants, and 176 rooms from $67-73 s, $74-84 d. The **Bellevue Hilton,** 100 112th NE, 455-3330, has an indoor pool, hot tub, sauna, 3 restaurants and lounges, and 184 rooms for $75-84 s, $85-93 d. For the ultimate in luxury, stay at the **Red Lion Inn** at 300 112th SE, just off I-405 exit 12 (northbound) or 13 (southbound), 455-1300. The 355 rooms start at a mere $95 s, climbing to $104-118 d; amenities include a heated pool, restaurant, and lounge with entertainment. Enjoy a home away from home at the **Residence Inn,** 14455 N.E. 29th Pl. (148th Ave. NE exit off Hwy. 520), 882-1222. One-and 2-bedroom suites go for $94-119 s, $94-

Old Bellevue

namon rolls (get them at the take-out deli in front) as for its dressed-up lunch and dinner menu; prices are moderate. For an even fancier dinner, **Fountain Court Off Main,** 22 103rd Ave. NE in Old Bellevue, 451-0426, specializes in pricey French-Northwest cuisine; enjoy dinner on the deck in summer. Open for lunch weekdays, dinner daily except Sunday.

Festivals And Fairs

The Bellevue Art Museum sponsors the annual **Pacific Northwest Arts and Crafts Fair,** held in Bellevue Square each July. Hear Northwest jazz at 3 days of outdoor concerts during the **Bellevue Jazz Festival,** held the third weekend in July at Bellevue Central Park, 451-4106.

Shopping And Services

At N.E. 8th St. and Bellevue Way NE, **Bellevue Square** is one of the Northwest's largest shopping malls—over 200 stores (including Nordstrom, The Bon, Frederick & Nelson, and J.C. Penney) and 16 restaurants, plus the Bellevue Art Museum in the 3rd-floor atrium, and glass-enclosed elevators for added panache. For a glimpse into Bellevue's past, visit the shops and galleries in **Old Bellevue's** restored business district on Main St. between 100th and Bellevue Way.

For additonal information on Bellevue and the surrounding area, contact the East King County Convention and Visitors Bureau, 515 116th Ave. NE, Ste. 111, Bellevue, WA 98004, 455-1926, or stop by the **Bellevue Public Library** at 11501 Main, 455-6889. For a medical emergency, dial 911 or **Overlake Hospital Medical Center,** 1035 116th NE, 454-4011 for the switchboard or 462-5200 for the 24-hour emergency room.

Transportation

To get to Bellevue by car, take either floating bridge (Hwy. 520 or I-90) from Seattle; from Sea-Tac, take I-5 to I-405 through Renton to Bellevue. **Metro,** 447-4800, has several buses serving Bellevue from Seattle. **Suburban Airporter,** 455-2353, serves the E side from Sea-Tac for $9-22.

129 d, and include a heated pool, whirlpools, sport court, and airport shuttle.

Food And Drink

At 10733 Northup Way, **Bravo Ristorante,** 827-8585, has received "Best Italian" awards from 3 local media. Enjoy Italian cuisine, fresh seafood, and gourmet pizza, plus piano bar music on weekends; open daily for dinner, weekdays for lunch. For American food, **C.I. Shenanigan's** on Lake Bellevue at 23 Lake Bellevue Dr., has fresh seafood, an oyster bar, beef, and pasta, plus an outdoor deck and a piano bar. One of the area's more popular restaurants, **The Thai Kitchen,** 14115 NE 20th St., 641-9166, has Thai vegetarian, chicken, and seafood dishes, prepared from mild to hot according to your specifications. **Marian's,** 777 108th Ave. NE, 451-7474, is as famous for its breakfast cin-

KIRKLAND

Surprisingly enough, Peter Kirk wasn't Kirkland's founding father—that honor belongs to Leigh Smith Jones Hunt. Hunt persuaded Kirk to build his steel mill, originally slated for Tacoma, in his town instead and offered to change the name to "Kirkland" as an added incentive. Kirk hoped to build the "Pittsburgh of the West"; fortunately or not, he never succeeded.

Outdoors

Moss Bay, on the E side of Lake Washington, hasn't been a bay since the Lake Washington ship canal was completed in 1916, lowering the water level 9 feet; and there's never been any moss. The name came from a bay in England, Peter Kirk's home. Nonetheless, Moss Bay features a small beach, marina, and shops. **Bridle Trails State Park,** 480 acres off 116th Ave. NE, has 28 miles of horse and hiking trails (more horses than hikers), including their Bridle Crest Trail which reaches to Redmond's Marymoor Park (see p. 67). Horses are available for rent at the park for $10 an hour with a day's notice; call Sandene's Horse Trail Rides, 822-1805. Just N of downtown on Lake Washington is **Juanita Beach Park** at 98th Ave. NE and N.E. Juanita Way, with an impressively long pier and one of the area's best beaches. Northwest of Juanita, **O.O. Denny Park,** Holmes Point Dr., has a small beach, picnic area, and a hiking trail leading to King County's largest Douglas fir, standing 255 feet in height, 8½ feet in diameter, and estimated to be 575 years old. Head farther N to N.E. 145th St. to **St. Edwards State Park,** a 316-acre retreat from civilization. This beautiful piece of property was part of a Catholic seminary until 1977; when the seminary closed, the diocese sold the land to the state and the park opened the following summer. St. Edwards boasts ¾ mile of forested, undeveloped Lake Washington shoreline and 5 miles of hiking trails, plus picnic areas, gymnasium, tennis courts, and a pool.

Winery

A new **Covey Run Winery** at 107 Central Way on Moss Bay, offers tastings, seminars, classes, and special events. Phone 828-3848 for a schedule of classes.

Accommodations

Kirkland's newest hotel, **The Woodmark at Carillon Point,** 1200 Carillon Pt., 822-3700 or (800) 822-3700, goes way beyond the comforts of home: fully-stocked mini-bar, a second TV *in the bathroom,* panoramic views of Lake Washington in most rooms, plus terry robes, full breakfast, VCRs, and an invitation to "raid the pantry" for late-night snacks. Of course, there's no such thing as a free breakfast: rooms start at $145 d, $175-500 for suites.

Those of us with tighter budgets can enjoy budget lodging at **Motel 6,** 12010 120th Pl.

Bridle Trails State Park

NE at I-405's 124th St. exit, 821-5618. Rooms are $27 s, $33 d, with a pool. The **Silver Cloud Motel,** 12202 N.E. 124th St., 821-8300, has 98 rooms for $33-36 s, $37-46 d, plus free laundry room and airport pick-up service, heated outdoor pool and jacuzzi. For a little more, stay at **Best Western Arnold's Motor Inn,** 12223 N.E. 116th St., 822-2300. Their 64 units go for $49-63 s, $55-69 d; pool, whirlpool, athletic club access, and airport transportation provided. **La Quinta,** 10530 N.E. Northup Way, 828-6585, or (800) 531-5900, has an outdoor pool, adjacent restaurant, and 120 rooms from $56-61 s, $64-69 d.

The **Shumway Mansion,** a 23-room B&B and reception center at 11410 100th Ave. NE, 823-2303, is a 3-minute walk from Juanita Beach. The antique-furnished inn was built in 1909; it was bought in 1982 by the Harris family and moved down the hill to its present location on 2.4 acres overlooking Juanita Bay. Two floors of the mansion are devoted to receptions and banquets; the 7 B&B rooms range in price from $60-95 s or d; all have private baths, 5 have water views, 2 have balconies. Please call regarding children; no smoking.

Food And Drink
Stop for a drink at **TGI Friday's,** part of the chain at 505 Park Place (kids are welcome in the restaurant). Then head to Moss Bay Marina for moderately priced, consistently good steak or seafood at **Anthony's Homeport,** 822-0225. Next door to Covey Run Winery, **Kirkland Roaster & Ale House,** 111 Central Way, 827-4400, roasts chicken, lamb, and other meats on a huge spit; moderate prices.

Shopping And Services
The **Old Heritage Place** is a collector's paradise. Located at 151 3rd St., this antiques mall has 65 shops filled with collectibles. Open daily 10 a.m.- 5:30 p.m., Sun. 1-5 p.m. The **Totem Lake Mall** (take the 124th St. exit from I-405) has 70 stores, restaurants, theaters, a post office, and a waterslide. At 620 Market St., the **Peter Kirk Building** houses shops and galleries in one of Kirkland's oldest buildings, constructed in 1891.

For maps or other information, visit the **Kirkland Chamber of Commerce,** 301 Kirkland Ave., 822-7066, or stop by the **Kirkland Public Library,** 406 Kirkland Ave., 822-2459. Throughout King County, dial 911 for medical, fire, or police emergencies; or, in Kirkland, phone **Evergreen Hospital,** 12040 N.E. 128th St. near the Totem Lake Shopping Center, 821-1111 for the switchboard or 823-7468 for 24-hour emergency service.

Transportation
From Seattle, take Hwy. 520 across the Evergreen Point Floating Bridge, then follow Hwy. 908 N to Kirkland for a total OW trip of about 10 miles. **Metro** provides daily service to Kirkland from Seattle and other points in King County; 447-4800.

REDMOND

Redmond, like neighboring Bothell and Woodinville, began as a boat landing along the Sammamish Slough from Lake Washington to Lake Sammamish. Foot travel in pioneer days was virtually impossible due to the dense forests and extensive marshland; inland travel was accomplished via river. Today the city is the self-proclaimed bicycle capital of the world, holding regular bicycle races at its Velodrome in Marymoor Park.

Parks
Marymoor Park on the West Lake Sammamish Pkwy. has 486 acres of open space on Seattle banker James Clise's 1904 estate. The mansion is now **Marymoor Museum,** 882-6401, featuring exhibits of local history; open Tues. through Thurs. and Sun., free. Marymoor Park is better known for its **Velodrome,** a 400-meter bike-racing track that draws competitors from across the United States. Bike races are held Fri. and Sat. evenings from May to Sept.; admission is $3, 882-0706. The park also features a 2¼-mile loop trail through woods and marshes with a Lake Sammamish view.

From Marymoor Park, bike or hike the paved 10-mile **Sammamish River Trail** to Bothell following the route of the Sammamish River. Sixty-eight acre **Farrel-McWhirter**

Park, 10400 192nd Ave. NE, has horse and hiking trails, picnicking, and a barnyard zoo. Charlotte's Trail is a paved path that extends the length of the park, ideal for disabled visitors.

Practicalities

The **Silver Cloud Motel,** 15304 N.E. 21st St., 746-8200, has 59 rooms with queen-size beds, free laundry room, and airport pick-up service for $32-36 s, $35-39 d. The **Redmond Motor Inn** at the intersection of Hwy. 520 and Redmond Way, 883-4900, has 137 rooms starting at $49 s, $54-58 d, plus a seasonal pool, jacuzzi, and adjacent pancake restaurant.

Lisa's, 8412 164th Ave. NE, 881-3250, features a moderately priced, varied (and variable) menu with a Southern accent. Open weekdays for breakfast and lunch, Wed. through Sat. for dinner.

The **Antique Connection,** 16701 Cleveland St., 882-3122, has 65 antique dealers under one roof. For more antiques, try **Days Gone Bye Antique Mall** on the lower level of the Ethan-Allen Bldg., 2207 N.E. Bel-Red Road.

From Seattle, take Hwy. 520 to Hwy. 920 to Redmond; or, hop aboard **Metro,** 447-4800.

WOODINVILLE

Woodinville, far enough away from Seattle to have its own identity, is a small (but rapidly growing), self-contained, unincorporated town with a lot to be proud of.

Wineries

Woodinville is home to the state's largest winery, **Chateau Ste. Michelle,** off Hwy. 202 at 14111 N.E. 145th St., 488-1133. Though the wine grapes are grown in eastern Washington (the vineyards here are experimental), the winery is among the nicest to visit: the original 1912 residence (once owned by Seattle lumber baron Fred Stimson) is surrounded by manicured grounds, an arboretum, and trout ponds, and features a full summer season of music and arts events in the amphitheater. Informative cellar tours and tastings are offered daily from 10 a.m.-4:30 p.m. Enjoy a basket lunch and a bottle of Chardonnay in the picnic area.

Columbia Winery, 488-2776, one of the state's oldest, is across the street from Ste. Michelle—the first castle on the left—on N.E. 145th Street (formerly Haviland's facility). Columbia's been in the varietal wine business since 1962, producing award-winning Chardonnay, Riesling, Cabernet Sauvignon, Semillon, and more, now available in 40 states. The tasting room is open daily, 10 a.m.-5 p.m.

French Creek Cellars, 17221 132nd Ave. NE, 623-WINE, is the newest member of the Woodinville wine family, having recently moved here from Redmond. French Creek started as an amateur wine-making group in 1973 and has since achieved international acclaim for its premium wines, which include Chardonnay, Riesling, Cabernet Sauvignon, Pinot Noir, and the less common Lemberger and ice wines. The tasting room and gift shop are open daily between noon and 5 p.m.

Outdoors

For a bit of fresh Woodinville air try the **Tolt Pipeline Trail,** a 10½-mile hiking and horse trail that passes through town just around the corner from Ste. Michelle as it extends from Norway Hill in S Bothell to Snoqualmie Valley near Duvall. The paved **Sammamish River Trail** passes through on the other side of Ste. Michelle on its way N to Bothell and S to Redmond for a 10-mile total. For *a lot* of fresh air take a balloon trip with **Lighter Than Air Adventures,** 21808 N.E. 175th St., 788-2454. If you've got the dough, the view of the Cascades, Puget Sound, Seattle, and surrounding countryside is worth the lofty prices: $115 pp for morning flights (1-1½ hours, includes Champagne brunch), $75 pp for evening flights (30-45 minutes, Champagne toast).

Accommodations

You'd think a town growing as fast as Woodinville, with 3 wineries drawing crowds every weekend, would have at least a handful of cut-rate motels. No doubt we'll see a Motel 6 or Super 8 sometime in the future, but for now, stay in Seattle or nearby towns, or better yet, enjoy a refreshing stay at a B&B. **Bear Creek Inn,** 19520 N.E. 144th Pl., 881-2978,

NORTHEAST KING COUNTY

SNOHOMISH COUNTY
KING COUNTY

522

BOTHELL

KENMORE

LOGBOOM PARK

BOTHELL WAY

405

BEAR CREEK INN

FRENCH CREEK CELLARS

WOODINVILLE

140 AVE NE

SAINT EDWARDS S.P.

NE 170 ST

JUANITA DR

100 AVE NE

SAMMAMISH RIVER

COLUMBIA WINERY

STE MICHELLE WINERY

WOODINVILLE-REDMOND RD

JUANITA BAY

JUANITA BEACH PARK

NE 124 ST.

NE 142 AVE.

SHUMWAY MANSION

KIRKLAND

405

SAMMAMISH RIVER TRAIL

202

REDMOND

WILLOW RD

AVONDALE WY.

TO FARREL-McWHIRTER PARK

LAKE WASHINGTON

908

REDMOND RD

520

BRIDLE TRAILS STATE PARK

MARYMOOR PARK

LAKE SAMMAMISH

0   1 mi
0   1 km

1. Teo's Mia Roma
2. Gerard's Relais de Lyon
3. Bothell Landing
4. Above-it-all
5. Evergreen General Hospital
6. Silver Cloud Motel
7. Totem Lake Mall
8. Best Western Arnold's
9. Peter Kirk Bldg.
10. Covey Run/Kirkland Roaster & Ale House
11. Old Heritage Place
12. Marina Park
13. TGI Friday's
14. Woodmark Hotel
15. library
16. Anthony's Home Port
17. Marymoor Museum
18. Velodrome
19. Redmond Motor Inn

© MOON PUBLICATIONS, INC.

features river-rock fireplaces, patios, fluffy comforters, hot tub, and a sunken tiled bathtub (shared by 2 guest rooms) surrounded by an acre of lawn and firs. Rooms are $48; no pets, no smoking (black lab in residence).

Food

Woodinville is far more than just Burger King and Dairy Queen (although they have those too); this unincorporated town boasts a remarkable variety of dining experiences. **Le Courtyard** offers nouvelle cuisine in a French country inn atmosphere at 17705 140th Ave. NE, 483-1088. The hunting lodge surroundings will gear you up for **Newman's** (13120 NE 177th Pl., 485-9372) menu: wild boar, antelope, bison, elk, quail, caribou, and more; pasta dishes for those who aren't "game." Open for dinner only. The **Creekside Restaurant,** upstairs at the same address, has American food—steak, chicken, seafood—in the $9-12 range; 485-0721. At **Armadillo Barbecue,** 13109 NE 175th St., 481-1417, you may not find armadillo, but you will find real Texas-style BBQ ribs, chicken, baked beans, and more, plus wine and beer; open for lunch and dinner daily. Feast on Mexican food at **Las Margaritas,** 13400 NE 175th, 483-5656. For diner-style food along with some gourmet surprises, try **Granni's Woodinville Inn** at 175th and 132nd; standard burgers and sandwiches are accompanied by French onion soup, crab quiche, and chocolate amaretto mousse. Breakfast is in the $3-4 range; lunches cost $4-6.

Shopping And Services

Molbak's, a nursery at 13625 NE 175th, is much larger than it looks—over 2,000 varieties of indoor and outdoor plants, garden tools, trees, bulbs, and conservatory/aviary fill for numerous green houses—and is as delightful for browsers as for serious gardeners; an espresso bar and gift shop add to the fun. Open daily. Visit **Hollywood Schoolhouse,** Hwy. 202 and 120th Pl. NE (head E from Ste. Michelle), for a novel shopping experience. You'll find antiques, arts and crafts shops, and galleries in this old-time country school. At the same intersection

(across the street), **Emerald City Antiques,** 485-5555, features 150 shops with over 12,000 square feet of antiques, collectibles, jewelry, prints, glassware, and more. Open daily 10 a.m.-6 p.m. **Pennsylvania Woodworks,** 17601 140th Ave. NE, 486-9541, sells furniture, quilts, woven rugs, wooden toys and more handmade by Amish craftspeople. The recently constructed **Towne Center** plaza on 175th has a grocery store, pharmacy, liquor store, fast food, and cleaners; across the street there's another grocery store (Albertson's), Payless Drugstore, and Urgent Care Medical Center for any medical problems (for a real emergency, dial 911).

Transportation

Metro has daily service to Seattle and environs even way out here in Woodinville. To drive to Woodinville from Seattle, either cross the lake and head N on I-405, turning E on Hwy. 522; or, take I-5 N from Seattle to Hwy. 522 through Bothell.

BOTHELL

Bothell was founded in 1884 by David Bothell and his family. Apparently without competition, they logged the area, built a hotel, platted the town, and sold lots to pioneers who wanted to get away from the bustle of the city. Located N of Lake Washington on the Sammamish River, Bothell is a small town about a half hour from Seattle, with one small distinguishing characteristic: **Bothell Landing,** 18120 Bothell Way NE, where a park, small shopping complex, and the **Bothell Historical Museum** mark the original steamboat berth. The museum, housed in the 1893 William Hannan house, is open Sun. afternoons from March to mid-December. The struggling shopping center is a disappointment, but you can pick up the **Sammamish River Trail** (see "Redmond," p. 67) here by crossing the footbridge behind the museum. **Country Village,** between Bothell Landing and I-405 at 23714 Bothell Hwy. SE, has 30 antique, food, jewelry, clothing, and gift shops open Tues. through Sun. till 4 p.m.

Lodging And Food

Open year-round, **Seattle North RV Park,** 22910 15th Ave. SE, 486-1245, has 227 tent and RV sites on 30 acres. Other than that, there's not much here for accommodations; try Kirkland, Lynnwood, or Edmonds.

One of Bothell's big surprises is **Gerard's Relais de Lyon,** a rather expensive French restaurant in an elegant house at 17121 Bothell Way NE, 485-7600; open for dinner only, daily except Monday. Other European tastes can be satisfied at **Teo's Mia Roma,** an Italian restaurant at 7614 N.E. Bothell Way in Kenmore, just W of Bothell. Open for dinner only; 486-6200 or 485-9545.

Transportation

To get to Bothell from Seattle, take Hwy. 520 across Lake Washington to Bellevue, then connect to I-405 N; or, take Hwy. 522 from I-5 N of Seattle. Better still, take **Metro,** 447-4800. Once in Bothell you can travel to Lynnwood, Edmonds, or Everett on **Community Transit,** 353-7433.

LYNNWOOD

Nothing much doing here, outside of the shopping centers and fast food joints strung together like popcorn. The **Alderwood Mall** on the E side of town hosts The Bon, Nordstrom, J.C. Penney, Sears, Lamonts, and many smaller stores; the mall is surrounded by other, smaller shopping plazas. Pick up a **Community Transit** bus here for Edmonds, Everett, or Bothell; 353-7433.

Lynnwood's **Silver Cloud Inn,** 19332 36th Ave. W, 775-7600, is one of the area's best deals with rooms from $33-36 s, $37-40 d. The **Best Western Landmark Motor Inn,** 4300 200th SW, 775-7447, has a heated indoor pool, hot tub, steam rooms, restaurant, and lounge, plus 102 rooms from $43-47 s, $47-53 d.

EDMONDS

Edmonds, 20 miles N of Seattle on Puget Sound, is a small city (pop. 28,700) surrounded by rolling hills and pine forests. Park your car along a downtown street and walk around—plenty of shops, galleries, bakeries, and restaurants to explore. When you tire of downtown, take off your shoes for a stroll along the narrow strip of Sunset Beach and watch the ferries cross the Sound to the Kitsap Peninsula.

Twenty shops and restaurants in an old-time atmosphere make up **Old Milltown** at 5th S and Dayton. For a more modern flavor, try **Harbor Square's** boutiques and galleries near the waterfront on W. Dayton. One of the more notable is the **Howard/Mandville Gallery,** with one of the largest inventories of collectible prints in the Northwest. The **Edmonds-South Snohomish Historical Museum,** 118 5th Ave., has a working shingle mill model, a marine room, and other displays depicting Edmonds' past. Open Tues., Thurs., and Sun. afternoons.

Outdoors And Underwater

Off the shoreline of Brackett's Landing (at the ferry dock) is **Edmonds Underwater Park,** where divers can explore the marine life that thrives in the 300-foot DeLion dry dock, sunk there in 1935 to serve as a breakwater. Since then, other underwater structures—including old tires, steel shelving, a model of the Evergreen Point Floating Bridge, and 2 tugboats—have been added for the enjoyment of both fish and diver, resulting in one of the Pacific Northwest's most popular underwater parks. From the shore, you'd never know anything was down there. The **Edmonds Fishing Pier,** just down the street from the ferry, was specifically constructed for fishing: the 2 enormous arms of the pier and parallel underwater structures direct migrating fish along the length of the pier and, with any luck, onto your hook. You can fish year-round, 24 hours; a bait shop, stores, and restaurants are adjacent. Edmonds' beaches are frequented by "Beach Rangers" (trained naturalists) as part of a nature program co-sponsored by the city of Lynnwood. **Sunset Beach** is visited by rangers most afternoons 2 hours before and after low tide; feel free to ask them any marine life questions you may have; groups can book an interpretive lecture or tour by calling the Edmonds Parks and Recreation Dept., 775-2525.

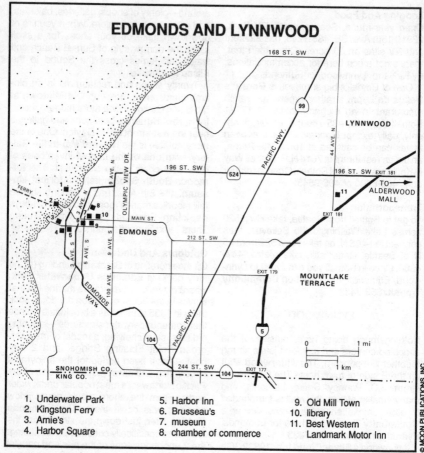

EDMONDS AND LYNNWOOD

1. Underwater Park
2. Kingston Ferry
3. Arnie's
4. Harbor Square
5. Harbor Inn
6. Brusseau's
7. museum
8. chamber of commerce
9. Old Mill Town
10. library
11. Best Western Landmark Motor Inn

© MOON PUBLICATIONS, INC.

Accommodations

Edmonds Harbor Inn, 130 W. Dayton, 771-5021, is close to the waterfront in Harbor Square. Their 60 rooms go for $43 s, $49-56 d, including continental breakfast. For a cheaper room, drive up 196th SW to Lynnwood (see above). **Heather House,** 1011 B Ave., 778-7233, is a B&B with Scottish influence: Scottish flags fly overhead and breakfast scones are a morning treat. Your king-size bed, private deck overlooking Puget Sound, and bath are only $35 s, $42.50 d, but breaking tradition, they charge $3 extra for breakfast. No kids or pets.

Food

Enjoy Northwest seafood with a view of the bay for lunch, dinner, or Sunday brunches at **Arnie's,** 2 blocks S of the ferry terminal. **Brusseau's,** 5th and Dayton, 774-4166, serves 3 moderately priced meals daily in this neighborhood cafe and bakery.

Other Practicalities

The **Edmonds Chamber of Commerce,** 120 5th Ave. N, 776-6711, will be happy to help you out with maps or other current information; or, try the **Edmonds Public Library** at 7th and Main, 771-1933. To get to Edmonds from Seattle, drive N on I-5 and follow the can't-miss signs. Once you're there, you can get around town and to Bothell, Lynnwood, and Everett via **Community Transit,** 353-7433.

Take the **Washington State Ferry** from Edmonds to Kingston, the Olympic Penin-sula's drop-off point. The crossing takes 30 minutes and leaves Edmonds about every 1½ hours off-peak (early mornings and late evenings), every 40 minutes during the day. Fares are $6.65 OW car-and-driver; (800) 542-7052 or (800) 542-0810 statewide.

TACOMA

Despite being the butt of Puget Sound jokes for many years, Tacoma is on the rebound and the next logical benefactor of western Washington's phenomenal growth. A world-class zoo, AAA baseball team, top-quality hotels and waterfront restaurants, a pro-posed University of Washington branch, es-tablished community colleges, and new bus-iness dollars provide a healthy base for what should become one of the '90s' fastest grow-ing cities. The new Frank Russell building just off the 11th St. bridge is a fine example of the shape of Tacoma to come. The city has been a leader in the containerized shipping busi-ness for many years, and also relies on wood products, shipbuilding, primary metal and chemical plants, health care, and a growing high-tech industry. Agriculture is also big bus-iness in Pierce County, particularly the Puy-allup bulb farms, which produce more bulbs than Holland. Like any city, Tacoma has its problems, not the least of which is bad press—the city's needle exchange program, for example, dominated national news for weeks, giving Tacoma the kind of exposure that doesn't do much for tourism—but there are enough oases of culture, fine dining, and pleasant parks to make Tacoma worth a visit.

History

English sea captain George Vancouver and his entourage first stumbled across the Puget Sound area in 1792 when Peter Puget, under Vancouver's order, sailed by Point Defiance and the Narrows. Members of Hudson's Bay Company came along and built Fort Nisqually in 1833, which has since been reconstructed at Point Defiance State Park. Another sea captain, Charles Wilkes, surveyed the Sound in 1841 and gave his starting point the name it still bears: Commencement Bay. The first settler, Job Carr, built his cabin on Com-mencement Bay and voila . . . Tacoma was born. Once the Northern Pacific Railroad reached the city in 1873, Tacoma's industries blossomed. Tacoma wasn't "Tacoma," (from "Tahoma" or "Takhoma," meaning "mother of waters," the Indian name for Mt. Rainier) until 1869; General M. M. McCarver had originally named it Commencement City.

SIGHTS

Point Defiance

Tacoma's most famous attraction is **Point Defiance State Park,** nearly 700 acres of gardens, foot paths, and shaded picnic areas plus the **Point Defiance Zoo and Aquarium,** home of beluga whales, polar bears, wal-ruses, elephants, and more. In summer, kids can ride an elephant; summer evening Zoo-sounds concerts are fun for the whole family (Tim Noah has appeared in years past). In December, come in the evening to see the twinkling animal Zoolights. Regular zoo ad-mission is $3.50 adults, $1.75 kids; 591-5335. Also at Point Defiance, **Never Never Land** has scenes from children's stories de-picted throughout a 10-acre wooded area. Visit the reconstructed **Fort Nisqually,** a mid-1800's Hudson Bay trading fort, and **Camp Six,** an old logging camp with a short steam railroad ride that the kids will love. A popular jogging route, **Five-Mile Drive** winds through the park, offering viewpoints and picnic stops along the way. **Owens Beach** on Com-mencement Bay offers summer sun or a plea-sant shoreline stroll any time of year. Rent a boat with a small motor and a tankful of gas for $36 a day at the Point Defiance Boat

downtown Tacoma and the 11th St. Bridge

House ($5 more gets you a rod and reel); the water off the point is always littered with fishermen, particularly during salmon season. Point Defiance is open every day, 10 a.m.-7 p.m. in the summer; some attractions charge a small admission fee. For more info call 591-5335.

Other Parks

Tucked away where you'd least expect it is the **Snake Lake Nature Center.** Their 54 acres of marshland and evergreens are just a stone's throw from busy 19th St. (1919 S. Tyler St., 591-5939), but 25 species of mammals and over 100 species of birds call it home. They've got 2 miles of self-guiding nature trails for the do-it-yourselfers, and offer guided tours the second Sat. of every month at 10 a.m. Don't let the name scare you off—the lake was named for its shape, not its inhabitants.

If you're in the downtown area and get the urge for a quick jog, head to **Wright Park** at S. 3rd and G streets. A small, shady park with gardens and paved paths, it also hosts the Seymour Conservatory. Built in 1907 and on the National Register of Historic Places, the conservatory hosts a stunning array of flowering plants.

Wapato Lake is a good practice pond for novice rowboaters. Located at S. 72nd St. and Sheridan Ave., the park also has picnic tables and some small flower gardens. House rules: if your boat fits on top of your car and doesn't have a motor, you're in; or, if

you forgot to pack yours, you can rent a boat there.

If you've wandered into NE Tacoma, **Browns Point Lighthouse Park** is a sunny spot for picnicking, ship-watching, or launching your own boat. Here you've got a great view of downtown Tacoma and Point Defiance, Vashon and Maury islands, the Olympics, and of course, the Sound. The trick is to find it (see map p. 86).

Narrows Bridge

Connecting Tacoma with the Olympic Peninsula, this bridge is an awesome sight—especially if you've seen clips of "Galloping Gertie," its predecessor, collapsing under severe winds in 1940. The Narrows is 500-plus feet above the ground, 6,000 feet long, and so far, quite stable.

Mt. Rainier

If you're in Tacoma on a semi-clear day, there are few places you can be without a view of 14,411-foot Mt. Rainier. It dominates the landscape with its permanent whitecap, and looks particularly dramatic from the Cliff House parking lot (see "Food," p. 75), the 11th St. bridge, Ruston Way, and Gig Harbor. The first peek of it will quicken your pulse, guaranteed. For a closer look, visit Mt. Rainier National Park (see p. 90).

Museums

The **Tacoma Art Museum** at S. 12th and Pacific Ave., 272-4258, is open daily with displays of American and French paintings, a children's gallery, library, frequent photography shows, and other traveling exhibits. Admission is $2 adults, $1 kids and seniors. The **Washington State Historical Society Museum,** 315 N. Stadium Way, 593-2830, has Eskimo, Native American, and Oriental artifacts, pioneer exhibits, and a little natural history thrown in. Admission is $2 adults, $1 kids and seniors.

Dome Tour

The **Tacoma Dome,** the giant blue geometric-patterned structure off I-5, offers 1-hour tours Mon. through Fri., June through Aug. (except when events are in progress); admission is $2 adults, $1 kids and seniors. The tour of the world's largest wooden dome includes info on the dome's history, construction, and how they convert from soccer to football to concert hall. For more info call 272-DOME (for event schedule, call 591-5318).

ACCOMMODATIONS

See the chart on pages 76-77 for hotels and motels in and around Tacoma.

For a change from the high-rises, spend a night at **Traudel's Haus,** 15313 17th Ave. Ct. E (off 152nd St. E—call for directions), 535-4422. Enjoy Old-World hospitality, antiques, and handmade lace along with private bath, fireplace, continental or full gourmet breakfast, all for just $30 s, $40 d, or $60 for the suite.

For info on camping and B & B's in Gig Harbor, Federal Way, and Vashon Is., see "Vicinity of Tacoma," p. 82.

FOOD

Ruston Way

Several of Tacoma's best restaurants are on the waterfront along Ruston Way and on N. 30th St., one street up from the water. At 2761 Ruston Way, **Harbor Lights** (the one with the tacky sign) is a very popular, moderately priced seafood restaurant. **C. I. Shenanigan's,** up the road at 3017 Ruston Way, is a tad pretentious for some tastes, but the food—moderately priced American—isn't bad and the upstairs bar is a lively place, frequently the site

of local radio stations' theme parties. **Katie Downs Tavern,** at 3211 Ruston Way, sits on a pier and offers pizza, a jeans-and-sneakers atmosphere, and a good-sized crowd with outdoor seating in the summer; over 21 only. Next to Katie Downs, **Hogan's Bay Co.** serves moderately priced seafood and steak. Farther N on Ruston, the **Lobster Shop South** is another popular, moderately priced seafood and steak restaurant, open daily for lunch and dinner plus an impressive Sunday brunch. At 2301 N. 30th St., one street away from the water, the **Grazie Cafe,** 627-0231, offers lunch, dinner, Sunday brunch, and a Sound view. A few doors down, **The Spar** has burgers, sandwiches, and great homemade soups, but it is a bar, so no kids.

An exercise course and bike path run along Ruston Way, good for a breezy post-lunch or dinner walk. There are also 2 public fishing piers here, complete with a bait shop and refreshment stand; the piers are a better bet for sightseeing than fishing, though, since Commencement Bay is one of Puget Sound's "hot spots," where the bottom fish and even salmon have shown unhealthy levels of toxins.

More Views

Johnny's Dock, on 1900 E. D St. (near the Dome), is located in one of Tacoma's less-attractive sections, but the view of the city and the boats docked outside is spectacular (particularly at night). The basic steak-and-seafood menu is reasonably priced, and *good;* the service is friendly, not overbearing. Don't miss it. Overlooking the Dome is **Stanley and Seafort's Saloon and Grill,** at 115 E. 34th, 473-7300, with another view that gets better as the sun goes down. The restaurant has a reputation for being overpriced, but that doesn't deter the crowds; if you're on a budget, just stop in for a beer and watch the sun set behind the Olympics.

If you want a sweeping Sound view plus a look at Mt. Rainier, try the **Cliff House,** 6300 Marine View Dr. at Browns Point, 927-0400. The atmosphere may be stuffy, but the steak and seafood are very good—though not cheap; the downstairs lounge offers the same view and a sandwich menu if you want to keep costs down. Farther N on Marine

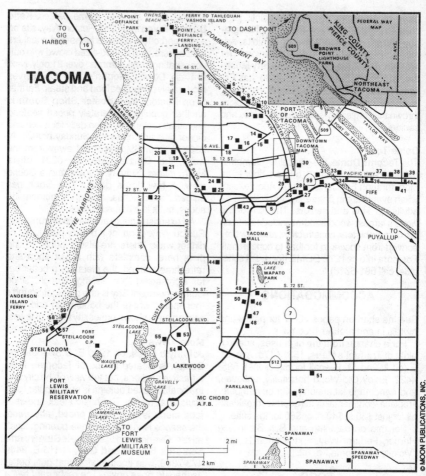

View Dr. (a.k.a. East Side Dr. and Dash Point Rd.) at Dash Point, you'll see a sign for the **Lobster Shop,** 6912 Soundview Dr. NE, 927-1513, sister to the Lobster Shop South across the bay. This is the original, more rustic version, where the steaks, seafood, and wine list are unequalled; open for dinner only, and reservations are always a good idea.

Downtown
Downtown Tacoma offers a number of lunch spots at Broadway Plaza and Tacoma Market.

The Judicial Annex, at 311 S. 11th (right at the corner of the Plaza) is a popular soup/sandwich/espresso stop with a full bar. One street up is the **Ark Delicatessen and Restaurant,** a small place tucked into the Market at 1140 Court C. In serve-yourself deli-style, they offer sandwiches, salads, and a nice selection of wines. **Bimbo's,** 1516 Pacific Ave., 383-5800, has been serving Italian specialties at this location for almost 70 years—the food's still great, but a change in locale is in order.

TACOMA

1. boat house
2. zoo and aquarium
3. Camp Six
4. Never-Never Land and Fort Nisqually
5. Antique Sandwich Co.
6. Lobster Shop South
7. Hogan's Bay Co.
8. Katie Downs Tavern
9. C.I. Shenanigan's
10. Harbor Lights
11. The Spar
12. Knapp's
13. Grazie Cafe
14. Bavarian Restaurant
15. Tacoma General Hospital
16. Lorenzo's
17. Engine House-9
18. Prosito's
19. Casa Bonita
20. Cloverleaf Tavern
21. Tacoma Community College
22. Cheers West
23. Cheney Stadium
24. Humana Hospital
25. Snake Lake Nature Center
26. Tacoma Salmon House
27. Tacoma Dome
28. Quality Hotel Tacoma Dome
29. Greyhound
30. Johnny's Dock
31. Amtrak Station
32. La Quinta
33. Portage Inn
34. Traveler's Inn
35. La Casa Real
36. Nendel's
37. King's Palace
38. King's Motor Inn
39. Royal Coachman
40. Best Western Executive Inn
41. Motel 6
42. Stanley & Seafort's
43. Java Jive
44. Days Inn
45. Shilo Inn
46. Sherwood Inn
47. Nendel's
48. Best Western Tacoma
49. Days Inn
50. Motel 6
51. Traudel's Haus
52. Black Angus
53. Best Western Lakewood
54. Lakewood Center
55. Sunnyside Beach Park
56. Bair Drug
57. Salter's Point Park
58. museum
59. E.R. Roger's

Others

The Old Spaghetti Factory at 1735 S. Jefferson, part of a small national chain, can fill you to capacity with an assortment of low-priced (under $8) pasta dishes and some terrific sourdough bread. This is a good spot to take noisy kids, but be prepared for a wait on the weekends. **Lorenzo's,** 2811 6th Ave., 272-3331, is a local favorite with its real Italian food at low to moderate prices. Just up the street, **Prosito's** serves good, low-priced Italian food and live jazz in a tiny little hole of a joint at 6th and Proctor.

The **Bavarian Restaurant** at 204 N. K St., 627-5010, specializes in "old country-style" German steaks and seafood, beer and wine, with live music on the weekends and a Sunday Champagne brunch. For a bite of the local catch, try the **Tacoma Salmon House,** near the Dome at 2611 Pacific Ave., 627-0141. Though salmon is their specialty, they have other seafood, prime rib, and beef dishes to choose from. **Stuart Anderson's Black Angus** restaurants are consistently good; there's one in Tacoma at 9905 Bridgeport Way SW, 582-6900. The **Cloverleaf Tavern** at 6430 6th Ave. cooks up—and delivers—some of the best pizza in town (rumor has it

actress Linda Evans gets her pizza here). Stay away from the chains and try a charming, casual, and inexpensive Mexican restaurant, **Casa Bonita,** at 6104 6th Ave., 565-1546. Another of the city's best Mexican restaurants is **Moctezuma's,** in a new location at 56th and Tyler.

Over in Proctor, **Knapp's** (2707 N. Proctor) offers casual dining and hearty, better-than-Mom's breakfasts; open 6 a.m. to 11 p.m. Pacific Hwy. E in Fife is lined with fast-food restaurants and budget motels; a good spot to stay if you're short on cash. Besides Burger King and McDonald's, there are a couple "real" restaurants here: **La Casa Real,** 3410 Pacific Hwy. E, 922-8877, is open daily for Mexican lunch, dinner, and Sunday brunch (with dancing in the lounge); **King's Palace,** 4903 Pacific Hwy. E, 922-0911, has Chinese food to eat in or take out, plus dancing in the lounge on weekends.

ENTERTAINMENT

Nightlife
There's plenty of nightlife in Tacoma: **Christie's** at the Executive Inn (Exit 137 off I-5 in Fife) has dancing Mon. through Sat. to Top-

TACOMA AREA LODGING

Name	Address	Phone	Rates	Comments
Best Western Executel	31611 20th Ave. S, Federal Way	941-5888	71-90 s 77-96 d	pool, hot tub, shuttle, restaurant, bar
Best Western Executive Inn	5700 Pacific Hwy. E, Fife	922-0080	48-56 s 53-62 d	pool, hot tub, sauna, exercise room, lounge, restaurant, airport limo
Best Western Lakewood	6125 Motor Ave. SW, Lakewood	584-2212	42-52 s 47-57 d	pool, lounge, restaurant nearby
Best Western Tacoma Inn	8726 S. Hosmer, Tacoma	535-2880	48-62 s 54-68 d	pool, hot tub, exercise room, restaurant, bar
Budget Inn	9915 S. Tacoma	588-6615	25 s, 28 d	laundry
Kings Motor Inn	5115 Pacific Hwy. E, Fife	922-3636	27 s or d	hot tub, laundry
La Quinta	1425 E. 27th St., Tacoma	383-0146	49-54 s 57-62 d	pool, hot tub, exercise room, restaurant, bar
Motel 6	5201 20th St. E, Fife	922-1270	24 s, 30 d	pool
Motel 6	1811 S. 76th St., Tacoma	473-7100	27s, 33 d	pool, jacuzzi
Nendel's	8702 S. Hosmer, Tacoma	535-3100	32-39 s 37-44 d	pool, bar, restaurant
Portage Inn	3021 Pacific Hwy. E, Fife	922-3500	26 s, 30 d	restaurant adjacent
Quality Hotel Tacoma Dome	2611 East E St., Tacoma	572-7272	50-60 s 60-70 d	near Dome; sauna, exercise room, restaurant, bar
Royal Coachman	5805 Pacific Hwy. E, Fife	922-2500	39-44 s 44-52 d	hot tub, library
Sheraton	S. 1320 Broadway Plaza, Tacoma	572-3200	75-99 s 85-110 d	hot tub, sauna, restaurant, bar
Sherwood Inn	8402 S. Hosmer, Tacoma	535-2800	30-34 s 32-36 d	pool, lounge, restaurant

TACOMA AREA LODGING (CONTINUED)

Name	Address	Phone	Rates	Comments
Shilo Inn	7414 S. Hosmer, Tacoma	475-4020	49 s 55-59 d	pool, hot tub, steam/sauna, exercise room
Super 8	1688 S. 348th, Federal Way	838-8808	35 s, 38-41 d	
Traveler's Inn	3100 Pacific Hwy. E, Fife	922-9520	26 s, 30 d	pool

40 bands. The lounges at C.I. Shenanigans and other Ruston Way restaurants (see above) come alive at night. A favorite with some of the locals is the unusual **Java Jive**, a teapot-shaped tavern on S. Tacoma Way; you won't want to come here for dinner, but the juke box features classics from the 60s and the live organ entertainment is, well, unique. **Engine House No. 9**, 611 N. Pine, is right around the corner from Lorenzo's on 6th Ave.; have a few brews and a pizza or plate of garlic bread sticks on the patio for a perfect end to a summer evening. **Cheers West**, 7102 27th St. W, alleged to be the hangout of the Tacoma Stars and Tacoma Tigers, is a spots-nuts bar with big weekend crowds plus weeknight trivia contests. The **Antique Sandwich Co.**, 5102 N. Pearl St. (right outside Point Defiance), offers acoustic and folk music (plus health-nut sandwiches) in a family, no-alcohol setting. For an exhaustive list of night spots, plays, concerts, etc., check the Tacoma *Morning News Tribune's* TGIF section on Fridays.

Sports
Tacoma's claim to fame is its Major Indoor Soccer League team, the **Tacoma Stars;** they play at the Tacoma Dome at 2727 East D Street. The Pacific Coast Baseball League is represented by the **Tacoma Tigers**, a AAA team that plays at Cheney Stadium, 2525 Bantz Blvd. (off Hwy. 16), and sometimes outdraws the Seattle Mariners!

Theater
The **Pantages Centre** at 9th and Broadway always has something going on—plays, acrobats, concerts—but unfortunately, a lot of their events sell out fast. Give them a call at 591-5894 to see what's on the agenda. The building itself is an ornate, restored vaudeville palace dating back to 1918. The **Tacoma Actors Guild (TAG)**, 1323 S. Yakima Ave., 272-2145, features nightly performances (except Mon.) through the winter season, with matinees on selected days. Every weekend in the summer, 565 Broadway (guess where it is) offers dinner theater. Dinner and the show go for $15; for $7.50 you can get the show with dessert only. Phone 272-8118 for info and reservations.

SHOPPING AND SERVICES

The **Tacoma Mall** is one of the largest shopping malls in the Northwest with over 140 stores, including Sears, J.C. Penney, Bon Marche, Nordstrom, and Frederick and Nelson, all on one exhausting level. From I-5 follow the signs for Tacoma Mall Blvd., at the S. 56th St. exit. Smaller shopping centers line S. 38th St., just N of the mall; closer to the center of town, 6th Ave. has KMart, Drug Emporium, and numerous other discount stores and small plazas.

The Tacoma area code is 206. If you need more info on Tacoma and the surrounding area while you're here or in advance, stop by or phone the **Tacoma-Pierce County Visitor and Convention Bureau** at 950 Pacific Ave., Ste. 300, 627-2836. The **Tacoma Public Library,** 591-5666, is operating out of temporary quarters at Broadway Plaza (on Broadway between 11th and 13th) until their main building at 1102 Tacoma Ave. S is renovated.

For fire, police, and other emergencies, dial 911. Plenty of hospitals in the area have 24-hour emergency room service: **Humana Hospital,** S. 19th and Union, 383-0011; **Tacoma General,** 315 S. K St., 594-1050; or **St. Joseph Hospital,** 1718 S. I St., 591-6660.

TRANSPORTATION

Getting Around By Car

Tacoma's street numbering system is relatively easy to follow—sometimes. The system that allegedly provides faster 911 response time would work much better on flat terrain with straight roads; as it is, some streets change names 7 or more times as they move in and out of boxes on an imaginary grid. But as a general rule, anything prefixed or suffixed by a "Northeast" is between Browns Point (Marine View Dr.) and Federal Way; "North" is up by Point Defiance; "South" is the tricky one, as it takes up the whole midsection of Tacoma, and sometimes looks more west or north than south; "East" is in the Dome area; and "West" is over by the University Place section, south of the Narrows Bridge. But pay attention: the "Avenue" or "Place" or "Street" appended to the number is *critical;* for example, there's a 42 St. S, a 42 Pl. S, and a 42 Ave. S, and as a general rule such streets never intersect or even come near each other.

By Bus

Pierce Transit, 593-4500 or (800) 562-8109 statewide, serves Tacoma, Puyallup, Gig Harbor, Lakewood, Steilacoom, Spanaway, Fife, and E to Buckley. **Greyhound,** 1319 Pacific Ave., 383-4621, provides cross-country service.

Arriving By Air

If you're flying into Tacoma, you'll probably arrive at **Sea-Tac Airport.** As the name suggests it's about halfway between Seattle and Tacoma. Sea-Tac is small enough so you can make all your connections but big enough to be a respectable international airport. The **Travelines Airporter,** 848-8788 or 839-2886, has service to Federal Way, Fife, and downtown Tacoma; fares are $8-10 OW. **Capital Aeroporter,** 572-9544, serves Fife, S. Tacoma, and S.W. Washington, starting from $6 OW. For up-to-the-minute information on airport parking, ground transportation schedules and rates, and weather and traffic conditions, dial (800) 544-1965 or 431-4444 from a touch-tone phone.

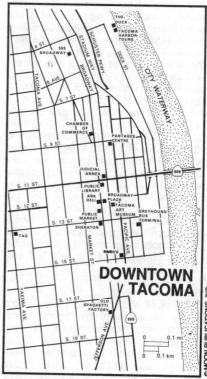

DOWNTOWN TACOMA

Java Jive

By Train

Amtrak serves Tacoma from its passenger station at 1001 Puyallup Ave., between the tideflat area and I-5 in the eastern part of the city. The *Coast Starlight* provides daily service to the Puget Sound area from Portland, San Francisco, and LA; the *Pioneer* also serves Seattle, Tacoma, and Olympia from Salt Lake City. Phone (800) 872-7245 for info.

By Ferry

The Washington State Ferry System is a heavily used method of everyday transportation around the Puget Sound region. From Tacoma, however, it can only get you to Vashon Island (see p. 83) departing from Point Defiance; fares are $2.15 RT for walk-ons, $7.50 RT for car and driver. For info on the ferry system call 464-6400 from Seattle, (800) 542-0810 or (800) 542-7052 from elsewhere in the state.

Harbor Tours

For a close look at Commencement Bay, Puget Sound, and The Narrows, take a cruise with **Tacoma Harbor Tours.** Evening dinner tours, offered from March through Sept., last 2 hours and feature baked salmon, prime rib, and chicken cordon bleu for $25-27 adults, $23-25 seniors. Sunday brunch tours, scheduled from March through Sept., depart at 10:30 a.m. and 1 p.m. and last 1½ hours; a full buffet is included in the price: $20 adults, $19 seniors, $13 kids 3-12. Enjoy a 4½-hour cruise to Tillicum Village on Blake Island for an alder-smoked salmon dinner and authentic Indian dance performance. These cruises depart every Sat. from March through Sept. at 10:30 a.m. and cost $30 adults, $28 seniors, $15 kids, and $10 toddlers. Sailing from May through Sept., their 1-hour harbor tour departs at 3 p.m. weekdays, 3:30 p.m. weekends; fares are $6.50 adults, $4.50 kids. Reservations are required; phone 572-9858 from Tacoma or 621-1941 from Seattle. The boat leaves from 535 Dock St. (just off Schuster Pkwy.); you'll see the long, barnlike McCormick Steamship Dock right on the water (there's also a bar, ice-cream shop, and galleries inside the drive-thru building).

VICINITY OF TACOMA

PARKLAND/SPANAWAY/LAKEWOOD

Technically separate towns, but in reality an extension of the Tacoma metropolitan area, the Parkland-Spanaway area hosts a few good restaurants and a beautiful park, while Fort Lewis and the McChord Air Force Base reside in neighboring Lakewood.

Sights

Twice a week the **McChord Air Force Base** opens for tours that include boarding their C-130 or C-141 cargo planes. The free 2-hour tours are held Tues. mornings and Fri. afternoons; phone 984-1910 for reservations.

Take Exit 119 from I-5 to the **Fort Lewis Military Museum,** one of the army's largest permanent posts. The museum emphasizes Northwest history, including artifacts from the Lewis and Clark expedition. Open Tues. through Sun., noon-4 p.m.; free.

One of Spanaway's summertime attractions is the **Spanaway Speedway,** with Sat., Sun., and Wed. night racing. The speedway is located at 159th and 22nd Ave. E; call 537-7551 for the week's schedule.

Located off Pacific Ave., **Spanaway County Park** is an ideal place to take a walk, go for a swim, or take out the boat. Back to back with Spanaway Lake Golf Course, the park has a beach, trails, lots of trees, and picnic areas.

Food

Just off I-5's 72nd St. exit, **The Olive Garden,** 475-1772, and **The Red Lobster,** 474-1262, first cousins in the chain, deliver consistently good, moderately priced, Italian and seafood dinners, respectively. The Olive Garden's non-stop breadsticks are legendary.

GIG HARBOR

Just across the Narrows Bridge from Tacoma, Gig Harbor definitely warrants a visit. The harbor is considered one of the best and most scenic on Puget Sound, with colorful boats, towering pines, and seaside houses, all against the picture-perfect backdrop of Mt. Rainier—a photo that graces many a calendar and magazine cover. The town itself is tiny, with a population of only 2,500 (probably 2,498 of them boat-owners) and a slightly touristy flavor, but the shops, galleries, good restaurants, and at least one great tavern will keep you busy. To get there, take the Soundview Dr. exit off Hwy. 16.

Kopachuck State Park

You'd never expect so much solitude so close to a major city! Located 12 miles NW of Tacoma off Hwy. 16 (just follow the signs), Kopachuck has 41 campsites ($7) shaded by skyscraping pines as well as a beach for swimming or fishing.

Kopachuck State Park

Accommodations

Built in 1901 by volunteers for the First Methodist Episcopal Church, **The Parsonage,** 4107 Burnham Dr., 851-8654, is a Victorian B&B within walking distance of Harborview Dr., Gig Harbor's main street. Their 2 guest rooms with shared bath go for $35 d. Another B&B, **No Cabbages,** 7712 Goodman Dr. NW, 858-7797, has 2 rooms with harbor views for $30 per room. For something more exotic, book a room aboard the **Krestine,** a 100-foot Baltic trading ketch built in 1903 and now moored "a mere monkey fist heave" from Gig Harbor's shops. The "Captain's Stateroom" is $60 s, $70 d, while 2 cozier crew cabins each go for $40 s, $50 d; full breakfast is included, dinners by special arrangement. Phone 858-9395 for reservations, or write Box 31, Gig Harbor, WA 98335.

Food

The **Tides Tavern,** 2925 Harborview, is alone worth the trip across the bridge. No waitress service—you order your beers and food at the bar, leave your name, and when your burger's ready it'll be delivered to your general vicinity . . . unless another "Bob" grabs it first! You can arrive by car or boat (dock right outside), and they've got a small deck for outdoor drinking and boat-watching. Besides burgers, the Tides offers pizza, sandwiches, soup, nachos, cheap beer, and weekend entertainment.

For a classier meal, these 3 steak-and-seafood restaurants all operate around the same price range—$10 dinners, on the average. The **Harbor Inn Restaurant,** 3111 Harborview Dr., 851-5454, has chicken and an occasional mako shark in addition to the standard steak and seafood. **W.B. Scott's,** 3108 Harborview Dr., 627-5446, adds some oddities like lamb stew and rabbit. **Neville's Shoreline Restaurant,** 8827 N. Harborview Dr., 627-1784, is the only 1 of the 3 that affords a view of Mt. Rainier.

Entertainment

Gig Harbor's **Performance Circle Theater** has performances in Celebrations Meadow during the summer months and at Burton Park Theater, 6615 38th Ave. NW, on winter weekends. Celebrations Meadow is on the L side of Peacock Hill Ave., about ½ mile up from Harborview; the theater is at the extreme N end of 38th Ave. NW. For info call 851-PLAY or 549-2661.

The **Breakfast-in-Bed Race,** a bizarre Gig Harbor tradition, is held every spring. A team of runners, generally in drag or otherwise unidentifiable, push an old-fashioned bed frame some 500 feet while the bedridden breakfast-eater must ingest oatmeal, soft-cooked eggs, and juice before the finish. Other annual events include a 4th of July bash and a summertime "Good Times Boat Cruise" around Vashon Island with a live band and dinner. For info on any of these events call the chamber of commerce at 851-6865.

VASHON ISLAND

Vashon Island is not the place to go if you're expecting a hot time on the ol' town; cows and horses probably outnumber humans. This rural, slow-paced, homey environment is fine for bike tours but not bar-hopping. The island was discovered in 1792 by (who else?) Capt. George Vancouver who, having named enough things after himself, decided to give this one to his Navy buddy, James Vashon. Maury Island, the piece of land east of Vashon, is connected to it by a natural sandbar and lots of manmade fill (and therefore not an island at all). Maury was separately named and identified by a member of the Wilkes survey party in 1841. The Vashon piece is 12½ miles N to S and a maximum 4 miles wide; Maury is only 5½ miles long and, at most, 2 miles wide—definitely bikeable, although the rolling hills may poop you out.

Things To Do

Vashon's biggest summertime event is the 2-day **Strawberry Festival** in mid-July. Parades, music, and crafts highlight the event, and since ferry traffic will be heavy, it's a good idea to arrive early. Other attractions include the **Beall Greenhouse,** on 91st Ave. SW, with its 1½ acres of orchids under glass, and **Wax Orchards** on S.W. 232nd and 131st Ave. SW, where the cider-making process is explained. **The Blue Heron Center for the**

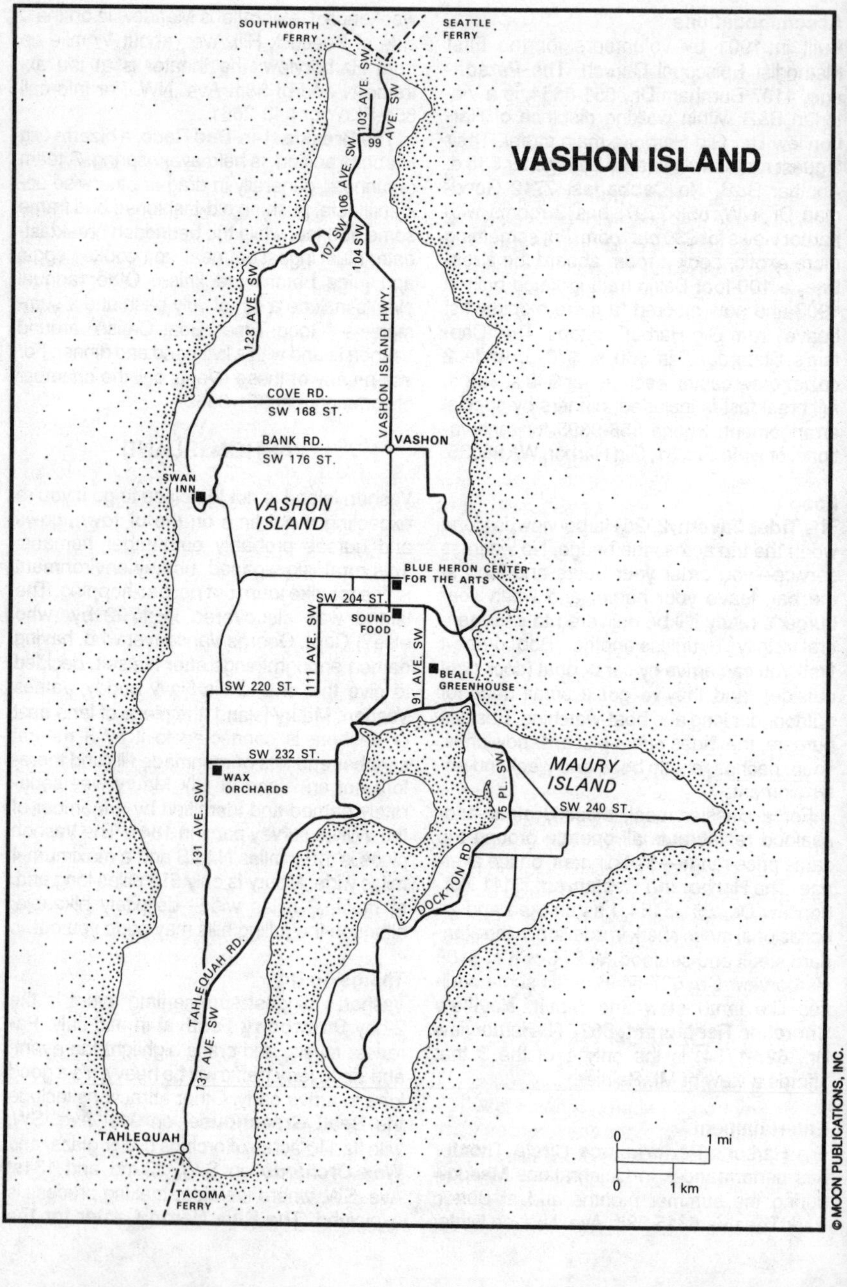

VASHON ISLAND

SOUTHWORTH FERRY

SEATTLE FERRY

99

103 AVE. SW

104 AVE. SW

106 AVE. SW

107 AVE. SW

123 AVE. SW

COVE RD.
SW 168 ST.

VASHON ISLAND HWY.

BANK RD.
SW 176 ST.

VASHON

SWAN INN

VASHON ISLAND

BLUE HERON CENTER FOR THE ARTS

SW 204 ST.

SOUND FOOD

111 AVE. SW

91 AVE. SW

SW 220 ST.

BEALL GREENHOUSE

SW 232 ST.

MAURY ISLAND

WAX ORCHARDS

SW 240 ST.

131 AVE. SW

75 PL. SW

DOCKTON RD.

TAHLEQUAH RD.

131 AVE. SW

TAHLEQUAH

TACOMA FERRY

0   1 mi

0   1 km

© MOON PUBLICATIONS, INC.

Arts, mid-island at Vashon Island Highway and S.W. 196th St., puts on various shows from time to time; call 463-5131 for info.

Accommodations
For a B&B in a quiet farm setting, try **The Swan Inn.** Rooms cost $40-65 s, $50-75 d, including a bacon-eggs-and-the-works breakfast. To get there, take Vashon Island Hwy. from either ferry dock to Vashon center; turn W at the light onto S.W. 176th St.; then watch for the blue mailbox (Box 454) and the swan sign.

Food
At least 2 restaurants on Vashon Island are worth a visit. **Sound Food,** mid-island on the Vashon Island Hwy., has a homey atmosphere and tasty food, not to mention a bakery and neighboring natural-foods store. The dinners are reasonably priced; there's a good lunch selection (try the hot sausage sandwich), lots of beer and wine options, and Sunday brunch (closed Tuesday).

Getting There And Around
A **Washington State Ferry** departs at least hourly from Point Defiance to Tahlequah on Vashon Island. The 15-minute trip costs $7.50 (no credit cards) for car and driver on the Point Defiance side; $2.15 for passengers or walk-ons; the return is free, whether you come back to Tacoma or opt for Southworth (S. Kitsap) or Fauntleroy (W. Seattle). Call the ferry system—464-6400 from Seattle, (800) 542-0810 or (800) 542-7052 statewide—for times, or get a schedule when you buy your ticket; there are chunks of time during mid-afternoon slow periods when the ferries just sit at the dock. For info on Vashon Island buses call 447-4800, or out-of-area, (800) 542-7876.

ANDERSON ISLAND

As quiet as it is, Vashon Island seems the thriving metropolis when compared to Anderson Island. Miles of roads and rural bike paths are the only attractions to draw mainlanders, with the possible exception of the **Johnson Farm,** founded by John Johnson in 1881. Tour the restored farmhouse, as well as the

pilot house from the *Tahoma,* the island's ferry from 1943 to 1954. Tours are conducted Sat. and Sun. afternoons from Memorial Day weekend through Labor Day.

Getting There
The **Pierce County Ferry System** is the proud owner of the tiny Anderson Island-Steilacoom ferry, which leaves Steilacoom Dock about every 2 hours from 6 a.m.-6 p.m. Round-trip fares are $4.30 for car and driver, $1.25 for a foot passenger, and $1.60 for a bicycle rider for the 20-minute run. Don't miss the last 6:30 p.m. departure; you'll be sleeping in the woods or knocking on doors, since there are no motels on the island.

STEILACOOM

The state's oldest incorporated city had established itself as the busiest port on Puget Sound by 1854. Today Steilacoom still clings to and respects its historic heritage. **Bair Drug and Hardware Living Museum** at 1617 Lafayette is an 1895 drugstore, complete with 1906 soda fountain where you can still get a soda or sundae. The museum also serves weekend breakfasts and lunch daily; open 9 a.m.-6 p.m. daily, 588-9668. The **Steilacoom Historical Museum** focuses on the town's pioneer period. Pick up their "Guide to Historic Steilacoom" for a walking tour. It's open Tues., Thurs., and Sun. afternoons, located in the Town Hall on Main and Lafayette; free.

Parks
Sunnyside Beach Park off Lafayette St. and **Salters Point Park** off 1st St. are both small waterfront parks with picnic facilities. **Fort Steilacoom County Park** on Steilacoom Blvd. has game fields plus good-sized Waughop Lake (drive down Dresdon Lane, then park by the barns and take a walk around the Waughop Loop).

Restaurant
Crystal chandeliers, antiques, and a Victorian home overlooking the Sound—an elegant setting for some of the best food around Puget Sound, at out-of-the-way **E.R. Rogers,**

1702 Commercial in Steilacoom, 582-0280.
The steak-and-seafood dinners are moderate to expensive, but well worth the money;
service is relaxingly slow. If you can't get
reservations, at least have a drink in the cozy,
upstairs-bedroom bar. Open daily for dinner
only, plus Sunday brunch.

FEDERAL WAY

Just N of Tacoma, over the line into King
County, is Federal Way. This newly incorporated city is one of the casualties of King
County's uncontrolled growth, as developers
race to fell the last tree, neighboring houses
are maybe 10 feet apart, and gridlock is a way
of life. But aside from the malls, fast food, and
traffic, Federal Way does hold a few worthwhile surprises.

Amusements

For a commercial form of entertainment, **Wild
Waves** and **Enchanted Village,** sister enterprises at 36201 Kit Corner Rd., will keep the
whole family amused. Wild Waves, 838-
8828, offers 400 feet of white-water rapids on
their Raging River Ride, waterslides, a
"beach" with artificial 5-foot waves for body
surfing, and scaled-down versions of the
adult attractions for the kiddies. All this for the
somewhat steep admission price of $13 ($11
for the kids). They're open from about Memorial Day through Labor Day. All the water is
heated so don't worry about the weather.
Neighboring Enchanted Village, 838-1700,
has rides, a children's museum, and a petting
zoo for $8 a head. Open April through Sept.
(hours and days vary by season, so call
ahead).

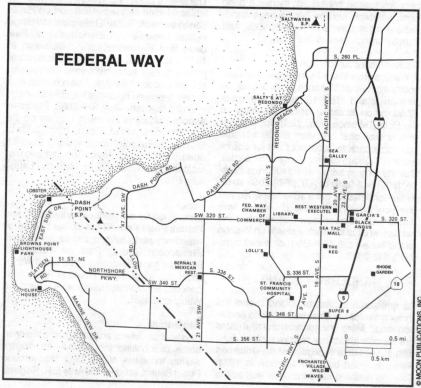

Gardens, Parks, And Camping

The Rhododendron Species Foundation Garden, Weyerhaeuser Way, has over 1,800 varieties of rhododendrons from around the world in a 24-acre garden—*something's* in bloom from March through September. Admission is $5 adults, under 13 free; call 927-6960 for days and hours.

Dash Point State Park is located on Puget Sound, on the Pierce-King County line on Hwy. 509, a.k.a. Dash Point Road. The wooded camping area, on the E side of the road, has 108 tent sites and 28 trailer hookups (from $7-$9.50). On the W, or Sound, side of the park, are a beach (the water here is warm enough for swimming—or at least wading—in summer), picnic tables, and trails that lead to the water. **Saltwater State Park,** 2 miles S of Des Moines (that's de-MOINZ, believe it or not) on Hwy. 509, has camping at 52 tent sites, a bigger beach, larger picnic area, and a refreshment stand.

Food

Redondo is just W of Federal Way, on Puget Sound; go W on 1st Ave. S, where you'll find a fishing pier, boat launch, and one of the area's best restaurants: **Salty's at Redondo.** Primarily a seafood restaurant (moderate to expensive), Salty's has one of the best sunset views around, and you can drink or dine outdoors on the pier in the summer months.

Federal Way seemingly has at least one representative from virtually every restaurant chain in the Northwest. There's a **Black Angus** at 2400 S. 320th, where you'll get a decent steak time after time. The **Sea Galley,** 30333 Pacific Hwy. S, specializes in crab legs, very reasonable prices, and fair-to-good food. **The Keg,** 32724 Pacific Hwy. S, specializes in prime rib dinners, but also features a long list of appetizers and sandwiches. **Garcia's,** 31740 23rd S, in back of the McDonald's on S. 320th, has reliable Mexican food and some good combination platters. The **Red Robin** at the E end of the Sea-Tac Mall on S. 320th has gourmet burgers, Sunday brunch, and a bar popular with the football crowd. Across 320th from the Sea-Tac Mall, the yuppified **Red Lobster** is quite good, but way too popular to attempt on a Saturday night without reservations—good choice for midweek.

A good place for a light meal is **Lolli's,** 32925 1st Ave. S (in the Quad), a restaurant/tavern that serves huge burgers and good sandwiches, along with an extensive selection of beers on tap; it might feel like a bar, but kids are legal and welcome. For homestyle Mexican food in a casual setting, try **Bernal's,** 2325 S.W. 336th (in the Safeway Plaza), 838-0448; the lounge features live entertainment every night.

Shopping And Services

The **Sea-Tac Mall** (on the S side of S. 320th St., about 2 lights into Federal Way from I-5) has a Sears, Mervyn's, Lamonts, and The Bon, plus numerous smaller specialty stores. Other shopping centers, drug, and grocery stores line S. 320th on both sides.

The **Greater Federal Way Chamber of Commerce,** at the corner of S. 320th and 1st at 32015 1st Ave. S, 838-2605, can help you out with maps and other area information. The **Federal Way Public Library** is at 848 S. 320th, 839-0257. **St. Francis Community Hospital** has 24-hour emergency care at 34515 9th Ave. S, 927-9700 or 838-9700; from Pacific Hwy. S, go W on 348th and follow the signs.

Transportation

Since Federal Way is in King County, it's served by **Metro,** (800) 542-7876 or 447-4800.

PUYALLUP VALLEY

Events

Puyallup (pronounced pyu-ALL-up), SE of Tacoma, is famous, at least in western Washington, for being the home of the **Puyallup Fair,** officially known as the western Washington Fair. One of the nation's 10 largest, the fair runs for 17 days in Sept. (starting the Friday after Labor Day) and attracts a crowd of more than 1 million to its concerts, livestock displays, rides, and refreshments. The fairgrounds are located at the intersection of Meridian St. and 9th Ave. SW.

The **Daffodil Festival** is another of Puyallup's well-known attractions. Sponsored by

Daffodil Princesses surrounded by Puyallup's bounty

the region's bulb farms, it's a 2-week series of events throughout Pierce County: the daffodil parade (the 3rd largest floral parade in the nation), a golf tournament, the "most magnificent mutt" show, a boat parade, and free daffodils everywhere you look. For info on any of the events call 627-6176. The **Van Lierop Bulb Farm** is one of the festival's sponsors; their spring garden display of over 150 varieties of crocus, iris, tulips, and, of course, daffodils, is something to see. Van Lierop's is located at 13407 80th St. E in Puyallup.

Yet another fair in the Puyallup Valley is the **Pierce County Fair,** held in Graham at 218th and Meridian (Hwy. 161) during the 2nd weekend in August. Highlighted by the infamous cow-chip throwing contest, there are also floral and photo exhibits, livestock displays, and a 5-km race. For info call 843-1173 before, or 847-4754 during, the fair.

Another big summer event is the outdoor production of **Jesus of Nazareth** in Puyallup's open-air amphitheater at 14422 Meridian S, performed at 8 p.m. every Fri. and Sat. night in July and August. One of 7 major passion plays in the country, the cast of over 200 is assisted by horses, cows, sheep, pigeons, and a donkey. For ticket info call 848-3577; the show's a bargain at less than $10.

Park

Speaking of animals, one of the region's biggest attractions is **Northwest Trek.** On Hwy. 161 near Eatonville (as you drive toward Mt. Rainier), this 600-acre wildlife park is a refuge for bighorn sheep, great blue herons, wild turkeys, bison, elk, moose, and more. An electric tram transports tourists on a 5½-mile, hour-long tour through the park; also available are 5 miles of nature trails. Share your picnic lunch with the tame deer in the visitor center's meadow, or join in a park-sponsored weekend festival, salmon bake, or photo tour. The park is open daily from Feb. through Oct. at 9 a.m. (closing times vary), weekends the rest of the year. The trams leave hourly beginning at 11 a.m. Admission is $5.50 adults, $3 kids; phone 832-6116.

Museums

Also near Eatonville, between highways 7 and 161, is the **Pioneer Farm Museum.** Here you can experience what pioneer life was really like as you grind grain, churn butter, and milk a cow. Hour-and-a-half guided tours leave every 45 minutes. The museum is open daily in summer, on weekends in spring and fall, for a small admission fee. The "world's largest" collection of Western artifacts is at the **Western Frontier Museum** at 2301 23rd Ave. SE (Trails End Ranch) in Puyallup, 832-6300. They're the proud owners of the "world's largest" longhorn as well as the "world's biggest" longhorn collection (who keeps track of these things?), not to mention carriages, arrowheads, guns, and all that other cowboy stuff. Open 9 a.m.-5 p.m. Wed. through Sun., or by appointment; admission $3.50 adults, $2.50 kids and seniors.

Furnished in 1890's style, the 17-room Victorian **Ezra Meeker Mansion** was built by the city's founder and first mayor. Located at 321 E. Pioneer in Puyallup, the mansion is open for tours Wed. through Sun. afternoons, March through mid-Dec.; admission $2 adults, $1 teens and seniors, 848-1770. The Ezra Meeker Days celebration, a week-plus celebration from the end of June through July 6, features a barbecue and extended mansion tour hours.

Accommodations

Puyallup has some of the least expensive lodging around at the **Northwest Motor Inn,** 1409 S. Meridian, 841-2600. Their 50 rooms start at $35 s, $39-43 d; whirlpool too.

ENUMCLAW

Home of the King County Fair, Enumclaw (or "place of the evil spirits") was established in 1885, and named for a nearby mountain where local Indians were once frightened by a severe thunderstorm. The views of Mt. Rainier, from just about anywhere in town, are outstanding.

Parks

Eighteen miles SE of town on Hwy. 410, **Federation Forest State Park,** 663-2207, has 619 acres of virgin forest, plus interpretive displays, hiking trails, fishing, picnicking, and part of the Naches Trail, a pioneer trail that connected eastern Washington with Puget Sound.

Twelve miles N of Enumclaw on Hwy. 169, **Green River Gorge State Park Conservation Area** is a 12-mile-long protected area of the Green River that includes wildflowers, caves, fossils, and **Flaming Geyser State Park.** Here old coal-mining test holes produce 2 geysers, one burning an 8-inch flame and the other sending methane gas bubbling up through a stream. Enjoy hiking, picnicking, fishing and boating, and a playground; no camping.

Mud Mountain Dam, 7 miles SE of Enumclaw off Hwy. 410, 825-3211, is one of the highest earth and rock flood-control dams. The park features a nature trail, wading pool, playground, picnic areas, and overlooks. The dam is open daily at 9 a.m.; free.

Bed And Breakfast

Enjoy English Hunt Club atmosphere in an elegant 1911 home at **Porter House B&B,** 3155 Porter St., 825-7671. Oriental carpets, European antiques, tapestries, and a blue enamel fireplace in the dining room complement the 4 upstairs guest rooms (2 shared baths with claw-foot tubs and shower). Rooms are $55-65 d (singles $5 less) including buffet-style continental breakfast. No pets, indoor smoking, or kids under 14.

Camping

Green River Gorge Resort, 886-2302, has 60 tent sites and 20 drive-through trailer or motorhome sites (30 feet max. length), plus sewer and electric hookups, piped water, flush toilets, showers, and laundromat. Fees are $8 per night (hookups extra). From Enumclaw, take Hwy. 169 N to Black Diamond Rd., then head 4 miles E on Green River Gorge Rd.; reservations accepted. Eleven miles NE of Enumclaw on Farman Rd., **Kanaskat-Palmer Recreation Area,** 886-0148, has 31 tent sites and 19 drive-thru sites (35 feet max. length) on the Green River. Electricity, flush toilets, showers, and boat rentals are available. Fees are $6 per night, no reservations necessary; open all year (limited facilities in winter).

Food

Delis are hard to find in the Northwest, but Enumclaw has a good one at **Baumgartner's,** 1008 E. Roosevelt, 825-1067. Pick up a croissant, sausage sandwich, or some wine and cheese for a picnic at Mt. Rainier. Up in Black Diamond at 32805 Railroad Ave., **Black Diamond Bakery,** 886-2741, bakes over 25 varieties of bread in a wood-fired oven, plus donuts, cookies, and other goodies. Closed Monday.

Events

The oldest county fair in the state, **King County Fair,** is held the 3rd week of July at Enumclaw's fairgrounds. A rodeo, live music, 4-H exhibits, food, crafts, and a logger's show highlight the event.

MOUNT RAINIER

The Indians wouldn't climb it; "Tahoma" was sacred ground, inhabited by a vengeful deity who didn't welcome visitors. But Hazard Stevens, the Union's youngest Civil War general, was determined to be the first to reach Rainier's summit. So in 1870 he began assembling his climbing party: an unemployed miner, Philomon Beecher Van Trump, and landscape artist Edward T. Coleman would accompany him to the summit; James Longmire, a local farmer, would guide them as far as Bear Prairie, at 2,630 feet; but the group needed someone with expertise. They found it in Sluiskin, a nomad Indian who had taken up residence at Bear Prairie, and whose grandfather, going against Indian tradition, had once attempted a summit climb—without success.

The first day out after Bear Prairie, Coleman turned back. He'd found himself in a precarious position on a precipice where he could go neither forward nor back with his 40-pound pack; so he chucked it, along with most of the party's food. Stevens, Van Trump, and Sluiskin continued.

As the climbers progressed, Sluiskin began losing his nerve. Stevens wrote about the Indian in an article for *Atlantic Monthly* in 1876: "Takhoma, he said, was an enchanted mountain, inhabited by an evil spirit who dwelt in a fiery lake on its summit. No human being could ascend it or even attempt its ascent and survive . . . at first, indeed, the way was easy . . . but above [the broad snow fields] the rash adventurer would be compelled to climb up steeps of loose, rolling rocks, which would turn beneath his feet and cast him headlong into the deep abyss below. . . . Moreover, a furious tempest continually swept the crown of the mountain, and the luckless adventurer, even if he wonderfully escaped the perils below, would be torn from the mountain and whirled through the air by this fearful blast." Begging off, Sluiskin promised to wait 3 days for the climbers to return; then he'd go to Olympia to tell their friends they were dead.

Sluiskin's description of the mountain wasn't far from the truth. Stevens wrote, "Our course . . . brought us first to the southwest peak. This is a long, exceedingly sharp, narrow ridge springing out from the main dome for a mile into mid-air. The ridge affords not over ten or twelve feet of foothold on top, and the sides descend almost vertically. . . . The wind blew so violently that we were obliged to brace ourselves with our Alpine staffs and use great caution to guard against being swept off the ridge."

After reaching the true summit of the mountain, Stevens and Van Trump found a volcanic steam cave where they spent the night. The next day the 2 men returned to Sluiskin, who was *really* surprised to see them, and expressed his deep admiration for the men who had conquered Takhoma: "Strong men," he said; "brave hearts."

Though the Indians called it "Tahoma" or "Ta-co-bet," Captain George Vancouver renamed the mountain in 1792 after his friend, Rear Admiral Peter Rainier (who had never seen it). About 10 years after Steven's climb, James Longmire built his mineral springs resort on what is now national park land, and the awesome beauty of the sleeping volcano has been drawing visitors ever since: over 1.5 million people visit Mount Rainier National Park every year. The park is located about 60 miles SE of Tacoma; visitor centers are open year-round at Longmire, May to mid-Oct. at Paradise, and during the summer at Ohanapecosh and Sunrise; here you can view exhibits (slide shows and films at Paradise), purchase assorted publications, or get additional information. The Paradise Visitor Center's circular glass-walled structure offers 360-degree views of the park. The visitor center at **Sunrise,** at 6,400 feet the highest auto-accessible point in the park, offers one of the best views. Admission to the park is $5 (good for 7 days).

Climate

Because of the incredible height of the mountain (recently recalculated at 14,411 feet), Rainier creates its own weather by interrupting the air flow around it, producing massive amounts of snowfall—a world-record 1,122 inches at Paradise in 1971-72. The mountain's height also accounts for its lenticular clouds—the upside-down, saucer-shaped clouds that obscure or hover just above the summit on otherwise clear days. Throughout most of the park, temperatures are not much different than those around Puget Sound; the nasty summer heat will sometimes follow you right up to Paradise, although generally the higher altitudes enjoy cooler temperatures. Spring and fall are the times to be careful; rain at Longmire can very often translate to snow at Paradise.

SIGHTS

Even when the mountain isn't "out," driving through the park provides numerous sight-

Longmire's mineral springs resort

seeing and photographic opportunities; the surrounding mountains, waterfalls, forests, and canyons alone justify the trip. Be sure to call ahead (206-569-2211) to see which roads are open. All park roads are closed from late Nov. to June or July, with the exception of the section from the Nisqually Entrance to Paradise, on which chains are frequently required.

Another way to view the mountain and surrounding area is from the **Mount Rainier Scenic Railroad,** 569-2588. The steam train leaves Elbe Station for a 14-mile, 1½-hour ride over bridges and through forests, with live music accompanying the spectacular views. The train runs weekends beginning Memorial Day, daily between June 15 and Labor Day; fares are $6.50 adults, $5.50 seniors, $4.50 teens, and $3.50 for kids, or buy a family pass for $17. The train leaves 3 times daily from Elbe on Hwy. 7.

Gray Line offers bus tours of the park; see "Getting There" below for details.

ACTIVITIES

Hiking

Rainier's hiking season is quite short: most trails are snow-free from mid-July to mid-Oct., though trails at the lower elevations may be clear earlier and later in the year. It's also advisable to dress for *all* seasons, with cotton under wool under rain gear, and strip as needed. A booklet of info for hikers and back-packers, called "Fragile, Handle With Care," is available at visitor centers or through the mail. About 305 miles of hiking trails criss-

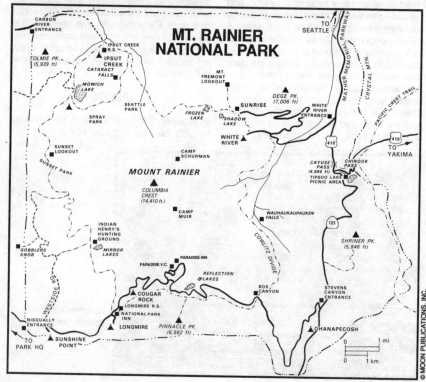

MT. RAINIER NATIONAL PARK

© MOON PUBLICATIONS, INC.

cross the park, many miles of which are suitable for day hikes. Best bet is to contact a ranger upon your arrival, who has up-to-date info on trail conditions and will be happy to suggest a trail suited to your experience and physical condition.

To get the best for less, here are 5 short (1- to 5½-mile) easy hikes that provide superior mountain views:

The **Pinnacle Peak** trail starts at the Reflection Lake parking lot (SE of Paradise) on Stevens Canyon Rd.; hike the 1½-mile trail to the saddle between Pinnacle and Plummer peaks.

For **Dege Peak,** start between Sunshine Point and the Sunrise parking area; this 1-mile trail climbs 7,006-foot Dege Peak in the Sourdough Mountains.

To get to **Mt. Fremont Lookout** from the Sunrise picnic area, follow the Wonderland trail 1½ miles to a junction of 5 trails; the lookout trail is well-marked. This 5½-mile trail takes about 3 hours RT.

From Mowich Lake in the NW part of the park, hike the 3-mile trail to the **Tolmie Peak** fire lookout (5,939 feet).

Gobbler's Knob is another fire lookout (5,500 feet) which can be reached from Round Pass on Westside Rd., near the Nisqually (SW) entrance. This 2½-mile trail passes Lake George.

More challenging day hikes with Rainier views: for **Shriner Peak** trail start from Hwy. 123, 3½ miles N of the Stevens Canyon entrance, or 7½ miles S of Cayuse Pass, and park on the W side of the road about ½ mile from the Panther Creek bridge. This 8-mile hike—about 5 hours RT—is almost completely devoid of shade, ending in a lookout/ranger station at Shriner Peak.

The 12½-mile **Sunset Lookout** hike begins from the end of Westside Road. Enjoy a 2-mile descent to a river, then climb 3½ steep miles to a fork at Sunset Park; take the right fork to Lookout Point. Allow about 8 hours RT.

Backpacking

The **Wonderland Trail** is a backpacker's dream: 93 miles of mountain passes, forests, streams, and alpine meadows, completely encircling the mountain. Campsites are stra-

Waterfalls are a common sight in Rainier's backcountry.

tegically placed about 10 miles apart, resulting in a good 10 days of hiking. You can start almost anywhere—Mowich Lake, Longmire, White River, Box Canyon—but Ipsut Creek may be the best choice, since you'd be hitting the only showers in the park at Paradise about halfway through. Also for marathon packers, the **Pacific Crest Trail** touches the E edge of the park at Tipsoo Lake on Hwy. 410, continuing N to British Columbia and S to Mexico. Backcountry permits are required for all overnight trips, and are available free from any ranger or visitor center.

For a rewarding overnight trip, **Seattle Park** trail starts from the far end of Ipsut Creek campground, continues along the Carbon River, approaches Cataract Falls (a quick side-trip), and crosses Marmot Creek. Camping is permitted about 1 mile below Seattle Park in Cataract Valley. Hike across a permanent snowfield into Spray Park, doubling back to return on the same route, or

A climbing party leaves Camp Muir for the summit.

continue to Mowich Lake, turning NE to follow Ipsut Creek back to the starting point. About 16 miles RT.

Another good overnighter, though not a circular route, is **Indian Bar.** This 14½-mile hike starts at Box Canyon on Stevens Canyon Rd., crosses Nickel Creek, then turns left to follow the Cowlitz Divide. At Indian Bar the Ohanapecosh River divides a meadow; the shelter is on the W side, just above Wauhaukaupauken Falls. Return by the same route.

Climbing

Despite Sluiskin's vengeful deity, more than 4,000 people reach Rainier's summit every year—of some 7,000 who attempt it. Two days are usually required for the trek: the first day involves a 4- to 5-hour hike over trails and snowfields to Camp Muir, the S side base camp at 10,000 feet, or Camp Schurman, on the N side at 9,500 feet; the 2nd day starts early (about 2 a.m.) for the summit climb and the return to the Paradise starting point. Reservations are not accepted for the high camps, so be prepared to camp outside: Muir's 25-person capacity is frequently filled, and Schurman has no public shelter—your only luxury is a pit toilet. Above the high camps climbers are roped, using ice axes and crampons to inch their way over glaciers to the summit. All climbers must register at a ranger station before and after their climb; solo climbers need the park superintendent's approval. But even inexperienced climbers can conquer the mountain: snow- and ice-climbing seminars are offered for climbers of all skill levels at Paradise by Rainier Mountaineering, Inc. They charge $50 for their 1-day snow and ice climbing school (no reservations necessary), $230-260 for a 3-day summit climb package (1 day of instruction plus the 2-day climb), and $350 for a 4-day Emmons glacier package (1 day of instruction plus a 3-day RT). RMI also offers seminars in crevasse rescue, mountain medicine, and basic rock climbing, plus winter ski programs and a 2-day avalanche course. Some of the required equipment is available for rental at Paradise. RMI recommends that persons under 15 not attempt the summit climb, and that climbers be in top physical condition. Call RMI at 627-6242 (535 Dock St., Ste. 209, Tacoma, WA 98402) in winter (Oct. to May) or 569-2227 (at Paradise) in summer.

Interpretive Programs

The National Park Service schedules nature walks, slide programs, and other organized activities from late June through Labor Day. Program schedules are posted at the visitor centers and campgrounds. Snowshoe walks are offered at the Paradise Visitor Center weekends and holidays from late Dec. through March.

Field Seminars

The Pacific Northwest National Parks and Forests Assn. offers 1- to 3-day seminars in glaciology, alpine ecology, photography, geology, and more at Mt. Rainier, plus similar courses at Mt. St. Helens. Tuition ranges from $85 to $100; participants are responsible for their own lodging, food, and equipment.

Seminars fill up fast; to get on the mailing list write Pacific Northwest Field Seminars, 83 S. King St., Ste. 212, Seattle, WA 98104, or phone (206) 442-2636.

Others
Fishing is generally disappointing at Rainier; the fish, if you get any, are small. Park waters are not stocked—the trout and charrs are gifts from Mom Nature—so restrictions are plentiful. Waters closed to fishing are Klickitat Creek above the White River entrance, Ipsut Creek above the Ipsut Creek campground, Frozen Lake, Shadow Lake, Reflection Lakes, and Tipsoo Lake; the Ohanapecosh River and its tributaries are OK for fly-fishing only. Lakes and ponds are open late-April through Oct.; rivers, streams, and beaver ponds from late-May through late-November. Bait fish, dead or alive, are forbidden, as are amphibians, roe, and non-preserved fish eggs. No license is required. Stop at any ranger station for info on limits and closures.

Non-motorized **boating** is allowed on all park lakes except Frozen Lake, Reflection Lakes, Ghost Lake, and Tipsoo Lake; row-boating is a great way to view the wildlife.

Facilities are open for **winter sports** at Paradise from Dec. to April. Soft platters and inner tubes may be used in designated play areas only. Most ski touring routes begin at Paradise, where rental equipment and instruction are also available; for maps and conditions contact a ranger. Growing weekend skiing and tubing crowds at Paradise—and the resulting parking problems—may force rangers to turn visitors away in the future, but so far no limits have been imposed.

ACCOMMODATIONS

Campgrounds
All campsites in the park (except Class-C group sites, which may be reserved) are available on a first-come, first-served basis only, with a limit of 14 days from June 15 through Labor Day, and 30 days from Labor Day to June 14. Class-A campgrounds (running water and flush toilets) are located at

---

PARK RULES AND REGULATIONS

- Pets must be confined or on a leash at all times; they are not allowed in the backcountry, on park trails, or in public buildings.

- No hunting. Firearms must be broken down and out of sight.

- No off-road vehicles.

- Leave rocks, plants, and animals where you find them.

- Firewood may be purchased at the Longmore service station or you can bring your own; collection of wood for fires is not permitted, except for dead wood from riverbeds at Ipsut Creek and Sunshine Point campgrounds.

- No trash in the toilets, please.

Ohanapecosh, White River, and Cougar Rock for $6/night. Class-B sites (running water and pit toilets) are at Sunshine Point and Ipsut Creek for $5/night. Class-C multiple-tent sites, at Ipsut Creek and Cougar Rock, have a central fireplace and tables for $1 pp. Sunshine Point is the only year-round camping area; the others are open only for the season. While no trailer hookups are available, holding-tank disposal stations are located at Ohanapecosh and Cougar Rock.

Inns
There are 2 inns within the park itself. The **National Park Inn** at Longmire is open daily year-round. This small inn has rooms with private baths from $49 s or d to $66 for the larger 2-room unit; rooms with shared baths go for $35 s or d. **Paradise Inn,** with unsurpassed mountain views from its altitude of 5,400 feet, and a spacious dining room, is open daily from late May to early October. Rooms with shared bath are $44 s or d; with private bath, $57-77. Contact Mount Rainier Guest Services, Box 108, Ashford, WA 98304, (206) 569-2275, for reservations.

For accommodations outside the park, see "Vicinity of Mount Rainier," p. 97.

Snow drifts permit skiing on roof of Paradise Lodge.

FOOD

The dining room at Paradise Inn opens at breakfast, lunch, and dinnertime, plus Sunday brunch during its season of operation. Paradise also offers a cafeteria, while Longmire has a sit-down restaurant. The snackbar at Sunrise operates only during the summer. Groceries can be bought during the summer at Longmire and Sunrise.

For food outside park limits, see "Vicinity of Mount Rainier," p. 97.

SERVICES

For brochures and information on camping, hiking, fishing, climbing, or other activities in the park, contact the National Park Service at Tahoma Woods, Star Route, Ashford, WA 98304, (206) 569-2211.

Backpackers can obtain topographic maps from the Mount Rainier Branch of the Pacific Northwest National Parks and Forest Assn., Longmire, WA 98397; for prices write or call (206) 569-2211, ext. 295. Camping supplies in the park are limited; better to bring yours

in from the outside. Public showers are available at Paradise, but there are no laundry facilities within park boundaries.

GETTING THERE

For year-round access to the park, take I-5 S to Hwy. 7; follow the Mt. Rainier signs as Hwy. 7 joins 706 and enters the park near Longmire. To get to the White River entrance (closed in winter) take Hwy. 18 E to Auburn; exit onto Hwy. 164 and follow that to Hwy. 410 and Mt. Rainier. From Yakima, take Hwy. 12, joining Hwy. 123 to the Stevens Canyon entrance, or Hwy. 410 over Chinook Pass.

Gray Line offers 10-hour Mt. Rainier bus tours for $29 adults, $15 for kids 5-12, daily from May through October. The bus leaves from downtown Seattle hotels—Sheraton, Westin, Crowne Plaza, and more—and the Space Needle. Backpackers can arrange to be dropped off at the park and picked up a day or two later for no additional charge. Their "Mt. Rainier Overnight," offered May through Sept., includes 1 night at Paradise Lodge for $106 s, $70 pp d, $61 pp triple. Call 626-5208 for info and reservations.

VICINITY OF MOUNT RAINIER

CRYSTAL MOUNTAIN RESORT

This year-round resort on Hwy. 410, just outside the N park boundary, has winter nordic and alpine skiing, plus hiking, fishing, swimming, tennis, horseback riding, and chairlift sightseeing rides the rest of the year. The ski resort boasts 3,120 vertical feet, 10 lifts serving 2,300 acres, plus 34 expert backcountry trails. With a top height of 7,002 feet, you'll have a fantastic view of nearby Mt. Rainier. Lift tickets are $26 adults, $16 kids, $12 seniors; under 5 and over 70 ski free. Adults can ski Mon. or Tues. for just $14. Forewarned is fore-filled: there's no gas at Crystal Mountain! Their **Summit House**, accessible only by chairlift, is the highest restaurant in the state and offers a phenomenal view of Mt. Rainier; watch for climbers approaching the summit. **Crystal Mountain Corral**, (206) 663-2589, has group trail rides, overnight barbecues, fishing, hunting, and photography trips; prices start at $25 for a short trail ride, $55-95 for a full day ride, and $135 for an overnight ride with steak fry and cowboy breakfast. You can stay at the **Crystal House Motel** for $40 d. For more info on the resort write Crystal Mountain, Box 1, Crystal Mountain, WA 98022, or phone 663-2265 or (800) 852-1444.

CHINOOK PASS

The highest of the mountain passes, Chinook Pass rises almost a mile above sea level (5,440 feet) on Hwy. 410. This is a fair-weather route, closed in winter and often dusted with snow as late as June.

Lake

At the summit of Chinook Pass, **Lake Tipsoo** is one of the most beautiful, easily accessed Cascade alpine lakes. Enjoy a picnic lunch here against a striking Mt. Rainier backdrop.

Accommodations And Food

Off Hwy. 410 in Goose Prairie, **Double K Mountain Ranch** is hidden in the William O. Douglas Wilderness, often under feet of snow. No pools, phones, or pavement here—just the indescribable natural beauty of the Cascades and high mountain lakes, with plenty of time for fishing, swimming, hiking, and skiing. The cabin and ranch house can accommodate up to 16 people; $275 per week gets you a room, meals, and use of the motorboat. Aside from July and Aug., when rooms are rented by the week only, you can stay for $60 per night with a 2-night minimum. Write Double K Mountain Ranch, Goose Prairie, WA 98929, for reservations.

Whistlin' Jack Lodge, 18936 Hwy. 410 at Chinook Pass, (509) 658-2433, borders on the sunny side of the mountains, with just 12-15 inches of rain annually and 312 days of sunshine. Open year-round, the lodge includes a motel, cottages, restaurant, lounge, gas, and groceries. Rooms cost $50-60 d for motel units, $65 d for a fireplace bungalow, and $75-100 d for cottages (the more expensive ones have hot tubs). In winter, rent cross-country skis or a snowmobile ($60-85 a day for one or 2); in summer, enjoy hay rides and trail rides. The food here is nothing to sneeze at: fresh blueberry pancakes for breakfast, a buffet lunch, and prime rib, mountain trout, or tenderloin tails for dinner.

WHITE PASS

Hwy. 12 between Yakima and Mt. Rainier traverses 4,500-foot White Pass. The route passes through heavily forested areas with a few clear views of Rainier.

Skiing

White Pass Ski Area, off Hwy. 12 about 55 miles W of Yakima, offers a 1,500-foot vertical drop and 650 acres of skiing, served by 4 double chairs, a poma, and rope tow. Amenities include a ski school, child care, cafeteria, bar, and privately owned condos. Lift tickets

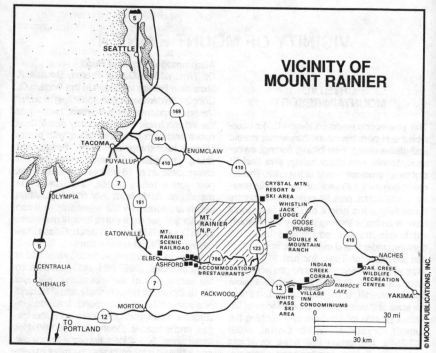

VICINITY OF MOUNT RAINIER

are $20 adults, $15 kids ($5 less midweek). Phone (509) 453-8731 for more information.

Horseback Riding

Eight miles E of White Pass Ski Area on Hwy. 12, **Indian Creek Corral** offers horseback rides from 1 hour to 3 days long, Memorial Day to Oct. 1. Take a guided trail ride for 1-3 hours for $10 an hour (kids must be over 12 or experienced), an all-day scenic trip for $50 per person, or a 3-day wilderness pack trip for $250. Groups are limited to 5 to keep it personal. Hikers can take advantage of their drop-camp service; they'll drop up to 75 pounds of gear at a selected site and pick it up whenever you like for $75. Write Star Route Box 218, Naches, WA 98937, or phone the owner at (509) 925-2062.

Lake

Traveling along Hwy. 12, you can't miss **Rimrock Lake,** just E of White Pass. The massive blue-green lake was created in 1927 by what was then one of the largest earth-filled dams in the country. Today Rimrock is popular with fishermen in search of good-sized Silvers, mid-May to late June, and with boaters, swimmers, and campers.

On the lake, **Twelve West** has 35 campsites (all but 4 with RV hookups), a marina with boat rentals, and a quality restaurant serving 3 meals daily, including steak and seafood dinners accompanied by Washington and imported wines. For reservations, phone (509) 248-2276 or write Star Route, Box 206, Naches, WA 98937.

Elk Feeding

During most winters, the large White Pass elk population and a small herd of bighorn sheep are fed at the **Oak Creek Wildlife Recreation Area,** 2 miles W of the intersection of highways 410 and 12 near Yakima. Keep an eye out for wildlife as you pass, particularly during early morning or late afternoon, when the animals are most active.

Backpacking

The **Pacific Crest Trail** intersects White Pass as it continues N to Chinook Pass and S through the Goat Rocks Wilderness, on its long path to Canada and Mexico.

The PCT follows the crest of the Cascades through the Goat Rocks Wilderness, passing through some alpine meadows but generally following rough terrain from 4,200 feet to 7,500 feet in elevation. Plan on 2 nights and 3 days to get through the Wilderness; the 2 miles between Elk Pass and Packwood glacier are the most hazardous, but the scenery here is the most spectacular. The trail is largely snow-free from late July to mid-Sept., but even in late Aug. you can expect to cross snowfields up to ½ mile across, so bring your ice axe and warm woolies—several hikers have died from hypothermia on these exposed ridges. Be sure to contact the Packwood Ranger Station, Box 559, Packwood, WA 98361, (206) 494-5515, when planning your trip for updated information on snow levels and trail conditions. You can send your supplies to yourself, General Delivery, White Pass Rural Branch, U.S. Post Office, Naches, WA 98937, marked "PCT Hiker" with your anticipated date of arrival; the post office is located in the Cracker Barrel store and may be reached by asking the operator for White Pass #5.

The trail from White Pass N to Chinook Pass is about 26 miles of more ridgetop hiking, passing a number of alpine lakes; allow 3 nights for this leg.

ASHFORD

Ashford is your last chance for food, lodging, and gas before you enter the national park. Rather than being a "last resort," some of the hotels, cabins, and restaurants here are as good or better than park facilities.

Accommodations

Lodging abounds in Ashford, just outside the SW park entrance. Listed on the National Register of Historic Places, **Ashford Mansion** is a 12-room turn-of-the-century inn on an old mountain road just 6 miles from the national park entrance. A wraparound porch, 2 2nd-floor verandas, and nearby Ashford Creek make this a delightful retreat. The 4 guest rooms share 2 baths; rooms are $48-80 d (singles $8 less). No kids or smoking. Write Box G, Ashford, WA 98304, or phone (206) 569-2739. **Alexander's,** (206) 569-2300, boasts immaculate rooms, handmade quilts, large fireplaces, stained-glass windows, a hot tub, free breakfast, and a quality restaurant featuring salmon fresh from Tacoma docks and rainbow trout from the pond out back. There are 11 rooms: $49.50 without bath, $66 with, and $82.50 for the "tower room," a 2-story, 2-room mini-paradise. **Growly Bear B&B,** (206) 569-2339, has 2 upstairs guest rooms with shared bath in an 1890s homestead; rates are $40-50 s, $50-60 d. **Rainier Country Cabins** has cedar cabins with fireplaces, electric heat, kitchens, and alpine views. A basic cabin goes for $36-39; with kitchen, $43- 46; with fireplace, $47-50. Call (206) 569-2355 or write Box IRS, Ashford, WA 98304 for reservations. The **Gateway Inn,** (206) 569-2506, features log cabins with rock fireplaces, a restaurant, cocktail lounge, and gift shop. Open year-round, the cabins are $31.50 s, $41.50 d. **The Lodge,** (206) 569-2312, has cottages capable of handling large groups, from $40-60 s or d with full kitchen and fireplace (add $5.50 pp, up to 6). **Mounthaven** has 9 cabins ($37-63, up to 4 persons) with kitchens and fireplaces as well as 20 full-utility RV hookups and a group lodge. Write Mounthaven, 38210 SR 706 E, Ashford, WA 98304, or phone (206) 569-2594.

Food

Alexander's, (206) 569-2300, specializes in homebaked bread and fresh salmon and trout. The **Copper Creek Restaurant,** (206) 569-2326, is open March through Oct. for breakfast, lunch, and dinner, with dinners starting at $10. For pizza, sandwiches, nachos, and over 60 beers and wines, try **Wild Berry Restaurant,** open 365 days a year—the food is better than you'd expect, and the prices are reasonable.

OLYMPIA

Olympia was settled in 1846 by Edmund Sylvester and Levi Smith, who filed claims of over 300 acres each under the Oregon Land Law. The town was named Smithfield until Smith died, leaving his share to Sylvester; then "Smithster" was born. Probably due to the awkward pronunciation, the city's official name was changed to Olympia, after the majestic mountains to the west. When Washington became a territory in 1853, Governor Isaac Stevens named Olympia the capital— and for the next 40 years, Olympia fought North Yakima, Vancouver, Ellensburg, Centralia, and other growing cities to retain the title. A bill was actually passed in 1861 moving the capital to Vancouver, but because of a minor flaw in wording and the omission of the date, the bill was ruled unconstitutional. (This faulty document is on display at the Washington State Capital Museum.) It wasn't until 1890 that Olympia was finally officially named Washington's state capital.

Although among the oldest of Washington's cities, Olympia certainly isn't one of the biggest, with a population of less than 30,000. Being at the southernmost end of Puget Sound would presumably mean an active shipping industry, but the Port of Olympia doesn't begin to compare to Tacoma or Seattle; Olympia's port is primarily a log-moving convenience, as lumber from the forests of the Olympic Peninsula is shipped to its destination. The Olympia brewery in nearby Tumwater is among the area's biggest businesses; oysters, berries, and mushrooms round out the county's agricultural business. But it's the capitol campus that gives Olympia its distinctive stately flavor.

SIGHTS

Capitol Campus
Clearly the highlight of the city, the landscaped grounds and majestic buildings of Olympia's capitol campus make it one of the country's most beautiful state capitals. Located between 11th and 14th avenues off Capitol Way, the campus consists of 55 acres of greenery, including an arboretum, a sunken rose garden, and an abundance of rhododendrons and cherry blossoms; a replica of Denmark's Tivoli fountain; and a number of historical buildings dating back to the early 1900s. The best place to start is at the **Visitor Information Center;** here you can get maps of the campus, brochures, tour information, plus a metered parking space. All of the on-street parking is leased, so visitors must park in one of the visitor lots; or, follow the signs from I-5 exit 105A to the free shuttle bus. The impressive **Legislative Building** is hard to miss: its 287-foot dome was the 4th largest in the world when it was completed in 1928. Tours of the capitol are offered hourly most of the year; call 586-TOUR. The **Governor's Mansion,** recently restored, is the oldest building on the campus, dating back to 1908. Tours are given Wed. afternoons by appoint-

---

DOWNTOWN OLYMPIA

1. Capitol Lake Park
2. Olympia Oyster House
3. Percival Landing & Budd Bay Cafe
4. Farmer's Market
5. Rainbow Restaurant
6. Golden Gavel Motor Hotel
7. Capitol Theatre
8. Crackers
9. Partlow Gallery
10. Washington Center for Performing Arts
11. Urban Onion
12. Execulodge/Governor House Hotel
13. Sylvester Park
14. Old Capitol
15. Carnegie's
16. Greyhound
17. Best Western Aladdin
18. Gardner's Seafood & Pasta
19. State Greenhouse
20. Governor's Mansion
21. Legislative Building
22. Insurance Building
23. Public Information Center
24. state library
25. State Capital Museum

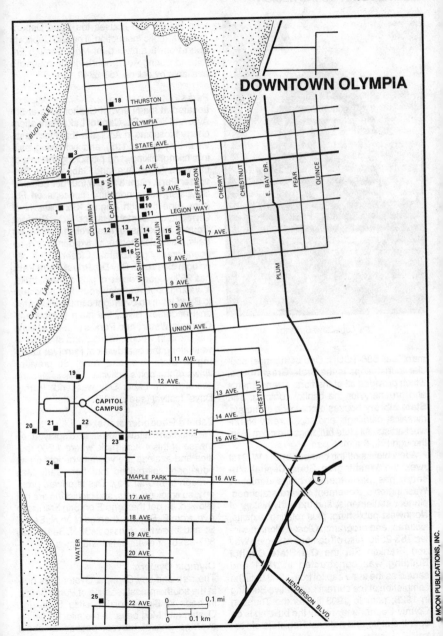

DOWNTOWN OLYMPIA

BUDD INLET

THURSTON
OLYMPIA
STATE AVE.
4 AVE.
5 AVE.
LEGION WAY
7 AVE.
8 AVE.
9 AVE.
10 AVE.
UNION AVE.
11 AVE.
12 AVE.
13 AVE.
14 AVE.
15 AVE.
16 AVE.
17 AVE.
18 AVE.
19 AVE.
20 AVE.
22 AVE.

CAPITOL LAKE

WATER
COLUMBIA
CAPITOL WAY
WASHINGTON
FRANKLIN
ADAMS
JEFFERSON
CHERRY
CHESTNUT
E. BAY DR
PEAR
QUINCE
PLUM
CHESTNUT

CAPITOL CAMPUS
MAPLE PARK
WATER

HENDERSON BLVD
5

0   0.1 mi
0   0.1 km

© MOON PUBLICATIONS, INC.

the Legislative Building

ment; call 586-TOUR. One of the most popular tourist stops is the **State Greenhouse,** which provides all of the floral arrangements and greenery for the capitol complex. The **State Library** houses a collection of murals, mosaics, paintings, and sculpture by Northwest artists. All state buildings are open Mon. through Fri., 8 a.m.-5 p.m.

A few blocks off the campus at 211 W. 21st Ave., the **Washington State Capital Museum** has permanent exhibits depicting Washington's movement toward statehood, pioneer settlements, and the early history of Northwest publishing, plus rotating exhibits, lectures, and programs. Closed Mon. in winter; 753-2580. Also off campus at Legion Way and Franklin St., the **Old State Capitol Building** was constructed in 1891 and served as the state capitol from 1903 until the completion of the current Legislative Building in 1928; prior to 1903 it was the Thurston County Courthouse. Today the building is on both the state and national Registers of Historic Places and houses the State Department of Public Instruction. The Old Capitol is open from 8 a.m.-5 p.m. Mon. through Fri. (closed during noon hour); group tours are available by calling 753-6740.

Parks
Located at the N end of Capitol Lake at 5th Ave. and Water St., **Capitol Lake Park** offers cherry blossoms in April, the "Lakefair" festival in July (see p. 105), and swimming, sailing, hiking, biking, and picnicking the rest of the year. At 7th Ave. and Capitol Way, **Sylvester Park,** named for city founder Edmund Sylvester, hosts noontime concerts on Fri. from June through August. Six miles N of Olympia on Boston Harbor Rd., **Burfoot County Park** has an interpretive trail, hiking trails, saltwater beach, playground, and an open, grassy picnic area. Closer to the city on both sides of E. Bay Dr., **Priest Point Park** has 253 wooded acres of picnic areas, trails, a wading pool, and playground, plus access to Budd Inlet; no overnight camping. Located on Henderson Blvd., the main attraction of **Olympia Watershed Park** is its 2-mile hiking trail through woods, marsh, and streams. A walk along the boardwalk at **Percival Landing** at State Ave. and Water St. provides views of the port's activities. This is also the scene of the Labor Day weekend "Harbor Days" festival (see p. 105).

Zabel's Rhododendrons
Washington's state flower is displayed en masse at this 4-acre park, where 1,200 rhodies and azaleas are yours to behold on an hour-long, self-guided tour from early May through Memorial Day. This is private property, so smoking, pets, and picnicking are not allowed. To get there, go E on San Francisco Ave. from E. Bay Dr., then go N on N. Bethel St. and follow the signs to 2432 N. Bethel; call 357-3370 for exact dates and times.

Olympia Oysters
The rare and tiny Olympia Oyster lives only in the southernmost reaches of Puget Sound in beds in Big Skookum, Little Skookum, Oyster, and Mud bays. In the mid-1920s the average annual harvest peaked at about

48,000 bushels, but then a Shelton pulp mill released pollutants that sharply decreased their numbers. The oyster population dwindled still further after the 1930s, when the importation of Japanese oysters began. These oysters brought with them two pests: the Japanese Oyster Drill and the Japanese Flatworm, harmful only to smaller oysters like the Olympia. By 1978 the Olympia Oyster harvest amounted to a mere 500 bushels. These little guys aren't heavy into socializing; they're bisexual in the truest sense, performing as males in the spring when they release a large quantity of sperm into the water, then changing into females and producing up to 300,000 eggs which become fertilized as the oyster takes in the sperm it had previously expelled.

To see how the rare Olympia oysters are raised, opened, and packed, visit the **Taylor United, Inc.** plant. Tours are by appointment only; 426-6178. To get there take exit 104 from I-5 onto Hwy. 101; take Hwy. 101 to Taylor Farm, S.E. 130 Lynch Rd., about 3 miles S of Shelton.

ACCOMMODATIONS

Bed And Breakfast
Built in 1910, **Harbinger Inn,** 1136 E. Bay Dr., 754-0389, has 3 rooms with shared bath from $42-48 s, $48-53 d, plus a 2-room suite with marina view and private bath for $73 s, $78 d. Enjoy late afternoon tea and cookies with a book from their library; no pets or kids under 12.

Hotels
Downtown at 909 Capitol Way, the **Golden Gavel Motor Hotel,** 352-8533, has 27 budget rooms from $27 s, $30-33 d. Just off I-5 at exit 105B, the **Carriage Inn Motel,** 1211 S. Quince, 943-4710, has 63 rooms from $32 s, $39-42 d. Within walking distance of the capitol, the **Execulodge Governor House Hotel,** 621 S. Capitol Way, 352-7700 or (800) 356-5335, has 120 rooms from $40 s, $46-52 d, in an 8-story building overlooking Sylvester Park and Capitol Lake. Also on the premises are a restaurant, bar, coffee shop, and heated

outdoor pool. **Best Western Aladdin Hotel,** 900 Capitol Way, 352-7200, is just 3 blocks from the Capitol Campus. Their 99 rooms are $42-52 s, $48-57 d, with outdoor pool, restaurant, and lounge; pets OK. Perched atop the hill on Evergreen Park Dr., the **Westwater Inn** has the city's best viewpoint, taking in the Capitol Dome, Capitol Lake, the Budd Inlet, and the Cascades. Rooms in this top-shelf hotel are surprisingly affordable: $48 s, $56 d in the "inner court" (no view); $56 s, $64 d for rooms on the lake side. For real luxury, jacuzzi suites ($75-85) and parlor suites ($120) are also available; pets are $10 extra. Standard equipment includes a heated outdoor pool, whirlpool, laundry facilities, and outdoor volleyball court; restaurant, lounge, and coffee shop on premises. Phone (800) 562-5635 statewide or 943-4000 locally to make reservations.

For other hotels and motels in the Olympia area see "Vicinity of Olympia," below.

Camping
Tenters and RVers can stay relatively close to town at **Black Lake RV Park,** 4325 Black Lake-Belmore Rd. SW, 357-6775, on the E shore of Black Lake 4 miles SW of downtown Olympia. Open year-round, the resort offers

the old state capitol

full hookups for $9 per night, non-hookup sites for $7, with weekly and monthly rates. Lake swimming, boat rentals, game room, hot showers, and groceries are also available.

Camping for hundreds of vehicles is available year-round at the **ORV Sports Park** on Hwy. 8, 16 miles W of Olympia. Fees are $5 per night on non-event days, $3 per night on event weekends (the $2 gate makes up the difference); hot pay showers and picnic tables are provided. See "Entertainment," below, for events held.

Open May through Sept., **American Heritage** at 9610 Kimmie St. SW, 943-8778, has over 100 campsites with full hookups, showers, heated pool; other amenities include free evening movies, arcade, kiddie farm, and go-karts. To get there, take exit 99 from I-5 and head east.

FOOD

Waterfront and view restaurants aren't as common in Olympia as in other Puget Sound cities. The **Ebb Tide Inn,** one of few, sits right on the water at the end of N. Washington St., past the none-too-busy Port of Olympia. Their steak-and-seafood menu is highlighted by a seafood bar and outdoor deck, and the lounge offers entertainment nightly; 943-7770. The **Budd Bay Cafe** at Percival Landing is open for lunch and dinner daily, with outdoor dining in summer featuring a peaceful marina view. **Seven Gables,** 1205 W. Bay Dr., 352-2349, looks across Budd Inlet toward Mt. Rainier, and the view isn't even the best part; the moderately priced menu features a wide variety, including steak, chicken, fettucine, and seafood. Open for dinner Tues. through Sat., Sun. for brunch.

Washington's oldest seafood restaurant, the **Olympia Oyster House,** has been serving the precious delicacies for over 50 years at 320 W. 4th Ave., 943-8020. Prices for a plate of Olympia oysters haven't changed much in that time; they're still about $20, though at lunchtime you can get a smaller portion for $10. Other dinners include fettucine, steak, chicken, and seafood-and-steak combinations.

Carnegie's, 7th and Franklin, 357-5550, serves moderately priced Northwest seafood, cajun food, and prime rib in the old Carnegie Library, a National Historic Site. **Gardner's Seafood and Pasta,** 111 W. Thurston St., 786-8466, is the place to go for local specialties—Dungeness crab, geoduck, Olympia oysters—at moderate prices; open for dinner daily. **Patrick's,** in the Execulodge Governor House Hotel at 621 S. Capitol Way, 352-7700, features Pacific Northwest seafood, steak, and veal, with a piano bar; closed Sunday. **Ceazans,** the restaurant at the Westwater Inn, has the best views in the area from its hilltop setting at 2300 Evergreen Park Dr., 943-4000, with a fancy steak-and-seafood menu in the moderate range. Dinner is served Mon. through Sat., with a Sunday Champagne brunch.

One of the city's most lively late-night eating spots is **Crackers,** in the Wards Building at 317 E. 4th Avenue. They're open Sun. through Thurs. till midnight, weekends till 3 a.m., and open daily at 7 a.m. for breakfast. The menu (loaded with puns) includes a number of breakfast omelettes in the $4-5 range, burgers and sandwiches around $5, and dinner entrees, including seafood, chicken, veal, pasta, and steak, from $7-14, in oak-and-hanging-plants decor.

For an all-natural breakfast, lunch, or dinner, try the **Urban Onion** at the corner of Legion and Washington, 943-9242. Their "wholesome cuisine," consisting of salads and sandwiches, pasta, stir-fries, and Mexican meals, is served daily from 7 a.m.-midnight.

The local pizza chain is **Brewery City Pizza,** with free delivery from 1621 Harrison Ave. NW, 754-7800, on the W side. For dinner with a horse show, see below.

ENTERTAINMENT

Nightlife
The classier restaurants and hotels (see above and "Tumwater," below) generally have subdued entertainment nightly (except Sun.) in the lounges. **Patrick's** at the Execulodge Governor House Hotel has live comedy on Sat. nights. The **Columbia St.**

Pub, 4th and Columbia, is known for its Sat. night jazz. **Trails End** at the Tumwater Trails End Arena is fully licensed with Tues. night comedy acts and dancing to Top 40 tunes on Fri. and Sat. nights; to get there, follow Capitol Blvd. S to Trails End Drive.

Equestrian Competitions

Follow Capitol Blvd. S to the **Trails Arena** at 7824 Trails End Dr. SE (technically in Tumwater), where horse shows of various types are held several times a week, as well as an occasional circus and BMX race. The **Trails Restaurant,** 753-8720, overlooks the arena, offering moderately priced lunch and dinner, including a build-your-own-dinner menu where you can select the side dishes to accompany your entree. Entry to the lower arena is generally free. Restaurant reservations are highly recommended.

ORV Sports Park

Thurston County provides an abundance of opportunities for off-roaders, with the ORV trails in Capitol Forest and 157 acres devoted to ORV usage in the **Thurston and Grays Harbor Counties ORV Sports Park,** located on the S side of Hwy. 8 about 16 miles W of Olympia. The park has a motocross track, hillclimb, trail riding area, kiddy motocross track, and camping (see "Camping" above). Motocross and 4-wheel-drive competitions are held nearly every weekend, year-round; admission is $2. Call 495-3243 for recorded information.

The Arts

Masterworks Choral Ensemble performs 4 concerts a year including Handel's *Messiah,* most of them at the **Washington Center for the Performing Arts,** 512 S. Washington Street. Tickets are $10 or less and are available in advance by writing Box 1091, Olympia, WA 98507. The WCPA also hosts an "Artists Series" featuring such performers as the Seattle Symphony, the Vienna Boys' Choir, ballet, theater, and the Peking Acrobats (from Oct. to April). Tickets are $12-23, depending on the performance and seating; to order ahead, write to the Washington Center for the Performing Arts at Box 202, Olympia, WA 98507. Tickets for all performances are also available at the box office (subject to availability) from 10 a.m.-6 p.m. Mon. through Fri., 10 a.m.-2 p.m. Sat., and 2 hours prior to the event.

Capitol Playhouse '24, located in the historic Capitol Theatre at 206 E. 5th Ave., 754-5378, produces 4 plays from Dec. to May as well as a summer Shakespeare Festival, consisting of 3 plays from June through August. Tickets may be purchased at the playhouse.

Gallery

Downtown Olympia has a number of art galleries and boutiques on 4th and 5th avenues good for browsing. The **Marianne Partlow Gallery** at 5th and Washington, 943-0055, is probably the most impressive, representing artists from the Northwest and beyond; open Tues. through Saturday.

Festivals And Fairs

The **Wooden Boat Festival,** 357-3370, held in mid-May at Percival Landing, includes a regatta and wooden boats open for public viewing. The first Sat. in June, Evergreen State College's **Super Saturday** features arts and crafts, food, and entertainment for all ages; phone 866-6000, ext. 6192, for information. The city's biggest summer festival is **Capital Lakefair,** held in mid-July, 943-7344. Activities include a bicycle road race, twilight parade, bed races, regatta, fireworks, and crowning of the Lakefair queen. The **Capital City Marathon** brings runners from across the U.S. to compete the fourth Sat. in July; phone RUN-1-RUN for information. Summer's end brings the **Harbor Days Festival** to Percival Landing over Labor Day weekend, highlighted by a regatta and tugboat races in the Sound; call 866-1988 for information.

Shopping And Services

Olympia's **Farmer's Market** at the corner of N. Capitol and Thurston has fresh fruit and vegies Thurs. through Sun., 10 a.m.-3 p.m. **Capital Mall,** 9th Ave. SW and Black Lake Blvd., is the area's largest shopping center with nearly 100 shops and restaurants, including Frederick & Nelson, The Bon, J.C.

Penney, and Lamonts. Just up Black Lake Blvd. is another shopping plaza, **Capital Village,** with grocery, drug, and hardware stores plus a sprinkling of fast-food restaurants. See "Lacey" below for South Sound Center.

The area code in and around Olympia is 206. For maps and general information stop by the **Greater Olympia Visitors and Convention Bureau,** 316 Schmidt Pl. in Tumwater, 357-3370, or write Box 7249, Olympia, WA 98507; or, try the **Olympia/Thurston County Chamber of Commerce,** 1000 Plum St., Olympia, WA 98501, 357-3362. Surrounding communities have their own chambers of commerce: **Lacey Chamber of Commerce,** next to Pay 'N' Save at 7 South Sound Center, Box 3206, Lacey, WA 98503, 491-4141; **Tumwater Area Chamber of Commerce,** 488 Tyee Dr., Tumwater, WA 98502, 357-5153; **Tenino Chamber of Commerce,** 208 Sussex Ave., Box 726, Tenino, WA 98589, 264-5075. Members of AAA can get guidebooks and area maps from their office at 1000 E. Union, 357-5561.

For medical emergencies, **St. Peter Hospital** has 24-hour emergency room service at 413 N. Lilly Rd., 456-7289. To get there, take exit 107 from I-5 northbound, exit 109 from I-5 southbound. **Black Hills Community Hospital** is near Capital Mall on Olympia's W side, 754-5858. For non-life threatening emergencies, try **Westcare Clinic,** on the W side at 3000 Limited Lane NW, 357-9392.

TRANSPORTATION

Arriving By Car

Olympia is about an hour S of Seattle (a half-hour S of Tacoma) on I-5, at the S end of Puget Sound.

Arriving By Air

To get to the capital city via a major carrier, you'll have to fly into Sea-Tac Airport (just S of Seattle) and get ground transportation into the city. **Capital Aeroporter,** 754-7113, serves Olympia 12 times a day from Sea-Tac; the OW fare is $17. Get up-to-the-minute information on ground transportation schedules and rates, weather and traffic conditions by calling the airport at (800) 544-1965 from a touch-tone phone.

Arriving By Train

Amtrak serves Olympia along its N-S *Coast Starlight* route from Seattle to Los Angeles and via its *Pioneer* route from Seattle to Salt Lake City. The Amtrak station is in E Olympia at 83rd and Rich Rd. SE. For schedule and fare info call (800) 872-7245.

Getting Around By Bus

Intercity Transit serves Olympia, Tumwater, and most of Thurston County from Mon. through Fri., 7 a.m.-5:30 p.m. The regular adult fare is $.35, kids $.25; day passes are available for $.75 adults, $.50 kids. Take advantage of the free zone covering downtown Olympia and the Capitol Campus area from 11 a.m.-2 p.m. weekdays. For route and schedule info call 786-1881, or stop by the customer service office at 526 S. Pattison during normal working hours.

Pierce Transit, 581-8000, offers an "Olympia Express" route from the Lakewood Park and Ride (S of Tacoma at I-5 exit 127) to the Capitol Campus. Geared toward commuters, the bus leaves Lakewood at 6:40 a.m. and 7 a.m., then departs the capitol for the return to Lakewood at 4:40 p.m. and 5:10 p.m. The OW fare is $1.25.

Greyhound connects Olympia to Seattle, Tacoma, Portland, and other cities along its N-S I-5 corridor, connecting to virtually anywhere in the country. For specific route and fare information call 357-5541 or visit the bus station at Capitol and 7th.

VICINITY OF OLYMPIA

LACEY AREA

A few miles NE of Olympia right off I-5, Lacey is primarily a suburban shopping area and retirement village. Just E and slightly N of Lacey proper is the Nisqually Delta, preserved wetlands geographically identical to Tacoma's industrial tideflat area.

Parks

Just off I-5 at exit 114, **Nisqually National Wildlife Refuge** is a protected home for 300 species of wildlife, including great blue herons, bald eagles, and red-tailed hawks, as well as a resting area for over 20,000 migrating ducks and geese. A 5.6-mile hiking loop trail, a 1-mile loop trail, a ½-mile interpretive trail, and photo blinds assist you in your bird-watching; be sure to bring binoculars and a field guide. A boat launch ramp is available at Luhr Beach; to use the landing you'll need a hunting, fishing, or trapping license, or a conservations decal, available from the State Game Dept., 516 N. Washington, Olympia, 753-5717. Visitors are welcome at the refuge 7 days a week during daylight hours; a $2 entry fee covers the permit holder and his spouse, children, and/or parents. No jogging, bicycling, motorbikes, pets, fires, or camping.

The **Audubon Nature Center**, 4949 D'Milluhr Rd. NE at Luhr Beach on Nisqually Reach, 459-0387, has marine animals and birds, a museum, fishing dock, boat launch, picnic area, guided tours, and raft trips. Open Wed., Sat., and Sun. afternoons.

Tolmie State Park, 5 miles from exit 111, has 1,800 feet of waterfront on Nisqually Reach with swimming, fishing, 3½ miles of hiking trails, and an underwater park with an artificial reef created by the intentional sinking of 3 wooden barges. Open for day use only, the park also provides an outdoor shower for swimmers and divers near the lower restroom. The park was named for Dr. William Frazer Tolmie, who spent 16 years at Fort Nisqually as physician, surgeon, botanist, and fur trader for Hudson's Bay Company. Tolmie also studied the languages of the Northwest people—his communication skills proved invaluable for negotiations during the Indian Wars of 1855-56.

Accommodations

Just 500 feet from the entrance to Tolmie State Park, **Puget View Guest House,** a B&B at 7924 61st Ave. NE, 459-1676, has 2-room waterfront cottage suites for $65 d (they'll hold 4) on peaceful Nisqually Reach—a beautiful, natural setting only 5 minutes from I-5. Breakfast is brought to your cottage door; overnight anchorage is available for boaters. For motel accommodations just 10 minutes from downtown Olympia, the **Super 8** at 4615 Martin Way, 459-8888, is just off I-5 at exit 109. Rooms are $36 s, $40-44 d.

Food

Lacey's **Brewery City Pizza** is at 4354 Martin Way, 491-6630. Next door, **O'Blarney's Pub,** 4411 Martin Way, has hard-to-find Irish music and sing-alongs on Tuesdays. Martin Way and Sleater-Kinney Rd. are lined with fast-food restaurants. **La Palma II** has Mexican food and a lounge at 523 South Sound Center, 459-9805.

Fairs And Festivals

Lacey's **Spring Fun Fair** is held in early May at St. Martin's College and South Sound Center; phone 491-4141 for details. The **Thurston County Fair,** held the first full weekend in Aug. at the County Fairgrounds in Lacey, is a 5-day festival with entertainment, food, and booths. Call 786-5453 for hours and information.

Shopping

Just off I-5 at exit 108 is **South Sound Center,** an enclosed mall with over 100 shops and restaurants, including Sears, Mervyn's, and Nordstrom Place Two. **Olympia Square,** just off I-5 on both sides of Pacific Ave., has a Ross Dress for Less, Food Pavilion, Sizzler's Restaurant, and more. Enjoy one-stop shopping for warehouse-priced groceries, clothes,

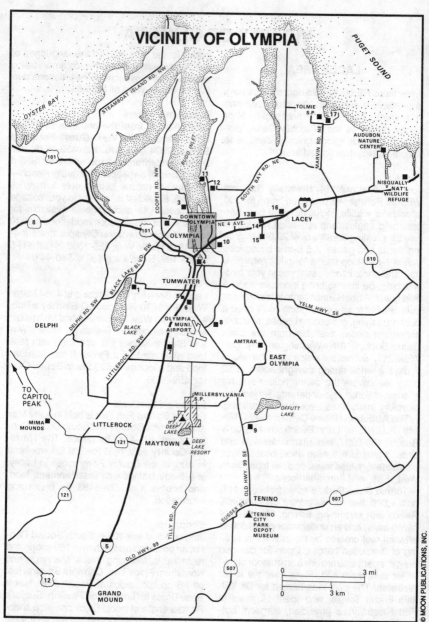

VICINITY OF OLYMPIA

OYSTER BAY

PUGET SOUND

TOLMIE S.P. ■ 17

AUDUBON NATURE CENTER

NISQUALLY NAT'L WILDLIFE REFUGE

STEAMBOAT ISLAND RD. NW

BUDD INLET

101

8

101

COOPER RD. NW

SOUTH BAY RD. NE

MARVIN RD. NE

■ 11
■ 12

3

2

DOWNTOWN OLYMPIA

OLYMPIA

NE 4 AVE.

■ 13

16 ■

■ 14

■ 15

10

LACEY

5

510

BLACK LAKE BLVD. SW

DELPHI RD. SW

■ 1

TUMWATER

5 ■
6

YELM HWY SE

DELPHI

Black Lake

OLYMPIA MUNI. AIRPORT

■ 8

LITTLEROCK RD. SW

TO CAPITOL PEAK

■ 7

AMTRAK

EAST OLYMPIA

MIMA MOUNDS

LITTLEROCK

MILLERSYLVANIA S.P.

Offutt Lake

121

DEEP LAKE

MAYTOWN

DEEP LAKE RESORT

■ 9

TILLY RD. SW

OLD HWY 99 SE

SUSSEX ST.

TENINO CITY PARK DEPOT MUSEUM

507

121

5

TENINO

507

12

GRAND MOUND

OLD HWY 99

0   3 mi

0   3 km

© MOON PUBLICATIONS, INC.

VICINITY OF OLYMPIA

1. Black Lake RV Park
2. Capitol Village Shipping Center and Capitol Mall
3. Seven Gables Restaurant
4. Olympia Brewery, Tumwater Historical Park, Crosby House, Henderson House, South Pacific, and Falls Terrace Restaurant
5. Tyee Motel
6. Motel 6
7. American Heritage KOA
8. The Trails Arena
9. Wolf Haven
10. Olympia Watershed Park
11. Priest Point Park
12. Zabel's Rhododendrons
13. St. Peter's Hospital
14. Brewery City Pizza and O'Blarney's Pub
15. South Sound Shopping Center
16. Super 8
17. Puget View Guest House

jewelry, and more at **Fred Meyer,** just off Sleater-Kinney Rd. across from South Sound Center.

TUMWATER

The home of Olympia Beer was Washington's first community—then named New Market—settled in 1845 along the Deschutes River at the end of the Oregon Trail. Starting at Independence, Missouri, the families in the Wagon Train of 1844 endured 19 months of cold, rain, and wearying travel through what's now Kansas, Nebraska, Wyoming, Idaho, and Oregon, en route to their final destination above Tumwater Falls. Members of Hudson's Bay Co., who had been stationed at Fort Nisqually since 1833, provided the settlers with the makings for the first sawmill N of the Columbia and traded army supplies for wood shingles.

Brewery
Heading down Deschutes Way toward Tumwater, you can't miss the **Olympia Brewery** immediately adjacent to Tumwater Falls Park (see below) at Custer Way and Schmidt

Place. A 40-minute tour of their facilities runs daily from 8 a.m.-4:30 p.m.

Parks
The **Tumwater Historical Park,** 602 Deschutes Way, is the site of the first American settlement in the Puget Sound region, founded in 1845. The neatly landscaped grounds include picnic areas, a boat launch into the Deschutes, an exercise trail, and lots of hungry ducks. Farther S on Deschutes Way, butting up against the brewery, you'll find **Tumwater Falls Park,** where you may see salmon heading upstream in the fish ladders.

Museums
Henderson House Pictorial Museum, 602 Deschutes Way, has photographic exhibits depicting life along the Deschutes River during the late 1800s, as well as recent photos of Tumwater's people and events; open daily in summer, Tues. through Sat. in winter. The **Crosby House,** adjacent to Tumwater Historical Park at Deschutes Way and Grant St., is Tumwater's oldest home; it was built in 1860 by Bing Crosby's grandfather, Capt. Nathaniel Crosby III, who came around the Horn to the Oregon Territory in 1847 and inspired the whole Crosby clan to follow him out West. Open by appointment only.

Accommodations
The **Tyee Hotel,** 500 Tyee Dr., provides a resort-like atmosphere to its guests with 20 landscaped acres of grounds, outdoor pool, and pickleball and basketball courts, while still offering reasonable rates from $53 s or d. Their restaurant, **Sutter's,** serves seafood, steak, and prime rib. For reservations call (800) 426-0670 or 352-0511.

For a distinctively non-resort atmosphere, **Motel 6,** near the brewery at 400 W. Lee St., 754-7320, has 119 standard motel rooms for $24 s, $30 d with an outdoor pool.

Food
In front of the Olympia Brewery and next to Tumwater Falls Park, **Falls Terrace** has a new peach paint job and some nice surprises inside. Lunches include sandwiches, fish,

burgers, steaks, and salads; moderately priced dinners feature chicken dishes, steak, seafood, veal, and traditional meals like pot roast and turkey dinners. A lower-priced early-bird menu is offered before the dinner crowds show up.

Migel's serves Mexican food at the Tumwater Valley Golf Course, 4611 Tumwater Valley Dr. SE. For Chinese and Polynesian food, try **South Pacific,** next to the brewery at 3507 Capitol Blvd., 352-0701. Or, have a **Brewery City Pizza** delivered free from 5150 Capitol Blvd., 754-6767.

Festival

The 3rd weekend in May, the **Tumwater Bluegrass Festival** brings fiddlers and banjo-pickers to Tumwater High School on Israel Road. Bluegrass concerts run from Fri. through Sun. with contests, booths, and Sunday morning Gospel music. Call 357-5153 for information.

Golf

Open to the public, the 18-hole **Tumwater Valley Golf Course,** 4611 Tumwater Valley Dr. SE, 943-9500, has a driving range, pro shop, and lessons.

TENINO

From downtown Olympia, follow Capitol Blvd. S onto Old Hwy. 99 to Tenino, a small, old, quiet town probably best known, in days of yore, for its sandstone quarry. The name Tenino has a handful of possible origins, from the Indian name for a fork or junction, to the more colorful Engine Number 1090 (ten-nine-oh) that ran on the Kalama-Tacoma railroad line in the 1870s.

Wolf Haven

This 30-acre wolf refuge is home to 39 wolves (plus coyotes and red foxes) who were no longer needed by researchers, were mistreated or unwanted by zoos and refuges, or were family "pets" who grew predictably wild. These former misfits are now loved and wanted—even introduced to visitors by name. The sanctuary offers guided tours and "howl-ins,"

featuring a marshmallow roast, reciting of Eskimo and Indian folk legends, singing, and howling with the wolves, 7 to 10 p.m. on Fri. and Sat. nights during the summer. Wolf Haven is located at 3111 Offut Lake Rd., just off Old Hwy. 99, 264-4695; open daily May to Sept., Wed. to Sat. in winter. Tours $3 adults, $2 kids; howl-ins $4 adults, $2.50 kids.

Park And Museum

One block off Sussex St., **Tenino City Park** has overnight camping and picnic areas plus the **Tenino Depot Museum,** 399 W. Park St., 264-4321, an original sandstone train depot housing a collection of historical Tenino and South Thurston County artifacts. Open Sun. 1 p.m.- 4 p.m or by appointment (264-4620).

Festival

The 4th weekend in July brings all kinds of commotion to quiet Tenino with the **Oregon Trail Celebration.** A parade, muzzle-loading camp, and kids' carnival highlight the fair.

DELPHI

Eight miles S of Tumwater is the **Mima Mounds Interpretive Area,** a Registered National Landmark with nature walks, an interpretive center, and picnic area. These grass-covered mounds, ranging in height up to 8 feet, are also scattered throughout southern Thurston County, parts of China, and Alaska. They're often referred to as "mysterious" because no one really knows how they got there; theoretical origins range from glaciers to pocket gophers.

From Mima Mounds continue N on Waddell Creek Rd. to **Capitol Forest,** a multi-use "working" forest (look out for logging trucks)

CAMPING IN THE STATE PARKS

- More than 90 Washington state parks have camping facilities. A large proportion of these have trailer hookups, and with a $9.50 maximum charge, the parks are a good value—and generally more aesthetically pleasing than private RV parks. The following information will help you to plan your trip and understand the individual park descriptions.

- Seventy-five percent of the state's campsites are classified as "standard." This means you get a picnic table, campstove, nearby running water, garbage disposal, and flush toilet, and in most parks (except Horsethief Lake, Wallace Falls, Mt. Spokane, and Spencer Spit), hot showers. Standard sites cost $7 per night.

- Many of the parks have "utility sites" with water, sewer, and/or electric hookups. Some of these can be as short as 35 feet in length (that's total length of RV or car plus trailer), so if you're traveling in an extra-long RV, be sure to get a copy of the guide below. Prices for utility sites vary with the type of hookup: add to the $7 standard site fee $.50 for water, $.50 for sewer, and $1.50 for electricity. If the utility sites are full or nonexistent, RVers may park in standard sites.

- Some parks also have "primitive" sites; that means no flush toilet, sometimes no running water. If you hike or bike in, the fee is $3; if you're in a motorized vehicle, it's $4.50.

- Camping is limited to 10 consecutive days per park from May through September.

- No chopping or gathering of firewood is allowed. Some parks sell campfire logs, but it's best to bring your own.

- Campsites are available on a first-come, first-served basis in all but 11 parks, where

reservations are accepted from the 2nd Mon. in Jan. until 2 weeks before Labor Day for the summer camping season. Reservations must be made at least 14 days in advance. Parks that allow reservations are Belfair State Park, Belfair; Fort Flagler State Park, Nordland; Moran State Park, Eastsound; Twin Harbors/Grayland Beach, Westport; Birch Bay State Park, Blaine; Ike Kinswa State Park, Silver Creek; Pearrygin Lake State Park, Winthrop; Fort Canby State Park, Ilwaco; Lake Chelan State Park, Chelan; Steamboat Rock State Park, Electric City; Lincoln Rock State Park, Wenatchee. Fort Worden State Park in Port Townsend has its own reservation system for campsites and other accommodations, year-round; phone (206) 385-4730 for a brochure or details. Call or write the State Parks Commission for a reservation application (address and phone below).

- Most parks are open all year, but some close from Oct. through March; those that remain open often have limited winter camping facilities. Be sure to phone the parks or parks commission (number below) if you're traveling in the off-season.

- No more than 8 people per campsite.

- Every camper should get a copy of the *Guide to Washington State Parks*. It lists each state park by region and includes information on number, type, and length of campsites, type of hookup, and other facilities. To get this guide, or detailed brochures on the parks you plan to visit, write the Washington State Parks and Recreation Commission, Public Affairs Office, 7150 Cleanwater Lane, KY-11, Olympia, WA 98504, or phone (206) 753-2027. In the summer you can phone (800) 562-0990 Mon. through Fri. during normal working hours for park information.

in the Black Hills. Free primitive campsites are available for tents and small trailers at 9 locations within the forest; hiking and horseback riding trails are clustered in the S end of the park while trailbikes may use those in the N end. Hunting and fishing are also permitted. To get a panoramic view of the area, follow the marked dirt road from Waddell Creek Rd. to 2,658-foot **Capitol Peak,** highest point in the Black Hills.

MAYTOWN

Maytown's most notable attraction is **Millersylvania State Park** on Deep Lake. Constructed between 1933 and 1939 by 200 members of the Civilian Conservation Corps, the park has facilities for swimming, boating, trout fishing, hiking, picnicking, and camping within its 840 forested acres on Tilly Road. Just S of the entrance to Millersylvania, **Deep Lake Resort** at 12405 Tilley Rd. S, 352-7388, has lakeside cabin rentals ($210-350 per week, $35-58 per day if available), camping (tents to full hookups) for $10-13 per night, lake swimming, playground, showers, laundry facilities, boating, and bike rentals on Deep Lake. Open late April through September.

ISSAQUAH

At the foot of the "Issaquah Alps," Issaquah (pop. 6,000) offers an escape to country-fresh air in a small town loaded with history, without sacrificing modern shopping centers and restaurants. Just 2 exits W of Bellevue on I-90, Issaquah's hills are within a half-hour drive of Seattle and Tacoma. These are very old, worn-down mountains; their lower elevation keeps them snow-free—and hikable—virtually year-round.

SIGHTS

Historical Tour

Issaquah was in its glory during its coal-mining and lumbering days around the turn of the century. Several buildings from this period are still in use; remains from the mine are also evident. Go down Newport Way to Park Blvd. and turn R onto Wildwood for a look at the original miners' homes, preserved and still occupied; at the end of the block, a depression in the ground near a grove marks the entrance to the mine's first shaft; to the R is the concrete bulkhead, used to anchor the mine's hauling machinery.

Downtown, a number of historically significant buildings face Front Street. **Odd Fellows Hall** is the oldest, built in 1888; the 2nd oldest commercial building is the **Grand Central Hotel,** dating from 1903; today it houses offices and apartments. Adjacent to the railroad tracks on Sunset Way, the old **Railroad Depot** was built in 1889 (the year Washington became a state), out of Washington Territory timber—note the "W.T." symbol. The depot is currently undergoing restoration for its 100th birthday. For more information on Issaquah's historical sights, follow the visitor information signs to the Chamber of Commerce at 160 Gilman Blvd. NW, 392-7024, or stop by the **Issaquah Historical Society Museum** at 165 S.E. Andrews, 392-3500, for a self-guiding tour map.

Parks

A mile and a half NW of Issaquah, **Lake Sammamish State Park** is one of the more popular Puget Sound area day-use parks. Swimming, waterskiing, and boating on the enormous lake combined with a large picnic area and concession stand attract summertime crowds—and traffic jams at the boat launch. Though there's no camping at the park, you can stay at one of 16 tent sites and 5 trailer hookup sites at **Vasa Park Resort,** on the W side of Lake Sammamish at 3560 W. Lake Sammamish Rd., 746-3260; rates start at $10.

Owners of smaller motorboats, canoes, and rafts may prefer **Pine Lake,** a county park off 228th SE with a 5-mph speed limit on the lake.

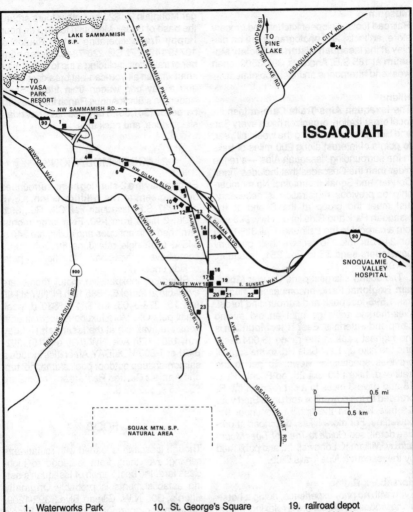

LAKE SAMMAMISH S.P.

TO VASA PARK RESORT

NW SAMMAMISH RD.

ISSAQUAH

E. LAKE SAMMAMISH PKWY. SE

NEWPORT WAY

NW GILMAN BLVD.

SE NEWPORT WAY

NE GILMAN BLVD.

RAINIER BLVD.

RENTON-ISSAQUAH RD.

WILDWOOD BLVD.

W. SUNSET WAY

E. SUNSET WAY

2 AVE. SE

FRONT ST.

ISSAQUAH-HOBART RD.

ISSAQUAH-FALL CITY RD.

ISSAQUAH-PINE LAKE RD.

TO PINE LAKE

TO SNOQUALMIE VALLEY HOSPITAL

SQUAK MTN. S.P. NATURAL AREA

0   0.5 mi
0   0.5 km

1. Waterworks Park
2. Motel 6
3. Holiday Inn
4. Meadow's S.C.
5. Heritage Square
6. Safeway/Pay 'N' Save
7. Harry O's
8. Gilman Station
9. La Costa
10. St. George's Square
11. Gilman Village
12. Originally Ellens
13. chamber of commerce
14. Issaquah Gallery
15. Boehm's Chocolates
16. Village Theatre
17. Odd Fellows Hall
18. Mandarin Garden
19. railroad depot
20. Grand Hotel
21. Issaquah Historical Society Museum
22. Greyhound
23. mine shaft and bulkhead
24. The Wildflower B&B

© MOON PUBLICATIONS, INC.

Museum

Railroad tools, a pioneer kitchen and grocery store, artifacts, and photographs are on display at the **Issaquah Historical Society Museum** at 165 S.E. Andrews, 392-3500, open weekend afternoons and by appointment.

Hiking

The **Issaquah Alps Trails Club,** a friendly, local organization, organizes hikes every Sat. and Sun. plus twice during the week, all year, to points of interest along 200 miles of trails in the surrounding "Issaquah Alps"—a range older than the Cascades that includes Tiger, Cougar, and Squak mountains. No membership or previous registration is necessary; just meet the group at the S end of the Issaquah Park and Ride lot on Hwy. 900 and join a carpool to the trailhead. Call 328-0480 for 24-hour info. To receive their quarterly newsletters send $5 to Box 351, Issaquah, WA 98027.

The county's largest park, **Cougar Mountain Regional Park,** encompasses most of this 1,595-foot peak and surrounding forest. Well-marked trails go past an old mining camp and waterfalls. **East Tiger Mountain** is the highest peak in the range (3,004 feet), and the hike up East Side Rd. to the summit provides spectacular views. To get to the trailhead, take I-90 exit 25; go R onto Hwy. 18 and drive 3 miles to a dirt road on the R; proceed to the powerline and park. Start your 6.9-mile hike on the uphill road under the powerline. For more hikes, described in precise detail, see *Guide to Trails of Tiger Mountain* by William K. Longwell Jr., and published by the Issaquah Alps Trails Club.

Horseback Riding

Even with no prior experience, riding a horse along wooded trails can be a relaxing, enjoyable way to view the scenery. **Tiger Mountain Outfitters,** 132nd Ave., 392-5090, offers guided 3-hour trips 3 times a day in Tiger Mountain State Forest; their ride to Poo Poo Point, a departure point for hang gliders, is $25 and is open to anyone over 10, though experienced riders under 10 are welcome. **Kelly Ranch,** 7212 Renton-Issaquah Rd., 392-6979, has guided trips to the top of Cougar Mountain for $20 and other tours around the base of Squak Mountain for $10 an hour. **Happy Trails,** operating out of Renton at 10719 142nd Pl. SE, 226-7848, offers a number of trail rides, including a trip to a coal mine shaft with an all-you-can-eat breakfast ($30), and a day-long wagon train trip to Stuart Anderson's Black Angus Ranch for a western barbecue ($41.50). They also have hay rides, sleigh rides, and pack trips.

ACCOMMODATIONS

Enjoy a stay in a 2-story log home surrounded by evergreens at **The Wildflower Inn,** a B&B at 25237 S.E. Issaquah-Fall City Rd., 392-1196, 2 miles from I-90. Four large rooms, furnished with antiques and quilts, are $40 s, $45 d (no single rate June through Aug.); some have a private bath. No smoking, pets, or kids under 12.

Standard, inexpensive motel rooms are available at **Motel 6,** 1885 15th Pl. NW at I-90 exit 15, 392-8405, for $24 s, $30 d; pool, small pets OK. More luxurious accommodations are available at the **Issaquah Holiday Inn,** 1801 12th Ave. NW (I-90 exit 15), 392-6421 or 1-800-HOLIDAY. Amenities include a salmon-shaped outdoor pool, sauna, hot tub, and **Annie's Garden Restaurant;** rooms are $53-56 s, $59-62 d.

FOOD

Though Issaquah is loaded with restaurants serving everything from fast-food to high-class fare, the best known of Issaquah's eating establishments is probably **Originally Ellen's,** 305 N.W. Gilman Blvd., 392-1209. Renown for gourmet hamburgers, Ellen's serves breakfast on weekends plus lunch and dinner daily; lunch is about $4-6 and dinner is generally under $10. **Cooper's Roost,** 120 N.W. Gilman Blvd., 392-5550, is a new and welcome addition to town. Owned by Mick McHugh (of F.X. McRory's and Jake O'Shaughnessey fame), Cooper's Roost offers an extensive seafood menu plus open hearth-roasted chicken, lamb, prime rib, and more, all at moderate prices. Reservations are a good idea. **Harry O's,** one of Issaquah's most elegant, has moderately priced lunches and dinners plus Sunday brunch at 719 N.W. Gilman Blvd., 392-8614. The **Mandarin Garden,** 40 E. Sunset Way, was voted the best Chinese restaurant around Puget Sound by the *Seattle P.I.* in 1984. Closed Mon.; call 392-9476 for take-out. For Mexican food try **La Costa,** 240 N.W. Gilman Blvd. at Gilman Station, open daily for lunch and dinner. Gilman Blvd. is also lined on both sides with fast-food restaurants and smaller bakeries, sub, and coffee shops at the numerous shopping centers.

ENTERTAINMENT

Festival
Every fall, salmon return to their birthplace at the state salmon hatchery, and Issaquah doesn't miss the opportunity for a celebration.

Gilman Village

The 2-day **Salmon Days Festival** is held the 1st weekend in Oct. with a parade, children's carnival, salmon bake (some "Welcome Home!"), arts and crafts displays, live music, hatchery tours, a Village Theatre performance, and 5- and 10-km runs; 392-0661.

Theater
From Sept. to May the semi-professional **Village Theatre** stages 5 musical performances at 120 Front St. N, 392-2202 (or call Ticket Master at 628-0888), in their original building (dating from 1914). Performances are held Wed. through Sun., and tickets cost $12-14 ($3 discount for seniors and under 18).

Water Park
Take exit 15 off I-90 to **Waterworks Park** for over a mile of waterslides on 22 runs including "The Black Hole," a 140-foot run in total darkness; other features include a picnic area, refreshments, gift shop, and video arcade. The park operates from mid-June to early Sept.; admission $11 adults, $8 kids, 392-8127.

SHOPPING AND SERVICES

Shopping
Before you start your Issaquah shopping spree, stop in at **Boehm's Chocolates** at 255 N.E. Gilman Blvd. for some high-calorie, low-nutrient, delicious energy. Chalet and candy factory tours are available by appointment, 392-6652, but the front counter is all you really need to see; you'll spend more than you planned.

Designed to trap the tourist dollar, **Gilman Village** at exit 17 off I-90 is a collection of early-1900s' Issaquah homes, all moved and restored to form a quaint collection of small shops. Restaurants and fudge shops, clothing and craft stores, gift and kitchenware boutiques, and jewelers abound; open daily. **St. George's Square,** 355 N.W. Gilman Blvd., has a bakery, gift shops, and clothing stores.

In historical downtown Issaquah, the **Issaquah Gallery** has paintings, photography, stained glass, pottery, and prints by Northwest artists at 49 Front St. N, 392-4247.

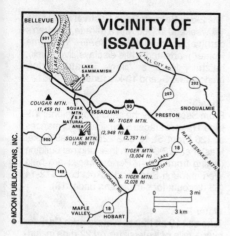

VICINITY OF ISSAQUAH

© MOON PUBLICATIONS, INC.

SERVICES

The Issaquah area code is 206. For maps and information contact the **Issaquah Chamber of Commerce,** 160 N.W. Gilman Blvd., 392-7024. For groceries, drugs, film, and the like, the shopping center at 12th and Gilman Blvd. has a Safeway, Pay 'N' Save, Ernst, and more. Across the street at Heritage Square

you'll find a liquor store, pizza place, and **Salvino Sports,** 392-8440, a sporting goods store with camping, fishing, and hunting equipment, bait, ammunition, and hunting and fishing licenses.

Call 911 for medical, fire, or police emergencies. **Snoqualmie Valley Hospital,** 1505 Meadowbrook Way SE in Snoqualmie, 888-1438, has 24-hour emergency room service.

TRANSPORTATION

By Car

To get to Issaquah from Seattle or Bellevue, take I-90 to Lake Sammamish State Park (exit 15) or exits 17 or 18 to get downtown. From Tacoma and points S, take I-5 to I-405 to eastbound Hwy. 900.

By Bus

Issaquah has no city transit system, but you can get to and from Seattle, North Bend, Redmond, and other points in King County via **Metro,** 447-4800. To connect to virtually anywhere in the country, take **Greyhound** from 55 Sunset Way, 392-7142.

1. Olympic Mountains, Olympic National Park (Washington State Tourism Division); 2. Mount Rainier from Cayuse Pass (D. Lyons) 3. Diablo Lake, North Cascades National Park (D. Lyons)

1. Rainbow Bridge, La Conner (D. Lyons); **2.** rafting on one of Washington's rivers (Wash. St. Tourism Div.);
3. Hell's Canyon excursion boats depart from Clarkston. (Wash. St. Tourism Div.); **4.** Port Orchard Marina on
the Kitsap Peninsula (D. Lyons); **5.** deep-sea fishing off Washington's coast (Wash. St. Tourism Div.);
6. freshwater fishing in mountain streams (Wash. St. Tourism Div.)

1. The University of Washington (Seattle-King County Convention and Visitors Bureau); 2. Mukilteo Lighthouse, Mukilteo (D. Lyons); 3. Track 29 Railroad Village in Yakima (D. Lyons); 4. Hoquiam's Castle, Hoquiam (D. Lyons); 5. Downtown Port Townsend is lined with historic buildings. (D. Lyons); 6. Port Angeles sightseeing trolley and shopping center (D. Lyons)

1. Riverfront Park, Spokane (Wash. St. Tourism Div.); 2. downtown Seattle and Elliott Bay (Seattle-King County Convention and Visitors Bureau); 3. Seattle's Space Needle (Seattle-King County Convention and Visitors Bureau)

EVERETT

On Puget Sound about 25 miles N of Seattle, Everett is a largely industrial city (pop. 57,000) with most people employed by the Boeing 747 plant but still economically dependent on lumber and wood products. The city is flanked by mountains, with Mt. Baker to the N, Mt. Rainier to the S, and 5,324-foot Mt. Pilchuck to the east. Coupled with its waterfront location, Everett is surrounded by recreational opportunities, as well as more indoor fun than most cities its size.

many in 1834, he immigrated to the U.S. in 1852, where he worked in an Illinois lumber mill and married a German woman, Elizabeth Bloedel. Weyerhauser was so hard working and thrifty that he was able to buy the mill a few years later, and then expanded his operation westward. His main Pacific coast lumber mill was built in Everett in 1903, becoming—and long remaining—the city's most important industry. When he died, Weyerhauser's lumber company was the biggest in the country.

HISTORY

Everett is one of the few Puget Sound areas that prompted Capt. George Vancouver to get off his boat. After coming ashore, Vancouver named the area "New Georgia" for King George III, and the English claim to this land lasted for more than 50 years.

The city of Everett was established in 1891 in boomtown fashion when John D. Rockefeller and other big Eastern investors planned to build the "New York City of the West," aided by rumors that the Great Northern Railroad would make Port Gardner its first Puget Sound stop. As much or more influential than Rockefeller in Everett's development was a man named Frederick Weyerhauser. Born in Ger-

SIGHTS

Mansions
In days of yore, Everett was home to some of the timber industry's most successful entrepreneurs. Not bashful about their financial success, these lumber barons built exquisite mansions in the N end of town on Grand and Rucker avenues that are still worth a drive by.

Boeing Tour
For kids over 12, touring Boeing's 747-767 assembly plant is the highlight of a visit to Everett. The plant itself, 115 feet high, has the largest cubic capacity of any building in the world; seeing one of these enormous airplanes indoors is an impressive visual experi-

Boeing's 747-767 assembly plant

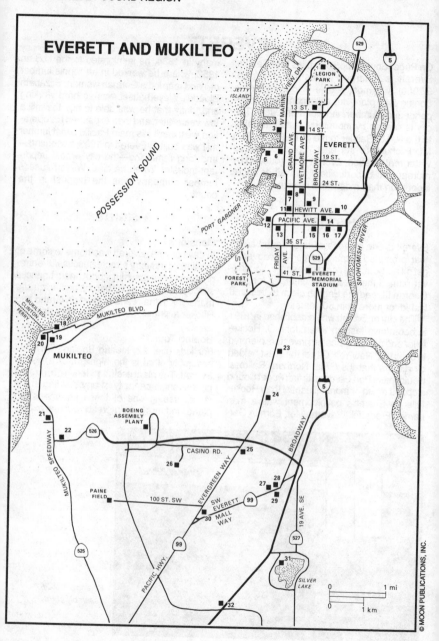

EVERETT AND MUKILTEO

© MOON PUBLICATIONS, INC.

EVERETT AND MUKILTEO

1. Legion Memorial Golf Course
2. Everett Community College
3. Firefighters Museum
4. General Hospital
5. Everett Marina Village: Pelican Pete's, Anthony's Home Port, Sea Charters, Bacchus by the Bay, Marina Village Inn, Bee Bee Fish & Chips
6. chamber of commerce
7. North Sound Harbor Tours
8. Civic Auditorium
9. YMCA
10. Klondike Kate's
11. public market
12. Amtrak Station
13. Providence Hospital
14. Snohomish County Museum
15. Petosa's
16. Nendel's
17. Everett Pacific Hotel
18. Seahorse Restaurant, Taylor's Landing, McConnel's Boathouse, Mukilteo-Clinton Ferry
19. Arnie's/Mukilteo Maritime Museum
20. Lighthouse and Mukilteo S.P.
21. Shamrock Shillelah & Shenanigan's
22. Charles at Smuggler's Cove
23. Gianni's Piccola Italia
24. Panivino
25. Cherry Motel
26. Walter E. Hall Golf Course
27. Everett Mall Inn
28. Northwest Motor Inn
29. Everett Mall
30. Motel 6
31. Silver Shores RV Park and Silver Lake Park
32. Holiday Inn

ence. Ninety-minute tours, held weekdays, include a slide show; 342-4801. To get there, take I-5 exit 189 W onto Hwy. 526. For a bus tour from Seattle, see "Transportation" p. 122.

Parks

Located on Alverson Blvd., **Legion Park** features a par course, tennis courts, and ballfield. **Forest Park** on Mukilteo Blvd. has a children's zoo, heated indoor public pool, and live music performed by local bands on Sun. afternoons June through August.

Museums

One of Everett's oldest commercial buildings, constructed in 1906, houses the **Snohomish County Museum**, 2915 Hewitt Ave., 259-8849. See a kitchen and bedroom typical of Everett at the turn of the century, plus photographs and Indian artifacts. Open Wed. through Sun. afternoons; free. At the 13th St. dock, see a collection of firefighters' equipment at the **Firefighters Museum** any time; the museum was designed for through-the-window viewing.

ACCOMMODATIONS

Motels And Hotels

Everett has a good selection of clean, cheap lodging: **Motel 6,** 10006 Evergreen Way, 347-2060, has 119 rooms and a pool for $24 s, $30 d; the **Royal Motor Inn** at Hwy. 99 and 10th St., 259-5177, has 35 rooms and a heated pool for $25-29 s, $29-38 d; and the **Everett Mall Inn,** 1602 S.E. Everett Mall Way, 355-1570, has a pool, coffee shop, and 63 budget rooms from $30 s, $34-35 d. The **Cherry Motel,** 8421 Evergreen Way, has complimentary continental breakfast and non-smoking rooms for $29-32 s, $33-41 d; call 347-1100. At 9602 19th Ave. SE, the **Northwest Motor Inn,** 337-9090, has 120 rooms across from the Everett Mall for $32-41 s, $38-46 d, with a pool, hot tub, and kitchen units available. At the **Cypress Inn-Everett,** 12619 4th Ave. W, 347-9099 or (800) 752-9981 statewide, enjoy king jacuzzi suites, continental breakfast, van service, outdoor pool, and more, starting at $40.

For something significantly nicer, the **West Coast Everett Pacific Hotel,** 3105 Pine St., has an exercise room, indoor pool, sauna, hot tub, lounge with nightly entertainment, some in-room refrigerators, children's activity center, room and poolside service, free airport, bus station, or railroad shuttle, and 254 rooms from $53 s, $58-60 d; (800) 833-8001 toll-free statewide or 339-3333 locally for reservations. Another larger facility is the **Holiday Hotel** off I-5 at 128th St., 745-2555, with an indoor pool, sauna, hot tub, tennis courts, shuttle, valet service, entertainment nightly except Sun., and 210 rooms starting

Everett's lumber barons lived in exquisite mansions.

at $50-60 s, $55-65 d. With many of the same features plus access to the local health club, **Nendel's Motor Inn** at 2800 Pacific Ave. has 133 rooms starting from $50-60 s or d; (800) 547-0106 in Washington or 258-4141 locally.

For exceptional lodging, stay at **Marina Village Inn** at the Everett Marina on W. Marine View Dr., 259-4040. Several of the 28 rooms overlook the water; other amenities include wet bars, bathroom phones, and refrigerator, with jacuzzis in the higher-priced doubles. Rates are $68 s, $74-82 d on the harbor side, $56 s, $62-68 d on the village side.

RV Park

Located at 11621 W. Silver Lake Dr., **Silver Shores RV Park**, 337-8741, has tennis, swimming, and fishing at Silver Lake, and water and electric hookups for $15, tent sites for $10.

FOOD

Everett Marina Village has 4 waterfront restaurants: **Anthony's Home Port**, 252-3333, has fresh Northwest and imported seafood flown in fresh daily to serve at lunch, dinner, or Sunday brunch, or on their New Orleans-style oyster bar; dinner prices are in the $9-19 range. **Bacchus By The Bay**, 258-6254, serves 3 meals (including lunch omelettes) and the widest wine selection in the area; take-out deli sandwiches are available for boaters or picnickers. **Pelican Pete's**, 252-3155, is a little more casual with seafood, steaks, pasta, and a fish-and-chips-and-burger bar, all at moderate prices; you can also dance at this popular singles spot from 10 p.m.-2 a.m. Tues. through Sat. nights, with Tues. night comedy at 9:30 p.m. **Bee-Bee's Fish and Chips,** is open daily for 3 meals, specializing in fresh fish and chips, onion rings, burgers, and more.

Panivino, 6309 Evergreen Way, 353-4635, serves moderately priced, top-quality pasta, sandwiches, and salads in unlikely shopping center surroundings. For more Italian cuisine including fresh pastas, seafoods, imported wines, and pizza-to-go try **Gianni's Piccola Italia,** 5030 Evergreen Way, 252-2435. Open for dinner only; closed Monday. **Gerry Andal's Ranch Restaurant,** 620 S.E. Everett Mall Way, 355-7999, features a full American ranch-style menu .

Down in Mukilteo, just W of the intersection of highways 525 and 526, **Charles at Smugglers Cove,** 8310 53rd Ave. W, 347-2700, serves highly praised yet moderately priced dinners in most elegant surroundings; closed Sundays. The **Seahorse Restaurant** at 707 Front St., 353-6477, has Northwest seafood, steak, prime rib, and pasta—and captive seahorses—with dancing on the weekends. Next door to the ferry dock is **Taylor's Landing,** 710 Front St., 355-2575, with waterfront dining featuring Northwest seafood, steaks, a popular clam chowder, and live entertainment Thurs. thru Saturday. One street up the hill, **Arnie's** has a view of the water at 714 2nd St., 355-2181. Enjoy moderately priced lunches and dinners of salmon, rockfish, ling cod, and steaks. To avoid the lunchtime crowds at the waterside restaurants, head up the hill to **Shamrock, Shillelah, and Shenanigans,** an Irish family restaurant at 8004 Mukilteo Speedway. Open for 3 meals, inexpensive lunches include burgers and sandwiches, Irish stew, and corned beef and cabbage; veal, chicken, and steak dinners are around $6. **Las Palmas,** 801 2nd, 355-6854, is a Mexican restaurant and cantina that's also open for breakfast.

ENTERTAINMENT

Jetty Island Days

A summer-long recreational event from July to Sept. sponsored by the parks department, the annual **Jetty Island Days** "celebration" includes free scenic ferry rides to the island departing from the Marina Village Visitors Dock, guided nature walks, sailing and rowing regattas, concerts, campfire programs, and picnicking, beachcombing, and birdwatching on a saltwater beach. For a program of events call Everett Parks and Recreation at 259-0300.

Baseball

The San Francisco Giants' Class-A farm team, the **Everett Giants,** plays at Everett Memorial Stadium from mid-June to Sept.; weekdays and Sat. games start at 7 p.m.; Sun. at 2 p.m. Call 258-3673 for schedule information.

Golf

There are 3 public 18-hole golf courses in the Everett area. In Everett proper, there's **Legion Memorial** at 144 W. Marine View Dr., 259-GOLF, and the **Walter E. Hall Golf Course** at 1226 W. Casino Rd., 353-GOLF. Up N a bit is the **Kayak Point Golf Course,** 13 miles W of Marysville at 15711 Marine Dr., 652-9676 or (800) 562-3094.

Festivals

Held in early June at the Everett Yacht Basin, **Salty Sea Days** features a parade, boat tours, carnival, kayak races, and booths. The **Washington State International Air Fair,** held at Paine Field in late Aug., has civilian aerobatics, military jet demonstration teams, and other flying displays in an exciting 2-day air show; 355-2266. Also held in Aug. at Forest Park, **Art In The Park,** 252-7469, features a juried arts show, craft booths, live performances, and hands-on activities and classes for children.

The Arts

Theatrical performances are held throughout the year at **Centerstage,** 252-7469, and the **College Playhouse,** 259-3355. Music lovers may enjoy a performance by the **Everett Symphony** at the Everett Civic Auditorium on Colby Ave. or on a Sun. afternoon at the Chateau Ste. Michelle Winery in Woodinville; concerts are scheduled from Nov. to May. Phone 259-7151, ext. 313, for more information.

For those more inclined toward the visual arts, **Northlight Gallery,** at 810 Wetmore in Everett Community College, **Farrens Gallery,** 2819 Wetmore, and the **Visual Arts Center,** at 2902 Colby, have large and varied displays.

Nightlife

Everett has a disproportionate number of dancing and drinking establishments for a city this small. At **Klondike Kate's,** 3120 Hewitt Ave., the lounge upstairs from the steak-and-seafood restaurant has live music on Fri. and Sat. nights. **Pelican Pete's** at Everett Marina Village is lively most of the week, with comedy on Tues. and dancing Tues. through Sat. till 2 a.m. **Bacchus By The Bay,** also at the marina, has live jazz on the weekends. **Hardy's Bar & Grill** is a popular happy-hour spot, with a piano bar and dance floor at the WestCoast Everett Pacific Hotel. **Filibeck's Chuck Wagon Inn,** 6720 Evergreen Way, also has live entertainment and dancing Tues. through Sat. nights. If it's a Monday hit the **Casbah,** 2222 Everett Ave., with live music every night. Wednesday through Sat. check out **Petosa's on Broadway,** 3121 Broadway, for live music in the lounge. **Henry's Lady,** up in Marysville at 6128 Marine View Dr., has dancing to live music Tues. through Sat. nights.

Shopping

The area's largest shopping center is **Everett Mall,** with over 150 small shops, giant department stores including Frederick & Nelson and The Bon, and 10 movie theaters under one roof. Along the bay at Everett Marina Village is an 1890s-style waterfront marketplace with restaurants, gift shops, clothing stores, and more. The **Everett Public Market,** 2804 Grand Ave., has antiques, fresh fish and produce, a coffee shop, and more in an out-of-the-way and visually unappealing location; future plans for the turn-of-the-century stable-and-storage building include restoring it to its original appearance. Open daily except Sun. in summer; 252-1089.

SERVICES

The area code for Everett and vicinity is 206. For maps and brochures, stop in or call the **Everett Area Chamber of Commerce,** on the 1st floor of the historic Weyerhaeuser office building at 1710 W. Marine View Dr., Box 1086, Everett, WA 98206, 252-5181. For specific information on the surrounding communities, contact the **Marysville Chamber of Commerce,** 1324 4th St., Marysville, 659-7700, or the **Snohomish Chamber of Commerce,** 116 Ave. B, Snohomish, 568-2526 (closed Fri. through Sunday).

Like most developed parts of the state, the Everett area is served by 911 emergency service. For less critical emergencies, call **General Hospital** at 14th and Colby, 258-6301, or **Providence Hospital** at 916 Pacific, 258-7555.

Health-conscious vacationers may be interested in a 1-day membership at the **Everett YMCA,** 2720 Rockefeller, 258-9211; for $5 you can use the rooftop track, racquetball and squash courts, weight room, and pool.

TRANSPORTATION

Everett is 30 miles N of Seattle, a straight shot on I-5. If you're flying into Sea-Tac airport, **Everett Airporter** departs hourly from the baggage claim area for the WestCoast Everett Pacific Hotel; fares are $20 RT, $11 OW. Call 258-1955 in Everett or 743-3344 in Seattle for reservations or information.

Amtrak serves the Everett area from their Terminal St. station; (800) 872-7245 or, from Seattle, 464-1930.

Everett Transit's buses and trolleys provide local transportation for $.30; phone 353-RIDE for schedule. To get out of town, **Community Transit** goes S to Edmonds and Seattle, N to Stanwood and Darrington, and E to Snohomish, Lake Stevens, and Granite Falls for $.50; call (800) 562-1375 or 778-2185 for information.

Gray Line of Seattle offers a 3-hour tour of the Boeing 747-767 plant, departing Mon. through Fri., May through mid-Sept., from downtown Seattle hotels. Available only to people over 12, the tour costs $15. For more info phone 626-5208.

The Mukilteo-Clinton ferry connects the Everett area to the S end of Whidbey Island every half hour or better. Fares are $2.15 RT for passengers or walk-ons, $3.75 OW for car and driver ($4.50 in summer), and $1.60 OW for bicycle and rider. Phone (800) 542-7052 or (800) 542-0810 toll-free statewide or 464-6400 in the Seattle area for schedule.

Charter Or Cruise

Docked at Everett Marina, **Sea Charters** on W. Marine View Dr. offers 1-hour sea lion tours for $9 (with occasional $5 weekend specials) from fall to early summer, when California's migratory sea lions are splashing around the bay. Their fishing charters with gear, bait, and coffee provided are $45-65 pp, depending on the boat. Phone 252-4188 or 776-5611 24 hours for information and reservations.

Everett Northsound Harbor and Island Tours, 2815 W. Marine View Dr., 339-1275, offers morning and afternoon salmon- and bottom-fishing charters for $30-50 pp.

By Boat
You can rent canoes, rowboats, and El Toro sailboats at **Silver Lake Park,** 259-0300. For adventuring into the Sound, stop at **McConnell's Boathouse,** 718 Front St. in Mukilteo, 355-3411, for boat rentals and fishing gear; 15-foot-long aluminum-and-wood boats rent for $16-18 per day, plus an additional $5-7 for a motor. Open March through October.

VICINITY OF EVERETT

MUKILTEO

Mukilteo was the site of the signing of the Point Elliott Treaty of 1855, whereby the leaders of 22 Indian tribes handed over their land to the white settlers. Today it's a pretty little suburb of Everett, with a scenic commute home along Mukilteo Blvd. for the city's employees. Because of Mukilteo's proximity to Everett, restaurants and hotels here are listed under "Everett," above.

Mukilteo Lighthouse

Parks
Adjacent to the Whidbey Island ferry terminal, **Mukilteo State Park** has a large picnic area, beach, and a boat launch with excellent fishing in Possession Sound; open for day use only. The **Mukilteo Lighthouse,** built in 1905, is still functional and open for free tours year-round on Sat. and Sun. afternoons; 355-2611.

Museum
At the corner of 3rd St. and Lincoln Ave., the **Mukilteo Maritime Museum,** 355-2514, depicts the history of Puget Sound's ferries with photographs and models. Open Wed. through Sun.; admission $1.50 adults, $.50 kids.

Entertainment
Held at the state park downtown, the mid-August **Mukilteo Pioneer Festival** has a parade, salmon seafood barbecue, arts and crafts display, sailing regatta, and the state chili cook-off. From Feb. to Oct. the professional **Lighthouse Repertory Theater** stages 5 productions; for ticket info call 347-6783.

SNOHOMISH

Early Indians called Snohomish "sdob-dwahlb-bluh," meaning "Indian moon," because that's where they believed their tribe came from. The town was settled in 1859 along the banks of the Snohomish and Pilchuck rivers, making it one of Washington's oldest communities. Numerous turn-of-the-century mansions in Old Snohomish bear witness to the town's earlier elegance.

Sights
Established in 1859, Snohomish has preserved a number of its elegant Victorian-era

homes, particularly in the area N of 2nd Street. Take a self-guided tour with a brochure available from the chamber of commerce at 116 Ave. B, or go inside on the annual Homes Tour held the first Sun. in October. The **Blackman Historic Museum**, 118 Ave. B, is an 1878 mansion built by a lumberman as a proud display of his cedar shingles; today it's filled with area artifacts and Victorian furniture. Open weekend afternoons.

Sundance Express offers an inexpensive horse-and-buggy tour of Snohomish for $1.50-5 pp, depending on destination, Fri. through Sun., beginning at noon and departing from the 1st St. bank clock. Just show up, or phone 334-6635 for reservations.

Bed And Breakfasts

Built in 1884 by A.H. Eddy, **Eddy's Bed & Breakfast**, 425 9th St., 568-7081, is a beautifully restored Victorian home with a panoramic view of the Cascades, Mt. Rainier, and the Olympics. The inn features a heated pool, gourmet breakfast, and canopy or 4-poster beds; rates are $55-65 d, ($10 less for singles). No indoor smoking, kids, or pets. At 119 Cedar St., **Countryman Bed and Breakfast**, 568-9622, was the town's first B&B. The 28-room Victorian mansion has rooms from $39 s, $45 d, including a guided tour of Snohomish, a packet of prints, and afternoon tea. **The Cabbage Patch Inn**, 111 Ave. A, 568-9091, is a farmhouse-style B&B with rooms from $35-45 d; the attached restaurant is open daily for lunch and dinner. **The Country Manner B&B**, above the Country Collector's shop at 1120 1st St., 568-8254, has 4 rooms for $49-59 behind an original 1880s storefront and overlooking the Snohomish River and sawmill. No pets, kids, or indoor smoking. **Harmon House B&B**, 322 Ave. C, 568-1078, has 4 rooms in an 1890 Victorian mansion, furnished in antiques and sharing one clawfoot tub, from $45-60. No pets or indoor smoking. At 312 Ave. D, **Noris House**, 568-3825, is an Edwardian B&B built in 1908 and furnished in period antiques. Rooms here are $54-65 d, including continental breakfast. No kids under 14, pets, or smoking.

Camping

Flowing Lake Park is a 42-acre county park located on 48th St. SE, a few miles E of Snohomish. Day-use facilities include a boat launch, swimming beach, picnic area, and playground; overnight camping is available at 29 hookup and 8 tent sites for $7. Ranger-guided nature hikes through the wooded portion of the park are given periodically. To reach the park take Hwy. 2 E from Snohomish; after 2 miles, turn L onto 99th St. SE, then turn L onto 171st Ave SE, and R onto 48th St. SE to the park at the end of the road.

Food

Located at 1st and B on the river in Old Snohomish, the **Silver King Restaurant** has a dreary, diner-like interior but specializes in steak and seafood, including Hood Canal oysters and the hard-to-find fried geoduck, with a view of the sawmill; prices are in the $8-16 range. For a coffee or light snack, the **Rivers Edge Cafe** on 1st St. has a comfortable, historic feeling enhanced by the absence of interior side walls—the restaurant is bordered lengthwise by the brick outer walls of the adjoining shops. For inexpensive Chinese food, try **Peking Duck**, 1208 2nd Ave., 568-7634. Open for lunch and dinner daily, the **Cabbage Patch Restaurant**, 568-9091, offers sandwiches, salads, pasta, beef, and seafood plus homemade desserts in multiple cozy dining rooms in an old home at 111 Ave. A. Prices are $4-8 for lunch, $7-11 for dinner. **Mardini's**, 1210 1st St., 568-8080, has pasta, quiche, steaks, seafood, stir-fry, and sauté dinners with a neat and pretty pink-and-antique-lace decor. For Mexican food, visit **Bernal's** at 515 2nd St., 568-7777.

Shopping

Snohomish is the self-proclaimed "Antique Capital of the Pacific Northwest." Collectors and browsers will want to spend a day at the **Star Center Antique Mall** at 821 2nd St., with 110 shops open daily till 5 p.m., a restaurant, and a children's play area. There are more than a dozen other antique shops within a 4-block walk of the mall.

Non-collectors might want to visit the **Old Snohomish Art & Craft Mall** at 121 Glen instead. Here over 90 area artists and craftspersons display their goods daily except Mon.; phone 568-9554 for hours.

MARYSVILLE

Though strawberries are Marysville's trademark, the economy is based on a number of other industries including lumber, dairy products, manufacturing, and high-tech enterprises.

Park
Eighteen miles N of Everett and 6 miles N of Marysville, **Wenberg State Park** on Lake Goodwin has excellent fishing with power boats permitted, a concession stand for fishing supplies and snacks, and 65 standard campsites ($6) and 10 electric-and-water hookup sites ($8) on 46 acres; 652-7417.

Accommodations
Best Western's Tulalip Inn offers moderately priced luxury at 6128 Marine View Dr., off I-5 at exit 199, with an indoor pool, restaurant and lounge with entertainment and dancing, airport shuttle, and 66 rooms starting at $48-58 s, $53-63 d, plus hot tub rooms for $120 s, $132 d; phone 659-4488 or (800) 528-1234.

Festivals
The 3rd week in June brings the **Strawberry Festival,** the town's tribute to one of its major crops and the area's biggest summer event, with a parade, carnival, art show, and adult trike races. Held in Oct., **Harvest Fest** has crafts, an open-air farmers' market, hay rides, and a big farmers' breakfast. At Christmastime, Santa Claus and the **Christmas Parade** head down festively adorned State Avenue.

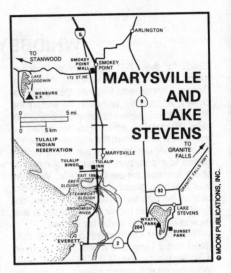

Bingo
Operated by the Tulalip Tribes, **Tulalip Bingo,** right off I-5 at exit 199, is open daily with 3 sessions daily from 11:30 a.m. and more than $100,000 in prizes every week, including special super-prize weekends where you can win campers, boats, cars, and trucks. No dingy, smoky Legion hall here—this is an enormous, landscaped, modern building with fresh air (no smoking allowed) and a restaurant. For times and other info 24 hours a day, call the Bingo Hotline at (800) 631-3313.

LAKE STEVENS

Two Snohomish County parks provide access to the waters of Lake Stevens. **Sunset Park,** on the E shore, has just a fishing dock and picnic tables on far less than an acre of land. On the W shore, **Wyatt Park** has a larger dock, boat launch for fishermen and water-skiers, picnic area, and swimming.

WHIDBEY ISLAND

Credit for the 1792 discovery of Whidbey Island goes to Joseph Whidbey, Master of George Vancouver's flagship, the HMS *Discovery*. Apparently, however, he wasn't the first one there: while exploring the island's W side, Whidbey stumbled upon the rotted remains of another ship, too weather-beaten to identify. Wandering wild oxen in the vicinity added to the mystery. When he stepped ashore in what is now Coupeville, Whidbey was met by a group of natives who couldn't believe he was so white! Whidbey was obliged to open his jacket to demonstrate that he was even white under his clothes.

The longest island in the continental U.S. (New York's Long Island has been declared a peninsula by the U.S. Supreme Court), Whidbey Island encompasses 208 square miles in its 45-mile length—no spot of which is more than 5 miles from the water. Today picturesque Whidbey Island is one of western Washington's biggest tourist attractions; attendance at Deception Pass State Park rivals that of Mount Rainier. Besides tourism, the island economy is supported by the Whidbey Naval Air Station in Oak Harbor and one of the country's largest loganberry farms near Greenbank. The movie "An Officer and a Gentleman" was filmed partly aboard the Whidbey-Port Townsend ferry *Kulshan*.

The climate is mild year-round: the temperature ranges from 40 to 60 degrees 80 percent of the time; temperatures above 75 and below 20 are rare. Autumn brings late-evening and early-morning fog; winter comes with light rain or mist every other day, though the total annual rainfall ranges from less than 20 inches in Coupeville and points N to 42 inches at Goss Lake in the S part of the island.

Services
For maps, brochures, and the like contact the chamber of commerce nearest your destination: **Central Whidbey Chamber of Commerce,** 262 W. Beach Lane, Box 152, Coupeville, 98239, 678-5434; **Clinton Chamber of Commerce,** 6231 Galbreath Rd., Clinton, 98236, 321-4545; **Freeland Chamber of**

Commerce, Box 361, Freeland, 98249, 321-5677; **Langley Chamber of Commerce,** Box 403, Langley, 98260, 321-6765; **North Whidbey Chamber of Commerce,** 2506 Hwy. 20, Oak Harbor, 98277, 675-3535.

Located mid-island in Coupeville, **Whidbey General Hospital** at Main St. and Hwy. 20 provides emergency care; 678-5151, 321-5151, or 911.

Getting There
To drive to Whidbey Island, you've got only one option: the Deception Pass Bridge at the island's N end. To get there, go W on Hwy. 20 from I-5. Otherwise, you'll have to come by **Washington State Ferry.** From the Seattle area, the Mukilteo ferry leaves for Clinton

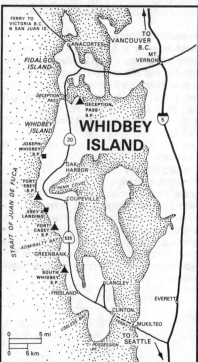

about every half hour; the 20-minute crossing costs $2.15 RT for passengers, $3.75 OW for car and driver, $1.60 OW for cyclists. From the Olympic Peninsula, board the ferry in Port Townsend to arrive in Keystone, at Fort Casey State Park. Ferries leave about every 50 minutes; fares are $3.30 RT for passengers, $5.55 OW for car and driver ($6.65 in summer), $2.30 OW for cyclists. For information on the state ferry system call (800) 542-0810.

OAK HARBOR

Settled first by sea captains, then the Irish, and at the turn of the century by immigrants from Holland, Oak Harbor's Dutch heritage is reflected in its festivals, a windmill at City Beach, and Holland Gardens. Today Oak Harbor is about the only place on the island you'll find fast food, traffic, and noise—but on an infinitely smaller scale than other Puget Sound cities.

Deception Pass State Park

When Capt. George Vancover first sighted this waterway in 1792 he called it Port Gardner. But then he realized he'd been deceived—the inlet was actually a tidal passage between two islands—so he renamed it "Deception Pass."

One of the state's most visited parks, Deception Pass has facilities that rival those of national parks: swimming at 2 lakes, 4 miles of shoreline, 18 miles of hiking trails, fresh- and saltwater fishing, boating, picnicking, rowboat rentals, viewpoints, and 251 campsites (no hookups) with hot showers and trailer dump stations. The park, 9 miles N of Oak Harbor on Hwy. 20, covers 3,000 forested acres on both sides of Deception Pass Bridge. Though only electric motors or rowboats are allowed on the park's lakes, you can observe beaver dams, muskrats, and mink in the marshes on the S side of Cranberry Lake, which also hosts a seasonal concession stand. A 15-minute hike to the highest point on the island, 400-foot Goose Rock, provides views of the San Juan Islands, Mt. Baker, Victoria, and Fidalgo Island, and possibly bald eagles soaring overhead. The trail

THE MAIDEN OF DECEPTION PASS

The Samish Indians told the story of the Maiden of Deception Pass, Ko-Kwal-Alwoot. The Samish beauty was gathering shellfish along the beach when the sea spirit saw her and was at once enamored; as he took her hand, Ko-Kwal-Alwoot became terrified, but the sea spirit reassured her, saying he only wished to gaze upon her loveliness. She returned often, listening to the sea spirit's declarations of love. One day a young man came from the sea to ask Ko-Kwal-Alwoot's father for permission to marry her. Her father, suspecting that living underwater would be hazardous to his daughter's health, refused, despite the sea spirit's claim that Ko-Kwal-Alwoot would have eternal life. Miffed, the sea spirit brought drought and famine to the old man's people until he agreed to give his daughter away, with one condition: that she return once every year so the old man could be sure she was properly cared for. The agreement was made, and the people watched as Ko-Kwal-Alwoot walked into the water until only her hair, floating in the current, was visible. The famine and drought ended at once. Ko-Kwal-Alwoot kept her promise for the next 4 years, returning to visit her people, but every time she came she was covered with more and more barnacles and seemed anxious to return to the sea. On her last visit her people told her she need not return unless she wanted to; and since that time, she's provided abundant shellfish and clean spring water in that area. Legend has it that her hair can be seen floating to and fro with the tide in Deception Pass.

Today this Samish legend is inscribed on a story pole on Fidalgo Island. To get there, follow Hwy. 20 to Fidalgo Island; go W at Pass Lake, following the signs for Bowman Bay and Rosario Beach, and hike the trail toward Rosario Head.

starts at the S end of the bridge, heading E from either side of the highway; take the wide trail as it follows the pass, then take one of the unmarked spur trails uphill to the top.

Other Parks

The newest addition to the state park system, **Joseph Whidbey State Park,** just S of the Naval Air Station on Swantown Rd., is largely undeveloped, with picnic tables, pit toilets, and 400 acres of beach for day use only. **Holland Gardens,** 500 Ave. W and 30th NW, site of the annual Holland Happening festival (see below), has shrub and flower gardens surrounding its white and blue windmill. **Oak Harbor Beach Park** has a sand beach, swimming, tennis and baseball facilities, and 54 campsites on the lagoon; 679-5551.

Enjoy the beaches year-round with a kite from **Pegasus Kite Shop** in the Old Town Mall on Pioneer Way, 675-4655. To explore the waters around the island, charter a boat from **J&J Charters,** 5191 N. Cornet Bay Dr., 675-9733. Sailboats and power boats are available to experienced boaters from $75 per day from April through Oct.; inexperi-

Holland Gardens

enced boaters can hire a skipper-guide for an additional $75 per day.

Whidbey Island Naval Air Station

The largest naval air base in the Northwest was situated here because Ault Field, the U.S. Navy Reserve's airstrip, has some of the best flying weather in the U.S.: it gets only 20 inches of annual rainfall, is out of the path of commercial flight routes, and is virtually isolated with little electrical interference. For information on air shows and driving tours through the base (2 weeks' notice is required), phone 257-2286.

Accommodations

Located at 5861 Hwy. 20, the **Auld Holland Inn,** 675-2288, has 28 rooms, a heated pool and whirlpool, tennis court, lawn games, and coin laundry. Rates are $34-63 s, $38-65 d. The **Coachman Inn,** 5563 Hwy. 20 at Goldie Rd., 675-0727, has 70 rooms from $40 s, $40-45 d, with a heated pool, whirlpool, exercise room, and laundry facilities. Top of the line is the **Best Western Harbor Plaza,** 5691 Hwy. 20, 679-4567. Their 80 rooms range from $37-52 s, $42-57 d (depending on the season), with a restaurant and pool.

Food

Oak Harbor's only waterfront restaurant, **Char's Cove,** 2068 200th Ave. SW, 679-2515, serves lunch weekdays, dinner daily, and Sunday brunch, with entertainment Tues. through Sat. nights in their lounge. **Two Sisters Pioneer Cafe,** 675-7981, offers lunch and dinner Mon. through Sat. plus Sunday Champagne brunch at the Old Town Mall. For something a little lighter, **Smiley's** has pizza, barbecued chicken and ribs, and steak teamed with silent movies and a big-screen TV at the corner of Pioneer Way and 60th Street. For Japanese food including a sushi bar, **Kyoto,** 9041 90th NW, 679-1433, is open for lunch and dinner daily except Monday.

If you plan to spend the day at Deception Pass, stop by **Two Sisters Picnic Basket** near the Pass on Hwy. 20, 679-0606, for family-priced picnic lunches to go, with homemade bread, salads, fruit, hardboiled eggs, even a tablecloth.

Festivals

The last weekend in April, Oak Harbor hosts **Holland Happening**—a folk parade, arts and crafts show, international dance fest, Dutch buffet, and tulip show in Holland Gardens at 500 Ave. W and 30th NW. In mid-Dec., the **Christmas Boatlight Parade** departs from Oak Harbor, proceeding around Penn Cove to the Coupeville Wharf; caroling and hot cocoa conclude the event.

COUPEVILLE

One of the oldest towns in Washington, the "Port of Sea Captains" was founded in 1852 when Capt. Thomas Coupe, after sailing through Deception Pass, dropped anchor and became one of the town's first white settlers (alongside 300 or so Skagit Indians). Today the little town sits amidst the nation's largest historical preservation district, operating modern businesses from Victorian-era buildings.

Parks

Fort Casey State Park, a historical army post site 3 miles S of Coupeville at the Port Townsend ferry dock, has 2 miles of beach, an underwater park, trails, picnic areas, spectacular Olympic views, and 35 campsites; good bottom, salmon, and steelhead fishing, accessible by boat launch in remarkably clear water. Check out their **Admiralty Point**

Lighthouse Interpretive Center, where you can learn about coast artillery and the 1890 defense post, and climb to the top for a view of Puget Sound. Much of the fort is open for public viewing, including ammunition bunkers, observation towers, underground storage facilities, and gun catwalks.

Fort Ebey State Park, W of Coupeville on Admiralty Inlet, has 50 campsites, a large picnic area, 3 miles of beach, and 2 miles of hiking trails. Due to its location in the Olympic rain shadow, the park is one of few places in western WA where numerous varieties of cactus can be found. Much of Ft. Ebey's popularity stems from Lake Pondilla, formed by a glacial sinkhole—a bass-fisherman's and swimmer's delight. Follow the signs from the N parking lot for a 2-block hike to the lake; half a dozen picnic tables and a camping area are reserved for hikers and bicyclists. Rockhounders frequent the area from Point Partridge to Ebey's Landing, often encountering gem-quality stones such as agate, jasper, black and green jade, plus quartz and petrified wood. The park's 226 acres serve as a wildlife preserve for bald eagles, deer, rabbits, raccoons, and ducks.

Ebey's Landing, 2 miles W of Coupeville center, with easily the most striking coastal view on the island, was the first National Historic Reserve in the country. As Ft. Ebey Rd. winds westward through acres of farmland, the glimpses of water and cliff might

Ebey's landing

remind you of the Northern California or Oregon coastline; the majestic Olympics add to the drama. From the small parking area at the water's edge, hike the 1-mile trail to Parego's Lagoon, then wade through the lagoon and climb Parego's Bluff for a view of the coastline, Olympics, and the Strait of Juan de Fuca that shouldn't be missed.

Historical Sights

The native Skagits didn't welcome the white settlers with open arms, and their northern neighbors, the Haida Indians, were even more hostile. To protect themselves from an attack that never came, the pioneers built 7 blockhouses by 1856. One of them, the **Alexander Blockhouse,** is at Alexander St. just off Front St.; another, the **Davis Blockhouse,** stands at the edge of the cemetery on Sherman Road. Call the Central Whidbey Chamber of Commerce, 678-5434, for more info. The **Island County Historical Society Museum** at Alexander and Coveland streets has displays of pioneer relics as well as a brochure describing a short walking tour of the town's Victorian buildings. **Chief Snakelum's Grave** in a grove 2 miles E of Coupeville commemorates the chief of the Skagit Tribe and one of the town's last Indian residents.

Accommodations And Food

Built in 1907 of madrona logs, the **Captain Whidbey Inn,** 2072 W. Captain Whidbey Inn Rd., 678-4097, has rooms, cottages, and houses on Penn Cove's wooded shores. Rates start at $55 s or d, going up to $105 for the 1- or 2-bedroom houses. Rowboat, sailboat, and bicycle rentals are available; breakfast, lunch, and dinner are served daily. **The Colonel Crockett Farm,** 1012 S. Fort Casey Rd., 678-3711, is an 1855 Victorian farmhouse overlooking Admiralty Bay at Ebey's Landing and surrounded by 2 acres of lawn and flower beds. Their 5 rooms are $55-75 d per night (singles $5 less), each with private bath; a buffet breakfast is served at 9:30 a.m. No smoking or kids under 14.

For more conventional lodging, the **Coupeville Inn,** 200 N.W. Coveland St., 678-6668, has 24 guest rooms with complimen-

tary continental breakfast, from $47-65 per night s or d, along with a view of Penn Cove and the Cascades.

Festivals And Fairs

Coupeville's annual **Arts and Crafts Festival** is held the 2nd weekend in Aug. with a salmon barbecue and music. If you're here the first weekend in Oct., don't miss the **Squash Festival,** celebrating the 30,000-ton squash harvest with canoe races, music, squash soup and main dishes, culminating in the crowning of the King and Queen of Squash.

GREENBANK

Don't be surprised if you never see Greenbank center—the general store and post office are easy to miss—but you can't miss the acres and acres of loganberries growing just N of town. Formerly the largest loganberry farm in the U.S., Chateau Ste. Michelle uses these berries for their Whidbey Island Liqueur. Stop by the tasting room on Hwy. 20 for a short self-guided tour and a taste of Ste. Michelle wines.

Parks And Gardens

Probably the island's most underrated park, **South Whidbey State Park** on Smuggler's Cove Rd. has hiking, picnicking, clamming and crabbing on a sandy beach, 54 (non-hookup) campsites, and striking Olympic views. The 87 acres of towering firs and alders protect resident black-tailed deer, fox, raccoons, rabbits, bald eagles, osprey, and pileated woodpeckers. Late summer means salmon in the Admiralty Inlet; a public boat launch is located 2 miles S of the park at Bush Point.

Meerkerk Rhododendron Gardens boasts a wide variety of rhododendron species and hybrids, plus other plants such as Japanese cherries, maples, magnolia, and more, on a 53-acre site on Resort Road. Max and Anne Meerkerk built a house and started the garden upon their arrival to Whidbey Island in 1963; Max died in 1969, leaving Anne to tend the garden until 1979, when she also died and bequeathed the gardens to the

Seattle Rhododendron Society. In response to one of Anne's last requests, an international rhodie test garden has been developed; plants from Germany, Japan, England, and other countries are added each year. The gardens are open Wed. through Sat. 9 a.m. to 4 p.m.; 321-6682.

Accommodations

The **Guest House,** 835 E. Christenson Rd., 678-3115, features a 3-room suite, 4 cottages, and 1 log home, all heavy on the romance, on 25 acres of forest and meadowland with marine and mountain views. The suite is $85; 3 cottages are $110, the 4th goes for $155, and the log home is $195. All accommodations except the suite include a fireplace, kitchen, VCR and complimentary movies, in-room jacuzzi, and are for 1 couple only. Other facilities include a pool, exercise room, and outdoor spa. Indoor smoking, kids, and pets are not allowed.

FREELAND

South Whidbey was seemingly designed for biking. The rolling hills, clean air, and beautiful weather are inspiring enough, but occasional deer and eagle sightings add to the pleasure. Rent a bike for a day (or week) from **The Pedaler** on Hwy. 525 at Tara Village, 221-5040. A boat launch and small sunny picnic area are found at **Freeland Park** on Holmes Harbor, about 2 streets over from "downtown" Freeland—just look for the water.

Accommodations

Get away from your troubles and your kids at the **Cliff House,** 5440 Windmill Rd., 321-1566. The entire house is yours for a 2-night minimum at $245 per night; a little pricey maybe, but look what you get: a gourmet kitchen, king-size feather bed, fresh flowers, CDs, jacuzzi, hammock for 2, fireplace, beach access and water views, and continental breakfast. No kids, pets, or smoking. Those with tighter budgets will enjoy **Sea Cliff Cottage;** same owners, same seclusion, same beach, at $135 per night with a 2-night minimum stay. The cottage features

a small kitchen, queen-size bed, fireplace, and continental breakfast.

Pillars By The Sea overlooks Holmes Harbor at 1367 E. Bayview Ave., 221-7738. The 3 rooms each have queen-size beds and private baths for $60 a night; add $10 for Sat. night only.

Harbor Hideaway, also on Holmes Harbor on E. Harbor Rd., 321-5180, sits on an acre of grass with panoramic water views. The 3 rooms are $45-55 d; add $5 for kids over 12, subtract $5 for single. **Chateau la Mer,** 4946 S. Scurlock Rd., 221-3753, is a contemporary B&B furnished in antiques, overlooking the beach at Bush Point. The 3 bedrooms are $35, $45, or $65 per night and include a gourmet breakfast, use of the jacuzzi, 2 bicycles, TV, stereo, VCR, compact-disc player, deck, and fireplace. An even lower-priced alternative is the **Harbour Inn,** 1606 E. Main St., 321-6900. Their 20 rooms are $35-40 s, $40-55 d during summer, less off-season. **Mutiny Bay Resort/Motel,** 5856 S. Mutiny Bay Rd. (Box 249), 321-4500, has chalets for $95 d ($75 in winter), cabins for $45-55 d ($35-45 in winter), and full-hookup trailer sites for $15-20 (no tents) on 450 feet of beachfront one mile W of Freeland at the end of Fish Road. Motel guests may not have pets.

Food

Mindy's in Harbor Village Square serves breakfast, lunch, and dinner daily and specializes in fresh strawberry and raspberry pies. For seafood and steaks, try the **Island Pub** on Harbor Ave.; they're open for lunch and dinner and have entertainment on Fri. and Sat. nights.

LANGLEY

If you only have time to visit one of Whidbey's towns, this is it. The shops lining the streets of this small waterfront artists' community make for good browsing, while the views of the Cascades and the Saratoga Passage provide an uplifting backdrop. Langley is the home of the **Island County Fair,** a 4-day event held in late Aug. with a logging show, local talent show, parade, music, and 4-H exhibits.

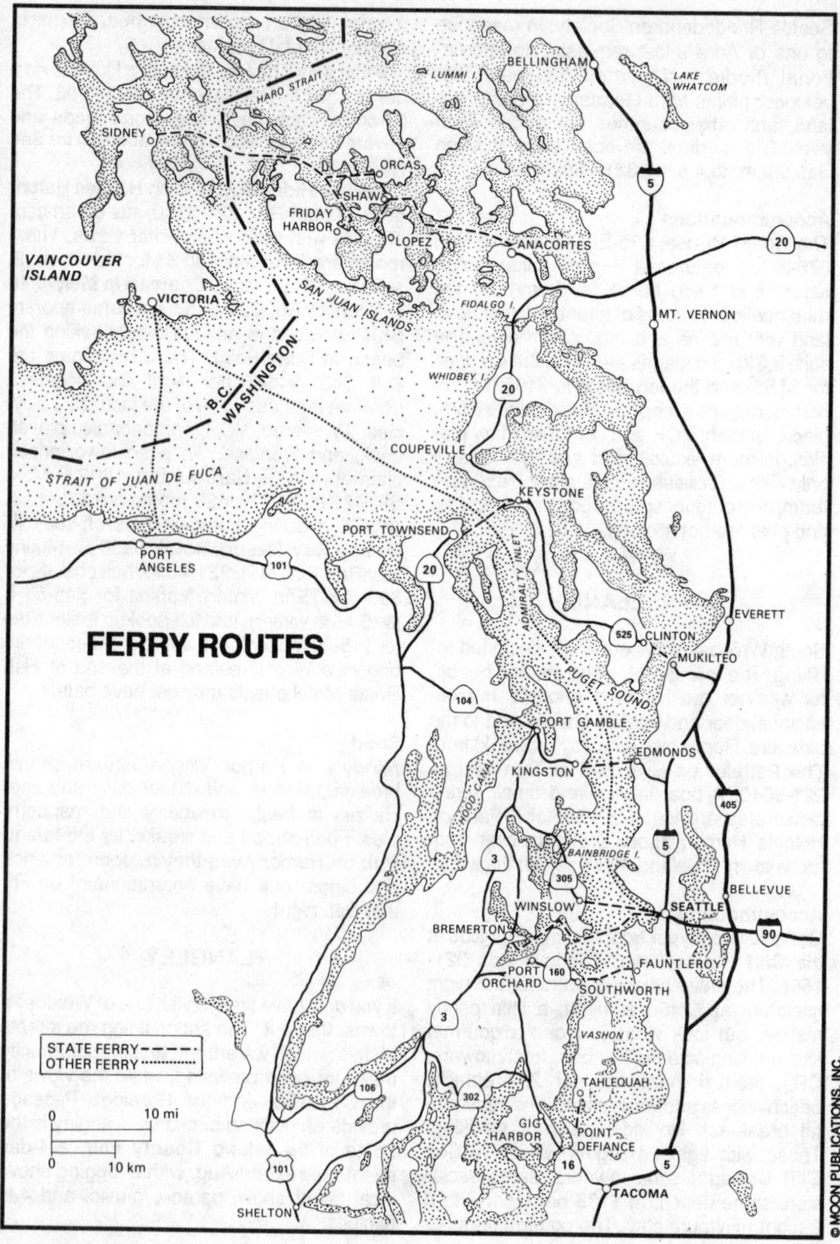
FERRY ROUTES
HARO STRAIT
LUMMI I.
BELLINGHAM
LAKE WHATCOM
SIDNEY
ORCAS
SHAW
FRIDAY HARBOR
LOPEZ
ANACORTES
VANCOUVER ISLAND
VICTORIA
SAN JUAN ISLANDS
FIDALGO I.
MT. VERNON
WHIDBEY I.
B.C.
WASHINGTON
COUPEVILLE
STRAIT OF JUAN DE FUCA
KEYSTONE
PORT TOWNSEND
PORT ANGELES
ADMIRALTY INLET
EVERETT
CLINTON
MUKILTEO
PUGET SOUND
PORT GAMBLE
EDMONDS
KINGSTON
HOOD CANAL
BAINBRIDGE I.
BELLEVUE
WINSLOW
SEATTLE
BREMERTON
PORT ORCHARD
FAUNTLEROY
SOUTHWORTH
VASHON I.
TAHLEQUAH
GIG HARBOR
POINT DEFIANCE
TACOMA
SHELTON
STATE FERRY
OTHER FERRY
0
10 mi
0
10 km
5
20
101
525
104
405
3
305
90
160
106
302
16

© MOON PUBLICATIONS, INC.

Accommodations

Langley's newest hotel, **The Inn at Langley,** 400 1st St., 221-3033, is a delightful getaway, overlooking the Saratoga Passage at the edge of downtown. The inn is a beauty, inside and out; the 24 guest rooms are elegantly decorated, and each has a fireplace and deck. The room rates are steep, but worth it: $115 d, $130 d for a corner room, up to $195 d for a suite. Continental breakfast is included; a 5-course dinner is $25. Also overlooking the Saratoga Passage, **The Whidbey Inn,** 106 First St., 221-7115, has 3 rooms and 3 fireplace suites, each with private bath and access to the sundeck, plus some of life's little luxuries—scented bath gels, chocolates on the pillows, and a breakfast basket of homemade breads, an egg dish, juice, and coffee brought to your door. Rooms start at $80 a night. No kids, pets, or indoor smoking. The **Saratoga Inn** is surrounded by 25 acres of forest and meadows at 4850 S. Coles Rd. (within walking distance of downtown), 221-7526. The inn has 5 rooms with views, private baths, and fresh flowers from $80-90; breakfast is continental, featuring muffins, croissants, and homemade blackberry jam. No pets, kids, or smoking. **Country Cottage,** a B&B on 3 acres at 215 6th St., 221-8709, has 3 rooms and 2 suites with private baths, a full breakfast, and a view of the Cascades and Saratoga Passage for $75-85 d; no kids, pets, or smoking. **Log Castle B&B,** on the waterfront at 3273 E. Saratoga Rd., 321-5483, was designed and built by the owners from material located on the property; of the 4 guest rooms, the 3rd-story turret—complete with widow's walk—is the most popular. Each room has its own bath and porch with Saratoga Passage and mountain views. Rooms cost $60-80; no pets or smoking.

Food

Don't miss the **Dog House Tavern and Backdoor Restaurant,** corner of 1st and Anthes on the waterfront. Nothing fancy— just a great place to grab a pork sandwich, nachos, or a burger and a couple beers while enjoying the view. Nothing else comes close.

Down the street a bit at 113 1st, **Cafe Langley** has a following of its own. Greek is the word: lamb kabobs, pita bread, soups, and other middle eastern dishes. Open for lunch and dinner daily. **Star Bistro** serves burgers, seafoods, salads, and more upstairs at 201½ 1st St.; open for lunch and dinner daily. Newly remodeled, **Mike's Place,** 215 First St., 321-6575, is another popular spot, serving lunch and dinner daily from an international menu, complete with home-baked bread and pastries.

CLINTON

Driving or biking around Clinton's rural, wooded back roads provides lungfuls of fresh air and some exhilarating vistas. Take Deer Lake Rd. (watch the signs—the road takes 90-degree turns without notice) to **Deer Lake Park** for swimming, boating, and fishing in a secluded, wooded area. From Hwy. 525, go L onto Campbell Rd., then L again on Maxwelton Rd. to **Maxwelton Beach,** where you'll find the island's best Dungeness crabbing.

Accommodations

Surrounded by Deer Lagoon and Useless Bay, **Home By The Sea** at 2388 E. Sunlight Beach Rd., 221-2964, has rooms for $75 d and cottages from $75-85 d with views of the Olympics and Admiralty Inlet. The cottages, one of which is available for families with children, require a 2-night minimum stay.

Food

Islander Restaurant, at the Clinton ferry landing, 321-4363, serves Italian and American food daily from 6 a.m.-2 a.m. plus Sunday brunch. For Chinese cuisine, **Hong Kong Gardens** is 1 mile from the ferry landing on Hwy. 525, 221-2828, with a view of Saratoga Passage. Open daily in the summer, closed Mon. in winter. **Le Quai,** a popular French restaurant on Hwy. 525, 321-1071, is open daily except Mon. for lunch and dinner.

ANACORTES

Visitors know Anacortes as the jumping-off point for the San Juan Islands, but this city of more than 11,000 people is far more than a ferry dock on the tip of Fidalgo Island. White men first resided on the island in the 1850s, but William Munks, who liked to call himself "The King of Fidalgo Island," claimed to be the first permanent settler and opened a store there in 1869. Amos Bowman tried to persuade the company he worked for, the Canadian Pacific Railroad, to establish their western terminus at Fidalgo—despite the fact that Bowman had never seen the island. When they refused, Bowman came down to check out the property himself, bought 168 acres of it, and opened a store, a wharf, and the Anna Curtis Post Office, named after his wife, in 1879. Bowman was so determined to get a railroad—any railroad—into Anacortes (pronounced "Anna Cortis") that he published a newspaper, *The Northwest Enterprise*, to draw people and businesses to his town. He was so convincing that the population boomed, even though, by 1890, the town's 5 railroad depots had yet to see a train pull up.

Residents gave up on the railroad idea and found financial success in lumber mills, a cannery, and box factory. The Burlington Northern Railroad eventually came—and went. Today Anacortes relies on its oil refineries, wood products, ship builders, food processors, and tourism for much of its income.

SIGHTS

Scenic Drive
Start at 36th St. and R Ave. for a scenic drive that takes you by the waterfront, through Washington Park, past Lake Erie, up Mt. Erie, and through old residential and industrial areas for an overall view of Anacortes' many faces. From 36th and R, go north on R and Q past Cap Sante Marina, then E to Cap Sante Park via 4th St. and V Avenue. Work your way over to 12th St. through the Causland Park residential area, loaded with well-kept houses, beautiful water views, and commercial buildings from the turn-of-the-century pre-railroad population boom. Head W on 12th Ave. to Oakes Ave. for water and island

views. Continue W to Washington Park via Sunset Ave., looping through the park on the scenic road; head S on Anaco Beach Dr., Marine Dr., and Rosario Rd. toward Lake Erie. Follow Heart Lake Rd. to Mt. Erie Dr., up to Mt. Erie's summit (described below). Upon your return to the base, follow Heart Lake Rd. N past Heart Lake and back to downtown Anacortes.

Parks
Three miles W of Anacortes, **Washington Park** is a strikingly beautiful picnic spot with 200 waterfront acres on the Rosario Strait affording views of the San Juans and Olympics. Walk, bike, or drive the 2.3-mile paved scenic loop, and pull in to 1 of many waterfront picnic areas. Other facilities include a boat launch, miles of hiking trails (see map), and a playground. Camp at one of the 46 hookup and 29 non-hookup wooded campsites from April through Oct. ($10, hookups

extra). The original park acreage was donated by 1 of Fidalgo Island's earliest pioneers, Tonjes Havekost, who said, "Make my cemetery a park for everybody." Additional acreage was bought by the Anacortes Women's Club in 1922 from the sale of lemon pies—they paid just $2,500 for 75 beachfront acres.

Five miles S of Anacortes, 1,270-foot **Mt. Erie** provides panoramic views from the Olympics to Mt. Baker to Mt. Rainier via a 1½-mile paved road to the partially wooded summit; the paths and fenced areas at the top point the way to clear viewing spots. Though the hill is small by mountain standards, the views are dizzying, perhaps because of its steep drop-offs and the oceans of water below. Take Heart Lake Rd. to Ray Auld Dr. and Mt. Erie Road.

For a good, low-altitude viewpoint of the Cascades and Skagit Valley, visit **Cap Sante Park** on the city's east side, following 4th St.

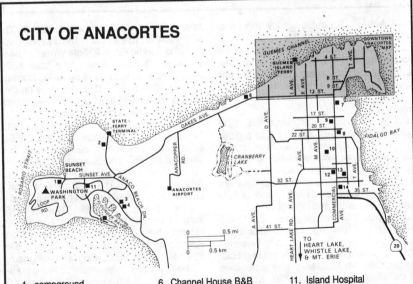

CITY OF ANACORTES

1. campground
2. Charlie's Restaurant
3. Burrow's Bay B&B
4. Skyline B&B
5. Slocum's Restaurant
6. Channel House B&B
7. chamber of commerce
8. Left Bank Antiques
9. Gateway Motel
10. Albatross B&B
11. Island Hospital
12. Anacortes Inn
13. Dutch Treat House B&B
14. Islands Motel and La Petite Restaurant

© MOON PUBLICATIONS, INC.

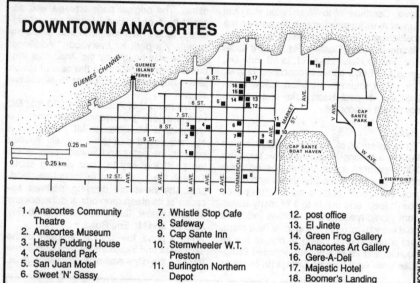

DOWNTOWN ANACORTES

1. Anacortes Community Theatre
2. Anacortes Museum
3. Hasty Pudding House
4. Causeland Park
5. San Juan Motel
6. Sweet 'N' Sassy
7. Whistle Stop Cafe
8. Safeway
9. Cap Sante Inn
10. Sternwheeler W.T. Preston
11. Burlington Northern Depot
12. post office
13. El Jinete
14. Green Frog Gallery
15. Anacortes Art Gallery
16. Gere-A-Deli
17. Majestic Hotel
18. Boomer's Landing

© MOON PUBLICATIONS, INC.

to W Avenue. Scramble up the mound of boulders for a better look.

Downtown, **Causland Park** covers a city block at 8th and N avenues; the ornate mosaic walls and gazebo were built in 1920 with colored stones from area islands.

Hiking

Stop by the chamber of commerce, 1319 Commercial Ave., and spend $3 for a guide to trails on 2,200 acres of Anacortes Community Forest Lands around Mt. Erie and Cranberry, Whistle, and Heart lakes. The city did a splendid job on these guides; all trails are numbered, rated for difficulty, and include mileage, elevation, and highlights.

Five loop trails, ranging from 2.3 to 3.5 miles, start at the topographic saddle between Mt. Erie and Sugarloaf on aptly named Mt. Erie Saddle Road. Despite the short distances, these are rated all-day hikes because of the steep climb up trails #26, #207, and #21 from the individual trailheads back to the Saddle Road. The longest of these, the **South-to-North Lake Loop,** circles Whistle Lake, passing an early 1900s' dam and old-growth Douglas fir and cedar. For this loop,

take trails #26, #207, and #21 to #22, #205, #20, #204, and back to #21. The shortest loop from the Saddle Rd. is **Middle Whistle Lake Loop** at 2.3 miles. Again, take trails #26, #207, and #21, then go N on #203, looping back on #204 to #21. This hike stays on the W side of Whistle Lake but offers lake views and a summertime mid-loop swim.

From the trailhead at the intersection of Mt. Erie and Heart Lake roads, hike the .6-mile **Pine Ridge Loop Trail,** #25 and #213, for views of Mt. Erie and Sugarloaf. This moderately difficult hike takes from 1 to 2 hours. Another short hike is the **Sugarloaf Trail,** starting on Ray Auld Dr. 6 mile from its intersection with Heart Lake Road. Take trail #215 from the marshy trailhead straight up, ignoring side trails, to views to the W of Port Townsend, the San Juan Islands, and the Strait of Juan de Fuca, and N to Bellingham.

The Cranberry Lake area also has a number of hiking trails, ranging from .2 to 2.6 miles. The **John M. Morrison Loop Trail** starts at the end of 29th St., following trail #104 for .9 mile; steep drop-offs in the middle section of the trail allow views of Cranberry Lake and old-growth Douglas fir forests. **Old**

Mine Trail is an easy, .6-mile OW hike to an old mine entrance. Park at the end of Georgia Ave., then follow trails #100, #102, and #103 to the mines; retrace your steps to return. For experienced hikers, the 1½-mile **Cranberry Lake Loop** circles the lake from the same Georgia Ave. parking lot via trails #100, #102, and #101; the narrow trail's difficulty lies in its poor footing and its disappearance into the lake in several spots. Allow 2 to 3 hours.

Museums And History

At 1305 8th St., the **Anacortes Museum,** 293-5198, has local history exhibits including a doctor's and dentist's office, photographs, and period furniture. Open Thurs. through Mon. afternoons; donation. Other remnants of earlier days are scattered throughout town, including the historic sternwheeler *W. T. Preston,* on display at 8th St. and R Ave., and the old Burlington Northern Railroad depot at 7th and R, now a refurbished community center. Speaking of railroads, don't miss the **Anacortes Railway.** Over a 20-year period, long-time resident Tommy Thompson created an authentically scaled 0-4-4 Forney-type steam locomotive that pulls 3 passenger cars between the depot at 7th and R and a turn-around at 9th and Commercial every weekend in summer.

The Causland Park area has a number of 1890s homes and buildings, many restored to their original splendor. The home owned and built by Amos Bowman and Anna Curtis Bowman in 1891 stands at 1815 8th St.; at 807 4th St., an architect's office is now housed in what was probably the finest bordello in the county in the 1890s. The Little Church at 5th and R was built by its Presbyterian congregation in 1889, and is undergoing restoration; still in use is the Episcopal Church at 7th and M, built in 1896.

ACCOMMODATIONS

Bed And Breakfast

Walking distance to downtown and the Cap Sante waterfront, the **Hasty Pudding House,** 1312 8th St., 293-5773, is an elegantly restored 1913 Edwardian B&B furnished in antiques and lace. Home-baked full breakfasts, afternoon tea, and a cozy fireplace add to the charm. Four guest rooms (2 with private bath) run $50-65 d; no pets or indoor smoking.

Scheduled to open in April 1990, the The **Majestic** is a European-style country inn in a restored 100-year-old building. The 23 guest rooms and suites, many with view decks, have private baths, cable TV, wet bars, and in-room coffee makers, and are accented with antiques. A continental breakfast basket is delivered to your room. The dining room features Northwest seafood, and their Victorian Pub offers casual dining and imbibing. Rooms range from $75-155.

Just opened in May 1989, **Albatross Bed and Breakfast,** 5708 Kingsway W, 293-0677, features 4 guest rooms, all with private bath, a block away from Skyline Marina and within walking distance of Washington Park. The well-kept contemporary home offers a view of the marina, home-baked breakfasts, free transportation to and from the ferries or airport, and designated smoking areas. Rooms are $59 s, $69 d, $79 t ($9 less in winter). At 2902 Oakes Ave., **Channel House,** 293-9382, was designed and built in 1902 for an Italian count, with 3 fireplaces and Puget Sound views from every bedroom. For today's guests, a gourmet breakfast, large hot tub, and antique-furnished rooms make this B&B a bargain at $38 s, $45 d. Shared bath; no pets, kids, or indoor smoking. **Dutch Treat House,** 1220 31st St., 293-8154, offers comfortable lodging in a 1930 Dutch Colonial home, with a full breakfast and rooms for $35 s, $50-55 d. They'll supply the wine glasses if you BYOB; kids over 8 OK, smoking outdoors only. **Burrows Bay,** 4911 Macbeth Dr., 293-4792, is a contemporary B&B with 1 luxury suite (it can accommodate up to 6) for $75 s, $85 d ($10 each additional person), with a fireplace, library, private deck and entry, and a sweeping view of the San Juans; breakfast is served in your room at your convenience. **Old Brook Inn,** 530 Old Brook Lane, 293-4768, has 2 guest rooms (1 can sleep 5) with private baths ($50-55 s, $60-65 d) and Fidalgo Bay views amidst an old orchard, complete with babbling brook. Children welcome.

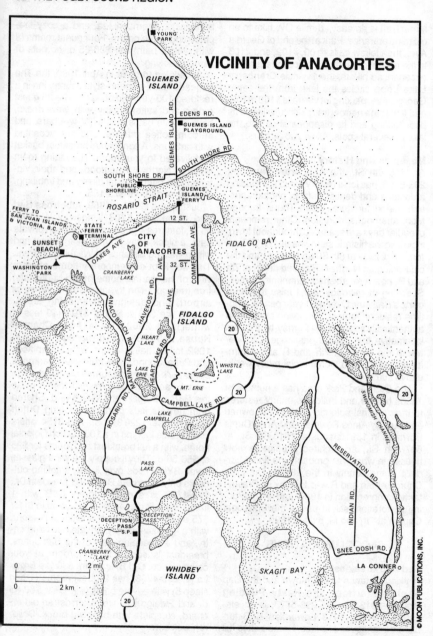

VICINITY OF ANACORTES

YOUNG PARK

GUEMES ISLAND

GUEMES ISLAND RD.

EDENS RD.

GUEMES ISLAND PLAYGROUND

SOUTH SHORE RD.

SOUTH SHORE DR.

PUBLIC SHORELINE

GUEMES ISLAND FERRY

ROSARIO STRAIT

FERRY TO SAN JUAN ISLANDS & VICTORIA, B.C.

STATE FERRY TERMINAL

12 ST.

CITY OF ANACORTES

OAKES AVE.

SUNSET BEACH

WASHINGTON PARK

CRANBERRY LAKE

D AVE.

32 ST.

COMMERCIAL AVE.

FIDALGO BAY

HAVEKOST RD.

H AVE.

FIDALGO ISLAND

20

ANACO BEACH RD.

ROSARIO RD.

MARINE DR.

HEART LAKE

HEART LAKE RD.

LAKE ERIE

WHISTLE LAKE

MT. ERIE

20

CAMPBELL LAKE RD.

LAKE CAMPBELL

20

SWINOMISH CHANNEL

RESERVATION RD.

PASS LAKE

INDIAN RD.

DECEPTION PASS

DECEPTION PASS S.P.

PASS

CRANBERRY LAKE

SNEE OOSH RD.

LA CONNER

0   2 mi

0   2 km

WHIDBEY ISLAND

SKAGIT BAY

20

© MOON PUBLICATIONS, INC.

Hotels And Motels

Holiday Motel, 2903 Commercial Ave., 293-6511, has 10 budget rooms from $24-35 s, $26-40 d. At 6th and O, the **San Juan Motel,** 293-5105, has 27 rooms for $26 s, $30 d. At 3006 Commercial Ave., the **Anacortes Inn,** 293-3153, has 44 rooms for $30-38 s, $34-46 d, with outdoor heated pool. Some rooms have water views. The **Cap Sante Inn,** 906 9th St., 293-0602, offers complimentary continental breakfast and rooms from $32-44 s, $36-46 d, within walking distance of the marina. The **Islands Motel,** 3401 Commercial Ave., 293-4644, is one of the city's nicest motels, with rooms starting at $40-60 s or d, and going up to $95 for the honeymoon suite, with fireplace, jacuzzi, and wet bar; prices for all rooms include pool, jacuzzi, and breakfast at **Le Petite Restaurant** (see below).

FOOD

At the Islands Motel, **La Petite Restaurant,** 34th and Commercial, 293-4644, serves some of the best dinners in Anacortes, plus a hearty Dutch breakfast; open daily for breakfast, dinner daily except Monday. On the waterfront at 209 T Ave., **Boomer's Landing,** 293-5108, is another of Anacortes' better restaurants, open daily for dinner, weekdays for lunch, specializing in lobster, steak, and seafood for $8-19; weekend entertainment in the lounge. Another nice one is **Slocum's Restaurant,** Skyline Way at Flounder Bay, 293-0644, with views of Skyline Marina. Specialties here are steak and seafood, up to $18; an extensive wine list includes everything from $9.95 Sutter Home blush to $75 Dom Perignon. The attached chowder house serves soups and sandwiches for lunch; also open for Sunday brunch. **Charlie's Restaurant,** at the ferry dock, has a moderately priced steak and seafood menu with water and dock views; a convenient place to stop for a drink while you're waiting for your ship to come in.

For less expensive eats, **Whistle Stop Cafe,** 818 Commercial, is open for breakfast and lunch, specializing in homemade cinnamon rolls. For take-out food for a bike or ferry trip or casual eat-in dining, stop by **Gere-a-Deli,** 502 Commercial, for sandwiches, salads, soups, or homemade desserts. **El Jinete** serves Mexican lunches and dinners at 509 Commercial, 293-2631.

ENTERTAINMENT

Festivals

Held the first 3 weekends in April in Anacortes, La Conner, and Mount Vernon, the **Skagit Valley Tulip Festival,** 293-3832, offers everything from boat rides to belly dancers to fireworks and the popular "Taste of Skagit" feed; see "Mount Vernon," p. 150, for tulip field auto/bike tours. The last weekend in July brings the self-explanatory **Anachords Annual Barbershop Concert and Salmon Barbecue.** If you missed this one, shoot for mid-August's **World's Largest King Salmon Barbecue.** Also held in Aug. is the **Anacortes Arts and Crafts Festival,** a 2-day event held downtown and at the depot at 7th and R that draws upwards of 35,000 people annually; phone 293-6211 for exact dates and times. Catch the holiday spirit, Puget-sound style: watch for the annual **Lighted Ships of Christmas Boat Parade,** held the 2nd Sat. in December.

Theater

The **Anacortes Community Theatre,** or ACT, stages 4 performances from March through Nov., plus annual performances of "A Christmas Carol" and "Broadway Melodies," at a 112-seat theater at 10th and M. For ticket information phone 293-6829.

SHOPPING

They don't call it "Commercial Avenue" for nothing. The **Anacortes Art Gallery,** 414 Commercial, 293-6656, has changing exhibits of area artists' work Tues. through Saturday.

Green Frog Gallery, 516 Commercial, 293-6661, has prints, etchings, gifts, and custom framing. Closed Sun. and Mondays. Pick up some Native American carvings, pottery, jewelry, prints, and more at **Samish Potlatch**

Gifts, 708 Commercial, 293-6404. Chocoholics won't want to miss **Sweet 'N' Sassy,** 710 Commercial, for chocolates, ice-cream bars, cards, and gifts. **Left Bank Antiques,** 1906 Commercial, 293-3022, has Victorian furniture, jewelery, prints, and toys. For groceries, there's a **Safeway** at 12th and Commercial, and a **Pay Less Drugstore** at 15th and Commercial.

SERVICES

The Anacortes area code is 206. For maps, brochures, or further information, contact the **Anacortes Chamber of Commerce,** 1319 Commercial Ave., 293-3832. For a medical emergency, **Island Hospital** at 24th and M, 293-3183, has 24-hour emergency room and ambulance service. For a tumble and spin-dry, try **Econo-Wash Laundry** at 2022 Commercial or **Thrifty Laundry** at 1502 Commercial.

TRANSPORTATION

By Car

Anacortes is about 80 miles N of Seattle, via I-5 and Hwy. 20. But it would be a shame to

drive to Anacortes without a quick sidetrip to La Conner (p. 154), especially in spring when the daffodils and tulips are blooming.

Ferries

To get to the San Juan Islands via state ferry, you've got no choice but to leave from Anacortes—and ferry traffic keeps a good portion of local businesses in business. For fares and other vital information see "San Juan Islands," p. 141, or phone the Washington State Ferry System toll-free at (800) 542-0810.

Skagit County operates a nearly new ferry to residential Guemes Island from 6th and I. The 7-minute crossing costs $4.20 for car and driver, $1 for passengers; the boat departs daily on the hour or better, from 6:30 a.m. most days to at least 6 p.m. Take your bicycle along for a scenic tour.

By Air

Departing from Anacortes Airport at 4000 Airport Rd. or Skagit Regional Airport, 1340 Peterson Rd., **West Isle Air** offers scenic, 45-minute San Juan Island flights year-round for $65 for 1-3 passengers, $115 for 4-6 passengers; 293-4691 in Anacortes or 757-6890 in Burlington.

SAN JUAN ISLANDS

Nestled between the Washington mainland and Vancouver Island, the San Juan Archipelago consists of 172 islands—as many as 400 when the tide goes out—with 376 miles of shoreline. Four of the largest—Orcas, Lopez, Shaw, and San Juan—are served by state ferry. The pace is slow and the dress is casual, so leave your ties at home, but don't forget your binoculars (for whale- and bird-watching), camera, and bike.

Climate

The San Juans do most of their tourist business between Memorial Day and Labor Day when the weather is warm—rarely above 85 degrees—and sunny, but for the locals September and October are the nicest months of the year: the tourists are gone, and the weather is still warm and dry, with highs in the 60s and lows in the 40s or 50s, and the salmon are running. Because the islands are shielded by the Olympic and Vancouver Island mountains, rainfall amounts to less than 25 inches per year; December is the wettest month, with 4½ inches of rain on the average and temperatures in the low 40s.

HISTORY

Because of inexact wording in the U.S.-Canada boundary treaty, the San Juan Islands were not only the subject of a territorial dispute, but also the stage for an international incident commonly referred to as the "Pig War." In June of 1859 one of 25 American settlers on San Juan Island, Lyman A. Cutler, shot and killed a pig that had wandered into his potato patch. The Englishman who owned the pig insisted that Cutler be brought to trial in Victoria, but the American refused to budge. Troops were dispatched on both sides to what are National Historic Sites today—the American Camp on the SE side of the island, and the English Camp in the NW corner—and remained there until the matter was settled by arbitration 13 years later, giving the San Juans to the U.S. Fortunately, the pig was the only casualty.

SERVICES

The area code in the San Juan Islands is 206. For maps and information, write or call the **San Juan Island Chamber of Commerce,** Box 98, Friday Harbor, WA 98250, 378-5240, or the **Orcas Island Chamber of Commerce,** Box 252, Eastsound, WA 98245, 376-2273.

Fitness fanatics might want to take advantage of the $10 1-day memberships offered by **San Juan Fitness and Athletic Club,** open daily in Friday Harbor; 378-4449. Facilities include racquetball courts, exercise equipment, sauna, steam room, spa, and juice bar.

For groceries, film, and other essentials stop by **King's Market** in Friday Harbor or **Templin's General Store** in Eastsound. You

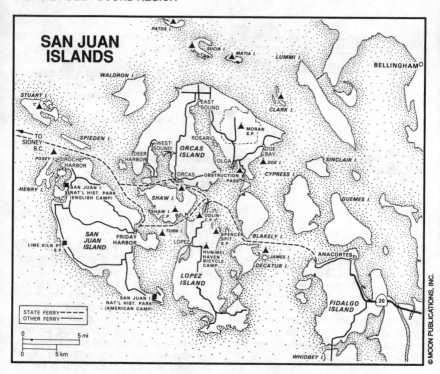

SAN JUAN ISLANDS

STATE FERRY — — —
OTHER FERRY ·········

0   5 mi
0   5 km

© MOON PUBLICATIONS, INC.

can do your laundry at **Wash Tub Laundromat,** San Juan Inn Boardwalk in Friday Harbor, 378-2070, or **Airport Center Self Service Laundry** in Eastsound, 376-2478.

For medical emergencies, call 911 in Friday Harbor or Lopez, or 376-2341 on Orcas Island.

TRANSPORTATION

By Air

San Juan Airlines connects to major carriers via Seattle, Bellingham, and Vancouver, B.C.; call them at 452-1323 or, toll-free in Washington, (800) 438-3880. You can also fly to Rosario Resort on Orcas Island from Seattle via seaplane twice daily with **Lake Union Air;** call 284-2784 collect in Washington. **West Isle Air,** 293-4691, flies daily from Anacortes to the San Juans, and as needed to Boeing or Sea-Tac Airport. **Kenmore Air,** (800) 832-9696 statewide or (800) 423-5526

outside Washington, serves the San Juans by float plane from Seattle. **Orcas Flight** offers scenic airplane rides from $45 for 30 minutes out of Orcas' Eastsound Airport; call 376-2771 for reservations or information.

By Ferry

If you can only take 1 ride aboard a **Washington State Ferry,** the trip from Anacortes to the San Juans should be the one. The scenery is so beautiful that even amateur photographers can get spectacular sunset-over-the-islands shots. Ferries leave Anacortes 5 times daily (7 times on Fri.) from 6:45 a.m.-9 p.m., stopping at Lopez, Shaw, Orcas, and Friday Harbor, in that order; it takes roughly an hour and 50 minutes from Anacortes to Friday Harbor. Fares to Friday Harbor are $4.65 for passengers, $15.85 car and driver ($19.00 in summer), and $6.25 bicycle and rider; car-and-driver fares to the other islands are a few dollars less, and carry-on kayaks go free. Once a day this ferry continues on to Sidney, B.C.; fares are $6.05 passenger, $26.05 car and driver ($31.25 in summer), and $8.55 bicycle and rider. For exact departure times or special fares call 464-6400 from Seattle or (800) 542-0810 statewide.

Day Cruises

Operating out of Bellingham, the **Maritime Heritage Center** offers 2 San Juan cruises from May through September. Their **Whale Search/Nature Watch** is a day-long 80-mile cruise between and around the islands in search of the orca, or "killer," whale. While whale sightings are common, porpoises, harbor seals, and bald eagles are practically guaranteed. Departing Mon., Wed., and Thurs. mornings, the cruises cost $45 pp. The Center also hosts **Rosario Resort Cruises** on Sun. for brunch ($35) and Fri. night for a seafood buffet ($45) at the Rosario Resort on Orcas Island. Onboard entertainment replaces the usual naturalist/tour guide. For information and reservations call 734-8866 from Bellingham or (800) 841-8866 in Washington.

Gray Line Water Sightseeing, 626-5208, provides daily 3½-hour San Juan Islands cruises, departing from Lighthouse Square at the Resort Semiahmoo in Blaine from May to mid-Oct. for $32 adults, $16 kids 5-12. The cruise route is quite a bit N of the Maritime Heritage route above, so you can do both without overlapping. This one heads S from Blaine, squeezing between Patos and Sucia islands and between Stuart and Spieden islands on its way to Roche Harbor, returning between Waldron and Orcas and E of Sucia, with lots of whale-sighting opportunities along the way. Binoculars are provided. Gray Line also offers an 11-hour San Juan Islands Cruise, also departing from the Resort Semiahmoo May through mid-Sept., for $56 adults, $40 kids. A San Juan overnight package is available for $212 d.

Once you're on San Juan Island, **Western Prince Cruises** offers trips for $35 aboard the 46-foot *Western Prince,* departing from the dock across Front St. from the museum. The cruises are narrated by a wildlife naturalist who knows all of the San Juans' 76 orcas by name. Prepayment is required for the 6-hour cruise, which includes lunch and a photo souvenir; for the shorter cruise, prepayment is nice but last-minute bookings are accepted as space allows. Phone 378-5315 for more information.

Longer Cruises

Catalyst Cruises, 515 S. 143rd St., Tacoma, 537-7678, offers several 5- to 14-day San Juan Island cruises, departing from Seattle, aboard their 55-foot motor cruiser *Sacajawea*. Catalyst is one of few Northwest charter outfits that offers scheduled cruises, meaning your group doesn't need to fill up the whole boat. Five- and 6-day cruises stop at several San Juan islands plus Victoria, B.C., and La Conner; a 2-week Canadian cruise visits the American San Juans and heads up to Campbell River, Big Bay, and Desolation Sound. Five- and 6-day cruises run June through Aug. ($662-95 pp); the 14-day San Juan/Canadian cruise is held once or twice each summer for $1590-1855 pp. Onboard meals are included with all cruises, and the fresh seafood is legendary.

One of the best deals for the money in the San Juans is an overnight sail offered by **Palmer's Chart House,** a B&B in Deer Harbor on Orcas Island (their inn is covered under "Orcas Island" below). For a minimum of 4 guests, you can spend the day—and night—aboard the 33-foot yacht *Amanate* for $125 pp, which includes dinner and a continental breakfast. Their day sails are a bargain, offered morning and afternoon for $25 pp (minimum 2, maximum 6 guests). For reservations call the Palmers at 376-4231 or write Box 51, Deer Harbor, WA 98243.

Departing weekly mid-July through Sept. from Vashon Island in S Puget Sound, **Gallant Lady Cruises** offers a 6-day San Juan Islands cruise aboard a 65-foot 1940s teak-and-mahogany yacht with stops at Rosario Resort, Friday Harbor, Sucia Island, and La Conner. The *Lady* is quite stable and the cruises are through protected waters, so seasickness is generally not a problem. The $699 pp pricetag includes all meals, featuring fresh seafood and low-fat meats served

Northwest, Continental, and Oriental style. For more information call or write Box 1250, Vashon, WA 98070, 463-2073.

Another 6-day cruise leaves from La Conner on the 62-foot fiberglass sailboat *J. Marie.* Sailing May through Oct., these cruises visit a number of the smaller islands, including Stuart and Sucia, with stops at Friday Harbor and Rosario Resort. All meals are included for $598; no kids under 12. For more information write or call **J. Marie Sailing Cruises,** Box 722, La Conner, WA 98257, 466-4292.

Take a 7-day sail in spring or fall aboard the *Norden,* an 83-foot-long wooden Baltic schooner. Departing from Friday Harbor, the cruise visits a number of smaller islands plus the larger resorts and, because of the size of the ship and the stillness of the water, even landlubbers won't get queasy. All meals are included for $685 pp, and families are welcome; call 842-2803 or write Box 10642, Bainbridge Island, WA 98110, for reservations or special family rates.

Sea Kayaking
Shearwater Sea Kayak Tours has half-day kayak trips paddling around East Sound or out to Point Doughty and overnighters to Matia, Sucia, or Jones Island; no experience necessary, but you must be at least 16. One-day tours start at $45; 2-day tours are $119-129; and 3-day trips are $169. Kayaking gear and most camping equipment is included.

Requiring somewhat more effort are the 3- and 6-day sea kayak tours offered from May through Sept. by **Northwest Sea Ventures,** Box 522, Anacortes, WA 98221. Led by an experienced guide well versed in local history and wildlife, these tours are open to anyone 15 or over in good physical condition; those with no previous experience will be assigned to stable 2-person kayaks. The group is limited to 8, covering 5-10 miles a day, with occasional sidetrips into small towns. The $165 and $325 prices include all camping and kayaking equipment, 3 meals a day, and instruction; just bring your sleeping bag. They also sell and rent kayaks and offer private and group lessons at their shop at 2114 Commercial St. in Anacortes. For more information call 293-3692.

Boat Rentals
Boat and kayak rentals are easy to find on the islands; rates are generally $30-40 a day for small outboard motor boats, increasing with the size of vessel. In Friday Harbor try **Different Strokes Boat Rentals,** 378-2342; on Orcas, **Black Bottom Boat Rental** in Eastsound, 376-4032.

By Bicycle
Bicycle rentals are available on the 4 major islands by the day, hour, or week; they're cheaper to bring on the ferry than a car. Rentals cost about $4 an hour, $12-16 a day; most shops also rent 15-speed mountain bikes (for trips up Mt. Constitution), panniers, child carriers, and helmets. On Lopez try **Lopez Bicycle Works,** Fisherman Bay Rd., 468-2847; on Orcas, **Island Chain Saw** in the Sears building in Eastsound, 376-2586; on San Juan, **Island Bicyles,** 180 West St. in Friday Harbor, 378-4941.

By Moped
For all the fun of biking without the effort, rent a moped from **Susie's Mopeds** in Friday Harbor, 378-5244, or **Key Moped Rentals** on Orcas Island at the ferry landing, Deer Harbor Marina, or in Eastsound, 376-2474.

Other
Shuttle bus service between Friday Harbor, Roche Harbor Resort, Lakedale, and other San Juan Island destinations is available from **San Juan Island Tow and Transit,** 378-5545. The 14-passenger vans make 3 loops of the island, departing hourly or so until 8 p.m.; OW fares start at $3 adults, half-price for kids. Taxi service is available before and after bus service.

SAN JUAN ISLAND

The largest island in the archipelago, San Juan Island is about 20 miles long and 7 miles wide, covering 55 square miles. Friday Harbor, the only incorporated town in the chain, is the county seat, the commercial center of the San Juans, and home to half of the island's 4,000 residents.

Sights

The American and English encampments from the 1859 "Pig War" are now National Historic Parks. The **American Camp** is located in the SE corner of the island, 5 miles from Friday Harbor, with 2 buildings and other remains of the original post and an interpretive trail; it's also home to the only nesting skylarks in the state. The **English Camp,** 8 miles from Friday Harbor on the NW side of the island, includes a restored hospital, blockhouse, commissary, and barracks, plus hiking trails to the top of Mt. Young which provide scenic vistas of the archipelago. Both sites have picnic areas and beach access for day use only. The grounds are open year-round with rangers at both sites in summer, but the buildings close in winter.

The **University of Washington** operates a marine biology research laboratory a mile N of Friday Harbor with an aquarium and display tanks. Free tours are given Wed. and Sat. afternoons in July and Aug.; phone 378-2165 for information.

Probably the most exciting sights in the San Juans, orca or "killer" whales are usually minding their own underwater business while tourists anxiously peer out their ferry windows. What some visitors think are schools of baby orcas escorting their boat are actually full-grown black-and-white Dall's porpoises. On the island, a good spot to watch for whales is from **Lime Kiln Point State Park** on Haro Strait on the island's W side; it's the only park in the country dedicated exclusively to whale-watching. Bald eagles also live on the island year-round; look for them between Eagle Cove and Cattle Point on the island's E side.

Museum

At 62 First St. in Friday Harbor, the **Whale Museum,** 378-4710, has whale and porpoise displays including full skeletons of a baby gray whale and an adult killer whale, paintings, photographs, and carvings. You can also adopt a whale for $20; you get your whale's photo and ID number plus a subscription to the museum's newsletter. Open daily till 5 p.m. in summer, till 4 p.m. in winter; admission is $2 adults, $.75 for kids. If you're intrigued by the museum and wildlife cruises (see "Cruises" above), consider attending the museum's week-long university-accredited "Whale School," offered 3 times in July and Aug. for $767. By the way, if you spot a whale anywhere around the San Juans, swimming

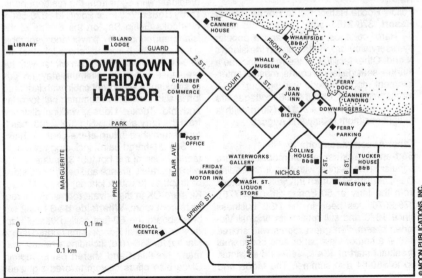

Sailboats provide photographic opportunities in the San Juans.

or stranded, be a sport and call the museum's 24-hour hotline: (800) 562-8832.

Winetasting
Sample San Juan Cellars' variety of wines created exclusively for **The Island Wine Company** at Cannery Landing (at the ferry dock) in Friday Harbor; open 10 a.m. to 6 p.m. daily, 378-3229.

Resort
Follow Roche Harbor Rd. to **Roche Harbor Resort,** 378-2155, with 100-year-old Hotel de Haro, cottages, condos, and a popular by-reservation-only restaurant on the island's N end. Other facilities at the resort include a marina, seaside tennis courts, musical entertainment, and a historic walking tour. Hotel rooms and suites cost $40-95, cottages are $75-95, and condos are $75-100 d, with a 4-night minimum in July and August.

Other Accommodations
Bed-and-breakfast accommodations are popular in the islands, with San Juan leading the pack. The **San Juan Inn,** just a half block from the ferry at 50 Spring St. (Box 776), 378-2070, has been in the B&B business since 1873 and still retains its original Victorian charm. Ten guest rooms with shared baths, a harbor view parlor, and continental breakfast start at $34 s, $45-49 d in winter, up to $60-64 d in summer. The **Moon and**

Sixpence, 3021 Beaverton Valley Rd., 378-4138, is a country inn with 3 guest rooms, a suite, and a rustic cabin from $65-95, with full Dutch breakfast, plus visiting eagles and swans outside for no extra charge. No pets; children by arrangement. Next to the American Camp at 4531-A Cattle Point Rd., **Olympic Lights,** 378-3186, has 5 rooms, 1 with private bath, for $55-80 including Olympic views, goose-down comforters, and full breakfast with eggs from the resident hens. **Duffy House,** 760 Pear Point Rd., 378-5604, overlooks Griffin Bay on the E side of the island surrounded by flower and vegetable gardens, with 5 rooms (shared baths) for $70-80 in summer, $60-70 in winter, with full breakfast. Two-night minimum stay; no kids or smoking. A waterfront cabin with laddered loft is also available in summer; call for rates and info. **Tucker House,** walking distance from the ferry at 260 B St., 378-2783, has 3 rooms furnished in turn-of-the-century charm for $65 d (shared bath), including full breakfast and use of the hot tub; 3 private rooms with separate entrance and bath, wood stove or fireplace (2 with kitchens) go for $80-90. Kids are OK in the private rooms. For a real waterfront room, **Wharfside B&B** has 2 cabins aboard the 60-foot sailing vessel *Jacquelyn,* docked at K dock at the Friday Harbor Marina, for $65-70 d, including a hearty seaman's breakfast and shared bath. Captain Clyde also offers custom-tailored sightseeing/whalewatch cruises and sportfishing charters ($60 pp for a half day of fishing) aboard his 27-foot cruiser. Call 378-3404 or 378-5661 for reservations and information.

For more conventional accommodations, **Friday Harbor Motor Inn,** 410 Spring St., 378-4351, has 72 rooms, some with kitchens, and a shared jacuzzi for $45-55 d in winter, $55-65 d in summer, within walking distance of the ferry dock. **Island Lodge,** 1016 Guard St., 378-2000, is a little less expensive at $36 d in winter, $52-60 d in summer, including a whirlpool, with moped and car rentals and free ferry or airport pickup.

Food
Cafe Bissett, 170 West St., 378-3109, serves elegant yet moderately priced dinners at this tiny sidestreet location. Open for dinner only, daily in summer, Thurs.-Mon. rest of year. For elegant dining, **Winston's,** 95 Nichols St. in Friday Harbor, has seafood, steak, and international cuisine plus a good wine and beer selection. Open for dinner only; 378-5093 for reservations. A tad more expensive, the **Duck Soup Inn,** 3090 Roche Harbor Rd., 378-4878, specializes in superbly done local seafood, chicken dishes, and regional wines. **Springtree Eating Establishment,** Spring St. in Friday Harbor, 378-4848, serves a varied menu including steak, seafood, chicken, pasta, salads, and more in a pretty Victorian setting; open for 3 meals daily. **Downrigger's,** 378-2700, at the Friday Harbor ferry landing, is open for lunch and dinner with seafood, steak, burgers, pasta including salmon ravioli, and a choice of 30 wines available by the glass. **The Cannery House,** overlooking the port at 174 First St., 378-2500, specializes in "homemade" Mexican meals, sandwiches, soups, and chowders. Open for lunch, dinner, and Sunday brunch in summer. For deep-dish pizza and Italian food in a family atmosphere, try **The Friday Harbor Bistro** in the Elite Hotel at 35 1st St.; phone 378-3076 for orders to go.

Entertainment
Friday Harbor and Roche Harbor gather 15 West Coast bands for their **Dixieland Jazz Festival,** held annually the 3rd weekend in July; 378-5509. A large, contemporary gallery in Friday Harbor, **Waterworks Gallery,** 315 Argyle at Spring St., 378-3060, has paintings, prints, watercolors, and sculpture by island and international artists.

ORCAS ISLAND

Orcas Island is reputedly the chain's most beautiful island, and definitely the hilliest: drive, hike, or bike to the top of 2,409-foot Mt. Constitution for a panoramic view from Vancouver, B.C., to Mt. Rainier. Orcas' most prominent mansion, Rosario Resort, regularly graces the pages of national travel magazines and employs almost 200 people, making it the county's largest private employer.

Park
Located near Eastsound, 5,000-acre **Moran State Park** is most popular for its paved road and hiking trails to the summit of 2,409-foot Mt. Constitution with views of the San Juans, Mt. Baker, and Vancouver Island. Other hiking trails include a 1½-mile straight downhill trek from the summit to Twin Lakes, and a 2 miler from Mountain Lake (park here) to Twin Lakes. Another option—with 3 waterfalls along the way—is the 2½-mile trail from Mountain Lake to Cascade Lake, following Cascade Creek. Or, hike the 4-mile loop trail around Mountain Lake for a chance to see some deer, particularly in the morning and early evening. The park's lakes also provide freshwater fishing and boating, with boat rentals and fishing supplies available at a concession stand. Campers can stay at one of 136 non-hookup sites, but all sites are preassigned, so check in at the pay station across from Cascade Lake when you first arrive, or call or write Moran State Park, Star Route Box 22, Eastsound, WA 98245, 376-2326, as much as a year in advance of your trip.

Museum
Located in Eastsound, the **Orcas Island Historical Museum,** 376-4840, has a collection of relics from 1880s pioneer homesteads. Open Tues. through Sat. afternoons in summer, donations gladly accepted.

Resort

The **Rosario Island Resort and Spa** is a nationally known getaway, and the largest resort in the state, housed in Seattle shipbuilder Robert Moran's turn-of-the-century mansion in Eastsound. Moran wasn't blessed with musical talent so he played the 1,972-pipe organ like a player piano and none of his guests were the wiser; organ concerts are still held Tues. through Sat. at 5 p.m. The building has been beautifully restored, offering fine dining, exercise equipment and classes, and salons featuring massage therapy, facials, body wraps, tanning beds, nail care, and more—all for a fee, of course. Room rates start at $85 s or d in summer with assorted winter packages, including a weekend "bargain" for $189 d for 2 nights' accommodations plus Fri. night seafood buffet and Sunday brunch. Phone 376-2222 or, toll-free statewide, (800) 562-8820 for reservations.

Other Accommodations

Situated on 80 acres in the shadow of Turtleback Mountain, **Turtleback Farm Inn** on Crow Valley Rd. in Eastsound, 376-4914, has 7 rooms, all with private bath, in a comfortable, farmhouse atmosphere. On warm days the full country breakfast is served outdoors on the valley-view deck. Rates are $65-130 d May to Oct., $60-100 d Nov. to May ($10 less for single). Kids by special arrangement, but no pets. The **Orcas Hotel**, on a knoll above the ferry dock in Orcas, 376-4300, is a 3-story Victorian resort built in the early 1900s overlooking Shaw Island and Harney Channel; extensively restored in 1985, it's on the National Register of Historic Places. Rooms, including continental breakfast, are $48-75 d, some with private baths, and kids are OK. The **Kangaroo House,** on approximately 2 acres N of Eastsound Village on N. Beach Rd. (Box 334), 376-2175, was built in 1907 and bought in the '30s by a sea captain, Harold Ferris, who picked up a young female kangaroo on one of his Australian voyages and tamed her with the music he frequently played onboard. Once home on Orcas, the captain found Josie could "dance," predict the weather, and keep the geraniums well-trimmed. The neighborhood kids gave Josie's house the name it still bears. Today the inn has 5 guest rooms from $60-70 d ($10 less off-season), plus a large sitting room with fireplace, period furnishings, and gourmet breakfasts. Sorry, no pets or indoor smoking. Over in Deer Harbor, **Palmer's Chart House,** Box 51, 376-4231, was the first B&B on Orcas Island when it opened for business in 1975, and still is one of the few with water views. Rooms here include a hearty breakfast, tea and coffee in your room, private entrance and bath, for $45 s, $60 d; dinner may be arranged for $7.50 pp. No pets, but they'll make arrangements with a local kennel. See "Longer Cruises," p. 141, for information on their overnight and afternoon sails.

For a resort atmosphere, try **Smuggler's Villa Resort** in Eastsound, 376-2297. Their 20 condominiums cost $88-94 (1-4 people) and include use of the hot tub, sauna, outdoor pool, tennis and pickleball courts, 400 feet of private beach, and moorage. The condos themselves have all the comforts of home: washer and dryer, microwave, fireplace, TV, and dishwasher, plus sunset views over Haro Strait. Weekly rates are available.

Around Eastsound from Orcas, past Moran State Park, is the little town of Olga and, farther S, **Obstruction Pass Resort,** 376-2472. Cabins on the protected bay start at $40 a night; for something a little different, their 104-foot tug has 5 private staterooms that sleep 2 comfortably from $50 d. Boat rentals are available.

Deer Harbor Resort, 376-4420, has motel units for $35, small cabins for $45, and larger guest houses for $50 and up available year-round on Deer Harbor, so named by the island's earliest settlers for its swift, black-tailed inhabitants. Deer still live on many of the islands and swim between them. The resort also has a heated indoor pool, restaurant, gift shop, and overnight moorage. In winter, your second night is free. Write Box 176, Deer Harbor, for more information. In the heart of Eastsound Village, **The Outlook Inn,** 376-2200, offers a bay view, comfortable country surroundings, restaurant, and bar, plus 30 rooms in a choice of styles: European-type (at the inn) with shared bath for $55 d, or American-style (in the annex) with

1. windsurfing in the Columbia Gorge (Wash. St. Tourism Div.); **2.** The Ellensburg Rodeo (Wash. St. Tourism Div.); **3.** exploring northeast Washington on horseback (Wash. St. Tourism Div.); **4.** Indian salmon bake at Tillicum Village on Blake Island (Mark Hewitt/Tillicum Village); **5.** Autumn Leaf Festival, Leavenworth (Wash. St. Tourism Div.); **6.** Fun Forest in Seattle Center (Seattle-King County Convention and Visitors Bureau)

1. Just driving through the park affords spectacular views (D. Lyons); **2.** Olympic National Park's forested shoreline (D. Lyons); **3.** Long Beach Peninsula (Wash. St. Tourism Div.); 4. Cape Disappointment Lighthouse at Fort Canby State Park, Ilwaco (D. Lyons); **5.** San Juan Islands (D. Lyons); **6.** sunset at Olympic National Park (D. Lyons)

1. Longacres Race Track, Renton (East King County Convention Bureau); **2.** golfing in eastern Washington (Wash. St. Tourism Div.); **3.** Fort Vancouver National Historic Site (Wash. St. Tourism Div.); **4.** hiking at Mount Rainier (Wash. St. Tourism Div.); **5.** Washington coast (Wash. St. Tourism Div.); **6.** cross-country skiing in the Methow Valley (Wash. St. Tourism Div.)

1. wildflowers at Mt. Baker (D. Lyons) **2.** rose gardens at Point Defiance Park, Tacoma (D. Lyons);
3. Mt. Vernon tulip fields (D. Lyons); **4.** Yakima Valley wine grapes (D. Lyons);
5. Tillinghast Seed Co., La Conner (D. Lyons)

private bath and TV for $68 d. Breakfast is not included but the Inn's restaurant opens at 8 a.m.

Food

The **Outlook Inn**, Main St. in Eastsound, 376-2200, serves 3 meals daily (moderately priced) in a relaxed and pretty Victorian setting with a bay view. Their world-class East Coast chef, Antony Vincenza Carbone, changes the dinner menu daily to insure the freshest seafood, and also shows considerable expertise in his beef, lamb, and poultry dishes, soups, and vegetarian fare. For Mexican food, **Bilbo's Festivo** on A St. in Eastsound is something of a local legend. They're open daily (except Mon.) for dinner, Thurs. through Sat. for lunch (summer only), plus Sunday brunch, with fresh-fruit margaritas and espressos; 376-4728. For inexpensive Italian meals and fresh seafood, try **La Famiglia Ristorante**, also on A St. in Eastsound. Open daily for dinner, lunch daily except Sun.; 376-2335 for reservations. Enjoy waterfront dining at **Christina's**, on Horseshoe Hwy. in Eastsound, 376-4904, with fresh seasonal cuisine including Crescent Bay oysters and a nice wine selection. Open for dinner daily in summer, Thurs. through Mon. in winter, plus Sunday brunch. Stop by **Cafe Oga** near Moran State Park for a beer and an inexpensive, homestyle lunch.

Theater

The newly completed **Orcas Theatre and Community Center** hosts a variety of events nearly year-round in Eastsound, from concerts to theatrical performances to lecture series; for ticket and schedule info, phone 376-4873.

Arts And Crafts

Orcas has a number of craft shops and galleries kept well supplied by the artists and craftspeople who live there. Olga's artist co-op is **The Artworks**, 376-4408, with an assortment of locally made arts and crafts; next door is **Cafe Olga**, a country cafe with homemade pies, beer, wine, and espresso. **Otters Lair Pottery** in Eastsound Square, 376-4708, specializes in functional stoneware

and porcelain pottery. See how candles are made from May to Oct. at **Orcas Island Candles**, Eastsound, 376-2645. **Darvill's Rare Print Shop** in Eastsound has, naturally, rare prints from the 18th and 19th centuries plus limited-edition prints by contemporary Northwest artists; 376-2351. **The Right Place** on West Beach, 376-4023, has an assortment of crafts from pottery to hand-knit and woven items to blown glass.

LOPEZ ISLAND

Because of its gently rolling hills, Lopez is the most popular with cyclists; views of the surrounding islands and mountains to the E and W poke out from every turn. Despite being one of the largest San Juan Islands, Lopez is probably the friendliest—waving to passing cars and bicycles is a time-honored local custom, and failure to wave will mark you as a tourist as surely as a camera around your neck and rubber thongs.

Parks

On the E side of the island, **Spencer Spit State Park** has a mile-long beach for good year-round clamming and beachcombing, 28 campsites, and a trailer dump station; camping is also available at **Odlin County Park** at the N end of the island.

Accommodations

For inexpensive camping far from civilization, bike out to **Hummel Haven Bicycle Camp**, 4½ miles from the ferry landing, off Center Rd. at Hummel Lake, 468-2217. No motor vehicles are allowed within the 40-acre campground (though parking spaces are available for those who arrive by car), and each secluded campsite is equipped with a firepit, picnic table, and bike rack for just $2.50 pp. If you need to, you can rent a bike for $10 a day; boat rentals are also available for trout fishing in the lake for $3.50 per hour.

For secluded log cabin living, try **Marean's Blue Fjord Cabins** at Elliott Rd. on Jasper Bay (Route 1 Box 1450). Nestled among 16 acres of forest, each cabin has a fully equipped kitchen and deck, and is situated to assure complete privacy just a short walk from the rocky beach. The smaller cabins, built for 2, are $55; a larger cabin with fireplace, water view, dishwasher, and space for 6 is $95 d ($10 per additional person). Call 468-2749 for reservations—they're required—and detailed directions (you'll need them to find the unmarked dirt road).

MacKaye Harbor Inn, a B&B on MacKaye Harbor Rd., 468-2253, has 5 antique-furnished rooms on the water for $60-85 d, including full gourmet breakfast.

Food And More

There's more than one way to make a living, and the owners of Jeanna's Seafood Gallery in Lopez Plaza, 468-2114, are trying 3 at once, with a seafood restaurant, art gallery, and fish market all rolled into one. Open daily 10 a.m.-9 p.m. The Bay Cafe, across Main St. from the post office in Lopez Village, 468-2204, opens Wed. through Sun. for Mexican, Indonesian, Thai, American—you name it—lunch and dinner. Also in Lopez Village, Gail's, 468-2150, serves soups, deli sandwiches, burgers, quiche, plus wine and beer; open for 3 meals daily (dinner on weekends only in winter).

SHAW ISLAND

The least visited of the ferry-served islands, Shaw is primarily residential and known mostly for the Franciscan nuns who operate the ferry dock and general store, "Little Portion." Shaw Island County Park, 2 miles S of the ferry landing, has 8 campsites, a picnic area, and a rope swing, but no drinking water.

OTHER ISLANDS

A number of the smaller islands in the archipelago are preserved as state parks, accessible only by private boat and largely undeveloped, with primitive campsites and no drinking water. Sea kayaks are a popular island-hopping mode of transportation, but since some of the smaller islands are several miles out, be careful not to overestimate your ability.

Blind Island State Park, on a small, unforested island about .2 mile from the N shore of Shaw Island in Blind Bay, has a rocky shoreline and 4 primitive campsites.

Doe Island State Park, about .1 mile SE of Orcas Island, has 5 primitive campsites on a small, secluded island with a rocky shoreline.

About .4 mile E of Decatur Island, James Island State Park has 13 primitive campsites on a small, forested island with sunny beaches on the Rosario Strait.

Two miles NE of Orcas Island is Clark Island State Park, with 8 primitive campsites—no garbage cans, so take it out with you—and beautiful beaches for walking, sunbathing, fishing, or treasure-hunting offshore. Matia Island State Park, 3 miles NE of Orcas Island, has 6 primitive campsites near the dock and is home to a large population of puffins. It also once was home to a hermit who got a regular workout rowing the 3 miles to Orcas and walking another 2 miles to Eastsound to buy his groceries. Sucia Island State Park, 2½ miles N of Orcas Island, is among the more beautiful of the "lesser" islands with crabbing, clamming, and scuba diving plus 51 primitive campsites. Popular for its hiking and good salmon and bottom fishing, Patos Island State Park has 4 primitive campsites about 5 miles N of Orcas Island and 2 miles NW of Sucia.

Close to San Juan Island are Posey Island State Park, about .6 mile W of San Juan's NW shore, recommended for kayaks and canoes with just 1 primitive campsite; Stuart Island State Park, 5 miles NW of Roche Harbor with good harbors for larger boats and 19 primitive campsites; and Turn Island State Park, .3 mile from San Juan's E shore, with 10 campsites, 2 beaches, and wooded hiking trails.

MOUNT VERNON

Disappointed gold miners settled for farming in an uneasy compromise, yet found a different kind of wealth in Mount Vernon's soil: 40 percent of the nation's peas are grown here, as are significant numbers of daffodils, tulips, irises, fruits, and vegetable seeds. Mount Vernon, 60 miles N of Seattle alongside I-5, was named after George Washington's plantation, both to honor him and because the town was founded on his birthday in 1877. The town grew quickly after an enormous natural logjam in the Skagit was cleared in 1879, allowing upriver travel; in 1884, Mount Vernon was chosen county seat, and by 1900, its population of 1,120 exceeded that of neighboring La Conner. Today, with a population of more than 15,000, the city is still the largest in the county, and in spring is certainly among the prettiest: tulips and daffodils are *everywhere,* from fields to yards to gas stations.

SIGHTS

Fields And Gardens
After March 1, get a map of tulip, iris, and daffodil fields (donation requested) from the chamber of commerce at the Mount Vernon Mall, corner of Riverside and College Way. The colorful spring layout is in bloom from mid-March to early May. Bring film! If you can't get a map, head W from Mount Vernon toward La Conner; most of the fields are in an area bounded on the N by Memorial Hwy. 536, on the W by La Conner-Whitney Rd., on the S by Chilberg Rd., and on the E by the Skagit River, intersected by McLean, Bennett, Calhoun, and Best roads. This is a great place to bicycle; nice, flat roads, very little traffic—except when the flowers are in bloom. A handful of farms invite the public to stroll through their display gardens; these include **Roozengaarde**, 1587 Beaver March Rd., 424-8531, open year-round, daily in April and May, with a show garden in bloom from Feb. to Oct., retail bulb sales, fresh cut flowers, and gift shop, and **West Shore Acres**, 956 Downey Rd., 466-3158, with a 1½-acre

show garden from mid-March to Mother's Day; they'll ship flowers or bulbs anywhere. Don't worry if you forget your map; the traffic jams will direct you to tourable fields.

If you miss the tulips and daffodils, all is not lost—**La Conner Flats,** 1598 Best Rd., 466-3821, has an assortment of flowers in bloom from March through September. This English country garden features daffodils, rhodies, tulips, azaleas, and dogwood in spring; roses, late rhodies, dahlias, glads, and herbs in summer; and mums, summer heather, and fall foliage in early autumn. The Granary in the Garden serves lunches and high tea (reservations recommended); adjoining Hart's Nursery sells everything that grows at La Conner Flats. Admission to the garden is $2.50 adults, kids free; open daily March through Oct., 10 a.m. to 6 p.m.

daffodil fields in bloom

Parks

At 13th St. and Blackburn Rd., **Hillcrest Park** has a zoo, oriental garden, tennis and basketball courts, picnicking, and a playground on 30 acres. Southeast of the city on Blackburn Rd. W, 927-foot **Little Mountain** affords views of the Olympics, San Juan Islands, and Skagit Valley farmland with 490 forested acres surrounding the summit observation area; to get there, follow Blackburn Rd. to Little Mountain Road.

Tours

Ask the chamber of commerce for their brochure, "Walking Tour of Historic Mount Vernon." It's a handy, if not thorough, guide to historic buildings, primarily along 1st and Main streets.

Get a free tour and sample the products of the **Washington Cheese Company,** 900 E. College Way, 424-3510, Mon. through Sat. 9 a.m.-5:30 p.m. Their cheese shop includes gift boxes, ice cream, and other dairy products.

ACCOMMODATIONS

Bed And Breakfast

Snuggled in the middle of 90 private acres of woods bordered by Weyerhauser timber, **Whispering Firs B&B,** 428-1990, offers shaded seclusion 3 miles S of Mount Vernon, 1 mile E of I-5 at 1957 Kanako Lane. Guest chambers have a private entrance and cedar deck, 2 queen-size beds (one's a waterbed), and private baths for $65-75 d. Prices include a big, country-style breakfast and use of the 8x8 hot tub. For more B&Bs, see "La Conner," p. 154.

Hotels And Motels

The Clear Lake exit off I-5 leads you to a number of lodging choices. For budget travelers, the **West Winds Motel,** 2020 Riverside Dr., 424-4224, has 40 rooms for $22 s, $28 d. A little more elegant is **Nendel's Inn,** 2009 Riverside Dr., 424-4141, with 88 rooms for $38-42 s, $43-50 d, plus a pool, jacuzzi, sauna, restaurant, and bar. The **TraveLodge,** 1910 Freeway Dr., 428-7020, has 70 rooms

for $38-42 s, $42-50 d, plus an indoor pool, jacuzzi, and exercise equipment. **Best Western Motor Inn,** 300 W. College Way, 424-4287, has 66 rooms, with a pool, for $35-50 s, $40-55 d; pets OK.

RV Parks

Riverbend Park, 305 W. Stewart Rd., 424-4480, has 120 RV and grassy tent sites for $14, plus laundry and hot showers, off I-5 exit 227; open all year. **Lake McMurray Resort,** 2294 McMurray Lane off Hwy. 9, has 45 grassy sites, 35 with water and electric hookups, for $10, with fishing, boat rentals, and swimming. Open April to Sept.; 445-4555.

Big Lake Resort, 1785 W. Big Lake Blvd., 422-555, has 8 RV hookups ($8), 4½ acres of tent sites ($8), and cabins ($150/week) on Big Lake at the foot of Little Mountain (what imaginative place names!). Big Lake is reputed to have the largest freshwater bass in western Washington, so rent a rowboat here and get free advice from the proprietor. For more camping see "Burlington," p. 156, or "North Cascades National Park," p. 275.

FOOD AND DRINK

The Longfellow Cafe, in the historic Granary Building at 120 First St., serves excellent seafood, sandwiches, and steaks at moderate prices, accompanied by an impressive selection of wines and beers, in an informal setting. Enjoy moderately priced fresh seafood, delicious baked goods, and more at **Wildflowers,** a Victorian house at 2001 E. College Way; open for lunch and dinner Wed. through Monday.

Mount Vernon's hotspot for lunch, **Cafe Europa** at 516 S. First St., serves great sandwiches on fresh-baked bread plus soup, salad, and pasta; open for lunch and dinner, Mon. through Friday. For inexpensive but terrific Mexican food try **La Tienda,** a combination grocery store/restaurant across the bridge at 602 Division Street.

Fast-food aficionados should follow 2nd St. onto Riverside Dr., where McDonald's and its clones await. **Cascade Pizza Inn,** 1825 Riverside or 2083 Hwy. 20 in Sedro Woolley, has

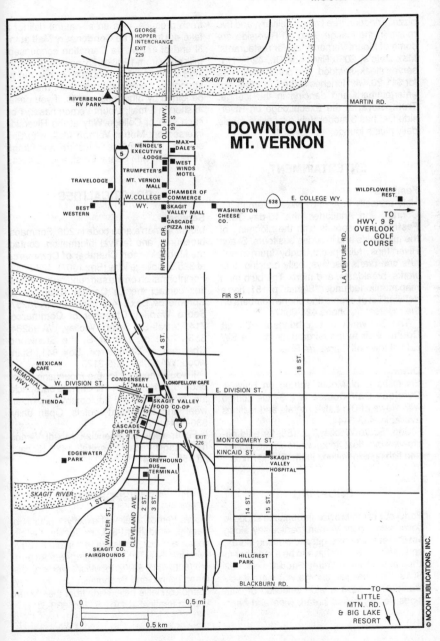

DOWNTOWN MT. VERNON

GEORGE HOPPER INTERCHANGE EXIT 229

SKAGIT RIVER

RIVERBEND RV PARK

MARTIN RD.

OLD HWY. 99 S

NENDEL'S EXECUTIVE LODGE

MAX DALE'S

WEST WINDS MOTEL

TRUMPETER'S

MT. VERNON MALL

TRAVELODGE

CHAMBER OF COMMERCE

W. COLLEGE WY.

E. COLLEGE WY.

538

WILDFLOWERS REST.

BEST WESTERN

SKAGIT VALLEY MALL

WASHINGTON CHEESE CO.

CASCADE PIZZA INN

RIVERSIDE DR.

TO HWY. 9 & OVERLOOK GOLF COURSE

LA VENTURE RD.

FIR ST.

4 ST.

18 ST.

MEXICAN CAFE

MEMORIAL HWY.

W. DIVISION ST.

CONDENSERY MALL

LONGFELLOW CAFE

E. DIVISION ST.

LA TIENDA

MAIN ST.

1 ST.

SKAGIT VALLEY FOOD CO-OP

5

CASCADE SPORTS

EDGEWATER PARK

EXIT 226

MONTGOMERY ST.

GREYHOUND BUS TERMINAL

KINCAID ST.

SKAGIT VALLEY HOSPITAL

SKAGIT RIVER

1 ST.

WALTER ST.

CLEVELAND AVE.

2 ST.

3 ST.

14 ST.

15 ST.

SKAGIT CO. FAIRGROUNDS

HILLCREST PARK

BLACKBURN RD.

TO LITTLE MTN. RD. & BIG LAKE RESORT

0   0.5 mi

0   0.5 km

© MOON PUBLICATIONS, INC.

pizza, grinders, free limited delivery, and live music in the lounge. Also on Riverside are some of Mount Vernon's fancier restaurants: **Max Dale's,** 2030 Riverside Dr., 424-7171, serves steak, seafood, and prime rib dinners for $11-20, with lunches in the $7 range, and entertainment and dancing in the lounge. **Trumpeters,** at the ExecuLodge on Riverside Dr., has 3 moderately expensive meals daily plus a lounge; 424-SWAN.

ENTERTAINMENT

Festivals
Held annually in April by Mount Vernon, La Conner, and Anacortes, the 10-day **Tulip Festival** corresponds with the blooming of the tulip fields and includes bus tours, Skagit River trips, tulip pedal, rugby tournament, arts and crafts displays, belly dancing, fireworks, breakfasts, and more. The bulb farm map mentioned under "Sights," p. 151, has a detailed list of events and phone numbers on the reverse; or, phone 428-8547.

The 2nd week in Aug. brings the **Skagit County Fair** to the fairgrounds on the SW side of town off Blackburn Road.

Other
Six miles E of Mount Vernon on Hwy. 9, **Overlook Golf Course** is a 9-hole course with views of Big Lake; rentals and lessons available, 422-6444.

See "Sedro Woolley," p. 158, for bald eagle-viewing float trips, white-water rafting, and fishing expeditions in the Skagit River.

SHOPPING

Park your car to browse through the shops in downtown Mount Vernon, particularly along 1st Street's bakeries, gift and clothing stores, and cafes. You don't have to be a member to shop at the **Skagit Valley Food Co-op,** 202 S. 1st. St.; they just charge you more if you aren't! They have a wide selection of bulk foods, locally baked bread, wine and beer,

fresh produce, plus an all-natural deli for a take-out lunch. The **Condensery Mall** at the N end of 1st was a Carnation condensed-milk plant from 1906-1975; now it's undergoing renovation and is largely empty, but its struggling bakery and restaurant may soon be joined by other businesses. If you prefer to shop in a mall, Mount Vernon has 2, 1 on each side of College Way at the Riverside intersection: **Mount Vernon Mall,** with Emporium and a Payless Drugstore, and **Skagit Valley Mall** with Sears, Ernst, and Payless.

PRACTICALITIES

Services
Mount Vernon's area code is 206. For maps, brochures, and festival information, contact the **Mount Vernon Chamber of Commerce** at 325 E. College Way (Box 1007), 428-8547. For information on the surrounding communities contact the **La Conner Chamber of Commerce,** Box 644, La Conner, WA 98257; **Sedro Woolley Chamber of Commerce,** 714 Metcalf St., Sedro Woolley, WA 98284, 855-0770, or, farther S, the **Stanwood Chamber of Commerce,** Box 641, Stanwood, WA 98292, 629-2123.

If you're headed for the mountains, **Cascade Sports,** 509 S. 1st St., has backpacking, bicycle, and ski equipment plus outerwear and equipment rentals. Open daily; 336-6641.

For medical emergencies, Mount Vernon has **Skagit Valley Hospital,** 1415 Kincaid, off 15th; 424-4111.

TRANSPORTATION

Mount Vernon is almost exactly 1 hour N of Seattle, straddling I-5; from Seattle, the city center and bulb fields are to the left. If you're flying into Sea-Tac, take **Bellingham Airporter,** (800) 235-5247, to Mount Vernon, Camano Island, and Snohomish County. Greyhound connects nationwide from their Mount Vernon terminal at 1101 S. 2nd; 336-5111.

VICINITY OF MOUNT VERNON

LA CONNER

La Conner is the most tourist-oriented town in Skagit County—too much so to suit the locals, but there's no denying it's a fun place to visit. Park the car and browse the old buildings, shops, restaurants, and bakeries all jammed into a tiny, very walkable downtown area—but do try to come on a weekday. During the Tulip Festival, La Conner looks like a beachfront tourist trap in July, with standing traffic, cyclists, mobs of pedestrians, full parking lots, and sidewalk hot-dog stands. This old fishing port, settled in the late 1800s with a current population of about 600, has a number of museums and 19th-century homes for history buffs to explore. Bright-orange Rainbow Bridge, crossing the Swinomish Channel, is a good spot for photographers to get a shot of the La Conner waterfront with a Mt. Baker backdrop.

Museums And Mansions

The **Gaches Mansion** at 2nd and Calhoun, is a restored Victorian mansion built in 1891 and partially furnished with period furniture; the 2nd floor houses paintings and sculpture at **The Valley Museum of Northwest Art.**

The mansion is open for guided tours weekend afternoons. Admission is $1; phone 466-4288 for information. The log cabin at 2nd and Morris was built in 1869 by Magnus Anderson, one of the area's first settlers, but is not open for tours. At 501 4th St., the **Skagit County Historical Museum,** 466-3365, has Northwest pioneer artifacts including farm and logging equipment, children's toys, clothing, and a farmhouse kitchen. Open Wed. through Sun. afternoons; admission $1 adults, $.50 kids.

Accommodations

At 2nd and Morris, **La Conner Country Inn,** 466-3101, boasts a fireplace in every room, a restaurant, **Barkley's** (see below), and a pub; rooms are $62-80 s, $67-85 d, including continental breakfast. The newly renovated **Hotel Planter,** a National Historic inn at 715 1st St., 466-4710, features 12 tastefully decorated guest rooms, all with private bath, plus a gazebo, hot tub, and garden courtyard. Rooms run $75-85 d for double and queen, $105 d for the deluxe jacuzzi room ($10 less in winter). No pets or smoking.

The Heron, a Victorian country inn off Hwy. 20 at 117 Maple St., 466-4626, has a whirlpool and 12 rooms from $45-74 s or d. **Ridge-**

Gaches Mansion

way House, a 1928 yellow brick B&B in the heart of the farmland, features 5 guest rooms, each with a sink (2 with private bath), plus complimentary appetizers and full breakfast for $45-75 d. No indoor smoking. **Rainbow Inn,** a B&B at 1075 Chilberg Rd., 466-4578, is a restored turn-of-the-century farmhouse surrounded by tulip fields, a Mt. Baker view, and a hot tub on the back deck. Antique-furnished rooms are $55 d with shared bath, $65 d with private bath. No smoking; pets are accommodated as space permits. Near the tulip fields at 1880 Chilberg Rd., **Downey House,** 466-3207, has 5 rooms; rates range from $60 s, $65 d, for the 2 rooms with shared bath to $75-80 s, $80-85 d for the 3 larger rooms with private bath. Amenities include a hot tub, full breakfast, evening blackberry pie, and a view of Mt. Baker. No pets or smoking. **Heather House B&B,** 505 Maple Ave., 466-4675, is a new (1979) house built to resemble a 1900s Cape Cod beach house, with bare oak floors and wainscoting; the 3 bedrooms, $45-65, share 2 baths. Terry robes, blow driers, flowers, candy, and a "help yourself" refrigerator add to the home's charm; continental breakfast is served at your convenience. **The White Swan Guest House,** 6 miles from La Conner at 1388 Moore Rd. on Fir Island (technically Mount Vernon), 445-6805, is a Victorian farmhouse with guest cottage. Three guest rooms share 2 baths ($65 d); the cottage has a private bath and can sleep 4 ($85). Enjoy the wood stove in the parlor and fresh-baked chocolate chip cookies. Breakfast is continental; no pets, smoking, or small children.

Campers and RVers are welcome at the **Potlatch RV Resort,** 415 Pearle Jensen Way, 466-4468, where you can relax in 1 of 2 hot tubs or the indoor pool while you're "roughing it" for $14 a night. **Pioneer Park,** adjacent to Rainbow Bridge, has camping and picnic tables.

Food And Drink

Barkleys's, 2nd and Washington at the La Conner Inn, is a local legend serving locally produced food: sockeye salmon, Dungeness crab, geoduck, red snapper, fresh vegetables, pasta, and steaks. Open for lunch Mon.

through Sat., dinner nightly, with a Sunday Champagne brunch; phone 466-4261 for reservations (highly recommended). Near La Conner, on Hwy. 20 between Anacortes and Mount Vernon, **The Farmhouse Restaurant,** 466-4411, is a busy family spot. Meals here, all under $11, include steak, fried seafood, chicken and turkey dinners, burgers, and all-day breakfast, with a buffet lunch in the lounge for $4.75. **La Conner Tavern,** on the Channel at 1st St., has world-famous burgers, plus dancing to live music. On the Swinomish Channel waterfront, **The Lighthouse Inn,** 466-3147, has outdoor-barbecued salmon, prime rib, fresh seafood, and picnic lunches to go. **The Black Swan,** 1st and Washington, 466-3040, is open for dinner only with moderately priced seafood, pasta, and more, made with the freshest Skagit Valley ingredients. **La Conner Seafood and Prime Rib House** has fine dining and a waterfront deck at 614 S. 1st St., 466-4014.

Festivals

The annual **Rotary Pig Roast** is held the 3rd Sat. in Aug. at Pioneer Park. September brings the **Fall Festival,** highlighted by a salmon barbecue, and Dec. brings the **Christmas Ships Parade** up the Swinomish Channel.

Bingo

Just W of the Swinomish Channel bridge on Hwy. 20, **Swinomish Indian Bingo** has bingo at 7 p.m. nightly, plus a matinee session Thurs. through Sun. (times vary—phone 293-4687).

Boat Rentals

The Swinomish Channel is a peaceful body of water for paddling or rowing; rent a boat from **La Conner Boat Rentals,** N. 3rd St., 466-3300. At the N end of 1st St., **Rainbow Enterprises,** 466-4054, rents everything from boats to bikes to cars.

Shopping And Galleries

The most fun way to shop in La Conner is just to meander through the downtown shops, stopping for lunch or a beer and heading out again. To get you started, **Pier 7,** on 1st St.,

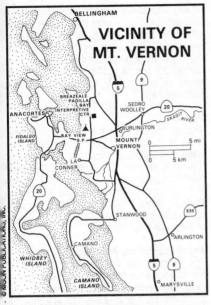

VICINITY OF
MT. VERNON

is a waterfront mall with gift shops, gallery, and other stores. **Town Square,** corner of 1st and Morris, combines modern shops and businesses with historic buildings, including the 1912 water tower and Magnus Anderson's 1869 log cabin. **Limedock Waterfront Mall** at the N end of 1st St. has still more shops including a gallery and seafood market. At 71750 1st St., **The Cheese and Wine Shoppe** is the place to go for Northwest wines, Walla Walla pickled vegetables, local cheeses, and smoked salmon.

Established in 1885, the **Tillinghast Seed House** is the oldest operating retail seed store in the Northwest; even brown thumbs will enjoy their gallery and gift shop on Chilberg Rd., at the S entrance to town.

Transportation

By car, La Conner is about an hour N of Seattle via I-5, and 10 minutes W across the tulip fields from Mount Vernon. You can take Hwy. 20 to La Conner-Whitney Rd. and head S; or, in spring, work your way through the tulip fields SW from Mount Vernon via

McLean, Best, and Chilberg roads.

La Conner Seaplanes, (800) 826-5580 or 671-1219, offers sightseeing flights over the San Juans, Mt. Baker, the Skagit Valley (another perspective on the tulip fields), the Olympic Peninsula, and the Cascades. Rates start at $20 for a 20-minute trip.

Built in Sweden in 1897, the 76-foot sailing vessel *Sylvia* still departs from La Conner, Seattle, Bellingham, and other docks for a number of scheduled and chartered cruises throughout Puget Sound. The several-day cruises can go up to $535 pp, but a number of inexpensive short trips are also available: 2-hour cruises during April's Tulip Festival are $20 pp; a half-day Elliott Bay cruise to watch Ivar's July 4th fireworks is $50 pp; a 2-day "Doe Bay Bash" celebrates the summer solstice for $168 pp. Write Box 524, La Conner, WA 98257, or phone 466-4929 for schedule.

BURLINGTON

Downtown Burlington is just a few minutes N of Mount Vernon, so close and indistinguishable it's difficult to tell where its borders are. But it does serve as "closest civilized point" to some interesting parks and natural features.

Parks

Eight miles W of Burlington on Padilla Bay, **Bay View State Park** is small—24 acres—but has 100 campsites (9 with hookups) for $7 across Bay View-Edison Rd. from the waterfront; the waterfront picnic area is well kept, with broad views of the bay, Anacortes' smokestacks, and Hat and Saddlebag islands. The **Breazeale-Padilla Bay Interpretive Center,** just N of the state park on Bay View-Edison Rd., has natural history and marine displays (including stuffed birds and fish), hands-on exhibits and books for kids, plus Sunday films, winter kayak trips, and workshops. Borrow a guide from the center for a .8-mile nature hike through the upland cedar forest and fields, where you might see bald eagles, herons, or Pacific black brants. The interpretive center is open Wed. through Sun. 10 a.m.- 5 p.m., 428-1558; free.

Accommodations

The **Cocusa Motel,** 200 W. Rio Vista, 757-6044, has 62 rooms for $32 s, $36-39 d (about $10 more in summer), with a heated pool and some refrigerators and balconies. The **Sterling Motor Inn,** 866 S. Garl, 757-0071, has 34 budget motel rooms for $29 s, $34-40 d, with a great little attached restaurant and bar (see "Food," below).

For campers who don't like to rough it, the **Burlington/Cascade KOA,** 646 N. Green Rd., 724-5511, is open all year with full hookup sites, grassy tent sites, an indoor heated pool, sauna, weight room, and many of the conveniences of 1st- class hotels for $12-16.

Food

The **Seven Countries Inn** at the Sterling Motor Inn, 866 S. Garl, is the kind of place most people glance at and drive past—but don't! The ramshackle exterior, complete with "today's special" readerboard, hides a wonderfully long menu: 42 omelettes, 20 burgers, 21 sandwiches, plus dinners, salads, and extensive beer/wine/drink list. Old-time logging and railroad photos line the walls, and they've got a bigger collection of travel brochures than the chamber of commerce; prices are moderate. For traditional Mexican food plus "fiesta hour" in the lounge, try **El Cazador,** 429 S. Garl, 755-9833. **Galley 5,** at I-5 and Hwy. 20, 757-4664, has a coffee shop, dining room, and Sunday brunch, next to the Cocusa Motel.

SEDRO WOOLLEY

Settlement of the area at the mouth of the Skagit River began as early as 1863, but a huge natural logjam prevented any upriver development until it was cleared in 1879. Mortimer Cook was one of the first pioneers to settle on the upper Skagit when he opened a general store in the town he named "Bug," supplying loggers and miners in the 1880s. Cook later succumbed to local pressure and changed the name to Sedro, his idea of Spanish for the "cedar" that covered the area. About the same time, P. A. Woolley built a sawmill a few miles away which became the economic basis of a small but thriving community. The towns were so close together it was difficult to determine their borders, so in 1898 the towns agreed to join forces yet retain both names. Today's Sedro Woolley is the commercial center for the farmlands that surround it and an outfitting town for adventurers on their way E into North Cascades National Park.

Parks

Though dwarfed by the nearby mountain lakes in the national park, **Clear Lake** has swimming beaches, boating, and fishing just 3 miles S of town. City parks include **Bingham Park,** a small city park with picnic tables at Hwy. 20 and Cook Rd., and **Riverfront Park,** McDonald Ave., somewhat larger with picnic tables and a playground on the banks of the fenced-out Skagit.

Accommodations And Food

The **Skagit Motel,** 1977 Hwy. 20, 856-6001, has 47 rooms for $25-27 d. Next door to the motel, **Angela's** serves sandwiches, fish, and steak dinners, all under $13, in a cheerful interior. Housed in the old Bingham Bank building at 210 Ferry St., the **Gateway Restaurant,** 855-0060, serves diners in a number of dark rooms, including 2 lounges, several dining rooms, a coffee shop, and bakery.

Festival

The 4th of July brings the week-long **Loggerodeo** to Sedro Woolley, an annual event since 1948 with logging contests, parades, and rodeos.

Outdoor Recreation

On Hwy. 20, just E of the Sedro Woolley town line, you'll find the **Mt. Baker Ranger Station/North Cascades National Park Service Complex,** with a N Cascades relief map, books and brochures for sale, and information on road closures and conditions (see "North Cascades National Park," p. 279).

For a day-long ride on horseback to Ross Lake, overnight camp trip in the North Cascades, or fishing trips on Josephine Lake or the Chiliwak River, contact **KM Ranch,** 946 Cockreham Rd., 826-3349. Daytime horseback rides cost $35-65; overnight camps are

$125, including a steak dinner and cowboy breakfast. Backpackers can have fresh food, beverages, and gear dropped off at North Cascades camps and packed back out for $50 per horse load—a nice alternative to lugging pots and pans or opting for gorp and instant cocoa.

The Skagit River is one of the best places in the country to view a large winter bald eagle population, with over 300 birds stopping by for a salmon feast on their journey S from Alaska and Canada. Eagles are particularly plentiful between Rockport and Marblemount (E of Sedro Woolley on Hwy. 20), but you'll also see them soaring overhead anywhere in the Skagit Valley. **Pacific Northwest Float Trips** offers bald eagle-watching trips as well as gold panning, sightseeing, and white-water trips on a number of area rivers, ranging from 5 hours to overnight. Prices start at $35. For more information write them at Box 736, Sedro Woolley, WA 98284, or phone 855-0535. Operating out of Kirkland, **Rivers Incorporated,** Box 2092, 822-5296, offers eagle-watching Skagit float trips and white-water rafting on the upper Skagit, Methow, Klickitat, and other rivers. Eagle trips are $35; white-water trips are $38-68 (depending on river and number of participants). Rivers Inc. also has 2-day Klickitat white-water trips, meals included, for $120-130. **Downstream River Runners,** operating out of Bothell (just N of Seattle), also offers eagle-watching float trips from Dec. through Feb. for $40, plus a full schedule of other white-water and float trips on Western and Eastern Washington rivers; they're one of the largest and most organized rafting companies around. Phone 483-0335 or, toll-free statewide, (800) 732-RAFT, or write 12112 N.E. 195th, Bothell, WA 98011 for more information.

If the idea of white-water rafting makes you shaky, take a 1-hour pontoon-boat trip up Swinomish Channel to Goat Island with **Ska-git Queen River and Channel Tours,** 855-0535, for just $10; or, take a longer trip to Hat Island for crab catching and lunch on Saddle Bag Island for $25.

Gallery
On Hwy. 9 about a mile N of Sedro Woolley at 2128 Bassett Rd., the **Lee Mann Gallery,** 856-0581, has a collection of photographs of the Pacific Northwest; open Mon. through Saturday.

STANWOOD

A small village just E of the bridge to Camano Island, Stanwood prides itself on having as its chief employer the largest independent frozen-pea processor in the world: Twin City Foods. The town also hosted the world's shortest railroad—7/8 of a mile—until it shut down in 1938.

CAMANO ISLAND

Primarily a residential island separated from the mainland by the shortest of bridges, Camano Island was originally inhabited by the Kikialos and Snohomish Indians and later, in the mid-1850s, by European loggers and settlers. Like Whidbey Island to the W, Camano receives less than 20 inches of rain annually because of the Olympic rainshadow effect. Besides vacation homes, the island boasts **Camano Island State Park,** with 134 acres and 6,700 feet of waterfront on Saratoga Passage. The picnic tables of the park's W side provide striking views of Whidbey Island and the Olympics; hiking trails, including a ½-mile interpretive loop, wind through 600-year-old Douglas firs with possible sightings of bald eagles, deer, raccoon, and opossum. Other activities here include scuba diving and fishing from the Point Lowell boat launch. The park's 2 camping areas have a total of 87 non-hookup sites, $6 per night.

BELLINGHAM

HISTORY

Bellingham Bay was named by Capt. George Vancouver for Sir William Bellingham, who provided Vancouver with supplies for his 1792 Puget Sound explorations. Capt. Henry Roeder and Russell V. Peabody established the first permanent settlement here in 1852; they came N from San Francisco in search of a sawmill site to supply their hometown's growing demand for lumber. When Roeder and Peabody met Lummi Indian Chief Cha-wit-zit in Olympia, they asked him if he knew of any place with "falling water all the time from a high hill." Cha-wit-zit apparently understood the Americans' broken English and, speaking in kind, suggested "at Whatcom, noise all the time." With the aid of the local Lummis, Roeder and Peabody built a mill at the foot of Whatcom Falls in 1853, producing lumber until it burned down in 1873.

William H. Prattle, another of Bellingham's earliest settlers, responded to Indian tales of local coal outcroppings by opening a margi-nally successful coal mine in the settlement called Unionville in 1853. The same year, San Francisco investors opened the Sehome mine, adjacent to the Whatcom settlement, and it became 1of the 2 largest employers in the area until the mine was flooded in 1878. Coal mining ceased until the Bellingham Bay Co. opened the largest mine in the state in the city's N end in 1918; it operated until 1951, when decreased demand led to its closure.

The 1850s also brought to Bellingham the aborted Fraser River Gold Stampede. About 10,000 people, most of whom traveled N from California, came to Whatcom to await the opening of a trail to British Columbia's new-found gold. The trail was never completed, and an order from Vancouver Island's governor James Douglas that all gold diggers obtain permits in Victoria before entering the province further squelched the would-be gold rush. One remnant from the gold boom is a brick building on E St.; the first brick building in the territory, it first served mercantile purposes and later as the Whatcom County Courthouse for 25 years.

The nearly simultaneous closures of the Whatcom sawmill and Sehome mine in the 1870s left the town floundering until the 1890s, when commercial attention again shifted to the timber and fishing industries. By the time the Whatcom and Fairhaven settlements combined to form Bellingham in the early 1900s, 8 saw- and shingle-mills and 4 salmon packing plants were providing the foundation of the city's economy. Today these industries combine with a heavy agricultural base, with dairy products, poultry, strawberries, and raspberries providing much of the county's income and supporting a population of nearly 46,000. In 1989, the Alaska Marine Highway Ferry System began docking its ships in Bellingham instead of Seattle, which should add considerably to Bellingham's tourist appeal and encourage economic growth.

Downtown Bellingham isn't among the most aesthetically pleasing of Puget Sound's cities; it's an old, squatty, congested city, much like Olympia would look without a Capitol Campus. Bellingham's treasures aren't immediately obvious, nor do they generally lie downtown; they're scattered along the Sound, or on the lakes, or in the parks, and are worth seeking out.

SIGHTS

Fairhaven

Ninth St.—formerly Railroad Ave.—was originally the point at which the Fairhaven and Southern Railroad grade entered the town from Skagit Valley. The men working on the railroad would follow the tracks back to 9th St. for an evening's entertainment, in rowdy bars and hotels such as "Miss Reno's" that provided much more than a bed for their patrons—and quite a hot reputation for Fairhaven. One unidentified man romanced himself into a state of exhaustion and dropped dead while walking up 9th Street. Another, John Moore, had a few too many at the Gilt Edge Saloon and decided to sleep it off on the tracks—poor John never heard the 2:30 a.m. train pulling into town.

Today Fairhaven is considerably more quiet. See old buildings and Victorian homes by taking a walking tour of the Fairhaven Historic District; maps are available from the Visitor and Convention Bureau, 904 Potter St., 671-3990. Several shops and galleries in the district are also worth a visit, including **The Glasserie,** 1306 11th St., 734-3638, with hand-blown and stained-glass art, and **Gallery West,** 1300 12th St., 734-8414, with fine art and crafts including oils and watercolors, sculpture, pottery, weavings, and jewelry. A new addition to Fairhaven, the restored **Marketplace** at 12th and Harris was built in 1890 and now houses shops and restaurants, including **Haven's Delight,** serving Chilean and Italian cuisine, and **Boehm's Chocolates.**

Parks

Seven miles S of Bellingham on Chuckanut Dr., **Larrabee State Park** has tidal pools for marine life viewing, 8 miles of hiking trails to 2 mountain lakes and viewpoints, boat launch, 61 standard campsites, and 26 hookup sites on more than 1,800 acres on Samish Bay. This became Washington's first state park when Charles Xavier Larrabee's family donated 20 acres in his honor in 1923.

A test site for the American Rose Society, **Fairhaven Park's** summer-blooming rose gardens are the highlight of the 16-acre manicured park at 107 Chuckanut Dr., which also has picnic areas, a playground, hiking trail, and tennis courts.

Samish Park, 673 N. Lake Samish Dr., is a 39-acre county park with 1,500 feet of Lake Samish shoreline for swimming, fishing, boating, picnicking, hiking, and a children's play area. Rent canoes, paddleboats, rowboats, sailboats, or a sailboard.

Whatcom Falls Park, near Lake Whatcom at 1401 Electric Ave., has hiking, tennis courts, a playground, picnic area, and state fish hatchery on 241 acres. With 12 acres on the lake itself, **Bloedel Donovan Park** has a swimming beach, boat launch, playground, and picnic area at 2214 Electric Avenue.

Lake Padden Park, 4882 Samish Way, has over 1,000 acres of hiking and horse trails, a golf course, picnic areas, and a playground, plus swimming, fishing, and non-motorized boating on the lake.

Thirty-eight acres of practically untouched canyon wilderness is yours for the hiking at

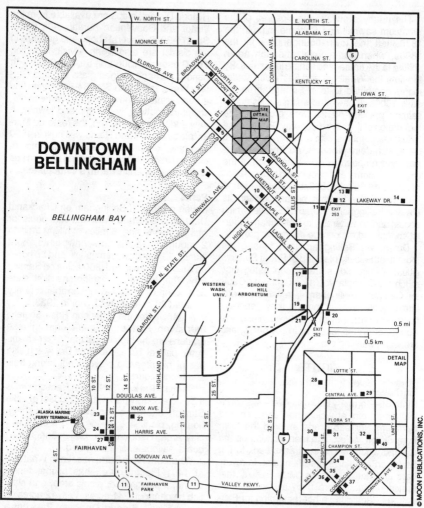

DOWNTOWN BELLINGHAM

BELLINGHAM BAY

WESTERN WASH. UNIV.

SEHOME HILL ARBORETUM

ALASKA MARINE FERRY TERMINAL

FAIRHAVEN

FAIRHAVEN PARK

DETAIL MAP

© MOON PUBLICATIONS, INC.

Arroyo Park on Old Samish Rd., with nature and horse trails and creek fishing.

Chuckanut Drive

For a scenic 7-mile driving tour with dazzling views of Puget Sound and the San Juans, **Chuckanut Drive** winds along the Samish Bay shoreline S of Bellingham on SR 11 from Fairhaven Park to Larrabee State Park and points S, intersecting with I-5 in Burlington (the scenery quits just S of Chuckanut Manor). Teddy Bear Cove is a nudist beach on Chuckanut Dr., just S of the city limits.

Western Washington University

This 224-acre campus is home to 9,500 students and a number of internationally acclaimed sculptures in an outdoor garden. Tours of the university and sculpture garden are given Mon. through Fri.; call 676-3440 for

DOWNTOWN BELLINGHAM

1. Decann House
2. Lion's Inn Motel
3. Bellingham Theater Guild
4. Maritime Heritage Center
5. Waterfront Tavern
6. Hamann's Gallery
7. Greyhound
8. Georgia Pacific Corp.
9. North Garden Inn
10. Bellingham Herald
11. Nendel's
12. Val-U-Inn
13. Visitors and Convention Bureau
14. A Secret Garden
15. KVOS TV
16. Cliff House
17. Aloha Motel
18. Pony Soldier Motor Inn
19. Park Motel
20. Motel 6
21. Bellingham Mall
22. The Castle
23. Fairhaven Bicycle shop
24. Speedy O' Tubbs and Dos Padres
25. Dirty Dan Harris/Marketplace
26. Gallery West
27. The Fairhaven
28. post office
29. library
30. Whatcom Museum of History and Art
31. Children's Museum Northwest
32. Cassidy's and Top of the Tower
33. Bristol Antiques
34. Aladdin's Lamp Antique Mall
35. Antique Mall
36. Bellingham Hardware Building/Boehm's
37. Parkade
38. Lord Cornwall
39. Il Fiasco
40. Pacific Cafe

times and reservations. For a self-guided tour, pick up a brochure at the university's visitor center or the Bellingham Convention and Visitor Center on Potter St. (see "Services," p. 167, for directions). Overlooking Bellingham Bay and accessible via a footpath from the university, the **Sehome Hill Arboretum** offers splendid views of the San Juans and Mt. Baker, plus 70 acres of 100-foot Douglas firs, wildflowers, and big leaf maples preserved in their natural state. The several miles of paved trails are smooth enough for wheelchairs and accessible year-round; other secondary trails may be slippery when wet.

Museums

Built as the Bellingham City Hall in 1892 at 121 Prospect St., the **Whatcom Museum of History and Art**, 676-6981, is recognized as one of the finest regional museums on the West Coast, with scheduled concerts and free, changing exhibits of regional history and contemporary art. The gift shop here is noteable on its own merits, with a large selection of arts and crafts, Northwest foods, and books. Open Tues. through Sun. afternoons; donation.

The **Children's Museum Northwest**, 106 Prospect St., 733-8769, has many participatory exhibits for kids of all ages, including a dental center with giant walk-in mouth, infant/toddler exploration center, TV station,

and puppet theater. Admission is $2 adults, $1 kids; closed Mondays.

Tours

See how a newspaper is produced at the *Bellingham Herald;* phone a week in advance for a tour of their facilities at 1125 N. State St., 676-2675. Media buffs will also enjoy a tour of the **KVOS Television Station** at 1151 Ellis St.; call 671-1212 3 days in advance.

ACCOMMODATIONS

Bed And Breakfast

High on a hill above Fairhaven, **The Castle,** 1103 15th St. (15th and Knox), 676-0974, offers old-world grandeur and 4 antique-furnished guest rooms in a 100-year-old historic landmark. Rooms go for $40 s up to $75 d; the 2 larger rooms have private bath. No pets, smoking, or kids under 12.

Housed in an ornate 3-story Victorian home, **The North Garden Inn** at 1014 N. Garden St., 671-7828 or (800) 922-6414, has 10 rooms (6 are available in winter), many with bay views, sharing 5 baths for $44-54 d, including a full breakfast. A Steinway grand piano is yours for the using; no kids, pets, or smoking.

Above Lake Whatcom surrounded by tall evergreens is **Schnauzer Crossing,** 4421

Lakeway Dr., 734-2808. This B&B has 2 rooms for $75 and $105, both with private bath; the master suite has a jacuzzi, double shower, sitting room, and fireplace. Special luxuries include a new outdoor spa, fresh fruit and flowers, and terry robes; borrow the owners' canoe to enjoy on Lake Whatcom, or get your exercise on their private tennis court. Children ($7.50) and pets ($10) can be accommodated with advance notice; no smoking.

A Secret Garden, 1807 Lakeway Dr., 671-7850, is one of Bellingham's newer B&Bs. Close to town, the turn-of-the-century inn offers 2 spacious suites with private baths and Victorian breakfast for $50 d; no pets or smoking.

The **DeCann House,** 2610 Eldridge Ave., 734-9172, is a Victorian B&B adorned by innkeeper Barbara Hudson's stained glass, etchings, and family heirlooms. Their 2 guest rooms with queen beds and private baths are $35-55, and feature a full breakfast and views of Bellingham Bay and the San Juans. No small children, pets, or indoor smoking. Five miles E of Bellingham at 2399 Mt. Baker Hwy., **Squalicum Ranch Bed and Breakfast,** 671-3868 or 733-2509, has over 300 acres of wooded hiking and riding trails, farm animals, fly fishing in Squalicum Lake, and a big country breakfast in a turn-of-the-century farmhouse, all for just $45 d.

In a pinch, call **Bab's,** 733-8642, a reservation service specializing in B&Bs with home and other lodging rentals. For B&Bs in the small towns N of Bellingham, see "Vicinity of Bellingham," p. 169.

Hotels And Motels

For tight-budget accommodations, the ever-present **Motel 6,** 3701 Byron St., 671-4494, has 60 rooms and a pool for $25 s, $31 d. Not much more expensive is the **Aloha Motel,** off I-5 exit 252 at 315 N. Samish Way, 733-4900; the 28 rooms are $26-29 s, $29-32 d, with free continental breakfast. Also inexpensive is the **Lions Inn Motel,** 2419 Elm, 733-2330, with 15 rooms with kitchens and refrigerators for $29-32 s, $36-44 d; pets OK. A new economy motel near the Bellis Fair Mall, **The Traveler's Inn,** 3570 Meridian St., 671-4600, charges $36 s, $40 d.

For a more moderately priced room, the **Pony Soldier Motor Inn,** 215 N. Samish Way, has 65 rooms from $45 s, $49-51 d, plus a heated pool; 734-8830 or, in Washington (800) 634-PONY. The **Park Motel,** 101 N. Samish Way, has 56 modern rooms for $42 s, $46 d, plus hot tub, sauna, and complimentary continental breakfast; 733-8280 or, in Washington (800) 732-1225. In the same price range is the **Val-U Inn,** 805 Lakeway Dr., with 82 rooms starting at $35-39 s, $39-46 d, including complimentary continental breakfast, guest laundry, and a hot tub room; 671-9600 or, statewide (800) 451-7766.

Done in colonial decor, the **Best Western Heritage Inn,** 151 E. McLeod Rd., 647-1912 or (800) 528-1234, has 61 rooms from $40-

Western Washington University

57 s, $45-62 d, with a pool, plus a restaurant and movie theater across the street. **Nendel's Inn,** 714 Lakeway Dr. (exit 253), 671-1011 or (800) 547-0106, is probably the most luxurious hotel in the area, with 132 rooms, an indoor pool, sauna, hot tub, exercise room, game room, barber, and beauty salon. Rooms here start at $60-72 s, $66-78 d. The piano bar features entertainment nightly except Sunday.

Cabin

The **Seagoat** is a reasonably priced, 3-bedroom cottage on the beach 2 miles from the Gooseberry Point ferry landing. For $65-75 for 1-3 people, $100 for 4, or $125 for 5-6 people, you get Mt. Baker views, a sunken rock fireplace, antique bedroom sets, and seclusion. Call 676-0974 or write 1220 Central Ave., Bellingham, WA 98225, for more information and reservations.

Sudden Valley Resort

As far as resorts go, this one isn't all that expensive. Located on 1,500 beautiful acres off Lake Whatcom Blvd., the lodging at Sudden Valley starts at $65-95 for a 2-person condo and goes up to $139-154 for a 6-person, 3-bedroom condo. There are no telephones in the rooms so harried executives can truly escape. Enjoy the resort for a lot less by camping: 89 campsites are $8 (no hookup) to $10 (full hookup), and you can use the facilities for an extra $5. Amenities include an 18-hole golf course, movies, play barn for the kids, basketball, ice skating, swimming pools, 6 tennis courts, and boating, swimming, and fishing on Lake Whatcom and Lake Louise. For a brochure or more information contact Sudden Valley Resort, 2145 Lake Whatcom Blvd., Bellingham, WA 98226, 734-6430.

See "Blaine," p. 171, for information on the new **Resort Semiahmoo.**

Campgrounds

See "Parks" above and "Vicinity of Bellingham" for the cheapest campsites. Private campgrounds in Bellingham include **Diamond S RV Park,** 5330 Guide Meridian, 671-2443, with 50 treed sites including electricity and showers from $12-14. Private campgrounds in neighboring towns are listed by town under "Vicinity of Bellingham."

FOOD

For the best Italian food in town, try **Il Fiasco,** across from the parkade at 1309 Commercial, 676-9136. The varied menu is accompanied by a good selection of Italian and regional wines, available by the glass. **The Pacific Cafe,** next to the Mt. Baker Theater at 100 N. Commercial, 647-0800, serves moderately priced steak, seafood, and teriyaki dishes in a warm atmosphere. Overlooking Samish Bay and the San Juans at 302 Chuckanut Dr., **Chuckanut Manor,** 766-6191, specializes in steak and fresh seafood from $7-30, Friday night smorgasbord, and Sunday Champagne brunch in an atmosphere more elegant than you'd expect from the bland exterior. Open for dinner year-round, lunch spring through fall; closed Mondays. One of Bellingham's best bay views can be yours at the **Cliff House,** 331 N. State, 734-8660; open for lunch and dinner, the specialty here is salmon but the menu also covers beef, chicken, and other seafood dinners from $8-17. **The Marina,** 985 Thomas Glenn Dr., 733-8292, has a terrific harbor view, indoor-outdoor lounge, and reasonably priced meals. For dinner from the rooftop, try **Top of the Tower** at 119 N. Commercial, 733-3443; lunch and dinners here include steak, veal, chicken, and seafood from $11-17, complemented by an extensive wine list. On a lower floor of the same building, the more casual **Cassidy's,** 734-4401, serves 3 meals daily from an American menu. Some of the area's best Southwest/Mexican food is at **Pepper Sisters,** 1222A Garden St., 671-3414. Open for dinner only, Tues. through Saturday. Or, have a gyro, souvlaki, or mousaka at **Eleni's Greek Restaurant,** 1046 Lakeway Center, 676-5555; also steaks, burgers, and chicken for your less adventurous companions.

Dirty Dan Harris', at 1211 11th St. in the Fairhaven district has prime rib and fresh seafood dinners in an 1800s-style saloon for $8-17; 676-1011. Fairhaven's finest dining is at **The Fairhaven,** 1114 Harris

Ave., 676-1520, where fresh seafood, veal, and steaks—even geoduck—highlight a 40-item menu and a wine cellar filled with over 230 varieties. Or, try the Mexican food at **Dos Padres,** 1111 Harris Ave. in Old Fairhaven; it was rated "best Mexican restaurant N of L.A." by the B.C. *Sun.*

ENTERTAINMENT

Annual Events

Bellingham's annual **Ski to Sea Race,** held Memorial Day weekend, tests the physical endurance and athletic skills of its participants over an 85-mile course which includes a downhill ski leg, running, bicycling, canoeing down the Nooksack River, and sailing across Bellingham Bay to the finish in the Fairhaven district. The race is the highlight of a week-long festival that includes a street fair, with crafts, live music and dancing, food, and a beer garden, on Sun. after the race. For specific dates call 734-1332.

The **Lummi Stommish Water Festival** is an annual mid-June event held at the Lummi Indian Reservation on Gooseberry Point. It includes war-canoe races, arts and crafts shows, Indian dancing, and a salmon bake; 734-8180.

Like other Puget Sound cities, Bellingham sponsors a Christmas **Lighted Boat Parade** in Bellingham Bay in early December; 733-7390.

Outdoor Recreation

Nearby 10,750-foot **Mt. Baker** offers downhill and cross-country skiing 7 months out of the year, due to its altitude and northern position in the Cascade range. For skiing, hiking, and other recreational opportunities in the Mt. Baker National Forest, see "Mt. Baker," p. 174.

The Arts

Western Washington University hosts a number of musical and theatrical groups in its auditorium. Some of the more notable events are the February **Jazz Festival,** 676-3130, the May concert by the **Whatcom Chorale & Symphony Orchestra,** 676-2170, and the Christmastime **Morca Nutcracker Ballet,** 676-1864. The **Mt. Baker Theatre** hosts musical and theatrical performances from Oct. to March at 106 N. Commercial; for ticket info call 734-4950. Staffed and performed entirely by local volunteers, the **Bellingham Theatre Guild** produces 5 plays a year from fall to spring at the old Congregational Church building at 1600 H St.; for ticket info call 733-1811.

At 1603 N. State, **Hamann's Gallery,** 733-8898, features original artwork, etchings, and limited-edition prints. In Fairhaven at 12th and Harris, **Gallery West,** 734-8414, displays paintings, sculpture, graphics, pottery, jewelry, glass, and more.

Nightlife

Harry O's, at Nendel's on Lakeway Dr. and I-5, has piano entertainment nightly (except Sun.) and a new dance floor. The **Lord Cornwall Restaurant** has dinner and dancing every night at 1408 Cornwall Ave., 671-2031. The **Black Angus,** 165 Samish Way, also has dancing. **Speedy O'Tubbs,** 11th and Harris in Fairhaven, has a variety of live music and dancing. Formerly The Digs, the place is said to have a resident ghost, who has appeared to a number of people between 3 and 4 a.m. in the foyer. Reputedly a woman, this spirit may have once been joined to the skeleton they found in a wall during reconstruction. More down to earth, the **Waterfront Tavern,** overlooking Bellingham Bay at 521 W. Holly St., has pool, poker, pull tabs, and punchcards.

SHOPPING

Bellingham's new 900,000-square-foot regional shopping mall, **Bellis Fair,** has 5 anchor stores—Bon Marche, Target, Mervyn's, J.C. Penney, and Sears—in addition to numerous smaller shops and a 500-seat Food Court. **Bellingham Mall** on Samish Way at I-5 exit 252, has just 25 stores selling apparel, jewelry, fabrics, candy, and services from hairstyling to tickets for area events. The downtown **Parkade** at Holly and Commercial has covered parking for a number of small shops along Commercial St., including Nordstrom Place Two on Cornwall. If you panic and drive through the Parkade accidentally (easy to do) they won't charge you for the trip—it happens to out-of-towners all the time. On W. Holly and Bay streets, the **Bellingham Hardware Building** houses apartments, businesses, and a couple retail shops.

Antiques
Whatcom County has a number of antique shops and malls. In Bellingham proper, **Bellingham Antique Mall,** 202 W. Holly St., 647-1073, is open daily till 5:30 p.m. and on Sun. afternoons with a wide selection of collectibles from 20 dealers. **Aladdin's Lamp Antique Mall,** 1318 Bay St., 647-0066, is open daily till 7 p.m. with heavy emphasis on comic books, furniture, glass, and books. **Bristol Antiques and Books,** 310 W. Holly St., 733-7809, has small collectibles and over 650 new books on antiques; open daily till 5 p.m.

SERVICES

The area code in the Bellingham area is 206. For maps, brochures, and general information contact the **Bellingham and Whatcom County Visitor and Convention Bureau,** 904 Potter St., 671-3990; open daily, year-round.

For 24-hour emergency care, contact St. Joseph's Hospital, 2901 Squalicum Parkway at exit 255, 734-5400.

TRANSPORTATION

By Air
Bellingham International Airport has service to Seattle and other West Coast cities via **Alaska Air, Horizon Air, USAir, and United Air Express.** If you're flying into Sea-Tac instead, **Bellingham/Sea-Tac Airporter** offers 5 roundtrips daily for $17 OW, $30 RT to Bellingham Mall or Bellingham Airport, 733-3600 or (800) BELLAIR. You can charter a sightseeing flight through **Cascade Flights,** 733-3727.

By Ferry
The **Alaska Marine Highway System,** 676-8445, recently moved up to Bellingham from Seattle; from here you can take the ferry to SE Alaska destinations. **AIT Waterways,** 671-1137, operates a foot ferry between Bellingham's Squalicum Harbor and Orcas and San Juan islands.

By Bus
Greyhound has nationwide service from its terminal at 1329 N. State St.; 733-5251 or (800) 528-0447. **Grayline of Seattle** travels between Seattle and Vancouver, B.C., with stops at the Bellingham Cruise Terminal, Bel-

The Alaska Marine Highway ferry system docks its ships in Bellingham.

lingham International Airport, and Semiahmoo. Locally, **Whatcom Transit** provides transportation to Ferndale and Lynden. **Lynden Stage Line** has 6 roundtrips daily between the Bellingham city bus terminal to Lynden and points in between; call 734-0520 for schedule, 354-1495 for other information.

By Car
Bellingham is about 86 miles due N of Seattle via I-5. If you're not in a big hurry, get off the highway near Burlington and head N on Hwy. 11, a.k.a. Chuckanut Dr., for some breathtaking vistas of the Sound after a few miles of straight 55-mph through farmland.

By Bicycle
Scenic Chuckanut Dr., historic Fairhaven, and peaceful Lake Samish are only a few places that cyclists will enjoy. If you didn't bring yours along, you can rent bicycles from **Fairhaven Bicycle Shop,** 1103 11th St., for

$10 a day or $15 a weekend. Mountain bikes are also available for $12 a day, $20 a weekend; 733-4433.

Cruises
For a sunset tour of Bellingham Bay coupled with a taste of local smoked salmon, cheese, and berries, take the 2-hour "Taste of Washington Cruise" offered from May through Sept. by the **Maritime Heritage Center,** 121 Prospect St., 734-8866 or, statewide (800) 841-8866. Held on Mon. and Wed. evenings, these cruises include a sampling of early Bellingham history and present-day uses of the bay. The Center also offers day-long and late evening whalewatching and dinner cruises to and around the San Juan Islands; **Gray Line Water Sightseeing** also offers a San Juan cruise, via a more northerly route from The Resort Semiahmoo in Blaine. For information on these 2 cruises, read "San Juan Islands," p. 141.

VICINITY OF BELLINGHAM

LUMMI ISLAND

The Lummi Indians were the first inhabitants of the island, but had abandoned their camp even before white settlers arrived in the 1870s. Today it's a quiet island, home primarily to salmon fishermen who use reef-nets in the style of the original Indians.

Hiking

Hiking trails lead to the points at the N and S ends of the island, as well as to the 1,500-foot summit of Lummi Peak.

To get to **Carter Point** at the island's S end, turn L onto Nugent Rd. from the ferry dock, and follow the paved road uphill to the L; then turn R onto Seacrest Dr., and R at the first fork in Scenic Estates onto Island Drive. Bear to the L as the road forks at a small lake, parking just past the lake on the abandoned quarry road. Walk along the road, taking an optional ¼-mile side trail heading to picturesque Inati Bay. After relaxing at the beach, return to the quarry road; it climbs uphill and to the R, providing good views of Reil Harbor to the east. Continue S to the knoll at the road's end for sweeping views of Bellingham, Mt. Baker, and the water below. Total hiking time is about 3 hours.

At the N end of the island, **Migley Point** can be reached via a 2-hour roundtrip loop along little-used roads. From the ferry dock, go L on Nugent Rd., then R on Legoe Bay for just over ½ mile to a fishing village on the bay; park here. Head N along the road, stopping to appreciate the westward views of Orcas Island, until you reach Migley Point; then head E down the other side of the island to Lummi Point, then back to the starting point.

For a 7-mile roundtrip hike leading to spectacular views of the San Juans, hike the 2½ hours to **Lummi Peak.** From the ferry dock go L on Nugent Rd., L again onto Sunrise Rd., and R on Seacrest Dr. for ½ mile to the top of the hill; park on a wide spot in the road a few yards up. Find the old logging road on the R, and follow it up the N side of Lummi Peak to sheer cliffs and panoramic views. As the trail progresses it gets harder to follow, as it splits and leads to knolls and viewpoints; at about the first mile, stay to the R at the fork, and at about 3½ miles, bear L to a clearing with views of Bellingham and points east. Head back here for a 7-mile roundtrip.

Accommodations

Located on the W side of the island at 2579 W. Shore Dr., **The Willows Inn,** 758-2620, has B&B accommodations from $90-120, including a full 3-course breakfast. The 2 dormer view rooms share a bath, while 2 rooms with antique double beds have private baths. The honeymoon cottage provides additional privacy and a magnificent view of the islands. Dining by reservation only. No kids, pets, or indoor smoking. **West Shore Farm,** 2781 West Shore Dr., 758-2600, offers B&B in their unique octagonal home with a 12-sided free-standing fireplace and sweeping Georgia Strait views. Guest rooms are $40 s, $50 d, including a full breakfast; lunch ($7 pp) and dinner ($15 pp) are available on request. No indoor smoking; kids are welcome, but call for specifics.

The Islander is a private campground with 10 sites, $4 up, on the water near the ferry landing at 2106 S. Nugent Rd., 758-2190.

Transportation

Getting to Lummi Island is easy, via a 7-minute ferry ride from Gooseberry Point aboard the *Whatcom Chief.* The boat departs for Lummi Island hourly or better from 7 a.m. to 12:10 a.m. For further information call the Lummi Island Ferry at 676-6730.

POINT ROBERTS

Bounded on 3 sides by water and on the 4th by British Columbia, it's only by political accident that Point Roberts belongs to the U.S., as the point was evidently ignored when the international boundary was drawn at the 49th parallel. The 450 Americans that live in Point Roberts year-round acknowledge the reality

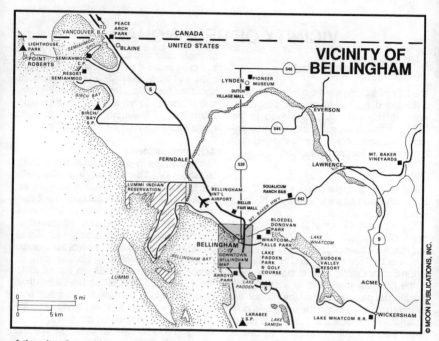

VICINITY OF BELLINGHAM

© MOON PUBLICATIONS, INC.

of the situation, with many businesses accepting Canadian currency at par value to encourage the mostly Canadian tourists, though the 5-square-mile point is only 23 miles (and 2 international borders) from Blaine.

Located on the SW tip of Point Roberts, Whatcom County's **Lighthouse Park** has 22 acres and a ½-mile beach, highlighted by a 600-foot boardwalk with a 30-foot lookout platform (whales are often spotted in August). The boat launch here sees a lot of use, with some of the Puget Sound's finest salmon fishing right off the point. In time-honored American tradition, the July 4th fireworks display is held here. The park is open all year with parking (no hookups) for campers and trailers; for camping reservations call (604) 945-4911.

On the point's E side, the beaches on Boundary Bay have some of the warmest water on the West Coast as the tide comes in over a square mile of sand bars, providing safe fun for kids and waders.

Check with the **Point Roberts Chamber of Commerce,** 945-2313, for the best places to eat and stay.

FERNDALE

Ferndale is one of those "Main Street, U.S.A." towns, with one main drag, a couple gas stations, 3 bars, and a drugstore. The best part of Ferndale is the postcard view of Mt. Baker from the end of the I-5 exit ramp.

Parks

Take a walk around a bog and interpretive displays at **Tennant Lake Natural History Interpretive Center,** 1¼ miles SW of exit 262 from I-5. One of the park's highlights is the **Fragrance Gardens,** designed so the sight impaired can experience the variety of plants by scent. Open Fri. through Sun. afternoons in summer, 733-2900; free. **Pioneer Park,** 2 blocks S of Main on 1st Ave., has museum displays in 7 log cabins in a beautiful park setting. The **Hovander Homestead** is a

1903 restored home on the Nooksak River with a barn, milkhouse, children's zoo, gardens, and picnic area. The park is open daily, but the homestead is open only on summer weekends. Admission is $3 for out-of-staters; 384-3444.

Accommodations

Overlooking Nooksack Valley farmland to the Cascades and Mt. Baker, **Hill Top Bed and Breakfast,** 5832 Church Rd., 384-3619, offers a twin bedroom with shared shower ($44), main-floor queen bedroom with private bath ($44), and fireside suite with private bath, shared shower, and room enough for 4 ($49 d). Continental breakfast. Kids are welcome (high chair and crib available); no indoor smoking. **Anderson House B&B,** 2140 Main St., 384-3450, is an 1897 banker's home with 4 guest rooms: 2 with shared bath are $42 s or d, 1 with private bath is $49, and the Tower Suite, with refrigerator, color TV, and private bath, goes for $69. No pets, smoking, or kids under 12.

Stay on a working dairy farm at **Grandview RV Park,** 3185 Grandview Rd., 366-5316. Other privately owned campgrounds in Ferndale include **Ferndale Campground,** 6335 Portal Way, 384-2622, with 45 sites with full hookups, showers, and laundry facilities for $10-13. **Bill's RV and Mobile Home Park,** 6006 Portal Way, 384-5700, is convenient if nothing else: it's 500 feet from the interstate. The 46 sites with full hookups are $15.

BIRCH BAY

Birch Bay is an awful lot of farmland and cow country with a huge ARCO refinery plopped right in the center. The park is the main attraction here, with over 300 species of birds—and almost as many campers—frequenting **Birch Bay State Park** on a mile-long waterfront on Birch Bay. Campsites are plentiful, with 147 standard ($6) sites and 20 hookups ($8.50), available by reservation from Memorial Day weekend through Labor Day. Other facilities include an underwater park, fishing (though there's no boat launch), a ¼-mile hiking trail, picnic area, and 40-acre Terrell Creek Estuary,

home to beavers, opossums, muskrats, and great blue herons. To get there, take exit 266 from I-5, following Grandview Dr.; take a R onto Helwig, then follow the signs to the park.

BLAINE

Way up N on the Canadian border, Blaine is evolving from a quiet waterfront town to a busy tourist destination.

Parks

Open for day use only, **Peace Arch State Park** at the Canadian border has beautifully landscaped grounds and gardens surrounding the Peace Arch, a symbol of friendship

between the U.S. and Canada that stands with 1 "foot" in each country. The parks were constructed by American and Canadian volunteers and funded by Washington and British Columbia school children, who contributed from 1 to 10 cents each for the project. Facilities include a picnic area, playground, and game sanctuary.

Semiahmoo County Park on the Semiahmoo Sandspit has restored salmon cannery buildings and an interpretive center open from Wed. through Sun. afternoons in summer, weekend afternoons the rest of the year; the park itself is open daily year-round.

Festival

The annual **Peace Arch Celebration,** held at the Peace Arch the 2nd Sun. in June, brings together veterans and scouts from the U.S. and Canada to celebrate our friendly relations; 398-1356.

Accommodations

Up where you'd least expect it is one of the Northwest's newest luxuries, **The Resort Semiahmoo.** A planned resort community, facilities include a 250-slip marina, athletic club, 18-hole golf course designed by Arnold Palmer, restaurants, lounges, and plenty of Puget Sound beachfront. Fortunately you don't have to buy a townhouse to stay here; you can get 1 of 200 rooms at **The Inn at Semiahmoo** for $105-165 s or d. The steep price also includes use of the tennis and racquetball courts, jogging trails, pools, sauna, steam room, and more. Their restaurant, **Stars,** features Northwest cuisine in a formal setting. Call (800) 854-2608 from anywhere in the U.S. or 371-2000 locally. **Semiahmoo Rentals,** 371-5700, rents motorboats, canoes, sailboats, sailboards, paddle boats, and mountain bikes at the marina.

The **Victorian Rose B&B,** housed in a 1905 Queen Anne-style cottage at 1274 Harrison Ave., serves a muffin-and-fruit breakfast with rooms priced at $30 s, $40 d; phone 332-8677 or write for reservations.

Private campgrounds in Blaine include **Richmond Resort,** near the bay at 8086 Birch Bay Dr., 371-2262; the 50 sites here with full utilities go for $15.50 a night. **U.S. Border RV Park** has 20 hookup sites and lots of others at 875 Johnson Rd., 332-8686. Sites cost $11-14.

LYNDEN AREA

Cows and chickens, berries, hops, potatoes, and—borrowing from the town's Dutch heritage—bulbs are all grown in this fertile agricultural region and taken to market in Lynden, the mini Bible Belt of the North. Calvinistic influences are seen in an unofficial ban on

Peace Arch at the U.S.-Canadian border

Sunday business and an infamous town ordinance prohibiting dancing wherever drinks are sold—leading to Sat.-night 12-mile pilgrimages to Bellingham's hot spots.

Lynden's **Dutch Village Mall,** opened in 1987, reflects the area's Dutch heritage. The mall features a 72-foot windmill, 20 retail shops, indoor canal, 200-seat theater, 6-room inn, restaurants, and more.

Museums

At 217 Front St., the **Lynden Pioneer Museum** exhibits Indian artifacts, horse-drawn buggies, early Chevies, and other remnants of pioneer life. Call 354-3675 for seasonally fluctuating hours; donations of $1 pp, $2 per family requested. Tractor buffs may enjoy a stop at the **Puget Sound Antique Tractor and Machinery Association** at 8825 Berthusen Rd., where a collection of steam-powered farm machinery can be viewed daily, for free; 352-3754.

Winery

Located SE of Lynden at 4298 Mt. Baker Hwy., **Mount Baker Vineyards** has tours and tastings Wed. through Sun. from 11 a.m.-6 p.m.; 592-2300.

Other Tours

Kids 12 and older can take a tour of **Mt. Baker Mushroom Farms,** also in Everson; call 966-5915 in advance of your visit. **Edeleen Dairy Products,** 9593 Guide Meridian in Lynden, is open to the public from 8 a.m. daily for tours of their facilities. Their most important function, ice-cream processing, is carried out Mon. through Thurs. after 2 p.m.; 354-5342.

Fairs

An international plowing match is the highlight of Lynden's **Spring Fair and Farmer's Day Parade,** held the 1st week of June at the fairgrounds. Mid-August brings the **Northwest Washington Fair** to Lynden, with rides, games, food, and events; held at the fairgrounds. In December, look for **Sinterklass's** arrival! For more information on these and other events phone 354-4111.

Accommodations

Spend a night in a windmill at the **Dutch Village Inn,** 655 Front St., 354-4440, at the Dutch Village Mall. Six hotel rooms (3 are in the windmill) feature Dutch furnishings, antiques, and Dutch-style breakfast for $50-80 d. Higher-priced rooms have private hot tubs. No pets or indoor smoking; kids are welcome. They also offer 7 full hookup RV spaces; inquire for details.

Farther E in Everson, **Wilkins Farm B&B,** 4165 S. Pass Rd., 966-7616, has 3 bedrooms with shared bath in a 100-year-old home for $20 s, $27 d, including a full breakfast and fresh flowers. The **Windmill Inn Motel,** 8022 Guide Meridian, 354-3424, has 15 budget rooms from $24-30 s, $31-39 d.

For campers, **Shenandoah** at 1640 E. Badger Rd., 354-5863, has 8 hookup sites and 5 acres of tent sites, hiking, and picnicking on a wooded lot.

ACME

Pass through the forests and farmlands of western Washington on an hour-long ride aboard a turn-of-the-century steam train with **Lake Whatcom Railway** in Wickersham on Hwy. 9. Normally operating Tues. and Sat. from June through Aug., the railway also hosts special "Santa Trains" 2 Saturdays in Dec.; all rides are $6 adults, $3 kids and students. Phone 595-2218 for reservations.

MOUNT BAKER

Mount Baker is the northernmost of the Cascade volcanoes. Like the others, it towers dramatically over the surrounding hills, bathed in glaciers and snowfields and serving as a scenic backdrop for Bellingham-area photographers. Besides improving the scenery, Mt. Baker-Snoqualmie National Forest is the site of a wealth of recreational activities, from skiing to hiking to white-water rafting, with over 200 miles of trails in over a half-million acres.

The 4 "life zones" on the mountain, from sea-level forest to alpine meadows, are home to a variety of wildlife including coyotes, black bear, black-tailed deer, porcupine, elk, marmots, and mountain goats. Forest birds include grouse, gray jays (the black and white equivalent of the eastern blue jay), ptarmigan, and a large winter population of bald eagles on the Skagit and Nooksack rivers. Five species of salmon spawn in the rivers, and the insect population is well-represented by 3 of its least popular members, the mosquito, black fly, and "no-see-um."

HISTORY

"Discovered" in 1792 by Capt. Vancouver's first mate, Joseph Baker, Mt. Baker had been known for centuries to local Indians as "Koma Kulshan," meaning "Broken One," a reference to an early eruption that blew out part of its summit. Like other Cascade volcanoes, Baker is asleep—but not dead. In 1843 it awoke from its slumber, spewing vast amounts of smoke and ash and causing a major forest fire on the E shore of Baker Lake. The mountain lay dormant from 1884 to 1975, when it again began to release steam.

The mountain has been a source for year-round recreation since 1868, when librarian-turned-mountaineer Edmund Coleman and his party climbed to the summit after 2 failed attempts. Either poor planners or extremely conscious of pack weight, the entire climbing party shared 1 plate and spoon and ate only bacon, bread, and tea during the 10-day ascent. By 1911, the mountain had become an integral part of the Mt. Baker marathon, a 118-mile roundtrip between Bellingham and the summit using any mode of transportation in addition to at least 24 miles on foot. The marathons were discontinued in 1913 after one competitor fell into a crevasse, though he did live to tell about it.

RECREATION

Mt. Baker-Snoqualmie National Forest covers an area far broader than just the peak and its immediate vicinity; it spreads E to the border of North Cascades National Park, and intermittently SE past the towns of Concrete and Darrington to Snoqualmie National Forest. As a result, it's difficult to draw a logical border between "Mt. Baker" and the North Cascades; so, for purposes of clarity, some trails and rivers that are technically in the Mt. Baker district will be included under "North Cascades National Park," p. 279, the most notable being the Skagit River area and Baker Lake. As a general rule, if you can get to it via Mt. Baker Hwy., it's in this chapter; anything accessed via Hwy. 20 is covered under North Cascades.

Skiing

Downhill skiing at **Mt. Baker** lasts from early Nov. to mid-May, the longest ski season in the state. Six chair lifts put 1,500 vertical feet of slope underfoot, from machine-groomed intermediate runs to open powder bowls. Nordic skiing is also available. Other facilities include child care, ski school, rentals, restaurant, and bar; no night skiing. Lift tickets are $20 adults, $14 youth (ages 7-15). For a ski report, phone 671-0211 from Bellingham or 634-0200 from Seattle; the business office number is 734-6771.

Glacier Nordic Ski School offers cross-country skiing along the Nooksack River at Salmon Ridge with trails, equipment rentals, lessons, and backcountry tours. Open Fri. through Sun. plus holidays, they're located in

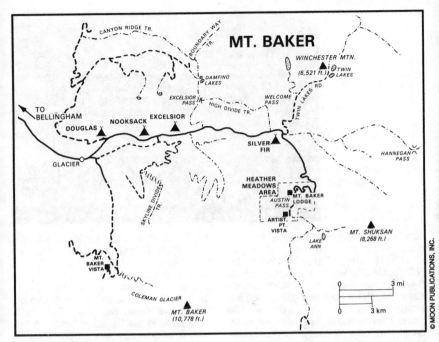

Glacier on the way to Mt. Baker. Call 671-4615 or write cross-country Resort-Salmon Ridge, Box 2974, Bellingham, WA 98227.

Rafting

North Cascades River Expeditions, (800) 634-8433 or 435-9548, offers advanced glacial white-water raft trips on the Nooksack from July to Sept. for participants over 12. A hearty lunch is included in the price, which ranges from $37-49 pp depending on day and group size. **Downstream River Runners,** 12112 N.E. 195th in Bothell, 483-0335, offers a white-water Nooksack trip (minimum age 12) for $45-60 pp; their prices may be a bit higher than other companies, but include wetsuits, lunches, and shuttle, and *all* guides have certified Swiftwater Rescue training.

Hiking

More than 200 miles of hiking trails meander through the Mt. Baker district, and, fortunately for hikers, all of them are closed to ORVs. The variety is enormous; backpackers and one-milers alike can find striking scenery within their reach. Hikers and photographers would do well to pick up a copy of Norm and Diane Perreault's *Photographers Guide To Mt. Baker.* This small, self-published book is the best Mt. Baker guide in print, fun to read and full of beautiful photos and been-there tips on hiking trails and scenic viewpoints. Send $2.95 plus $1 postage to Norm and Diane Perreault, Box A, Glacier, WA 98244, or buy a copy at the Glacier Creek Motel, Forest Service Information Centers, or Village Books in Bellingham.

First the short, though not necessarily easy, hikes. Take Rd. #3060 off Mt. Baker Hwy. to the trailhead for a 1.8-mile OW hike to **Welcome Pass;** this route gains 2,200 feet in elevation via 67 switchbacks to an open meadow with sweeping views of the surrounding area. From the end of Mt. Baker Hwy. at Artist Point, follow the 1.8-mile loop trail up lava cliffs to the appropriately named flat-topped **Table Mountain;** a complete redo in 1988 made this trail, though still steep,

Mount Baker from Chain Lakes Trail

accessible to most hikers. One of the most popular—and overused—hikes is the 2½-mile OW **Heliotrope Ridge Trail** to the edge of **Coleman Glacier,** the starting point for Mt. Baker summit climbs. The trail starts from Rd. #39 off Mt. Baker Hwy. and gains 1,500 feet along the way. An easy 2-mile OW hike leaves from the end of Twin Lakes Rd. off Mt. Baker Hwy. to a lookout atop **Winchester Mountain,** with excellent views of mounts Baker and Shuksan and the North Cascades.

Popular with equestrians and hikers is the 6-mile RT **Skyline Divide** trail, beginning 13 miles up Rd. #37 and providing ample Baker views and wildflower meadows. Starting at Austin Pass near the end of Mt. Baker Hwy., the 4-mile OW hike to **Lake Ann,** one of the Cascades' most beautiful high-country lakes, is a popular route with day-hikers and the major approach trail to Mt. Shuksan. Physically fit day-hikers should try the 9-mile RT hike to **Excelsior Pass** for spectacular views of Baker and Shuksan after a 3,800-foot gain in elevation.

Backpacking

Only a few loop trails are suitable for overnight trips; most Mt. Baker trails are in-and-out propositions. Still, the scenery here is good enough to see twice.

One loop, perhaps too short for the more robust, starts on Mt. Baker Hwy. for a 4.5-mile hike to **Excelsior Pass** (see above), follows

the **High Divide** trail for 4 miles, and returns to Rd. #3060 via **Welcome Pass** for 1.8 miles (see above). To stretch it out, travel N for 3 miles past the Excelsior Pass/High Divide junction to **Damfino Lakes** and Rd. #31. To continue N, take the poorly maintained old bootleggers' route, **Boundary Way,** for 3 more miles to the Canadian border. A trail turns W off Boundary Way just past Damfino Lakes; this is **Canyon Ridge,** heading back to Rd. #3140, but the trail is hard to follow and the rangers discourage its use.

From the campground at the E end of Rd. #32, **Whatcom Pass** trail starts with 4 level miles, climbing abruptly up to Hannegan Pass, then back down to a fork at the entrance to North Cascades National Park. The R fork continues E over Whatcom Pass and eventually to Ross Lake. Permits are required for overnight stays in the national park; you can get one in Glacier at the Public Service Center.

Climbing

Thousands of people annually reach the snow-and-ice summits of Mt. Baker and smaller, but no less challenging, Mt. Shuksan (elev. 9,127 feet). Inexperienced climbers can register for a 6-day summer alpine mountaineering class with **American Alpine Institute** and acquire all the skills they need, starting on gentle terrain and working up to more challenging slopes, for the end-of-week summit climb. Cost is $380. Contact them at 1212 24th St., Bellingham, WA 98225, 671-1505, for information on this and other Mt. Baker and Mt. Shuksan climbs.

Northwest Wilderness Guides offers 2-day ascents of Mt. Baker for $85 or less, depending on group size, in July and August. Included in the price is all climbing gear, instruction, tents and stoves, ice axe practice, breakfasts and dinners; you supply clothing, lunches, pack, sleeping bag, and boots. All that's required is *good* physical condition—don't kid yourself on that one—and proficiency in ice axe self-arrest, which you'll acquire through the practice sessions. Call 733-7014 at least a week in advance for reservations or more info.

Picnicking

Sightseeing and sandwich-chomping are as athletic as some of us like to get. Picnic areas are located at the **Mt. Baker Viewpoint,** past the trailhead on Rd. #39; **Shuksan Picnic Area,** at the beginning of Rd. #32; and at **Austin Pass,** a.k.a. Heather Meadows, at the end of Mt. Baker Highway. **Heather Meadows,** stuck between Baker and Shuksan, has been drawing tourists since the first lodge was built here in the 1920s, although it has since burned to the ground. The lakes, meadows, and rock formations surrounded by snowcapped peaks were the setting for Clark Gable's *Call of the Wild* and Robert DeNiro's *The Deer Hunter.* The view of Mt. Shuksan across Picture Lake is one of the world's most photographed scenes.

ACCOMMODATIONS

See "Bellingham" and "Vicinity of Bellingham" for a wide selection of B&Bs, motels, hotels, and campgrounds within an hour of Mt. Baker; accommodations at or near the mountain are quite limited.

Bed And Breakfast

Twenty-six miles E of Bellingham in Maple Falls, **The Yodeler Inn,** 7485 Mt. Baker Hwy., 599-2156 or (800) 642-7334, is a countrified B&B, built by an early settler in 1917. The inn's 5 guest rooms share 3 baths, a hot tub, and a living room with a fireplace; rates are $48 s, $55 d.

Cabins

Open year-round, **Glacier Creek Motel,** 599-2991, has 9 motel rooms and a number of small creekside cabins accommodating up to 6 people on Hwy. 542. Rates are $29 d for the motel rooms, $43 d for cabins.

Camping

There are 4 campgrounds maintained by the ranger district, although one, **Excelsior,** is open only to large groups with reservations. Two offer camping for a small fee: **Douglas Fir,** 2 miles E of Glacier on Mt. Baker Hwy., has 30 sites; **Silver Fir,** 13 miles E of Glacier, has 21 sites. **Nooksack,** just E of Douglas Fir, is now closed except for overflow.

gold panning on Glacier Peak

FOOD

For fine dining after a tiring romp in the woods, **The Cookhouse,** 7521 Kendall-Sumas Rd. in Kendall, 599-2594, is open for 3 meals, daily, with country cooking and a good beer and wine selection. Also on the classier side is the **Innisfree Restaurant,** 31 miles E of Bellingham on the Mt. Baker Hwy., 599-2373, serving regional foods with seasonally changing hours. The **Chandelier** in Glacier, 599-2949, has family dining and the largest dance floor at Baker. **Paisano's** has pizza (for there or to go) and Italian food at 6186 Mt. Baker Hwy. in Deming, 599-2380.

SERVICES

The area code in the Mt. Baker area is 206. For further information, contact the **Mt. Baker Ranger District,** Box 232, Sedro Woolley, WA 98284, 856-5700. In case of emergency, call the ranger district at 856-1324, or the Mt. Baker/Snoqualmie National Forest Supervisors Office, 442-5400. The Whatcom County Sheriff, 676-6911 or 384-5390, or the Skagit County Sheriff, 336-3146, can also help. To report a forest fire call (800) 562-6010.

The Outpost in Glacier, 599-2991, rents cross-country skis, backpacking equipment, gold pans, mountain bikes, and more. Outdoor equipment, clothing, maps, and cross-country ski rentals are available in Bellingham at **Base Camp, Inc.,** 901 W. Holly, 733-5461.

THE OLYMPIC PENINSULA

OLYMPIC NATIONAL PARK

The diversity of climate and geography in Olympic National Park's 908,720 acres of wilderness is one reason it was among the 100 parks in the world named a "World Heritage Park" by the United Nations in 1981: rugged glaciated peaks, damp low-lying rain forests, and 57 miles of virgin shoreline provide some of Washington's most spectacular (and most photographed) scenery. Paved roads only skirt the park, allowing the largest coniferous forest in the Lower 48 to remain the undisturbed home of 180 species of birds and 50 species of animals, including Roosevelt elk, black bear, deer, bald eagles, and Olympic marmots. Noticeably absent are the grizzly bear, red fox, pika, porcupine, and other species common to the Cascade range. The reason for this difference between the ranges dates back to the Pleistocene Ice Age, when a Canadian glacier isolated the Olympics from the rest of Washington. It's taken 11,000 years for the red fox and porcupine to advance to the park's southern boundary; the mountain goats native to the Cascades were artificially introduced to the Olympics in the 1920s and now thrive in the park's interior.

Today Olympic National Park ranks 10th in attendance among U.S. national parks, with over 3 million visitors in 1984 and 1985; but because of its enormous size and preserved interior, it's not hard to find peaceful solitude on its lakes and trails.

Climate

The weather in Olympic National Park is as varied and unpredictable as its geography. Rain is an ever-present threat, particularly on the western "wet" side, although three-quarters of the park's precipitation falls from Oct. through March. In summer, park temperatures may be in the 80s—or the 60s; at sea level mild temperatures prevail, summer 70s to winter 40s.

SIGHTS

Highway 101 circles the park, with paved or dirt roads leading to attractions around the park's periphery. The park is open year-round, although some roads may be closed in winter. A $3 park entrance fee, good for 7 days, is charged at Staircase, Hoh, Heart o'

enjoying the sun and sand at Olympic National Park

the Hills, Mora, Elwha, and Soleduck entrances in summer.

Hurricane Ridge

One of the park's most scenic areas and by far the most visited, Hurricane Ridge rises over 5,200 feet seemingly straight up from the Strait of Juan de Fuca, providing an awesome contrast from sea level and breathtaking 360-degree views from the summit. The paved road starts at Race St. in Port Angeles, becoming Hurricane Ridge Rd. as it snakes up mountainsides for 17 miles at an easy 7 percent grade; frequent turnouts allow for photo breaks. At the top, **Hurricane Ridge Lodge** provides food service, a gift shop, summer naturalist programs, winter ski rentals and ski-tow service; summer hiking trails and winter cross-country ski and showshoe trails start here as well (see "Activities" p.

182). One of the park's best areas for spotting wildlife, black-tailed deer often bound across the parking lot and black bear are sometimes visible from a distance. The ridge's name isn't without basis in fact: the first lodge at the summit lost its roof in a strong winter blast.

If the dropoffs and absence of guardrails on Hurricane Ridge Rd. made your palms sweat, you're in for a real treat on **Obstruction Point Road.** Starting from the Hurricane Ridge parking lot, this narrow gravel road follows the ridge for 8 miles without a rail or fence, providing spectacular views for the strong-hearted. The road, constructed in the 1930s by the Civilian Conservation Corps, went as far as it could until a steep talus slope prohibited any further roadmaking; that point is still an "obstruction" today.

Hoh Rain Forest

Nearly 140 inches of rain per year keep this slug haven perpetually green and damp under towering conifers over 200 feet tall and up to 10 feet wide. The **Hoh Visitor Center,** located 18 miles E of Hwy. 101 on the Hoh River, offers interpretive exhibits and summer guided walks; nearby are 3 short-interpretive trails.

Lake Crescent

According to Indian legend, Mount Storm King once became so fed up with the bickering between the Clellams and Quileutes that he broke a rock off his head and threw it down at the warring tribes, damming a river and thereby creating Lake Crescent. The scientific view of the lake's origin isn't much different, though attributed to an ancient landslide blocking the Lyre River. Today, freshwater Lake Crescent, 624 feet deep and 8½ miles long, is locally famous for its Beardslee trout. Swimming, boating, camping, picnicking, and, of course, fishing are popular lake activities.

Marymere Falls

This 90-foot unspoiled waterfall is 20 miles W of Port Angeles. To get there, hike the ¾-mile trail starting behind the Storm King Ranger Station or from Lake Crescent Lodge.

OLYMPIC NATIONAL PARK
STRAIT OF JUAN DE FUCA

© MOON PUBLICATIONS, INC.

Sol Duc Hot Springs
Bask in 102- to 109-degree natural hot springs, throwbacks to the area's volcanic ancestry. Located 12 miles from Hwy. 101 just S of Lake Crescent, facilities include 84 year-round campsites, nature trails, and summer evening programs at the amphitheater.

Quinault Valley
Surrounded by steep mountains and dense rain forest, **Quinault Lake** is bordered on the NW by Olympic National Park and on the SE by Olympic National Forest; the lake and land to the SE are part of the Quinault Indian Reservation and subject to Quinault regula-

tions. The Quinault Rain Forest is 1 of 3 major rain forests on the Peninsula; here the annual average rainfall is 140 inches, manifested in enormous trees and lush vegetation. Quinault Valley Loop Auto Tour, a 25-mile trip connecting South Shore Rd., North Shore Rd., and Hwy. 101, boasts views of Quinault Lake, the rain forest, and possible glimpses of Roosevelt elk; not recommended for those with trailers in tow.

The Pacific Coast

To preserve the natural habitat, automobile access to the park's Pacific Ocean beaches is severely limited, but the picturesque cliffs and sea stacks are certainly worth the effort to get there. At the NW corner of the park, 3-mile hiking trails lead from the Ozette Visitor Center to Cape Alava and Sand Point on the Pacific coast. Cape Alava and the beaches near Lake Ozette and La Push are known for fruitful beachcombing, particularly for collectors of the colored glass balls used in the Orient to float nets. All along the coast are millions of flat, round rocks, remarkable in their uniformity, worn smooth by the ceaseless pounding of the surf—perfect for skipping in Quinault Lake! At the park's southern coastal reaches, beach access, summer naturalist programs, and tidepool walks are available at Mora and Kalaloch campgrounds.

Near the N park boundary, Point of Arches is a testimony to the relentless pounding of the Pacific where, with a force of 2 tons per square inch, the ocean carves giant arches out of ancient rock. Neighboring Shi Shi (pronounced shy-shy) Bluffs provide a vantage point for watching the spring and fall gray whale migrations; the best viewing season is from March to May. Both Shi Shi Bluffs and Point of Arches are accessible only through Neah Bay, after a mile hike from road's end. The Arches, legendary children of Destruction Island and Tatoosh Island, were pushed from Mother Tatoosh's canoe when she deserted her husband because, she said, "You'd probably grow up just like your father!"

Be prepared for soggy, windy weather; 100 inches of annual rainfall combine with sometimes-violent winds for less-than-pleasant

hiking weather, although thanks to the Japanese Current the temperatures are mild year-round.

ACTIVITIES

Naturalist Programs

Guided walks, campfire programs, and demonstrations are held daily or on weekends at Elwha, Fairholm, Heart O' the Hills, Hoh, Kalaloch, Mora, Soleduck, and Staircase campgrounds, July 4th through Labor Day. Check the campground bulletin board for times and topics.

Field Seminars

Olympic Park Institute, a nonprofit educational organization, offers field seminars for would-be naturalists, photographers, and anyone interested in the ecology or geography of the park. Course offerings in the past have included Birds of the Olympic Peninsula, Nature Photography, Wilderness Medicine, Watercolor in the Olympics, Geology of Olympic National Park, and more. Seminars last 2-5 days (over a weekend), cost $110-220, and may be taken for college credit. For information and registration, write Olympic Park Institute, HC62 Box 9T, Port Angeles, WA 98362, or phone 928-3720.

Hiking

Over 600 miles of hiking trails criss-cross the park, covering the park's virgin forest core. These short trails provide maximum reward for minimum hiking effort (mileages are OW):

From Lake Crescent Lodge, follow the **Marymere Falls Trail** 1/4 mile for a spectacular view of the 90-foot falls. For a similar experience, try the **Soleduck River Trail** from the Sol Duc Ranger Station; after 1 mile you reach Soleduck Falls and a footbridge over a deep gorge.

Take the Elwha River Trail for 2 miles to **Humes Ranch,** built in 1889 by Grant Humes, who made his living leading wilderness expeditions and by hunting and trapping game. Today his cabin is on the National Register of Historic Places.

A 4-mile hike starting at Lyre River Rd. or N. Shore Rd. at opposite ends of Lake Crescent, the **Spruce Railroad Trail** follows the tracks of the 1918 Spruce Railroad, built to supply spruce for WW I aircraft. The war was over before the railroad was completed, however, and the spruce was no longer needed. Two tunnels and depressions from the never-used railroad ties remain. Besides a taste of local history, the hike provides a view of Lake Crescent.

A number of trails begin at Hurricane Ridge, including 1½-mile **Hurricane Hill Trail,** a paved walk to the top of 5,757-foot Hurricane Hill passing picnic areas, marmot colonies, and spectacular vistas. A longer hike, the **Klahanee Ridge Trail,** follows the ridge's summit for 2 miles after leaving the paved trail near the marmot colonies.

For an all-day hike, the 14-mile RT **Colonel Bob Trail** provides views of Mt. Olympus, Quinault Valley, and the Pacific Ocean from

Giant trunks covered with moss are a rain forest staple.

its 4,492-foot summit. Drive past Quinault Lake on South Shore Rd. till you see the trailhead on the right.

The 4-mile **Quinault Loop Trail,** accessible from Willaby and Falls Creek campgrounds and the Lake Quinault Lodge, provides an easy 2-hour trek along the shore and into the rain forest. Easier still is the ½-mile **Quinault Rain Forest Nature Trail,** where signs explain the natural features. A good hike for those traveling with small children begins at North Fork Campground, following the **Three Lakes Trail** for the first mile to Irely Lake.

Backpacking

The only way to cross the park is on foot; auto roads barely penetrate it. Backcountry use permits are required for trail or beach camping; pick one up at the ranger station nearest your point of departure. Because of overuse, reservations are required for Flapjack Lakes and Lake Constance trails; call the Staircase Ranger Station at 877-5569.

For a S to N 44-mile hike, start at the North Fork Ranger Station (follow North Shore Rd. from Quinault Lake); the North Fork Trail follows the North Fork Quinault River for 16½ miles, then joins the Elwha River Trail terminating at Lake Mills near Elwha (just W of Port Angeles). You'll be hiking in reverse the route of James Halbold Christie, leader of the Seattle Press expedition across the then-unexplored Olympic Peninsula. It took Christie and his party 6 months and 1 black bear to complete the route in 1890; it should take you only 4 days and a packful of gorp. Bring binoculars for a closer look at the mountain goats near Elwha.

A somewhat shorter loop trail follows the Soleduck River Trail to Seven Lakes Basin, then shifts uphill to the summit of Bogachiel Peak and out for a RT of 22 miles. For a 24-mile OW, relatively level hike on the more remote E side, start at Graves Creek on the S side of the park, follow the E fork of the Quinault River for 13 miles, passing Enchanted Valley Ranger Station and Anderson Pass, then travel alongside the Dosewallips River to the Dosewallips Ranger Station and campground.

Climbing

When English sea captain John Meares first sighted Mt. Olympus from aboard ship in 1788, he reputedly said, "If that be not the home where dwell the gods, it is certainly beautiful enough to be, and I therefore will call it Mt. Olympus." He seemed to have forgotten (or never knew) that Juan Perez named the four peaks "Sierra Nevada de Santa Rosalia" in 1774. George Vancouver used Meares' name for the mountain, following a trend caused by the waning of Spanish influence in the Northwest.

Climbing 7,965-foot Mt. Olympus is a 44-mile RT proposition. From the Hoh Ranger Station—the closest and most popular departure point—hike 12 flat miles along the Hoh River Trail, then another 4 to the Olympus base camp, Glacier Meadows. Crossing Blue Glacier and the Snow Dome requires rope, ice axe, crampons, and mountaineering skills; a hard hat is advised because of rock falls near the summit. The 8-mile climb from Glacier Meadows to the summit takes about 10 hours. The best months for climbing are late June through early Sept., driest months in the park; prior to that time mud and washouts may slow you down. *A Climber's Guide to the Olympic Mountains,* published by The Mountaineers, gives detailed information on this and other climbs in the park. This book, other trail guides, and quadrangle maps can be obtained from The Pacific Northwest National Parks and Forests Assn., Olympic Branch, 3002 Mt. Angeles Rd., Port Angeles, WA 98362; write for prices.

Fishing, Boating, And Rafting

The clear, turquoise waters of Lake Crescent are open to fishing and boating; rowboats can be rented from Lake Crescent Lodge. Salmon fishing is popular in the Strait of Juan de Fuca and along the coast; no license is necessary within park limits, though salmon and steelhead punch cards are required. These punch cards are not available in the park, but sporting goods stores statewide have them.

Boating is permitted at 9-mile-long Ozette Lake (the state's largest totally natural lake) in the park's NW corner; in fact, boating in is the only way to get to Ericson's Bay Campground on the W shore. Boat over to the lake's S end and hike the 2.3-mile trail to Norwegian Memorial, a tribute to the victims of a 1903 shipwreck on the Pacific coast. You're practically assured of isolation, since the only other way to get there is by miles of beachwalking.

Olympic Raft and Guide Service offers summer raft trips on the Elwha River for $25 adults, $15 kids, leaving from Elwha Resort. For reservations and information, phone 457-7011 or write Box 846, Port Angeles, WA 98362.

Winter Sports

Ski rentals, 2 rope tows, poma lift, and cross-country ski trails provide Nordic and Alpine skiing at Hurricane Ridge; non-skiers can enjoy the sights via a naturalist-led snowshoe walk (snowshoes provided). Snow-tubing is another popular winter activity at the Ridge. The road is plowed and the lodge and ski facilities are open for holiday and weekend day-use only from mid-Dec. to late March; 452-9235.

ACCOMMODATIONS

Indoors

The following accommodations are located in or very near the park. For meals, lodging, and sights in Sequim or Port Angeles, see pages 187 and 196.

At the base of Storm King Mountain, **Lake Crescent Lodge** has fireplace cottages (built for Franklin Roosevelt's visit in 1937), modern motor lodge rooms, and new cottages with views of the mountains and Lake Crescent. Rates start at $35 s, $40 d for historic lodge rooms with shared bath; $53-57 d for motor lodge rooms; $64-84 for 3-person Roosevelt cottages. Open May to Nov., write National Park Concessions, Lake Crescent Lodge, HC 62, Box 11, Port Angeles, WA 98362-9798, or call 928-3211 for reservations. **Log Cabin Resort,** at the NE end of the lake, has motel units, cabins, campground, and boat rentals 3 miles from Hwy. 101 on E. Beach Road. Lodging rates range from $35-40 d for cabins, $48 for motel rooms, and $55 for waterfront A-frame chalets. Open all year; contact Manager, 6540 E. Beach Rd., Port Angeles, WA 98362, 928-3245.

About 12 miles S of Hwy. 101 and 28 miles W of Port Angeles, **Sol Duc Hot Springs Resort** has a restaurant and cabins from $54 and up, s or d, and trailer hookups for $9. Swim in warm mineral pools and a freshwater pool for $3.75 a day, or enjoy a massage. Handicapped cabins are available; the lodge, 2 pools, and 3 cabins are wheelchair accessible. Open mid-May through Sept.; write Sol Duc Hot Springs Resort, Box 2169, Port Angeles, WA 98362-0283, or call 327-3583 for reservations.

Kalaloch Lodge, 35 miles S of Forks or 70 miles N of Aberdeen on Hwy. 101, has motel and cabin accommodations overlooking the Pacific. Open year-round, cabins range from $54-82 d; motel and lodge rooms go for $34-68 d. Pets are allowed in the cabin area for an additional $4 charge. Contact Kalaloch Lodge Reservation Clerk, HC Route 80, Box 1100, Kalaloch, WA 98331, 962-2271 for reservations.

RULES, REGULATIONS, AND GOOD THINGS TO KNOW

- Use extreme caution when hiking the beaches; round the headlands on the outgoing tide to avoid being trapped between the cliffs and the unforgiving incoming tide.

- Submerged drift logs can make beachwalking dangerous during storms or heavy surf. Keep a good distance from the water.

- Weekday bicycling around Lake Crescent can be hazardous; fast-moving logging trucks use most of the narrow roadway. Sundays are safer.

- Dogs and cats are prohibited in the park except on roads, in parking lots, or within a quarter mile of an automobile campground or overnight facility; no pets in public buildings or on park trails. Where permitted, they must be on a leash.

- No wheeled vehicles (except wheelchairs) are allowed off established automobile roads.

- Firearms must be broken down, sealed, or cased to make them unusable.

- Dead and downed wood may be collected for fires unless otherwise posted; cutting from live trees or plants is prohibited.

- Don't attempt to approach the wildlife; observe from a distance for your own safety. Feeding animals is prohibited as it disturbs their natural, healthy dietary habits.

- In the backcountry, boil all water for 1 minute; even pristine Olympic National Park has giardia.

Seventy miles S of Forks and 40 miles N of Aberdeen on S. Shore Rd., the **Lake Quinault Lodge** has an indoor pool, sauna, jacuzzi, and rooms ranging from $58-78 s, $61-85 d. Write to them at S. Shore Rd., Box

Olympic National Park's rugged coastline

7, Quinault, WA 98575, or call 288-2571 or, toll-free in WA, (800) 562-6672 for reservations. Also on Quinault Lake with some of the least expensive lodging in the area is **Rain Forest Resort Village,** 3½ miles off Hwy. 101 on S. Shore Road. Rooms at the inn, with private bath and TVs, are $28-34 s, $38-40 d; simple wooden cabins range from $38-79 d, some with fireplaces and/or jacuzzis; 31 trailer hookups are available for $9 a night. Write them at Route 1, Box 40, Lake Quinault, WA 98575, or call 288-2535 or, toll-free in WA, (800) 562-0948. Around the other side of the lake, 4 miles N of Hwy. 101 on N. Shore Rd., **Lochaerie Resort,** 288-2215, has 6 cottages, all different, built from 1926-1941 for $40-60 d per night. All have lake views and fireplaces; some also have porches and lofts.

Outdoors

Camping in the park is available on a first-come, first-served basis for $5 a night (free in primitive campgrounds). No showers or laundry facilities are available at any campground; if you really miss bathing, Sequim Bay State Park, Bogachiel State Park, and Dosewallips State Park have showers you can use. Although lacking trailer hookups, some campgrounds do have trailer dumping stations. Trailers over 21 feet in length will have a tight fit. The camping limit is 14 days.

The following campgrounds are open year-round for tents and trailers: Elwha, 41 sites;

Fairholm, 87 sites; Heart O' the Hills, 95 sites; Hoh, 95 sites; Kalaloch, 179 sites; Mora, 91 sites; Ozette, 14 sites; and Staircase, for small trailers only. Open year-round for walk-in campers are Erickson's Bay, 15 sites, and July Creek, 31 sites.

These campgrounds for tents and trailers are classified as closed-if-it-snows: Graves Creek, 45 sites, and Soleduck, 84 sites. Same category, no trailers: Deer Park, 18 sites. Boulder Creek's 50 sites are walk-in only.

Summer-only campgrounds for tents are Dosewallips, 33 sites; North Fork, 8 sites; Queets, 26 sites. The only summer-only campground for trailers is Altaire, with 29 sites.

FOOD

Lake Crescent Lodge, 20 miles W of Port Angeles on Hwy. 101, serves moderately priced salmon, steak, scallop, and oyster dinners as well as daily breakfast and lunch in the Lodge Dining Room; the cocktail lounge opens daily at 5 p.m. The restaurant at **Sol Duc Hot Springs Resort** serves breakfast, lunch, and dinner daily, with limited service early and late in the season. **Lake Quinault Lodge** offers gourmet dining and cocktails with a broad lake view; neighboring **Rain Forest Resort Village** serves fresh seafood, steaks, and cocktails year-round.

TRANSPORTATION

Arriving By Car

From Tacoma take Hwy. 16 N to Hwy. 3 in Bremerton; join Hwy. 104 at Port Gamble, connecting with Hwy. 101 to Port Angeles. Highway 101 continues to circle the park, finally joining I-5 near Olympia.

Arriving By Ferry

From the Seattle area, access to the Olympic Peninsula is provided via the Seattle/Winslow and Edmonds/Kingston ferries; take your pick. The Kingston ferry runs a little more often, leaving about every 40 minutes as opposed to Winslow's more-or-less hourly schedule. From the N, the Keystone/Port Townsend ferry leaves Whidbey Island about every 50 minutes. The fares are the same for all three: $3.30 RT passenger, $5.55 OW car and driver ($6.65 in summer).

The MV *Coho* sails between Victoria, B.C., and Port Angeles 4 times a day (twice daily off-season); the 1½-hour crossing costs $22 for car and driver, $5.50 for passengers, $2.75 for kids, and $2.40 for bicycles OW. For more info on the *Coho* contact Black Ball Transport, 106 Surrey Bldg., Bellevue, WA 98004, 622-2222, or check at the ferry dock at the foot of Laurel St. in Port Angeles, 457-4491.

Arriving By Air

San Juan Airlines, 452-9500, offers scheduled flights from Seattle to Fairchild International Airport in Port Angeles.

Bus Tours

Seattle's **Gray Line,** 624-5813, offers 2-day bus tours of the Olympic Peninsula. Included in the $114 pp double-occupancy price are overnight accommodations at the Red Lion Bayshore Inn in Port Angeles and lunch at the Alderbrook Inn Resort on Hood Canal. Departing from downtown Seattle hotels, the tour circles the Peninsula on Hwy. 101, providing views of Hurricane Ridge, the Pacific Ocean, and a rain forest.

SERVICES

The area code on the Olympic Peninsula is 206. For additional information, phone the visitor center or ranger station nearest your destination: on the N side, Pioneer Memorial Visitor Center, 452-4501; on the W, Hoh Visitor Center, 374-6925; and on the E, Hoodsport Ranger Station, 877-5254. For general information on camping, hiking, accommodations, etc., write the Superintendent, Olympic National Park, 600 E. Park Ave., Port Angeles, WA 98362, or stop by the Pioneer Memorial Visitor Center, about 1 mile from Hwy. 101 on Race Street.

PORT ANGELES

A population of 17,100 makes Port Angeles the largest city on the northern Olympic Peninsula. Its busy harbor, protected by the strong arm of Ediz Hook, is visited daily by logging ships, fishing boats, and the MV *Coho* from Victoria. The view from the Port Angeles city pier is breathtaking: rocky Hurricane Ridge, made more ominous by a wispy cloud cover, seems to rise straight out of the turbulent waters of the Strait of Juan de Fuca, creating an overwhelming contrast of land and water, height and depth.

In 1610 this strait was discovered by Greek pilot Apostolos Valerianus, sailing under the Mexican flag and the Spanish name Juan de Fuca. De Fuca's claim was thought to be something less than the truth until 200 years later when Capt. John Kendrick, an American, found the Greek's observations to be quite accurate. The town of Port Angeles was named by an early Spanish explorer—literally "Port of Our Lady of the Angels"—and although it changed names a number of times in the interim, Port Angeles was organized under its original name in 1890. The town's first white settler, Angus Johnson, traded with Hudson's Bay Company in Victoria across the Strait in 1857; in 1862 President Lincoln named Port Angeles and Ediz Hook as military reservations. Port Angeles was the 2nd town site (after Washington D.C.) to be planned by the federal government, probably because of the attractiveness of its deep harbor—though the town's population at the time was only 10. The military influence held on for decades, as parts of the Pacific Fleet anchored in Port Angeles every summer in the 1920s and '30s, providing the town with 30,000 eligible bachelors and attracting unattached women from all over for a little summer fun. Today the city caters to tourists; it feeds, shelters, and entertains many of Olympic National Park's 3 million annual visitors.

SIGHTS

Municipal Pier And Marine Laboratory

The best part of Port Angeles, outside of its proximity to Olympic National Park, is clearly the city pier. An observation tower at pier's end provides 360-degree views of the city, harbor, and majestic Olympic mountains, while a sandy beach with picnic area is available for day use. Also located on the pier near the *Coho* ferry dock, the Arthur D. Feiro Marine Laboratory, operated by Peninsula College, has hands-on displays and exhibits of the area's sealife with volunteers to answer questions. Open daily in summer, weekend afternoons the rest of the year. Admission is $1 for adults, $.50 kids under 13. For specific hours or a guided tour call 452-9277, ext. 264.

Ediz Hook

Drive W on Marine Dr. to a mile-long natural sandspit protecting one of the world's deepest harbors. Watch as freighters are guided in, or take out your own boat for fishing or sightseeing; motorboat rentals are available at Thunderbird Boathouse for $6 per hour ($20 minimum) or $45 per day including fuel. Picnicking and beachcombing are also popular activities. The U.S. Coast Guard Air Station occupies the far end of the spit; slightly closer to the mainland, the Puget Sound Pilots Association assigns a pilot to each com-

mercial ship passing this point to steer it on its way through Puget Sound.

Parks

Eighty-seven campsites, a marine life sanctuary, hiking trails, beach, and picnic areas occupy 196-acre **Salt Creek Recreation Area** off Hwy. 112, W of Port Angeles. Open year-round.

Near the William R. Fairchild International Airport at W. Lauridsen Blvd. and Bean Rd., **Lincoln Park's** authentic pioneer cabins and an Indian longhouse accompany tennis courts, baseball diamond, campsites, nature trails, picnic area, and children's fishing pond at this 144-acre park.

The 17-acre county park at **Freshwater Bay** on the Strait of Juan de Fuca is primarily a saltwater boat launch with minimal recreational facilities.

Clallam County Courthouse And Historic Museum

A State Historic Site (built in 1914), the county courthouse houses the Clallam County Museum's displays of Olympic Peninsula history. Located at Lincoln and Fourth streets, the museum is open Mon. through Sat. 10 a.m.-4 p.m.; donation.

Municipal Pier and observation tower

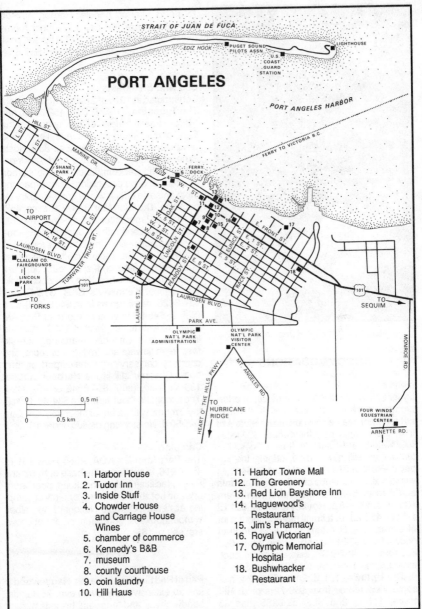

1. Harbor House
2. Tudor Inn
3. Inside Stuff
4. Chowder House and Carriage House Wines
5. chamber of commerce
6. Kennedy's B&B
7. museum
8. county courthouse
9. coin laundry
10. Hill Haus
11. Harbor Towne Mall
12. The Greenery
13. Red Lion Bayshore Inn
14. Haguewood's Restaurant
15. Jim's Pharmacy
16. Royal Victorian
17. Olympic Memorial Hospital
18. Bushwhacker Restaurant

© MOON PUBLICATIONS, INC.

sculpture outside Feiro Marine Laboratory

ACCOMMODATIONS

Hotels

Lodging is plentiful in Port Angeles, and fortunately much of it is inexpensive. If you're not too particular, a few downtown motels of truck-stop quality post their under-$20 rates on readerboards outside their offices. For familiar, yet still inexpensive, lodging, the **Super 8 Motel** at 2104 E. First St., 452-8401, is within walking distance of several restaurants and 3 miles from the B.C. ferry; rooms are $35-40 s, $38-48 d. **Royal Victorian,** 521 E. 1st St., 452-2316, a small motel without a lot of extras, has 11 rooms in a wide range of prices, from $32-64 s or d. **Aggie's Inn,** 602 E. Front St., 457-0471, has an indoor pool, sauna, and 114 rooms for $34-40 s, $42-60 d. The **Uptown,** 101 E. 2nd, 457-9434, has some view rooms from $36-72 s or d. **Hill Haus,** 111 E. 2nd St., 452-9285, has 23 rooms (some with balconies) going for $36-

75 s or d. On Port Angeles Harbor, the **Red Lion Bayshore Inn** has 187 guest rooms (some with bayside balconies), a heated pool, and adjacent restaurant; rooms are $57-83 s, $67-91 d.

Bed And Breakfasts

Constructed in 1910 of English Tudor design, **The Tudor Inn,** 1108 S. Oak, 452-3138, has 5 bedrooms with views of the Olympics or the Strait of Juan de Fuca, a lounge, library, and private baths; room rates are $42-68 d. Hosts Jane and Jerry Glass have made arrangements with local companies offering salmon charters and guided hiking or backpacking trips, and also offer a winter cross-country ski package. The **Glen Mar,** 318 N. Eunice, 457-6110, has 2 rooms for $45 d—one overlooking the water, one with a mountain view—and a 2-room suite with a harbor view for $70 d. Breakfast on the patio, use of the grand piano, and coffee or tea in your room are among the options here; but no indoor smoking, please. **Kennedy's B&B,** 332 E. 5th, 457-3628, has 5 rooms from $40 s, $50-60 d ($35 s, $45-55 in winter) in one of Port Angeles' oldest homes, built in 1896. Included in the price is a full bacon-and-eggs breakfast, fresh flowers and fruit in your room, and courtesy car service to the airport or ferry dock. Cheaper still is the **Harbour House,** 139 W. 14th, (800) 654-5545 or 457-3424. The 2 rooms without views are $34-40 d, while the 2 rooms with harbor or mountain views are $45-50 d. No smoking or kids under 10.

Camping

The **Port Angeles KOA,** 2065 Hwy. 101 E, 457-5916, is nestled at the base of Hurricane Ridge; facilities include hookups, pool, laundry, and hot showers. There's plenty of camping at nearby Olympic National Park, albeit *without* hookups, pool, laundry, or hot showers; see p. 186.

FOOD

Part of Red Lion Bayshore Inn, **Haguewood's** has an extensive menu with over 75 salads, sandwiches, and entrees; breakfast runs about $4, lunch $4-8; dinners, $8-15, feature crab and steak. Forget atmosphere—Denny's is more elegant. The challenge here is to take more than 40 seconds to finish your food, though getting a harbor-view window seat will remove you from most of the hash-slinging commotion. Served at a more relaxed pace, the specialties at the **Bushwhacker,** 1527 E. 1st St., 457-4113, include seafood, steak, chicken, and a chowder bar; open from 5 p.m. **The Greenery Restaurant,** in the midst of the downtown shopping area at 117-B E. 1st St., 457-4112, serves 3 meals a day Mon. to Sat., specializing in cioppino, fresh-baked French bread, and homemade pasta in a plants-and-wood decor catering to the city's businesspersons; prices here are about the same as Haguewood's, but what a difference! This place even *smells* good. **Birney's Restaurant,** 1st and Eunice streets, 457-4411, serves all meals daily and all-you-can-eat Sunday Champagne brunch. If you prefer diner-style, the tiny **Chowder House,** 117 N. Oak St., offers breakfast all day, plus clam chowder, chili, soups, and sandwiches till 4:30 p.m. **First Street Haven,** 1st and Laurel, serves hearty breakfasts and inexpensive sandwiches, quiche, and salads for lunch. Just E of Port Angeles at 2300 Hwy. 101 E, highly acclaimed **C'est Si Bon** prepares local seafood with a French accent, with Olympic and rose garden views adding to the ambience; fortunately, you can't see the dark-flamingo paint job from the inside. Open for dinner Tues. through Sun.; call 452-8888 for reservations. And for the old reliable, **Pizza Mia,** 3033 Hwy. 101 E, 452-3131 or 452-1111, is open till 2 a.m. and delivers.

RECREATION

Fishing
Depart at 6 a.m. for a 5-hour salmon-trolling trip on the Strait of Juan de Fuca with **Carousel Charters,** 1030 Mt. Pleasant Rd., 457-3000. No fishing expertise is required; the knowledgeable skipper provides fishing tackle, salmon punchcard and stamp, coffee and doughnuts (even nets and cleans your catch) for $55 per person.

    Fish Bear Charters, Box 1424, 457-7029, operates daily from mid-June to mid-Sept. (and some April and May weekends) with an all-day fishing excursion, including gear, cleaning, and bagging, for $60 (no kids under 12), maximum 6 persons; 457-7029. If it's salmon you're after, July through mid-Aug. is the best time, according to Fish Bear's Skipper John Willits.

    One of the most popular charter trips is offered by **Satin Doll Charters,** operating every day, year-round with winter blackmouth, halibut, and ling cod fishing in Port Angeles waters, and summer deep-sea fishing for salmon, bottom fish, halibut, or ling cod from Big Salmon Resort in Neah Bay, about 60 miles W of Port Angeles. All tackle is furnished; bring your own lunch. A full day of fishing costs $50, plus a buck for a 1-day license. For information on the winter Port Angeles trips write Box 2108, Port Angeles, WA 98362, or call 457-6585 after 5 p.m.; for summer charters, write Big Salmon Resort, Neah Bay, WA 98357, or call 645-2374.

    Blue Dolphin Charters runs salmon and bottom fish charters year-round (weekends only Sept. to June) for $55 per person, with everything but lunch included (they provide continental breakfast) aboard their 32-foot cruiser with heated cabin. Call 928-3709 for reservations.

    For more fishing charters departing from towns W of Port Angeles along the Strait of Juan de Fuca, see "West of Port Angeles," p. 193.

    Experienced anglers may want to participate in **Derby Days,** a 10-day late-Aug. festival highlighted by 2 parades and culminating in a 2-day salmon fishing derby with prizes totaling $50,000.

Horse Riding
Four Winds Equestrian Center, 787 N. Arnette Rd., 3 miles SE of Port Angeles off Monroe Rd., has guided trail riding by appointment only for $10 per hour with a $20 minimum; call 457-4385 for reservations.

Auto Racing
From May through Sept. **Port Angeles Speedway,** 5 miles E of Port Angeles on Hwy. 101, has stock and hobby-car races every Sun. afternoon. Gates open at 11 a.m., with

time trials at 1 p.m. and races at 2 p.m. For prices and additional info call 457-6063.

Symphony

The **Port Angeles Symphony Orchestra** begins its 6-concert season in Oct. but holds other special-occasion concerts throughout the year at various locations. Tickets can be purchased at Angeles Music in Port Angeles or Carlson's Hallmark in Sequim; season tickets and other info are available from PASO, Box 2148, Port Angeles, WA 98362, 457-5579.

SHOPPING AND SERVICES

Port Angeles' downtown shopping district is centered around 1st St., where shops, restaurants, galleries, and movie theaters can keep your wallet out all day. **Inside Stuff,** 301 W. 1st, carries out-of-the-ordinary, innovative home and bath accessories. Across the parking lot from the Red Lion and just off the waterfront, **Harbor Towne** at 222 N. Lincoln is a small shopping mall with clothing shops, a candy store, and assorted boutiques. Wine lovers won't want to miss **Carriage House Wines,** located in a tiny old white house just off the waterfront at 219 N. Oak. They have a good selection of imported and domestic wines, a winetasting area, and home winemaking and brewing supplies. Open Mon. through Sat. till 5:30 p.m.; call 452-WINE for their extended summer hours.

The area code on the Olympic Peninsula is 206. For maps, brochures, and further information on Port Angeles contact the Chamber of Commerce, 121 E. Railroad Ave., 452-2363. Olympic National Park Headquarters at 600 Park Ave. can give you hiking, camping, and other park info, but first read "Olympic National Park," p. 179.

Campers and backpackers will appreciate **Peabody Street Coin Laundry** after getting back to nature in Olympic National Park; open 7 days a week, 24 hours a day, at 212 S. Peabody.

For medical emergencies, contact **Olympic Memorial Hospital,** 939 Caroline St., 457-8513.

TRANSPORTATION

By Air

San Juan Airlines, 452-1323, provides daily commuter service to Victoria, B.C., and Seattle's Sea-Tac Airport from Fairchild International Airport on the city's W side.

Getting Around By Bus

Greyhound Bus Lines, 452-7611, departs twice daily for Seattle from 215 N. Laurel Street. **Clallam Transit,** (800) 858-3747, provides hourly service throughout Port Angeles, E to Diamond Point and as far W as Forks, Neah Bay, and Clallam Bay, including Olympic National Park's Sol Duc Hot Springs and Lake Crescent. Connect with **Jefferson Transit** in Sequim for Port Townsend, Port Ludlow, Quilcene, and other Jefferson County points.

Trolley Tours

Clallam Transit operates 2 50-minute trolley tours: the "Waterfront Tour" shows you Ediz Hook, the port, paper and wood mills, and marina, while the "Panorama Tour" takes you to the Olympic National Park Visitor's Center with views of the Strait of Juan de Fuca, Vancouver Island, San Juan Islands, and the Olympics. Tours leave hourly in the summer, less often in the off-season, from the chamber of commerce office on Railroad Ave. at the waterfront. Fares are $2 adults, kids under 12 free when accompanied by an adult. For more information call the chamber of commerce at 452-2363 or Clallam Transit, (800) 858-3747.

Arriving By Ferry

The Port Townsend, Kingston, Winslow, and Bremerton **Washington State Ferries** deposit you at various points on the W side of Puget Sound for $5.55 OW car and driver ($6.65 in summer), $3.30 RT passenger, or $2.30 OW bicycle rider; from each of these destinations you can connect, after varying amounts of driving, with Hwy. 101 to Port Angeles. From Seattle, the most direct route is via the Kingston ferry, over the Hood Canal

Bridge, and onto Hwy. 104, connecting to Hwy. 101 near Discovery Bay. For specific info on departure times or fares call the ferry system at (800) 542-0810, or (800) 542-7052 toll-free statewide.

Ferry To Victoria
For a side-trip, the MV *Coho* leaves Port Angeles for Victoria, B.C., 4 times daily in summer, twice daily in winter. One-way fares for the 1½-hour crossing are $22 car and driver, $5.50 passengers, $2.75 kids, and $2.40 for bicycles. This route across the turbulent Strait has been known to make landlubbers severely seasick; stop by **Jim's Pharmacy,** 221 S. Peabody St., for *free* seasick pills before you go. For specific departure times contact the ferry terminal at the foot of Laurel St. in Port Angeles, 457-4491, or Black Ball Transport, 106 Surrey Bldg., Bellevue, WA 98004, 622-2222.

WEST OF PORT ANGELES

JOYCE

Joyce is the easternmost in a series of small towns on the Strait that cater primarily to commercial and recreational fishermen. Accommodations and restaurants here and in neighboring fishing towns are no-frills enterprises.

Museum
Housed in a former railroad station on Hwy. 112, the **Joyce Museum,** 928-3568, has relics from the town's early days plus logging and railroad equipment, photos, and driftwood carvings. Open afternoons Tues. through Sunday.

Accommodations
Five miles W of Joyce, **Harrison Beach,** 928-3006, has furnished cabins and trailers for $22-45 d (no bedding supplied in the trailers). Right next door, **Lyre River Park,** 928-3436, has 60 hookup sites for $11-12 and 15 non-hookup campsites for $10-11 on the Strait and Lyre River. Other facilities include hot showers, laundry, dump station, and boat ramp. **Whiskey Creek Beach,** 3 miles W of Joyce, 928-3489, has primitive (no electricity, pit toilets) camping on the beach for $5; trailers are available for $13-15 a night. Cabins are available on a monthly or yearly basis only.

CLALLAM BAY

Once a commercial logging center, today Sekiu (pronounced SEE-kew) and Clallam Bay, like the other Strait towns, depend on fishermen for their livelihoods.

Parks
The Clallam County parks department has 2 parks in the Clallam Bay area: **Clallam Bay Spit** is a 33-acre waterfront park for day use only; **Pillar Point Fishing Camp,** just E of Clallam Bay, is a 4-acre park with 35 campsites (small fee) and boat launch, open for camping from mid-May through mid-September.

Resorts
Curley's Resort, 963-2281, has lodging in motel units for $28-55 or cabins for $20-26; trailer space, with full hookups, is also available at $8 a night. More importantly in these parts, Curley rents 14- and 16-foot fiberglass boats for $16 bare, $45 with motor and a tank of gas.

Herb's Motel and Charters, 963-2346, has 12 motel rooms from $24-52. Their 6-person charter boat runs from March through Sept.; a 6-hour trip costs $55 pp with all gear included.

NEAH BAY

At the end of Hwy. 112, 72 miles from Port Angeles, Neah Bay sits on the Makah Indian Reservation in virtual isolation, at the northwesternmost point of the continental United States. Fishing is the big business here as well, with charter boats, commercial fishermen, and vacationing anglers competing for the resident salmon and bottom fish.

In 1970 tidal erosion unearthed old Ozette Indian homes that had been preserved in a mudslide some 500 years earlier. After 11 years of digging by Washington State University archeologists the excavation site was closed, and the thousands of artifacts thus uncovered are now on display in the **Makah Cultural and Research Center** in Neah Bay. The museum is open 10 a.m.- 5 p.m. daily in summer, Wed. to Sun. rest of the year, for a $3 admission; 645-2711.

Makah Days is the town's big annual festival, celebrating its citizenship grant. Held in

Charley Swan dressed to impress for Neah Bay's Makah Days

late Aug., dances, a parade, fireworks show, salmon bake, canoe races, and Indian gambling highlight this 3-day event.

FORKS

The westernmost incorporated city in the Lower 48, Forks is the economic center and logging capital of the western Olympic Peninsula—a big handle for this town of 3,000 with one main drag. The town's big selling point is its proximity to the W side of Olympic National Park and Pacific coast beaches.

Sights

Forks proudly displays the world's largest western red cedar—19 feet wide, 170 feet tall, and still growing in a cleared field. To see the tree go E on Nolan Creek Rd., about 6 miles S of the Hoh River Bridge on Hwy. 101. Stay on Nolan Creek Rd. for about 1¼ miles, then go R for 1½ miles on forest road N-1100. Turn R for ½ mile, then take another R for another ½ mile—it's hard to miss.

The **Forks Timber Museum,** 374-9663, will reopen in spring of 1990 in a new facility at the S end of town, built by the high school carpentry class with donated funds. The museum has historical logging and Indian cultural exhibits; call for new hours.

Park

Six miles S of Forks on Hwy. 101, **Bogachiel State Park** (Indian for "muddy waters") encompasses almost 200 acres on the usually clear Bogachiel River. Enjoy the short nature trail through a rain forest, or swim, paddle, or fish in the river—famous for its summer and winter steelhead, salmon, and trout. The park has 41 standard ($7) campsites; no hookups, but RVs up to 35 feet long will fit.

Accommodations

There's actually a B&B way out here! **Miller Tree Inn,** just E of Forks' only stoplight, 374-6806, has 6 rooms (2 with private half-baths, 1 with full bath) in a comfortable 3-story homestead on 3 acres. Rates are $30-35 s, $40-60 d, including a full breakfast. Kids over 6 welcome; smoking limited to 1 bedroom and kitchen area, or outdoors. The **Forks Motel,** 4 blocks S of town on Hwy. 101, 374-6243, has a heated pool and 58 rooms from $38 s, $38-47 d, plus 8 rooms with kitchens for an additional $6.

Food
Get the best Chinese food for miles at **South North Gardens,** Sol Duc Way. For pizza, lasagne, spaghetti, and deli sandwiches try **Pacific Pizza** at Forks Ave. and C Street. Open daily; call 374-2626 for take-out. **Clark's Vagabond,** 142 Forks Ave. N, is open daily for all meals (24 hours on Fri. and Sat.) offering steaks, seafood, and dancing in the lounge. A mile N of Forks at the La Push Rd. junction on Hwy. 101, the **Smokehouse Restaurant,** 374-6258, is open daily for lunch and dinner with a full menu specializing in seafood.

Fishing
Operating near Forks out of the virtually uncharted town of Beaver, **West Side Guide Service,** 327-3671, runs year-round steelhead and salmon charters on Olympic Peninsula rivers. All tackle and bait is furnished as part of the $100 for 1, $170 for 2 price tag.

stained-glass art displayed at the chamber of commerce

SEQUIM

The weather in Sequim (pronounced SKWIM) is odd for the soggy Olympic Peninsula: 17 inches of annual rainfall and habitually clear skies are caused by the town's location in the "blue hole," a locally famous weather pattern. As storms pass over the peninsula, they split in 2; part clings to the Olympics, the rest is blown along by the Strait's air currents, bypassing Sequim like an island in the stream. The pleasant temperate climate and lack of hustle and bustle make this town of 3,180 an ideal retirement community, while the tourist trade and natural features of the area provide a disproportionate number of visitor attractions.

SIGHTS

Parks

The **Dungeness National Wildlife Refuge** provides habitat for 250 species of birds on the world's longest natural sandspit: 6-mile-long Dungeness Spit. As many as 40,000 birds rest at this saltwater lagoon during their migratory journeys. Admission is $2 per party. Hike the 6-mile trail to the lighthouse at the spit's tip, or rent a horse. **Quarter Moon Ranch,** Spath Rd., 683-5863, rents horses for trail, beach, or mountain riding for $7.50 per hour, including a mandatory lesson. Clamming, fishing, and canoeing are permitted in the protected bay, but not camping, dogs, firearms, or fires.

Dungeness Recreation Area, a 216-acre Clallam County Park at the base of the refuge, has camping from Feb. through Oct. in 65 campsites ($6 county residents, $8 nonresidents) with showers and a dump station; 683-5847.

Sequim Bay State Park, just E of Sequim on Hwy. 101, has 60 wooded tent sites ($6), 26 hookup sites ($8.50), a boat launch, scuba diving, hiking, tennis courts, and superb views of Sequim Bay.

Museums

One block N of Hwy. 101 at 175 W. Cedar, the **Sequim-Dungeness Museum,** 683-8110, is home to 12,000-year-old bones and artifacts unearthed at Sequim's world-famous Manis Mastadon Site (see "History," p. 11, for background on the dig). Other displays

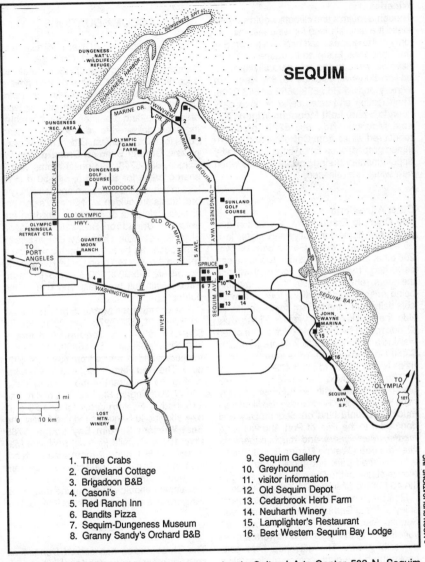

1. Three Crabs
2. Groveland Cottage
3. Brigadoon B&B
4. Casoni's
5. Red Ranch Inn
6. Bandits Pizza
7. Sequim-Dungeness Museum
8. Granny Sandy's Orchard B&B
9. Sequim Gallery
10. Greyhound
11. visitor information
12. Old Sequim Depot
13. Cedarbrook Herb Farm
14. Neuharth Winery
15. Lamplighter's Restaurant
16. Best Western Sequim Bay Lodge

© MOON PUBLICATIONS, INC.

include Indian and Eskimo artifacts, pioneer farming, and timber exhibits. Open Wed. through Sun., noon to 4 p.m.; donation. **Sequim Natural History Museum** in the Peninsula Cultural Arts Center 503 N. Sequim Ave. room. 4, features dioramas of Olympic Peninsula birds and wildlife from seashore to the sub-alpine zone. Donation requested.

Wineries

Though Sequim's arid climate would seem to make it a natural place for wineries, the majority of the grapes used here are grown E of the Cascades. Maria and Eugene Neuharth have been producing only naturally fermented fine dinner wines since 1978 at **Neuharth Winery** on Still Rd., 683-9652 or 683-3706. Their tasting and sales cellar is open daily noon to 5 p.m. **Lost Mountain Winery,** 730 Lost Mountain Rd., 683-5229, produces robust red wines from California and Washington grapes; open for tastings and tours by appointment or during special periods when new wines are released.

Other Attractions

The **Olympic Game Farm,** a vacation and retirement home for Hollywood stars, is a 90-acre preserve where Gentle Ben and over 200 other animals of TV and movie fame can be visited. If you're lucky, you may witness the stars rehearsing their lines or actually being lensed. Guided walking tours are available daily from June to Sept. for $4 adults, $3 kids; the park is open all year for driving tours (2 loop roads) for the same prices. Combined walking and driving tour tickets are $5 adults, $3.50 kids. Follow the signs from Sequim 5 miles NW to Ward Rd.; 683-4295.

"The Duke" loved the Strait; he often explored the waters with his refurbished Navy mine sweeper, the *Wild Goose.* He liked it so much he bought land on Sequim Bay and donated it to the Port of Port Angeles for a marina. Many years and much paperwork later, the **John Wayne Marina** has 422 slips, a landscaped park and picnic area, and a bronze statue of the Duke as he appeared in the 1949 flick, *She Wore A Yellow Ribbon.*

Gourmet cooks and craftspeople might enjoy a visit to **Cedarbrook Herb Farm,** 986 Sequim Ave. S, 683-7733, where over 150 varieties of herbs, teas, and flowers are organically grown. The gift shop here sells books, herb vinegars, potpourri, decorative straw hats, catnip mice, and herbal moth repellents. Open daily March through Sept., weekends Oct. through December.

ACCOMMODATIONS

Five miles from Hwy. 101 and ½ mile from the beach, **Groveland Cottage,** 1673 Sequim Dungeness Way, 683-3565, features 4 comfortable guest rooms (2 with private bath) from $55-75 s, $60-80 d (lower in winter), plus a country store with gifts by local artists, wine, and groceries. Enjoy the morning paper delivered to your door, then head down for a full breakfast. Older children only, please. **Granny Sandy's Orchard,** 405 W. Spruce, 683-5748, has guest rooms with 2 shared baths for $35-45 s, $40-50 d ($10 less in winter); fresh flowers and family-style breakfasts are evidence of Granny's personal touch. No pets or smoking. Children are welcome. **Brigadoon B&B,** 105 Brigadoon Blvd., 683-2255, is a fairly new B&B in a 1920 farmhouse, set back from the highway on a knoll on the way to Three Crabs Restaurant. Rooms are $45-60 s, $50-65 d ($5-10 less in winter), with full breakfast and use of the outdoor spa.

The **Greathouse Motel,** .5 mile E of town on Hwy. 101, 683-7272, has 20 rooms for $32-42 s, $34-48 d. **Sequim West Motel,** 740 W. Washington St., 683-4144, has a restaurant and 21 rooms from $39-50 s, $39-60 d. **The Red Ranch Inn,** 683-4195, adjacent to the restaurant of the same name at 830 W. Washington St., has 31 motel rooms furnished in Western decor for $44-50 d. A new addition to Sequim's lodging family, the **Best Western Sequim Bay Lodge,** 1788 Hwy. 101 E (¾ mile from John Wayne Marina), 683-0691, offers 2-room suites with hot tubs and/or fireplaces, plus on-site restaurant and pool, from $ 50-105 d.

Campers should check out the numerous campgrounds at Olympic National Park, p. 186.

FOOD

The Three Crabs has served Dungeness crab and other local seafood specialities such as red snapper, halibut, and salmon for over 25 years at their waterfront location on Three Crabs Rd.; they also have a retail seafood market. Open daily at noon; take Sequim-Dungeness Way from Hwy. 101, then go R on Twin View Dr. at the Three Crabs sign. Reservations are recommended, 683-4264. The **Oak Table Cafe,** 292 W. Bell, 683-2179, serves gourmet breakfasts and light lunches. For pizza and beer, sandwiches, and spaghetti in a family atmosphere, try **The Bandit's Pizza Parlor** at 392 W. Washington, 683-3388. **Casoni's,** 105 Hooker Rd., 683-2415, offers something a little fancier: seafood, veal, steak, and sautees. Open for lunch and dinner at the intersection of Hwy. 101 and Carlsborg Road. **The Lamplighter Restaurant,** 1292 Hwy. 101 E, 683-4134, serves moderately priced Mexican and American lunches and dinners. The **Dungeness Inn,** 683-3331, overlooking the Dungeness Golf Course at 491A Woodcock Rd., serves breakfast, lunch, and dinner Tues. through Sun., specializing in prime rib, steak, seafood, and bouillabaisse. Another steakhouse, **The Red Ranch Restaurant,** has a 50-item salad bar to accompany their mesquite-broiled grain-fed beef. On Hwy. 101 in Sequim, they're open daily for dinner, 683-6622.

The area's only dinner theater is the **Old Sequim Depot,** 710 S. Sequim, 683-6840, where your choice of 3 dinners precedes the live production in a 76-year-old restored railroad station. Open for lunch and dinner Tues. through Saturday.

ENTERTAINMENT AND INFORMATION

Festivals
Established over 90 years ago and still going strong, the **Sequim Irrigation Festival** celebrates the beginning of Dungeness Valley agriculture thanks to the hand-dug ditch that first brought water from the Dungeness River to the arid prairie in 1896. The first festival (May 1, 1896) was a picnic in a shady grove; today a parade, art and flower shows, and the crowning of a May Queen commemorate the annual event.

Gospel Jamboree
For something a little different, hear old time Southern Gospel music every night except Mon. at 7 p.m. (weekends only Oct. through April) at the **Olympic Peninsula Retreat Center,** 309 Kitchen Dick Lane, 683-2780.

Gallery
Olympic Peninsula artists are represented at **Sequim Gallery,** 130 N. Sequim Ave., 683-6503. Drawing and watercolor classes are taught by resident artist Judy Priest.

Golf
Two 18-hole public golf courses in the area are: the **SunLand Golf Course,** 683-6800, just N of Sequim at 109 Hilltop Dr., and the **Dungeness Golf Course,** 683-6344, adjacent to the Dungeness Inn Restaurant, N of Carlsborg on Woodcock Road. Green fees are $11 weekdays, $12-13 weekends.

Fishing
Departing from the John Wayne Marina at daylight, **Lucky Strike Charter Service,** Box 2288, 683-2416, provides tackle and gear (but not lunch) for an 8-hour salmon, halibut, or bottom-fishing excursion. Trips cost $55; punchcards are available on the boat.

Information
The area code in Sequim and all of the Olympic Peninsula is 206. For maps, brochures, and further information contact the **Sequim-Dungeness Valley Chamber of Commerce,** 1192 E. Washington, 683-6197.

For fire, medical, or police emergencies, dial 911. The nearest hospital with 24-hour emergency service is **Olympic Memorial**

Dungeness crab

Hospital, 939 Caroline in Port Angeles, 457-8513.

TRANSPORTATION

Arriving By Car
From the Puget Sound area, take Hwy. 16 N from Tacoma to Hwy. 3 in Bremerton; cross the Hood Canal Bridge (Hwy. 104) at Port Gamble, then connect with Hwy. 101 to Sequim.

Arriving By Air
Coastal Airways, 683-4444, has daily half-hour flights from Sequim Valley Airport to Seattle's Sea-Tac Airport. Farther W, Port Angeles' Fairchild International Airport offers daily scheduled commuter service to Sea-Tac, Bellingham, Hoquiam, the San Juan Islands, Vancouver and Victoria, B.C., via **San Juan Airlines,** 452-1323 or (800) 438-3880.

Getting Around By Bus
Clallam Transit, 452-4511 or (800) 858-3747, operates a daily commuter route between Sequim and Port Angeles, including a stop at Fairchild International Airport, and regular routes as far W as Forks and Neah Bay. **Greyhound,** 683-4343, offers nationwide service from their station at 117 E. Washington.

PORT TOWNSEND

Nestled in the northern tip of Quimper Peninsula—an offshoot of the NE portion of massive Olympic Peninsula—Port Townsend is best known for its generous helping of Victorian architecture, with more authentic remnants of this period than any other town N of San Francisco. Wealthy merchants of the late 1800s built these beauties, many of which have been restored and are located in one of the town's 2 National Historic Districts.

The main port of entry to Puget Sound and the first townsite on the Olympic Peninsula, Port Townsend started off with a bang. Platted in 1852, by the late 1880s the town prospered as a busy seaport; it reached its all-time peak population of 7,000 in 1890. An official port of entry, Port Townsend hosted consulates and agencies from Chile, Sweden, Norway, Germany, France, Great Britain, and Hawaii during its prime. From there it was all downhill: the transcontinental Union Pacific railroad opted for a Seattle junction rather than a Port Townsend one, and Seattle and Tacoma ports siphoned off much of the town's shipping. Over the years, military bases and a pulp and paper mill restored Port Townsend's economic stability; today, tourism accounts for a good deal of the town's prosperity.

SIGHTS

Parks
On Point Wilson on the Strait of Juan de Fuca, **Fort Worden State Park** (the only army fort named for a navy man), houses a collection of Victorian homes, historical army barracks, and hidden bunkers. Modern facilities include a campground with 50 hookup sites, underwater park, boat launch, tennis courts, and hiking trails, including a 30-minute self-guided historic walk. If it looks familiar, it may be because the movie, *An Officer and a Gentleman,* was filmed here. Also at the park is the **Port Townsend Marine Science Center,** 385-5582, located on the dock. "Wet tables" offer intimate, hands-on relationships with local sea creatures; beach walks, evening slide shows and lectures, seaweed workshops, and fish-printing classes are given for an optional donation. Lodging is available in the officers' quarters and camping is permitted with advance reservation or pre-registration upon arrival; write Fort Worden State Park, Box 574, Port Townsend, WA 98368, or call 385-4730.

Chetzemoka Park on the Admiralty Inlet at Jackson and Roosevelt streets remembers

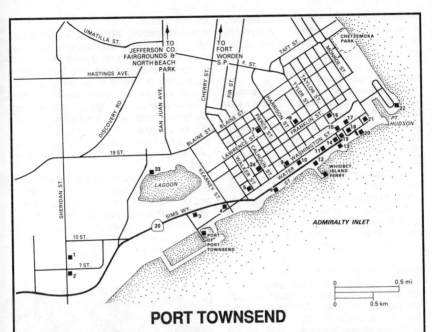

PORT TOWNSEND

1. Jefferson General Hospital
2. Manresa Castle
3. chamber of commerce
4. La Fonda
5. Old Consulate Inn and Port Townsend Motel
6. Tides Inn
7. Lizzie's B&B
8. Inn Deering
9. Heritage House
10. James House
11. Earthenworks Gallery
12. Palace Hotel
13. Lido Restaurant
14. Water St. Deli
15. Puffin and Gull Apartment Motel/ Sport Townsend
16. Rothschild House
17. Bishop Victorian Guest Suites
18. China Restaurant
19. North by Northwest
20. police
21. city hall and museum
22. Shanghai Restaurant
23. Kai Tai Lagoon Nature Park
24. Jefferson County Courthouse

© MOON PUBLICATIONS, INC.

Chief Chetzemoka, friend to the town's earliest settlers. Today the small, shady park offers picnicking, gardens, a bandstand (often used for weddings), and beach access.

At 12th St. near Sims Way, **Kah Tai Lagoon Nature Park** encompasses 85 acres of wetlands, grasslands, and woodlands—great for birdwatching—plus picnic and play areas, exercise equipment, and 2½ miles of trails. No camping or swimming.

Four miles S of town, 377-acre **Old Fort Townsend State Park** has 7 miles of hiking trails and 40 shady tent sites under tall firs,

sloping to a 150-foot cliff on Port Townsend Bay. The fort was established in 1856 to guard against possible Indian attacks, and in 1859 troops were sent from the fort to assist England in the San Juan Island boundary dispute commonly known as "The Pig War" (see San Juan Islands, p. 141). Old Fort Townsend saw sporadic activity through the 1800s until a fire, started by an exploding kerosene lamp and unstoppable due to lack of water, destroyed the barracks in 1895 and the fort was decommissioned. During WW II the fort was used as an enemy munition defusing station; in 1958 it was turned over to the State Parks Commission. A short historic self-guided walk starts at the display board near the park entrance.

Museums And Homes

Housed in the city's 1891 City Hall Complex, **Jefferson County Historical Society Museum,** 210 Madison St., 385-1003, has 3 floors of marine antiques, 5,000 historical photographs, a Victorian bedroom, and a research library. Open daily 11 a.m.-4 p.m., Sun. 1 p.m.-4 p.m.; donation requested.

The **Rothschild House** on Franklin and Taylor streets was built by D.C.H. Rothschild, a Port Townsend merchant, in 1868. Notable for its simplicity of style, the house belonged to the Rothschild family for nearly 90 years; the last remaining son, Eugene, donated it to Port Townsend in 1959 and it is on the National Register of Historic Places. Now restored, housing period furniture and surrounded by herb and flower gardens, the Rothschild house is open to the public daily from May to Oct., weekends the rest of the year, for a donation; 385-2722.

Historic Home Tours are held the 1st weekend in May and the 3rd weekend in Sept.; owners of private Victorian residences open their doors to the public. Tickets are $10 adults, $5 kids under 12, and may be purchased up to 1 month in advance from the Visitor Information Center, 2437 Sims Way, Port Townsend, WA 98368, 385-2722.

ACTIVITIES

Excursions

Inn Deering, a Victorian B&B at 1208 Franklin St., 385-6239, offers personalized excursions in and around Port Townsend for $250 per couple. Let them do the planning while you kick back and enjoy! For the price of 2 nights' lodging at other inns, here's what you get: 2 nights' accommodations plus breakfast at Inn Deering, 1 picnic lunch, 1 dinner, and 1 activity of your choice: windsurfing, fly-/cruise to the San Juans, fishing on Puget Sound, massage therapy, Champagne moonlight cruise, or music and theater.

On The Water

Sport Townsend, 215 Taylor S., 385-6470, offers kayak tours, windsurfing lessons, bicycle tours and rentals, a video library, and an assortment of outdoor gear. No kayaking experience is necessary to enjoy a 3- to 4-hour Mystery Bay wildlife paddle ($35 pp), a 2-hour historical tour ($25 pp), or a day-long Dungeness National Wildlife Refuge trip ($65 pp). Or, come home from vacation with a new skill—learn to windsurf in 2 full lessons, guaranteed! Try it out with a 2½- hour mini-lesson for $25.

Sea Sport Charters, Box 805, Port Townsend, WA 98368, 385-3575, offers salmon and bottom fishing charters, marine wildlife cruises to Protection Island, evening cruises with dinner at a waterfront restaurant, plus special excursions aboard the 42-foot *Cheyenne.* Phone for dates, prices, and reservations.

Jefferson County Courthouse, 1892

Anderson Lake, S of Port Townsend on Anderson Lake Rd. off Hwy 20, is an isolated lake surrounded by trees; it's a future state park site. Meanwhile, the lake is open for fishing only during the season; no camping, picnicking, hunting, or swimming.

Bicycling

Tour historic Port Townsend on a bike from **Coast to Coast** at 1102 Water St., 385-5900, or **Sport Townsend,** 215 Taylor S., 385-6470.

ACCOMMODATIONS

Cabin

Enjoy a romantic getaway at **The Cabin,** 839 N. Jacob Miller Rd., 385-5571. Surrounded by woods and water views, the cabin features a complimentary bottle of Champagne, fire pit, fresh-baked goods and a stocked refrigerator for a full make-it-yourself breakfast, all for $70 d.

Bed And Breakfasts

A Victorian B&B at 731 Pierce St., **Lizzie's,** 385-4168, has 8 guest rooms from $45-85 d ($6 less s), some with private bath. Enjoy the 2 parlors with fireplaces, leather sofas, library, and grand piano. Smoking permitted; kids over 10 welcome. Two night minimum weekend stay.

James House, 1238 Washington St., 385-1238, a Victorian mansion built in 1891, was the first B&B in the Northwest and is still going strong. Commanding views of the town and waterways, 11 guest rooms and suites range from $47-120, with shared or private bath; a secluded cottage with 2 beds and private bath goes for $75 d, $85 t. Limited accommodations for children in garden suites and cottage; no pets.

Another Victorian B&B, **The Old Consulate Inn,** 313 Walker St., 385-6753, overlooks Port Townsend from atop a high bluff, providing mountain and water views in comfortably elegant surroundings. The inn was built in 1889 by F.W. Hastings, son of Port Townsend's founding father Loren B. Hastings. Enjoy the fireplaces in 2 parlors or hone your skills in the large billiard and game room. Eight guest rooms all have private bath; rates range from $59-95 d. No smoking or pets.

Three short blocks from downtown, the elegant **Ravenscroft Inn,** 533 Quincy St., 385-2784, features a gourmet breakfast (served when *you're* ready), a great room with an always-lit fireplace, columned piazza with Sound and mountain views, and 5 guest rooms, all with private bath, for $63-85 d. No pets or kids under 12.

An annual part of the Historic Homes Tour, **Heritage House,** 385-6800, furnishes its rooms with museum-quality antiques and offers unparalleled views of the surrounding waters and mountains from its location at 305 Pierce Street. The 6 guest rooms are $50-83 s or d. No pets or smoking, but kids over 8 are welcome.

Built in 1871 by Captain Henry L. Tibbals as a home for his family, the house and guest quarters at 1208 Franklin were completely renovated in 1984 and became **Inn Deering** 3 years later. Three bedrooms in the main house are decorated with antiques and Victorian furnishings; the 2 rooms with shared bath are $50, the 3rd, with private bath, is $60. The self-contained guest house ($70) features private bath, kitchen, double bed and rollaway. Kids are welcome, non-smokers preferred; 385-6239. See "Tours" above for Inn Deering Excursions.

Holly Hill House, 611 Polk, 385-5619, built in 1872, has been beautifully maintained and renovated to provide 4 guest rooms, each with queen bed (Lizette's room can accommodate 3 persons) and private bath ($66-98 d, singles $5 less). Full breakfast included. No pets or kids under 12; smoking outdoors only.

Built in 1889, the historic Victorian mansion at 744 Clay St. is now an elegant B&B, the **Starrett House Inn** (385-3205). Five of the 9 guest rooms have private bath; some boast Sound and mountain views. Rates are $50-85; no kids under 12, pets, or smoking.

Arcadia Country Inn, 1891 S. Jacob Miller Rd., 385-5245, was built in 1908 and operated as a brothel, speakeasy, boarding house, and restaurant in the intervening

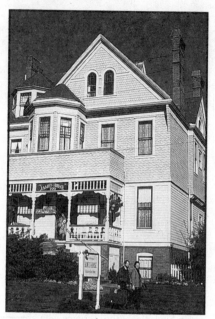

James House (1881)
was the Northwest's first B&B.

years. Today it's a B&B, offering 5 rooms with private bath for $60-80; children are welcome, but no pets or indoor smoking please.

Inns And Motels

Somewhere between a hotel and a B&B is the **Palace Hotel,** 1004 Water St., 385-0773 or (800) 962-0741. Newly renovated in Victorian style, the 100-year-old inn features a variety of accommodations, from small rooms with a shared bath ($42 s, $47 d) to kitchenette suites ($74 s, $79 d). Each room has a name and a unique identity: some are decorated with antiques and ceiling fans, some have water views or exposed brick walls. All include cable TV and continental breakfast. Children are welcome; non-smoking rooms available.

In the heart of the historic district, **The Port Townsend Motel,** 2020 Washington St., 385-2211, has 25 units, scenic and water view rooms, and free continental breakfast

for $48-78 s or d; pets are allowed. Just up the road at 2333 Washington St., **Aladdin Motor Inn,** 385-3747, has rooms starting at $58-80 s, up to $75-85 s or d for rooms with refrigerators and microwaves; every room has a Sound view. **Tides Inn,** 1807 Water St., 385-0595, has 21 units with complimentary breakfast, also allows pets, and was part of the filming of *An Officer and a Gentleman;* prices start at $48-78 s, $58-98 d. **The Bishop Victorian Guest Suites,** 714 Washington St., 385-6122, offers 13 1- or 2-bedroom suites with mountain and water views, complete kitchens, and continental breakfast from $60-78 d.

Puffin and Gull Apartment Motel, 825 Washington St., 385-1475, can accommodate up to 6 people for $50-58 d, $10 each additional double bed; no smoking or pets.

The **Manresa Castle,** an 1892 mansion at 7th and Sheridan, 385-5750, has 39 rooms modernized only by the addition of color TVs, private baths, phones, and electric heat. Prices run from $64-110 d; many rooms have bay views. Restaurant and lounge on the premises. Tours of the castle are $1.25 adults, $1 kids, which may be applied toward your room charge.

Lido Restaurant and Inn, 925 Water St., 385-7111, is a 100-year-old Victorian inn with 4 rooms from $49-75 d—or, better yet, enjoy the Take-Over-The-Inn Special with your loved one and 4 other couples for $240. If you can't make the inn, be sure you don't miss the restaurant (see below).

FOOD

Lido Restaurant and Inn on the waterfront at 925 Water St., 385-7111, is a 100-year-old establishment serving lunch and dinner daily (no lunch on Sat.) featuring fresh seafood and Italian specialties, plus a 4-room inn upstairs. The **Fountain Cafe,** 920 Washington St., 385-1364, is popular with visitors and locals alike, specializing in seafood (most notably oysters); open for lunch and dinner daily.

For a Mexican lunch or dinner, try **La Fonda,** 2330 Washington St., 385-4627, offering

Mexican and seafood specialties, margaritas and Mexican beers. The **Shanghai Restaurant** at Point Hudson, 385-4810, is the place to go for good, inexpensive Chinese food. If you're biking or enjoying a summer picnic, design your own sandwich at the **Water Street Deli,** 926 Water St.; wine, beer, salads, and homemade desserts also available. Stop by **Elevated Ice Cream,** 627 Water St., for espresso, Italian ices, chocolates, and fresh, homemade ice-cream treats.

Just out of town, the **Hadlock House,** 141 Chimacum Rd., Hadlock, 385-3331, specializes in jumbo prawns and weekend-only prime rib. Open daily for lunch and dinner. **The Discovery Bay Restaurant and Lounge,** 5781 Hwy. 101 in Discovery Bay, 385-1711, serves lunch and dinner with dining and dancing on the waterfront.

ENTERTAINMENT

The **Centrum Foundation,** a nonprofit arts organization, sponsors 7 major festivals and events from mid-June through Labor Day including Jazz Port Townsend, American Fiddle Tunes, Port Townsend Writers' Conference, dance workshops, and performances by the Tacoma Actors' Guild, all at Fort Worden State Park. Phone 385-3102 or write Box 1158, Port Townsend, WA 98368, for information.

Festivals
The **Rhododendron Festival** is held the 3rd weekend in May, with parades, dances, antique and art shows, a carnival, rhododendron displays, and the crowning of the Rhododendron Queen, whose handprint and signature are forever captured in the cement sidewalk downtown. The end of July brings the 2-day **Jazz Festival,** a Centrum event held at Fort Worden State Park. The 2nd weekend in Aug. is reserved for the **Jefferson County Fair,** the old-fashioned kind with livestock shows and 4-H displays. The **Wooden Boat Festival** is held the 2nd weekend in Sept., an educational affair with displays, lectures, and classes to promote interest in the dying art of wooden boat building

and restoration. Early Oct. brings the **Kinetic Sculpture Race** to Port Townsend; human-powered mechanical sculptures race over land *and water* to the finish. This race is a derivation of the Ferndale, California 3-day 37-mile world championship contest.

SHOPPING AND INFORMATION

Galleries
Water and Lawrence streets house numerous art galleries and antique shops. **North By Northwest,** 918 Water St., 385-0995, features Indian and Eskimo art, artifacts, baskets, and jewelry. **Earthenworks,** 1002 Water St., 385-0328, has native photography and other works of American art. Other galleries offer original bronze, wood, and stone sculptures, pottery, custom jewelry, prints, porcelains, and plates. Gallery Walks are held the first Sat. of each month, from 5:30-8 p.m. March through Dec., during which galleries hang their new shows, serve refreshments and often have artists on hand.

The Main Street Project
Not on Main St. at all but covering Water St. and intersecting Tyler, Taylor, Adams, and Quincy streets, this waterfront historic district houses antique and gift shops, bookstores, restaurants, clothing stores, and an ice-cream emporium.

Military Surplus
It's fitting that an area surrounded by old forts and military installations would be a good source of army surplus material; there are a few such shops along Hwy. 20 approaching Port Townsend.

Info
The Port Townsend area code is 206. For a self-guiding historic tour map or other information contact the **Port Townsend Chamber of Commerce,** Tourist Information Center, 2437 Sims Way, Port Townsend, WA 98368, 385-2722. For medical emergencies, dial 911 or contact **Jefferson General Hospital** at 9th and Sheridan, 385-2200.

*wooden boats
at Port Townsend*

TRANSPORTATION

Arriving By Ferry
Port Townsend is served directly by the Keystone ferry, departing from the W side of Whidbey Island about every 50 minutes. Fares are $3.30 RT passenger, $5.55 OW car and driver ($6.65 in summer), $2.25 OW cyclist. Other cross-Sound connections are the Edmonds/Kingston, Seattle/Bremerton, and Seattle/Winslow ferries; the fares are the same as the Keystone/Port Townsend route, but considerable driving is involved; cross the Hood Canal Bridge, then take Hwy. 104 W to Hwy. 20 N to Port Townsend.

Ferry To The San Juans
Calm Sea Charters, 385-5288, provides charter-passenger service between Port Townsend and Friday Harbor on San Juan Island. The boat leaves Port Townsend twice daily, May through Sept.; fares are $27.50 RT, $18.50 OW.

Bus Service
Jefferson Transit, 385-4777, serves Port Townsend and Jefferson County, connecting with Clallum Transit to Port Angeles and Greyhound to Seattle and Port Angeles.

Arriving By Air
Ludlow Aviation, 385-6554, flies to Seattle and elsewhere from Jefferson County International Airport; sightseeing flights are also available for $68 per hour for 1-3 people.

VICINITY OF PORT TOWNSEND

MARROWSTONE ISLAND

The island's biggest attraction is **Fort Flagler State Park,** at the northern tip of Marrowstone Island and surrounded by water on 3 sides. Boating, picnicking, crabbing, salmon and bottom fishing, wooded hiking trails, and camping in 116 beach sites are available in this 783-acre park. Located in the Olympic rain shadow, the park only gets 17 inches of rain per year. Along with Fort Worden and Whidbey's Fort Casey, Fort Flagler helped protect Puget Sound from would-be attackers in the late 1800s; today the fort is on the National Register of Historic Places. Campsites may be reserved in advance; write Fort Flagler State Park, Nordland, WA 98358, for information.

On the road to Fort Flagler, the park on **Mystery Bay** has a picnic area, beach, boat moorage, and protected waters for small boaters, along with striking Olympic views.

Lodging
The Ecologic Place, 10 Beach Dr. in Nordland, 385-3077, has 11 rustic cabins with Oak Bay and Olympic views, accommodating 1-6 people for $30-65 per night, $180-395 by the week; each comes with complete kitchen and bath facilities, plus a wood stove. The owners stress that they are not a motel and prefer not to rent cabins for a single night. No pets, campers, or trailers, and only small boats can be launched at the beach; kids under 8 are OK in July and August. Canoes are available for rent for Oak Bay paddling, where waterfowl and other wildlife can be seen.

CHIMACUM

Fifteen minutes S of Port Townsend, this wide-open, slow-paced farming community doesn't have a great deal to offer; but **The Summer House,** 2603 Center Rd., 732-4017, provides B&B luxury without a B&B price. The 2 guest rooms in this Victorian farmhouse share a bath for $30 s, $40 d, including a simple fresh fruit and pastry breakfast. Smoking is not permitted, but children over 3 are welcome.

PORT LUDLOW

The Resort at Port Ludlow *is* Port Ludlow. The resort offers the utmost in luxury: heated outdoor and indoor pools, jacuzzi, saunas, squash and tennis courts, paved bike paths, an award-winning golf course, a marina on Port Ludlow Bay complete with rental sail-

The Resort at Port Ludlow

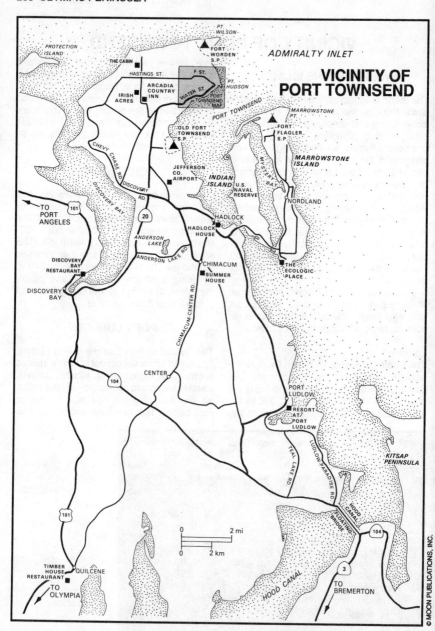

PROTECTION ISLAND

PT. WILSON

FORT WORDEN S.P.

ADMIRALTY INLET

VICINITY OF PORT TOWNSEND

THE CABIN

HASTINGS ST.

ARCADIA COUNTRY INN

IRISH ACRES

F ST.

WATER ST.

PORT TOWNSEND MAP

PT. HUDSON

PORT TOWNSEND

MARROWSTONE PT.

CHEVY CHASE RD.

DISCOVERY RD.

OLD FORT TOWNSEND S.P.

FORT FLAGLER S.P.

MARROWSTONE ISLAND

JEFFERSON CO. AIRPORT

INDIAN ISLAND

U.S. NAVAL RESERVE

MYSTERY BAY

NORDLAND

DISCOVERY BAY

TO PORT ANGELES

101

20

ANDERSON LAKE

ANDERSON LAKE RD.

HADLOCK

HADLOCK HOUSE

CHIMACUM

THE ECOLOGIC PLACE

DISCOVERY BAY RESTAURANT

DISCOVERY BAY

CHIMACUM-CENTER RD.

SUMMER HOUSE

104

CENTER

PORT LUDLOW

RESORT AT/ PORT LUDLOW

KITSAP PENINSULA

TEAL LAKE RD.

LUDLOW-PARADISE RD.

HOOD CANAL FLOATING BRIDGE

104

101

0   2 mi

0   2 km

TIMBER HOUSE RESTAURANT

QUILCENE

TO OLYMPIA

HOOD CANAL

3

TO BREMERTON

© MOON PUBLICATIONS, INC.

boats, and the **Harbormaster** restaurant, serving breakfast, lunch, and dinner with entertainment nightly (except Mon.) in the lounge. Room rates are as you might expect: $90 d for economy rooms, $99 d for a view bedroom, and 1- to 4-bedroom suites start at $130 d. But hey, kids under 12 are free in their parents' room! Call (800) 732-1239 toll-free statewide, or 437-2222 for reservations.

You don't have to be a guest at the resort to take advantage of some of their offerings, however. **Bicycle rentals** are available for $3 per hour; 437-2222. **Rowboat rentals** are $2 per hour, $6 for a half day, $10 full day; **sailboats** are $6, $18, and $35, while **power boats** are $10, $30, and $60. Six people can employ **Captain Mel** for a full-day sightseeing trip aboard his 40-foot sailboat for $100; call 437-2222 for info.

QUILCENE

The **Olympic Music Festival** is an annual summertime concert series held weekends from late June to mid-August. The Philadelphia String Quartet and guest artists perform their "Concerts in the Barn" ¼ mile S of Hwy. 104 on Center Rd.; tickets are sold through Ticketmaster, at the Timber House (see below), or at the gate when available. For a free festival brochure write Friends of the PSQ, Box 45776, Seattle, WA 98145, or call 527-8839.

Prime rib, seafood, and Mexican food on Monday distinguish the **Timber House,** a restaurant on Hwy. 101 ½ mile S of Quilcene, 765-3339. Open for lunch and dinner daily except Tuesday.

KITSAP PENINSULA

The Kitsap Peninsula is a quiet, somewhat anonymous appendage to the Olympic Peninsula—in fact, visitors and locals alike sometimes confuse the 2, thinking that anything W of Seattle must be the Olympic Peninsula. The only cross-Sound connections are via ferry or Tacoma's Narrows Bridge, preventing the Kitsap Peninsula from becoming another Bellevue. While the Kitsap Peninsula shares the inaccessibility of Whidbey Island, it doesn't share that island's striking natural beauty, so its tourism potential is also limited. If you had to draw the peninsula, you'd only need 2 crayons: forest green, since most of it is heavily wooded, and battleship gray, for Bremerton's shipyards.

tact the individual towns' chambers of commerce and public relations departments: **Central Kitsap Chamber of Commerce,** 9191 Bay Shore Dr. NW, Silverdale, 692-6900; **Greater Poulsbo Chamber of Commerce,** 19044 Jensen Way NE, Poulsbo, 779-4848; **Bainbridge Island Chamber of Commerce,** 123 Madrone Lane W, Bainbridge Island, 842-3700; and for Port Gamble info, contact **Pope and Talbot,** Public Relations Dept., Box 217, Port Gamble, WA 98364, 297-3341.

For fire, police, or medical emergencies, dial 911. The area's major medical center is **Harrison Memorial Hospital,** 2520 Cherry Ave., Bremerton, 377-3911.

SERVICES AND INFORMATION

The area code on the Kitsap Peninsula is 206. The people at the **Bremerton/Kitsap County Visitor and Convention Bureau** at 120 Washington Ave., Suite 101, Bremerton, 479-3588, can answer most of your questions and provide you with maps and brochures. For more specific information, con-

TRANSPORTATION

Arriving By Air
Serving Port Orchard, Bremerton, Silverdale, and the Tacoma area, **Bremerton-Kitsap Airporter,** 876-1737 or (800) 562-7948, provides transportation to and from Sea-Tac Airport for $10-18 OW; reservations are required.

Arriving By Car

From Tacoma, take Hwy. 16 across the Narrows Bridge and follow it to Port Orchard and Bremerton on the Kitsap Peninsula. Highway 3 takes over at this point, leading you to Poulsbo (off Hwy. 3 onto Hwy. 305) and Port Gamble, where the Hood Canal Floating Bridge connects the Kitsap and Olympic peninsulas.

Arriving By Ferry

Three points in Kitsap County are served by the **Washington State Ferry** system. From the Seattle waterfront you can take a 60-minute trip to Bremerton or a 35-minute crossing to Winslow on Bainbridge Island; or, from the Fauntleroy dock in West Seattle, take the 35-minute ride to Southworth on the SE side of the peninsula. Ferries depart about 70 minutes for Bremerton, every 50 minutes for Winslow, and every 40 or 50 minutes for Southworth. Fares are the same for all 3 crossings: $5.55 OW for car and driver ($6.65 in summer), $3.30 RT for passengers, and $2.30 OW for bicycle riders.

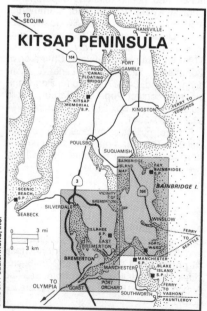

Horluck Transportation Co., Inc., 876-2300, provides ferry service across the Sinclair Inlet between Bremerton and Port Orchard for foot traffic only; the 10-minute crossing costs 60 cents OW, available daily.

Getting Around By Bus

Kitsap Transit, 373-2877 or 697-2877, provides daily service to Bremerton, Silverdale, Bangor, and Poulsbo.

Bus tours of the Kitsap Peninsula are available from **Open Rode Tours,** 738 Bay St., in Port Orchard. Among the offerings are 4 museum tours ranging from 6 hours to 2 days, a 2-day Kitsap Circle tour, and an 8-hour Hood Canal/Shelton tour. For specific information on dates and prices call 876-9305.

Getting Around By Bicycle

Lack of traffic and congestion make Kitsap County an excellent place for cyclists. A map of recommended bike routes throughout the county is available for $1 from the Bremerton-Kitsap County Visitor and Convention Bureau (see above). This "Kitsap County Bike Map" shows bike routes, other good roads, circular bike tours, uphill sections, difficult intersections, bike shops, campgrounds, and other points of interest, plus rules of the road.

BREMERTON

Surrounded by water on 3 sides, Bremerton seems a likely place for the Puget Sound Naval Shipyard, the "Welcome Aboard City's" economic mainstay since 1891. Since the U.S.S. *Missouri* no longer uses Bremerton as its home port, there isn't much for the tourist to see here, with the exception of the **Naval Shipyard Museum,** in the Ferry Terminal Bldg. at 151 1st Street. The museum has American and Japanese naval artifacts, ship models, and historical naval displays. Open Tues. through Sun.; donation. Call 479-7447 for information. The only other taste of the Navy that visitors can enjoy is during Armed Forces Week in May, when a parade, memorial services, softball tournament, and crowning of Miss Armed Forces highlight the festivities.

© MOON PUBLICATIONS, INC.

Bremerton and Port Orchard are served by Horluck Transportation's passenger ferry.

Parks

Eighty-one acre **Belfair Park,** 15 miles SW of Bremerton on Hwy. 3, has camping and trailer hookups, and swimming, and fishing on Hood Canal. Make reservations by mail from Memorial Day through Labor Day: N.E. 410 Beck Rd., Belfair, WA 98528, 478-4625.

Illahee State Park, 3 miles NE of Bremerton on Hwy. 306, has 25 campsites on 75 acres close to the urban area, with swimming beaches, boat launch, and pier for salmon and bottom fishing.

Hikers will enjoy the 2-mile trek to the summit of 1,700-foot **Green Mountain** for spectacular views of the Kitsap Peninsula, Puget Sound, and the Seattle skyline. From Seabeck Hwy. go W on Holly Rd., then take a L onto Tahuyeh Rd. for 1¼ miles to Gold Creek Rd.; turn L onto Gold Creek and follow it for 1½ miles to the trailhead on the L, before Gold Creek Bridge. Be sure to wear proper footwear: the trail is rocky and often wet.

Accommodations

Once the private residence of Colonel Julian Wilcox, the 1936 10,000-square-foot waterfront **Wilcox House,** 2390 Tekiu Rd., 830-4492, was described in historical accounts as "the grand entertainment capitol of the Canal region." Five marble and copper fireplaces and the original oak parquet floors are accented by antique and period furniture, and every room is angled to capture a water and Olympic view. Outdoors, a 300-foot pier can accommodate guests' boats. Clark Gable once stayed in the room that now bears his name. Five rooms each have private bath and king bed for $90-145 d. No pets, indoor smoking, or kids under 15.

At **North Bay Inn,** E. 2520 Hwy. 302 in Belfair, 275-5378, enjoy a stay in an antique-furnished farmhouse on the N end of Case Inlet. A fireplace, shoreline view, and sweeping lawn enhance your visit. Three guest rooms share a bath for $50-60 d. No kids or pets.

For budget lodging, rooms at the **Super 8 Motel,** 5068 Kitsap Way, 377-8881, start at $31 s, $34-36 d, and pets are allowed. The **Midway Inn,** next to the Black Angus on Hwy. 303 at 2909 Wheaton Way, 479-2909, is just as cheap: their 60 rooms cost $33 s, $35-39 d, with free continental breakfast, laundry facilities, and some kitchen units. **Oyster Bay Inn,** 4412 Kitsap Way, 479-2132, is a step up in quality with 100 rooms, a heated pool, and small balconies overlooking tranquil Oyster Bay. Rooms start at $38 s, $42-44 d. **Nendel's,** 4303 Kitsap Way, 377-4402, has free continental breakfast, pool, and adjacent restaurants; their 102 rooms cost $35-58 s, $46-64 d. **Quality Inn Bayview,** 5640 Kitsap Way, 373-7349 or (800) 422-5017, is the town's classiest hotel, with Mt. Rainier views, restaurant, 2 lounges with nightly entertainment, 2 movie theaters, an indoor pool, jacuzzi, and free child care for kids 3-12. They offer a

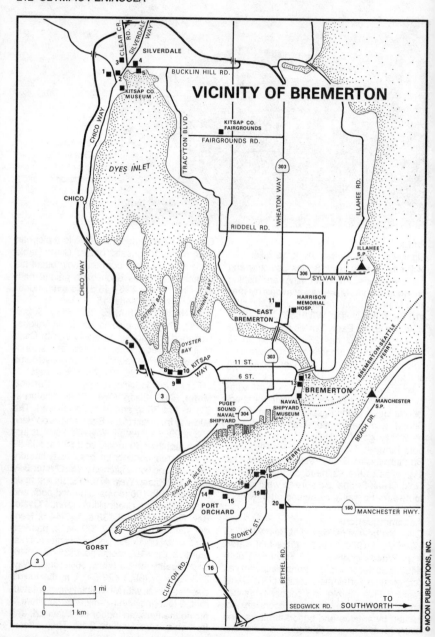

VICINITY OF BREMERTON

© MOON PUBLICATIONS, INC.

VICINITY OF BREMERTON

1. Kitsap Mall
2. O'Mally's Pub
3. Silverdale Cinemas
4. Poplars Motel and Restaurant
5. Best Western
   Silverdale Hotel and Resort
6. Bayview Inn
7. Super 8 Motel
8. Oyster Bay Inn
   and Hearthstone Restaurant
9. Best Western West Gate
10. Yee's Restaurant
11. Midway Inn
12. visitor information
13. Sinclair's
14. Clambake
15. Ogle's B&B
16. Tweten's Lighthouse
17. Farmer's Market
18. Olde Central Antique Mall
19. Log Cabin Museum
20. Vista Motel

variety of weekend discount rates with Champagne and other amenities; their standard room rates start at $35-45 s, $41-51 d.

Food

Next to the Oyster Bay Inn, the **Hearthstone** restaurant at 4312 KitsapWay, 377-5531, has moderately priced lunches and dinners specializing in prime rib, seafood, and steak; entertainment and dancing in the lounge daily except Sunday. **Sinclair's,** a block from the ferry landing at 232 Washington Ave., 479-7799, features moderately priced seafood with a waterfront view; open for 3 meals. For a Chinese Sunday Champagne brunch, or a daily selection of over 200 Cantonese and Mandarin items plus steak and seafood, try **Yee's,** overlooking Oyster Bay at 4180 Kitsap Way, 479-8222. Have nachos, a sandwich, or salad over the water at the **Boat Shed,** a mile from the ferry dock at 101 Shore Drive.

Theater

The oldest outdoor theater in the Northwest, **Mountaineers' Forest Theater** on Seabeck Hwy. holds outdoor productions in late May or early June. The amphitheater's log terraced seats are beautifully backdropped by rhododendrons, Douglas firs, and hemlocks; be prepared for a 1/3-mile hike from your car to the theater. For tickets and information write 300 3rd Ave. W, Seattle, WA 98119, or phone 284-6310.

Fairs

Every Aug. the **Kitsap County Fair and Rodeo,** 692-3655, comes to the Kitsap County Fairgrounds 5 miles N of Bremerton center off Hwy. 303. Highlighted by a rodeo, the fair also includes a carnival, circus, and entertainment. Younger cowboys and cowgirls display their talents at the annual **Little Britches Rodeo,** held at the Fairgrounds in mid-June; 876-2040.

PORT ORCHARD

Across the Sinclair Inlet from Bremerton, Port Orchard is a small waterfront community with an antique mall and other shops within walking distance of the marina and "foot ferry" dock.

Park

Follow Beach Dr. from Port Orchard for a scenic approach to Manchester State Park, at the entrance to the Sinclair Inlet, 6 miles NE of Port Orchard and just N of Manchester. The park's 111 acres include 50 campsites, trailer dump stations, hiking and interpretive trails, and swimming, fishing, and scuba diving in Rich Passage. You can rent a 13-foot aluminum boat with motor for $35 a day or $12.50 for the 1st hour, $5 each additional hour, from Manchester Boatworks, 9001 Main St. E, Manchester, 871-4040, daily in summer, weekends and holidays in winter. To fish from a pier, try the Harper Fishing Pier on Hwy. 160 on the way to the state park.

Winery

East of Port Orchard on Banner Rd., **Coolen Wine Cellars,** 871-0567, produces sulfite-free premium red wines and an estate-bottled Champagne. The tasting room is open weekends, noon to 5 p.m., or by appointment.

Museum

Housed in a 1913 pioneer log home, the **Log Cabin Museum** has rotating exhibits of Kitsap Peninsula history. At the corner of Sidney and DeKalb, the museum is open Sun. afternoons and Mon. mornings; free.

Accommodations

Overlooking the Sinclair Inlet, **Ogle's Bed and Breakfast,** 1307 Dogwood Hill SW, 876-9170, has 2 guest rooms in a comfortable, rambling 1-story home in wooded hills; breakfast is served indoors before view windows or on the outdoor deck. You can't beat the price: $35 s, $45 d. Kids over 10 OK; no pets or indoor smoking. The **Vista Motel,** 1090 Bethel Ave., 876-8046, has spartan, inexpensive rooms from $27 s, $32 d.

Food

For a semi-scenic view of the Bremerton shipyards with your breakfast, lunch, dinner, or Sunday brunch, try **Tweten's Lighthouse,** on the water at the intersection of Bay St. and Port Orchard Blvd., 876-8464. Their steaks, seafood, veal, chicken, and pasta dinners are around $12; for breakfast, be sure to try one of their enormous cinnamon rolls. The **Clambake,** on Hwy. 160 just W of Port Orchard, 876-3545, serves dinner every day and lunch daily except Sun., featuring steak-and-seafood combinations, oysters, red snapper, salmon, and prime rib in less-than-elegant surroundings.

Shopping

The **Olde Central Antique Mall,** 801 Bay St. at Sidney, 895-1902, has 60 shops specializing in collectible glassware and furniture; open daily from 10 a.m. Every Sat. morning from April to Oct. brings the **Farmer's Market** to Port Orchard, where fresh Northwest produce can be purchased at the waterfront on Frederick Street.

BLAKE ISLAND

Accessible only by boat, Blake Island has 476 acres of state park land with 30 standard campsites and 11 primitive sites, with excellent bottom fishing, scuba diving, a ¾-mile loop nature trail and 8 miles of other hiking trails. To get there, rent a boat from **Manchester Boatworks** (see "Port Orchard" above). Organized tours to Tillicum Village for an Indian salmon bake, craft displays, and interpretive dances depart daily from Seattle (p. 59) and Tacoma (p. 81), but only by special charter from Kitsap departure points. These charters are generally offered by **Open Rode Tours,** 738 Bay St., Port Orchard, 876-7292, or **Horluck Transportation,** Sidney Dock, Box 87, Port Orchard, 876-2300.

SILVERDALE

Silverdale's Kitsap Mall (see below) and surrounding restaurants and plazas have helped turn the town into the peninsula's commercial center. Just N of town is the Bangor Annex, a nuclear submarine base.

Park

West of Silverdale in the small town of Seabeck, **Scenic Beach State Park** has 50 campsites, salmon fishing and oyster gathering in season, with Olympic Mountain views on Hood Canal. To get there take Anderson Hill Rd. W to Seabeck Hwy., particularly pleasant when the spring rhodies are in bloom.

Museum

Kitsap County Historical Society Museum, 3343 N.W. Byron St., 692-1949, has musical instruments, photographs, toys, clocks, and nautical artifacts from the Kitsap Peninsula plus area information; open daily, free. After visiting the museum have a picnic lunch at the adjacent waterfront park on Dyes Inlet.

Accommodations And Food

Just S of the Bangor Submarine Base, **Seabreez Cottage,** 16609 Olympic View Rd. NW, 692-4648, features 2 loft bedrooms, sleeper sofa, washer/dryer, fully equipped kitchen, TV, spa, continental breakfast, and Olympic views, all for $99 d weekends, $89 d weekdays ($20 less in winter), with a 2-night minimum stay (or add $20 for a 1-night stay).

The **Poplars Motel,** 9800 Silverdale Way, 692-6126, has 53 rooms at $36-41 s, $44-56 d, heated pool, and attached steak-and- seafood restaurant, appropriately named the **Poplars Restaurant,** 692-5564, with dinners in the $8-13 range and dancing in the lounge. A giant step up in price and quality, the **Best Western Silverdale on the Bay Resort Hotel,** 3073 N.W. Bucklin Hill Rd., 698-1000, has 151 rooms from $65-75 s, $70-80 d, plus a glassed-in heated pool, sauna, jacuzzi, exercise room, pickleball and tennis courts, and room and patio service. Their **Mariner Restaurant** features excellent Northwest seafood; open for 3 meals.

At Silverdale Village, **O'Malley's Pub and Eatery,** 9447 Silverdale Way NW, 692-6976, features Irish food and drink plus steaks and seafood.

Festival

Silverdale's **Whaling Days** festival, held in late July, is the town's biggest event: a parade, arts-and-crafts displays, boat races, air show, sidewalk sales, 5- and 1-mile runs, and carnival.

Shopping

The first major shopping mall on the Kitsap Peninsula, the **Kitsap Mall,** just S of the junction of highways 305 and 3, has over 200 stores, including Sears, Lamonts, and The Bon. The mall is surrounded by smaller shopping centers, fast-food restaurants, and **Silverdale Cinemas,** a 4-theater complex at 9923 Clear Creek Rd. NW, 698-1510.

POULSBO

Poulsbo's first settler was a Norwegian who rowed across the Sound from Seattle and was reminded of his homeland's mountains, fjords, and valleys. Today, Scandinavian architecture and festivals perpetuate the culture of "Little Norway's" first immigrants, at least enough to add the tourist dollar to its mainstay industries of fishing and oystering. Poulsbo is also the "Geoduck Capital of the World." Pronounced "gooey-duck," the large, obscene-looking clam commonly weighs in at 3-12 pounds and lives up to 50 years or longer. Because of its less-than-appetizing appearance, the geoduck is largely used in chowders. In an effort to make it somewhat

more appealing, there's been a movement to change the geoduck's name to "King Clam," following the line of thought that changed the Spider Crab into Alaskan King Crab—but so far the name hasn't stuck.

Poulsbo wants to give the geoduck a good name.

Sights

Get friendly with a sea cucumber in its saltwater touch tank or learn about other Puget Sound sea creatures at the **Marine Science Center,** 215 3rd Ave. S, 779-5549. Open Tues. to Sun. in summer, Mon. through Fri. during the school year; donation.

Stroll down the boardwalk at the edge of Liberty Bay connecting **Liberty Bay Park** to the small arboretum at **American Legion Park.** Both parks have picnic areas, restrooms, and water access.

Sea Kayaking

Tours, kayak rentals, and instruction are available from **Poulsbo Sea Kayaking Co.,** Liberty Bay Marina, 17791 Fjord Dr. NE, 697-2464, including a kayak tour of the Dungeness Wildlife Refuge (see "Sequim," p. 196) with all equipment and lessons provided for $26.

Accommodations

Poulsbo's **Evergreen Motel,** 18680 Hwy. 305, 779-3921, has 60 rooms, some with kitchens and/or mountain and water views, from $32-38 s, $38-48 d, plus a heated pool, whirlpool, and playground. **Cypress Inn,** 19801 N.E. 7th, 697-2119, has 65 rooms for $41-49 s, $46-54 d, plus a small pool. For a more luxurious stay, try the **Manor Farm Inn,** a B&B at 26069 Big Valley Rd. NE, 779-4628, where fresh-squeezed orange juice, a hot tub, and a 3-course farm breakfast are just part of the pampering you'll receive at this working farm. The 8 guest rooms (all but 2 with private bath) are $90-120 d. A 2-bedroom farm cottage across the street goes for $165 d; a 2-bedroom beach cottage 2 minutes up the road has Olympic views, private beach, fireplace, and more for $230 d. Four- and 6-course dinners are available from $25-25 pp. No kids, pets, or indoor smoking.

Food
Open daily for breakfast, lunch, and dinner, **The Viking House,** on the waterfront at Poulsbo's Wharf, 779-9882 or 283-0920, serves steak, pasta, and seafood with the town's best-stocked liquor cabinet. **Larry's Best BBQ,** 19559 Viking Way at the S end of town, barbecues pork, chicken, beef and more in old West style.

Festivals
Poulsbo is a lively little town, with festivals and fairs taking place year-round. Over 50 bands compete in the annual **Viking Jazz Festival,** the largest event of its kind in the state. Held at the N Kitsap Community Center Auditorium, bands compete for 2 full days in Feb. starting at 9 a.m.; finals begin at 7:30 p.m. Admission is $3.50 adults, $2.50 kids; 779-5777. The **Viking Fest,** held in mid-May, has a parade, food, and games. The **Scandia Midsommarfest** in June brings Scandinavian food, music, and folk dancers to Frank Raab Park. The **Poulsbo Boat Rendezvous** in late July is a gathering of Poulsbo-built wooden boats at the marina, while the holiday season brings the annual **Yule Log Ceremony,** held sometime after Thanksgiving, featuring Norwegian folk dancers and a guest appearance by Santa Claus.

SUQUAMISH

The name "Suquamish" came from the Indian word "d'suq'wub" (apparently after much mispronunciation) meaning "place of clear salt water." The Suquamish were a peaceful people, spending their days fishing, digging for clams, playing with their children on the beach, generally minding their own business. As the white man took over, they were forced to surrender their own culture: children were sent to Tacoma schools, where boys learned trades and girls provided cheap kitchen labor, while the Suquamish men went to work at Port Madison lumber mills.

Historical Sights
The **Suquamish Museum** off Hwy. 305 is a good place to start a tour of Suquamish and the Port Madison Indian Reservation. Chief Seattle, his Suquamish descendants, and Pacific Northwest history come to life in this shoreline museum with award-winning exhibits and slide presentation, narrated by Suquamish elders. Open daily spring and summer, Tues. through Sun. the rest of the year; admission is $2.50 adults, $1 kids under 12, 598-3311.

Chief Seattle's Grave overlooks Puget Sound with a glimpse of Seattle's skyscrapers in a small, peaceful cemetery on the Port Madison Indian reservation. It's not hard to tell which grave is his: painted canoes are positioned high above the headstone to hon-

Chief Sealth's (Seattle's) grave

or this leader of the Suquamish Nation and friend to the early settlers.

A cedar longhouse 500-1,000 feet long and 60 feet wide, the communal home of 8 Suquamish chiefs and their families, stood at the waterfront site now called "Old Man House" until 1870, when federal agents torched it in an effort to subtly discourage this form of accommodation. Today a Washington State Heritage site, a small historical display marks the location of the original longhouse on a lot surrounded by housing developments at the W end of Agate Passage. After seeing the slide show and displays at the Suquamish Museum depicting the peaceful, everyday Suquamish life, this tiny historical remembrance will break your heart.

Festival

Chief Seattle Days, an annual weekend affair held in August at the downtown Suquamish waterfront park, has been going strong since 1911 with canoe racing, arts and crafts, traditional Indian dancing, storytelling, and salmon bake.

BAINBRIDGE ISLAND

When Vancouver sailed through Puget Sound in 1792, he never realized that Bainbridge Island was an island; it wasn't until 1841 that Charles N. Wilkes (of the famous Wilkes expedition) found Agate Pass, the waterway separating the island from the Kitsap Peninsula. Wilkes named the island for Capt. William Bainbridge, a Naval hero from the U.S.S. *Constitution*. Within 15 years of its charting, Bainbridge Island was home to one of Puget Sound's greatest lumber mills, and soon thereafter its ports were world renowned. Port Blakely had the biggest sawmill in the world, employing over 1,000 men, and the shipyard there built the largest sternwheeler at that time in the Pacific Northwest, the *Julia*.

Today the 4- by 12-mile island is almost entirely privately owned, by millionaires, politicians, artists, and a few fishermen, a full 85 percent of whom commute by ferry to their Seattle-area jobs.

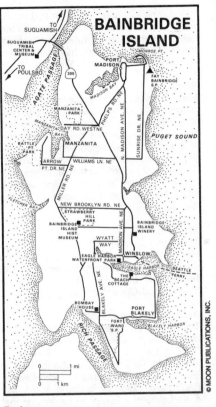

Parks

Two state parks make this island worth a visit: **Fort Ward State Park,** 6 miles from the Winslow ferry terminal at the island's S end, has 137 acres for day-use picnicking, boating, and scuba diving on a mile-long beach; **Fay Bainbridge State Park,** with a mere 17 acres, has 26 hookup campsites, hot showers, and beach access with scuba diving and boating facilities at the island's NE end.

City and district parks include **Strawberry Hill Park** on High School Rd., 18 acres with ball fields and a museum; **Battle Point Park,** on the island's W side on Battle Point Dr. NE, with 90 acres of jogging trails, ballfields, tennis courts, gardens, and a pond; **Manzanita Park,** on Day Rd. on the NW side of the island, with 120 acres of hiking and equestrian trails, but, unfortunately, no horse rentals; and **Eagle Harbor Waterfront Park** with picnic tables, play areas, trails, and a boat launch on the waterfront in Winslow.

Winery

Family-operated **Bainbridge Island Winery,** ¼ mile from the ferry terminal at 682 Hwy. 305 in Winslow, is the only place (outside of a restaurant) to buy their limited-run western and eastern Washington wines, including their increasingly popular "Ferryboat White." The outdoor picnic area is a refreshing spot for a lunch break. Tours and tastings are held Wed. through Sun. from noon to 5 p.m.; 842-9463.

Museum

The history of former mill towns Port Madison and Port Blakely is preserved in exhibits and displays at the **Bainbridge Island Historical Museum** at Strawberry Hill Park on High School Road. Open Sat. 11 a.m.-4 p.m.; free.

Accommodations

The Captain's House, 234 Parfitt Way (4 blocks W of the Winslow ferry terminal), 842-3557, is a turn-of-the-century B&B overlooking Eagle Harbor with rowboats, tennis courts, and an old-fashioned porch swing. Rooms are reasonably priced at $35 s, $40 d, and include a European pastry and fruit breakfast.

For a vacation from the kids try **The Beach Cottages,** 5831 Ward Ave. NE on Eagle Harbor, 842-6081. Their 2-night minimum stays are $75 d per night, but look at what you get: 1 of 4 cottages, either right on the water or 40 feet back, with Olympic and Cascade views; a queen-size bed, TV, stereo, fireplace, robes, and ingredients for a cook-it-yourself breakfast; and a waterfall outside your door. Weekly rates are $422, and off-season specials include a 3-nights-for-the-price-of-2 midweek deal. No kids or pets.

The Bombay House in SE Bainbridge Island at the corner of Beck and W. Blakely roads overlooks Rich Passage; country antiques, flowers, and a widow's walk add to the home's turn-of-the-century charm. Rooms are $50-68 d; phone 842-3926 or write 8490 N.E. Beck Rd., Bainbridge I., WA 98110.

Food

Noted for serving some of the best Mexican food in the Northwest is the **San Carlos Restaurant,** 2 blocks from the Winslow ferry terminal at 279 Madison N, 842-1999. Open for lunch Tues. to Fri., dinner daily. On the waterfront at the Winslow Wharf Marina, the **Saltwater Cafe,** 403 Madison Ave. S, 842-8339, features seafood, pasta, and Cajun dishes daily from 11:30 a.m. The **Streamliner Diner,** Winslow Way and Bejune, is famous for its hearty breakfasts.

Festival

May brings the **Scotch Broom Festival** to Bainbridge Island, highlighted by a Rotarian-Kiwanian Tiddlywink contest held in the middle of Winslow's main street.

PORT GAMBLE

A native of East Machias, Maine, Captain William Talbot founded North America's oldest continuously operating sawmill here in 1853. Modeling the city after his own hometown, he built traditional New England-style homes and imported trees from back East. The town has since been restored by the Pope and Talbot Lumber Company and preserved as an historic district. Walking down these quiet streets, shuffling through the fallen leaves, you'd swear you were in Vermont.

Park

Located 4 miles S of town on Hwy. 3, **Kitsap Memorial State Park** has saltwater swimming, hiking, fishing, oyster- and clam-gathering, boating, picnicking, scuba diving and 43 campsites on 58 acres; 779-3205.

Hood Canal

The 80-mile-long Hood Canal is not a canal at all, but a tidal channel; Capt. George Vancouver originally named it "Hood's Channel" when he sailed through it in 1792, but faulty records copying resulted in the name change. Today a 6,471-foot-long bridge, the

The Pope and Talbot Lumber Co. is still Port Gamble's economic mainstay.

Hood Canal Floating Bridge, connects the Kitsap and Olympic Peninsulas. The world's 3rd-longest floating bridge (the longest over tidewater) was opened in 1961 and served the peninsulas well until Feb. 13, 1979, when a violent storm with 100-mph gusts broke off and sank nearly a mile of the western portion of the bridge. Ferry service took over the job for the more than 3 years it took to rebuild the structure. Today you can cast a line for salmon or bottom fish from the fishing pontoon; there's a special angler's parking lot at the Kitsap end of the bridge. Just N of the bridge, **Salsbury Point County Park** has a boat launch.

For information on towns on the W side of the canal such as Hoodsport, Union, and Shelton farther S, see "Shelton And The Lower Hood Canal," p. 220.

Museums
The **Port Gamble Historic Museum,** downhill from the General Store on Hwy. 104, 297-3341, houses exhibits from the timber company, original rooms from hotels and houses, and a Forest of the Future display. Open daily from Memorial Day to Labor Day.

Of Sea and Shore Museum, housed in the General Store, has a book shop and the largest shell collection in the country. Open daily in the summer, weekends only the rest of the year; donations requested.

Nursery
The **Cyrus T. Walker Tree Nursery and Forest Research Center,** on the edge of town off Hwy. 3 (follow the signs), was established in 1976 to grow more than 3 million trees annually on Pope and Talbot lands. Tours of the facility include a look at 4 greenhouses, a water reservoir, pump house, a tree shade house, and a film about tree growing. Free; 297-3292.

HANSVILLE

The **Hansville Recreation Area** occupies the northernmost tip of the Kitsap Peninsula, NE of Port Gamble and the Hood Canal Bridge. This is *the* place to catch salmon in Puget Sound—most fishing is done quite close to shore, rarely more than a half-mile out. The facilities here are all geared toward fishermen: the accommodations are sparse and the lone restaurant isn't fancy. The historic **Point No Point Lighthouse** is here, so named by the Wilkes expedition because the point that was visible from one approach disappeared from the other. Tours of the light station are available Wed. through Sun. afternoons with a day's notice required; call 638-2261. The beach here provides good views of Hood Canal, the Admiralty Inlet, and Whidbey Island, but picnicking and fires are not allowed.

Accommodations
Captain's Landing has rustic cabins, a trailer and RV park, waterfront restaurant, pub with weekend entertainment, and boat and

fishing equipment rentals. Open year-round, the cabins run from $47-60 with a maximum 6 persons in each. Trailers and RVs can park for $18.50 for waterfront space, $14 off waterfront; non-hookup spaces are available for $10-12 per night. Boat rentals are $75 per day with motor, $25 without motor. Call 638-2257 or write Box 113, Hansville, WA 98340.

SHELTON AND THE LOWER HOOD CANAL

Mason County, of which Shelton is the county seat, is 1 of the nation's largest Christmas tree producing areas; every year, over 3 million trees are shipped worldwide. Originally named Sheltonville, the town was founded in 1855 by David Shelton, although its plat wasn't officially recorded until 1884. Forestry, farming, fishing, and oystering were and still are the primary industries here, beginning in 1878 when the first shipment of oysters left Kamilche. Shelton, a blue-collar town of about 7,600, is the only incorporated city in the county. Lake Cushman is a popular fishing and summer recreation spot, just E of the Staircase entrance to Olympic National Park (p. 179), and the dam at the lake's SE end produces a part of Tacoma's electricity. Hoodsport's winery and Union's waterfront resort attract some visitors, but for the most part the lower Hood Canal area is largely undeveloped.

SIGHTS

Parks
Eight miles W of Belfair on Hwy. 106, **Twanoh State Park** is a popular spot for swimming and waterskiing on Hood Canal. The park also has tennis courts, a concession stand for snacks and groceries, and camping at 30 standard ($7) and 9 hookup ($9.50) sites.

Enjoy diving, clamming, crabbing, and fishing in Hood Canal at **Potlatch State Park,** 12 miles N of Shelton on Hwy. 101. Have a picnic on the water, or explore the underwater park; camp across the street at 17 standard ($7) and 18 full-hookup ($9.50) sites.

You'll need a boat to get to 2 other Shelton-area state parks: **Squaxin Island State Park,** between Shelton and Hartstene Island, has 20 primitive campsites ($3 plus a boat moorage fee from $4-6); **Stretch Point State Park,** 12 miles N of Shelton, has no camping, showers, toilets, or drinking water, but has 1 of the best sandy beaches around Puget Sound.

Lake Cushman was a popular resort area at the turn of the century, offering fishing, hiking, and hunting. By the 1920s, the 2 lakeside resorts had shut down and the City of Tacoma had planned a dam on the Skokomish River. When completed, the dam increased the lake's size tenfold to 4,000 acres. Though private summer homes are springing up around the lake, the area still has a decidedly remote feel, thanks in part to its protected neighbor, Olympic National Park, about 10 miles up the road. **Lake Cushman State Park,** 7 miles W of Hoodsport, is a popular spot with fishermen: cutthroat, kokanee, and rainbow trout inhabit the lake, the home of the only known entirely freshwater king salmon run. Hikers will enjoy the 4 miles of hiking trails at the park, leading from lake's edge to deep woods; swimming, water skiing, and, in winter, cross-country skiing, are also popular. Camp at 1 of 50 standard ($7) campsites or 30 hookup ($9.50) sites.

A mile S of Brinnon on Hwy. 101, **Dosewallips State Park** covers 425 acres at the foot of the Olympic Mountains, offering both fresh- and saltwater activities at the confluence of Hood Canal and the Dosewallips River. Enjoy fishing for salmon and bottom fish in the canal, steelhead in the river, or clamming, crabbing, and oystering on the shores of the canal; there's a public boat launch 6 miles N of the park at Whitney Point. Stay at 1 of 113 campsites, 40 with full hookup, for $7-9.50 per night. Two miles S of Brinnon, **Pleasant Harbor State Park** has a dock adjacent to a private marina; no camping, boat launch, or swimming facilities.

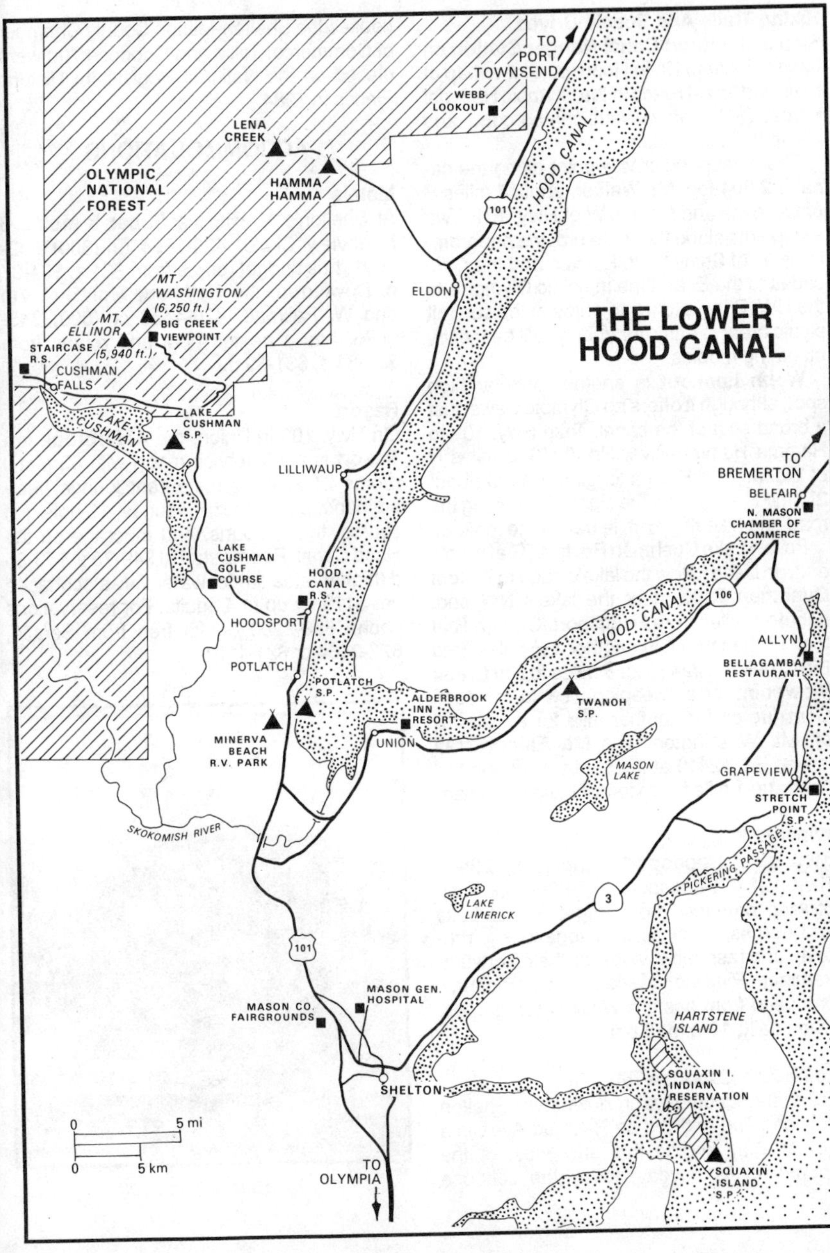

TO
PORT
TOWNSEND

WEBB
LOOKOUT

LENA
CREEK

HAMMA
HAMMA

OLYMPIC
NATIONAL
FOREST

ELDON

HOOD CANAL

101

MT.
WASHINGTON
(6,250 ft.)
BIG CREEK
VIEWPOINT

MT.
ELLINOR
(5,940 ft.)
STAIRCASE
R.S.
CUSHMAN
FALLS

LAKE CUSHMAN

LAKE CUSHMAN
S.P.

**THE LOWER
HOOD CANAL**

LILLIWAUP

TO
BREMERTON

BELFAIR

N. MASON
CHAMBER OF
COMMERCE

LAKE
CUSHMAN
GOLF
COURSE

HOOD
CANAL
R.S.

HOOD CANAL

106

HOODSPORT

ALLYN

POTLATCH

BELLAGAMBA
RESTAURANT

POTLATCH
S.P.

ALDERBROOK
INN
RESORT

TWANOH
S.P.

GRAPEVIEW

MINERVA
BEACH
R.V. PARK

UNION

MASON
LAKE

STRETCH
POINT
S.P.

SKOKOMISH RIVER

LAKE
LIMERICK

3

PICKERING PASSAGE

101

MASON GEN.
HOSPITAL

HARTSTENE
ISLAND

MASON CO.
FAIRGROUNDS

SQUAXIN I.
INDIAN
RESERVATION

SHELTON

SQUAXIN
ISLAND
S.P.

0   5 mi
0   5 km

TO
OLYMPIA

© MOON PUBLICATIONS, INC.

Hiking Trails And Scenic Drives

Stop at the **Hood Canal Ranger Station** on Lake Cushman Dr. in Hoodsport for a map of trails and forest roads in the Olympic National Forest ($1), and current campground and hiking trail information.

The most popular viewpoint along the canal is 2,804-foot **Mt. Walker,** about 5 miles S of Quilcene and 5 miles W of Hwy. 101. Two viewpoints along the route provide panoramic views of Seattle, Mt. Rainier, and the Cascades to the E, and the majestic Olympics to the NW. Bring a lunch to enjoy at the summit picnic area; in early summer, you'll be met by blooming rhodies.

Webb Lookout is another popular high spot, although it offers no Olympic views, just a broad shot of the canal. Take Hwy. 101 to Hamma Hamma River Rd. #249, 2 miles N of Eldon. Turn R on a logging road at about 2½ miles and follow the signs. Park along the road and hike the ½-mile trail to the lookout.

Follow Lake Cushman Rd. to a "T" at road's end; go L and follow the lake's edge to 70-foot **Cushman Falls,** near the lake's NW end, about 11 miles from Hoodsport. Or, turn R at the "T," then turn L in another 1½ miles onto Big Creek Rd. #2419 for 6 miles to **Big Creek Viewpoint** for a sweeping view to the east. Continue on for another mile for a waterfall off Mt. Washington. The **Mt. Ellinor Trail** leaves Rd. #2419 at the 5-mile point; the trail heads up 1 mile for a view of Lake Cushman.

Winery

Stop in at **Hoodsport Winery,** N. 23501 Hwy. 101 in Hoodsport, 877-9894, for a sip of wine produced from Puget Sound fruits and berries, such as their loganberry, rhubarb, and raspberry wines, or their Gerwürztraminer, Riesling, Merlot, or Chardonnay, produced from eastern Washington grapes. Open daily, 10 a.m.-6 p.m.

Tollie And Caboose 700

Tollie, the locomotive in downtown Shelton between 2nd and 3rd on Railroad Ave., is a 90-ton shay engine that saw most of the country in its heyday; today the caboose houses the Shelton-Mason County Chamber of Commerce. Tollie and Caboose 700 were placed on the National Register of Historic Places in 1984.

ACCOMMODATIONS

Motels

At Shelton's N exit, the **Super 8 Motel,** 6 Northview Circle, 426-1654 or (800) 843-1991, has budget rooms from $31 s, $34-37 d. Downtown, the **Hallmark Motel,** N. 7th and W. Railroad, 426-4468 or (800) 345-5676, has a heated pool and rooms from $27-31 s, $31-39 d.

Resort

On Hwy. 106 in Union, the **Alderbrook Inn Resort** is a full-service resort with 83 motel rooms, 21 cottages, restaurant, lounge, heated indoor pool, jacuzzi, saunas, 18-hole golf course, tennis courts, and moorage on the Hood Canal. Rooms start at $49-75 s, $53-85 d (higher rates are for water views); cottages are $110 for up to 4 adults. For reservations phone 898-2200 or, toll-free from Seattle, 622-2404 or 621-1119.

Tollie and Caboose 700

Bed And Breakfast

Stay close to the Alderbrook for a fraction of the price at **Highland House,** E. 31 Hyland Dr. in Union, 898-4862. Enjoy the resort's golf, tennis, and other facilities while you stay at this cozy B&B for $24-36 d in winter, $30-45 d in summer, including continental breakfast; the highest-priced master bedroom has a private bath.

Campgrounds And RV Parks

Glen-Ayr RV Park, N. 25381 Hwy. 101 in Hoodsport, 877-9522, has RV parking and motel rooms on a rocky Hood Canal beach, good for clamming and oyster gathering. Open year-round, rates for RV parking are $14 d including hookups; motel units are $40-50 per night. Pets are not allowed in the motel; RVers must keep their dogs on a leash. About 3½ miles S of Hoodsport on Hwy. 101, **Minerva Beach RV Park,** 877-5145, is open all year with sites from $11 per night across the highway from the Hood Canal.

Real campers may prefer to stay at the free or very inexpensive national forest campgrounds, though these are usually closed during the off season. **Collins,** 8 miles W of Brinnon, has free camping at 9 tent and 5 trailer sites; on Hamma Hamma Rd., stay at **Hamma Hamma,** 7 miles in, or **Lena Creek,** 9 miles in, for $3. None of the national forest campgrounds charge more than $8, and most are in the $3-6 range; get a complete list, including location, fees, and numbers and types of sites, from the ranger station in Hoodsport.

FOOD

Shelton's **Capital Restaurant,** 102 W. Railroad, 426-1101, serves 3 meals daily, specializing in low-priced steak and seafood; the food is much better than the atmosphere. For Chinese food plus lunch and dinner buffet, try **Dragon Palace,** also near McDonald's at 2503 Olympic Hwy. N; phone 426-7975 for orders to go. Enjoy Mexican lunches and dinners Tues. through Sat. at **Hacienda,** 1927 Olympic Hwy. N, 426-7070. On Lake-

land Dr. at the Lakeland Golf and Country Club in Allyn, **Bellagamba,** 275-2871, serves moderately priced steak, seafood, veal, and pasta for lunch and dinner Tues. through Sunday. The restaurant at the **Alderbrook Inn Resort** in Union, 898-2200, serves 3 meals daily from a varied menu that includes steak, seafood, chicken, and veal dishes. Lunch runs $4-9, dinner $8-20.

ENTERTAINMENT

Festivals

Early June's **Mason County Forest Festival** in Shelton began as an effort to prevent forest fires; today the event includes a Paul Bunyan parade, an appearance by Smokey the Bear, a carnival, musical entertainment, an arts-and-crafts show, and logging competition.

The **Mason County Fair** is held annually the last weekend in July at the fairgrounds, ½ mile N of downtown Shelton off Hwy. 101. Highlights of the fair include the Olympic Peninsula Draft Horse Show, live entertainment, and traditional county fair favorites such as 4-H exhibits and cake and preserve competitions.

The **West Coast Oyster Shucking Championship and Seafood Festival,** a.k.a. "Oyster Fest," is held annually in early Oct. at the Mason County Fairgrounds. The fair's main event, high-speed oyster shucking, lasts about 2 minutes; the national record, set here in 1984, is held by Diz Schimke, who shucked 24 oysters in 2:41.31 minutes. Surrounding the competition are 2 days of wine-tasting, a cook-off, art and boating exhibits, dancers, bands, and magicians. Admission is $2 adults, $1 kids.

The holiday season brings Santa to Shelton during the annual **Christmas Parade and Bazaar,** held the 1st weekend in December. Santa lights the Christmas tree, then visits the kids at the 100-booth bazaar; the parade is set for Sat. at 5 p.m.

Golf

Golfers can enjoy the summer sunshine at the 18-hole courses at the **Alderbrook Inn,**

898-2200, or the **Lake Cushman Golf Course,** 4 miles W of Hoodsport on Lake Cushman Rd., 877-5505.

GETTING THERE

By Car

Shelton is about 50 minutes from Tacoma via I-5 and Hwy. 101; continue N on Hwy. 101 to downtown Hoodsport, then turn L to Lake Cushman and Olympic National Park's E side. An alternate route from Seattle would be to take the ferry to Bremerton (see "Bremerton," p. 210), then head S on Hwy. 3.

By Boat

For a scenic alternative to driving, take the *Spirit of Alderbrook* from Seattle's Pier 56 for a day-long excursion through Hood Canal with a stop at the Alderbrook for lunch; fares are $30 adults, $20 kids. Phone 623-1445 or see "Seattle," p. 59, for more details.

SERVICES AND INFORMATION

The Shelton and Hood Canal area code is 206. For maps or festival information, contact the **Shelton-Mason County Chamber of Commerce** (located in the caboose on Railroad Ave. between 2nd and 3rd streets), Box 666, Shelton, WA 98584, 426-2021, or the **North Mason Chamber of Commerce,** Theler Center, Box 416, Belfair, WA 98528, 275-4898.

For ambulance, police, or fire emergencies, dial 911. **Mason General Hospital,** 2100 Sherwood Lane in Shelton, 426-1611, has 24-hour emergency-room service.

SOUTHWESTERN WASHINGTON

MOUNT ST. HELENS

Prior to May 18, 1980, Mt. St. Helens had the most perfectly shaped cone in the Pacific Northwest volcanic chain. Often called "the ice-cream cone in the sky," 9,677-foot Mt. St. Helens was viewed as a sleeping beauty, popular with hikers, climbers, and other outdoor adventurers. It was silent for as long as any of them could remember—the volcano had been dormant for 123 years. On March 20, 1980, Mt. St. Helens began to rumble. By March 30, steam was rising from 2 brand-new craters, which had merged by April 4 into 1 huge crater measuring 1,700 feet across. Seven weeks of minor earthquakes followed. At 8:32 a.m. on May 18, 1980, Mt. St. Helens blew her top; the eruption had the explosive power of several atomic bombs.

Triggered by an earthquake that measured 5.1 on the Richter scale, the eruption blew 1,312 feet off the volcano's summit in a vertical plume of ash that rose 16 miles. Temperatures 15 miles away reached 572 degrees; the heat, volcanic ash, and debris killed 57 people and destroyed over 220 homes and 17 miles of railroad. The wildlife death toll was upward of 5,000 black-tailed deer, 1,500 Roosevelt elk, and millions of birds and fish; the economic loss included 4½ billion board feet of usable timber.

The damage wasn't limited to this 15-mile radius: 60,000 acres not destroyed by the blast were covered with over 8 inches of ash. Six hours after the eruption, the water at Castle Rock, 40 miles downstream, was over 100 degrees; towns in eastern Washington were coated with 2-3 inches of ash, clogging carburetors and shrouding the towns in thick darkness at noon. Traces of ash were detected as far away as mid-Montana, Vancouver, B.C., and the Washington and Oregon coasts.

Mt. St. Helens isn't ready for another long nap. Since the eruption, the volcano has had numerous smaller, dome-building eruptions and irregular spurts of activity. Plant and animal life is slowly returning to the devastated area. Hiking trails are being cleared, and a new visitor center relates the mountain's volatile history. But the mountain has permanently shed its light-hearted "ice-cream cone" reputation.

SIGHTS

Scenic Drives And Viewpoints

Until 1987, the area immediately surrounding Mt. St. Helens' crater was closed to the public because of sporadic volcanic activity, logging, and constructon, but now the "forbidden zone" is open. You don't have to be a climber to enjoy the view; you can get close enough for some striking photographs without even leaving your car. The close-up views are all on the E and S sides of the volcano, so you'll have to loosen your I-5 apron strings to get the really good shots. Be sure to fill your gas tank before you start your final approach to the visitor center or any of the St. Helens access roads; gas stations are few and far between.

Forest Rd. #26 and some of the viewpoint roads are not recommended for trailers or boats; these are narrow, single-lane roads with turnouts. For easier driving, drop off your trailer at the Woods Creek Information Station or Iron Creek Picnic Site on Forest Rd. #25 if traveling from the N, or at the Pine Creek Information Station if you're coming from the south.

For a quick trip, or for a good starting point from the N, take exit 49 to the new visitor center on Silver Lake for maps and current trail and road conditions. From there, continue E on Hwy. 504 to the end for a W-side viewpoint. If you get off I-5 at exit 68 instead, you'll find the old visitor center is closed, but follow Hwy. 12 toward Randle for a binocular view of the crater opening and lava dome, 3 miles W of Morton on Short Road. From Hwy. 12, shoot down Rd. #25 to #99; this will lead you past several viewpoints, picnic areas, trailheads, and Spirit Lake on its way to **Windy Ridge,** the closest access on the E side at the very edge of the restricted zone,

just 3 miles from the crater. Prior to the #99 cutoff you'll see Rd. #2516 to **Strawberry Mountain;** another good viewpoint, but not recommended for those in bulky motor homes. Continuing S on #25 (after backtracking from the Windy Ridge lookout), get a good view of mudflow deposits along **Muddy River.** If you're not in a motor home, take Rd. #2588 to the **Lahar** viewpoint, located on a mudflow close to the mountain's SE side. From Lahar take Rd. #83 SW—or, if you skipped this one, stay on #25 and go W at the Rd. #90 junction, *then* take #83 N—to everyone's favorite, **Ape Cave.** You don't want to miss this one; see "Spelunking" and "Hiking" below. From here you can take #83 S to #90, continue S to Hwy. 503, and eventually return to I-5 at Woodland, exit 21. Start early for this long loop trip: it takes about 2¾ hours to get from exit 68 to Windy Ridge, and another 2½ hours to get to Woodland—not including cave explorations, photo stops, and potty calls. Forewarned is forearmed: the only concession along the way is at Independence Pass in summer, so pack some Cokes and cookies. The all-important restrooms are located at the visitor center and information stations (see below), plus Ryan Lake (Rd. #2612), Bear Meadow (Rd. #99), Windy Ridge, Lava Cast (Rd. #83), and Ape Cave.

Winter travelers will likely be thwarted in their loop attempt; roads #25, #26, and #99 are generally closed by snow from Nov. to May, and the Ape Cave road is closed till April 1, regardless of weather, to protect deer and elk in their winter range. Call the visitor center's 24-hour info line at 274-4038 for road conditions before you set out. A parking lot, shuttle bus staging area, and ticket booth are located at the intersection of roads #99 and #26. Buses run daily in summer (including holidays), departing about every 20 minutes; fares are $1.50, kids under 6 free.

A new Spirit Lake Memorial Highway is planned to extend the present W side Hwy. 504 eastward to Coldwater Lake, with completion scheduled for 1991. The road will climb 3,800 feet above the valley floor, providing panoramic viewpoints and hiking access to Johnston Ridge, where you'll be able to peer into the volcano's crater.

Visitor Centers

The $3 million **Visitor Center** on the shores of Silver Lake, completed in 1986, features an impressive, $800,000 walk-in model volcano, a theater featuring an 8-minute slide show, a mural, and numerous displays. This center, at exit 49 (Castle Rock) off I-5, replaces the visitor center (now closed) at exit 60 or 68 near Lewis and Clark State Park—regardless of what the highway signs say. From late June to early Sept., park rangers give talks and lead nature hikes and car caravans from various information stations and viewpoints throughout the day; get a copy of the *Volcano Review* at the visitor center or information stations for schedule. At **Windy Ridge,** a ranger tells the story of the eruption hourly, every summer afternoon. The **Pine Creek Information Station** is open daily in summer on the mountain's SE side with educational videos and books for sale; the **Iron Creek Information Station** on Rd. #25 also has up-to-date information on conditions and viewpoints. At **Ape Cave,** naturalists lead a lantern walk through the lava tube every summer afternoon.

ACTIVITIES

Spelunking

Located on the S side of the mountain, **Ape Cave** is the longest lava tube cave in N and S America, and among the longest in the world at about 12,810 feet. Despite widely circulated stories to the contrary, there are no apes nor Bigfoots around Mt. St. Helens; the "ape-like creatures" that threw rocks at Mt. St. Helens miners in 1924 turned out to be a pair of local youths, not Sasquatch. Prior to the 1980 eruption, there were reports of 12- to 18-inch footprints attributed to Sasquatch, but no such evidence has surfaced since the eruption. The cave actually got its name from a group of local conservationist Boy Scouts in 1952 who liked to call themselves the "Mt. St. Helens Apes," in fond memory of the creatures of rock-throwing fame.

Tube caves are formed when fluid basaltic lava, called pahoehoe (pah-hoey-hoey), is crusted over with cooler lava during an eruption; afterward, the more liquid pahoehoe drains out, leaving a tunnel. Ape Cave is of the "unitary" or "throughway" type; other tube caves, such as the ones at Lava Beds National Monument in California, are of a more complex, intertwining structure.

The roof of Ape Cave is as much as 60 feet thick in some places and quite thin in others—spots which will eventually give way (a few thousand years from now), creating a trench. The cave's most famous feature is the "Meatball," a round ball of lava that got stuck above the present floor level when the lava was flowing through the cave; it's located about 2,500 feet from the metal stairway.

The main entrance to the cave is a lava sink, with cemented stairs leading down to the small upper level, and metal stairs down to the main level. The temperature in the cave is about 42 degrees, year-round, so wear warm clothing, gloves, and hiking boots, or comfortable walking shoes if you intend to stay only in the dry, lower part. This is not a tacky, well-lighted, guided tour; you're on your own, so bring *at least* 2 sources of light (a headlamp will free your hands). Avoid torches and flares because the smoke harms cave-dwelling insects and thoroughly annoys

other visitors; same goes for smoking. Keep food, beverages, and pets out of the cave; removing pieces of the cave for "souvenirs" is thoughtless and strictly prohibited. Ape Cave now has its own **visitor center,** offering sound spelunking advice and lantern rentals.

Hiking

Mt. St. Helens hiking trails are still undergoing clearing, reconstruction, and rerouting. Don't use an out-of-date guidebook or map (particularly pre-1980!), and check in at a ranger station for current trail conditions and routes. Fresh water for canteen-filling is available at Meta Lake, Norway Pass, and Pine Creek.

A short, 1/8-mile paved trail at **Meta Lake** on the NE side of the mountain takes you through a grove of trees that survived the 1980 blast by virtue of a deep snowcover. Another easy trail is the 1-mile loop at **Cedar Flats,** 3 miles N of the Pine Creek Information Station on Rd. #25. Here you'll see a preserved old-growth forest, with Douglas firs and western red cedars topping 600 years old.

On Rd. #26 on the E side you'll find the **Norway Pass** trailhead. This new, 2.2-mile OW hike takes about 1¾ hours each way and passes a "blowdown" forest (leveled by the force of the eruption) on its way to spectacular views of crater waterfalls, the lava dome, and Spirit Lake. **Ape Canyon Trail** is a long, 5½-mile OW hike well worth the effort. Starting at the Lahar viewpoint, the trail climbs a ridge to the pumice Plains of Abraham, upward to the treeless top of Ape Canyon, with striking views of mounts Adams, Rainier, Hood, and St. Helens.

Not far from Mt. St. Helens is **Goat Rocks Wilderness,** about an hour E of Randle on Hwy. 12; see "Mt. Rainier," p. 99, for hiking and camping here. Mt. Adams, due E of Mt. St. Helens on the opposite side of Gifford Pinchot National Forest, is covered in a separate chapter beginning on p. 233.

Climbing

After the eruption, Mt. St. Helens' summit was closed to climbers until early 1987, although scores of climbers, clad in white to blend in with the snow, completed the illegal ascent in the interim. The earliest "legal" climbers described the accomplishment as a good winter day hike, with no technical climbing involved, although a snow precipice at the crater rim invites disaster as it tempts you further and further over the edge for a closer look.

A permit is required for travel above 4,800 feet or for entry into the crater. Travel on the crater floor is permitted when the ground is snow-covered, but camping in the crater is not allowed. From Nov. to mid-May, climbers need only register before and after their climb at Yale Park, 2 miles W of Cougar on Lewis River Rd.; from mid-May through Oct., 100 permits will be issued per day. Thirty of these will be available at Yale Park on the day of the climb; the other 70 may be reserved in advance by mail or in person at the Monument Headquarters. Even with a permit, climbers must still sign in and out at Yale Park.

Even though the climb is not technically difficult, don't underestimate the steep slopes and severe weather. Climbing boots, ice axe, sunscreen, crampons, rope, and a hard hat are suggested, and climbers should rope up near the crater rim.

Winter Sports

Forest Road #83's 2 **Sno-Parks** offer a wide area for winter activities from cross-country skiing and snowshoeing to snowmobiling. To use the area you'll need a Sno-Park permit, available at Cougar area stores. **Shoestring Glacier Lahar,** 4½ miles E of the Sno-Park, is another popular cross-country skiing and snowmobiling spot, made more exciting by dangerously steep gullies. For good skiing and beautiful views, take Rd. #81 W for 1 mile beyond the #83-#81 junction, then go N on Rd. #8100830. On the park's N side, **Ryan Lake** is usually accessible year-round on Rd. #26, 20 miles S of Randle, with open, flat areas for skiing or snowmobiling.

Seminars

If you're clever enough to plan ahead, you can get in on 1 of the field seminars at Mt. St. Helens offered by the Pacific Northwest National Parks and Forests Association. Scheduled in late summer, these 3-day weekend seminars cost $60-100 and include such topics as Mt. St. Helens photography, geology, and elk recolonization. For a descriptive brochure write or phone Pacific Northwest Field Seminars, Mt. Rainier National Park, Longmire, WA 98397, 569-2211 ext. 295.

Fishing
Salmon, trout, steelhead, bass, sturgeon, and smelt fishing is popular along the Lewis River from the Columbia to Mt. Adams, with access to Yale, Swift, and Merwin reservoirs and numerous recreation sites (contact a ranger for current limits and regulations). Unfortunately, boat rentals are rare in these parts; best bet is to rent from 1 of the RV parks or motels below.

Area Parks
If you get to the monument and the roads are closed, or the mountain's covered by a thick cloud, don't despair! Get yourself a picnic lunch and visit the parks and dams along Hwy. 12 instead. **Lewis and Clark State Park,** home to the defunct visitor center, has a 1¼-mile nature trail, plus 25 campsites. Across the street is **Jackson House,** a log cabin built in 1844 that was a popular stopping place for Oregon Trail travelers. **Mayfield Lake County Park,** about ¼ mile off Hwy 12 just before Mossyrock, is open for day-use only with a boat launch, small picnic area, and playground. Follow Hwy. 12 E to Mossyrock and the **Mayfield Dam;** there's a nice roadside viewpoint about 3 miles E of Mossyrock on 12. To get to **Mossyrock Dam Park,** turn S at the Mossyrock light and follow the signs 3 miles east. Here you'll find hundreds of campsites, picnic tables, and boat launches on beautiful green-blue Riffe Lake. The 23½-mile-long lake was dam-created in 1968; originally named Davisson Lake after Ira S. Davisson, a public power pioneer. The lake was renamed Riffe Lake in 1976 to honor the settlers of Riffe, founded in 1898 and now covered by about 225 feet of water. If you turn N at the Mossyrock light you'll eventually get to **Ike Kinswa State Park,** about 3 miles off the highway. The park is open year-round for trout fishing on Mayfield Lake, with swimming, picnicking, and 101 campsites on the lake (41 with hookups).

Across from the new visitor center on Silver Lake, **Seaquest State Park** has 54 tent sites and 16 hookup sites on one of the best bass fishing lakes in the state.

All state park campgrounds charge $7-9.50 per night. For other specific information on camping in the state parks, see p. 111.

ACCOMMODATIONS

Bed And Breakfast
Six miles E of Morton on Hwy. 12, **St. Helens Manorhouse,** 498-5243, is a 1910 3-story Douglas fir home, with 4 bedrooms (private and shared baths) for $36 s, $49 d. A full breakfast is included. No kids, pets, or indoor smoking.

Resort
Five miles N of Morton on Hwy. 7, **Resort of the Mountains** is a natural health center with motel accommodations, a natural foods store and restaurant, exercise room, and organic garden—definitely not for the Cheetos-and-beer crowd. Rooms all have fireplaces, kitchens, and dishwashers for $40 s, $50 d. Reservations are required; write 1130 Morton Rd., Morton, WA 98356, or phone 496-5885.

Cabins And Motels
In Morton, the **Evergreen Motel,** 496-5407, has budget rooms for $21 s or d. On Hwy. 12, 13 miles E of exit 68, the **Lake Mayfield Motel and Restaurant,** 985-2484, has 8 rooms for $30 d, with a full-service family restaurant specializing in homemade rolls and desserts. The **Mt. St. Helens Motel,** 227 Spirit Lake Hwy. in Castle Rock, 274-7721, has 32 rooms for $30 s, $32 d, and laundry facilities just 5 miles from the visitor center. At 3201 Spirit Lake Hwy. in Silver Lake, **Silver Lake Motel and Resort,** 274-6141, has motel rooms, rustic 2-bedroom cabins, RV and tent sites, plus boat rentals for fishing. Open year-round. Rooms are $45 d, $60 for 2-4 persons, with a porch over the water; full RV hookups

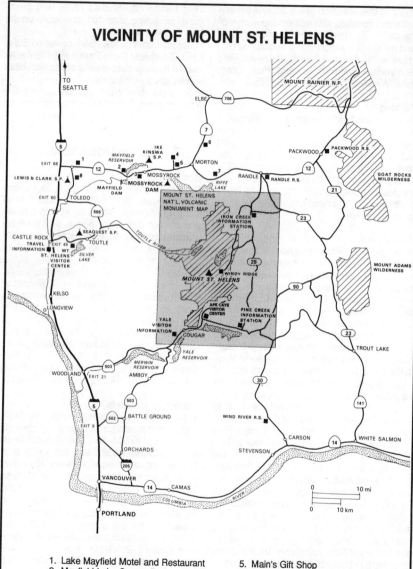

VICINITY OF MOUNT ST. HELENS

1. Lake Mayfield Motel and Restaurant
2. Mayfield Lake County Park
3. Mountain Road Inn
4. Short Road Viewpoint
5. Main's Gift Shop
6. Resort of the Mountains
7. St. Helens Manorhouse
8. Jackson House

are $12.50, tent spaces $9; motorboats are $30 per day, rowboats $12.50.

Camping

Forest Service campgrounds are concentrated on the S and SE sides of the monument. Near the town of Cougar, **Cougar** and **Beaver Bay** provide tent camping, first-come, first-served, for $4 a night on the Yale Reservoir on Rd. #90; go N on #81 to **Merrill Lake,** a Department of Natural Resources campground; **Speelyai Hill** has camping and an RV park. Go E on #90 to **Swift** campground, for $4 tent and RV sites just S of the Pine Creek Information Station; reserve a spot by calling Pacific Power and Light, (503) 243-4778. Farther E, **Lower Falls** has camping on Rd. #90. The only park campground on the N side is **Iron Creek,** open in July with 96 sites ($5 per night) 10 miles S of Randle on Rd. #25. **Tower Rock,** near Iron Creek on Rd. #76, has 22 sites. Cougar, Swift, and Iron Creek all have summer campfire programs from June or July through Aug., when a park naturalist gives talks, shows slides, or leads sing-a-longs.

Private RV parks in the area include **Harmony RV Park,** 2½ miles N of the Mossyrock caution light on Harmony Rd. in Silver Creek. They have 52 trailer sites plus 14 tent sites for $9, overlooking manmade Mayfield Lake on the Cowlitz River; for reservations phone 983-3804. On the SW side of the mountain, **Volcano View Campground,** 230 Hwy. 503 in Ariel, 274-7087, is open all year with 26 trailer sites and 15 tent sites for $12 near Merwin Lake.

See "Area Parks" above for camping in state and county parks on the N and W sides of the monument.

FOOD

You'll have to go into 1 of the neighboring towns to find something to eat; the monument has just 1 snack bar, at Independence Pass, open only in summer. In Morton, the **Wheel Cafe** has steaks, seafood, a salad bar, and chicken and sandwiches to go, plus a lounge, and is almost always open (7 a.m.-2 a.m.).

Also in Morton, the **Roadhouse Inn** is strictly sit-down, serving steak and seafood dinners plus breakfast and lunch; 496-5029. In Mossyrock, the **Mountain Road Inn** at the caution light on Hwy. 12 has nightly dinner specials and live entertainment Fri. and Sat. nights. On the W side, Toutle has a restaurant, drive-in, souvenirs, groceries, and gas on Hwy. 504. See "Longview/Kelso," p. 244, for more food and lodging on the W side of the monument.

SHOPPING

It wouldn't be a trip to Mt. St. Helens without picking up some ceramic or glass ornaments made from St. Helens' ash. **Marti's Ceramics,** 630 Westlake Ave. in Morton, has a wide assortment of souvenirs and also conducts tours of the ash-ceramic factory. Open daily April to Sept. till 4:30 p.m. **Mains Gift Shop,** 4 miles W of Morton on Hwy. 12 at the foot of the Hopkins Hill viewpoint, has a variety of St. Helens glass ornaments, ceramics, petrified wood, gemstones, and the usual T-shirts, with a free video showing the eruption.

SERVICES AND INFORMATION

The **Visitor Center** at Silver Lake has all the maps and current trail and road information you'll probably need; they're open daily, year-round, and have a 24-hour recording for road conditions and other information at 274-4038. Another visitor center at Ape Cave can provide assistance and lantern rentals. The ranger stations can also help; they're located at **Packwood,** NE of the monument, 494-5515; at **Randle,** 497-7565; and at **Wind River,** 427-5645. For emergencies, 911 only works from the phone at the Pine Creek Information Station; otherwise, call the Washington State Patrol at 577-2050 or the Skamania County Sheriff at 427-5047, 24 hours. All St. Helens area phone numbers are preceded by area code 206.

For more general area information, visit the small travel information building just W of I-5 exit 49 in Castle Rock.

TRANSPORTATION

By Car
The Silver Lake Visitor Center is about 2 hours S of Seattle via I-5, or about 1½ hours N of Portland, Oregon.

Bus Tours
With pickup points in Olympia, Castle Rock, the old visitor center, and Randle, **Capital Aeroporter** has narrated bus tours to Windy Ridge from June through Sept. for $20-30, depending on point of departure. This is a good deal for people who don't want to take their enormous motor homes over miles of gravel roads, or anyone who'd rather soak up the scenery than drive; 754-9544 or (800) 225-3966 toll-free.

Departing from Tacoma, **Cascade Trailways** offers a full-day Mt. St. Helens motorcoach tour about every 2 weeks from late June through Aug. for $28 pp, including a box lunch; 383-4615 or (800) 824-8897 statewide toll-free.

A little later in the season, **Gray Line of Seattle** offers a 2-day "Mountain Connection" trip to Eatonville's Northwest Trek, Mt. Rainier, and Mt. St. Helens' Windy Ridge with overnight accommodations at Rainier Country Cabins (see "Mt. Rainier National Park," p. 99). Offered about every other week from mid-Sept. to early Nov., the excursion costs $133 pp d or s; phone 624-5813 in Seattle or write 720 S. Forest, Seattle, WA 98134 for more details.

Scenic Flights
A number of small aviation companies offer scenic flights over Mt. St. Helens for $25-35 pp, depending on the type of aircraft and length of flight, affording passengers a view of the crater and lava dome that you just can't get any other way. **Sunrise Aviation** is the closest to the mountain, operating out of Morton from 9 a.m. to dark; phone 496-5510 or 496-5207 for information and reservations. Departing from Vancouver, WA, **Vancouver Aviation,** 695-3821, offers 1-hour flights from Pearson Airpark. Departing from the same airport, **Aircraft Specialties, Ltd.,** 694-8971, also has 1-hour flights on an appointment basis. Aero West Aviation, 423-4902, departs from Kelso, and also offers Columbia Gorge and Pacific Coast air tours.

MOUNT ADAMS

Measuring in at 12,276 feet, Mt. Adams is no peanut; its snow-covered peak is as worthy of oohs and aahs as Rainier's. If it stood alone, Adams would be a prime recreation site, silhouetted on license plates and keychains. But from a Seattle viewpoint, Adams is geographically behind and below its attention-getting neighbors: Mt. Rainier, a heavily used national park, and Mt. St. Helens, a rumbling national volcanic monument. The lack of any good access roads (you've got to drive behind Mt. St. Helens along gravel forest roads) and the Yakima Indian Reservation bordering on the E, make Adams an isolated, under-utilized mountain. Those willing to venture out onto remote forest roads will find trails, unusual geologic formations, and scenic areas; if your goal is to escape civilization, this is the place to do it—load up your 4-wheeler and frame pack and go!

SIGHTS AND RECREATION

Viewpoints

Approaching Trout Lake on Hwy. 141, the **Indian Sacred Viewpoint** provides a spectacular view of Mt. Adams. For a closer look, take Forest Rd. #23—the main Mt. Adams access road—about 8 miles from Trout Lake. Just before the pavement gives way to gravel, you'll have a good view of the mountain to the east.

Ice Cave

Ancient volcanic activity formed this 650-foot-long, 4-section lava tube cave, which during pioneer times supplied ice for the towns of Dalles and Hood River. Accessible from Ice Cave Forest Campground, 10 miles W of Trout Lake, the cave entrance is a collapse sink, 15 feet across and 14 feet deep, connected to 3 other collapse sinks by passageways of varied diameter. Wear warm clothing and boots, and bring at least 2 light sources and a helmet or other head protection.

Lava Beds

The **Big Lava Bed Geologic Area** encompasses 12,500 acres of lava beds, remains of an ancient volcano. In the N section of the beds, the crater, now covered by trees, rises 800 feet; inside, the walls slope down almost to lava-bed level; a small meadow covers the bottom of the bowl. Another visually interesting feature is the 100-foot-deep trough or sink of unknown geologic origin, NE of the crater. When exploring the lava beds, be sure to bring your own water; by mid-June, all the creeks are dry. Take Hwy. 14 from White Salmon to Cook; at Cook, go N on the county road for 7 miles to Willard; then take Forest Rd. #66 N for 7 miles along the E side of the lava bed.

Hiking

Mt. Adams Wilderness, N of Trout Lake, and **Indian Heaven Wilderness,** just NW of the lava beds, offer miles of little-used hiking trails; you won't find Mt. Rainier's crowds here because the average day hiker isn't willing to drive this far into the woods on beat-up forest roads. So if it's seclusion you want, check at the ranger station (see "Services" for locations) for a map ($1) and rudimentary—but free—trail guide.

For a good view of the area's peaks, take a short hike to the top of **Little Huckleberry Mountain,** best hiked mid-July to October. Take Forest Rd. #66 (along the E edge of the lava bed) to the #49 trailhead; climb the steep grade for 2½ miles to the summit and a refreshing berry break.

The most heavily used trail in the Mt. Adams Wilderness is **South Climb,** a 2.2-mile trail from Cold Springs campground to timberline, where climbers depart for routes to the summit. Take Forest roads #80, #8040, and #500 (about 13 miles) to Cold Springs campground at road's end.

Beginning at Morrison Creek Horse Camp on the S side of Mt. Adams, 2.7-mile **Crofton Butte** trail follows the mountain's lower

Novice mountaineers often use Mt. Adams as a first climb.

slopes for scenic views of the butte. Take Forest roads #80 and #8040 for about 10 miles from Trout Lake.

Thomas Lake is a well-used 3.3-mile trail through Indian Heaven Wilderness, starting near Dee Lake and passing Thomas, Naha, Umtux, and Sahalee Tyee lakes before intersecting with the Pacific Crest Trail near Blue Lake. Head N on the main road from Carson, then turn R onto Forest Rd. #65 for about 17 miles to the trailhead.

Backpacking

The **Pacific Crest Trail** passes through Indian Heaven, Mt. Adams, and Goat Rocks wilderness areas—some of Washington's most scenic and God-forsaken real estate—on its way to the Canadian border. The PCT hooks up with civilization near Bridge of the Gods on the Columbia River on the S, and at White Pass on the north. The 18 miles of the trail that pass through Mt. Adams wilderness are accessible from Forest Rd. #23, near its intersection with Forest Rd. #8810, on the S; on the N, the PCT crosses Forest Rd. #5603 near Potato Hill. Subalpine meadows, glacial streams, dense forest, wildflowers, and scenic viewpoints reward the adventurous hiker. The PCT traverses Indian Heaven Wilderness from S to N: start at Crest Horse Camp, just S of the wilderness boundary on Forest Rd. #60 (R off Forest Rd. #65); the trail

passes lakes, meadows, and forest for 17 miles through the wilderness area, then connects with Forest Rd. #24 near Surprise Lakes on the N side.

Climbing

Mt. Adams is 1 of the easiest Northwest volcanic peaks to climb; in fact, it's often used as a first climb by area mountaineering clubs. Before you begin, be sure to register with the Mt. Adams Ranger Station in Trout Lake. The S slope route is least difficult: it begins at the end of the road at Cold Springs Camp, at an elevation of 6,000 feet; follow the old road for 2 miles to Timberline Camp. From here the trail leads to a large snowfield. Bear R across the snowfield to the ridge, following the ridge to the false summit at 11,500 feet. A zigzag trail leads through pumice to the summit, for a 6- to 8-hour OW trip. Other, more difficult routes are described in the American Alpine Club's *Climber's Guide*.

ACCOMMODATIONS

Ranch

Glenwood's 160-acre **Flying L Ranch** sits in a secluded valley on the eastern slope of the Cascades, with a spectacular skyline dominated by Mt. Adams. Open from April through Oct., the electric-heated inn and adjacent

MOUNT ADAMS AND VICINITY

© MOON PUBLICATIONS, INC.

cabin can accommodate at least 15 people. Inn rooms start at $49 d for a small room, up to $64 d for the suite, including a family-style breakfast; the 2-room cabin goes for $50 per night. Dinners may be arranged for large groups; otherwise, you can eat in Glenwood or cook your own in a kitchenette unit. Kids can swim or raft in their small lake, or take a short ride on the owners' horse. Special summer naturalist programs are held by **Mount Adams Institute,** a nonprofit organization dedicated to the preservation of Mt. Adams; also, an annual **Artists' Retreat** features a slide show, 2 nights' lodging, 2 days' breakfasts and dinners, and plenty of time for painting and sketching the majestic mountain, all for just $75. Phone or write Route 2, Box 28, Glenwood, WA 98619, (509) 364-3488 for more information.

Camping

The Mt. Adams ranger district has 20 developed campgrounds. Most are free; there is a $4 fee at the larger campgrounds, including **Cultus Creek,** with 53 trailer and 10 tent sites, **Moss Creek,** with 18 trailer sites, **Oklahoma,** 23 trailer and 3 tent sites, **Peterson Prairie,** 19 trailer sites, and **Tillicum,** with 37 trailer and 12 tent sites. See the ranger at Trout Lake for a complete list of campground locations and facilities.

PRACTICALITIES

Trout Lake has minimal services, in the form of 1 restaurant, a small grocery store, and a gas station. For more dining variety and other services, head S to White Salmon or, better still, The Dalles, Oregon.

The area code for the Mt. Adams ranger district and surrounding area is 509. Get maps, camping information, and current trail conditions at the Mt. Adams District Ranger Station in Trout Lake, 395-2501.

GETTING THERE

There are 2 ways to approach Mt. Adams: from Seattle, take I-5 S to I-205 near Vancouver, then follow I-205 to Hwy. 14 and head east. At Underwood, take Hwy. 141 N to Trout Lake. An alternative is to take I-5 S past Chehalis, then head E on Hwy. 12 to Randle and take Forest Rd. #23 S for 56 miles to Trout Lake. The 2 ends of Forest Rd. #23 are paved, but the middle section—about 25 miles worth—is gravel. It's also about the most isolated road you'll ever experience, and any mechanical problem will be a major catastrophe out here, so be sure your vehicle is in sound working order and full of gas before you set out.

CENTRALIA

At first glance, Centralia and Chehalis seem like overgrown rest areas on the long stretch of highway between Seattle and Portland. Though these working-class towns aren't known as vacation destinations, they do share a rich and colorful history, some of the best antique and factory-outlet shopping around, and are 1 of the biggest baseball centers in western Washington. Centralia's population of nearly 12,000 makes it about twice as big as Chehalis, the county seat.

HISTORY

Centralia is the only city in Washington founded by a black man. George Washington was the slave of James C. Cochran, a Missouri man who, in 1850, filed a claim on the land where Centralia now sits. Washington, set free and adopted by Cochran, later bought the land for $6,000. He platted a town, sold lots, built a home, and donated a parcel of land for the development of George Washington Park. Within 15 years, Washington had sold 2,000 lots and named the thriving town "Centerville." During the 1893 depression, Washington hauled supplies up from Portland for his neighbors, offered interest-free loans, found work for Centerville's residents, and saved the town from economic disaster. Though a respected businessman, not everyone liked him, or his color: someone tried to kill him by putting carbolic acid in his wine. But Washington lived to be 88, when he died from being thrown out of a buggy.

Centralia is best known for what is often referred to as the "Centralia Case." The early 1900s brought a long, hard-fought labor struggle to the Pacific Northwest. Dominated by a Chicago union, the Industrial Workers of the World were called "Wobblies" after a Chinese member reputedly tried to pronounce I.W.W., and came up with "Eye-Wobbly-Wobbly." The radical Wobblies wanted to unite the workers of the world into 1 great union, take possession of production machinery, and abolish the wage structure. Though they tried to relieve the horrible working conditions of the times, the Wobblies allegedly resorted to violent means and spread out into political affairs. They strongly urged members not to enlist when the U.S. declared war on Germany in WW II. Their stance drew fire from the *L.A. Times* and others, who stated that I.W.W. stands for "I won't work" and "I want whiskey." In September, 1918, 100 Wobbly leaders were convicted of obstructing the war effort, and the Wobblies were finished as a major labor force.

Wesley Everest was a Wobbly leader who died a hero's death. In 1919, lumbermen decided to rid Centralia of Wobblies, and warned the organization through ads in the local paper. On Armistice Day, 1919, Everest was sitting in the I.W.W. Hall, on Tower Ave. between 2nd and 3rd streets, when members of the American Legion marched through the streets, armed; Legion members claim it was part of the Armistice Day Parade. Someone fired a shot; each side said the other fired first. The Legion stormed the building, Everest shot into the crowd, and was chased into the woods by the mob. He waded up to waist in the turbulent Skookumchuck River and surrendered. The crowd came after him, dragged him back to town tied to a car's bumper, and put him in jail. After dark, they came back for him, and castrated, hanged, and shot him at the Chehalis River bridge. Only Wobblies were tried for the massacre that left 4 Legionnaires dead; no one was tried for Everest's lynching. Three witnesses that claimed the Legionnaires stormed the hall were arrested for perjury.

SIGHTS

Historic Sights And Museums

Take exit 81 off I-5, then follow Mellen St. W for ¼ mile to the bridge where Wesley Everest was hanged on Nov. 11, 1919.

Mrs. George Washington named Iron, Maple, Pearl, Silver, and First streets, on which you can now find elegant turn-of-the-century homes, though often not restored to their earlier splendor.

The **Magyar Museum,** 2228 Harrison Ave., 736-4178, is open daily from April through Oct. with displays of Indian artifacts, wood carvings, antiques, dolls, and ivory.

Murals
Fourteen murals decorate the outside walls of downtown Centralia's buildings, modeled after historic photographs. The murals depict Buffalo Bill Cody, Centralia's founder George Washington, railways, ferries and sternwheelers, and buildings and scenes from Centralia's past. Get a map and guide to the murals from the chamber of commerce.

Parks
George Washington Park, downtown between Pearl and Silver streets, was donated by the city's founder and houses a library and playground.

At **Fort Borst Park,** a mile W of town off Harrison Ave., visit the 1852 Borst Blockhouse that was a strong defense against Indian attacks, originally built at the confluence of the Chehalis and Skookumchuck rivers. The house that Joseph Borst, an early Centralia settler, built for his young bride

Murals decorate Centralia's downtown buildings.

CENTRALIA
1. Casey's Pizza Mill
2. Country Cousin Restaurant
3. Motel 6
4. Park Motel
5. Ferryman's Inn
6. Casa Ramos Restaurant
7. Hallmark Motel
8. Lake Shore Motel
9. Peppertree West Motor Inn
10. Centralia College
11. Centralia Square and Antique Mall Cafe
12. Washington Park and Library
13. Candalite Mansion
14. factory outlets

Mary in 1860 still stands here; Borst boasted that the house was so well built it would last for 80 years! Tours of the home are given Mon. through Fri. by appointment only, 736-7687. The park is open daily, and also offers an arboretum, rhododendron garden, playground, and trout fishing for kids under 14.

Though Centralia has a number of noteworthy parks, they can be difficult to find, tucked behind shopping centers and motels. **Riverside Park,** on the Skookumchuck River, has a large grassy play and picnic area, hidden behind the Hallmark Motel on Harrison Avenue.

Power Plant Tour
Lewis County is the largest producer of electric power in the state, thanks to **Pacific Power and Light Co.,** a coal-fired plant 12 miles N of town. Phone 736-9901 to reserve a spot in their 2-hour guided tour, given Tues. and Thurs.; kids under 12 must be accompanied by an adult.

ACCOMMODATIONS

Bed And Breakfast
The 6,500-square-foot home built in 1903 for lumber baron J.P. Gurrier is now Centralia's only B&B, the **Candalite Mansion,** 402 N. Rock, 736-4749. Six guest rooms with full breakfast run from $50-100 d; lower rates

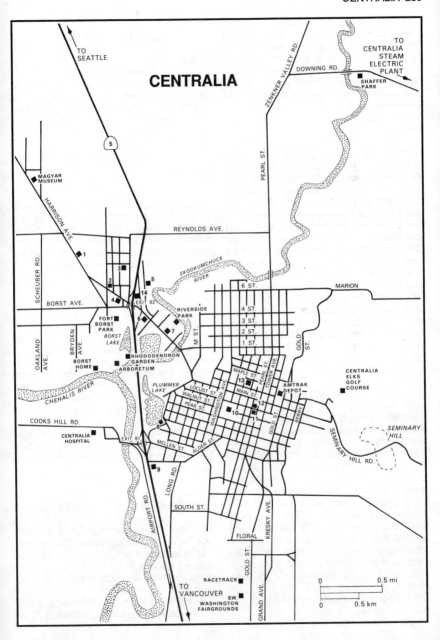

have double beds and shared bath, higher rates are for larger rooms with king-sized bed and private bath. Enjoy the ping pong and pool tables or just cozy up by the fireplace. No smoking or pets. Well-behaved kids OK only by arrangement; not a good place for rambunctious toddlers (breakables and handmade rugs!).

Motels

Just off I-5 at 1310 Belmont, **Motel 6,** 330-2057, is always the cheapest: rooms here are $21 s, $27 d, including a pool. **Peppertree West Motor Inn and RV Park,** 1208 Alder just off exit 81, 736-9362, also has budget rates ($20-22 s, $22-26 d) plus RV parking and a pool; pets are welcome. Across from Fort Borst Park, the **Park Motel** at Belmont and Harrison, 736-9333, has 31 rooms for $22-24 s, $25-29 d. Another bargain is the **Lake Shore Motel,** 1325 Lake Shore Dr., 736-9344, with 34 rooms for $25-27 s, $29-31 d, on Plummer Lake. The **Hallmark Motel,** 702 Harrison Ave., 736-2875 or (800) 345-5676, has a heated pool and 93 rooms starting at $31 s, $35-39 d. The **Ferryman's Inn,** just off I-5 at 1103 Eckerson Rd., 330-2094, charges $34 s, $36-40 d, and has a pool and spa; pets OK for a fee.

FOOD

Centralia caters to the tight-budget diner; expensive restaurants are scarce. At 1054 Harrison Ave., the **Country Cousin** serves 3 meals daily at inexpensive prices, specializing in chicken and steak; 736-2200. At 202 W. Locust next to Centralia Square, the **Antique Mall Cafe** is among the best, serving steak, seafood, pasta, and chicken from $7-13, plus Sunday brunch for $9; open daily for lunch and dinner, 736-1183. **Casey's Pizza Mill** has pizza, lasagne, and a salad bar at 2 locations: in Centralia at 1326 Harrison, 736-1156, and in Chehalis at 1340 N.W. Maryland, 748-7111. For Mexican food, try **Casa Ramos,** just off I-5 at 929 Harrison, 330-2045; open 7 days for lunch and dinner. For more dining, see "Chehalis" below.

ENTERTAINMENT

Fairs

Late July's **Pioneer Days** brings a street fair, arts and crafts, sidewalk sales, and music to downtown Centralia; 736-0300. Since 1909, the **Southwest Washington Fair** has been one of the largest summer festivals in the state, attracting crowds of over 125,000 annually on the 3rd weekend in Aug. to the fairgrounds at the S end of town on Gold Street.

Golf

Three golf courses serve the area: **Centralia Elks,** 1012 Duffy, 736-5312, has 9 holes; **Newaukum Valley,** 3024 Jackson Hwy. in Chehalis, 748-0461, and **Riverside Golf Course,** near Centralia's airport at 1451 N.W. Airport Rd., 748-8182, are 18-hole courses.

SHOPPING

Centralia's newest designation is Factory Outlet Capital of the Northwest. Just off I-5, 28 factory-owned and -operated stores include London Fog, Gitano, Corning Glass, and Hanes, and an additional 40 stores will be added to the Centralia/Chehalis area by the end of 1990 in an effort to draw shoppers to the developing downtown cores. Downtown's **Centralia Square Antique Mall,** 201 S. Pearl, 736-6406, is an antique collector's paradise, with 50 dealers displaying estate jewelry, furniture, and other collectibles; open daily till 5 p.m.

SERVICES AND INFORMATION

The area code in and around Centralia is 206. The **Twin Cities Chamber of Commerce,** I-5 and National Ave., Chehalis, 748-8885, or tollfree statewide, (800) 525-3323, has information on both Centralia and Chehalis and all of the surrounding area.

For police and fire emergencies, dial 911. For medical emergencies, **Centralia Gen-**

eral Hospital, 1820 Cooks Hill Rd., 736-2803, has 24-hour emergency service.

TRANSPORTATION

Steam Railroad
Take a ride on the **Centralia/Chehalis Steam Railroad,** either between Centralis and Chehalis or out to a railroad junction called "Ruth" in the Boistfort Valley. The railroad expects to operate on weekends, May through Sept.; phone the chamber of commerce for details.

By Car
Centralia is halfway between Seattle and Portland (about 85 miles each way), with Chehalis about 5 miles farther south. Driving S from Seattle, you'll know you're near Chehalis when you see the Hamilton Farms readerboard, proclaiming a generally obnoxious political message on either side.

By Train
Amtrak, 736-8653 or (800) 872-7245, serves Centralia from Union Depot, located (appropriately enough) on Railroad Avenue.

By Bus
Centralia's bus service is provided by **Greyhound,** 2604 N.E. Kresky Rd., 736-9811. **Twin Transit,** 330-2072, has service connecting Centralia and Chehalis hourly.

VICINITY OF CENTRALIA

CHEHALIS

Like Centralia, Chehalis earns much of its income from the logging industry, though it has a better sampling of restaurants than its neighbor to the north. This small town boasts the oldest church in the state.

Historical Sights

Visit the **Lewis County Historical Museum,** 599 N.W. Front St., for extensive local history displays including genealogical histories, photographs, and pioneer and Indian relics, all housed in a restored depot. Open Tues. through Sat., 748-0831.

The **Pennsylvania Historic District** covers 5 blocks on West St., featuring elegant turn-of-the-century historic homes.

Three miles W of town on Hwy. 6, the **Claquato Church** is the state's oldest, built on this site in 1858. The interior boasts handcrafted pews, while the bronze bell was shipped from Boston via Cape Horn. The church is open on selected holidays; contact the chamber of commerce for more information. The **John R. Jackson House State Historic Site,** 3 miles E of I-5 exit 68 on

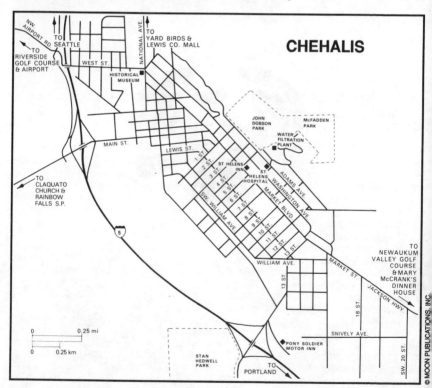

CHEHALIS

Jackson Hwy., is a half-acre park surrounding one of the oldest structures N of the Columbia, a log cabin built around 1845 that served as the Jackson Courthouse in 1850. The park is open daily, but the cabin is kept locked; free.

Parks
Swim or fish in the Skookumchuck River, hike, or enjoy a picnic lunch at **Schaefer County Park,** ½ mile N of town on Hwy. 507. **Stan Hedwell Park,** by the Newaukum River on Rice Rd., is a 176-acre park with hiking trails, fishing and swimming areas, 6 athletic fields, and overnight camping, plus ornamental gardens. **McFadden Park** has 24 acres for picnicking, a good Mt. Rainier view, and the McFadden Log House, built in 1859 and Chehalis's oldest home. **Dobson Park,** just outside of downtown, is also 24 acres with hiking trails, playground equipment, and a picnic area.

West of Chehalis, 18 miles down Hwy. 6, is **Rainbow Falls State Park.** Constructed by the Civilian Conservation Corps in the 1930s, it features a swinging bridge over the Chehalis River, hiking trails, and play equipment, plus 47 standard ($7) campsites (no hookups).

Rainbow Falls State Park

Accommodations
Nine miles S of Chehalis, **Whispering River Inn,** 149 Mosley Rd., 262-9859, is a 2-story colonial home near the Newaukum River. Relax in the porch swing, enjoy the parlor fireplace, or take a walk along the river. Two rooms share a bath, and breakfast is continental; rates are quite reasonable at $35 s, $40 d. No kids or smoking.

The **Cascade Motel,** 550 S.W. Parkland Dr., 748-8608, has 29 budget rooms for $31-37 d. The **Best Western Pony Soldier Motor Inn,** 122 Interstate Ave. at exit 76, 748-0101, offers free continental breakfast, a heated pool, and 69 rooms with queen-size beds for $38-50s, $42-54 d.

Food
Mary McCrank's Dinner House, 4 miles S of town at 2923 Jackson Hwy., 748-3662, has

been serving home-style cooking in a farmhouse atmosphere since 1935. Open for lunch and dinner daily except Monday. The **St. Helens Inn,** 440 N. Market Blvd., serves lunch and dinner, plus great desserts, in elegant surroundings (for moderate prices) in an 1890s hotel.

Festivals
In mid-June, rose growers arrive from all over the state to compete in the **Lewis County Rose Show.**

Shopping
The **Lewis County Mall** is the area's major shopping center, hosting 26 stores including Sears and J.C. Penney. It's at the N end of Chehalis, 1½ miles from town; take National Ave. N to Kresky Road.

LONGVIEW/KELSO

Though Longview's first settlers paddled up the Columbia River in 1849, it wasn't until the 1920s that the city experienced its first growth spurt. Engineers from the Long-Bell Lumber Company sought a new supply for timber as their resources were running out in Texas and Louisiana. Southwest Washington had an abundant supply of old-growth timber and, from a logging viewpoint, Longview's location—on a major river and rail lines—was ideal. Lumber baron R.A. Long founded the city in 1923, and Longview became the first planned city in the Pacific Northwest, designed with ample room for future development and an eye toward the aesthetic. Today, Longview boasts a population of over 31,000. Besides a thriving lumber business, Longview and its close neighbor, Kelso, comprise one of southwest Washington's largest retail shopping centers.

Kelso (pop. 11,000) got its start in the 1840s when the Hudson's Bay Co. used Cowlitz and Columbia river ports to export beef from the Kelso Wharves. Settlement began in 1847, with Peter Crawford's donated land claim on the Cowlitz River giving rise to the town of Crawford, renamed Kelso in 1884 after the founder's Scottish birthplace. Kelso was incorporated in 1889, became county seat in 1923, and has since been an important logging, milling, and fishing town, called "The Smelt Capital of the World" in honor of the abundant winter run of these fish up the Cowlitz River. The first Cowlitz County cannery was built in 1886, and the smelt are still a dominant force in Kelso's economy as tons of fish are shipped annually to the Orient.

SIGHTS

Parks

Longview's early planning is made evident by **Lake Sacajawea Park,** a 120-acre park that bisects the city along Nichols Blvd. with a string of serene lakes surrounded by grassy hillsides, shady trees, and a jogging path.

The **Civic Center** is a grassy green in the city's core, at the intersection of Olympia and Washington ways. Surrounding the green are many of the city's oldest buildings, including the **Public Library,** finished in 1926 and now on the National Register of Historic Places, and the **Monticello Hotel,** built in 1923 and still sporting some of its original elegance.

A small park at 18th, Maple, and Olympia avenues in Longview marks the **Monticello Convention Site,** where Washington resi-

Lake Sacajawea Park

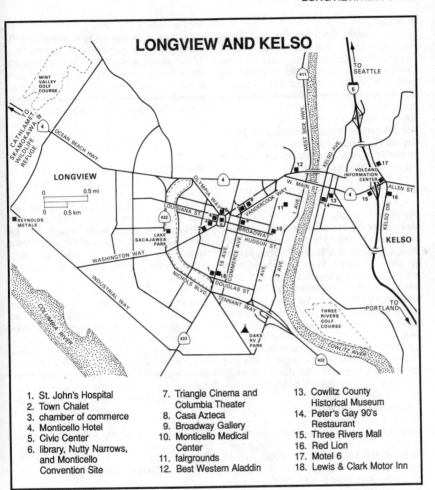

LONGVIEW AND KELSO

1. St. John's Hospital
2. Town Chalet
3. chamber of commerce
4. Monticello Hotel
5. Civic Center
6. library, Nutty Narrows, and Monticello Convention Site
7. Triangle Cinema and Columbia Theater
8. Casa Azteca
9. Broadway Gallery
10. Monticello Medical Center
11. fairgrounds
12. Best Western Aladdin
13. Cowlitz County Historical Museum
14. Peter's Gay 90's Restaurant
15. Three Rivers Mall
16. Red Lion
17. Motel 6
18. Lewis & Clark Motor Inn

dents met to petition the government to separate Washington Territory from Oregon.

The Nutty Narrows

Just up Olympia Way from the Civic Center, the Nutty Narrows is the world's only skybridge for squirrels. Builder and developer Amos J. Peters built it in 1963 to save the critters as they attempted to cross the busy street. Peters is honored for his effort with a many-times-greater-than-life-size squirrel sculpture between the library and skybridge.

Mt. St. Helens

The **Kelso Volcano Tourist Information Center,** ½ mile E of town on Minor Rd. (next to the Kelso Chamber of Commerce), is a small-time exhibit for those who may have missed the *real* St. Helens visitor center up near Castle Rock. This one has a 15-foot model of the volcano and Toutle River valley, plus photos and exhibits of the 1980 eruption. Open daily; adults $.50, kids free, 577-8058. For more information on the national monument, see p. 225.

Museum

Visit the **Cowlitz County Historical Museum,** 405 Allen St. in Kelso, to see Chinook and Cowlitz Indian artifacts, relics from the Oregon Trail, war items, dolls, and changing exhibits. Open Tues. through Sat. till 5 p.m.; 577-3119.

Tour

The **Reynolds Metal Company,** 4029 Industrial Way, 425-2800, offers a free tour of its aluminum-reduction plant every Thurs. at 1 p.m. for kids over 12.

ACCOMMODATIONS

Motels And Hotels

Quality lodging in Longview is scarce. The **Monticello Hotel,** 17th and Larch in Longview, 425-9900, is a stately building flanked by gardens across from the Civic Center green. The hotel is largely offices and apartments, but rooms in the adjacent motel are inexpensive—$31 s, $35 d, with 2 fireplace rooms for $39 d—with an elegant restaurant (see below). **Town Chalet,** 1822 Washington Way, Longview, 423-2020, has budget rooms for $25-28 s, $29-34 d; many rooms have kitchens. In the same price range, **Lewis and Clark Motor Inn,** 838 15th Ave., 423-6460, has 32 rooms for $28-30 s, $32-36 d, opposite the Medical Center.

Kelso is the better choice for quality accommodations, largely because its location along I-5 has drawn some of the larger chains to the area. The predictable but inexpensive **Motel 6,** 106 Minor Rd., 425-3229, has 64 budget rooms for $26 s, $32 d, plus heated pool. The **Best Western Aladdin,** 310 Long Ave., 425-9660 or (800) 528-1234, has an indoor pool, whirlpool, and guest laundry, plus 79 rooms starting at $34-50 s, $40-53 d. The **Red Lion,** 510 Kelso Dr., 636-4400 or (800) 547-8010, is the best in town, with a heated pool, room and poolside service, restaurant, and dancing in the lounge; rooms start at $60-64 s, $60-70 d.

RV Parking

RV campers can stay at **Oaks Trailer and RV Park,** open year-round at 636 California Way in Longview, 425-2708. Facilities include more than 60 hookups, laundry, kids' play area, and free cable TV for $10.50 a day; monthly rates available. For more camping in the Mt. St. Helens area, see p. 231.

FOOD

Henri's, 4545 Ocean Beach Hwy. in Longview, 425-7970, is a popular spot for business lunches or an evening out, specializing in moderately priced steak and seafood dinners and an impressive wine collection; open weekdays for lunch, Mon. through Sat. for dinner. The dining room at the **Monticello Hotel,** 17th and Larch in Longview, 425-9900, serves primarily steak and seafood in an elegant 1920s decor; open for lunch and dinner (dinners run $7-14). **Hillman's Restaurant,** 1125 Commerce Ave. in Longview, 423-7040, also serves moderately priced seafood and steak for lunch and dinner daily, with dancing nightly in the lounge. For Chinese food, try **The Paragon,** 1311 15th Ave. in Longview, 423-7830; closed Mondays. Enjoy Mexican lunches and dinners at **Casa Azteca,** 1124 Washington Way, Longview. Over in Kelso, **Peter's Gay '90s Restaurant,** 310 S. Pacific, 423-9620, specializes in steaks in a gay-'90s atmosphere highlighted by a solid marble bar, antique lamps, and stained glass.

ENTERTAINMENT

Festivals

After the annual winter smelt run comes to a close, Kelso hosts a season finale in the form of a comical **Smelt Eating Contest** the first Sun. in March. The Independence Day **Go-4th Celebration** is 1 of the largest in the country. Held at the fairgrounds in Longview in late July or early Aug., the **Cowlitz County**

Fair has exhibits and entertainment; 577-3121. The **Kelso Highlander Festival,** held in Aug. each year, features a parade, Scottish bagpipe music, truck pull, and more.

Golf
The area's 2 major public golf courses are **Mint Valley,** 4002 Pennsylvania in Longview, 577-3395, and Kelso's **Three Rivers,** 2222 S. River Rd., 423-4653. Both are 18-hole courses with covered driving ranges, restaurants, and equipment sales and rentals.

Symphony And Movies
The **Columbia Theater,** 1231 Vandercook Way, 423-1011, is another legacy from the prosperous 1920s. Now undergoing a massive restoration effort, it will soon host local theater and dance groups as well as national acts. For now, the **Southwest Washington Symphony** gives a handful of performances there from Nov. through May; 425-5346 or 425-5887.

The **Triangle Cinema,** 1228 Washington Way, 425-5448, has 4 screens showing first-run films.

SHOPPING

Kelso's newest shopping center is the impressive **Three Rivers Mall,** just off I-5 at Longview/Kelso exit 39. Still under construction in early 1988, the mall will feature The Bon, J.C. Penney, Emporium, and scores of smaller specialty shops. It's feared that the mall will leave downtown Longview's retail core, now located primarily along Commerce Ave., a ghost town of deserted storefronts.

Stop by downtown Longview's **Broadway Gallery,** 1418 Commerce Ave., 577-0544, to see an outstanding collection of southwest Washington art produced by more than 30 area artists, including jewelry, pottery, watercolors, weaving, baskets, sculpture, and more. Open Mon. through Sat. till 5:30 p.m., with extended Christmas hours.

SERVICES AND INFO

The Longview/Kelso area code is 206. For more information, contact the **Longview Chamber of Commerce,** near the Civic Center at 1563 Olympia Way, Longview, 423-8400, or the **Kelso Chamber of Commerce,** just E of the I-5 entrance ramp at 105 Minor Rd., Kelso, WA 98626, 577-8058.

For medical, fire, or police emergencies, dial 911. For other medical problems, the **Monticello Medical Center,** Broadway and 7th in Longview, 636-7253, has a 24-hour physician-staffed emergency room; or, try **St. John's Hospital,** 1614 E. Kessler Blvd., Longview, 636-4818 for emergencies, 423-1530 for the switchboard.

TRANSPORTATION

By Car
I-5 passes right over Kelso on its way to Portland; Longview sits just to the west. The cities are about 125 miles, or just over 2 hours, from Seattle.

By Bus
Community Urban Bus Service (CUBS), 254 Oregon Way, provides local service; phone 577-3399 for schedule information. **Greyhound,** 423-7380, provides cross-country connections from their 1109 Broadway station.

By Train
Take **Amtrak's** *Pioneer, Coast Starlight,* or *Mount Rainier* into Kelso from Seattle, Los Angeles, and other major West coast cities; (800) 872-7245.

VICINITY OF LONGVIEW

WEST OF LONGVIEW

Wildlife Refuge

Just E of Skamokawa, the **Columbian White-tailed Deer National Wildlife Refuge** is home to an endangered species of white-tailed deer found only along the lower Columbia River near Cathlamet and the Umpqua River near Roseburg, Oregon. Lewis and Clark reported large numbers of these deer from The Dalles W to the Pacific, but the conversion of woodlands and grasslands to agricultural use nearly caused the deer's extinction. The 440-acre refuge was established in 1972 to protect the estimated 230 remaining animals, which have since increased to nearly 400. Birds such as red-tailed hawks, bald eagles, Canada geese, and great blue herons also frequent the refuge.

The best time for viewing the deer is early morning and dusk between Sept. and May, from Steamboat Slough Rd. and Brooks Slough Rd.; your car serves as a blind. Center Rd. is a 2½-mile OW hiking trail through the middle of the refuge, starting at refuge headquarters just off Hwy. 4, at the area's W end; please don't hike off the road as this disturbs the deer. For more information contact the refuge at Box 566, Cathlamet, WA 98612, 795-3915.

Park

Thirty miles from the Pacific, **Skamokawa Vista Park** is a 28-acre facility on what was once the home of the Wahkiakum Indians, led by Chief Skamokawa, whose name means "smoke on the water," in honor of the morning fog. The park borders the Columbia, where you can watch ships crossing the treacherous Columbia River bar. Camp at 1 of 15 RV sites or 4 tent sites, and enjoy the tennis and basketball courts, playfields, paths, and viewpoint.

Museum

The **Wahkiakum County Historical Museum,** 65 River St. in Cathlamet, 795-3954, is a small museum with photographs and exhibits of pioneer days in SW Washington. Open daily except Mon., 1 p.m.-4 p.m., in summer; in winter, 1 p.m.-4 p.m., Thurs. through Sunday.

Bed And Breakfast

About 20 miles W of Longview, **The Country Keeper Inn,** 61 Main St. in Cathlamet, 795-3030, overlooks the Columbia River and Puget Island. The relaxing, well-kept inn is within walking distance of Cathlamet's downtown area and features 5 guest rooms (3 with river view) for $40-60 d, including full breakfast. No pets or indoor smoking; quiet, well-behaved children OK.

Gallery Bed and Breakfast, 4 Little Cape Horn, 425-7395, commands a majestic view of the Columbia River and features parlor fireplace, view deck, sandy beach, and gift shop. Four guest rooms are priced according to your breakfast order: $50 d with continental, $60 d with a full brunch-type breakfast. Well-behaved kids over 10 OK; outdoor smoking only; some pets with prior approval.

VANCOUVER

A 2-time winner of the All-America City Award, Vancouver's population of over 43,000 is supported by wood products, electronics, and the neighboring Portland economy, where many of Clark County's 215,000 residents are employed. Besides serving as a Portland suburb and Washington's I-5 gateway city, Vancouver enjoys a colorful history, kept alive by the Fort Vancouver National Historic Site, Officers' Row, and recreational opportunities at nearby Mt. St. Helens and the Columbia River.

SIGHTS

Fort Vancouver

The United States and Great Britain had been unable to come to terms on the ownership of Oregon Country, a fur- and lumber-rich land that included the Northwest coast of North America. By 1818, the 2 powers had agreed to share the land until an agreement could be reached—but in 1825, the British Hudson's Bay Co. moved its headquarters from Fort George, at the mouth of the Columbia, to Fort Vancouver, 100 miles inland, in hopes of solidifying the British claim to the region. Fort Vancouver became the Pacific Northwest's commercial center for fur trading from Utah to Hawaii; shops, fields, pastures, and mills made the fort a self-sufficient, bustling pioneer community. Droves of pioneering Americans were drawn to Oregon's fertile farmland in the 1830s and '40s, leading to the division of the territory along the 49th parallel in 1846—a boundary that put Britain's Fort Vancouver squarely on American soil. By 1860 all of Fort Vancouver was in the hands of the U.S. Army, but decay and a fire in 1866 destroyed all of the remaining structures.

Beginning in 1948, archeologists recovered more than a million artifacts, leading to the accurate reconstruction of 5 of Fort Vancouver's buildings on the original location, now preserved as a National Historic Site. The 3-story-tall bastion, the fort's unofficial trademark, was originally built in 1845 as protection from Americans and to salute arriving ships with its 8 cannons. Other reconstructed buildings include a blacksmith's shop, bakery, Indian trade shop, and the elegant residence of John McLoughlin, Columbia Dept. head. Fort Vancouver is open daily year-round. Guided tours are given by park service rangers throughout the day as demand requires, and visitors may also enjoy the slide programs and exhibits at the interpretive center. From downtown, drive E for a half mile on E. Evergreen Blvd.; 696-7655, $1 fee mid-May to September.

Parks, Birds, And Trees

The **Ridgefield National Wildlife Refuge,** just off I-5 in Ridgefield, has over 4,615 acres of fields, woodlands, and marshes for the protection of otters, deer, beaver, as many as

Fort Vancouver National Historic Site

1. Amtrak
2. The Crossing Restaurant
3. Columbia Arts Center
4. Esther Short Park
5. Slocum House Theater
6. Red Lion Inn at the Quay
7. Who-Song and Larry's Cantina
8. TraveLodge
9. Hidden House Restaurant
10. Clark County Historical Museum
11. Shilo Inn
12. Greater Vancouver Chamber of Commerce
13. Chart House

© MOON PUBLICATIONS, INC.

180 species of birds and, in winter, up to 10,000 geese and 40,000 ducks. Hiking and fishing are permitted—the mile-long "Oaks to Wetlands Wildlife Trail" is popular with all ages; no fires or ORVs.

Vancouver Lake Park is a local hot spot for both windsurfers and fishermen. The nearly 300-acre strip of land on the S and W shores of 2,800-acre Vancouver Lake offers picnicking, swimming, grassy and shady areas, plus fishing for shad, sturgeon, steelhead, and more. Take Hwy. 501 (a.k.a. Fourth Plain Blvd.) W for about 3 miles; bear R at the giant arrow, just after you see the huge lake on your R, a few hundred feet to the parking lot.

Five miles S of Woodland just off I-5, **Paradise Point State Park** offers fishing in the E. Fork Lewis River, a 2-mile hiking trail, and camping at 70 standard ($7) sites. **Battle Ground Lake State Park** is the more popular summer getaway, 21 miles NE of Vancouver on Hwy. 503. The sandy beach and snack bar attract swimmers; riders will enjoy the equestrian trails. Camp at 1 of 35 standard ($7) sites.

Museums And Historic Buildings
The only fully restored row of officers' homes in the nation is at Vancouver's **Officers' Row National Historic District.** The City of Van-

couver paid the hefty $10 million price tag for the restoration of these 21 turn-of-the-century homes, the 2 most famous of which are the **Marshall House** and **Grant House,** named for their 1-time residents General George C. Marshall and President Ulysses S. Grant. The Marshall House, 1313 Officers' Row, 693-3103, is open for touring (free); the Grant House, 1101 Officers' Row, 696-9699, is a fine restaurant (see below).

The **Clark County Historical Museum,** 1511 Main St., 695-4681, is open Tues. through Sun., afternoons; free exhibits include an 1890 country store, 1900 doctor's office, Indian artifacts, and the 1st piano in Washington Territory, built in 1836.

The **Covington House,** 4201 Main St., 693-9571, is 1 of the state's oldest log cabins. Built in 1848, it housed the area's 1st school: open to the public June through Aug., Tues. and Thurs. 10 a.m.-4 p.m.; free.

Exhibits at **Pearson Air Museum,** 101 E. Reserve St., include Lindbergh's 1927 flight and the 1937 Soviet landing in Vancouver from the world's first transpolar flight, plus operating vintage aircraft. Admission is $2 adults, $1 kids, 694-7026.

Out in Yacolt, the **Pomeroy House/Living History Farm,** N.E. Lucia Falls Rd., gives visitors a look into Clark County's rural lifestyle in the 1920's. Tour the working blacksmith shop, herb garden, and historic log home the 1st full weekend of each month, May through Oct.; 686-3537.

Winery

Just N of Vancouver, **Salishan Vineyards,** North Fork Rd. in La Center, 263-2713, produces dry wines including award-winning Pinot Noirs and Rieslings. Open for tours and tastings Sat. and Sun. 1 p.m.-5 p.m. from May through Dec., or by appointment. Take I-5 exit 16 onto N.W. La Center Rd., following it N onto Main St. and N. Fork Road.

ACCOMMODATIONS

At I-5 exit 4, the **Value Motel,** 708 N.E. 78th St., 574-2345, has over 100 rooms starting at $16-18. The **Guest House Motel,** 11504 N.E.

2nd St. (off I-205 and Chkalov Dr.), 254-4511, has 47 rooms starting at $31 s, $36 d. **Nendel's Suites,** 7001 N.E. Hwy. 99, 696-0516, has a pool, guest laundry, and all kitchenette rooms from $32-39 s, $37-44 d.

The **Vancouver Lodge,** downtown at 601 Broadway, 693-3668 or (800) 255-3050, has moderately priced lodging for $36-40 s, $42-50 d. Off I-5 exit 4 at 7901 N.E. 6th Ave., the **Best Western Ferryman's Motel,** 574-2151, has 132 rooms from $39-54 s, $44-59 d, plus a heated pool, spa, and laundry facilities. At 221 N.E. Chkalov Dr., the **Mark 205 Motor Inn,** 256-7044 or (800) 562-2205, has 120 rooms from $43 s, $50 d, plus an indoor pool and jacuzzi, near the Vancouver Mall. Downtown's **Shilo Inn,** 401 E. 13th St., 696-0411 or (800) 222-2244, has 120 rooms from $46 s, $52-58 d, plus a heated pool, hot tub, sauna, laundry, valet service, and free continental breakfast. Another **Shilo Inn,** this one at 13206 Hwy. 99 (the 134th St. exit off I-5) in Hazel Dell, 573-0511 or (800) 222-2244, has 66 rooms from $44 s, $49-55 d, indoor pool, hot tub, steam room, sauna, valet service, coin laundry, and free continental breakfast.

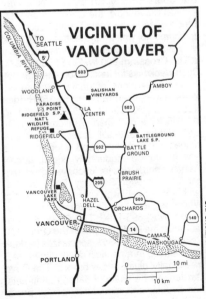

Enjoy top-of-the-line accommodations at the **Red Lion Inn at the Quay,** 100 Columbia St., 694-8341, overlooking the Columbia River. The 160 rooms here cost $63-90 s, $73-100 d, but include a heated pool with poolside service, restaurant (see below), bar with dancing nightly (except Sun.) and a Columbia River view, room service, and bellhops. For a home away from home, try **The Residence Inn,** near the Vancouver Mall at Hwy. 500 and N.E. Thurston Way, 253-4800 or (800) 331-3131. Apartment-style rooms include fully equipped kitchens (complete with popcorn popper), separate living rooms (some with fireplaces), free continental breakfast and newspaper, pool, hot tub, sport court, and guest laundry. Rates start at $53-63 per night; $10 extra for rollaway, $5 for a pet.

FOOD

Enjoy black-tie service in an elegant historic setting at **The Grant House,** 1101 Officers' Row, 696-9699. Antiques, fireplaces, and a list of 250 regional wines complement the high-priced Northwest and continental menu. **The Chart House,** 101 E. Columbia Way, 693-9211, overlooks the Columbia and features moderate-to-expensive steak, seafood, and prime rib, with an oyster bar and a good wine list. Have dinner in a railroad diner car at **The Crossing,** 900 W. 7th St., 695-3374. Open weekdays for lunch, Mon. through Sat. for dinner; entrees of prime rib, seafood, steak, and chicken run from $9-15. **Hidden House,** 100 W. 13th St., 696-2847, was built in 1885 for a prominent Vancouver citizen, L.M. Hidden, and still retains the original stained glass, shutters, and woodwork—but now it offers a moderately priced, largely French menu. Open for lunch weekdays, dinner Tues. through Saturday. Enjoy the Columbia River view with your Mexican food at **Who-Song and Larry's Cantina,** 111 E. Columbia Way, 695-1198. **The Quay,** the restaurant at the **Red Lion Inn at the Quay,** 100 Columbia St., 694-8341, specializes in steak and seafood in a nautical decor. Open for 3 meals daily, plus Sunday brunch. **The Olive Garden,** 1 of a chain of Italian restaurants, has popular and moderately priced pasta, veal, chicken, and seafood dishes, plus their famous breadsticks, at 8000 N.E. Parkway Dr., Orchards.

ENTERTAINMENT AND SHOPPING

Festival

The **4th of July** celebration held at Fort Vancouver has one of the best fireworks displays in the Northwest, food, crafts, and live music. Held the last Sun. in July, the **International Festival** has ethnic food, dancing, and entertainment, and best of all, it's free. August's **Clark County Fair** is the 5th largest in the nation, held at the fairgrounds at 17402 Delfel Rd. in Ridgefield; phone 573-1921 for a schedule of events.

The Arts

At 400 W. Evergreen Blvd., the **Columbia Arts Center** offers a full, year-round schedule of theatrical productions, art shows, and concerts. For information on current events or a copy of their latest newsletter with calendar, phone 693-0351 Mon. through Saturday. Listed on the National Register of Historic Homes, the 60-seat Slocum House Theater was built in 1867 and moved to Esther Short Park at W. 6th and Esther in 1966. The theater is now most famous for its August Victorian Festival, though it stages productions year-round.

Shopping And Movies

The 2-level **Vancouver Mall** has over 115 shops, restaurants, and services, including 5 major department stores—J.C. Penney, Nordstrom, Mervyn's, Sears, and Meier and Frank—at the junction of I-205 and Hwy. 500, or from downtown, follow Fourth Plain Blvd. E. Just outside the mall, the **Vancouver Mall Cinemas** features 4 first-run films; phone 254-0000 for listing.

SERVICES AND INFORMATION

The Clark County area code is 206. For maps or other information, visit the **Vancouver/ Clark County Visitor and Convention Bureau** at 404 E. 15th St. (L off the I-5 Mill Plains exit 1D), 693-1313.

For all fire, police, or medical emergencies, dial 911. For emergency room services, try **St. Joseph's Hospital,** 600 N.E. 92nd Ave., 256-2064, or **Vancouver Memorial,** 3400 Main St., 696-5232.

TRANSPORTATION

Horse And Buggy
Take a covered wagon or horse-drawn carriage ride through Officers' Row with the **Palmer House Carriage Company.** Horse-drawn carriages pick up at the Grant House; covered wagon rides start from the front of Fort Vancouver on E. 5th Street. For current schedules and fares phone (503) 284-5893.

Scenic Train
Enjoy a 2½-hour train ride through the Cascade foothills and along the Lewis River to Moulton Falls County Park with the **Lewis & Clark Railway Co.,** 1000 E. Main St., Battle Ground, 687-2626. Along the way you'll pass through a 340-foot rock tunnel, travel over 3 wooden trestles, and see waterfalls and acres of countryside. Fares are $9 adult, $5 kids; trains run Feb. through Nov. (phone for schedule). A special December Christmas Tree Train takes passengers to an E Amboy tree plantation, where they can cut their own tree to take back home; fares are $12 adults, $6 kids, not including tree.

By Car
From Seattle, Vancouver is about 165 miles S on I-5. The speed limit shifts back and forth from 55 mph to 65 mph, so stay alert—the metropolitan areas are heavily patrolled.

By Bus
The local transit system is **C-TRAN,** 108 E. 7th, 695-0123, providing service throughout Clark County. For cross-country trips, phone **Greyhound,** 512 Columbia St., 696-0186 or (800) 528-0447.

By Train
Amtrak provides daily service to Vancouver from its station at the foot of W. 11th St.; phone (800) 872-7245 or 694-7307 for information.

By Air
The Vancouver area is served by most major carriers at **Portland International Airport.** Make cross-country or international connections with **United,** 696-0155, **American,** (800) 433-7300, or **Continental,** (800) 525-0280; **Alaska Airlines,** (800) 426-0333 primarily serves West Coast cities.

THE COLUMBIA GORGE

Driving along Hwy. 14 on the Washington side of the Columbia River, the scenery takes a dramatic turn, from the green, forested hills of the western section to the dry, yellow, barren hills of the eastern half. Temperature extremes on the E side range from zero or less in winter to 110 degrees of dry heat in summer. The area between the Maryhill Museum near Goldendale and the Ste. Michelle Winery in Paterson is a region most travelers hurry through on their way to more civilized areas. However, the Gorge (from Washougal to Maryhill, and from both sides of the Columbia) offers some of the Northwest's most photographed scenery.

HISTORY

When Capt. George Vancouver's 1792 expedition sailed up the Northwest coast, they must've been napping as they passed the Columbia River—George never saw it. That same year, American trading captain Robert Gray discovered this great river on his journey to become the first American to sail around the world. Gray claimed the river and its huge drainage area for the U.S., naming the river after his ship, the *Columbia Rediviva,* "Columbus lives again." After Gray's discovery, Vancouver sent William Broughton out to explore the upriver territory; Broughton asserted that Gray hadn't found the true channel, and claimed the river for England. Canadian traders searched western Canada for the Columbia's source. Finally, in 1811, David Thompson found it, and canoed to the confluence of the Snake and Columbia where he erected a sign, stating, in part, "Know thereby that this country is claimed by Great Britain." The conflicting claims weren't settled until the U.S.-Canada boundary treaty of 1846.

The most famous Columbia River explorers were Meriwether Lewis and William Clark. Selected by Thomas Jefferson in 1803 to lead an expedition from St. Louis to the Pacific Coast, they were to keep extensive logs of the flora, fauna, and geography of this unknown territory, and to establish friendly relations with the native Indians. The 33 members of the expedition set out on May 13, 1804, in a 55-foot barge powered by 22 oars. When they ran out of river, the party got horses from the Indians and headed for the mountains, where they nearly starved to death. The Plateau Indians helped them find the Columbia River, where they built canoes and paddled downstream, arriving at Fort Clatsop on the Pacific Coast in late November, 1805. Seattleites won't be surprised to hear that Lewis and Clark recorded 31 consecutive days of rain during their visit to the Northwest! In March, 1806, the party headed home. After a 2-year absence, many had given them up for dead, but only one member of the 33-man party died enroute, apparently of appendicitis.

SIGHTS

Parks, Dams, And Viewpoints

If you have a boat, visit **Reed Island State Park** on the Columbia River, 3 miles E of Camas-Washougal Marina. There are 5 primitive campsites here (no water).

On Hwy. 14 between Washougal and North Bonneville, the **Cape Horn Viewpoint** offers a good spot for photographing the dramatic W entrance to the Gorge.

Beacon Rock State Park is 35 miles E of Vancouver on Hwy. 14 (near North Bonneville). The core of an ancient volcano, 848-foot-high Beacon Rock is the largest monolith in North America and the 2nd largest in the world (after Gibraltar). The rock was named by Lewis and Clark in 1805. It was a "beacon" informing river travelers that there were no further obstructions in the river from here to the Pacific Ocean, 150 miles away! Henry J. Biddle bought the rock in 1915 to preserve it, and spent 2 years blazing the trail to the summit; his heirs donated the rock to the state in 1935. Hike Biddle's 1-mile trail for spectacular views of the Gorge; the trail boasts a 15 percent grade, but handrails make the hiking both easier and safer. This and other trails provide 14 miles of hiking in the park. Advanced climbers may attempt to climb on the S side of the rock only; register at the trailhead. Fishermen can launch their boats here to catch Columbia River sturgeon, and campers can stay in 1 of 33 standard forested sites (no hookups).

Visit the **Bonneville Second Powerhouse** visitor center, opened in 1983 on the Washington side of the Bonneville Dam, to see the inner workings of the powerhouse and informative displays. You'll feel dwarfed by the enormity of the river, dam, and surrounding hills. The dam is referred to as "the bottleneck of the Columbia," but a proposed new lock will bring Bonneville's capacity up to that of other Columbia River dams. Cross "The Bridge of the Gods" into Oregon and visit the original **Bonneville Lock and Dam,** a popular tourist spot with continuous presentations, exhibits, and a fish-eye view of the Columbia's inhabitants. The bridge crosses the river at the site of the former Cascade Rapids. According to Indian legend, a stone arch once spanned the river at this point, and its collapse created the Cascade Rapids, damming the Columbia and causing considerable trouble for upriver travelers until the creation of the Cascade Locks in 1896. You can see these locks, no longer in use, at **Cascade Locks Marine Park,** on the Oregon side of the river. A small museum here relates Columbia River history, and includes the Northwest's first steam locomotive, the *Oregon Pony.*

The **Klickitat Gorge,** just N of Lyle, is a strikingly scenic area accented by rope bridges, where you can often see local Indians fishing with dip nets.

Cross over into Oregon via Hwy. 197 to see **The Dalles Dam.** Take the free train for a guided tour of the dam, displays, and fish ladders. "The Dalles" is from the French "Le Dalle," meaning "the trough," the most dangerous point in the river for early navigators. Just E of The Dalles on Oregon's I-84, the **Fort Dalles Historical Museum** boasts a number of intact 1850s structures, including the 1856 Surgeon's Quarters that now houses the museum, and the original 1859 Wasco County Courthouse, now housing the visitor's center. Stop here for a free walking-tour map.

Horsethief Lake State Park, 28 miles W of Goldendale on Hwy. 14, has good trout and bass fishing from your boat or 1 of the park's rentals, with 2 boat launches—1 on the lake, 1 on the river. The park is surrounded by Indian petroglyphs on natural rock formations; other facilities include a divers' underwater park and 12 standard (non-hookup) campsites.

Just E of Horsethief and 12 miles S of Goldendale on Hwy. 97, **Maryhill State Park** offers Columbia River access for boating, windsurfing, and fishing, plus 50 full-hookup campsites.

A mile N of Goldendale, **Goldendale Observatory State Park,** (509) 773-3141, has the country's largest telescope open to public viewing, a 24½-inch reflecting Cassegrain. Take a tour and enjoy free audiovisual programs, displays, and demonstrations Wed. through Sun., 1 p.m.-5 p.m. and 7 p.m.-11 p.m.; (winters Fri. through Sun. only). The

Beacon Rock

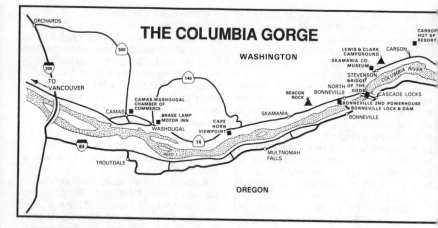

THE COLUMBIA GORGE

camping facilities here are for group use only, but you can stay instead at **Brooks Memorial State Park,** 15 miles N of Goldendale on Hwy. 97, with 22 standard sites and 23 hook-up sites on 700 forested acres. Enjoy the 9 miles of hiking trails and good trout fishing in the Klickitat River, or snowmobiling in winter; 773-4611.

The **John Day Lock and Dam,** 24 miles upriver from The Dalles, gave birth to Lake Umatilla and produces enough electricity for 2 cities the size of Seattle. Here you'll find 1 of the largest single-lift locks in the world, hefting vessels 113 feet. At the dam on Oregon's I-84, enjoy the fish viewing room, visitor's gallery, and Giles French Park with a boat launch, fishing, and picnic area.

Farther W on the Columbia, **Crow Butte State Park** also offers boating, fishing, and waterskiing, with 50 hookup sites, 30 miles W of the McNary Dam along a virtually unpopulated stretch of Hwy. 14.

Scenic Drive
Oregon's **Scenic Highway,** built in 1915, runs parallel to I-84 from Lewis and Clark State Park, 17 miles E of Portland, to Ainsworth State Park, across the Columbia from Beacon Rock. If you have the time or inclination to cross over, this road passes the most beautiful waterfalls in the Gorge, including 620-foot **Multnomah Falls.** For a detailed guide to the Scenic Highway and other Oregon attrac-

tions, pick up a copy of *Columbia River Gorge: An Enjoyment Guide,* a bargain at $2, available at the Skamania County Museum.

Museums
The well-known **Maryhill Museum of Art,** 773-3733, was billed by *Time* magazine as "the loneliest museum in the world" when it opened in 1940. Housed in Sam Hill's 1926 "Castle on the Columbia" 100 miles from any major city, the museum is 1 of the country's finest, drawing more visitors than either the Seattle or Portland art museums with an impressive collection of drawings and plasters by French sculptor Auguste Rodin, French fashion mannequins, paintings, Russian icons, antique chess sets, and Native American artifacts. The museum's cafe serves lunch and snacks to eat in or take on the road. Open 9 a.m.-5 p.m., daily from mid-March to mid-Nov.; admission $3 adults, $1.50 kids.

Three miles E of Maryhill is the nation's first WW I memorial, an exact replica of England's Stonehenge, built by Sam Hill between 1918 and 1930.

Stevenson's **Skamania County Historical Museum,** (509) 427-5141, has displays of pioneer life, Indian artifacts, and the world's largest collection of rosaries—nearly 4,000, gathered from around the world and fashioned from a variety of materials—in the Courthouse Annex basement on Vancouver Ave.; open every afternoon, free. The histori-

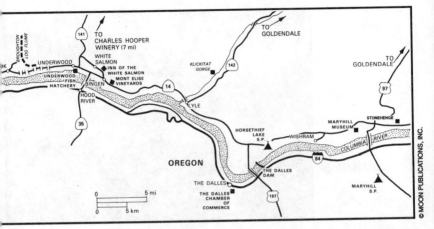

cal society also has an outdoor museum, at Rock Creek Park and Fairgrounds on 2nd Ave., with a Corliss steam engine and caboose.

Goldendale's 20-room **Presby Mansion,** 127 W. Broadway, (509) 773-4303 or 773-5779, is the home of the Klickitat County Historical Museum. Accurately restored and filled with pioneer furniture and other exhibits, it's open Tues. through Sun., May through Oct., the rest of the year by appointment.

Log Flume

The 9-mile long **Broughton Log Flume,** though no longer in use, is still visible from Hwy. 14, E of Bingen, at the mouth of the White Salmon River. The flume, built in the 1920s, carried roughsawn lumber from the Willard mill to a planing mill on the Burlington Northern Railroad line, via a Douglas fir trough with a 1,000-foot drop.

Wineries

Mont Elise Vineyards, 315 W. Steuben in Bingen, specializes in Pinot Noir and offers tours and tastings Thurs. through Sat. afternoons; (206) 493-3001. Eleven miles N of White Salmon on the road to Trout Lake, the family-run **Charles Hooper Winery** produces 2,000 gallons of Riesling, Chardonnay, Gewürztraminer, and Pinot Noir Blanc every year; open weekends, 10 a.m.-6 p.m, and most summer weekdays, (509) 493-2324.

On the Columbia River in Paterson, the state's largest winery, **Chateau Ste. Michelle,** offers tours and tastings of its Columbia Crest line daily, 10 a.m.-4 p.m.; (509) 875-2061.

ACCOMMODATIONS

Hotels And Motels

Take Hwy. 14 to Washougal's **Brass Lamp Motor Inn,** 544 6th St., (206) 835-8591. The 14 rooms start at $32 s, $34.50 d, and include a heated pool, whirlpool, sauna, and laundry facilities.

The **Inn of the White Salmon,** 2 miles E of the bridge at 172 W. Jewett in White Salmon, (509) 493-2335, is a 50-year-old European-style B&B featuring an outdoor hot tub and antique-furnished rooms starting at $59 d with breakfast, up to $116 d for the deluxe suite; weekday singles are a bargain at $44. Enjoy the locally famous country breakfast without lodging for $13—but be sure to phone ahead for reservations. Kids are not encouraged; call ahead for restrictions.

Also in White Salmon, **Orchard Hill Inn,** (509) 493-3024, is a secluded country inn surrounded by forests and apple orchards. Rooms are $33 s, $48 d, including a sideboard breakfast of breads, cheeses, cereal, and fruit, and use of the whirlpool and 1,000-book library; kids are welcome ($3 extra for toddlers and babies, $15 extra for older kids), but pets are not. Groups or large families can

Columbia Gorge

rent a 6-bed bunkhouse. Smoking is allowed in the sitting room or outside. Take Hwy. 141 from White Salmon to Husem, then turn R on Oak Ridge Rd. for 1.8 miles to the inn.

The Grand Old House, across the bridge from Hood River in Bingen, (509) 493-2838, is a Victorian B&B built in 1860. Rooms are $30-65, including a full breakfast and hot tub, and the proprietors will be happy to help you arrange for sailboard rentals and lessons, or cross-country ski tours. The inn serves dinners Tues. through Sun., emphasizing fresh seafood, steak, and chicken entrees.

The historic **Carson Hot Springs Resort,** (509) 427-8292 in Carson, has been drawing visitors to its 126-degree natural mineral baths since the springs were discovered in 1876. At that time, the baths were seen as a cure for everything from arthritis to kidney disorders. The St. Martin Hotel was built in 1897 to replace the tents that had accommodated the droves of guests; cabins were added in the 1920s. Today you can stay in the same lodgings—and enjoy the same relaxing bath *plus* a massage. Hot baths are $5 each, $12-18 for a massage; rooms start at $22-27 s, cabins are $24-29 s (add $5 each additional person), and hot tub suites are $90 d. Full-hookup RV spaces are $8 per day, with tent spaces available for just $3 a day. The restaurant here serves 3 home-style meals daily.

Three Creeks Lodge has individual, duplex, and 4-plex chalets and Creekhouses (hillside condos that sleep 2-6) scattered through 60 acres of forest and streams in the Simcoe Mountains on Hwy. 97 near Goldendale, (509) 773-4026. All units have color TVs, skylights, hand-crafted pine furniture, and an outdoor deck or patio; most have private spas, fireplaces, and kitchenettes. Rooms start at $46 d, up to $135 d for a deluxe unit and $155 d for a Creekhouse; with a 7-course, candlelit, European-style dinner included, rates are $213-245 d. This is a wildlife protection area: no pets, no hunting, no ORVs.

For budget Goldendale lodging, stay at the **Ponderosa,** 775 E. Broadway, (509) 773-5842; the 28 rooms here are $28 s, $32-34 d.

At 333 Vancouver Ave. in Stevenson, **Evergreen Inn B&B,** (509) 427-4303, offers cozy comfort in the heart of the Columbia Gorge. Kids are welcome—a rollaway or crib is available upon request—and a room with full breakfast is $45 d. Lunches and dinners by arrangement; no pets or indoor smoking.

You can also find plentiful mid-Columbia food and lodging in The Dalles, Oregon; visit The Dalles Area Chamber of Commerce, 404 W. 2nd St., (503) 296-2231, for suggestions and Oregon information.

Camping

Aside from state park campgrounds and resorts mentioned above, camping and RV parking in the Columbia Gorge is available at

Beacon Rock Trailer Park 12 miles E of Stevenson on Hwy. 14, (509) 427-8473, for $8.50; open all year.

FOOD

Three Creeks Lodge, Hwy. 97 in Goldendale (see above for lodging), is 1 of the finest restaurants you'll find in the Columbia Gorge area. Local fresh seafood, steak, and produce are complemented by Yakima Valley and Columbia Basin wines. Open for 3 meals daily, with Sunday Champagne brunch; (509) 773-4026. Other inns listed above also serve meals.

The Camas/Washougal area features a number of small restaurants and pizza places, including a Dairy Queen (527 N.E. Cedar in Camas). Mexican food aficionados will enjoy **Juanita's,** 231 3rd in Camas, 834-5856; open for lunch and dinner Mon. through Saturday.

ENTERTAINMENT

Festivals And Events

July 4th brings the usual fireworks, picnics, and concessions to Skamania County; the best way to see the fireworks is aboard the sternwheeler *Columbia Gorge* (see below). July also brings the **Columbia Gorge Bluegrass Festival,** with foot-stompin' music, gospel and stage shows, and plenty of food all day long at the Rock Creek Fairgrounds. The annual **Skamania County Fair and Timber Carnival,** held the 4th weekend in Aug., offers entertainment, contests, exhibits, and food. The **Klickitat County Fair and Rodeo** is held annually in Goldendale over Labor Day weekend; contact the City Clerk, 773-4288, for specific information.

Windsurfing

The wind blowing through the Columbia Gorge provides some of the best windsurfing conditions in the country—but not for beginners. Gusty winds, large waves, a strong current, and frigid water make the Gorge challenging for even experienced sailors. The most protected waters in the Gorge are at Horsethief Lake, but even here strong winds may make it difficult for the beginner to

return to the upwind launch area. If you're sitting this one out, expert-level conditions at **Swell City,** 4 miles W of the Bingen Marina, and the **Fish Hatchery,** 3½ miles W of Hood River, make for exciting sailboard-watching, as does **Maryhill State Park,** where the river is less than a half mile wide.

SERVICES AND INFORMATION

For more information on Columbia Gorge area towns and events, stop at the downtown Stevenson visitor center (open year-round) or

contact the **Goldendale Chamber of Commerce,** Box 524, Goldendale, WA 98620, (509) 773-3400, the **Skamania County Chamber of Commerce,** Box 1037, Stevenson, WA 98648, (509) 427-8911, **Camas-Washougal Chamber of Commerce,** 422 NE 4th Ave., Camas, WA 98607, (206) 834-2472, or the **Skamania Parks and Recreation Dept.,** (509) 427-5141, ext. 217. For more information on the Oregon attractions along the Columbia, contact the **Columbia Gorge Visitors Association,** Box 118, Hood River, OR 97031, (503) 386-6262.

For emergencies, phone 911 in the Camas-Washougal area, (509) 427-5626 in Skamania County. You'll have to travel to Vancouver for a hospital: **St. Joseph Community Hospital,** 600 N.E. 92nd Ave., (206) 256-2064, or **Vancouver Memorial Hospital,** 3400 Main St., (206) 696-5232.

TRANSPORTATION

By Car

While the trip along Hwy. 14 does offer some beautiful Gorge scenery, by the time you arrive at Maryhill Museum you'll realize this Columbia River trek is a lot longer than it looks on the map—especially if your destination is Tri-Cities, more than 200 miles from Camas. The crowds at Maryhill probably have less to do with art appreciation than with sore fannies. This is truly a God-forsaken part of the state, so stock up on Cokes, chips, or whatever gets you through the drive.

Scenic Drive

A drive from Carson to the E side of Mt. St. Helens provides ample photographic and recreational opportunities. See the Mt. St. Helens map on p. 230 for access roads.

Scenic Cruises

Take a cruise on the Columbia, with views of steep basalt cliffs and stops at Cascade Locks, Bonneville Dam, and Stevenson, aboard the sternwheeler **Columbia Gorge,** (503) 374-8427 or (503) 223-3928. The boat can accommodate 599 people (400 indoors),

and has full food and beverage services. Cruises depart daily, mid-June to Sept., from Cascade Locks, Oregon, across the toll bridge between North Bonneville and Stevenson, Washington. Daily 2-hour cruises depart 3 times a day and cost $9 for adults; Thurs. through Sat., enjoy a sunset dinner cruise for $26 adults, or watch the fireworks aboard a special July 4th cruise.

For a longer cruise, check out 1- and 2-day tours aboard **The Whatever,** Box 3, North Bonneville, WA 98639, (509) 427-4347. Take an 8-hour cruise for $60, including 2 meals, to Sauvies Island and Portland Harbor, Longview via Sauvies Island, or Jantzen Beach to Beacon Rock; for $75, with 3 meals, see the Columbia Gorge from Camas, through the Bonneville Dam, on to Bradford Island. Two-day tours travel from Portland to Astoria or the Columbia Gorge from Portland for $169 s, $149 pp d; if time and money are no object, take the 7-day tour from Portland to Lewiston (return by chartered bus) through 8 locks for $749 s, $649 pp d.

Board **YachtShip CruiseLine's** 4-deck *Executive Explorer* for a 6-day cruise following Lewis and Clark's route through the Columbia and Snake rivers. Starting in Portland, the cruise takes you to Astoria, Tri-Cities, Whitman Mission, Lewiston and Hells' Canyon, Maryhill Museum, and the Columbia Gorge, starting at $995 pp. Cruises run April through May and Sept. through early Nov.; write YachtShip CruiseLine at 523 Pine St., Suite 808, Seattle, WA 98101, or phone (206) 623-4245 for more information.

By Train

Bingen/White Salmon is the closest **Amtrak** station to the Columbia Gorge. Contact the station at 800 N.W. 6th, 248-1146, or phone Amtrak's toll-free number, (800) 872-7245, for information.

By Bus

The cruises listed above are as close as you'll come to an organized tour of the Gorge. Bus service to these parts is close to non existent: Vancouver's **C-Tran,** 695-0123, will get you as far E as Camas.

THE PACIFIC COAST

The northern half of Washington's coastline—from the state's northwest corner at Neah Bay to the Quinault Indian Reservation—is a picture of how the Pacific coast *should* look: pristine beaches, pounding waves, bent pines sculpted by relentless sea breezes. This area looks natural because it's protected: the Quinault beaches are off-limits to the public; farther north, most of the coastline is part of Olympic National Park (see p. 179) and thereby immune to "progress."

The coastline south of the reservation is a different picture entirely. Most of the beaches have sand hard enough to drive on, with numerous legal access points from Moclips to Long Beach; look both ways before heading for the surf! Beach driving leaves debris: from oil slicks to food wrappers and beer cans strewn across the sand. In summer, horse manure piles up. People find it "romantic" to rent horses and gallop along the beach, like a scene from a Grade-B tear-jerker. But horses don't defecate in the movies. Periodic clean-up efforts help, but this 70-mile expanse of heavily used beach is just too much to maintain. Fortunately, new legislation is in the works to close the Ocean Shores peninsula and 40 percent of the Long Beach peninsula to vehicular traffic from mid-April through Labor Day, beginning in 1990—a good start toward a cleaner, more inviting coastline.

Investors haven't even done a good job of commercializing these areas. Ocean Shores, at the south end of what's referred to as "North Beach," was purposely developed as a summer resort area in the '60s and '70s. Perhaps because of its newness, it still lacks the beach-resort atmosphere that you'd find on the East Coast, Florida, or California. The failure of these Pacific coast towns to develop may be due in part to lousy beach weather; western Washington is not the best place to go for a tan, and thanks to the California current, summer temperatures are cooler than one would expect at this latitude. But weather alone doesn't explain why Washington residents often spend their vacations at the cleaner Oregon coast, where you *can't* drive on the beach.

OCEAN SHORES TO TAHOLAH

Quinault Indian Reservation beaches, from just S of Queets almost to Moclips, have been closed to the public since 1969, in an effort to forestall further destruction of the natural landscape. Good for them! However, you can arrange for an escorted tour of Point Grenville or Cape Elizabeth, 2 good birding spots, by calling 276-8211, ext. 323. As you drive N from Ocean Shores toward Moclips, you'll notice that the beaches look better and better all the time. The area from Moclips to Pt. Brown, "North Beach," includes the hub of summer activity, Ocean Shores.

Situated on a 6,000 acre, 6-mile-long peninsula, Ocean Shores was strictly Indian clamming ground until May 7, 1792, when Robert Gray's ship *Columbia Rediviva* found the harbor entrance. Gray's discovery led to a slow settlement of the area, started in 1860 by the peninsula's original homesteader, Matthew McGee, and followed shortly thereafter by A.O. Damon, who bought the southern tip of the peninsula from McGee. It wasn't until 1970 that Ocean Shores became an incorporated city, after investors bought the

6,000 acres from Damon's grandchildren and started selling lots. There's still plenty of beachfront property available! The nicer homes are all at the southern tip, near Pt. Brown; Ocean Shores' commercial center is closer to the city's stone arch entryway.

Farther N, Copalis Beach and Ocean City are "Home of the Razor Clam." The State Department of Fisheries sponsors clam digging clinics throughout the summer at Ocean City State Park and neighborhood schools to better prepare you for the short, intense razor clam season; phone 249-4628.

Parks And Beaches

To get to any of the central or southern Washington beaches, just follow the green or brown "Beach" signs pointing seaward from the beachfront highway, in this case Hwy. 109. The advantages of state parks are restrooms, camping facilities (usually), and sometimes no vehicle access to the beach—a plus or a minus depending on your perspective.

Starting from the S—a logical point since Ocean Shores is the center of North Beach civilization—**Ocean City State Park,** 2 miles N of Ocean Shores on Hwy. 115, has 178 campsites (29 with hookup) close to Ocean Shores' restaurants and shops. No beach access for vehicles here, however there are numerous access points in Ocean Shores; from the end of Chance a la Mer, you can drive onto the beach or rent a horse. With all that ocean out there, it's easy to overlook Ocean Shores' 6-mile-long **Duck Lake,** but it's a haven for small boats, fishermen, and waterskiers. You can launch your boat from City Park, at Albatross and Chance a la Mer, or Chinook Park Boat Launch on Duck Lake Drive.

Just W of Copalis Beach, **Griffiths-Priday State Park** is a day-use facility for picnicking, kite flying, beach combing, and birdwatching at the mouth of the Copalis River. The Copalis Spit is 1 of 3 snowy plover breeding grounds on the Washington coast; in 1985, only 15 pairs nested in the state. These birds are very sensitive to human intrusion. To protect them, large areas of the beach N of the park entrance are closed to the public, from the high tide mark to the dunes, from mid-March to

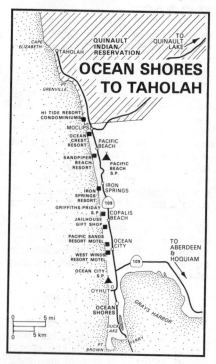

late August. The restricted areas are marked on the map at the park entrance.

Pacific Beach State Park in Pacific Beach offers surf fishing, clamming, and beachcombing with 138 beachfront campsites (20 with hookups).

Accommodations

Hotels, motels, and RV parks are abundant in and around Ocean Shores; as you proceed northward the pickings are slimmer, but there are still a handful of quality resorts.

Ocean Shores has quite a few motels to choose from, but the best are booked up in advance—phone ahead. Starting with the least expensive, the **Oceanside Motel,** Ocean Shores Blvd., has a pool, sauna, and rooms from $20-36; (800) 562-6373 or 289-3323. The **Sands Resort,** Ocean Shores Blvd., 289-2444, has 80 rooms starting at $38-42, up to $42-45 for kitchenettes, plus a game room, heated pool, hot tub, and sauna. At the **Discovery Inn,** 5 miles S of town on Point Brown Ave., 289-3371, prices start at $42 d for a motel-type room, $50 for a studio, and $55-60 for a 1-bedroom fireplace suite; facilities include a pool, hot tub, and playground. In the same price range, **The Polynesian,** 291 Ocean Shores Blvd., 289-3361, starts at $49 for a motel unit, $66 d for a studio with view balcony, up to $89-109 for 1- and 2-bedroom suites (lower in winter); amenities include an indoor pool, lounge, and restaurant serving seafood, steaks, and Polynesian cuisine. On the beach at Ocean Shores, **The Canterbury Inn,** 289-3317 or (800) 562-6678, has luxury accommodations with an indoor pool, hot tub, and private balconies, and suites with full kitchen and fireplace. Summer rates (April through Sept.) are $64-76 for a studio, $80-90 for a 1-bedroom suite, $120-130 for 2 bedrooms; winter rates are $13-23 less. **The Grey Gull,** 289-3381 or (800) 562-9712, has efficiencies ($70-75 d), 1- and 2-bedroom suites ($100-150 d), and penthouses ($200 d), all facing the ocean with kitchens, fireplaces, heated outdoor pool, and sauna. Winter rates (Oct. through March) are $13-40 less. If all else fails, call **Ocean Shores Reservations Bureau,** (800) 562-8612 or 289-2430, or

Ocean Front Beach Rentals and Reservations, (800) 544-8887, for information and reservations.

Just N of Ocean Shores at Ocean City, the **West Winds Resort Motel** has budget accommodations from $28-32 d. Open all year; 289-3448. Also in Ocean City, **Pacific Sands Resort Motel,** 289-3588, has rooms with no kitchen from $35 d, with kitchen $40-45 d.

Three miles N of Copalis Beach on Hwy. 109, **Iron Springs Resort,** 276-4230, is open all year with fireplace cottages ($40-68 d) and studio apartments ($34-42 d) nestled among spruce trees on a low bluff overlooking the ocean. Facilities include a heated indoor pool, gift shop, and playground, though kids generally prefer to splash in the shallow creek running out to sea.

Open year-round, the **Sandpiper Beach Resort,** 276-4580, 1½ miles S of Pacific Beach on Hwy. 109, has studio apartments from $42 d and suites from $59 d up to $132 for 3 bedrooms, right on the beach; most rooms feature fireplaces and full kitchens. A kite shop at the office guarantees cloudy-day fun.

Ocean Crest Resort, on Hwy. 109 at Sunset Beach in Moclips, 276-4465, has economy rooms with no view for $34-45 d; studios with fireplaces, ocean view balconies, and refrigerators for $46-81 d; and 1- and 2-bedroom apartments for $71-95 d; prices substantially lower in winter. Facilities include a recreation center with indoor pool, sauna, hot tub, exercise equipment, tanning bed, and children's play area, plus a restaurant (see below) and ocean-view lounge. On the ocean 3 miles N of Moclips on Hwy. 109, **Hi Tide Resort Condominiums,** 276-4142, has 24 1- or 2-bedroom suites with kitchens for $44-64 s or d, some with view balconies, most with fireplaces; larger 2-bedroom housekeeping units are $84-94 s or d.

Camping And RV Parks

Campers can park their tents or RVs for $7 at 1 of the state parks (above), or these commercial RV parks: **Tidelands,** $12 a night, on the beach at Copalis Beach, 289-8963; **Surf and Sand RV Park,** $14, also at Copalis Beach, 289-2707; **Blue Pacific Mo-**

Rent a moped
at Ocean Shores.

tel and Trailer Park, $10, Ocean City, 289-2262; **Marina View RV Park,** $9, at the Ocean Shores marina, 289-3391.

Food
Most of the notable food on this stretch of beach is in Ocean Shores. At Ocean Shores Blvd. and Chance a La Mer, **Ocean Shores Inn** serves 3 meals daily and Sunday brunch overlooking the beach, with live weekend entertainment and dancing in the lounge; 289-2407. The **Misfit Restaurant** at the municipal golf course is open for lunch and dinner with prime rib, steak, and seafood; 289-3376. **The Homeport Restaurant,** just past the city entrance on Pt. Brown Ave., 289-2600, serves 3 meals; specialties include salmon, Dungeness crab, steak and lobster dinners ($8-16), and fish and burger lunches ($4-7). For Chinese food, try **Look's Village Chinese Restaurant,** Pt. Brown Ave., 289-2152; open for lunch and dinner daily (closed Mon. in winter).

For ocean-view quality dining at the N end, try **Ocean Crest** at the resort in Moclips, 276-4465. Open for 3 meals, the varied dinner menu features Northwest specialties such as Willapa Bay oysters, trout, quail, steak, and seafood for $9-18, with entertainment weekends in the lounge.

Mopeds
Scoot around town on a moped rented from **O.W.W. Inc.** on Chance a la Mer, 289-3830. Mopeds and bicycles can also be rented at the Shores Mall in Ocean Shores (see below).

Fishing
Although Westport is usually thought of as Washington's fishing capital, Ocean Shores Marina also hosts a number of charter boats offering fishing, whale- and birdwatching, and sightseeing cruises; phone (800) 562-7720 for reservations and information. Or, take the summer passenger ferry from Ocean Shores to Westport and depart from there. **Olympic Adventures,** headquartered in Copalis Beach, offers steelhead, salmon, and trout fishing excursions in the Copalis River; (800) 824-0936.

Golf
At Canal and Albatross in Ocean Shores, the 18-hole **Ocean Shores Golf Course** is open to the public, with restaurant, lounge, and complete pro shop; 289-3357.

Events
Ocean Shores hosts an annual **Beachcombers Fun Fair** at the Convention Center in March. See displays of glass floats and drift-

wood art, or listen to speakers on marine topics. **"Undiscovery Day"** or the "Hey George Festival" is an annual April 27 event, commemorating the fact that Capt. George Vancouver *didn't* discover Ocean Shores on his 1792 exploration; patrons of local taverns run to the beach at midnight and shout "Hey, George!" April brings the **Kite Flying Festival** to Griffiths-Priday State Park in Copalis Beach; another kite flying and **Sandsculpture Contest** is also held here in July. A kite festival is part of Ocean Shores' annual **Festival of Colors,** held each May; another kite flying contest is held here each October. Ocean City sponsors the area's 4th of July fireworks and picnic.

Shopping

Ocean Shores' **Shores Mall** has bike and moped rentals, kite shop, bank, clothing store, and state liquor store on Chance a la Mer, just before the beach. In Homeport Plaza on Pt. Brown Ave., Ocean Shores' **Gallery Marjuli,** 289-2858, is open daily with art and gifts created by Northwest artists. **Tide Creations Gift Shop,** near the marina on Pt. Brown Ave., has thousands of items, from kites and windsocks to fudge; 289-2550. On Hwy. 109 in Copalis Beach, **The Jail House Gift Shop** is housed in a jail built in 1937, and sells Washington arts and crafts plus kites and toys.

Services And Info

With an information center at Hogan's Corner on Hwy. 109, the **Ocean Shores-Olympic Coast Chamber of Commerce,** 289-4552, can provide maps and current festival and tour information. Across the street from Shores Mall on Chance a la Mer in Ocean Shores, the **Ocean Shores Convention and Information Center,** 289-2451, has brochures, local menus, and other information, as does the **Ocean Shores Chamber of Commerce** on Pt. Brown Ave., just inside the entry archway.

For medical emergencies, 911 territory extends as far as the 289 exchange. Near Pa-

cific Beach and Moclips, 911 won't work; phone 276-8375 for emergencies. In less dire situations, the **North Beach Health Care Clinic,** Hwy. 109 in Copalis Beach, has doctors on call 24 hours a day, plus a dentist; 289-2427.

Transportation

To drive to the coast from Seattle, take I-5 S to Olympia, then follow the "Ocean Beach" signs to Hwy. 101, then join Hwy. 8, which merges into Hwy. 12 at Elma. Despite the route changes, it's a straight shot. At Hoquiam, take Hwy. 109 north. For Ocean Shores, turn L at Hogan's Corner onto Hwy. 115; for all other North Beach cities, follow Hwy. 109. Ocean Shores is about 130 miles from Seattle, 102 from Tacoma.

Grays Harbor Transportation Authority route 50 serves North Beach from Ocean Shores to Taholah from Aberdeen and Hoquiam; route 51 is the local Ocean Shores service. Fares are $.25 adults, kids under 5 free; (800) 562-9730 or 532-2770.

ABERDEEN/HOQUIAM

Aberdeen and Hoquiam are twin cities on the easterly tip of Grays Harbor; Aberdeen is the larger of the 2, with a population of 18,700

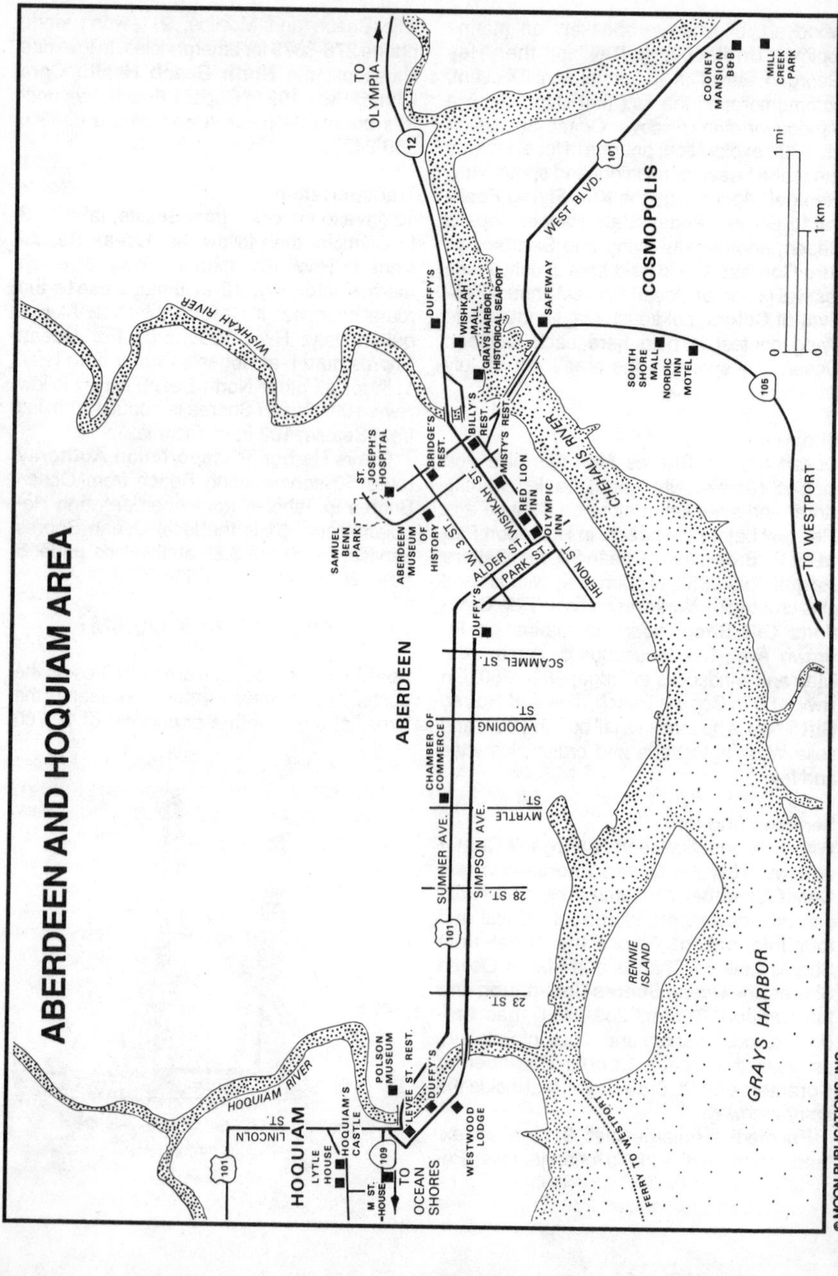

ABERDEEN AND HOQUIAM AREA

TO OLYMPIA

12

COONEY MANSION B&B

MILL CREEK PARK

WEST BLVD.

101

COSMOPOLIS

1 mi

1 km

WISHKAH RIVER

DUFFY'S

WISHKAH MALL

GRAY'S HARBOR HISTORICAL SEAPORT

SAFEWAY

SOUTH SHORE MALL

NORDIC INN MOTEL

105

TO WESTPORT

BILLY'S REST.

MISTY'S REST.

BRIDGE'S REST.

ST. JOSEPH'S HOSPITAL

SAMUEL BENN PARK

ABERDEEN MUSEUM OF HISTORY

RED LION INN

OLYMPIC INN

PARK ST.

WISHKAH ST.

W. 3 ST.

ALDER ST.

HERON ST.

CHEHALIS RIVER

ABERDEEN

DUFFY'S

SCAMMEL ST.

CHAMBER OF COMMERCE

WOODING ST.

MYRTLE ST.

SUMNER AVE.

SIMPSON AVE.

28 ST.

101

23 ST.

RENNIE ISLAND

GRAYS HARBOR

FERRY TO WESTPORT

HOQUIAM RIVER

POLSON MUSEUM

LEE ST. REST.

DUFFY'S

WESTWOOD LODGE

LYTLE HOUSE

HOQUIAM'S CASTLE

LINCOLN ST.

M ST.

K ST.

HOQUIAM

101

109

TO OCEAN SHORES

© MOON PUBLICATIONS, INC.

doubling that of Hoquiam. Heading W from Olympia, you'll notice acres and acres of clearcut; this is the most heavily logged area of the state—some of these hills have been cleared 3 times.

To celebrate the state's centennial in 1989, a full-scale replica of Robert Gray's *Lady Washington* was constructed to serve as the central part of Aberdeen's new **Grays Harbor Historical Seaport;** a replica of Gray's *Columbia Rediviva* may be added in the future. Plans for the seaport include a maritime museum, motels, convention center, and shopping village at the confluence of the Chehalis and Wishkah rivers.

Mansions And Museums

In 1897, lumber baron Robert Lytle built **Hoquiam's Castle,** a 20-room Victorian beauty at 515 Chenault Ave. in Hoquiam. The mansion has been restored to its original luster, completely furnished in antiques, Tiffany lamps, and cut-crystal chandeliers, and is open for tours daily in summer, weekends in winter, closed in Dec.; $3 adults, $2 kids, 533-2005. Another wealthy lumber magnate, Alex Polson, owned the 26-room mansion at 1611 Riverside Ave. in Hoquiam. **Polson Museum,** 533-5862, housed in the mansion, is filled with Grays Harbor history and logging exhibits, and is surrounded by a small park with rose gardens and exotic trees. Open Wed. through Sun. in summer, weekends in winter; donation.

In the National Guard Armory at 111 E. 3rd, the **Aberdeen Museum of History,** 533-1976, has exhibits of local history including a turn-of-the-century kitchen and bedroom, pioneer church, photographs, antique fire trucks, canoe collection, and a continuous slide show; open Wed. through Sun. in summer, weekends in winter. Donation.

Wildlife Refuge

Due W of Hoquiam off Hwy. 109, **Grays Harbor Wildlife Refuge,** 533-5228, is a 500-acre wetland in the NE corner of Grays Harbor Estuary that attracts up to half a million migrating shorebirds in spring and fall. The 2 dozen shorebird species that visit the basin include the western sandpiper, dunlin, short- and long-billed dowitcher, and red knot; other birds seen here are the peregrine falcon, northern harrier, and red-tailed hawk. The best viewing time is 1 hour before and 1 hour after high tide. The arrival of the spring shorebirds in mid-April is cause for the annual **Festival of Shorebirds,** featuring slide programs and displays by state and local wildlife organizations, usually held in 1 of the city's shopping malls.

Parks

At E. 9th and N. I streets, Aberdeen's **Samuel Benn Park** has rose and rhododendron gardens, tennis courts, playground, and picnic facilities. **Lake Aberdeen** at the E entrance to town has swimming and non-motorized boating plus play equipment.

East of Aberdeen, about a mile N of Montesano off Hwy. 12, **Lake Sylvia State Park** has swimming, trout fishing, boat launch and rentals on a small lake, plus 35 wooded campsites. Follow the signs for 10 miles N of Elma to **Schafer State Park** on the Satsop River. Formerly a park for Schafer Logging Company employees, today it has 47 public campsites (6 with hookups), riverside picnic areas, and a fine collection of mossy trees. Weyerhauser's **Swinging Bridge Park** is also about 10 miles from Elma in the middle of nowhere, forking L off the road to Schafer; here you'll find free camping with a 5-day limit, free firewood, and secluded picnic and play areas.

Accommodations

Lytle House, 509 Chenault in Hoquiam, 533-2320, is a Victorian B&B next door to Hoquiam's Castle with 4 non-smoking guest rooms (expanding to 7 in summer 1990) with shared bath for $40 s, $50 d, including full breakfast buffet. More than just a B&B, the antiques, collectibles, and furniture here are for sale, as are small gifts of lace, flowers, and potpourri. No indoor smoking; call regarding kids under 10.

The M Street House, 82 M St., 532-4262, has 2 guest rooms with private entrance in a 1912 home. Breakfast is served in your room or the dining room. Rates are reasonable: $35 s, $40 d.

Also in Hoquiam, the **Westwood Lodge,** 910 Simpson Ave., 532-8161 or (800) 562-0994, has 65 motel rooms starting at $36-42 s, $43-55 d, with some kitchens and 2-bedroom suites.

The **Nordic Inn Motel,** next to the South Shore Mall at 1700 S. Boone in Aberdeen, 533-0100, has 66 rooms from $28-36 s, $34-44 d, attached restaurant, coffee shop, and lounge with live entertainment 6 nights a week. The **Red Lion Motel,** 521 W. Wishkah just off Hwy. 101 in Aberdeen, is a little nicer; rooms here are $42-55 s, $52-65 d; 532-5210 or (800) 547-8010. The **Olympic Inn,** 616 W. Heron in Aberdeen, 533-4200, has some kitchens, laundry facilities, and rooms starting at $30-40 s, $37-46 d.

Just S of Aberdeen, **Cooney Mansion B&B,** 802 E. 5th in Cosmopolis, 533-0602, was built by lumber baron Neil Cooney at the turn of the century, and sits adjacent to woods and a golf course on a dead-end street. Five of the 9 guest rooms have private bath; rates are $55 d, including use of the whirlpool, sauna, and common fireplace.

Food

At 112 N. G St. in Aberdeen, **Bridge's,** 532-6563, has prime rib, steak, and seafood dinners, including razor clams, from $7-18; lunch runs about $4-9. The atmosphere is elegant but not stuffy, with a wide selection of non-alcohol drinks in addition to a full bar; open for lunch and dinner daily plus Sunday brunch. **Billy's,** a restored saloon at 322 E. Heron, also serves delicious steaks, seafood, and sandwiches; with that gold and bright green paint job you can't miss it. At 116 W. Heron in Aberdeen, **Misty's,** 533-0956, has a good assortment of Washington wines and micro-brewery beers, plus American-menu lunches and dinners; kids are welcome. Aberdeen's **Nordic Inn,** at the motel of the same name at 1700 S. Boone St., serves moderately priced steak and seafood; open for 3 meals. **Duffy's** is the local family restaurant, featuring a varied, inexpensive-to-moderate menu and great pies. There are 3 Duffy's in an incredibly small area: 1605 Simpson Ave.

and 1212 E. Wishkah St. in Aberdeen, and 825 Simpson Ave. in Hoquiam. Also in Hoquiam, the **Levee Street Restaurant,** 709 Levee St., 532-1959, serves fine sautés, fettucine, and steaks with a European flair and a river view.

Festival

Hoquiam's **Loggers Playday,** held the 2nd weekend in Sept., is an opportunity for sedentary executives to see what real work is all about. After kicking off the event with a parade, loggers compete in ax-throwing, log-chopping, tree-climbing, and more. Thelma is Elma's **Slug Festival** mascot, welcoming thousands to the annual event in August. Elma is also home to the Grays Harbor fairgrounds, where you can take in horse racing in July, the county fair in Aug., and horse shows and auto races year-round.

Shopping

In Aberdeen, follow Hwy. 105 over the bridge and around the corner to **Safeway,** at Boone and Scott, and the **South Shore Mall,** featuring Sears, J.C. Penney, KMart, and 4 cinemas. The smaller **Wishkah Mall,** on Hwy. 12 at the E end of Aberdeen, has 30 stores including Ernst, Pay 'N' Save, and Lamonts.

Services And Info

The **Grays Harbor Chamber of Commerce,** 532-1924, is open weekdays at 2704 Sumner Ave. in Aberdeen. For emergencies, dial 911 or head for **St. Joseph's Hospital,** 1006 N. H St. (near Samuel Benn Park), for 24-hour service; 533-0450 or (800) 634-0030.

Transportation

Aberdeen and Hoquiam are well served by **Grays Harbor Transportation Authority,** 532-2770 or (800) 562-9730. Route 20 is the local service, running from W. Hoquiam to Aberdeen and Cosmopolis. You can take bus 40 E to Olympia, 60 to Quinault Lake, 55 to Westport, 50 to North Beach, and 51 to Ocean Shores. The **Grays Harbor Passenger Ferry** operates daily from Memorial Day through Labor Day, with weekend service in Sept., connecting Aberdeen and Hoquiam with Westport; 268-0047.

WESTPORT TO NORTH COVE

This section of coastline is known as "The Cranberry Coast"; the bogs E of Hwy. 105 near Grayland produce the bulk of the state's berries from plants imported from Cape Cod in the early '30s. Westport, the principal Cranberry Coast city, calls itself "The Salmon Capital of the World," and it does seem that there's nothing to do there but fish: charter boat services line the waterfront, where locations are marked not by street address but by proximity to numbered floats. You'll be hard pressed to find a luxurious hotel room here; the bare-bones, bed-and-shower motels cater to sportsmen who are out to sea by 5 a.m.

Parks And Viewpoints

Open for day use only, **Westhaven State Park,** on Hwy. 105 just N of Westport, is popular with rock hounds, beachcombers, and divers; look for agates and Japanese glass floats. The jetty was built here to increase the velocity of the seagoing water, collected from 6 rivers flowing into Grays Harbor. Prior to the construction of the jetty, deposits of sediment mandated annual channel dredging. The jetty worked—the channel hasn't required dredging since 1942. **Westport Light State Park,** about a mile S of Westhaven off Hwy. 105 (continue straight when 105 goes L), is another day-use park good for kiteflying, rock hounding, and fishing for ocean perch. The lighthouse here was built in 1898. There's vehicular beach access here, but the sand is considerably softer than at other driveable beaches; be careful if you don't have 4WD. **Westport Observation Tower and Ramp,** on opposite ends of Revetment Dr. N of Westport Marina (head for the neon Islander Restaurant sign), are good places to view freighter activity, scenery, sunsets, or an occasional whale.

On Hwy. 105, 2 miles S of Westport, **Twin Harbors State Park** has over 17,000 shoreline feet in its 317 acres; facilities include 332 campsites (49 with full hookup), a ¾-mile sand dune nature trail, picnic areas, and playground. Between Grayland and North Cove on Hwy. 105, **Grayland Beach State Park**

has 4,000 feet of ocean frontage, a self-guided nature trail through huckleberry, sitka spruce, and lodgepole pine, and 200 acres for picnicking and camping with 60 full-hookup sites. Other beach access points are marked with "Beach" signs on Hwy. 105.

Historical Sights

A historical bus tour departs Sat. afternoons in summer from the Westport Observation

WESTPORT AND LONG BEACH PENINSULA

© MOON PUBLICATIONS, INC.

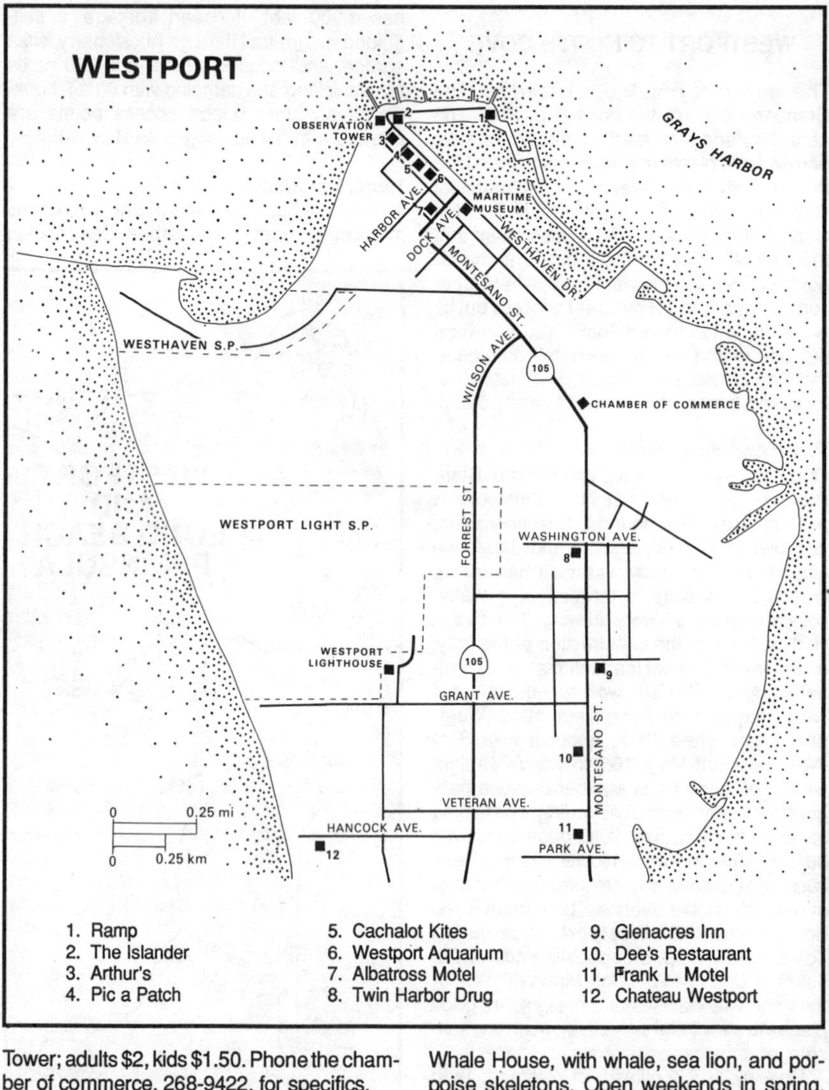

WESTPORT

1. Ramp
2. The Islander
3. Arthur's
4. Pic a Patch
5. Cachalot Kites
6. Westport Aquarium
7. Albatross Motel
8. Twin Harbor Drug
9. Glenacres Inn
10. Dee's Restaurant
11. Frank L. Motel
12. Chateau Westport

Tower; adults $2, kids $1.50. Phone the chamber of commerce, 268-9422, for specifics.

At 2201 Westhaven Dr. in Westport, the **Historical Maritime Museum** is housed in a former Coast Guard station and includes photographs of the early Aberdeen-Westport plank road, cranberry and logging industry exhibits, Coast Guard memorabilia, and The

Whale House, with whale, sea lion, and porpoise skeletons. Open weekends in spring, Wed. through Sun. afternoons in summer, and by appointment in fall and winter; 268-9692.

Aquarium

The **Westport Aquarium,** 321 Harbor St., 268-0471, is open daily from April through

Dec. with large display tanks holding octopus, sharks, bottom fish, and anemones, plus performing seals and a gift shop.

Accommodations

Bed-and-breakfast establishments aren't as common on the newly commercialized coast as in other, older parts of the state. **Glenacres Inn,** built around 1898 on 9 acres at 222 N. Montesano, 268-9391, is 1 of few. This B&B has 5 beautifully decorated inn rooms, all with private bath ($55-65), 3 motel-like rooms with TVs and private bath ($45-50), and 4 cottages that can sleep up to 14 people. Continental breakfast and use of the outdoor hot tub included for inn guests only.

Most Cranberry coast accommodations are in motel-form, closer to Motel 6 than the Sheraton. Expect a heavy summer surcharge after Memorial Day. **Chateau Westport Motel,** 710 Hancock, 268-9101, offers the only luxury accommodations in Westport, with 110 rooms (some with kitchens or view balconies) from $55 s or d to $125 for a 3-bedroom suite, with indoor heated pool, hot tub, and free continental breakfast; winter rates are half off. For less expensive, fisherman-style lodging in the $20 range try the **Frank L. Motel,** 725 S. Montesano St., 268-9200, 1 of many low-priced motels lining Montesano. The **Albatross Motel,** 200 E. Dock St., is a short walk to the floats, with rooms for $35-45 d (some with kitchens); 268-9233. **The Islander,** Westhaven and Revetment, 268-9166, combines a budget motel, RV park, restaurant, lounge, and charter service; rates start at $37 s, $46-47 d in winter, up to $60 s, $63-67 d in summer. South of Westport, **Ocean Gate Resort** in Grayland has cabins ($27-37 d) and RV spaces ($10) on the ocean; 267-1956. Other than that, there's virtually nothing but houses between Westport and Tokeland (see below).

Food

At the corner of Westhaven and Cove, tiny **Arthur's,** 268-9292, is *the* quality restaurant in town, open for lunch and dinner daily with seafood, prime rib, and burgers. **Dee's Restaurant,** 203 S. Montesano St., 268-9737, is open for 3 meals and popular with locals and

guidebook writers alike; grab a box lunch here for your fishing trip, or have just-caught seafood for dinner. **The Islander** is across the street from Arthur's, with an overpriced dinner menu ($10-15) considering the so-so cooking; to keep it cheap, order from the Java Shop sandwich menu and stay late for the musical entertainment.

Festivals

The 3rd weekend in March, Grayland-area artists display their driftwood and shell creations at the town's **Driftwood Show.** Westport's **Blessing of the Fleet,** held annually in May, includes a memorial service for people lost at sea and demonstrations of Coast Guard sea-air rescues. The **Cranberry Blossom Festival,** held annually in June, celebrates the blooming of the tiny pink flowers with festivities including the crowning of "The King of the Bog." Held in early June, the 2-day **Westport Kite Meet** has contests for the youngest and oldest kite flyers, best crash event, longest train of kites, and more, sponsored by Pic a Patch Kites, 268-0877. Westport's 2-week-long **Saltwater Festival** starts with a late-June parade and ends with July 4th fireworks, interspersed with kite-flying contests, treasure hunt, bicycle race, and more.

Fishing And Whalewatching

You don't have to charter a boat to go fishing; the whole stretch from Westport to North Cove is popular for surf fishing. The jetty near Westhaven State Park (see above) is a good spot for catching salmon, rockfish, ling cod, surf perch, and crabs. Clam digging is seasonal and requires a license. The 1,000-foot-long **Westport Fishing Pier,** off the end of Float 20 at the Westport Marina, is another landlubber fishing option.

Offshore rocks and reefs are feeding grounds for salmon, bottom fish, even halibut; take a charter boat to find the best spots, not to mention having your fish cleaned and ready to cook by the time you get back to shore. The charter services all charge about the same amount, so when you call for reservations be sure to check whether the price includes bait and tackle, cleaning, sales tax,

Charter boats operate year-round.

etc., to see if your "bargain" is really a good deal. All of the following charters depart from Westport. **Westport Charters** schedules trips for salmon, bottom fish, or albacore tuna from April through Oct., plus winter Puget Sound and Strait of Juan de Fuca salmon and bottom fish charters from Neah Bay, Sequim, Everett, and Seattle, aboard a fleet of 40- to 50-foot charter boats. Their office is across the street from Dock 8; (800) 562-0157 or 268-9120. **Neptune/Rainbow Charters,** (800) 562-0165 or 268-0124, also has charters for salmon, tuna, sea bass, and bottom fish, in addition to spring and fall Gray whale-watching trips. **Deep Sea Charters,** across from Float 6, (800) 562-0151, has salmon fishing June through Sept., bottom fishing March through Oct., and whalewatching excursions from March through May. Other Westport outfits offering similar services are **Cachalot Charters,** across from Float 12, 268-0323; **Sea Horse Charters,** across from Float 5, 268-9100 or (800) 562-0171; **Bran Lee Charters,** Westhaven Dr., 268-9177 or (800) 562-0163; and **Salmon Charters, Inc.,** 268-9150 or (800) 562-0145.

Shopping

Across from Westport's Float 12, **Cachalot Kites** has kites of every description, plus windsocks and toys, as does **Pic a Patch,** almost next door, reputedly the best kite shop on the coast. For 1-day film processing, prescriptions, seasickness pills, and camping supplies, stop by **Twin Harbor Drug,** 421 N. Montesano in Westport; 268-0505. There's very little else here for the shopper.

Poor fishing in previous years led to an economic depression in town, with the numbers of shops and charter services dwindling; changes in fishing seasons and limits have made vast improvements in both fishing and the tourist trade, so you should see growth in tourist shops and services here before long.

Services And Info

At 1200 N. Montesano St. in Westport, the **Westport-Grayland Chamber of Commerce,** 268-9422, is open daily in summer, weekdays in winter, and has maps, brochures, and festival and tour information.

Transportation

The **Westport-Hoquiam Passenger Ferry** operates in summer only, providing service to Hoquiam and Ocean Shores with 3 trips each way daily; (800) 562-9730. **Grays Harbor Transit** route 55 serves Westport, Grayland, Aberdeen, and Hoquiam for $.25 adult, kids under 5 free; (800) 562-9730 or 532-2770. If you're driving to Westport, take Hwys. 101, 8, and 12 W from Olympia; then head SW on Hwy. 105 to Westport. The trip takes about 2 hours from Tacoma; 2½ hours from Seattle.

WILLAPA BAY

Raymond, on the Willapa River just E of the bay, began as a booming milltown, with 20 lumber mills processing Pacific Coast trees. Today they're still harvesting the same hills, thanks to years of reforestation, with just 2 mills, including a new Weyerhauser plant. Just south of Raymond, South Bend, the city that calls itself "The Oyster Capital of the West," is the highlight of the Willapa Bay area. Founded in 1869, South Bend started out as a sawmill town; when the Northern Pacific Railroad extended a spur to South Bend in the late 1880s, it became "the Baltimore of the Pacific." Victorian homes, churches, and an ornate glass-domed courthouse attest to the prosperity of the times. The Panic of 1893 put an end to South Bend's grandiose logging plans, while the Willapa Bay oysters that had brought great sums of wealth to a few shrewd businessmen were just about farmed out. Aquaculture had its start in the early 1900s, when 95 carloads of Chesapeake oysters were "planted" in the bay. Oyster processing plants flourished until 1919, when a mysterious pestilence wiped out the crop. In 1924, the Japanese oyster was introduced, spawning faster than they could be harvested. When the Great Depression finished off South Bend's lumber business, the oyster plants were still going strong—as they are today. South Bend's other major contribution to the state is Helen Davis; she composed the state song, "Washington, My Home."

Historic Sights
In South Bend, follow the "Courthouse" signs up the hill to the **Pacific County Courthouse,** built in 1911 and covered by an immense, multi-colored glass dome over mosaic-tile flooring. The parklike grounds surrounding the courthouse offer views of Weyerhauser-shaved hills and the town below. Tours of the courthouse may be arranged in advance by phoning the Pacific County Historical Society, 875-5224, or just explore on your own during normal working hours.

Also in South Bend, the **Pacific County Historical Museum** has an impressive collection of local artifacts at 1008 W. Robert Bush Dr.; 875-5224.

Just E of Raymond, off Hwy. 6 in Menlo, **Willie Keil's Grave** is testimony to a father's devotion to his son. Willie's dad promised the boy he would lead a wagon train west; when Willie died in Bethel, Missouri, in 1855, his father put the body in a lead-lined, alcohol-filled casket and carried his remains to Washington in honor of his pledge.

Tokeland, protruding into the N end of Willapa Bay off Hwy. 105, is the site of a number of turn-of-the-century homes and commercial buildings, including the **Tokeland Hotel.** Built as a home in 1885, it became an inn in 1899 and is now on the National Register of Historic Places.

Parks
The 12,000-acre **Willapa National Wildlife Refuge** encompasses all of Long Island plus parts of Leadbetter Point State Park and Shoalwater Bay. Long Island can be reached only by boat from launch areas at refuge headquarters (12 miles N of Ilwaco on Hwy. 101, 484-3482), Nahcotta, or other points on the Long Beach Peninsula. Getting there can be tough due to tidal fluctuations—during low tide, you can practically walk out to it—but the island has 5 primitive campgrounds. The resident deer, elk, grouse, and bear may argue with the "refuge" designation, since archery hunting is allowed. No motorized travel is permitted. You don't have to get out to the island to enjoy the wildlife, though; there are numerous turnouts along highways 105 and 101 where you can pull off and watch herds of elk or black-tailed deer.

Just W of South Bend, **Bruceport County Park** has RV parking ($6) and Willapa Bay beach access.

Accommodations And Food
South Bend is the big city around Willapa Bay, but the food here isn't particularly notable. Best bets are **Boondocks,** Willapa and W. Robert Bush Dr., 875-5155, a steak and seafood restaurant on the bay (open for 3 meals), and **O'Sheridan's** next door at 1011 W. Robert Bush Dr., a tavern that serves the ever-present oysters on the half shell.

Festivals
South Bend's Memorial Day weekend **Oyster Stampede** starts off with a winetasting to get you in the spirit, and continues with oyster shucking and eating contests, oyster cook-

BEACH DRIVING

Most of Washington's Pacific shoreline S of the Quinault Indian Reservation is open to vehicular traffic. This fact causes considerable debate among the natives, many of whom feel it's unnatural to have to look both ways before going for a swim, or don't want to have their kids flattened by RVs. In any case, it's legal; so here are a few rules, regulations, and driving tips.

- The shoreline is considered a state highway; therefore, only registered vehicles driven by licensed drivers are allowed.

- Pedestrians have the right of way; cars and horses must yield.

- Drive only on the higher hard sand, not in the water, on the clam beds, or in the dunes, and observe the 25 mph speed limit.

- If you get stuck, put boards or other hard, flat material under your tires and pull out slowly.

off, Reno night, and dancing. Menlo, SE of Raymond on Hwy. 6, sponsors the annual **Pacific County Fair,** a 4-day event in late August. Naselle, E of the refuge on Hwy. 4, sponsors the 2-day **Finnish-American Folk Festival,** with dramatic performances, dancing, food, music, and arts and crafts, in late July; 484-7759. Fifteen miles E of Raymond, Frances is a ghost town that comes to life twice each year for Swiss festivals: **Schwingfest** in July, a tribute to Switzerland's national sport, wrestling, and autumn's **Oktoberfest,** with beer, polka music, and lots of bratwurst; 934-6321.

Services

The **South Bend Chamber of Commerce,** W. 1st and Alder, 875-5231, has maps and other current information on the Willapa Bay area. For medical emergencies, South Bend has **Willapa Harbor Hospital** at Alder and Cedar, 875-5526.

Getting There

For most people, the Willapa Bay area is something you pass through on your way to Long Beach, Westport, or Ocean Shores. Highways 105 and 101 outline the bay, affording occasional wildlife spottings and some fast, relaxing roads.

LONG BEACH PENINSULA

The Long Beach Peninsula feels a lot like North Beach at first, with the drive-on, littered beaches and waterfront hotels, but on closer inspection you'll see something that's missing from Ocean Shores: character. The town of Long Beach has the only walkable downtown area on the coast, with little shops and tacky souvenir joints—like a *real* beach town. At the N end of the peninsula, things are drastically different too: beautifully restored turn-of-the-century homes in Oysterville, and an isolated natural area at Leadbetter Point.

Parks

At the N end of Long Beach Peninsula on Hwy. 103, **Leadbetter Point State Park** is a protected natural area and wildlife refuge, providing sanctuary for waterfowl, particularly during spring and fall migrations; birdwatchers will enjoy the foot trails through dunes and woods. The ocean side of the point is off-limits from April to Aug. to protect the fragile nests of the snowy plovers, but you'll see thousands of black brant in the marshes during their spring migration from Mexico to Alaska. Getting there can be an adventure; the bumpy road seems endless, but keep your chin up— the gravel part goes for 2 miles, followed by ¾ mile of hardpacked dirt. There are hiking trailheads at road's end and at end of the gravel section. The mosquitos are thick out here—bring insect repellent! No fires, camping, or off-road driving allowed.

Fort Canby State Park, 2½ miles W of Ilwaco, is the peninsula's most scenic state park, as well as home to the **Lewis and Clark Interpretive Center,** with photos, authentic journal entries, and multi-media presentations of the explorers' historic trip from Illinois to Cape Disappointment at the southern tip of the Long Beach Peninsula. The Cape got its name from British fur trader John Meares, after a number of failed attempts at crossing the Columbia River bar. It's not that Meares was a lousy sailor; over 230 ships were wrecked or sunk here before jetties were constructed to control the bar. You can see the mouth of the Columbia by turning R at the concession area and driving to the road's end; park here and walk through the sand to the lookout atop North Jetty. The Cape Disappointment Lighthouse is the Northwest's oldest, built in 1856; follow the quarter-mile path from the Coast Guard Station or a quarter-mile trail from the Interpretive Center. The North Head Lighthouse was built in 1898 and stands above Dead Man's Hollow, commemorating the sailors of the ill-fated *Vandelia* that sunk here in 1853; it's a short walk from the upper parking lot or a 2.1-mile hike from the trailhead. Another hike, the Waikiki Trail, climbs the bluffs for 1 mile to an old radar station and lookout, affording great ocean views. The beach was named Waikiki in honor of a Hawaiian sailor whose body

North Head Lighthouse

washed ashore here after a failed attempt to cross the bar in 1811, aboard Capt. Jonathan Thorn's *Tonquin*. Other park activities include camping at 250 sites (60 hookup), surf and jetty fishing, hiking trails, and a concession for snacks and fishing supplies.

Loomis Lake State Park, S of Klipsan Beach, has picnic tables and restrooms on the ocean, not the lake; the *real* Loomis Lake is about a quarter mile N, open at 4 a.m. for public fishing. No camping at either facility.

Two miles SE of Chinook on Hwy. 101, **Fort Columbia State Park** is a National Historic Site, constructed in 1895 but never engaged in battle; an interpretive center in the enlisted men's barracks features coastal artillery. Hike up Scarborough Hill behind the fort for a view of the Columbia River. Open for day use only.

Museums And History
Oysterville boomed in the late 1800s with the discovery of Willapa Bay oysters; a number of homes constructed during this era have been restored and are included in a self-guided historic walking tour. For a map, stop by the Oysterville Church or phone 665-4575. Take a weekend guided tour through the Tom Crellin House, built in 1869; also 665-4575.

Visit the **Ilwaco Heritage Museum,** just E of Hwy. 101 at 115 S.E. Lake St., 642-3446, for a look into Pacific Coast history via models, exhibits, and photographs of early settlers' fishing, oystering, and forestry methods and Cape Disappointment shipwrecks.

Rhododendron Garden
The **Clark Rhododendron Nursery** is a visual treat with over 1,000 varieties of rhodies in bloom in spring and early summer, 6½ miles N of Long Beach on the bay. The nursery is open daily in spring and summer, weekdays fall and winter; 642-2241.

Tours
Nahcotta has several oyster canneries, all kept in business by the abundance of Willapa Bay oysters. Tour the **Nahcotta Shellfish Laboratory** weekdays and hear a tape about oyster biology. Sorry, the actual oyster beds are closed to the public. About a mile NE of

Long Beach, the **Washington State University Research Center**, Pioneer Rd., studies the private lives of cranberries; take a tour to see the bogs, picking equipment, and slide show. Try to time your visit for June, the peak bloom season, or October, to see the harvest. Open 9 a.m.-4 p.m., Mon. through Friday.

Inn

The highly acclaimed **Shelburne Inn,** Hwy. 103 and 45th St. (Box 250) in Seaview, is an elegant 1896 Victorian hotel and restaurant definitely worth at least a mealtime visit, if you can't swing an overnight stay. The 16 guest rooms are cheerfully furnished in antiques, 5 have private bath; rates range from $69 for a double with shared bath, $79-100 for a double with private bath, to $135 for a suite with private bath. A full country breakfast is included; for many, it's the highlight of their stay. Dinners here are superb as well, with Northwest seafood and game enhanced by in- season vegetables and berries, Northwest wines, and homemade breads, pastries, and desserts. Open in summer for Sunday brunch, and daily for lunch and dinner; closed Wed. in winter, open for lunch Thurs. through Saturday. For room reservations, phone 642-2442; for dinner, 642-4142.

A 1926 Presbyterian church was restored by 2 Seattle couples and converted into **The Inn at Ilwaco,** 120 Williams St. NE, 642-8686. The inn's guest quarters occupy the old Sunday school rooms and the santuary is now a playhouse, welcoming concerts and theater as well as receptions, reunions, and other events. Ten guest rooms run $45-70 d; well-behaved children are welcome, but no smoking or pets. **Scandinavian Gardens Inn,** a block W of Hwy. 103 between 16th and 17th (Rt. 1 Box 36), 642-8877, is a quiet hideaway featuring a Scandinavian breakfast buffet, 4 double rooms and a 2-room suite, all with private bath, plus sauna and spa for $75-145 d.

Motels

Even the nicest beachfront motels and resorts in Long Beach are reasonably priced.

The Breakers, a mile N of town on Hwy. 103, 642-4414, is 1 of the largest, with 106 rooms, heated pool, hot tub, and private balconies starting at $39 d, $44 d with kitchen, and $65 for a 1-bedroom suite. **Chautauqua Lodge,** a block W of Hwy. 103 at 304 14th St. NW, 642-4401, has 120 rooms from $28 d (no view) to $40 with an ocean view and $50 with a kitchen, plus an indoor pool, hot tub, sauna. Their **Potlatch Restaurant** serves fine seafood for lunch and dinner, and the bar has weekend dancing. The **Surfside Inn,** 3 miles N of Ocean Park at 31512 J Pl., 665-5211, has 96 rooms starting at $32 d, an indoor pool, hot tub, restaurant and bar with weekend dancing, view balconies, and golf course. The new **Super 8,** 500 Ocean Beach Blvd., 642-8988, has 51 rooms for $37-40 s, $41-49 d. **Nendel's Inn,** 409 10th St. SW, 642-2311 has similarly priced rooms: $38-52 s, $41-52 d.

Resorts

About midway on the Long Beach Peninsula, **Ocean Park Resort,** 259th Ave. and R St. in Ocean Park, 665-4585, has accommodations to suit everybody, with 12 motel rooms ($34-39 s or d), 8 cabins, 140 tent and RV spaces, pool, jacuzzi, and other extras like clam digging equipment rentals, kids' play area, and sports courts.

Food

Some of the best food on the peninsula is at the **Shoalwater Restaurant** at the Shelburne Inn (see above). **The Sanctuary Restaurant,** corner of Hazel St. and Hwy. 101 in Chinook, 777-8380, serves fresh local seafood, (including Willapa oysters), steaks, veal, and homemade desserts in a converted Methodist Episcopal church built in 1906. Open for dinner Wed. through Sunday. **The Ark Restaurant,** 665-4133, is another local legend, located in Nahcotta on Willapa Bay 12 miles N of Long Beach on Sandridge Rd., or just turn R at the Ocean City light. The building is rustic at best but the seafood is famous, especially after publication of *The Ark Cookbook* and attendance at food fairs and festivals. **B.J.**

a good day's catch at Ilwaco

Squidley's in Ocean Park, 665-5261, features fresh seafood and home-baked goods, $12 and less; open for 3 meals daily.

Shopping

Long Beach is the commercial core of the peninsula, with all the typical beachfront services including bike and moped rentals, candy stores, an amusement park, and the oh-so-tacky **Marsh's Free Museum,** a huge souvenir shop. **Gray Whale Gallery & Gifts,** 105 Pacific Ave., has Northwest art, cards, jewelry, and cranberry products made from the local crop. **Bergkvist Scandia Gifts,** 504 Pacific Ave. S., sells Scandinavian imports, crystal, jewelry, and more. Don't miss **Pastimes,** a collectibles shop and espresso bar at S. 5th and Pacific Hwy., 642-8303. Clocks, china, and glassware for antique hounds; cappuccino, hot chocolate, iced egg creams, and baked goods for the rest. The **Charles Mulvey Gallery,** a few doors N of the Shelburne, is open weekends with Northwest coast watercolors. In Ocean Park, the **Potrimpos Gallery,** Bay Ave. between Hwy. 103 and Sandridge Rd., 665-5976, features watercolors, sculpture, and photography in a Victorian house.

Festivals

Long Beach hosts the annual Independence Day **Fireworks on the Beach,** as well as the week-long **International Kite Festival** in late August (bring color film!). The annual **Cranberry Festival,** held in Ilwaco in Oct., celebrates more than a century of coastal cranberry farming. Cranberries were originally called "crane berries" by early settlers, who thought the blossoms resembled cranes' heads.

Fishing

Ilwaco is a scaled-down version of Westport, with charter boats leaving daily for deep-sea rockfish, flounder, sole, and ling cod, migrating albacore tuna, and sturgeon and salmon near the mouth of the Columbia. Salmon punch cards are available on the boats themselves or in the charter offices. A few charter services include **Pacific Salmon Charters,** 642-3466, **Ilwaco Charter Service,** 642-3232, and **Coho Charters,** 642-3333.

Services And Info

For information on area festivals, maps, and other information, stop by the **Megler Information Center,** 777-8388, a mile E of the Astoria Bridge on Hwy. 401, or the **Long Beach Peninsula Visitors Bureau** at the junction of highways 101 and 103, 642-2400. You can't miss Ilwaco's **Ocean Beach Hospital,** just off the main drag; 642-3181 or 642-2316 for fire or ambulance only. Long Beach is the place to go to do your laundry, buy groceries, get your car washed, or rent a moped; bike rentals are also available in Seaview.

Transportation

Unlike North Beach, the Long Beach peninsula is served by 2 parallel main roads: Hwy. 103, going through the commercial centers on the ocean side, and Sandridge Rd., passing the largely residential sections on the bay side. The roads intersect at Oysterville, where only 1 road continues up to Leadbetter Point. To get to Long Beach from Seattle, you can take the scenic route along Hwy. 101, after traveling on Hwy. 12 to Aberdeen, or the freeway route, S to Longview/Kelso on I-5, then W on Hwy. 4; it's about the same distance either way.

A public bus system runs every hour, Mon. through Saturday. For personalized service, call **Beach Cab,** 642-3905.

NORTH CENTRAL WASHINGTON

THE NORTH CASCADES AND LAKE CHELAN

North Cascades National Park is an outdoor lovers' paradise. Few roads spoil this pristine wilderness, where rugged peaks, mountain lakes, and waterfalls greet the determined back-country hiker. Three hundred eighteen glaciers—more than half of those in the Lower 48—are found on this national park's half million acres. Although Hwy. 20 is one of the country's most scenic routes, the park and surrounding national forests can best be experienced close up, on foot or horseback; in fact, many campgrounds and 1 resort are not accessible by car. So don't just drive through; bring your hiking boots, map, and a flexible schedule to really experience the North Cascades.

Climate

The weather on the W side of the North Cascades is cooler and wetter than the eastern portion, protected by the rainshadow effect. The middle section of Hwy. 20 is closed in winter, usually from mid-Nov. to late April or beyond, although it is open to snowmobile traffic from Colonial Creek to Early Winters. Lower-elevation hiking trails, such as those along Ross Lake and Lake Chelan, are generally accessible from April through mid-Oct.; at higher elevations, trails are open from mid-July through September. The glacier-fed waters of Ross, Diablo, and Gorge lakes are too cold for swimming, but boating and fishing are popular activities.

HISTORY

The earliest white men to explore the North Cascades were Alexander Ross and his party, who crossed today's southern park boundary at Cascade Pass in 1814. In 1859, Henry Custer, working as an assistant of reconnaissances for the International Boundary Commission, traversed the region and commented: "Nowhere do the mountain masses and

Liberty Bell at Washington Pass in the North Cascades

peaks present such strange, fantastic, dauntless and startling outlines as here . . . [It] must be seen, it cannot be described." From 1880 to 1910, prospectors struck gold, platinum, lead, and zinc, but mountain travel was too difficult to justify the modest return. Though logging and early settlement of the area began around 1900, the potential of the Skagit River wasn't harnessed until 1924, when the 1st of 3 dams was built by Seattle City Light. This rugged area was preserved as the North Cascades National Park Service Complex in 1968, incorporating Ross Lake and Lake Chelan National Recreation Areas, and North Cascades National Park.

SIGHTS

Scenic Drives

Highway 20 joins Hwy. 153 at Twisp, Hwy. 97 near Pateros, and Hwy. 2 near Wenatchee to form the NW portion of the "Cascade Loop." This 400-mile scenic drive winds through the North Cascades, past Ross Lake and Lake Chelan, through Leavenworth on its approach to Stevens Pass and returns to western Washington and Whidbey Island. Highway 20, the **North Cascades Scenic Highway,** was originally commissioned in 1893, when state legislators set aside $20,000 for the completion of the Cascade Wagon Route.

Some 79 years and $4.5 million later, the highway was completed. Along the route are numerous pull-offs for viewing the striking scenery, plus access to self-guiding trails, campgrounds, and informational displays. Be sure to make at least 2 stops: at **Diablo Lake,** for lunch in a cozy lodge with a lake view, and at 5,447-foot **Washington Pass Overlook,** where a short paved trail leads to over-the-highway viewpoints of Liberty Bell, the symbol of the North Cascades Hwy., and surrounding mountains. There are no gas stations, restaurants, or other facilities (except restrooms at Washington Pass) for the 75 miles between Ross Dam and Mazama; but those with fuel-efficient cars can fill up in Sedro Woolley and have plenty of gas to get to Lake Chelan.

On the N shore of Lake Chelan, drive the 12-mile scenic loop from downtown Manson along the shore of Lake Chelan, up into apple orchards and past smaller lakes in the foothills, with striking views all along the way. From Manson drive W on Lakeshore Dr. and Summit Blvd., N on Loop Ave. and Manson Blvd., E on Wapato Lake Rd., then S on the Chelan-Manson Hwy. back to Manson. Another scenic spot is on the S shore of the lake; follow Hwy. 97 for 9 miles W of Chelan to **Chelan Butte Lookout,** across the street from the Park Lake Motel. The road curves upward with pullouts for photos of the lake, surrounding hills, and acres of apple orchards.

Baker Lake

Nine-mile-long Baker Lake was created by the upper dam on the Baker River; the Lower Baker Dam created Lake Shannon, just off Hwy. 20 near Concrete. Baker Lake is very popular with campers, boaters, and water-skiers, despite the enormous stumps that lurk just below the water's surface. To get there,

take Baker Lake-Grandy Lake Rd. N from Hwy. 20.

Ross, Diablo, And Gorge Lakes

The 2nd largest lake in the North Cascades after Lake Chelan, **Ross Lake** is 24 miles long and up to 2 miles wide, covering 12,000 acres from the Skagit River up to and beyond the Canadian border. You can see the lake from the Ross Lake Overlook on Hwy. 20 or area hiking trails (see below), but the only

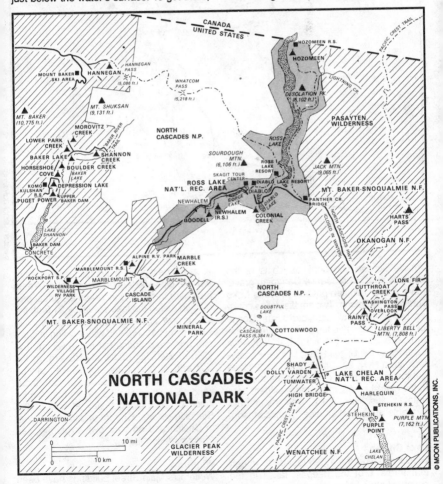

© MOON PUBLICATIONS, INC.

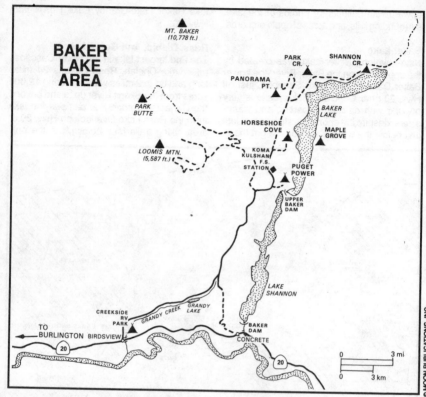

BAKER LAKE AREA

MT. BAKER (10,778 ft.)

PARK BUTTE

LOOMIS MTN. (5,587 ft.)

PARK CR.

SHANNON CR.

PANORAMA PT.

HORSESHOE COVE

BAKER LAKE

MAPLE GROVE

KOMA KULSHAN F.S. STATION

PUGET POWER

UPPER BAKER DAM

LAKE SHANNON

CREEKSIDE RV PARK

GRANDY CREEK

GRANDY LAKE

TO BURLINGTON

BIRDSVIEW

BAKER DAM

CONCRETE

20

20

0   3 mi

0   3 km

© MOON PUBLICATIONS, INC.

vehicle access and boat launch is at the lake's N end, via a 39-mile Canadian gravel road. A boat taxi can get you to **Ross Lake Resort** (see below). Two smaller lakes created by Seattle City Light dams are **Gorge Lake,** 210 acres, and the emerald-green **Diablo Lake,** covering 910 acres just W of Ross Lake along the Skagit River; both are accessible from Hwy. 20. Diablo and Gorge lakes get their deep-green color from the minerals in the glacial runoff, much more evident here than at bluer Ross Lake. Boat rentals are available at all 3 lakes; see "Transportation" below.

Lake Chelan
Glaciers carved the 1,500-foot-deep trough that forms 1 of the deepest lakes in the country: Lake Chelan (pronounced shel-AN).

At its deepest point, the glacier- and stream-fed lake dips 400 feet below sea level. A dam built here in 1927 to increase electrical production raised the lake's level by 21 feet; the lake is now a popular year-round resort; with swimming, boating, and water-skiing in summer and cross-country skiing in winter. The town of Stehekin (that's ste-HE-kin), at the NW end of the 55-mile-long lake, can be reached only by boat, plane, or foot; thousands of visitors take the 4-hour boat trip for lunch or an overnight stay at one of the Stehekin resorts. Or, rent and launch a boat in Chelan and do your own exploring; see "Transportation" below.

Winthrop
Winthrop's Main Street buildings have been remodeled with an "Old West" theme to re-

flect the town's 1890s mining boom—and to encourage hungry, tired Hwy. 20 drivers to stop for a meal, gas, and souvenirs. A visitor information building on the corner can help you with lodging, camping, restaurants, and other area facilities. Winthrop also hosts annual festivals and rodeos (below) that reflect the western mood.

Seattle City Light Tours

Seattle City Light has been offering regularly scheduled tours of their Skagit facilities since 1928. Today, a 4-hour guided tour begins with a slide presentation at the Skagit Tour Center in Diablo, followed by a 560-foot ride up Sourdough Mountain on an antique incline railway used to haul supplies during the construction of the Diablo Dam. Then, enjoy a cruise across deep-green Diablo Lake and back to an all-you-can-eat dinner. Tours leave 3 times a day, Thurs. through Mon., from late June to early Sept; the total cost of the tour and dinner is $18 adults, $15 kids and seniors, kids under 5 free (but mention them when making reservations). Contact the Seattle City Light Tour Desk, 1015 3rd Ave., Seattle, WA 98104, (206) 684-3030, or from late June to Labor Day, stop by the Skagit Tour Center.

A 90-minute tour is also given Thurs. through Mon. afternoons. This 1½-hour version includes a slide show, ride on the incline lift, and tour of the Diablo Powerhouse (sorry, no boat ride) for $5 for everyone over 12.

State Parks

About 10 miles E of Baker Lake on Hwy. 20, **Rockport State Park** has 5 miles of wooded hiking trails (including 1 with wheelchair access), Skagit River steelhead fishing, and camping at 50 hookup sites and 8 standard sites under an old-growth Douglas fir forest.

Pearrygin Lake State Park, 5 miles N of Winthrop off Hwy. 20, offers a sandy beach, fishing, and boat launch on a small lake, winter snowmobiling, plus camping at 57 full- or water-only hookup sites and 26 tent sites.

Another park popular with the summer crowd is **Alta Lake,** 2 miles SW of Pateros off Hwy. 153. Fish, swim, and boat in east-of-the-mountains sunshine, and enjoy the mile-long trail for a scenic view. Lots of camping

here: 16 partial hookup sites, 164 tent sites.

Two state parks provide camping along Lake Chelan. **Lake Chelan State Park** is right on the lake, 9 miles W of Chelan, with an underwater park, docks for campers, boat launch, and concession stand. Camp at 1 of 127 tent sites or 17 full-hookup sites. **Twenty-five Mile Creek State Park,** 18 miles N of Chelan, has camping at 52 tent sites and 33 hookup sites, plus a swimming pool for campers and Lake Chelan boat launch.

All state park campgrounds charge $7 for a standard site, up to $9.50 for a full-hookup site. For more information on camping in the state parks, see p. 111.

Museums

Winthrop's **Shafer Museum** on Castle Ave., (509) 996-2817, is housed in an 1897 log cabin built by the town's founder, Guy Waring. Displays include pioneer farming and mining tools, bicycles, furniture, and other relics from the early days in the Methow Valley. Open daily, Memorial Day through mid-Oct.; donations appreciated. Visit the **Lake Chelan Museum** at Woodin Ave. and Emerson St. in Chelan, (509) 687-3470, to see displays of pioneer and Indian relics. Open Mon. through Sat. afternoons June through Sept., by appointment the rest of the year.

ACCOMMODATIONS

Inns And Resorts

Six miles past the Koma Kulshan Guard Station on the W shore, **Baker Lake Resort** has cabins, camping, boat rentals, a store, and a restaurant. The resort is generally open from the 1st day of fishing season in April through October. Cabins with bathrooms are $35 s, $40 d; without bathroom, $25 s, $30 d; camping is $10 d, plus $3 per day for hookups. Write Box 100, Concrete, WA 98237, or phone (206) 853-8325 or 424-0943 for reservations.

Seven miles E of Newhalem, **Diablo Lake Resort** has lodging in housekeeping cottages supplied with linens, pots and pans, and electric heat. Rates are $45-50 s or d for cabins; camping is available for $8 per night; Visa/MasterCard accepted. You'll also find a snack bar, restaurant, grocery store, and mo-

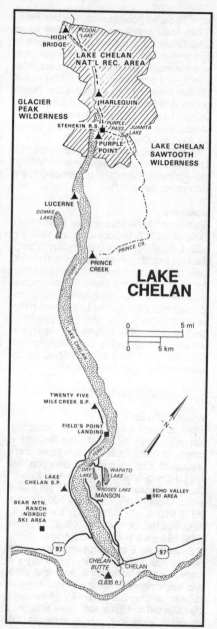

LAKE CHELAN

torboat and canoe rentals. No public telephone; pets OK for an additional $5. Open year-round. Write Diablo Lake Resort, 503 Diablo, Rockport, WA 98283, or phone (206) 386-4429.

You can't drive to **Ross Lake Resort;** you'll have to hike in, boat in from Hozomeen, or take the boat taxi that leaves the Ross Dam Powerhouse parking lot twice a day. Lodging comes in "modern units," housing up to 6 people for $52, "rustic units" that can fit 4 people for $33, and "bunkhouse units" for $75 for 1-6 people, $7 for each additional person up to 10. You can rent a motor boat or canoe here (see "Transportation" below for details), but there are no telephones, groceries, food service, or pets, and they don't take credit cards. Write Ross Lake Resort, Rockport, WA 98283.

North Cascades Lodge in Stehekin can be reached only by floatplane or tour boat from Chelan (see "Transportation" below). Lodge rooms cost $46-68 s or d; furnished housekeeping units are $82 s or d (available Oct.-May). Amenities include a restaurant, bar, boat rentals, gasoline, and groceries; credit cards OK, but no pets. Write Box W, Chelan, WA 98816, or phone (509) 682-4711 for information and reservations. For general information on these 4 resorts, write or phone North Cascades National Park, 800 State St., Sedro Woolley, WA 98284, (206) 855-1331.

The **Mazama Country Inn,** just off Hwy. 20 in Mazama, (509) 996-2681, has 10 guest rooms in the newly completed lodge plus additional rooms in the restored farmhouse. Winter may be the best time to visit; miles of cross-country ski trails are accessible from the door of the inn, and a full line of rental equipment, guided tours, and lessons are available. Summer rates are $65 s, $75 d; winter rates are $95 s, $145 d, and inlcude all meals, served family-style. All rooms have private bath; outdoor hot tub and sauna available. No smoking, pets, or kids under 10. For more information, write Box 223, Mazama, WA 98833.

Atop a low summit, **Sun Mountain Lodge,** Patterson Lake Rd. 9 miles S of Winthrop, (509) 996-2211, has 50 rooms, all with mountain views. Nordic skiers will enjoy the 50

miles of groomed trails; there's also a heated pool, 4 tennis courts, horseback riding, and a restaurant. Rooms are $72 s or d in summer, $60 s or d after Labor Day.

At **Stehekin Valley Ranch,** your meals, lodging, and local transportation are included in the price of your cabin: $49 per person, $10-39 for kids under 12 (depending on age). The ranch is open from late May through Sept. and offers a variety of activities: 2½-hour horseback rides for $25, 10-mile raft trips down the Stehekin River for $35, several-day mountain hiking and horseback trips, day hikes, fishing, boating, and more. For more information write Stehekin Valley Ranch, Box 36, Stehekin, WA 98852, or phone the answering service during normal working hours at (509) 682-4677.

Bed And Breakfast

The **Cascade Mountain Inn,** 3840 Pioneer Lane, Concrete-Birdsview, (206) 826-4333, has 6 guest rooms, each furnished in the theme of a different country. Most rooms have views of Sauk Mountain, and each has a private bath. Rooms are $52-58 s, $68 d; no pets or kids under 10. Lunch and dinner are available to guests and others with reservations.

At Stehekin's **Silver Bay Inn,** enjoy broad views of the lake and mountains while breakfasting in the solarium. Couples can enjoy the master suite for $78 d; families will enjoy 1 of 2 waterfront cabins, $78 d ($7.50 each additional up to 4 total). Two night minimum; no pets or credit cards. Transportation to and from the boat landing is provided. Write Box 43, Stehekin, WA 98852, or phone (509)

682-2212 Mon. through Fri. during working hours.

Relax in Victorian splendor at the romantic **Whaley Mansion,** 415 3rd St., Chelan, (509) 682-5735. The 1911 frame house has been restored with French wallpapers, custom carpeting, and elegant draperies, plus modern conveniences like private baths. Rooms are $65-95 d; Champagne breakfast included. No kids, pets, or smoking. In Manson at Rt. 1 Box 424, **Lee's,** (509) 687-3942, is a modern-day B&B just off Totem Pole Road. Enjoy Lake Chelan and mountain views, plus privacy and low rates: $40 s, $55 d.

The town of Pateros also has B&Bs; these are described, along with Lake Pateros, Bridgeport, and Brewster, under "Vicinity Of The North Cascades," below.

Motels And Hotels

At the S end of Winthrop on Hwy. 20, the cedar-log **Virginian,** 996-2535, has motel rooms and cabins (some with fireplaces) and a heated pool in summer; rooms are $40-75 d, up to $150 for a 1-bedroom house and $200 for a 3-bedroom fireplace unit.

In Chelan, the Apple Inn Motel, 1002 E. Woodin Ave., (509) 682-4044, has a heated pool, hot tub, and budget rooms from $26-48 s or d.

Most of the rooms in Chelan are considerably more expensive. The **Caravel Motor Hotel,** 322 W. Woodin, (509) 682-2715, has 61 rooms from $78 d in summer (down to $58 d after Labor Day and lower still in winter), including a pool, boat moorage, playground, airport and bus depot transportation, on the

Diablo Lake

waterfront. **Campbell's Lodge,** 104 W. Woodin Ave., (509) 682-2561, has 106 rooms plus 17 cottages; rates are $52-86 s, 54-96 d in summer, $28-64 s, $32-68 d after Labor Day. Amenities include 2 heated pools, hot tub, poolside service, boat moorage, and a sandy beach. See "Food," below, for the hotel restaurant, the **Campbell House.**

Darnell's Resort Motel, off Hwy. 150 on the lake's N shore, (509) 682-2015, features luxury accommodations with heated pool, hot tub, sauna, exercise room, lighted tennis courts, putting greens, rowboats, bicycles, moorage, kids' play area—you name it. One-bedroom suites are $108-115 per day for a family of 4; 2-bedroom suites for a family of 6 are $133; the budget 2-person loft is $60, and the 4-6 person penthouse, complete with 2 fireplaces, jacuzzi, wet bar, and sundeck is $250 a day. Off-season rates—before Memorial Day and after Labor Day—are $50-80 d, $200 for the penthouse. No pets.

Hotels at Lake Chelan fill up fast in summer, even at these outrageous prices, so be sure to have reservations if you're determined to stay on the lake. Bargain hunters who don't mind traveling can pick and choose from several reasonably priced hotels in Wenatchee, a half hour S on Hwy. 97, even when Chelan is booked solid; for example, the Wenatchee's Red Lion Thunderbird is a 1st-class hotel (room service, pool, restaurant, and the all-important shower caps and sewing kits) with rooms for about $50 s, $60 d.

Camping And RV Parks

The W side of Baker Lake has numerous campgrounds: **Boulder Creek, Baker Lake, Lower Park Creek,** and **Shannon Creek** are right on the main drag, while **Puget Power, Depression Lake, Horseshoe Cove,** and **Morovitz Creek** are off the beaten path. Campgrounds accessible by car on the North Cascades Hwy. include **Goodell, Newhalem, Colonial Creek, Rainy Pass, Cutthroat Creek,** and **Lone Fir.** Fees from $3-5 are collected at the larger campgrounds: Goodell (22 sites, open year-round), Newhalem (116 sites, mid-June to Labor Day), and Colonial Creek (162 sites, mid-April through Oct.). No hookups are available. Along Cascade River Rd., camp at **Cascade Island, Marble Creek,** or **Mineral Park.** Brave the 39-mile gravel road from Canada and camp at **Hozomeen** at the N end of Ross Lake, from mid-May through Oct., or take a boat up Lake Chelan and camp at **Stehekin.** In summer, a shuttle bus drives campers from Stehekin to **Harlequin, High Bridge, Tumwater, Dolly Varden, Shady,** and **Cottonwood** campgrounds along the Stehekin River for a real escape from the crowds. Enjoy summer naturalist activities including nature walks and evening programs at Colonial Creek, Newhalem, Hozomeen, and Stehekin.

Private RV parks include **Creekside,** 761 Baker Lake Rd. in Birdsview, (206) 826-3566, with 25 trailer sites for $8 on the banks of Grandy Creek. **Wilderness Village,** on the Skagit River in Rockport, (206) 873-2571, has RV parking for $8-9, $2-3 additional for hookups; leashed pets are welcome. Marblemount's **Alpine RV Park and Campground,**

1½ miles E of town on Hwy. 20, (206) 873-4142, has 30 full-hookup trailer sites for $8 a night; open all year. At **Rocking Horse Ranch** in Mazama, (509) 996-2768, stay at 1 of 25 tent sites (10 suitable for RVs) for $8 from April through October. Two miles N of Twisp on Hwy. 20, **River Bend Trailer Park,** (509) 997-3500, is open from mid-April through Oct. with 56 trailer sites for $9; hook-ups extra. In Pateros, the **Outpost RV Park** on Hwy. 97, (509) 923-2200, is open all year with 20 trailer sites for $9.

Check out "State Parks" above for more camping.

FOOD

Food is hard to come by between Sedro Woolley and Winthrop. For a midday stop, try the **Hidden Inn** at Diablo Lake Resort for pizza, sandwiches, and other low-priced items with a lake view; open for 3 meals daily.

Most Hwy. 20 travelers stop at Winthrop for lunch, as evidenced by the town's parking problem even on midweek summer afternoons. For casual dining, downtown's **Duck Brand Restaurant,** (509) 996-2192, serves moderately priced Mexican food, on the deck on sunny days; open for 3 meals daily. To find it, look up from the "Hotel and Restaurant" sign on the E side of the street. For pizza, snacks, sandwiches, and ribs, the over-21 crowd will enjoy **3 Fingered Jack's Saloon,** also downtown. **The Virginian,** the restaurant at the motel just S of Winthrop on Hwy. 20, (509) 996-2536, serves 3 meals daily from a menu that includes pork, seafood, steak, and chicken; dinner runs $8-13.

The **Stehekin Valley Ranch Restaurant** is open every night from mid-June through Sept., Fri. and Sat. nights from late May to mid-June. The menu includes steaks, burgers, salad bar, and homemade desserts— all of which will taste pretty good after a week of backcountry travel or a long day in the saddle! Reservations are required. The restaurant is 9 miles up the valley from Stehekin, but free transportation is provided from the Stehekin Valley Ranch.

There are a number of restaurants to choose from in Chelan. For Mexican food

---

NORTH CASCADES NATIONAL PARK

RULES AND REGULATIONS

- Vehicles are not permitted in the park except on the North Cascades Hwy. and Cascade River Road.

- No dogs or other pets, except on the Pacific Crest Trail, Ross Lake, and Lake Chelan National Recreation Areas, and vehicle access campgrounds, where they must be on a leash.

- No hunting or firearms in the national park; hunting is allowed according to state seasons and regulations at Ross Lake and Lake Chelan National Recreation Areas.

- No backpacking groups over 12.

- Backcountry permits—required for all overnight trips—are issued on a first-come, first-served basis. Areas that fill up fast are Fireweed, Copper Ridge, Thorton Lakes, Basin Creek, Monogram Lake, and McAllister Camp.

- Don't bury your trash; pack it out.

- Campground quiet hours are 10 p.m. to 6 a.m.

- Don't pick, dig, cut, or remove any plants or trees; berry and fruit picking for your personal consumption is OK.

---

overlooking the lake, try **Cosina del Lago** on the Manson Hwy. next to Chelan Shores; (509) 682-4071. The **Campbell House** at Campbell's Lodge, 104 W. Woodin Ave., (509) 682-2561, offers elegant dining from a a continental menu specializing in steak and seafood; prices are moderate, with dinners in the $7-18 range. Open for 3 meals; closed Dec. to March. **Katzenjammers** on Wapato Point in Manson, (509) 687-9541, serves moderately priced steak and seafood; open weekdays for lunch, daily for dinner, plus Sunday brunch.

ACTIVITIES

Hiking

More than 300 miles of maintained trails provide ample opportunities to explore this rugged wilderness area. Trails below 3,000 feet are generally open by mid-April or May; higher up, you may meet snow in July so be prepared. Wear bright colors when hiking in the recreation areas so hunters won't mistake you for a deer.

In the Baker Lake area, hike through a rain forest along the **Baker River.** To reach the trailhead for this 6-mile RT hike, drive N on Baker Lake-Grandy Lake Rd. for 14 miles to the Komo Kulshan Guard Station. Follow the forest service road for 11½ miles, then L a mile, then R on the 1st side road for half a mile to the start of trail #606. This level, low-elevation trail affords views of glaciers and beaver ponds on the way to Sulphur Creek. Stop at the creek and retrace your steps for a 3- to 4-hour hike, snow-free from early spring to late fall.

Another Baker Lake hike takes you to **Park Butte,** a 5,450-foot summit with views of Mt. Baker glaciers. This summer-only trek is 7 miles RT, but with an elevation gain of over 2,200 feet, it'll take a good part of the day to complete. Go N for 12½ miles on Baker Lake-Grandy Lake Rd., then turn L on Loomis-Nooksack Rd. #13 for 9 miles to road's end. The trail is W of the road, crossing Sulphur Creek before the switchbacks begin.

Some of the park's most spectacular scenery can be seen at **Cascade Pass.** This is a day-use-only area; no camping is allowed between the end of Cascade River Rd. and Cottonwood camp on the S side of the pass. Drive to the trailhead at the end of Cascade River Rd., a 25-mile trip from Marblemount. The first 2 miles of the 7-mile RT hike climb steadily through forest and meadows to the 5,400-foot pass at 3½ miles. Allow about 5 hours for this summer-only hike.

Drive to Hart's Pass from Mazama, then go R for 1½ miles on Slate Peak Rd. to the **Windy Pass** trailhead for another high summer-only hike. This 7-mile RT hike starts at 6,800 feet with little additional elevation gain

for striking views of peaks and meadows all along the route. Get an early start; hiking at this elevation may be a little slower than your normal pace.

To hike to **Cascade Pass** from the S side of the park, take *Lady of the Lake* to Stehekin and hop the shuttle bus to road's end at Cottonwood campground. From here climb the talus slope to Doubtful Creek (that is, doubtful if you can cross it in spring); continue uphill for a OW trek of 5½ miles to the pass, with a total elevation gain of 2,600 feet. For a shorter Stehekin-based trip, take the shuttle to High Bridge for a 1¼-mile uphill hike to **Coon Lake** for excellent views of Agnes Mountain and good birdwatching.

For detailed descriptions of these and many other North Cascade hikes, see Ira Spring and Harvey Manning's *101 Hikes in the North Cascades,* published by The Mountaineers in Seattle. Fifteen hikes accessible by the Stehekin shuttle are described in the park brochure, "Day Hiking in Stehekin," available at any ranger station; be sure to pick up a map to accompany the brochure.

Backpacking

A backcountry permit is required for all overnight trips, in an effort to reduce overcrowding and preserve the fragile alpine environment. Pick one up at the information or ranger stations at Marblemount, Hozomeen, Chelan, Stehekin, Early Winters, or Concrete (summer only). The North Cascades are among the most rugged mountains in the Lower 48, so plan accordingly: lots of wool clothing, extra food, a waterproof tarp, and a flexible schedule for waiting out storms and resting feet and muscles sore from all the ups and downs.

From June to Nov., enjoy the 31-mile trip from Panther Creek to Hozomeen along Ross Lake's **East Bank Trail.** The trailhead is on Hwy. 20, 8 miles E of the Colonial Creek campground at the Panther Creek bridge. The trail leads through low forest and along the lake shore for 18 miles, when you have the option of continuing to Hozomeen or taking a side trip up 6,085-foot **Desolation Peak.** The RT up the peak is 9 miles, *almost* straight up, with an elevation gain of 4,400 feet; you'll be rewarded with views of Mt. Baker, Shuksan, Jack Mountain, and The Pickets. To get right to the peak, skip the first 18 miles of hiking by taking the water taxi to the Desolation Peak trailhead; stay overnight at Lightning Creek campground, since you probably won't return in time to catch the boat.

Use the *Lady of the Lake* to make a 38-mile loop trip from Prince Creek, past Lake Juanita and 6,900-foot Purple Pass, to Stehekin. Lot of ups and downs on this hike, through forests and alpine meadows with striking views of mountain peaks, including 8,690-foot Star Peak. The upper Lake Chelan area has a fair number of rattlesnakes, so watch your handholds.

The **Pacific Crest Trail** enters the park from the S from Glacier Peak Wilderness, crossing Hwy. 20 at Rainy Pass and heading N through the Okanogan National Forest to the Canadian border.

The North Cascades are among the most rugged mountains in the U.S.

Climbing

The **American Alpine Institute** offers 6- and 12-day alpine mountaineering courses in the North Cascades for those with little or no climbing experience; tuition is $380 and $670. Their basic rock course, also for beginners, is $100 for 2 days. The group also offers scheduled guided climbs, individual instruction, and classes in other climbing-related subjects. For a brochure or more information, write 1212 24th St., Bellingham, WA 98225, or phone (206) 671-1505.

Hunting And Fishing

You can rent a small motorboat at Baker Lake Resort, Diablo Lake Resort, Ross Lake Resort, Stehekin's North Cascade Lodge, or from private operators in Chelan (see "Transportation" below). Diablo Lake has boat launch ramps at Diablo Lake Resort and Colonial Creek Campground; at Gorge Lake, there's a small ramp near Diablo. At Lake Chelan, launch from Chelan, Manson, or Twenty-Five Mile Creek or Lake Chelan state parks. Catch rainbow, brook, golden, and Dolly Varden trout in mountain lakes and streams, or Kokanee salmon in Lake Chelan.

Hunting is not allowed within national park boundaries; however, hunting is permitted in season at Ross Lake and Lake Chelan national recreation areas. Licenses are required and all state laws apply.

Pack Trips

North Cascade Outfitters leads horseback trips into the Pasayten Wilderness. "Economy" trips include riding horses and a guide; you provide food, tents, kitchen gear, and sleeping bags, for $60 a day. With a "1st-class" trip, pay $90 a day and get riding horses, guide, meals, tents—everything but your sleeping bag and toothbrush. Kids 8 and over are welcome; some exceptions are made for younger children. For more information write Box 397, Brewster, WA 98812, or phone (509) 689-2813 during normal working hours or (509) 689-3131 evenings and weekends.

Sightseers, photographers, hunters, and fishermen will all find a package to suit their needs from **Early Winters Outfitters.** Day-long horseback trips start at $60. For more information write or phone Star Route Box 28, Winthrop, WA 98862, (509) 996-2659.

Claude Miller Pack Trips offers horseback trips into the Pasayten and Sawtooth wilderness areas. Hiking trips, where the outfitter carries the equipment, start at $65 per day; saddle horse trips, including tents, start at $75 a day if you do the cooking, $95 if they do. For more information write Box 250, Winthrop, WA 98862, or phone (509) 996-2350.

If you're traveling with young children, your best bet may be a trip with **Back Country Burro Treks,** Box 150, Malo, WA 99150, (509) 779-4421 (evenings). A burro is gentle and cooperative enough to carry a 2-year-old on its back, relieving you of having to carry the child on long trips or settle for 2-mile hikes. The outfitters will supply you with a burro for the child, packing all of your camping equipment and meeting you at a designated campsite; at camp, you can cook your own meals ($35 per person per day) or leave the food preparation to the outfitters ($75 per person per day). Kids are $5 per day under 50 pounds, $10 per day up to 75 pounds. Scheduled treks last from 3-14 days, averaging 9-10 miles of hiking per day.

Eagle Float Trips

Just E of Rockport, the **Skagit River Bald Eagle Natural Area** is a haven for wintering bald eagles. The eagles arrive in Oct. and feast on the Skagit River salmon run through March. The best way to see the eagles is on a scenic-float trip down the Skagit with 1 of the area organizers. One of these, **Downstream River Runners,** claims to encounter at least 50 of these majestic birds perched in trees along the route. Their 9-mile trip from Marblemount to Rockport is held Dec. through February. The river is so gentle that wet suits are not necessary (just warm winter clothing), and kids over 5 are welcome; $40 pp includes a post-float picnic lunch. Write 12112 N.E. 195th, Bothell, WA 98011, or phone (206) 483-0335 for more information.

Other companies offer essentially the same scenic-float trip, with varying prices and departure dates. **Pacific Northwest Float Trips,** operating out of Sedro Woolley, (206) 855-

0535, offers a Skagit River float for $35 adults, from Dec. through Feb. or early March. Rivers Inc., Box 2092 in Kirkland, WA 98083, (206) 822-5296, also offers Dec. through March eagle-watching trips on the Skagit for $35. **North Cascades River Expeditions,** Box 116, Arlington, WA 98223, (206) 435-9548, or (800) 634-8433 has 10½-mile Skagit River trips, year-round, for $37-49 with a riverside lunch included; minimum age 6.

Winter Sports

The Methow Valley, from Mazama to Pateros, is known throughout the state for its fine cross-country skiing. The Methow Valley Ski Touring Assn. maintains over 150 km of trails, many of which are accessible from area inns (see above), as well as providing rentals, lessons, and hut-to-hut skiing. Phone (800) 422-3048 for information.

The Lake Chelan Valley is another heavily skied area. Ten minutes from Chelan, **Bear Mountain Ranch Nordic Ski Center** offers 40 km of groomed trails and 2,500 acres of forest and meadows for your cross-country skiing enjoyment. Open Fri. through Sun. and holidays from Dec. through Feb., daily during the Christmas holiday season. For ski conditions, phone (509) 682-5444 or (206) 453-5785. Other Chelan-area nordic ski trails include 5 km of groomed runs at **Lake Chelan Golf Course** and another 5 km of groomed trails plus *plenty* of backcountry touring at Stehekin; the *Lady of the Lake* runs all winter (see "Transportation" below). In Echo Valley, 12 miles NW of Chelan, **Lake Chelan Nordic Skiers** has 20 km of groomed cross-country trails for every skill level. Rent cross-country equipment for $10 a day or $25 for 3 days at **Lake Chelan Sports,** 137 E. Woodin Ave., (509) 682-2629. In Echo Valley, **Lake Chelan Ski Club** has day and night downhill skiing on 3,000-foot Echo Mountain, served by 3 rope tows and a poma lift; open Wed. and weekends.

Liberty Bell Alpine Tours, (509) 996-2250, offers helicopter downhill skiing for the truly adventurous, flying skiers to deep powder on over 80 downhill runs in the Okanogan National Forest. Ski from Dec. to May; 5 runs will set you back $245.

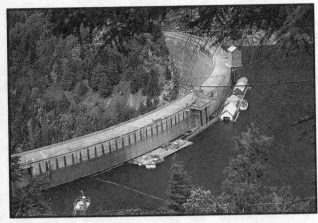

Diablo Dam

For information on skiing at Mission Ridge, see "Wenatchee," p. 313; for Okanogan Valley skiing, see "Vicinity Of The North Cascades," below.

Snowmobilers will enjoy the 125 miles of trails on both sides of Lake Chelan, accessible from 3 Sno Parks, or the 150 miles of trails in the Methow Valley, with 5 Sno Parks and snowmobile rentals; for information contact the Lake Chelan Ranger Station, (509) 682-2576, or the Okanogan County Engineers, (509) 422-3350.

Festivals

May is the start of Winthrop's rodeo season and **49ers Days,** with a parade, drawings, dance, and baseball tournament. **River Rat Days,** held in Winthrop on the July 4th weekend, features a 12-mile race on the Methow River from Winthrop to Twisp on rafts, inner tubes, and canoes. Enjoy the **Apple Blossom Festival,** held the 2nd weekend in May in Manson (on the N shore of Lake Chelan). The 4th of July brings fireworks and a watermelon seed-spitting contest to Manson. See Chelan's **rodeo** the 3rd weekend in July, or visit their **Harvest Festival** in mid-September.

Water Slide

Take advantage of Chelan's sunshine and enjoy the water slides, hot tub, sunbathing, games, and concessions at **Slidewaters,** 102 Waterslide Dr. on the lake's S shore,

(509) 682-5751. Open Memorial Day weekend through Labor Day; admission is $9 adults, $6 kids 4-7.

Golf

Winthrop's **Bear Creek Golf Course** is a 9-hole course; (509) 996-2284. In Pateros, **Alta Lake Golf Course** on Alta Lake Rd. also has 9 holes; (509) 923-2359. For 18 holes, try **Lake Chelan Golf Course,** a championship course at 1501 Golf Course Dr., (509) 682-5421.

SHOPPING AND SERVICES

At the North Cascades Visitor Center in Concrete, visit the **Saturday Market,** where fruit, crafts, houseplants, and baked goods are offered for sale from 9 a.m.-5 p.m. every Sat. from Memorial Day to Labor Day. Visit **The Mountain Gallery,** 114 Riverside Ave. in Winthrop, (509) 996-2166, for paintings, wood carvings, photographs, and prints of Western and North Cascades scenery and wildlife.

For up-to-date information on trail conditions and weather forecasts, contact the ranger stations at Marblemount, (206) 873-4500, or Chelan, (509) 682-2549. Maps and other information may be obtained at these and other ranger stations at Stehekin, Early Winters, Concrete, and Sedro Woolley.

On the N side, gasoline and oil are available at Marblemount, Diablo Lake Resort, and

Ross Lake Resort. Do your laundry at Diablo Lake Resort. Marblemount, Newhalem, and Diablo Lake Resort also stock limited groceries and supplies. **Methow Valley Central Reservations,** (800) 422-3048, can help you find lodging from cabins to motels and provide information on helicopter skiing, ski rentals, steelhead fishing, and more. On the S side, Chelan is a bustling tourist town with all the services you'll ever need. For maps or other information, contact the **Lake Chelan Chamber of Commerce,** Box 216, Chelan, WA 98816, (800) 4-CHELAN in Washington or (509) 682-2022.

For medical emergencies, contact a ranger station in the more remote areas or **Lake Chelan Community Hospital,** 503 E. Highland, (509) 682-2531, in Chelan. Though "safety first" is always good advice, be especially careful when hiking in the Stehekin area; there are no doctors or medical facilities outside the ranger's first-aid kit, and it's a long boat ride to Chelan.

TRANSPORTATION

By Car
North Cascades National Park and Ross Lake National Recreation Area are about 100 miles, or 2½ hours, from Seattle via I-5 and Hwy. 20. Remember to gas up at or before Diablo Lake (Sedro Woolley is cheapest if you get lots of miles per tank), since there are no services for 75 miles between the dams and Mazama.

By Bus
No bus service goes to the N side of the park; the closest you'll get is Mount Vernon. On the S side, however, Chelan is served twice daily from Wenatchee by **Empire Bus Lines,** (509) 682-2022, connecting with Greyhound and Trailways for country-wide service.

Take the boat up Lake Chelan (see below) and the summer shuttle bus from Stehekin to campgrounds and hiking trails along Stehekin Valley Rd. for an extensive, no-car journey into the Cascades backcountry. The shuttle runs to the end of the road near Cascade Pass 3 times daily; the RT fare is $8 adults, $4 kids and seniors, or buy an annual pass for $20 adults, $40 for the family. Be sure to get a shuttle schedule at the Chelan or Stehekin ranger station before setting out; seats are not reserved or guaranteed for the return trip, so be prepared to spend the night in case you miss the late afternoon bus.

By Boat
The *Lady of the Lake II* departs from Chelan for Field's Point, Lucerne, and Stehekin in the heart of the Cascades. In summer, the boat leaves daily at 8:30 a.m., arriving in Stehekin at 12:30 p.m.; after a 1½-hour layover for lunch and exploring, the boat heads back for a 6 p.m. return to Chelan. From mid-Oct. to mid-April, the boat departs on Sun., Mon., Wed., and Fri., shortens the layover to ½ hour, and returns to Chelan by 4:30 p.m. No reservations are necessary. Fares to Stehekin are $19 RT adults, $9.50 kids 6 to 11, to Lucerne, fares are $16 adults, $8 kids. The boat will stop at any Forest Service campsite upon request. No pets allowed in summer; in winter, they must be in travel cages. One barge trip a week is made to transport cars, bicycles, horses, pets, canoes, and other large cargo. Shorter dinner cruises popular in the past have been discontinued, but may start up again in 1988 or later. For more information, write the Lake Chelan Boat Company, Box 186, Chelan, WA 98816, or phone (509) 682-2224.

Boat Rentals
Baker Lake, Diablo Lake, Ross Lake resorts rent small boats, with or without motor, for about the same fee: $30-35 a day or $7-8 an hour for a boat with motor, $15-17 per day or $3-4 per hour for a row-it-yourself model. Ross Lake also rents 17-foot canoes for $15 per day, $4 per hour. At Lake Chelan, **Chelan Boat Rentals** on the lake's S shore at 1210 W. Woodin Ave., (509) 682-4444, rents motorboats, Hobie cats, jet skis, and mopeds. Boats cost $40-50 per hour, and include gas, skis, life jackets, and knee boards, and require a $100 cash deposit. Hobies are $20

per hour, jet skis are $25-40 per hour, and mopeds are $12 per hour, all requiring a deposit of $20-30.

By Air
Chelan Airways offers daily seaplane service to Stehekin, Domke Lake, and other up-lake destinations aboard 4- and 6-passenger planes. Fares to Stehekin are $35 OW, $70 RT; to Domke Lake, popular with fishermen,

fares are $40 OW, $80 RT. Both require a 2 passenger minimum. Or, fly 1 way and take *Lady of the Lake* the other direction for $45 pp, minimum 2 people. Sightseeing flights of the Chelan basin start at $15; the Stehekin Valley tour is $25, and a 110-mile tour of all of Lake Chelan with a stopover at Stehekin is $50. For more information write Box W, Chelan, WA 98816, or phone (509) 682-5555 or (509) 682-5065.

VICINITY OF THE NORTH CASCADES

OKANOGAN VALLEY

Omak and Okanogan, the valley's largest cities, are separated by a distance of 4 miles, from center to center. Nestled between the E and W sections of the Okanogan National Forest, they serve as the commercial hub for a sparsely populated area dominated by apple orchards in Bridgeport and Brewster and outdoor recreation in the national forest. Okanogan, the older of the 2 towns, was established in 1907 and serves as the county seat as well as headquarters for governmental and state departments. Omak, the modern-day commercial center, was chartered in 1910 but slow to develop until a sawmill was built there in 1922. Omak now boasts a slightly larger population—almost 4,000 residents, compared to Okanogan's 2,400—though the entire county consists of just 31,500 people. The Okanogan Valley is a dry area surrounded by mountains, with 28 inches of annual snowfall and a hot, sunny summer.

Okanogan National Forest
The Okanogan National Forest offers a plethora of recreational activities, from hiking to camping to cross-country skiing. The area from the eastern border of North Cascades National Park, from Rainy Pass to Winthrop and S to Chelan, is covered under "North Cascades And Lake Chelan," p. 279, but the Okanogan National Forest Headquarters is located in Okanogan, just over the bridge from the Cedars Inn on Hwy. 97, 422-2704;

stop here for backcountry permits, maps, or other information if you're entering the forest or national park from the east.

Parks
For camping, fishing, and swimming at 2 lakes, visit **Conconully State Park,** 22 miles NW of Omak on Hwy. 97. Seventy-five campsites ($6) include 10 with water hookup ($.50 extra); hike the half-mile nature trail. Okanogan's **Legion Park** offers overnight camping on the Okanogan River and a Farmer's Market in summer.

Three miles NE of Bridgeport on Rufus Woods Lake, **Bridgeport State Park** offers boating, fishing, golf, and 28 standard ($6) campsites. Nine miles farther N on Hwy. 17, **Fort Okanogan State Park** is open for day use only from late June through Aug.; enjoy a picnic lunch and visit the fur-trading post at the interpretive center.

St. Mary's Mission
This Jesuit mission was founded in 1896 by Father Steven Etienne DeRouge to bring Christianity to the Okanogan and Chelan Indians. DeRouge's presence met with resistance until he saved an Indian child who had fallen into the swift waters of the creek; the priest was then accepted. The church was completed in 1915, with local settlers and Indians cooperating in the building of the altar; the side altars were shipped around the Horn from France. Take Hwy. 155 E of Omak for 4 miles, then go 1½ miles south. Open daily; 826-2097.

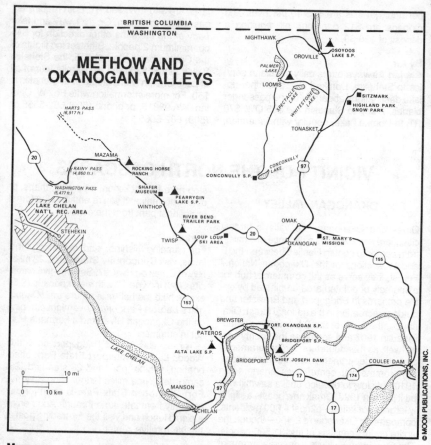

BRITISH COLUMBIA
WASHINGTON

**METHOW AND
OKANOGAN VALLEYS**

NIGHTHAWK

OROVILLE

OSOYOOS
LAKE S.P.

PALMER
LAKE

LOOMIS

SITZMARK

HIGHLAND PARK
SNOW PARK

HARTS PASS
(6,917 ft.)

TONASKET

SPECTACLE LAKE

WHITESTONE LAKE

20

MAZAMA

RAINY PASS
(4,860 ft.)

ROCKING HORSE
RANCH

CONCONULLY
LAKE

97

CONCONULLY S.P.

WASHINGTON PASS
(5,477 ft.)

SHAFER
MUSEUM

PEARRYGIN
LAKE S.P.

LAKE CHELAN
NAT'L. REC. AREA

WINTHROP

RIVER BEND
TRAILER PARK

OMAK

STEHEKIN

TWISP

LOUP LOUP
SKI AREA

20

OKANOGAN

ST. MARY'S
MISSION

155

153

BREWSTER

FORT OKANOGAN S.P.

PATEROS

BRIDGEPORT S.P.

ALTA LAKE S.P.

BRIDGEPORT

CHIEF JOSEPH DAM

COULEE DAM

LAKE CHELAN

17

174

0   10 mi

0   10 km

MANSON

97

17

CHELAN

© MOON PUBLICATIONS, INC.

Museum
The **Okanogan County Historical Museum,** 1410 2nd N in Okanogan, (509) 422-4272, is open from May through Sept. with displays depicting pioneer life in the county; free.

Dam
Though overshadowed by the Grand Coulee to the E, Bridgeport's **Chief Joseph Dam** boasts a 2,000-foot-long powerhouse—the largest in the world. There is no visitor center as yet, but visitors are welcome to enjoy the sights from the designated viewpoint. The dam was named after Chief "I shall fight no more forever" Joseph, leader of the Nez Perce

Indians during a skirmish with the U.S. Army in 1877 that led to the capture of 200 Indians just 30 miles from the Canadian border.

Accommodations
The **Cedars Inn,** at the junction of highways 97 and 20 in Okanogan, (509) 422-6431, has 78 rooms for $36 s, $41 d, plus a heated pool, restaurant and bar, and free airport and bus station transportation. Across the bridge into Okanogan, the **Ponderosa Motor Lodge,** 996 2nd S, (509) 826-9971, has modest motel rooms with kitchenettes plus RV hook-ups; rooms are $25 d, with or without kitchen. The **Motel Nicholas,** a half mile N of Omak

on Hwy. 215, 826-4611, has 22 rooms for $30 s, $30-40 d.

Campers and RVers can stay in town at **Log Cabin Trailer Court,** Hwy. 215, 826-4462. Open year-round; sites cost $8. Three resorts NW of Tonasket near Loomis are open from April through Oct. or Nov., for $9-10 per night: **Spectacle Lake Resort,** 12 miles NW of Tonasket on Loomis Hwy., 223-3433; **Rainbow Resort,** 14 miles NW of town on Loomis Hwy., 223-3700; and **Spectacle Falls Resort,** another mile NW on Loomis Hwy., 223-4141.

Pateros has an abundance of lodging for Methow Valley cross-country skiers and fishing enthusiasts. One of the area's best places to stay is **The French House,** 206 W. Warren in Pateros, (509) 923-2626. The country home is decorated with antiques, crafts, and handmade quilts, and room rates of $32 s, $45-50 d, include a full breakfast. Kids under 4 are free; for older kids ($4 additional), bring a sleeping bag and pillow and the owners will provide a foam pad or cot. No pets or indoor smoking.

Another Pateros B&B is **Amy's Manor,** 5 miles NW of town on Hwy. 153, (509) 923-2334, (Box 411, Pateros, WA 98846). The 170-acre estate overlooks the Methow River and features 4 guest rooms, fireplace, basketball and tennis courts, and a small farm with goats, chickens, rabbits, and cows; rooms are $40 s, $50 d, with continental breakfast. No kids under 12, indoor smoking, or pets.

Whistlin' Pine Resort, off Hwy. 153 on the W shore of Alta Lake in Pateros, (509) 923-2548 or (509) 923-2448 (winter only), has accommodations ranging from tent spaces to deluxe cabins, and entertainment from boating to windsurfing to pack trips. Camp for $7 a night in a tent space, $9 per night for an RV hookup, or stay in a primitive cabin for $15 or a cabin with modern conveniences, like kitchen and bath, for $39 per night. Rent a sailboard for $8 an hour, $11 an hour with a lesson, or rent a rowboat or canoe for $12 a day to fish or explore in Alta Lake. Horse enthusiasts can enjoy a guided trail ride ($6.50 an hour) or a pack trip for $80-95 per day.

A professional rodeo is part of the annual Omak Stampede.

For conventional motel accommodations, try the **Lake Pateros Motor Inn,** 115 S. Lakeshore Dr. in Pateros, (509) 923-2203. Their 30 lakeshore rooms cost $29-44 s, $33-52 d.

Food

Most of the area's restaurants, including the only Dairy Queen for miles, are in Omak. Omak's **Breadline Cafe,** 102 S. Ash, 826-5836, serves inexpensive lunches and dinners of soups and sandwiches Mon. through Sat., and Fri. night ethnic dinners. **Cafe di Midi,** 17½ N. Main St. in Omak, serves an inexpensive breakfast and lunch daily, with heavy emphasis on vegetarian fare. Out in Loomis, **Palmer Mountain Barbecue,** 116 E. Palmer Ave., 223-3311, serves barbecued steak, chicken, brisket, seafood, and ribs; open for 3 meals daily.

Festivals

Omak is famous for its annual **Stampede and Suicide Race,** held in Aug. at East Side Park. Festivities include 2 parades, Western art show, carnival, a professional rodeo, and a horse race down a steep cliff and across the Okanogan River. Animal welfare organizations speak out against this race every year because often a horse will break a leg during what's seen as a cruel and senseless form of entertainment; but the race goes on. Tickets for the 3-day event cost $4-10 and are available in advance from Omak Stampede, Inc., Box 916, Omak, WA 98841, 826-1983. The weekend before the Stampede, Omak's **Not Quite White Water Race** is a slow float down the lazy Okanogan River. Rafters display their creative talents in their costumes and raft design while spectators bomb the participants with water balloons.

Skiing

The Okanogan Valley boasts an abundance of winter sports areas. **Loup Loup,** between Okanogan and Twisp on Hwy. 20, has alpine skiing on a 1,250-foot vertical drop served by 2 pomas and a rope tow, plus 2 km of groomed cross-country trails. Rentals and lessons are available. Open Wed., Sun., and holidays, (509) 997-5334. About 12 miles NE of Tonasket, **Sitzmark** offers alpine skiing on a small, 650-foot vertical drop served by 1 chair, 1 poma, and 1 rope tow, plus 6 km of groomed cross-country trails. Open Wed.-Sun., and holidays, (509) 488-3323. **Highland Park Snow Park,** 10 miles NE of Tonasket, has 12 km of groomed cross-country trails; open daily.

Snowmobilers will enjoy over 100 miles of groomed trails at 6 snow parks in the Okanogan Valley; for specifics, phone the Okanogan County Engineers, (509) 422-3350.

Information

The area code on this side of the mountains is 509. For groceries, gas, and other necessities, Omak, the area's thriving metropolis, is the better choice. For more information on Okanogan County events, contact the **Omak Chamber of Commerce,** 401 Omak Ave., Omak, WA 98841, 826-1880. For medical, fire, or police emergencies, dial 911.

OROVILLE

Oroville lies just S of the Canadian border on Hwy. 97. One of the county's oldest cities,

Oroville's first pioneer, Hiram Okanogan Smith, settled here in 1858, planting apples and mining for gold. Apple orchards are still a prominent feature in the valley, as 10,000 acres of farmland are irrigated from Oroville to Tonasket.

Parks

A mile N of Oroville center on Hwy. 97, **Osoyoos Lake State Park** offers year-round fishing, swimming, water-skiing, and concessions on a lake shared with our Canadian neighbors. Stay at 1 of 80 campsites for $7; no hookups. **Palmer Lake,** S of Nighthawk, a popular spot with fishermen, is managed by the Bureau of Land Management; a boat launch and picnic area are at the S end of the lake.

Accommodations And Food

Visit **Sun Cove Resort** on 2-mile-long Wannacut Lake for a family retreat. The remote area offers hiking, swimming, and fishing in a trout-stocked mineral lake, plus a playground, heated swimming pool, boat, kayak, and canoe rentals, and guided horse-trail rides. Groups up to 8 can stay in a large cottage for $395 per week; up to 6 people, $310 per week. The smaller cabins require a 2-day minimum stay for $48 d. Tent campers can stay for $10, $11 for trailers (hookups extra). Open April-October. Write Rt. 2, Box 1294, Oroville, WA 98844, or phone 476-2223, for reservations.

For conventional motel accommodations, try the **Red Apple Inn,** Hwy. 97 and 18th, 476-3694. Rooms are $20-29 s, $27-35 d (the higher-priced rooms have kitchenettes) and include a heated pool, riverfront picnic area, and laundry facilities. Down in Tonasket, another **Red Apple Inn** at Hwy. 976 and 1st, 486-2119, charges $28-31 s, $32-37 d for similar facilities.

Try **Don Ernesto's,** 806 Central, 476-2339, for Mexican and American lunch and dinner daily, breakfast on the weekends.

Festival

Early May means **May Day,** a 2-day festival with parades, dancing around the May Pole, arts and crafts, race, and more.

DARRINGTON/GRANITE FALLS

Darrington, in the foothills of the Cascades NE of Everett, was home to the Sauk and Suiattle Indians until white miners arrived in the late 1800s and early 1900s, in search of silver and gold. Though some deposits were found, the real money in this area was in logging; Swedish, Irish, Welsh, and Norwegian loggers, as well as those from the southern U.S., founded a community that still reflects its ethnic origins.

Granite Falls, with a population of just over 1,000, sits at the SW end of the "Mountain Loop Highway," an impressive title for a half-paved, half-gravel road connecting Granite Falls and Darrington. This rainy logging town at base of the Cascades provides a jumping-off point for hikers, campers, cross-country skiers, and snowmobilers exploring the Mt. Baker National Forest.

Monte Cristo, S of Darrington and E of Granite Falls, was established in the 1890s when gold and silver strikes lured over 1,000 people to the boom town, connected by rail to the port of Everett. The ore turned out to be of poor quality, and within 20 years Monte Cristo had become a ghost town. The fireplace and foundation of the Big Four Inn, a luxurious turn-of-the-century resort that burned to the ground in 1949, stand as reminders of the town's earlier glory. During the Depression, the railroad to Monte Cristo was replaced by the Mountain Loop Highway; today, the only access to the town is via a 4-mile hike from the end of the paved section of "highway"—the neglected bridges into town can't stand up to vehicular traffic.

Climate

The Darrington district is an anomaly in the Cascades. Whereas the Seattle area receives 30-40 inches of rain per year, Darrington gets an average of 80 inches while Monte Cristo gets over 140 inches, creating a dense rain forest much like those of the Olympics. The low altitude here means questionable snowfall, though cross-country skiing and snowmobiling are popular area activities.

RECREATION

Hiking

There are over 300 miles of trails within the Darrington Ranger District. Due to budget cuts, many of these trails are maintained by volunteers, so do your part to keep them clean. Parking area theft is becoming a real problem in this isolated area. Don't assume your valuables are safe in the trunk—leave them at home or carry them with you whenever possible, and report all thefts to a ranger station or the county sheriff.

The closest of the area peaks to Granite Falls is 5,324-foot **Mt. Pilchuck,** offering a number of good day hikes. For a 360-degree view of the Cascades and Puget Sound from an abandoned lookout atop Mt. Pilchuck, head toward the tiny Mt. Pilchuck ski area via Mt. Pilchuck Rd. #3014, a half-mile E of the Verlot ranger station, and park near the sign marking the trailhead. Allow 4 hours for the 2-mile OW hike, and be prepared for a 2,300-foot gain in elevation; best in late summer.

The virgin forest is as much the attraction as the clear mountain lake on the 4-mile RT hike to **Heather Lake.** To reach the trailhead, take Rd. #3014 for 1½ miles, then hike up an old logging road before reaching the forest and then open meadows. Allow 3 hours; elevation gain 1,100 feet.

Late spring is a good time to hike the 2½ miles to **Lake 22,** to see the numerous waterfalls along the way in their most turbulent state. The trail, starting 2¼ miles E of the Verlot ranger station, also passes through an old-growth cedar forest to the mountain lake. Allow 4 hours for the mild 1,400-foot elevation gain.

For a short, ¾-mile hike, take Rd. #3013 for 1½ miles to the trailhead for **Maiden of the Woods.** A Seattle sculptor, Dudley Carver, carved this woman (who was to be accompanied by various animals and wood spirits) into the side of a giant cedar as part of a proposed park. The park plan was abandoned, as was the sculpture.

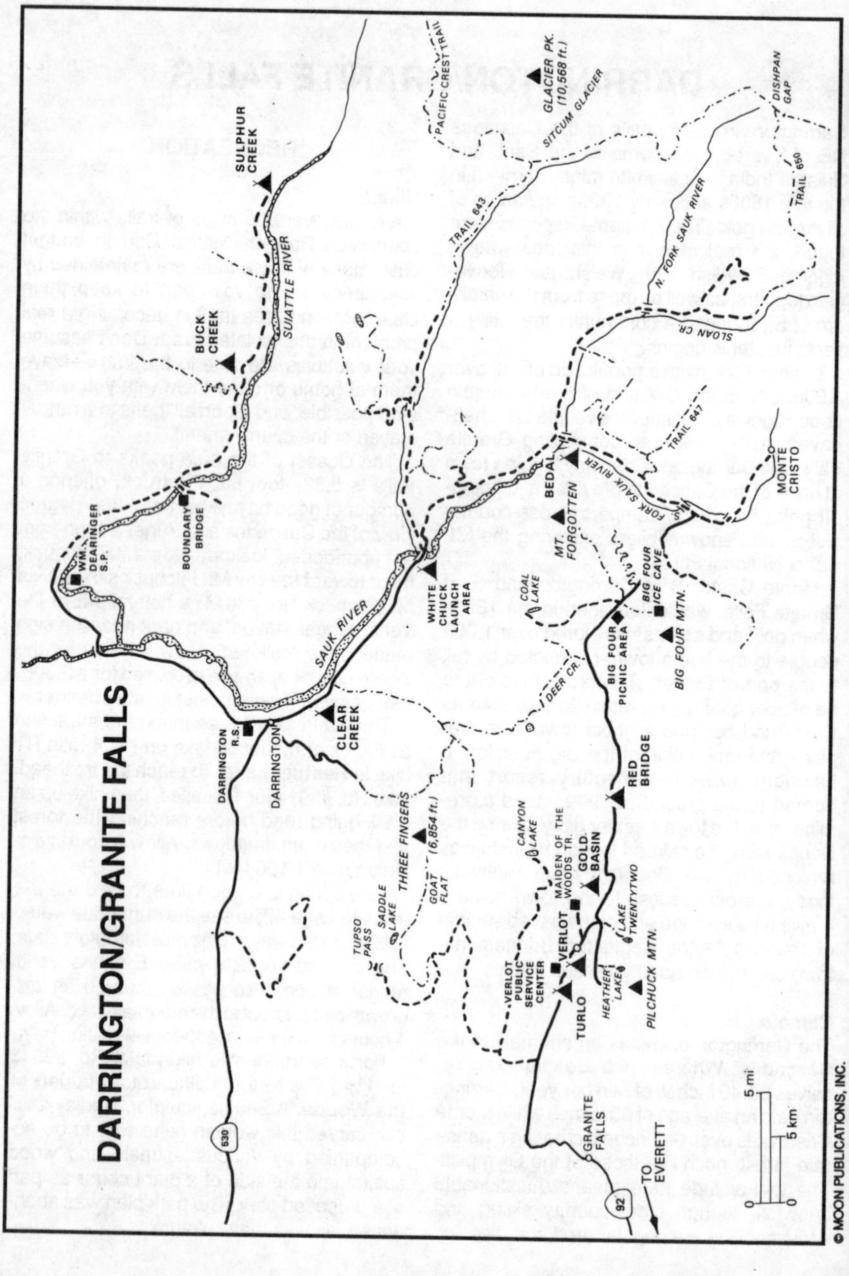

DARRINGTON/GRANITE FALLS

Labels on map:
SULPHUR CREEK
BUCK CREEK
SUIATTLE RIVER
GLACIER PK. (10,568 ft.)
SITCUM GLACIER
PACIFIC CREST TRAIL
TRAIL 643
N. FORK SAUK RIVER
SLOAN CR.
TRAIL 649
DISHPAN GAP
WM. DEARRINGER S.P.
BOUNDARY BRIDGE
SAUK RIVER
WHITE CHUCK LAUNCH AREA
COAL LAKE
BEDAL
MT. FORGOTTEN
TRAIL 647
S. FORK SAUK RIVER
BIG FOUR ICE CAVE
BIG FOUR PICNIC AREA
BIG FOUR MTN.
MONTE CRISTO
DARRINGTON R.S.
DARRINGTON
CLEAR CREEK
DEER CR.
RED BRIDGE
SADDLE LAKE
THREE FINGERS
GOAT (6,854 ft.) FLAT
CANYON LAKE
MAIDEN OF THE WOODS TR.
GOLD BASIN
TUPSO PASS
VERLOT PUBLIC SERVICE CENTER
TURLO
VERLOT
HEATHER LAKE
LAKE TWENTYTWO
PILCHUCK MTN.
GRANITE FALLS
TO EVERETT
530
92

5 mi
5 km

© MOON PUBLICATIONS, INC.

The **Big Four Ice Caves** are a popular 2-mile RT hike, starting 22½ miles from Granite Falls at the Big Four Picnic Area. The hike begins at a marshy area inhabited by beavers, then heads through a dense forest and over the S Fork of the Stillaguamish River to the ice caves and a view of 6,135-foot Big Four Mountain. The caves are generally exposed in Aug. and are visible through Oct., but admire them from afar: the caves are very dangerous to enter, as tons of ice may separate from the ceiling at any time, and in winter and spring the snowfield is susceptible to avalanches.

A full-day hike to alpine meadows starts 26 miles from Granite Falls and heads up **Mt. Forgotten** for an 8-mile RT hike. Take the Mountain Loop Hwy. for 15¼ miles from the Verlot Public Service Center, then go N on Perry Creek Rd. #4063 for a mile to the trailhead. The trail passes waterfalls at about 2 miles, heading through an old-growth forest for another 1¾ miles to the first meadow. Allow 7 hours to reach the meadows at 5,200 feet, an elevation gain of 3,100 feet. The trail continues through meadows to Mt. Forgotten's climbing route (for experienced alpine climbers only).

The rangers at the **Darrington Ranger Station** or the Verlot Public Service Center (see "Services" below) can provide you with excellent printed material on these and many other trails in the Darrington District.

Backpacking

The ultimate backpacking experience, the **Pacific Crest Trail,** crosses the Glacier Peak Wilderness at Dishpan Gap, accessible via Bald Eagle Trail #650. Drive E on Mountain Loop Hwy., 27 miles from the Verlot Public Service Center to Sloan Creek Rd. #49; turn L, and stay on Rd. #49 for 8½ miles to Cadet Creek Rd. #4920. Go R, staying on the road for 2 miles to Sloan Creek. Park here and cross the bridge by foot, hiking another 2½ miles to the trailhead. From here, it's 9½ miles to Dishpan Gap through clearcut, forest, and meadows with a 2,300-foot gain in elevation. In the Wilderness, you're likely to see deer, blue grouse, and hoary marmots,

plus an occasional lynx, mountain goat, and cougar.

The 6.7-mile OW trail to **Tin Pan Gap** and Three Fingers Mountain is a popular overnight hike. From Verlot, go W on Mountain Loop Hwy. for 4 miles, then head N on Tupso Pass Rd. #41, following it for 18 miles to the trailhead. The trail passes through dense forest for 2½ miles to 4-acre Saddle Lake; continue for another 2½ miles through meadows to Goat Flat, a popular camping spot. Use only a campstove; fire rings leave near-permanent scars in these fragile meadows. The trail reaches Tin Pan Gap after about 6 miles; from here, the hike becomes a technical climb over Three Fingers Glacier and a scramble to the top of Three Fingers Mountain and lookout.

Climbing

The Pacific Crest Trail approaches 10,541-foot **Glacier Peak,** a popular alpine climb in summer and fall. Climbers typically take White Chuck Trail #643 to the Pacific Crest Trail #2000, scrambling to the timberline and following the Sitkum glacier to the summit; consult with a North Cascades climbing guide (see "Booklist," p. 386) for a detailed description of the route. In spring, phone 527-6677 for avalanche information.

Boating And River Running

Enjoy a half- or full-day white-water or scenic float trip on the Sauk, Suiattle, or Skagit rivers with **Downstream River Runners.** A full-day white-water trip on the Suiattle, including all gear, costs $50-65 adults, (minimum age 12); a 10-mile Class III-IV white-water trip on the Sauk costs $55-70 (minimum age 14). In winter, enjoy a half-day float trip on the Skagit to see the wintering bald eagles for $40 adults; OK for kids as young as 5. (For more Skagit River eagle trips, see "The North Cascades And Lake Chelan," p. 279.) Prices include wetsuits (drysuits $10 extra), lunch, and shuttle. For a brochure or reservations, write 12112 N.E. 195th, Bothell, WA 98011, or phone (206) 483-0335.

Rivers Incorporated, Box 2092, Kirkland, WA 98033, (206) 822-5296, offers a Suiattle

The Darrington area is popular with hikers and backpackers.

the river is considerably calmer and is popular for canoeing.

Paddlers and rubber rafters will enjoy exploring 6-acre **Coal Lake,** a subalpine lake at 3,600 feet elevation. Go E on the Mountain Loop Hwy. for 15 miles from the Verlot Public Service Center, then go N on Coal Lake Rd. #4060 for 4½ miles to the trailhead. Carry your boat for about 50 feet to the lake, where you'll find a toilet and a limited number of campsites (that fill up very quickly).

Another lake with easy canoe and raft access is 5-acre **Canyon Lake.** From the Verlot Public Service Center, drive 4 miles on the Mountain Loop Hwy. to Rd. #41; turn R, continuing for 2 miles to Green Mtn. Rd. #4110. Turn R again (heading E now), driving 1.3 miles to Rd. #4111; follow this road for 10¾ miles to the trailhead on the L side of the road. Carry your boat along the 50-foot trail to Canyon Lake, surrounded by trees and a few campsites; fair fishing.

The Darrington District boasts a large number of small lakes, some of which provide excellent fishing. Check at the ranger station or public service center for a list of lakes and suggestions on the best for boating, fishing, or paddling.

Cross-country Skiing And Snowshoeing

Skiers and snowshoers can count on solitude when exploring the Darrington District; most roads aren't plowed and snowfall is unpredictable at this low elevation, and what snow there is is often wet and difficult to ski through. Still determined? Take these routes as suggestions; if the roads themselves aren't snow-covered, keep driving along the route until you come to some.

From Hwy. 530 on the way to Darrington, go S on French Creek Rd. #2010 through dense forest and switchbacks for great views and a fast, downhill trip back. Or, from the Darrington Ranger Station, drive N on Hwy. 530 for 6½ miles to Suiattle River Rd. #26; ski on the road or follow the road till you hit snow.

On the Granite Falls side, the Big Four Area is very popular with skiers, snowshoers, snowmobilers, and winter hikers; take the Mountain Loop Hwy. 23 miles from Granite Falls to the end of the maintained road at

trip for novice or advanced river runners in July and Aug. for $38-60, depending on group size (lunch and wetsuit available but not included in price). They also offer Upper Skagit white-water ($38-60) and Skagit eagle trips ($35), plus runs on the Wenatchee, Methow, and Klickitat rivers.

Experienced, do-it-yourself river runners will enjoy the challenges of the Sauk and Suiattle rivers. The Suiattle is the more tame of the 2, rated Class II to III from Boundary Bridge to the Sauk River; it's unnavigable within the National Forest boundary due to logjams, hidden stumps, and debris. Put in at Boundary Bridge or William Dearinger State Park. The Sauk River ranges from Class I to V; from the White Chuck launch area to Clear Creek it's a IV or V, with difficult rapids through narrow passages. From Bedal to White Chuck, the river is classified as a Class III to IV, and below Clear Creek it ranges from Class III to I. North of Darrington,

Deer Creek Rd. #4052. Ski 2 miles from the parking area to Big Four Picnic Area, following the S Fork of the Stillaguamish River; continue another mile to the snowfield near the Big Four Ice Caves. The avalanche danger here is severe; don't travel beyond the edge of the clearing—it's the force of avalanches that created and maintain that clearing! Allow 3-5 hours RT; suitable for beginner skiers.

ACCOMMODATIONS

Motels

Darrington's **Stagecoach Inn,** 1100 Seaman St., 436-1776, is an attractive, though small, motel with rooms from $32 s, $43 d. A greater variety of lodging is available in Arlington, about 25 miles W on Hwy. 530. **Smokey Point Motor Inn,** 17329 Smokey Point Dr. at Arlington exit 206 off I-5, 659-8561, has rooms from $30 s, $35-50 d, plus a year-round heated pool and whirlpool. The **Arlington Motor Inn,** 2214 Hwy. 530 off exit 208, 652-9595, has rooms from $29-32 s, $38-42 d. Granite Falls doesn't offer much; best to stay in Marysville or Everett (see p. 117), or better yet, go camping.

Camping

The Forest Service operates 13 campgrounds in the Darrington district, most on a first-come, first-served basis; no electrical hookups or dump stations. Campgrounds are open from Memorial Day through Labor Day weekends, and campers are limited to a 14-day stay in campground.

From Granite Falls, neighboring **Turlo** and **Verlot** campgrounds have 19 and 26 spaces respectively near the Verlot Public Service Center; **Gold Basin** campground, 2½ miles E of the service center, has 93 campsites. All 3 have piped well water, trailer space, flush or vault toilets, and garbage service and charge a $6 fee. **Red Bridge** campground, 7 miles E of the Verlot service center, has 16 sites with vault toilets; no well water or garbage collection, but no fee either.

From Darrington on the Mountain Loop Hwy., **Clear Creek** campground has 10 sites and trailer space 3½ miles from the Darring-

ton Ranger Station; **Bedal** has 18 units and trailer space 18 miles from the ranger station. Both have vault toilets; no fee. From Darrington via Suiattle River Rd. #26, **Buck Creek,** 23 miles in with 51 spaces, and **Sulphur Creek,** 28 miles from Darrington with 29 campsites, have trailer spaces and vault toilets; no fee.

These 4 campgrounds are available by reservation only (contact the Darrington office, 436-1155): **Esswine,** 5 miles E of the Verlot service center, $15; **Boardman Creek,** about 6 miles E of Verlot, $25; **Marten Creek,** 9 miles E of Verlot, $15; **Coal Creek Bar,** 12½ miles E of Verlot, $15; and **Beaver Creek,** 13½ miles E of Verlot, $15. These are smaller campgrounds, with 3 to 8 campsites each; Boardman and Coal Creek have trailer spaces.

FOOD

Aside from a handful of diner-style restaurants and backwoods taverns in Darrington and Granite Falls, food in these parts is scarce. Head back to Arlington for good food in surprising surroundings: 2 restaurants right off I-5 at the Hwy. 530 exit, **Weller's Chalet Inn** and **O'Brien's Manor,** are remarkably good considering their right-off-the-interstate location. Weller's has good sandwiches for about $5, steak and seafood dinners for $6-14, in surroundings that look like an uneasy mix of rest stop and restaurant. O'Brien's has sandwiches, salads, and light dinners (heavy on the turkey) for under $6. Travel E on Hwy. 530 for fast food in downtown Arlington. Off I-5 exit 206 (Smokey Point), the shopping center adjacent to the Smokey Point Motor Inn offers pizza, Mexican food, and a family restaurant, plus banks, state liquor store, drugstore, and mini-post office.

ENTERTAINMENT

The last weekend in June brings the annual **Timber Bowl Rodeo** to the rodeo grounds 4 miles W of Darrington. In mid-July, enjoy Darrington's 3-day annual **Bluegrass Festival and Street Fair.**

SERVICES AND INFORMATION

The area code in Darrington, Granite Falls, and surrounding area W of the Cascades is 206. For up-to-date information on trail conditions, campgrounds, fishing, and other outdoor activities contact the **Verlot Public Service Center,** 691-7791, or the **Darrington Ranger Station,** 436-1155. For other area information, call or write the **Granite Falls Chamber of Commerce,** Box 28, Granite Falls, WA 98252. Hikers and campers can stock up on forgotten supplies at **Forrister's Sport Shop** on Hwy. 530 in Darrington; for groceries, the **IGA** is across the street. The closest hospital to Darrington is **Cascade Valley Hospital,** 330 S. Stillaguamish in Arlington; call 911 or 435-2133.

TRANSPORTATION

By Car

The **Mountain Loop Highway** from Darrington to Granite Falls is a 55-mile-long, largely unpaved road through valleys and forests, offering numerous glimpses of snowy peaks. From Darrington, the road is paved for the first 9⅓ miles, becoming a narrow dirt road for the next 23½ miles; the remaining 22 miles to Granite Falls are paved. The "highway" and area logging roads are popular snowmobile routes in winter.

By Bus

Based in Everett, **Community Transit** goes S to Edmonds and Seattle, N to Stanwood and Darrington, and E to Snohomish, Lake Stevens, and Granite Falls for $.50; (800) 562-1375 or 778-2185.

SKYKOMISH

The little towns of Skykomish and, to the E, Index, Gold Bar, and Monroe, serve mainly as jumping-off points for the wealth of recreational opportunities in the nearby Cascade wilderness areas. The Skykomish District encompasses over 315,000 acres of National Forest land and 41,000 acres of state and private lands, with striking natural features from glaciers and alpine meadows to dense forests intersected by clear, clean rivers. The Alpine Lakes and Henry M. Jackson Wilderness Areas and the Mt. Index Scenic Area are within the district's boundaries; access to Glacier Peak Wilderness Area is via the Pacific Crest Trail. Much of the area's beauty can be seen through your car windows and from short roadside paths, but over 140 miles of hiking trails let you experience its splendor at close range.

RECREATIONAL ACTIVITIES

Scenic Drives

U.S. Hwy. 2, the main access to the area, is a spectacular drive in and of itself. From the Skykomish Ranger Station, 1 mile E of Sky-

komish center on Hwy. 2, W to the small town of Scenic, the 2-lane road gains 1,000 feet in elevation; from there to the summit of Stevens Pass it gains another 2,000 feet to reach a height of 4,061 feet, passing rugged snow-covered peaks and waterfalls along the way.

Other scenic drives in the Skykomish District are on numbered gravel forest roads. Create your own loop route from the roads on the map below, or try the **Maloney-Sobieski Mountain Rd.** for views of Glacier Peak and deep valleys. To get there, head E from the ranger station for ½ mile, then turn L onto Foss River Rd. #68. Drive about 5½ miles to the intersection of #68 and #6840; go R onto #6840. When you reach the next fork, stay to the R onto #6846 until the next fork; then go L to Sobieski Mountain or R to Maloney Mountain, with spectacular views on either route.

Waterfalls

The Hwy. 2 planners must have loved waterfalls: several raging falls are right along the roadside. **Bridal Veil Falls,** ¼ mile E of the Index junction, vary with the season: summer

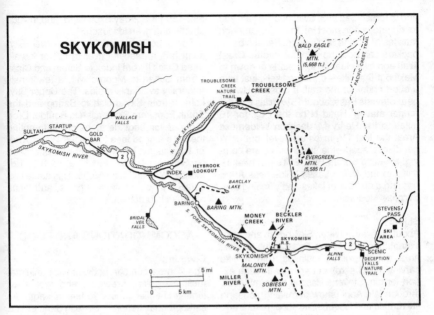

SKYKOMISH

brings 2 distinctive "veils" while winter freezes the falls into a glistening sheet of ice. Five miles E of the ranger station, **Alpine Falls** drop 50 feet into the Tye River below; park on the S side of the highway and follow the can't-miss path. About 1½ miles from Alpine Falls are **Deception Falls,** right on the S side of the highway. Be careful here—it's easy to lose your footing on the mossy rocks. To see the biggest falls you've got to exert a little more effort: **Wallace Falls,** a 265-foot waterfall, is a 7-mile RT hike from the trailhead 2 miles NE of Gold Bar.

Nature Trails

If you're not up for a long hike, these 2 half-mile nature trails through Douglas fir forests will give you a breather from mountain driving. **Deception Falls Nature Trail** begins at the N end of the picnic area about 6½ miles from the ranger station on Hwy. 2; **Troublesome Creek Nature Trail** starts 10.8 miles NE of Index next to the Troublesome Creek campground on North Fork Skykomish Rd. #63.

Hiking Trails

Check in at the ranger station for information on trail conditions before you start any of the longer hikes described below.

For a short trip, try the 1-mile OW hike from Hwy. 2 just E of Index to **Heybrook Lookout** for views of Mt. Index, Baring Mountain, and the Skykomish Valley. Another lookout, **Evergreen Mountain,** can be reached via a 1.5-mile OW hike from the end of Evergreen Mountain Rd. #6554. The trail gains 1,300 feet in elevation, but on a clear day the 360-degree view includes Glacier Peak and Mt. Rainier. Regrettably, this trail is open to ORVs. Slightly longer (2.2 miles OW) but with little elevation gain is the **Barclay Lake** trail, following the course of Barclay Creek to the lake with a nice view of Baring Mountain. To get to the trailhead, take Barclay Creek Rd. #6024 for 4 miles.

Backpackers have quite a few options. A good 2-day RT hike (9.7 miles OW) starts from North Fork Skykomish Rd. #63 to **Bald Eagle Mountain,** via a loop from trail #1050 N to trail #650, E to trail #1051, and SE to the end of forest road #63. Switchbacks take you to ridgetops for most of the hike, through masses of hillside wildflowers. Serious backpackers can hook up with the **Pacific Crest Trail** and hike clear up to Canada or down to Mexico if they like—or, more likely, just hike a short chunk of the trail. It crosses Hwy. 2 near Stevens Pass, about 15½ miles E of the ranger station. Head N on the PCT for 16 miles to the Henry M. Jackson Wilderness Area; the first 1½ miles are level, but don't get discouraged—the switchbacks are coming! Heading S from Hwy. 2, it's just over 19 miles to the Alpine Lakes Wilderness Area, passing a number of lakes and climbing over Surprise Mountain.

Skiing

About halfway between Skykomish and Lake Wenatchee is **Stevens Pass,** a full-size ski area, popular with Seattleites, with 10 lifts serving 1,125 acres of beginner through expert terrain. Stevens Pass is open mid-Nov. through late April (snow permitting), offering ski rentals and lessons, ski shop, restaurant, cafeteria, cocktail lounges, and weekend child care. Lift tickets are $24 adults, $18 kids, $20 seniors; 6 and under, 70 and older ski free. Phone (206) 973-2441 or (206) 634-1645 for conditions.

See "Wenatchee," p. 313, for information on **Mission Ridge Ski Area.**

Raft Trips

Operating out of Bothell, **Downstream River Runners** offers 1- to 5-day white-water or float trips on numerous rivers throughout eastern and western Washington and Oregon, including the popular and challenging Skykomish River with its class V "Boulder Drop" ($55-70, minimum age 14) and an Upper Skykomish trip on an inflatable kayak ($70, minimum age 16). These guys are pros! Write them at 12112 N.E. 195th in Bothell, WA 98011, or phone (206) 483-0335, for a brochure.

North Cascades River Expeditions, Box 116, Arlington, WA 98223, (206) 435-9548 or (800) 634- 8433, also offers a variety of 1- and 2-day river trips, including the Skykomish, Wenatchee, Skagit, Klickitat, and more. Prices are $37-40 pp for 1-day trips,

$82-159 for a 2-day expedition, and include shuttle and riverside lunch.

For a do-it-yourself trip, the lower Skykomish is a peaceful river to raft or kayak, rated Class II from Index to Sultan and Class I from Sultan to Monroe with a few small, generally avoidable rapids. The Upper Skykomish from Skykomish to Baring and the South Fork from Skykomish to Boulder Drop are *not* for beginners; before attempting them it's a good idea to consult *Water Trails of Washington* by Werner Furrer, published by Signpost Books, 8912 192nd SW, Edmonds, WA 98020, for $5.95. This guide has detailed maps, cautionary notes, and loads of useful information.

ACCOMMODATIONS AND FOOD

Camping

The 4 area campgrounds provide minimal facilities—toilet, fireplace, and table—for tents and trailers under 15 feet in length. All campgrounds generally close in Sept. after a late spring opening; all sites are available on a first-come, first-served basis for a small nightly fee. **Beckler River,** 2½ miles from the ranger station, has 24 sites; **Money Creek,** just over 4 miles away, also has 24; **Miller River,** about 6½ miles from the station, has 15; and **Troublesome Creek,** 20 miles away, has 35 primitive sites (no well water or garbage pickup) for no fee. As in virtually all natural areas today, giardiasis is a problem; boil all drinking water for 3-5 minutes to prevent this "backpacker's diarrhea."

Motels

Virtually deserted "downtown" Skykomish has a gas station, 2 motels, 2 restaurants, a tavern, and a liquor store. Take your pick! Following the Skykomish River W along Hwy. 2, you'll pass a number of other bare-bones establishments between Skykomish and Monroe that consider a 4-foot sign reading "MOTEL" or "RESTAURANT" sufficient advertising. One of the cleaner and more modern is the **Dutch Cup Motel** at 918 Main St. in Sultan, with rooms going for $31 s, $35-41 d; 793-2215.

Food

The **Dutch Cup Restaurant,** up the street at 927 Hwy. 2, is open daily from 5 a.m.-2 a.m. (a courtesy to the skiers passing through) with steaks and weekend specials. When you arrive in the thriving commercial center of Monroe (pop. 3,000) you'll be overwhelmed by the choices: Dairy Queen, McDonald's, and Rax have brought fast-food to the foothills, but locally owned establishments provide a welcome change of tastes. **Nina's Soup Kitchen,** 113 E. Fremont, is open daily for breakfast and lunch, and the **Holiday Inn Country Eatery and Lounge,** 612 E. Stevens Pass Hwy., serves homemade chili, steaks, soups, and desserts.

SERVICES

The Skykomish Ranger Station provides recreation and topographic maps, books, and current information on trail conditions and campground closures. The ranger sta-

tion is open daily in summer, Mon. through Fri. in winter.

The Skykomish area code is 206. For medical emergencies call 2222 in Skykomish; for first aid or search and rescue, call the King County Sheriff at (800) 344-4080 or the Snohomish County Sheriff at 1-258-2484. To report a forest fire, call the Skykomish Ranger Station at 677-2412 or the Dept. of Natural Resources at (800) 562-6010.

TRANSPORTATION

Skykomish is on the good-road-conditions side of Stevens Pass, often a challenge to traverse (and sometimes closed) in winter. If you're going to ski at Stevens Pass Ski Area or continue W to Leavenworth or Wenatchee, be sure to phone 976-7623 (there's a $.35 toll for the call) for road conditions before you set out; you don't want to have to buy chains at the only gas station in Skykomish.

LEAVENWORTH

HISTORY

Although preceded by prospectors and Hudson's Bay fur traders, the first settlers in the Leavenworth area didn't arrive until the late 1880s, with the news that the Great Northern Railway planned to lay tracks through the valley. The resulting population "boom" brought Leavenworth about 300 people by the turn of the century. They were mostly railroad men or lumberjacks employed by the Lamb-Davis Lumber Co., operators of 1 of the state's largest sawmills. The after-hours rowdiness of these laborers gave little Leavenworth a somewhat unrefined reputation that took years to live down. Even so, by the early 1920s a wave of families bought tracts of land to grow "Wenatchee Big Red" apples. When the railroad moved its switching yard from Leavenworth to Wenatchee, and the sawmill closed its doors after logging all its waterfront land, these family-based fruit farms provided much of the town's income. But by the 1960s, it was clear that Leavenworth needed more than apples to survive. The newly formed committee on tourism suggested a fall festival and a major remodeling job. Suggestions ranged from a Gay '90s theme to a Western town, but with the impressive mountain backdrop, an Alpine village seemed the best answer. The renovation was financed with private funds, and backed by local bankers. A look at the bustling village today shows how much a dying town can accomplish with cooperation and elbow-grease.

SIGHTS

The Bavarian Village
Start your tour of the Bavarian Village on Front St., the heart of town, where there's plenty of on-street parking. Shops, restaurants, taverns, and hotels are squeezed side-by-side, all beautifully decorated with carved wood, flower boxes, and murals—even the automated teller machine is surrounded by a painted alpine scene! There are shops that sell wooden toys, clocks, music boxes, wool clothing, and a bakery, **Hoelgaard's** (731 Front St.), that will tempt even the strongest-willed. Work your way back through the numbered side streets and onto Commercial for more shops. Don't miss **Obertal Mall** on 9th St.; it contains galleries, high-quality craft and gift shops, boutiques, and a coffee shop.

Parks
Riverfront Park, on the banks of the Wenatchee River off 8th and Commercial, has walkways over and around the river, benches for a respite from shopping, plus beautiful views of the peaks surrounding Icicle Canyon. Cross-country ski from here to the golf course. **City Park,** across Front St. from the shops, is a relaxing, sunny spot for a picnic lunch or noontime break.

Twenty-three miles N of Leavenworth on Hwy. 207, **Lake Wenatchee State Park** is a popular year-round recreation area, with cross-country skiing in winter, plus swimming, fishing, and canoeing on over 12,000 feet of spectacular Lake Wenatchee waterfront, set against a backdrop of majestic snow-covered peaks. Other facilities include boat rentals, weekend-evening interpretive programs, and 197 wooded campsites (no hookups). Summer camping is $6 per site; a number of sites are plowed for winter camping at $4.50 a night. Rent a horse from **Icicle Outfitters and Guides** for a guided 1- or 2-hour ride from their barn at the park for $8 an hour, Memorial Day through Labor Day; no reservations necessary.

ACCOMMODATIONS

Bed And Breakfast
Housed in the Old Blewett Pass Stage Stop that served as a B&B in the early 1900s, the **Old Blewett Pass Bed and Breakfast,** 548-4475, came back to life in 1986, offering food and lodging "country-western style" about 10 miles S of downtown at 3470 Hwy. 97. Rooms are $30 s, $38 d with shared bath, $40 s, $48

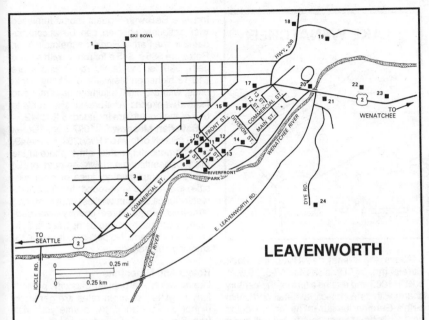

LEAVENWORTH

TO SEATTLE
TO WENATCHEE

1. Haus Rohrbach Pension
2. Der Ritterhof Motor Inn
3. Enzian Motor Inn
4. Casa Mia
5. Gustav's Onion Dome Tavern
6. Hoelgaard's Bakery
7. Cascade General Hospital
8. Hansel 'n' Gretel Deli and Reiner's Gasthaus
9. chamber of commerce
10. city park
11. Der Sportsman, Edelweiss Restaurant and Europa Hotel
12. Obertal Mall and Baren Haus
13. Edel Haus Inn
14. Haus Lorelie Inn
15. U.S. Forest Service
16. Evergreen Inn
17. Greyhound Station
18. Brown's Farm B&B
19. Bavarian Meadows
20. Bayern Village Motor Inn
21. Chalet Trailer Park
22. Pine Village KOA
23. River's Edge Lodge
24. Mountain Home Lodge

© MOON PUBLICATIONS, INC.

d with private bath; a 4-person family suite is also available for $60. A full breakfast is served; children are welcome to enjoy the enclosed playground, and babysitting is available with advance notice. Other extras include a pool, sauna, and recreation room.

Brown's Farm B&B, 548-5863, is a 3-gabled log home surrounded by woods and farm animals at 11150 Hwy. 209. Antique-furnished rooms are $55-65 d; kids ($5-10 more) are welcome to hike the wooded trails, gather farm-fresh eggs, or play with Barney, the family dog. Winter guests can rent cross-country skis, then warm up with hot cider by the rock fireplace. Bring a sleeping bag and pillow for the kids; foam pads are provided. No pets or smoking in the guest rooms.

Haus Rohrbach Pension, 12882 Ranger Rd., 548-7024, is a European-style inn overlooking the Leavenworth Valley. Their 10 rooms are $55-75 s, $65-85 d. The complimentary breakfast features sourdough pancakes and home-baked cinnamon rolls, and an outdoor pool and hot tub are also available. Their Alm Haus offers a bedroom, dining area, kitchen, and bath, and can accommodate 6-8 people for $98-118. Kids are welcome; outdoor smoking only, and no pets.

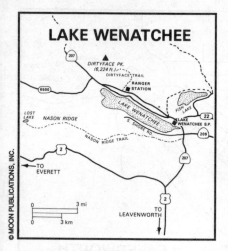

Above the Wenatchee River, the **Haus Lorelei Inn,** 347 Division St., 548-5726, was built in 1903 and retains a turn-of-the-century charm with its architectural detail and Elisabeth's German furniture. The inn is located on the riverfront cross-country ski trail and a short walk from a sandy swimming beach, just 2 blocks from downtown. The 6 rooms (4 with private bath) are $65 d, including a full breakfast and use of the hot tub and tennis court. No smoking.

Mountain Home Lodge, 548-7077, (Box 687), is in a category by itself: located just 3 miles from downtown, this lodge is a true escape, particularly in winter when transportation from parking lot to lodge is via snowcat. Half a mile up into the Cascades, winter rates—$148-188 d—include 3 meals a day (add $10 pp for the snowcat RT); there's no need to go into town when cross-country skiing, snowshoeing, and sledding are right out the back door! Other activities, such as downhill skiing, horseback riding, snowmobiling, white-water rafting, and mountain tours can be arranged. Summer room rates—$78-108 d—are without meals; meals cost $8.25 for breakfast, $6 for lunch, and $18.50 for dinner, and meal reservations must be made in advance. No pets or kids; smoking outdoors only.

Located between Waterfront Park and the shopping district at 320 9th St., **Edel Haus Inn** is a B&B with 5 guest rooms furnished with antiques; children can be accommodated in the Family Room on the main floor. Rates are $35 s, $45 d for rooms with shared bath, $50 for the family room; prices are $10-15 higher on festival and holiday weekends, with a 2-night minimum on winter and festival weekends. A full breakfast and private use of the hot tub are included; 548-4412.

Bavarian Meadows, 11097 Eagle Creek Rd. 3 miles N of town off Hwy. 209, 548-4449, offers a peaceful country atmosphere in the midst of beautiful meadows. An outdoor hot tub, with complimentary juice or cider tubside, is available year-round; the full breakfast includes Belgian waffles, bratwurst, and farm-fresh eggs. Three country-style bedrooms each have private bath; 1 bed is $55-65, $85 for 2 beds. No pets or kids under 13; smoking outdoors only.

Hotels And Motor Inns

Leavenworth is a popular getaway, particularly in winter, so room rates are generally higher on weekends; try to time your visit from Sun. through Thursday.

The **Enzian Motor Inn,** 590 Hwy. 2, 548-5269 or (800) 223-8511, is a cross between a conventional motel and B&B: its 77 rooms, convention facility, and heated pool and hot tub are standard hotel equipment, but the German architectural design, imported furniture, continental breakfast, and complimentary cross-country ski rentals give the inn a warm, homey feeling. Rates are $49-75 s, $56-75 d. The **Europa Hotel,** downtown at 833 Front St., 548-5221, has 12 rooms with full baths, TV, and continental breakfast in European style for $36-46 s or d. **Der Ritterhof Motor Inn,** Hwy. 2, 548-5845, has 52 rooms, heated pool, hot tub, outdoor volleyball, horse shoes, and badminton areas, and a putting green from $45-47 s, $51-53 d. **Bayern Village Motor Inn,** 1505 Alpen See Strasse, 548-5875, has rooms with private decks overlooking the Wenatchee River, swimming pool, and barbecue pits for $45-60 s or d. The **Evergreen Inn,** 1117 Front St., (800) 327-7212 or 548-5515, is less than 2 blocks from the downtown commercial center and has cottage-like rooms from $30-50 s,

Leavenworth's streets have a Bavarian flair.

$45-75 d, with midweek discounts in winter. Between Leavenworth and Cashmere on Hwy. 2, **The River's Edge Lodge,** 548-7612, has 23 rooms on the Wenatchee River with outdoor pool and hot tub starting at $40-60 s or d; some rooms include kitchenettes.

Camping
Located on the Wenatchee River at 11401 River Bend Dr., the **Leavenworth Pine Village KOA,** 548-7709, operates from April through mid-Oct. with a heated pool, cabins, laundry, groceries, and Sat. hay rides; rates are $13.50 per night; hookups extra. The **Chalet Trailer Park,** ½ mile E of town on Hwy. 2, has 24 sites for $10.50, including all hookups. Open from May to Oct.; 548-4578. About 15 miles NW of Leavenworth near Lake Wenatchee, **Midway Village RV Park** has 10 tent sites and 23 hookup sites for $8. Open all year; 763-3344. For camping in Lake Wenatchee State Park, see "Parks" above.

FOOD

The village has a number of restaurants, all very Bavarian from the outside but often with largely American menus fortified by a token bratwurst or Wiener schnitzel. You'll get the real thing at **Reiner's Gasthaus,** 829 Front St., 548-5111, serving authentic Austrian, Bavarian, and Hungarian cuisine with live accordian music, all at low to moderate prices.

The **Edelweiss Restaurant,** 843 Front St., 548-7015, is open for 3 meals with a mixed American/German menu; lunch runs $2-9, dinners up to $22 for twin lobster tails, but generally $12 or less. Grab a beer and burger at **Gustav's Onion Dome Tavern,** at the W end of town on Hwy. 2. **Hansel 'N' Gretel Deli,** 819 Front St., has German sausages, sandwiches, homemade pies, 18 flavors of ice cream, and picnics-to-go. Perhaps a little out-of-place, **Casa Mia** has Mexican food (under a Bavarian disguise) across from the fire station at 703 Hwy. 2; 548-5621. Or, for pizza, try **Baren Haus** at 9th and Front streets. If you're headed up to Lake Wenatchee, try the **Cougar Inn Resort** at the end of Hwy. 207 for steaks, seafood, prime rib, chicken, and Sunday Champagne brunch with stunning lake and mountain views; 763-3354 for reservations.

ENTERTAINMENT

Festivals
The people in Leavenworth always find something to celebrate, with festivals and fairs circling the calendar. January brings **The Great Bavarian Ice Fest,** with a snowman contest, kids' cross-country ski day, fireworks, and Sasquatch dance in mid-month. Smaller festivals fill the months until the big **Maifest,** held on Mother's Day weekend, when costumed Bavarian dancers circle the May Pole, and concerts, a fun run, volksmarch, and Sat. night

street dance are accompanied by oompa music from the band stand. This weekend marks the start of **Art in the Park,** with area artists displaying their talents every weekend from May through Oct. in City Park. The **Washington State Autumn Leaf Festival,** a week-long event held at the end of Sept., starts with a grand parade and includes daily oompa music, a street dance, hootenanny, fun run, flea market, and casino night. But Christmas is Leavenworth's most festive holiday: the **Christmas Lighting Festival,** held the 1st and 2nd Sat. in Dec., when all the Christmas lights go on simultaneously at dusk. Mr. and Mrs. Claus appear in their house in the park, and caroling, sleigh rides, concerts, and food booths add to the holiday festivities.

Sleigh Rides And Hay Rides

The people at **Red-Tail Canyon Farm** at 11780 Freund Canyon Rd. operate hay rides and sleigh rides year-round through scenic Red-Tail Canyon. One-hour sleigh rides are $7 adults ($10 in the evening), $4 for kids; hay rides are $6 and $4. To get there, take Hwy. 209 N for 2½ miles; 548-4512 for reservations. **Eagle Creek Ranch,** 548-7798, also offers hay and sleigh rides over the meadows and through the woods surrounding the ranch 2 miles N of town off Hwy. 209.

Snowmobile Tours

See the Cascades and the Leavenworth valley from a unique perspective on one of **Cascade Snowmobile Safaris'** snowmobile tours. All cold-weather clothing from snowsuits to boots to helmets is included in the price of $35 for a 2-hour tour, $45 for a 3-hour tour, starting off Hwy. 2 and heading almost to the top of Wedge Mountain and/or Boundary Butte. Two tours are scheduled every day, weather permitting, with occasional twilight tours; riders must be 16 or over. For reservations call 548-5162 or 548-4337.

Cross-country Skiing

Leavenworth is a popular spot with cross-country ski enthusiasts, with over 30 km of groomed trails within minutes of downtown. Four ski areas are maintained by the Bavarian Nordic Club: 1 mile from Leavenworth on Icicle Rd., 13 km of groomed tracks traverse a golf course and gravel pit with mountain and river views. A few miles out of town at the mouth of Icicle Canyon, a 10-km level trail goes through meadows and forests above the Fish Hatchery. Ski Hill Dr. has a 5-km track, with 2 km lighted for night skiing, rolling over the hills adjacent to the downhill ski area. Here you get the added benefit of a lodge and weekend food service. Lake Wenatchee State Park, 23 miles N of Leavenworth, has a minimum of 5 km of maintained trails. Trail fees for the first 3 areas are $4 per day for adults, kids under 12 free; skiing is free at Lake Wenatchee State Park. For more information contact the Bavarian Nordic Club at Box 573, Leavenworth, WA 98826, 548-5983.

Eagle Creek Ranch has 10 km of groomed trails, ski rentals, and instruction on Eagle Creek Rd., 2 miles N of town on Hwy. 209, as well as wilderness hut-to-hut ski trips and Sat. night "moonlight ski and barbecues" in Jan. and Feb.; call 548-7798 for specifics.

The **Leavenworth Nordic Center** on Hwy. 2 just E of the downtown area offers ski equipment rentals and lessons in everything from the basics to telemark techniques, plus a Kiddies Kamp where your 4- to 8-year-old can learn to ski from a patient expert.

Cross-country ski rentals are available from the ski areas themselves or the following retail outlets: **Der Sportsman,** 837 Front St., 548-5623, or **Gustav's Onion Dome Tavern,** Hwy. 2, 548-4509.

For overnight cross-country skiing or alpine hiking in the high Cascades, stay in semi-luxury at **Scottish Lakes Nomad Camps,** 548-7330. Two rustic camps, 1 halfway up and 1 at the top of 5,000-foot McCue Ridge, provide warmth, company (up to 35 people), and a ride down for $56 d at Midway (no meals) and $120 d at High Camp (3 meals); prices ⅓ off in summer. Write Box 312, Leavenworth, WA 98826, for details.

Downhill Skiing

Leavenworth has its own tiny ski area, Leavenworth Ski Bowl, with 2 rope tows providing uphill transportation for the handful of runs.

The ski season here is generally shorter than at the bigger areas because of the lower elevation; call 548-5115 for conditions.

Two larger ski areas are close by: **Stevens Pass,** 35 miles to the W on Hwy. 2 (see "Skykomish," p. 302), and **Mission Ridge,** 35 miles in the other direction near Wenatchee (see p. 313).

Raft Trips

The rivers in the central Cascades support a number of white-water outfitters in the Leavenworth-Skykomish area. **Quiet Water Outfitters & Guides** operates out of Leavenworth over Gustav's Onion Dome, providing scenic float trips for people 4 and over on the upper Wenatchee from April to Aug. and exciting white-water trips for adults from mid-April to about mid-July; prices are in the $30-45 range. Canoe rentals are also available, with the outfitters getting you started and picking you up at a predetermined point downriver. For info and reservations call 763-3733.

The **Northern Wilderness Co.,** a somewhat bigger operation, provides all the necessary equipment and a gourmet lunch for their river trips, ranging from slow float trips to wild white-water rides on the Wenatchee, Skykomish, Naches, Tieton, and other rivers throughout central and western Washington. Call them toll-free at (800) 848-8001 for specific trip dates and reservations.

For more central Cascade raft trips see "Skykomish," p. 302.

Pack Trips

From July through Sept. **Eagle Creek Ranch** offers a number of pack trips to Alpine Lakes, Glacier Lakes, and Henry M. Jackson wilderness areas in the Cascades. Their standard pack trips and their "you hike & we pack" trips—meaning you provide and cook the food—cost $60-70 pp per day. "Drop camp" packages, where the wrangler takes you to a favorite spot for as long as you like and then comes back to get you out, include pack and saddle horses and cost $250 pp. They also offer day-long horseback rides along mountain trails from April through Sept. at 9 a.m. everyday. For a brochure or additional info contact them at Box 719, Leavenworth, WA 98826, 548-7798.

Icicle Outfitters and Guides offers hourly horse rides at Lake Wenatchee State Park for $8 an hour, guided day rides into the Cascades for $45 a day, and an assortment of 2-5 day pack trips, including combination horseback-and-raft or -canoe trips, from $50 pp per day for the hike-and-pack trips, $160 for an overnight campout and barbecue in the high country, to $350 for a 5-day horseback trip. Write or call them at Box 322, Leavenworth, WA 98826, 784-1145 or 763-3647.

Hiking

The Lake Wenatchee Ranger District, centered around Lake Wenatchee and Fish Lake at the N end of Hwy. 207, has an extensive system of hiking trails. Popular with hikers and photographers is the **Dirtyface Trail,** a steep 4½-mile OW trail from the Lake Wenatchee Ranger Station to the Dirtyface Lookout at 6,000 feet, with views of the lake and surrounding scenery. Backpackers may want to try the **Nason Ridge Trail,** a 22-mile OW scenic trail along the length of the Nason Ridge, starting at South Shore Rd. off Hwy. 207; check at the ranger station for possible closures due to trail reconstruction. A number of other 1-day or longer hikes start from various points along a complicated network of numbered forest roads; best bet is to check at the ranger station for detailed maps and printed trail descriptions. This is black bear country; hikers and campers should use standard bear precautions (see "Flora and Fauna," p. 4).

Climbing

Good physical condition is the only requirement for participation in 1 of **Leavenworth Alpine Guides'** guided climbs and rock- and ice-climbing courses. Prices range from $25 for the half-day basic rock course to $310 for a 5-day alpine climbing camp with an ascent of 9,415-foot Mt. Stuart. A number of other courses and climbs are offered, including other central Cascade peaks, Mt. Baker, the Alps, and Mt. Everest. For a brochure write Box 699, Leavenworth, WA 98826, 548-4729.

SERVICES AND INFORMATION

All Leavenworth-area phone numbers are preceded by area code 509. For maps, brochures, and additional information contact the **Leavenworth Chamber of Commerce,** Box 327, Hwy. 2, Innsbrucker Bldg., Leavenworth, WA 98826, 548-7914.

Hikers and campers will find **Die Waschrei** on Front St. a relief: laundry facilities *and* hot showers in the same place! Open daily, 7 a.m.-10 p.m. A place as beautiful as Icicle Canyon should be heavily photographed; take your rolls to **Der Darkroom,** 819 Front St., for 1-hour processing.

The Leavenworth area, unlike some mountain communities, is equipped with emergency 911 service. For less critical medical emergencies, contact **Cascade Hospital,** 817 Commercial St., at 548-5815.

TRANSPORTATION

Getting There
Driving to Leavenworth via Hwy. 2 through Stevens Pass has been described as "driving through a Christmas card." Rocky, snow-covered peaks surround the highway as you approach the 4,061-foot pass; then, closer to Leavenworth, the Wenatchee River rushes alongside the road. The trip from Seattle is about 125 miles. From late fall to early spring, be sure to call 976-7623 (there's a $.30 toll) for pass conditions before setting out—and

have your chains ready! As an alternate route, take I-90 over Snoqualmie Pass to Hwy. 97 N over Swauk Pass; these passes are generally drier, and snowfree earlier, than Stevens. From Wenatchee the trip is an easy one: 30 miles NE on Hwy. 2.

Greyhound Bus Lines serves Leavenworth from their Kountry Kitchen "station" at the E end of town on Hwy. 2; they have 3 eastbound and 3 westbound departures every day, year-round. The nearest real airport (outside the airstrips at Lake Wenatchee and Cashmere) and railroad station is in Wenatchee; see p. 317 for information.

Bus Tours
Gray Line of Seattle offers tours from Seattle to Leavenworth for Maifest ($34) in early May and the Christmas Tree Lighting Ceremony ($30) on the first 2 Saturdays in December. Prices for both 1-day trips include a snack on the bus. For more information call Gray Line at (206) 624-5813. Also operating out of Seattle, **Don & Diane Funtours** has 1-day bus tours in late Sept. or early Oct. to the Autumn Leaf Festival, and the first Sat. in Dec. to the Tree Lighting Festival; both tours are $34. For reservations or information call (206) 282-3508.

Departing from Tacoma, **Cascade Trailways** offers 1-day Autumn Leaf Festival tours for $28.50, including snack; call (206) 383-4615 (Tacoma) or (206) 838-3465 (Seattle), or toll-free statewide (800) 824-8897 for information and reservations.

WENATCHEE

Driving E on Hwy. 2 from the damp Puget Sound area, the transition to the "dry side of the mountains" is an abrupt one. The heavily forested, snowcapped Cascades give way to bone-dry hills, blanketed by snow in winter but covered only by dry brown grass in summer. None of Puget Sound's mostly cloudy days here: Wenatchee gets over 300 sunny days—only 10-15 inches of rain—per year. The warm sunny days, cool nights, and volcanic ash soil combine to provide ideal apple growing conditions.

Phillip Miller was Wenatchee's pioneer apple grower. In 1872, Miller took squatter's rights on a parcel of land in the Wenatchee Valley and planted a handful of apple seedlings. The trees flourished, and when the railroad came to Wenatchee in 1892, Miller drove in the silver spike to link the last rails—and to help determine Wenatchee's economic future. Miller's ranch shipped its first full carload of apples to Seattle in 1901. Irrigation projects, beginning with the Highline Canal in 1904, brought much-needed water to this arid region, and helped the apple industry blossom. Today, an average of 30,000 carloads of apples are shipped from the Wenatchee Valley every year.

SIGHTS

Ohme Gardens

Located just N of Wenatchee on a bluff overlooking the Wenatchee Valley, **Ohme Gardens** is a testimony to over 50 years of watering and weed-pulling by the Ohme family that transformed a barren hillside of sagebrush into one of America's most highly acclaimed gardens. Originally created for the Ohmes' personal use, the patch of green on the otherwise desolate hillside attracted visitors' attention. Now covering 9 acres, the gardens resemble natural alpine scenery: evergreens, grass, ponds, and waterfalls blend with the existing rock—a cool reprieve from the scorching Wenatchee sunshine. A lookout from the gardens' highest point provides broad views of the valley, Cascades, and Columbia River. The gardens are near the junction of Hwys. 2 and 97, 3 miles N of Wenatchee, at 3327 Ohme Rd., 662-5785; open daily from 9 a.m. to dusk, early April through October. Admission is $3 adults, $1.50 kids under 18; steep dropoffs make this a hazardous place for uncontrollable toddlers.

Rocky Reach Dam

The 4,800-foot-long **Rocky Reach Dam,** 7 miles N of Wenatchee, has been damming the Columbia since 1962. Picnic on 15 acres of landscaped grounds, visit the fish viewing room, and check out the 2 exhibits. **The Gallery of the Columbia,** contains the pilothouse of the late 1800s steamer Bridgeport and replicas of Indian tools and villages, lumbermen, and turn-of-the-century railroaders; **The Gallery of Electricity** relates the history of electricity in displays and photos, and allows visitors to generate their own electricity. To get there, follow Hwy. 97 N from Wenatchee.

Museum

The **North Central Washington Museum,** 127 S. Mission, 662-4728, has 2 floors of exhibits pioneer life in the Wenatchee area, the first transpacific flight, and the Great Northern Railway are the main attractions. Joined to the museum by a skybridge, the Apple Industry Exhibit includes a working antique apple sorter and assembly line. Open weekdays 10 a.m.-4 p.m., weekends 1 p.m.-4 p.m.; donation.

More Apples

At 2900 Euclid Ave., the **Washington State Apple Commission Visitor Center,** 663-9600, has a film and displays about the apple industry, and, better still, samples of a variety of apples and juices. Open daily May through Oct.; free.

Parks

On the E side of Rocky Reach Dam, 6 miles N of Wenatchee on Hwy. 2, **Lincoln Rock State Park** has swimming and a boat launch

Ohme Gardens

popular with fishermen and water-skiers. Camping facilities here include 27 non-hookup sites. Nine miles SW of Wenatchee on Squilchuck Rd., **Squilchuck State Park** has winter cross-country skiing amidst a forested mountain setting, plus a small downhill ski area with 2 rope tows, ski school, and coffee shop. Camping here is limited to large groups with advance reservations; call 662-1651.

ACCOMMODATIONS

Hotels And Motels

For budget lodging (from $22-25 s, $28-36 d) with a year-round heated pool and sauna, try **Scotty's Motel,** 104 N. Wenatchee Ave., 662-8165. The **Imperial Inn,** 700 N. Wenatchee Ave., 663-8133 or (800) 368-4400, is also inexpensive, with 40 units from $20-23 s, $26-35 d. Among the nicest of the area's budget motels is the **Orchard Inn,** 1401 N. Miller across from the Valley North Shopping

Center, 662-3443 or (800) 368-4571. Rooms start at $32 s, $35-41 d, and include a heated pool and hot tub, available year-round.

Nendel's Inn, on the Columbia River in E. Wenatchee at 11 W. Grant Rd., 884-6611, has 101 rooms from $34-36 s, $42-46 d, with a pool, sauna, whirlpool, and adjacent restaurant and lounge. The **Chieftain,** 1005 N. Wenatchee Ave., 663-8141 or (800) 572-4456, has a heated pool, hot tub, attached restaurant, and 105 rooms from $34-38 s, $41-50 d. The **Best Western Rivers Inn,** 580 Valley Mall Parkway in E. Wenatchee, 884-1474 or (800) 528-1234, has 55 rooms from $38-48 s, $43-53 d, with jacuzzi, heated pool, restaurant, and lounge. Even more elegant is the **Red Lion Motor Inn,** 1225 N. Wenatchee Ave., 663-0711. Rooms are reasonably priced—$48-58 s, $55-65 d—and include all the niceties of more expensive hotels: a heated indoor pool and jacuzzi, room service, and a restaurant and lounge with nightly entertainment. Another quality hotel is the **West Coast Wenatchee Center Hotel,** 201 N. Wenatchee Ave., 662-1234, with 146 rooms and suites from $49-61 s or d. Extras include free airport shuttle, swimming pools and jacuzzis indoors and out, exercise room, glass elevators, room and valet service, and a rooftop restaurant serving breakfast, lunch, and dinner with mountain and river views.

Camping

About 15 miles N of Wenatchee, **Entiat Park** has tent and trailer camping on the Columbia River. The **Wenatchee River County Park,** 6 miles W of Wenatchee on Hwy. 2, has playgrounds, picnic areas, and camping for 64 trailers and RVs (40 full hookups, 24 water and electric only) and 20 tent sites; overnight fees are $7-9. The park is open from April through Oct., and all camping is on a first-come, first-served basis.

FOOD

The **Horan House Restaurant,** 2 Horan Rd., 663-0018, serves international cuisine in a home built in 1896 by John Horan, the val-

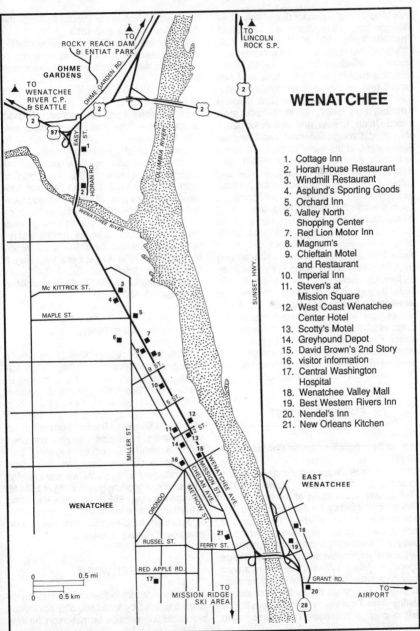

WENATCHEE

1. Cottage Inn
2. Horan House Restaurant
3. Windmill Restaurant
4. Asplund's Sporting Goods
5. Orchard Inn
6. Valley North Shopping Center
7. Red Lion Motor Inn
8. Magnum's
9. Chieftain Motel and Restaurant
10. Imperial Inn
11. Steven's at Mission Square
12. West Coast Wenatchee Center Hotel
13. Scotty's Motel
14. Greyhound Depot
15. David Brown's 2nd Story
16. visitor information
17. Central Washington Hospital
18. Wenatchee Valley Mall
19. Best Western Rivers Inn
20. Nendel's Inn
21. New Orleans Kitchen

© MOON PUBLICATIONS, INC.

ley's "Apple King"; open for dinner only, Tues. through Sat.; reservations are suggested. **The Windmill,** 1501 N. Wenatchee Ave., 663-3478, has been one of the Northwest's prime steakhouses for the past 65 years, featuring char-broiled steak, pork, and seafood. Open for dinner Tues. through Saturday. At 928 S. Mission, the **New Orleans Kitchen,** 663-3167, serves moderately priced Cajun, Creole, and catfish for dinner only, Wed. through Saturday. **The Chieftain Restaurant,** at the motel of the same name at 1005 N. Wenatchee Ave., 663-8141, specializes in moderately priced seafood and prime rib ($7-13), and is open for 3 meals daily; they also feature live entertainment Tues. through Sat. nights. **Magnum's,** 1112 N. Wenatchee Ave., 662-9121, serves prime rib, seafood, pasta, and steaks at family prices, generally under $10; open for 3 meals daily. **The Cottage Inn** has been serving chicken, steak, and seafood at the 134 Easy St. location since 1940. Open for dinner only, Tues. through Sat.; 663-4435. **Steven's at Mission Square,** 218 N. Mission, 663-6573, serves fresh seafood, steaks, and pasta for lunch weekdays, dinners Mon. through Saturday. Enjoy live Maine lobster plus other seafood, steak, and pasta at **David Brown's Second Story,** 23 S. Wenatchee Avenue. Open daily; 662-1508 for reservations.

ENTERTAINMENT

Festivals

The self-proclaimed "Apple Capital of the World" is the only proper place to hold the annual **Apple Blossom Festival,** going strong since the "Blossom Days" of 1919. This 10-day event starts at the end of April and is highlighted by the Apple Blossom Parade on the first Sat. in May; other festivities include carnivals, circuses, horse shows, gem and mineral exhibits, and a production staged by local talent. The **Wenatchee Youth Circus** opens in July in Wenatchee, then travels throughout the Pacific Northwest all summer. The end of summer brings the **Wenatchee Valley Arts Festival,** a juried sidewalk fine arts display, to downtown Wenatchee in late

September. For more information call the Allied Arts office at 662-1213.

Leavenworth, the Bavarian village nestled in the Cascades just 22 miles away, hosts numerous festivals throughout the year; see p. 306.

Skiing

Just 12 miles from Wenatchee, **Mission Ridge** is one of the area's bigger ski areas, with 4 double chairs serving 33 runs—70 percent of which are intermediate—and a 2,140-foot vertical drop. One chair and the beginner's rope tow serve the area lighted for night skiing on Wed. through Sat. and holidays. There are also 42 km of marked cross-country trails on rolling terrain, and spaces available for RVers. All the big-time ski area extras—ski school, cafeteria, rentals and repairs—are available here. For snow conditions call 663-7631; to get there, take Hwy. 2 to S. Mission Street.

For information on the tiny **Squilchuck Ski Bowl** see "Parks" above.

SHOPPING

The **Wenatchee Valley Mall** is the area's largest, with 47 stores including Sears, Lamonts, and Ernst, across the bridge in E. Wenatchee. The **Valley North Shopping Center,** Miller St. in N. Wenatchee, is a smaller version, highlighted by J.C. Penney. At 2nd and Mission, **Mission Square** has an assortment of boutiques, including a kitchen shop, fine art and custom framing shop, craft supply store, deli, and restaurant. Skiers and other outdoors enthusiasts will want to visit **Asplund's,** a sporting goods store at 1544 N. Wenatchee Ave., 662-6539. Here you'll find everything from swimsuits to bicycles to backpacking supplies, plus cross-country ski equipment, rentals, and lessons.

SERVICES

All phone numbers in Wenatchee and points E are preceded by area code 509. For maps, brochures, or specific information on the Wenatchee area, contact the **Wenatchee Area Visitor and Convention Bureau,** Box 850, 2 S. Chelan Ave., Wenatchee, WA 98801, or call 662-4774 or toll-free statewide (800) 57-APPLE.

For fire or police emergencies, dial 911. For medical emergencies or problems, phone **Central Washington Hospital,** 1300 Fuller, 662-1511.

TRANSPORTATION

Arriving By Air
Wenatchee's airport, Pangborn Field, was named in honor of Clyde Pangborn, a pilot who piled up aviation record after record in the '20s and '30s. Pangborn's most notable feat was accomplished on Oct. 6, 1931, when he and Hugh Herndon completed the first non-stop flight over the Pacific Ocean, landing at the Wenatchee Airport—minus the landing gear they had intentionally dropped when excess weight threatened to shorten their flight. The trip was an eventful one—the pair was charged with spying and held in Tokyo for several weeks before being released with a hefty fine; then, while crossing the Pacific, icy wings and an empty gas tank nearly did them in.

Today Pangborn Field connects Wenatchee with Seattle, Spokane, Tri-Cities, and Portland by commuter airlines such as **Horizon Air,** (800) 547-9308.

Arriving By Bus
Greyhound, 662-2183, provides daily service to Seattle, Spokane, and other cities from their depot at 301 1st Street.

Bus Tours
Gray Line of Seattle has 2-day bus tours from downtown Seattle to Wenatchee for the May Apple Blossom Festival; prices of $137 s, $110 pp d include RT transportation, hotel accommodations, dinner, and a snack. For information and reservations call (206) 624-5813.

Arriving By Train
Amtrak serves Wenatchee daily via their Seattle/Chicago train, *The Empire Builder,* connecting to Ephrata and Spokane to the E and Everett, Edmonds, and Seattle to the west. For reservations and information call (800) USA-RAIL.

VICINITY OF WENATCHEE

CASHMERE

Tucked between Wenatchee and Leavenworth on Hwy. 2, the tiny town of Cashmere (pop. 2,300) is famous—at least statewide—for its Aplets and Cotlets and Grapelets. These gooey, all-natural confections are made of fruit juices (apple, grape, and apri-COT) and walnuts and coated with powdered sugar.

Sights

Tours of the downtown Cashmere **Aplets and Cotlets** plant (just off Hwy. 2) include free samples and are available Mon. through Fri., and most summer weekends, from 8 a.m.-11:45 a.m. and after lunch from 1 p.m.-5 p.m., 782-2191.

Reputedly among the top 5 restored pioneer villages in the country, the **Chelan County Historical Museum,** 5698 Museum Dr., 782-3230, has restored and furnished 18 of the oldest buildings in Chelan County, all built prior to 1900, to create an authentic old-West atmosphere. A blacksmith shop, school, gold mine, mission building, and hotel are part of the Pioneer Village; there's also a sizable collection of Indian artifacts. Open 10 a.m.-4:30 p.m. weekdays, and Sun. afternoons; closed mid-Oct. to April 1. Donation.

Food

Among Cashmere's more elegant restaurants is **The Pewter Pot,** a colonial-style restaurant featuring fresh baked bread and locally grown produce. Open for lunch and dinner; 782-2036. The **Coachman Inn,** 128 Cottage Ave., 782-3213, is open daily from 6 a.m.; prawns, steaks, and prime rib are the specialties here. The lounge, open till 2 a.m., features live country-western music nightly. Open weekdays from 5 a.m., the **Parkside Restaurant** at Cottage and Division serves 3 meals daily from an omelette/sandwich/seafood/steak menu; 782-4317.

To ship some eastern Washington apples home to your relatives, stop in at **Bob's Apple Barrel** on Hwy. 2 for a gift pack; 782-3341.

Festivals

Celebrated the 1st week in July, **Founder's Days** are a creation of the local chamber of commerce, inspired by the 1979 celebration of Cashmere's 75th year of incorporation, the "Diamond Jubilee." The town had such a good time they made the fair an annual event. One of the highlights is the "Stillman Miller Hill Climb," inspired by an early resident who claimed he could pour himself a beer in the local tavern, run up Numbers Hill, and be back before the head settled. Whether or not he actually made it is anybody's guess; but the concept was so appealing that runners are still trying it today. Other events include a parade, barbecue, arts and crafts show, and street dance.

Cashmere is also home to the **Chelan County Fair,** a 4-day event beginning the first Wed. after Labor Day, highlighted by rodeos, musical entertainment from area bands, a carnival, and youth group exhibits.

The 2nd weekend in Oct. brings **Cashmere Apple Days,** the primary fund-raising event of the Chelan County Museum. Apple bin races, an apple pie baking contest, music, dancing, and staged shoot-outs are all part of the pioneer days fun.

For specific festival dates, maps, or other info contact the **Cashmere Chamber of Commerce,** 99 N. Division, Cashmere, WA 98815, 782-1511.

Raft Trips

Rafters from the daring to the scared-skinny can find a raft trip to their liking with **Wenatchee Whitewater and Scenic River Trips.** Real white-water enthusiasts will enjoy their Sept. Tieton River trip, the fastest, narrowest river they run, plunging 50 feet per mile over its 15-mile course; children and more timid rafters may prefer their 2-hour to 2-day scenic float trips, with plenty of photographic, birdwatching, and gold-panning opportunities in the Upper Wenatchee River. Prices range from $21 for a 2-hour meander, $25-33 for a full-day scenic, $39-49 for a full-day white-water, to $249 for a 3-day white-water trip on Oregon's Deschutes River; Visa and MasterCard are OK. Wetsuits, tents, and sleeping bags may be rented for a small fee. For a brochure or reservations, call 782-2254 or write Box 12, Cashmere, WA 98815.

SNOQUALMIE AREA

When most Washington residents hear "Snoqualmie," they think first of the pass and ski areas, then the falls; the tiny town is only an afterthought. Snoqualmie Pass is the easiest way through the Cascades in winter, sporting the widest highway and lowest elevation of any of the mountain passes; the 4 ski areas at the summit bring a lot of vehicular traffic through the region. Snoqualmie Falls is an attraction both for the falls themselves and for the restaurant and new hotel that sit atop it. But the little town of Snoqualmie, with about 2 blocks of civilization on either side of the tracks, draws tourists only for its scenic railroad. The bigger town in the rural Snoqualmie area is North Bend, a pseudo-Bavarian village at the foot of Mount Si, one of the state's most hiked mountains.

SIGHTS

Snoqualmie Falls

One hundred feet taller than the ones at Niagara, Snoqualmie Falls in Fall City has been awe-inspiring since probably the last Ice Age, and electricity-generating since 1898, when Puget Power built the world's first totally underground generating facility. Though the land is all owned by the utility, they've made a great deal of it available for public use with a landscaped park and picnic area, hiking trail, view platforms, and a snack bar. To get there, drive about 4 miles N on Hwy. 203 from Snoqualmie; open all year.

Carnation Research Farm

North of Snoqualmie and Fall City on Hwy. 203 is the Carnation Research Farm, owned and operated by the Carnation milk-and-ice-cream, dog- and cat-food people. Free, self-guided tours of the plant include the milking carousel, maternity barn and recovery room, and research kennels where beagles, Scotties, and fox terriers sample new flavors of dog food. Because of their susceptibility to airborne illnesses, the kitties are kept in a cattery closed to visitors. The rest of the place is open Mon. through Sat. 10 a.m-3 p.m.; 788-1511.

Museum

In North Bend, the **Snoqualmie Valley Historical Museum**, 320 N. Bend Blvd. S, has

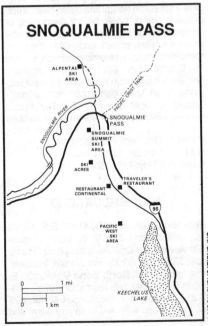

SNOQUALMIE PASS

ALPENTAL SKI AREA

SNOQUALMIE RIVER

PACIFIC CREST TRAIL

SNOQUALMIE PASS

SNOQUALMIE SUMMIT SKI AREA

SKI ACRES

TRAVELER'S RESTAURANT

RESTAURANT CONTINENTAL

90

PACIFIC WEST SKI AREA

0   1 mi

0   1 km

KEECHELUS LAKE

© MOON PUBLICATIONS, INC.

permanent displays of Indian artifacts, pioneer and logging history, and a small gift shop. Open weekend afternoons from April through Oct.; 888-3200 or 888-0062.

Winery

The **Snoqualmie Winery,** 1000 Winery Rd. in Snoqualmie (take a R off the Snoqualmie Falls exit from I-90), produces 7 varieties of wine, including Johannisberg Riesling, Merlot, and Cabernet Sauvignon. Besides the usual gift shop, this one has a big picnic area with panoramic views of the Cascades and Snoqualmie Valley. Open for tours and tastings 10 a.m.- 4:30 p.m. daily, year-round, with occasional extended hours during the summer and ski seasons; 888-4000.

Herbfarm

Fourteen years ago, Lola Zimmerman put out a few pots of her home-grown herbs at a roadside stand. Today, The Herbfarm boasts over 400 kinds of live herb plants, 120 species of succulents, and classes in everything from Medicinal Gardening to Herbal Vinegars. Pick up an herbal flea collar, beer bread mix, live plants, book, herbal deodorant, or gourmet coffee bags at the farm's country store. Or, plan ahead and enjoy their immensely popular weekend luncheon, served Fri. through Sun., April through Christmas. The 2-hour luncheon is a 6-course meal featuring fresh local game and fish, accompanied by vegetables from The Herbfarm's garden; $24.95 per person, and reservations are required. The Herbfarm is open daily, March to Oct., with reduced days and hours in fall and winter; 32804 Issaquah-Fall City Road, Fall City, 784-2222.

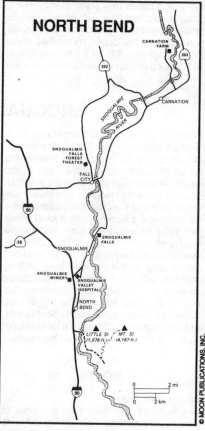

ACCOMMODATIONS

Hillwood Gardens B&B, 41812 S.E. 142nd St. in North Bend, 888-0799, features mountain views in an Oriental atmosphere; rooms cost $35, no children. For simple, inexpensive lodging, the **North Bend Motel,** 322 E. North Bend Way, has rooms for $27 d; 888-1121. Cheaper still, the **Sunset Motel,** 227 W. North Bend Way, will keep you warm and dry for $22 d; 888-0381. On the way to Snoqualmie Pass, just off I-90 at exit 34, the **Edgewick Inn,** 14600 468th Ave. SE in North Bend, 888-9000, has 43 modern rooms plus a whirlpool and laundry facilities for $33 s, $37-42 d.

In 1988, the long-awaited **Salish Lodge,** (800) 826-6124, opened at Snoqualmie Falls. This luxury hotel features a wood-burning fireplace, spa, and refrigerator in every room, plus a balcony in most. A great place for a honeymoon or a getaway weekend, the rooms here are pricey: $150 s or d for a courtyard room, $165 s or d for a room with a river and mountain view.

FOOD

The Salish Lodge Restaurant atop Snoqualmie Falls has been in operation (under various names) since 1916. The new dinner menu features 6 entrees in the $15-24 range, and the farm-style Sunday brunch has always been a regional favorite. The homey lodge atmosphere, with overstuffed chairs surrounding a warm fire in the lounge, is worth the price of admission. Don't waste it on the kids. Reservations are recommended: (800) 826-6124.

Atop Snoqualmie Pass, the **Restaurant Continental**, 434-6343, specializes in fondues; open daily for breakfast, lunch, and dinner. Also at the pass, **Traveler's Restaurant** has inexpensive sandwiches, burgers, light meals, take-out food, and—God bless 'em—plenty of public restrooms.

ENTERTAINMENT

Skiing

Snoqualmie Pass offers probably the best skiing in the state, with more choices than in any other region. There are 4 major ski areas here, virtually side by side. Three of them operate as one, calling themselves "The Big 3" and requiring only 1 lift pass: **Alpental, Ski Acres,** and **Snoqualmie Summit.** Snoqualmie, in the center, emphasizes beginner and intermediate terrain serviced by 8 chairs and 5 rope tows. Ski Acres is the next step up in difficulty, with a good showing of intermediate and expert as well as beginner terrain, with 7 chairs and 6 rope tows. Alpental is the big guy, with a 2,200-foot vertical drop, and while novices and intermediate skiers have some territory, the emphasis here is clearly on difficult and expert-only slopes, serviced by 4 chairs, 4 ropes, and a platter. You can ski between Ski Acres and Snoqualmie via expert-level terrain, but you'll have to board the free shuttle bus to get to Alpental. Lift tickets are $15 weekends, $12.50 midweek; night skiing, available on almost all of Snoqualmie and Ski Acres' slopes and about a third of Alpental's, costs $11-12. Child care is available at Ski Acres for kids 2 and over, daily except Tues. and by appointment; call 434-6400 for reservations. Naturally, all 3 areas provide ski school, equipment rentals, restaurants and/or snack bars; in addition, Ski Acres has 20 km of cross-country trails, including 1 ½ km of lighted track for night skiing. Snoqualmie and Alpental are closed Mon., Ski Acres is closed Tues., except during the Christmas season. Call 236-1600 for the Snoqualmie report; or from Seattle, call 634-0200; from Tacoma, 572-4300; and from Everett, 353-7440.

Pacific West Mountain Resort, otherwise known as Pac West, is just W of The Big 3. Members of the Pac West Sport & Racquet Club receive a 25 percent discount on the $12 day lift pass, but you don't have to be a member to ski here. The mountain has a 1,143-foot vertical drop, making it slightly higher than Ski Acres and Snoqualmie; the beginner through expert terrain is served by 4 double chairs and 2 rope tows. Night skiing goes on till midnight. Besides the usual ski school, rentals, restaurant, and lounge, Pac West has extensive cross-country ski terrain. For info call 633-2460.

Hiking

North Bend's 4,167-foot **Mount Si** is one of the most climbed mountains in the state; 10,000 people a year take the 8-hour RT hike. It's not just the length of the hike that's tough—the elevation gain of 3,100 feet keeps you puffing. The views W to Puget Sound, Seattle, and the Olympics, however, are worth the effort. To get there go L on 432nd SE (Mt. Si Rd.), about a mile from the E edge of North Bend. After you cross the Middle Fork Snoqualmie River, go R at the first intersection, then drive 2 ½ miles to the parking lot, trailhead, and picnic area. The trails are generally snowfree from April to November.

Theater

Set amongst towering evergreens at the foot of the falls, the **Snoqualmie Falls Forest Theater** in Fall City has stage performances every weekend from late June to about Labor Day, plus a special Easter Passion Play. For current productions and ticket info call 222-7044.

SERVICES

The area code in the Snoqualmie area is 206. For maps, brochures, and other information contact the **Snoqualmie Falls Chamber of Commerce,** Box 356, Snoqualmie, WA 98065, 888-2320, or the **North Bend Chamber of Commerce,** 320 S. Bendego, North Bend, 888-1678.

Dial 911 for medical, fire, and police emergencies. **Snoqualmie Valley Hospital** is easy to find from the I-90 Snoqualmie Falls exit, at 1505 Meadowbrook Way SE, for 24-hour emergency service; 888-1438.

TRANSPORTATION

Arriving By Car
Carnation, Snoqualmie, Fall City, and North Bend lie to the W of the mountains, actually just E of Bellevue and Issaquah, so getting there from Seattle isn't a problem in winter. Although Snoqualmie Pass is the easiest pass to traverse, it does get snowy up there and sometimes closes during heavy storms; call 976-7623 (there's a $.30 toll) for road conditions and information on snow tire or chain advisories or requirements.

Arriving By Bus
The Big 3 ski areas offer bus service from Seattle and Bellevue via the *Snoqualmie Fly-*

er. For information call 232-8182. Seattle's **Metro** serves Fall City (right to the falls), Snoqualmie, and North Bend; call 447-4800 for schedule.

Bus Tours
For a "Wines and Antiques" tour, call **Gray Line of Seattle** at 624-5813. The bus leaves downtown Seattle for a tour of Snoqualmie Winery, then, well-oiled, you head for the Putnam Antique Mall, making a final stop at Woodinville's Chateau Ste. Michelle for more vino. This tour operates monthly from Jan. through June for $28.

Steam Train Tour
The **Puget Sound & Snoqualmie Valley Railroad** operates steam trains between Snoqualmie and North Bend, at the base of Mount Si, through the Snoqualmie Valley, passing the top of Snoqualmie Falls and offering other viewpoints along the way. The 1¼-hour ride departs about every 1½ hours on Sun. from April through Oct., and on Sat. from Memorial Day through Sept.; fares are $5 adults, $3 for kids 5-15, and lap-sitters under 5 are free. Two special "Santa Trains" run the first 2 weekends in Dec. for $2; also, a Halloween "Spook Train" operates the last weekend in Oct.—anyone dressed in full costume rides for half-price. Call 888-3030 weekends, or 746-4025 24 hours a day.

EASTERN WASHINGTON

SPOKANE

HISTORY

Spokane's population of 172,000 makes it the largest city between Seattle and Minneapolis and the 2nd-largest city in Washington. Though Spokane is less than half as large as Seattle, and has little of that city's suburban sprawl, the 2 cities have had much in common from their earliest days: both were leveled by great fires, after which both towns were rebuilt in brick; both cities attribute some of their early growth to outfitting gold and silver miners; both have impressive park systems designed by the same firm; and both cities hosted a World's Fair.

Probably the most exciting event in Spokane's history was witnessed by no one: the Spokane Flood, which occurred 18,000 to 20,000 years ago. As the Ice Age came to an end, the glaciers melted and water backed up behind the ice-dammed Clark Fork River, near the Idaho and Montana border, forming an enormous lake covering more than 3,000 square miles—larger than today's Puget Sound. As the ice dam melted, the great pressure from the backed-up water caused it to suddenly collapse, sending an unimaginable rush of water over all of eastern Washington, flattening the landscape, digging coulees, washing away soil, and emptying the great lake in as little as 2 days. What a white-water raft trip!

The next several thousand years were relatively uneventful ones for Spokane, but the first white settlers came to the area in 1810—very early in Washington's history—when David Thompson built Spokane House, the first trading post in the state. The War of 1812 and turbulent times that followed led to the abandonment of the post in 1826, and white settlers didn't return until 1838, when Elkanah Walker and Cushing Eels established a Protestant mission that lasted until 1847. Though Spokane County was created in 1859, which included all of the land between the Columbia River and Rocky Mountains, N of the Snake River, the first permanent settlers didn't arrive at "Spokane Falls" until 1871. By 1880, Spokane's population had grown to only 350, and the town competed hotly with neighboring Cheney for the county seat. Vote counters announced Spokane as the winner, but Cheney residents suspected the officials of lying about the results, so they came at night, kidnapped the election official and his records, and proclaimed Cheney as the winner of the ballot. Spokane's population grew dramatically by the next election, and in 1886 the city had the votes it needed to win the county seat back.

Like Seattle, Spokane experienced tremendous growth when the railroad came to town: from a population of 350 in 1880 to almost 20,000 by 1890. The Northern Pacific was the Northwest's first railroad, but its monopoly drove transportation prices sky-high; though eastern Washington was the cheapest place to grow wheat, the farmers paid the highest prices getting it to market. The city of Spokane was so determined to get a 2nd railroad, they gave the land, free of charge, to the Great Northern Railroad Co. to be sure

Looff Carousel

it would pass through town—and loosen the Northern Pacific's grip on the farmers.

As in Seattle and Ellensburg, a devastating fire ripped through Spokane in the summer of 1889. The 3 fires put an end to the all-wood construction that had previously been so popular in these forested regions, and the downtown areas were all rebuilt in brick. Though farming was a large part of the Spokane economy, the turn-of-the-century gold and silver strikes throughout the Northwest also sparked the city's economic growth.

The event that put Spokane on the map for most of the country was Expo '74, the city's World's Fair. The theme for the fair, "Celebrating Man's Fresh, New Environment," was a real problem for the developers, since the location chosen was Havermale Island in the middle of the polluted Spokane River, in a dirty, run-down section of town. The governing bodies of Washington and Idaho combined their efforts to clean up the river, while grass and trees were planted and buildings torn down to prepare for the fair. The result was a world-class expo that won international attention and served to gear up the country for the bicentennial celebration.

SIGHTS

Riverfront Park

The site of Expo '74 has been preserved as a striking city park covering over 100 acres in downtown Spokane, with many of the original displays still intact on both sides of the Spokane River. Outdoors, visit the Japanese Garden, Canada Island, and suspension bridge and skyride over **Spokane Falls,** illuminated at night. Indoors, enjoy the **Eastern Washington Science Center,** featuring a planetarium and 150 hands-on exhibits; open Memorial Day through Labor Day, admission is $2.50 adults, $1.50 kids. The 5-story-high **IMAX Theater,** 1 of only 40 in the world, has shows on the hour from 1 p.m., featuring dazzling, sharp images and stereo sound for $3.75 adults, $2.75 kids; phone 456-5511 for schedule. Riverfront Park boasts the **Spokane Opera House,** home to the Spokane Symphony Orchestra. The **Pavilion** amusement park features the Dragon

Coaster and other rides for the daring, plus tamer attractions for the kids. Be sure to take a spin on the hand-carved 1909 **Looff Carousel** on the park's S side; the fare is $.60. Take a gondola ride over the Spokane River, park, and falls from the W side of the park for $2.50 adults, $1.50 kids. The park also features an ice-skating rink, miniature golf course, restaurant, picnic areas, and more. All-inclusive park admission is $8.50 adults, $7.50 kids.

Every weekend from May to Sept., Riverfront Park hosts an arts and crafts show, and every Wed. and Sat. it sponsors a public market with fresh produce near the N park entrance. The **Flour Mill**, adjacent to the park at W. 621 Mallon, was the most modern mill W of the Mississippi when it was built in 1890; today it houses shops, restaurants, and galleries; 838-6541.

Historical Sights And Museums

Visit the magnificent sandstone **Cathedral of St. John the Evangelist**, 1125 S. Grand Blvd., 838-4277, to see an impressive example of Gothic architecture complete with stained-glass windows and stone and wood carvings. Forty-nine bell carillon concerts are held Thurs. at noon; Aeolian-Skinner organ recitals are scheduled regularly (phone for times). Take a guided tour on Sun. following morning services or most summer afternoons; phone 838-4277 for times. The bookstore and gift shop are open daily; admission is free.

Browne's Addition, on the city's W side along W. Pacific and W. 1st, boasts some of the city's finest homes from the 1890s; stroll through the tree-lined neighborhood and stop at **Patsy Clark's** (see "Food" below) for a drink at the grandest mansion on the block, or let the kids enjoy the Big Toys and swings at shady **Coeur d'Alene Park** on W. 2nd Street. Also in the neighborhood, the **Eastern Washington State Historical Society,** W. 2316 1st Ave., houses its enormous collection in 2 buildings: the **Cheney Cowles Memorial Museum** has regional artifacts dating to prehistoric times as well as rotating exhibits in the Fine Arts Gallery; the **Campbell House,** built in 1898, is a restored mansion from Spokane's turn-of-the-century "age of elegance." Open Tues. through Sat. 10 a.m.-5 p.m. and Sun. afternoons; free, 456-3931.

At E. 200 Cataldo Ave., the 5-story **Museum of Native American Cultures** houses the largest collection of Indian artifacts in the Northwest, including beads, paintings, ceramics, plus Western art. Admission is $3 adults, $2 kids, or $7 for the family. Open Tues. through Sun.; 326-4550.

The **Crosby Library,** E. 502 Boone Ave. at Gonzaga University, houses a large collection of Bing Crosby records, trophies, awards, and other memorabilia. The library was Crosby's gift to his alma mater. Open daily Sept. to April, Mon. through Fri. rest of the year; phone 328-4220, ext. 6133, for hours or a campus tour.

The **Fort Wright Museum and Cemetery,** W. 4000 Randolph Rd., 328-2970, is on the site of the Fort George Wright army post built in 1899. The museum displays include military memorabilia and a totem pole relating the history of the fort. Open weekend afternoons.

GREATER SPOKANE

BIGELOW GULCH RD.

ARGONNE RD.

TRENT RD.

Super 8

TO IDAHO

DISHMAN-MICA RD.

UPRIVER DR.

FREDERICK AVE.

Blakely Estates B&B

Longhorn BBQ

Days Inn

290

Niko's Greek Rest.

Felts Field

Arbor Crest Winery

EUCLID AVE.

Esmeralda Muni. Golf Course

FREYA ST.

FANCHER WAY

Broadway Ave.

Spokane Fairgrounds

Spokane Indians Ball Park

90

MARKET ST.

GREENE ST.

ILLINOIS AVE.

Playfair Race Track

Peking Garden

THOR ST.

Trent Ave.

Sprague Ave.

Gateway Hotel

FREYA ST.

Lincoln Park

Hillside House B&B

PERRY ST.

18 AVE.

1 mi

1 km

0

FRANCIS AVE.

NEVADA ST.

Azar's Cafe

WELLESLEY AVE.

B.W. Tradewinds

Dewey, Cheatam, & Howe

Marianna Stoltz House

DIVISION ST.

Northtown Shopping Center

Corbin Park

Waverly Place B&B

INDIANA AVE.

MONROE ST.

MAPLE ST.

Downtown Spokane Map

WASHINGTON ST.

DIVISION ST.

2 AVE.

LINCOLN ST.

BERNARD ST.

GRAND BLVD.

Manito Park

395

Quality Inn

Liberty Motel

Town & Country Cottage

ALBERTA ST.

NORTHWEST BLVD.

DRISCOLL BLVD.

291

TO RIVERSIDE S.P.

Downriver Muni. Golf Course

Downriver Dr.

Ft. Wright Museum

Durocher House B&B

Broadway

Fotheringham House B&B

The Blair

Patsy Clark's

Eastern Wash. State Museum

Coeur d'Alene Park

Indian Canyon Park

395

TO SPOKANE INT'L. AIRPORT, FAIRWAYS GOLF COURSE, & WORDEN'S WINERY

Indian Canyon Golf Course

Finch Arboretum

Last Chance Riding Stables

Sunset Blvd.

© MOON PUBLICATIONS, INC.

Twelve miles NW of Spokane on Aubrey White Parkway, the **Spokane House Interpretive Center,** 325-4629, is built on the site of the first structure built by white men in the Pacific Northwest. Erected in 1810, the fur-trading post sat at the confluence of the Spokane and Little Spokane rivers; today's interpretive center relates the trading post's history in photos and artifacts. Open Wed. through Sun., free; 466-4747. See **Indian Painted Rocks** 30 miles NW of Spokane, between Spokane House and the Spokane Country Club near Rutter Bridge.

Eastern Washington University

Sixteen miles W of Spokane on Hwy. 904 in Cheney, EWU enrolls 8,000 undergraduates and 1,600 graduate students in over 100 majors, both on the 350-acre campus and by extension in downtown Spokane. One of the university's major points of interest is the fact that the NFL's Seattle Seahawks practice there for 6 weeks each July and Aug., and visitors are welcome to attend. The Gallery of Art is another attraction, with changing exhibits throughout the school year. Phone 359-6200 for information on these or other university events.

Parks

Stroll through the **John A. Finch Arboretum,** 3404 Woodland Blvd., to see 65 acres of maples, rhododendrons, and ornamental trees along Garden Springs Creek, or walk the interpretive trail with signs in braille and print. Open daily; free.

See more blooms and bushes at **Manito Park,** Grand Blvd. at 18th Ave., 456-4331. Have a picnic and enjoy the changing fountain displays, rose, lilac, and Japanese gardens, duck pond, and conservatory.

For a view from the highest point in the city, visit Review Rock at **Cliff Park,** 13th Ave. and Grove St., 456-4381. The rock, ½-acre wide at the base, was once a volcanic island.

Mt. Spokane State Park, 30 miles NE of the city on .Hwy. 206, encompasses over 16,000 acres including 5,878-foot. Mt. Spokane and 5,306-foot Mt. Kit Carson. Enjoy downhill skiing at Mt. Spokane (see below),

or cross-country skiing, snowmobiling, hiking, and huckleberries throughout the park. Have lunch at **Vista House,** a restaurant atop Mt. Spokane; drive up in summer, take the chairlift in winter. Camping at this enormous park is limited to 12 standard ($7) campsites.

Riverside State Park, 6 miles NW of town, rents horses for trail rides and has an ORV area. A lava formation in the river here is typically referred to as "bowl and pitcher." Camping is plentiful, with 101 standard ($7) sites.

Liberty Lake, near the Idaho border at the I-90 Liberty Lake exit, has public swimming, picnicking, and boating.

Wildlife Refuge

Twenty-one miles S of the city, 17,000-acre **Turnbull National Wildlife Refuge,** 235-4723, has miles of trails and roads for walking, skiing, horseback riding, or driving through the protected lake area. This refuge, unlike others in eastern Washington, is not open to hunting; this is strictly an observation-only area, and nature lovers will be rewarded with sightings of grebes, hawks, shorebirds, deer, coyote, owls, badgers, herons, and an occasional bald eagle or peregrine falcon. The refuge is open every day during daylight hours.

Wineries

Enjoy a picnic with a bottle of award-winning wine at **Worden's Winery,** Washington's oldest at 7217 W. 45th, 455-7835. Open daily noon to 5 p.m. for tours and tastings. **Latah Creek Winery,** off the I-90 Pines exit at E. 13030 Indiana Ave., also features tours, tastings, and a picnic courtyard. Open daily from 10 a.m., Sun. from noon; 926-0164. **Arbor Crest,** E. 4506 Buckeye, 927-9894, also has a tasting room and gift shop open daily from noon to 5 p.m.

Zoo

Nine miles E of the city at 12600 Euclid Ave., just off Pines Rd., **Walk in the Wild** is a 240-acre zoo and park with nature trails, animal petting area, and weekend trained parrot shows. Though not a world-class zoo, you can see flamingos, eagles, bears, bison, and more. Open daily, year-round. Admission is $2.50 adults, $1.50 kids; 924-7220.

ACCOMMODATIONS

Bed And Breakfast

Enjoy homelike surroundings in 1 of 2 guest rooms at the **Blakely Estate B&B,** E. 710 Hodin Dr., 926-9426. The reasonable rates—$38 s, $43 d—include continental breakfast and use of the hot tub and shared sitting room with fireplace. No pets, smoking, or drinking on the premises; 2-night minimum stay on weekends and holidays.

Stay in an 1891 Victorian home in historic Browne's Addition at the **Fotheringham House B&B,** across the street from Patsy Clark's at 2128 W. 2nd Ave., 838-4363. The home was built by the first mayor of incorporated Spokane. Rooms have queen or double beds and period furnishings; rates are $40-45 s, $45- 50 d (the higher-priced rooms have private bath) including continental breakfast. No kids, pets, or indoor smoking.

Three doors down from the Clark Mansion, **The Georgian,** W. 2118 2nd Ave., 624-7107, offers 2 guest suites in a home built for Moses Phelps in 1901 and now listed on the National Historic Registry. The Lunette Suite has a parlor with fireplace, queen-sized bed, and bath, overlooking Coeur d'Alene Park; the Americana-Lee Suite features a 100-year-old oak bedroom set (double bed), tile bath, and extra bedroom for a guest or children over 12. Both include full breakfast; rates are $75 s, $85 d in summer, $65 in winter. Smoking on the veranda only; no pets.

Marianna Stoltz House, 427 E. Indiana, 483-4316, was built in 1908 on a tree-lined street 5 blocks from Gonzaga University. Today the B&B features 4 guest rooms with private or shared bath from $40 s, $50 d, with a full breakfast and complimentary evening wine or homemade liqueurs. No pets (there's a kennel nearby) or indoor smoking; kids over 6 OK.

Waverly Place, 709 Waverly Place off Division, 328-1856, is a Victorian B&B on Corbin Park. Built in 1902, the home features hardwood floors, gas chandeliers, and a wrap-around porch, plus 3 guest rooms for

$35-55 s, $40-60 d. Kids are OK (for an extra $10); no pets, but smoking is allowed in the living rooms.

Hillside House B&B, E. 1729 18th St., 535-1893 or 534-1426, is a cozy country home on Spokane's South Hill, near Lincoln Park. Antique-furnished rooms cost $38 s, $48 d, with shared bath, and feature a gourmet breakfast (served in bed if you like). No smoking, pets, or kids under 10.

Durocher House B&B is part of the Holy Names Center at Fort Wright, W. 4000 Randolph Rd., 325-4739, used for conferences, retreats, and seminars. The B&B has lodging for $35 s, $40 d, with private bath for $5 more; continental breakfast is included, and weekly or monthly rates are available. No indoor smoking; pets and children by arrangement.

Just N of Spokane in Deer Park, enjoy **Bed and Breakfast with Love's,** N. 31317 Cedar Rd., 276-6939. The Victorian-style home with wrap-around porch sits amidst 5 acres of pine trees for peaceful seclusion just minutes from bustling Spokane. Two rooms with shared bath go for $40 s, $45 d, with a full breakfast, evening snack, library, and private hot tub room. No indoor smoking or pets; kids by prior arrangement. From Spokane, take Hwy. 395 N to Dennison Rd., then follow Dennison for 2¾ miles.

Twenty minutes to downtown and 15 miles to Mt. Spokane skiing, **Town and Country Cottage,** N. 7620 Fox Point Dr., 466-7559, offers reproduction nostalgia pieces and oak-period furniture alongside a sitting room with a cozy fireplace and TV. Rooms are inexpensive—$28 s, $38 d—including continental breakfast (served in your room if you like). No pets, smoking, or small children.

Hotels And Motels

Be it ever so humble, the **Motel 6,** 1508 S. Rustle St. (on the W side of Sunset Hwy., near the airport), 459-6120, is still the cheapest in town: the 122 rooms cost $24 s, $30 d, and include a pool. The **Super 8 Motel,** N. 2020 Argonne Rd., 928-4888 or (800) 843-1991, has a game room and coin laundry, plus rooms from $34 s, $36-42 d. Other lodging bargains include the **Days Inn,** 1919 Hutchinson Rd. (at the I-90 Argonne Rd. exit),

DOWNTOWN SPOKANE

BOONE AVE.

SPOKANE COLISEUM

CATALDO AVE.

NATIVE AMERICAN CULTURE MUSEUM

GONZAGA UNIV./ CROSBY LIBRARY

BROADWAY

SPOKANE FALLS

RIVERFRONT PARK

SPOKANE RIVER

SPOKANE FALLS BLVD.

TRENT AVE.

RIVERSIDE AVE.

SKYWALK

SPRAGUE AVE.

1 AVE.

2 AVE.

3 AVE.

5 AVE.

7 AVE.

8 AVE.

PIONEER PARK

MAPLE ST.
MONROE ST.
WALL ST.
HOWARD ST.
STEVENS ST.
WASHINGTON ST.
BERNARD ST.
BROWNE ST.
DIVISION ST.
SHERMAN ST.
GRAND BLVD.

CLIFF PARK

0   0.2 mi
0   0.2 km

1. Civic Theater
2. Flour Mill and Clinkerdagger's
3. Cavanaugh's Inn at the Park
4. Cavanaugh's River Inn
5. Imax Theater
6. Looff Carousel
7. Sheraton
8. Casa Blanca
9. River Park Square
10. Morelands

11. C.J. Timothy's Comedy Underground
12. Cyrus O'Leary's
13. Niko's
14. Sherwood Mall
15. Azar's Cafe
16. Auntie's Bookstore and Cafe
17. Henry's Pub
18. Greyhound Depot
19. Ankeny's Restaurant and Ridpath Hotel
20. Old Spaghetti Factory

21. Europa Pizzeria
22. Amtrak Station
23. Gatsby's
24. Best Western Tradewinds
25. Deaconess Hospital
26. Best Western Thunderbird Lodge
27. Holiday Inn
28. Sacred Heart Medical Center
29. St. Lukes Hospital

© MOON PUBLICATIONS, INC.

926-5399, with 92 rooms from $40 s, $45 d, and the **Liberty,** N. 6801 Division St., 467-6000, with a heated pool and rooms from $32 s, $35-44 d.

A step up the ladder is the **Best Western Thunderbird Lodge,** W. 120 3rd Ave., 747-2011, with 90 rooms from $36-46 s, $36-52 d, plus a heated pool and hot tubs. The **Best Western Trade Winds-Downtown,** W. 907 3rd Ave., 838-2091, features rooms for $36-44 s, $36-52 d, plus a hot tub, weight room, and continental breakfast. The **Best Western Trade Winds-North,** N. 3033 Division St., 326-5500, is a bit more expensive ($48-56 s, $50-56 d) but has a year-round pool, hot tub, and continental breakfast. Make reservations at any Best Western hotel by phoning (800) 528-1234. The **Quality Inn,** E of town at N. 905 Sullivan Rd., 924-3838, and the **Quality Inn Oakwood,** 7919 N. Division St., 467-4910, have rooms from $51-52 s, $55- 56 d, plus a heated pool; the N. Division inn also has an exercise room. The **Quality Inn Spokane House,** 4301 W. Sunset Hwy., 838-1471, has 90 rooms from $45-49 s, $50-54 d, as well as a heated pool, hot tub, sauna, room and poolside service, restaurant and bar, and driving range. The **Holiday Inn-Downtown,** E. 110 4th Ave., 838-6101, has 153 rooms from $45-54 s, $49-60 d; amenities include a heated pool, poolside and room service, and bellhops. Downtown's **Shilo Inn,** E. 923 3rd, 535-9000, has a restaurant, exercise room, hot tub, indoor pool, and sauna; rooms start at $41-46 s, $46-58 d. Another quality hotel is the **Ridpath,** W. Sprague and 1st Ave., 838-2711 or (800) 426-0670, with 350 rooms from $50-65 s, $60-85 d, plus all the usual features as well as a barbershop, drugstore, and some bathroom phones.

Stepping up in price, **Cavanaugh's River Inn,** N. 700 Division St., 326-5577, features 2 heated pools, a wading pool, whirlpool, and sauna, restaurant, bar, and room and poolside service, tennis courts, and dancing nightly except Sun.; rooms start at $55-60 s, $59-64 d. Its sister operation, **Cavanaugh's Inn at the Park,** W. 303 N. River Dr., 326-8000 or (800) 843-4667, has rooms from $66-93 s, $75-102 d, most of the other Cavanaugh's amenities, plus an exercise room. At I-90 and

Sullivan Rd., the **Red Lion Inn,** 924-9000 or (800) 547-8010, has 241 rooms, a heated pool, restaurant, lounge with dancing, barbershop and beauty salon; rates start at $54-66 s, $64-76 d. The enormous **Sheraton,** N. 322 Spokane Falls Ct., 455-9600, has 388 rooms, a heated pool and exercise room, restaurant, bar, dancing, and more on the Spokane River; a good weekend getaway, rates here are $75-95 s, $84-104 d weekdays with regular weekend specials for about $60 d.

Camping

Spokane is an urban area, but it's amazing how abruptly the city stops and the country begins. **Picnic Pines on Silver Lake,** 3 miles W of Spokane on Medical Lake Rd., 299-3223, is open all year with 29 trailer sites from $9. **Peaceful Pines Campground,** a mile SW of Cheney on Hwy. 904, is also open year-round with 20 sites from $9. Other resorts and trailer parks in the area are off I-90 exits 264, 270, and 272, though most are closed in winter. See "Parks" above for more—and cheaper—camping.

FOOD

One of the most elegant mansions in the Northwest is now home to **Patsy Clark's Restaurant,** W. 2208 2nd St., 838-8300. Patsy came to America in 1870, made millions in mining, and commissioned an architect to build him a nice little home—and money was no object. The resulting structure features stained-glass windows from Tiffany's, Italian marble, and carved wood from England. Enjoy a dinner of duck, lamb, prime rib, or seafood (at about $20 a head), or just have a drink in the bar and tour the interior. Open daily for dinner plus Sunday brunch.

In the Flour Mill near Riverfront Park, **Clinkerdagger's,** 621 W. Mallon Ave., 328-5965, serves up a well-prepared American menu with a view of Spokane Falls. **Moreland's,** on the skywalk at 216 Howard St., 747-9830, features a varied, moderately priced French menu. **Ankeny's,** at W. 515 Sprague Ave. atop the Ridpath Hotel, 838-6311, specializes in prime rib with a panoramic view; open for lunch and dinner daily

Patsy Clark's Restaurant

except Sunday. Another hotel restaurant with a view is the **Spokane House,** at the Quality Inn at 4301 W. Sunset Hwy., 838-1475, serving steak, seafood, veal, and chicken; open for 3 meals daily plus Sunday Champagne brunch. For a varied menu from burgers to seafood, try **Dewey, Cheatam, and Howe,** E. 12909 Sprague, 928-7688, or N. 3022 Division, 326-7741; lunch runs about $5, dinners $7-13. **Auntie's Bookstore and Cafe,** 313 Riverside Ave., serves a good home-made lunch (breakfast and dinner on weekends) in a bookstore! Across Spokane Falls Blvd. from Riverfront Park, **Cyrus O'Leary's,** W. 516 Main, 624-9000, has a book-length, moderately priced menu with everything from seafood and pasta to burgers and quiches in a light-hearted atmosphere; fun for lunch, dinner, or just some beers and appetizers. For cheap eats, try the **Old Spaghetti Factory,** S. 152 Monroe St., 624-8916. Like its Seattle and Tacoma clones, the converted warehouse features a pasta menu that stays under $8; open daily for dinner only.

Spokane is not without its ethnic restaurants as well. **Azar's Cafe,** N. 3818 Nevada, 487-0132, or W. 410 Sprague, 838-4783, serves inexpensive Lebanese sandwiches and kebabs; open for 3 meals daily except Sunday. **Peking Garden,** E. 3420 Sprague, 534-2525, is among the city's best Chinese restaurants—and inexpensive to boot. For pizza, calzones, and Yugoslavian treats, try the **Europa Pizzeria And Bakery,** S. 125 Wall St., 455-4051. Mexican food is the mainstay at **The Casa Blanca,** next to the Sheraton at W. 200 Spokane Falls Blvd., 456-0350. Enjoy Greek food in spartan surroundings at **Niko's Greek and Middle East Restaurants.** Open for lunch and dinner at S. 321 Dishman-Mika Rd., 928-9590, and for breakfast and lunch at W. 720 Sprague, 624-7444, the food at this popular spot is inexpensive, and lamb is their specialty; enjoy belly dancing on Thurs. or a Moroccan dinner on Sunday.

SHOPPING

Downtown, a **skywalk** connects 15 blocks of shopping and dining on 2 levels, including 2 shopping malls plus large department stores such as Nordstrom, The Bon, The Crescent, Lamonts, and J.C. Penney. **River Park Square** is at the NE end of the skywalk at Main and Post, and connects to **Sherwood Mall** at Riverside and Stevens. Parking is available at Main and Stevens, and Howard and Sprague.

The restored **Flour Mill** overlooking the Spokane River at Riverfront Park is home to 26 shops, including galleries, restaurants, gifts, and candy stores. At Wellesley and Division, the **Northtown Shopping Center** has a Sears, The Crescent, and a number of smaller shops.

ENTERTAINMENT

Festivals

Enjoy the roping and riding at the **Diamond Spur Rodeo,** held in the Spokane Coliseum in March; 328-6761. Also in March, the **Western Art Show and Auction** brings hundreds of paintings to the Convention Center for browsers and buyers to enjoy. Mid-May's **Lilac Festival** features parades, exhibits, a flower show, and concerts. The **Bloomsday Run,** also in May, attracts over 30,000 runners and up to 100,000 spectators with a downtown 7.5-mile course. Cheney's mid-July **Rodeo Days** features bronc and bull riding, calf roping, and a parade at 1 of the largest amateur rodeos in the Northwest; 235-4848. The **Spokane Interstate Fair,** 535-1766, held for 9 days in mid-Sept. at the fairgrounds at Broadway and Havana, features live musical entertainment and a rodeo; admission is $4 adults, $3 students, $.50 kids.

Nightlife

Enjoy music from the '60s plus a good beer and cooler selection at **Henry's Pub,** W. 230 Riverside. **Gatsby's,** S. 152 Browne, has rock 'n' roll nightly except Sunday. For Top 40 and jazz, try **Ankeny's** atop the Ridpath Hotel at W. 515 Sprague, nightly except Sunday. Other hotel bars with entertainment include the **Ramada Inn** at the airport with a sing-along piano bar; J.J.'s Lounge at the **Sheraton** with local bands on Sun. and Mon. and dancing the rest of the week; and light jazz and music from the '50s and '60s at the **Spokane House Restaurant,** W. 4301 Sunset Highway. Hear Top 40 dance tunes at **Casa Blanca,** W. 200 Spokane Falls Blvd., next door to the Sheraton. Country and western music lovers will want to head E to **Kelly's,** 773-5003, at the Idaho state line, for Grand Ole Opry-style music Wed. through Sat. and free dance lessons on Wed. nights. Try **C.J. Timothy's Restaurant and Comedy Underground,** across from Riverfront Park at W. 525 Spokane Falls Blvd., for live comedy Tues. through Sun.; 456-6565 for reservations.

Music And Theater

Riverfront Park sponsors concerts and other entertainment during the summer months; phone 456-5511 for schedule. The **Spokane Symphony Orchestra** presents classical and pops concerts and "The Nutcracker" at the Spokane Opera House, W. 334 Spokane Falls Blvd., plus a number of free summer concerts in city parks; 624-1200. The **Spokane Civic Theater,** 1020 N. Howard, hosts performances from drama to comedy nearly year-round; phone 325-1413 or 325-2507 for schedule and ticket informa-

Spokane Opera House

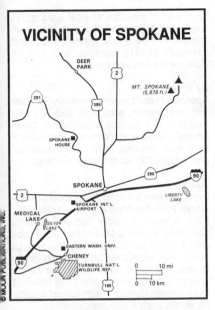

VICINITY OF SPOKANE

DEER PARK
2
291
395
MT. SPOKANE (5,878 ft.)
SPOKANE HOUSE
290
90
SPOKANE
LIBERTY LAKE
2
SPOKANE INT'L. AIRPORT
MEDICAL LAKE
SILVER LAKE
EASTERN WASH. UNIV.
CHENEY
90
TURNBULL NAT'L. WILDLIFE REF.
195
0   10 mi
0   10 km

© MOON PUBLICATIONS, INC.

tion. For information on the **Spokane Interplayers Ensemble,** a resident professional theater group, phone 455-PLAY.

Baseball
The Northwest League's **Spokane Indians** play Class-A ball at the Interstate Fairgrounds Stadium, on Havana St. between Sprague and Broadway. The stadium, which seats 10,000, was designed for Class-AAA ball, played here until 1982; it's now the classiest ballpark in the league. The Indians play 38 home games each season; phone 535-2922 for ticket and schedule information.

Horse Racing
From May to Oct., take a chance on a horse at the **Playfair Race Course,** Altamont and Main streets, every Wed., Fri., Sat., Sun., plus holidays; phone 534-0505 for post times. Admission is $1.75 general, $4 turf club; kids under 10 free.

Trail Riding
Enjoy a trail ride with **Last Chance Riding Stable** from Indian Canyon Park, 4812 W.

Canyon Dr., 624-4646. The 1-hour ride costs $7 and includes Spokane views, waterfalls, and creeks; open every day from 9 a.m. to dark.

Skiing
Thirty miles NE of town on Hwy. 206 at Mt. Spokane State Park (above), 5,883-foot **Mt. Spokane** offers alpine skiing, including a 1½-mile-long run, from 5 chair lifts and a 2,000-foot vertical drop. Night skiing draws the crowds here, as does the dry snow and 360-degree view of the Cascade, Selkirk, and Rocky mountains. Other features include ski school and rentals, restaurant, and bar (no child care). Cross-country ski trails are adjacent, as are **Snowblaze Condominiums,** 238-4543. Lift tickets are $18 adults, $12 kids; ski midweek for just $5! Phone 238-6281 for more information. For information on **49 Degrees North** in Chewelah, see "The Northeast Corner," p. 380.

Golf
Spokane is proud of its 3 beautiful city-owned 18-hole golf courses, all within 10 minutes of downtown. **Downriver,** N. 3225 Columbia Cir., 327-5269, is just S of Riverside State Park and affords views of the Spokane River. **Esmeralda,** E. 3933 Courtland, 487-6291, is a relatively new course suitable for all skill levels. **The Fairways,** off I-90 exit 272 on Milville Rd., 747-8418, is Spokane's newest 18-hole course. **Indian Canyon,** S. Assembly and West Dr. at the top of Sunset Hwy., 747-5353, was rated among the top 10 public courses in the U.S. by *Golf Digest,* and is the site of many major golf tournaments.

SERVICES AND INFORMATION

The Spokane area code is 509. Visit the **Spokane Regional Convention and Visitors Bureau,** W. 926 Sprague, 624-1341, for up-to-date information on festivals and events, maps, brochures, and other information.

In case of emergency, dial 911 for police, fire, or ambulance, or 456-4100 for the Washington State Patrol. Medical emergencies can be handled at **St. Luke's Memorial Hos-**

pital, S. 711 Cowley, 838-7278, **Sacred Heart Medical Center,** W. 101 8th Ave., 455-3344; or **Deaconess Medical Center,** W. 800 5th Ave., 458-7100. For non-emergency medical questions, dial 455-RN11, 24 hours, for "Ask a Nurse."

TRANSPORTATION

Arriving By Air
Spokane International Airport, just W of town, is served by several major commercial airlines, including **United,** 838-4711, with international service; **Alaska Airlines,** 838-6320, serving Seattle, Pasco, and western states from Alaska to Arizona; and **Horizon Air,** (800) 547-9308.

Arriving By Train
Amtrak's *Empire Builder* serves Spokane with daily service from Chicago, Minneapolis, and other midwest cities, continuing W to Wenatchee, Everett, and Seattle or SW to Pasco, Vancouver, and Portland, Oregon. Stop by their station at W. 221 1st St. or phone 624-5144 or (800) 872-7245 for schedule and fares.

Getting Around By Car
Spokane is about 250 fast highway miles from Seattle via I-90, most of which is 65 mph after leaving the densely populated Puget Sound area. Spokane is not as taken with the numbered street system as Seattle and Tacoma, so a good map is a necessity; Rand McNally's Spokane street map is one of the best, and is available at most area drug-, book-, and department stores. Spokane addresses can be a little confusing, but rest assured—W. 410 Sprague and 410 W. Sprague are one and the same.

By Bus
Spokane Transit serves downtown Spokane and the Cheney area; call 328-7433 for routes and schedule information. **Greyhound** provides nationwide connections from their terminal at W. 1125 Sprague; phone 624-5251 for schedule and fares.

Tours
Departing from the Flour Mill adjacent to Riverfront Park, the **Spokane Tour Train,** 455-5921, features a 1-hour tour of Spokane's attractions aboard a 1890-style train. Trains depart 4 or 5 times daily from June through Labor Day, weekends only through Sept.; fares are $3 adults, $1.50 kids under 12.

Gray Line, 624-4116, offers 2½-hour bus tours through Spokane, with special emphasis on the city's museums and parks. Tours depart from downtown hotels Tues. through Sun. mornings from June through Aug.; fares are $6 adults, $3 kids under 12. A combined bus and train tour includes both of the above trips on the same day for $7.50 adults, $3.75 kids.

From June through Aug., **Gray Line** also offers a 4½-hour winery tour, with 45-minute stops at Worden's, Arbor Crest, and Latah Creek wineries. Tours depart on Mon. only, from June through August. Fares are $6 adults, $3 kids; 624-4116.

CLARKSTON AND THE PALOUSE REGION

Clarkston is Washington's most inland seaport, more than 450 miles E of the Pacific via the Columbia River and its chief branch, the Snake. The region's first settlers were cattle ranchers, taking advantage of the nearly endless grazing lands. The Asotin Creek irrigation project of 1895 brought much-needed water to the parched region; the wagon bridge built in 1896 between Clarkston and Lewiston provided access to Lewiston's railroad. These projects, as well as the dams that turned the wild lower Snake into a navigable waterway, paved the way for agriculture, industry, and population growth.

Clarkston's first containerized shipment departed for Japan in 1975; today's primary exports are peas to Europe and paper products to Japan. However, agriculture and forest products, not international shipping, are the mainstay of the city's economy.

Clarkston is situated in the portion of eastern Washington often referred to as "The Banana Belt," because it has, as early Indians put it, "no wind, no snow." Some may take exception to the "no snow" part, but the climate is generally milder than that of other areas E of the Cascades. When driving to Clarkston or Pullman from the N or W, you can't help but notice the wheat fields, covering the land with intriguing patterns of gold and brown as far as the eye can see. Early French fur traders called this area of green grassland "pelouse" (lawn). The name was soon given to the land, the Indians who lived here, and the river that runs through it. The Indians rode spotted horses that the white settlers dubbed palouse or palousey horses; "a palousey" eventually became "appaloosa." Today, the national headquarters of the Appaloosa Horse Club is a few miles E of Pullman, and the Palouse region yields more wheat per acre than any other dry-land farming region in the United States. To travelers, the towns in this region are little more than pit stops on a journey to Hell's Canyon or Idaho, but the wheat fields provide an unexpected scenic diversion.

SIGHTS

Hell's Canyon

The highlight of any trip to SE Washington is a jet-boat ride through the deepest river gorge in the world, the Snake River's 5,500-foot-deep Hell's Canyon, separating Oregon and Idaho. Along the way you'll see mysterious petroglyphs, an ancient lava flow, abundant wildlife, and rugged canyon scenery.

Beamer's Landing Jet Boat Tours offers 1- to 5-day excursions to Dug Bar, Hells Canyon National Recreation Area, or Copper Creek Lodge, plus a white-water boat-and-float combination. Rates start at $55, including lunch, for a 1-day excursion from Hellsgate State Park Marina to Dug Bar, where Chief Joseph and his band of Nez Perce crossed the Snake as they fled the Cavalry. A 1-day Hells Canyon scenic excursion goes for $75. Enjoy the 2-day mail run, with an overnight stop at Copper Creek Lodge, for $185. Other trips include a 3-day, 2-night Copper Creek getaway ($325) and a 5-day jet-boat tour with white-water rafting on Hells Canyon rapids ($695). A special Saturday-night cruise from Hellsgate Marina to Heller Bar Lodge, 30 miles upriver, includes a prime-rib dinner and winetasting on the deck for $35 pp. For more information write Box 1223, Lewiston, ID 83501, or phone (208) 743-4800.

Snake River Adventures, 717 3rd St., Lewiston, ID 83501, (208) 746-6276 or (800) 248-1045, offers 3 1-day Hell's Canyon jet-boat tours, starting at $75 pp for a 184-mile RT to $120 for a 216-mile RT to Hell's Canyon Dam. Lunch and soft drinks are provided. They also offer overnight excursions to rustic Sheep Creek Ranch from $160 pp, and overnight hunting and fishing excursions for $220 pp.

Snake Dancer Excursions, 614 Lapwai Rd., Lewiston, ID, (800) 234-1941 or (208) 743-0890, offers a 1-day, 182-mile RT jet-boat tour into Hell's Canyon, beginning at

Swallows Nest Park boat launch in Clarkston. They follow the traditional mail route, without delivering the mail. The $75 pp fare ($40 kids under 12) includes lunch and snacks (bring your own pop or beer) and swimming as weather permits.

For an even more exciting trip, take a 3- to 6-day, 34- to 85-mile camping and float trip through Hell's Canyon with **Row River Odysseys West**, Box 579, Coeur d'Alene, ID 83814, (208) 765-0841. Meals, tents, and equipment are provided for $360 pp for the 3-day trip, $695 for the 6-day trip.

Parks

Five miles S of Clarkston, **Chief Looking Glass Park** provides boat access to the Snake River with launch ramps, docks, and moorage, plus picnic tables and a playground. The 16-mile wheelchair-accessible **Clearwater and Snake River National Recreation Trail** connects parks, historic sites, and attractions from Chief Looking Glass Park N to Hells Gate State Park, Swallows Nest Rock, and up· to West Pond. Hiking, biking, fishing, swimming, and picnicking are permitted along portions of the the trail. Eight miles W of town on Hwy. 12, **Chief Timothy State Park** sits on Silcott Island in the middle of the Snake River. The park was named for a Nez Perce Indian chief who befriended the early white settlers. The area's history is depicted in the park's Alpowai Interpretive Center in exhibits and audio-visual programs. Enjoy the limited shade and cool breeze off the river, and camp at 1 of 33 standard ($7) sites or 33 full-hookup ($9.50) sites. Other facilities include a boat launch, playground, swimming beach, and concession stand in summer.

Head S on Hwy. 129 for 4½ miles past Anatone to **Fields Spring State Park** for a panoramic view of 3 states, the Snake River basin, and the Wallowa Mountains from the summit of 4,500-foot Puffer Butte, reached by a 1-mile hike. Along the way you'll see numerous birds and 150 varieties of wildflowers, at their best in late spring. Camp in one of 20 standard ($7) sites; winter visitors will enjoy the miles of cross-country skiing.

Museum And Artifacts

Visit the **Asotin County Historical Museum**, 3rd and Filmore in Asotin, 243-4659, to see early Asotin artifacts and buildings such as the 1882 Forgey log cabin and a pole barn housing carriages and a collection of branding irons. Open Tues. through Sat. afternoons.

Stop by the Clarkston Chamber of Commerce, 731 5th St., for directions to several Indian petroglyphs that can be seen from the road or from Hell's Canyon tour boats. These carvings are over 5,000 years old (and difficult to find).

Events

The small **Asotin County Fair,** held the last weekend in April, features a rodeo, parade, cowboy breakfast, and stock show and sale. Late April through mid-May, the **Dogwood Festival** celebrates spring's flowering dogwoods with concerts, Art in the Park, historical walking tours, and the Bing Band Ball. June's **I Made The Grade** 13-mile bicycle ride starts at Chief Timothy State Park, crosses the Snake River, and heads up the old Lewiston grade for a total ascent of 1,000 feet. Mid-December's **Reflections on the Confluence** is a lighted boat parade on the Snake River, from Swallows Nest Park. Phone the **Clarkston Chamber of Commerce**, 758-7712, for further information on these events.

The **Valley Art Center,** 842 6th St., features rotating exhibits and sales, including a Valentine's Day art show in which all works sell for $100 or less, and offers workshops and classes in all media.

ACCOMMODATIONS AND FOOD

The **Golden Key,** 1376 Bridge St., 758-5566, has 17 budget rooms for $21 s, $25 d, and a pool. **Nendel's Valu Inn,** 222 Bridge St., 758-1631 or (800) 547-0106, has 83 rooms from $29-38 s, $36-40 d, plus pool, restaurant, and bar. The **Best Western Rivertree Inn,** 1257 Bridge St., 758-9551 or (800) 528-1234, has 47 rooms for $36-46 s, $42-52 d (higher rates apply during football season), with a heated pool, hot tub, sauna, and free airport and bus station shuttle.

Henry's, just over the bridge at 200 Bridge St., 758-9613, serves sandwiches, steak, pasta, seafood, and chicken for $7-14; open 7 days for lunch and dinner. **Fazzari's,** 1281 Bridge St., 758-3386, features pizza, spaghetti, and sandwiches; open daily for lunch and dinner. **Peking Restaurant,** 907 6th St., 758-5555, serves Chinese food and an all-you-can-eat lunch buffet. Cross the state line into Lewiston for more food and lodging options.

SERVICES AND INFORMATION

The Clarkston area code is 509. For maps or other current information contact the **Clarkston Chamber of Commerce,** 731 5th St., Clarkston, WA 99403, 758-7712, or for Pullman information, the **Pullman Chamber of Commerce,** N. 415 Grand Ave., Pullman, WA 99163, 334-3565.

All of Asotin County has 911 service for fire, police, and medical emergencies. Phone (800) 626-6780 for the State Patrol. Medical assistance is available at **Tri-State Memorial Hospital,** 1221 Highland Ave. in Clarkston, 758-5511, or **Memorial Hospital,** Washington Ave. in Pullman, 332-2541.

TRANSPORTATION

By Air
The Lewiston Airport is served by 3 regional airlines with connections and joint fares with 5 national airlines. Call AAA, (208) 746-0407, or AIA Travel, (800) 635-1519, for reservations or information.

By Car
Clarkston is about 100 miles S of Spokane; take Hwy. 195 past Pullman and across the Idaho border, then follow the signs for Hwy. 12 and Clarkston. The Idaho stretch follows the top of a ridge, providing spectacular views of Lewiston, Clarkston, and the Snake and Clearwater rivers as you descend; stop at one of the scenic viewpoints for a better look.

By Bus
Greyhound serves the Palouse region from their station at 1002 Idaho St. in Lewiston; phone (208) 746-8108 for schedule and fares.

VICINITY OF CLARKSTON

PULLMAN

Pullman was founded by Bolin Farr, who came from Missouri to settle at the confluence of Dry Fork Creek, Missouri Flat Creek, and the S fork of the Palouse in 1876. By 1881, the town had grown—to a population of 3. The citizens decided to call their "city" Pullman, after Chicago industrialist George Pullman, who funded their $50 4th of July celebration. A railroad branch extended to the town, the "crossroads of the Palouse," in 1883; by then Pullman boasted 2 stores, a hotel, post office, and blacksmith shop. Two fires devastated the downtown district in 1887 and 1890; structures were rebuilt in brick, and many of these turn-of-the-century buildings are still standing.

The Washington Agriculture College and School of Engineering opened in Jan. 1892, with 26 students. Today, Washington State University has 1,700 faculty members and a student body of more than 16,000, distributed throughout one graduate school and 8 undergraduate colleges. Pullman feels like a typical small college town, with an abundance of we-deliver pizza and sub shops and beer by the keg.

Washington State University

The WSU Cougars field teams in football, basketball, baseball, gymnastics, and track and field; for a schedule of athletic events, phone 335-9626. The 12,000-seat **Beasley Performing Arts Coliseum** stages events from rock concerts to opera; for a schedule phone 335-1514. The new **Pullman Summer Palace Theater** in Daggy Hall performs in June and July; 335-7236. Other places to visit on campus include the **Connors Museum of Zoology** (in the Science Building) with the largest public collection of animals and birds in the Pacific Northwest, the Museum of Fine Art (in the Fine Arts Center), and the Museum of Anthropology (in College Hall).

Ferdinand's Bar in Troy Hall is a soda fountain run by the university's agricultural school and the campus's most popular tourist attraction; have some university-made ice cream or pick up a tin of WSU's Cougar Gold Cheese to take home. A 9-hole golf course and 2,000-square-foot putting green on the W edge of the campus are open to the public. For a campus map or other information, stop by the visitor information center in the Safety Building on Wilson Rd., or phone 335-3564 for general information.

Parks

On the W side of town, **Sunnyside Park** has hiking trails, picnic areas, tennis and basketball courts, and playgrounds; this is the site of Pullman's annual 4th of July picnic and fireworks.

Follow the signs from Hwy. 195 and drive to the top of **Steptoe Butte,** about 25 miles N of Pullman, for panoramic views of the

PULLMAN

TO SPOKANE 27

TO HILLTOP MOTEL & RESTAURANT

270 DAVIS WAY

CHAMBER OF COMMERCE

2 3 MAIN ST.
PARADISE ST.
4 5

GRAND AVE.

WASHINGTON STATE UNIVERSITY

STADIUM WAY

6

8

7

1

NOT TO SCALE

9

10

11

27

1. Travel-Inn American Hotel
2. Alex's Restaurant
3. Greyhound Depot
4. The Seasons
5. police department
6. city playfield
7. Nendel's Inn
8. Memorial Hospital
9. Mr. Steak
10. Quality Inn
11. Pelican Pete's

© MOON PUBLICATIONS, INC.

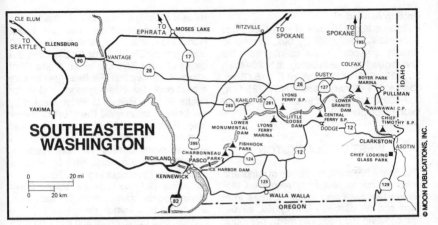

Palouse River farmland and Idaho's mountains to the east. The state park has picnic areas, but no water or overnight facilities. Three-hundred-acre **Kamiak Butte County Park,** about 15 miles NE of Pullman on Hwy. 27 near Palouse, has camping, picnicking, and a one-mile hiking trail to the top of the 3,360-foot butte.

Hot Air Balloon Rides
For an exciting way to view the scenery, try a hot-air balloon ride with **Fantasy Flights.** Departing year-round from Pullman, a 1½-hour ride costs $75 pp, and a ½-hour flight is just $45, including complimentary Champagne. For reservations or more information write them at N.W. 1250 State Hwy. #4, Pullman, WA 99163, or phone 332-7676.

Accommodations
The lodging in Pullman leaves a lot to be desired. By far the best in town is the **Quality Inn Motel,** S.E. 1050 Johnson Rd., 332-0500, with 66 rooms from $36-60 s, $50-67 d, plus a pool, hot tub, sauna, and an adjoining dressed-up Mr. Steak restaurant. **Nendel's Inn,** S.E. 915 Main St., 332-2646, has 60 rooms near the entrance to WSU and adjacent to the railroad tracks—still used by thundering locomotives at odd hours of the night. Rates are $29-37 s, $34-40 d (higher during college events), plus a pool. The **Travel-Inn**

American Motel, S. 515 Grand Ave., 334-3500, has 34 rooms from $30 s, $32-40 d, with a pool. The **Hilltop Motel,** on top of the hill on Colfax Hwy., 334-2555, has budget rooms that look it for $21 s, $26 d. Take a short drive to Moscow, Idaho, for more lodging options.

Campers can stay at **Pullman RV Park** at the city playing field, corner of South and Riverview streets., for $8 a night from April through Nov.; for reservations call the Parks and Recreation Dept., 334-4555, ext. 227.

Food
Enjoy authentic Mexican cuisine at **Alex's Restaurante,** N. 139 Grand Ave., 332-4061. The **Hilltop Restaurant,** Colfax Hwy., 334-2555, serves steak and seafood, plus Sunday brunch, with a panoramic city view but not much for atmosphere. **Pelican Pete's,** next to the Quality Inn at S.E. 1100 Johnson Ave., 334-4200, serves burgers, steaks, and salads for lunch and dinner daily with a lounge open till 2 a.m. **The Seasons,** S.E. 215 Paradise St., 334-1410, serves a broad variety of moderately priced dinners, including seafood, chicken, and lasagne, accompanied by Washington wines. Open daily for dinner, weekdays for lunch, and Sunday brunch. **Rusty's Tavern,** N.E. 1515 Merman Dr., is popular with WSU students for its beer, wine, and burgers.

Getting Around

Pullman is about 75 miles of wheatfields S of Spokane via Hwy. 195. By bus, connect to virtually any point in the country from the **Greyhound** stations in Colfax, at N. 804 Main St., 397-4524, or Pullman, at E. 115 Olsen, 334-1412. **Pullman Transit,** N.W. 725 Guy, 332-6535, provides scheduled bus service throughout town.

WEST OF CLARKSTON

The Snake River offers a variety of parks and boat launches for year-round recreation. **Wa-wawai County Park,** about 25 miles from Clarkston on Whitman County Rd. #9000, has camping (no hookups) for $4 per night, picnic areas, playground, and hiking trails. Just S of the park, **Wawawai Landing** has a launch ramp and dock on Lower Granite Lake, created by the Snake River's **Lower Granite Dam,** 25 miles N of Pomeroy. The dam has a visitor center and restrooms. On Lake Bryan, just W of Lower Granite Dam, **Boyer Park and Marina** has launch ramps, moorage, docks, swimming area and bath house, picnic area, and camping. **Central Ferry State Park,** on Hwy. 127 about 12 miles N of Dodge, features a swimming area with lifeguards, boat launches and docks, picnic area, snack bar, and camping in 60 hookup sites ($9.50). **Little Goose Dam,** the cause of Lake Bryan, is about a mile W of Starbuck on Hwy. 261. Facilities here include a boat dock, fish-cleaning room, and visitor center. In Lake Herbert G. West, created by the Lower Monumental Dam, **Lyons Ferry State Park** has good fishing, swimming, and boating at the confluence of the Snake and Palouse rivers, 8 miles NW of Starbuck on Hwy. 261. Enjoy a picnic here by Palouse Falls, or stay overnight in one of 50 standard campsites ($7); no hookups. **Lyons Ferry Marina,** across the river from the state park, also has a boat launch, dock, boat fuel and service, plus picnic areas and camping from $7 (hookups extra).

Palouse Falls State Park, about 6 miles N of Lyons Ferry, offers picnicking and a scenic view of 190-foot Palouse Falls, plus 10 primitive campsites ($3-4.50). The **Lower Monumental Dam,** about 6 miles from Kahlotus on Devils Canyon Rd., has a visitor center, picnic area, and boat dock.

For information on Ice Harbor Dam and Lake Sacajawea at the W end of the Snake River, see "Tri-Cities," p. 345.

WALLA WALLA

Walla Walla is in a class apart from most of its eastern Washington neighbors. Whereas many cities on the dry side of the mountains are hot, dry, and without character, Walla Walla is a refreshing change. Here, trees have been cultivated for decades and offer much-needed shade and visual relief from the sameness of the eastern Washington landscape; parks are cool and well cared for; old homes and commercial buildings add to the city's elegance, Whitman College supplies the youthful influence, and the famous Walla Walla sweet onion gives the town of 25,600 a unique identity. The restaurants may not be 1st class, but some of the motels are as accommodating as any in Seattle or Spokane.

Walla Walla boasts—and endures—4 distinct seasons, with an average of 4 days over 100 degrees in summer and 2 winter days below zero, with about 20 inches of snow. The Walla Walla Valley also enjoys a variation in height that much of Eastern Washington lacks; the western end of town lies at 300 feet above sea level, while the Blue Mountain foothills to the east rise to 3,000 feet. The weather, trees, and historic buildings combine to give the city a distinctive New England flavor. The valley enjoys a long growing season, with wheat, potatoes, barley, asparagus, alfalfa, and the Walla Walla sweet onion the big money crops; livestock and dairy products are also significant parts of the Walla Walla economy.

HISTORY

In 1805, Lewis and Clark passed through the Indian hunting ground at the confluence of the Columbia and Walla Walla rivers, and in 1818, Fort Walla Walla was established here as a fur-trading post. Dr. Marcus Whitman, a medical missionary, built the first white man's home in the Northwest in 1836, in a spot called Waiilatpu (wy-EE-la-poo), "Place of the Rye Grass." His attempts to teach Christian principles to the Cayuse Indians met with little success, as they had no real interest in religion or books. Whitman's daughter was the first white girl born W of the Rockies and N of California; the Whitmans also adopted the 7 Sager children whose parents had died on the trail. The whole family was massacred by Indians in 1847, after the Cayuse had grown suspicious of the white man's intentions. There was no further white settlement in Walla Walla until after the Indians and white men agreed to the terms of the treaties laid out by Isaac Stevens' Great Council.

In 1856, Colonel Edward Steptoe built an army barracks at Mill Creek to keep the peace; "Steptoeville" rose up around it and was later named Walla Walla, or "many waters." In 1859, the city was named county seat; no small honor, since the county included half of Washington, all of Idaho, and parts of Montana. When gold was discovered in Idaho in the 1860s, prospectors came to Walla Walla for supplies, and the town prospered. Like a number of other Northwest cities, Walla Walla suffered a substantial loss when a series of fires swept through the wooden downtown area in the 1880s. Most of the oldest buildings still standing date back to the late 1880s, when the town was rebuilt in brick. Walla Walla was the site of the Northwest's first railroad, and the state's first bank and college.

SIGHTS

Whitman Mission

You can get the whole story of Marcus and Narcissa Whitman's pioneer mission on the Oregon Trail at the Whitman Mission, a National Historic Site 7 miles W of Walla Walla on Hwy. 12. No buildings remain, but you can walk the self-guiding trails to the mission site, grave, monument, and sites of the first house, blacksmith shop, and grist mill. The visitor center is open daily except major holidays; admission $1.

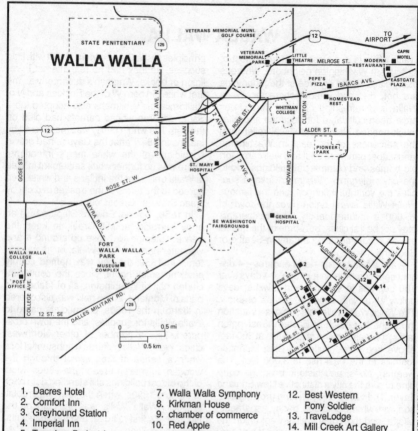

WALLA WALLA

1. Dacres Hotel
2. Comfort Inn
3. Greyhound Station
4. Imperial Inn
5. Tapadera Budget Inn
6. Whitman Hotel
7. Walla Walla Symphony
8. Kirkman House
9. chamber of commerce
10. Red Apple
11. Liberty Theater
12. Best Western Pony Soldier
13. TraveLodge
14. Mill Creek Art Gallery
15. Carnegie Center

© MOON PUBLICATIONS, INC.

Museums

Step back in time with a visit to the **Fort Walla Walla Museum Complex** at Fort Walla Walla Park on Myra Rd., 525-7703. The museum features 14 original and re-created pioneer buildings, including the 1880 Babcock Railway Station and the cabin built by Ransom Clark just S of Walla Walla in 1859. A large horse-era agricultural display, including a 33 mule-team combine, fills 5 buildings. Open 1-5 p.m., weekends only in May and Oct., daily except Mon. in June through Sept.; admission is $2 adults, $1 kids.

Visit the **Kirkman House,** a mansion built in 1880 by entrepreneur William Kirkman and the town's only period house museum at Main and Colville. The ornate structure features a beautiful widow's walk and figurehead keystones; open Thurs. and by appointment, 529-4373.

Walking Tour

Pick up a brochure from the chamber of commerce, 29 E. Sumach, for a walking tour of the historic downtown area. Some of the sites you'll pass are the 1917 **Liberty The-**

atre, built on the site of Steptoe's fort at W. Main and Colville, and the **Dacres Hotel,** built in 1899 at W. Main and 4th to replace the burned-down Stine House built in 1873; historians speculate that the brickwork on the 4th St. facade is part of the original structure, while the W. Main pressed-metal columns were added in the reconstruction. The **Sheriff's Office,** built in 1906, is a classic building with ornate rooftop balustrade. It's hard to miss the 10-story **Marcus Whitman Hotel,** built in 1928 at 2nd and W. Rose.

Parks And Camping

Fort Walla Walla Park, Dalles Military Rd., has camping with hookup sites, showers, and fireplaces, plus the Fort Walla Walla museum, described above; 525-3700. Other city parks include the well-kept, 47-acre **Pioneer Park,** with aviary, duck pond, play equipment, picnic tables, and gardens, and **Veterans Memorial Park,** Sumach St. E, with a jogging and exercise trail. Outside of town, **Lewis and Clark Trail State Park** has 30 standard campsites on treed land—a rarity in these parts—4 miles E of Waitsburg on Hwy. 12; fish in the river and enjoy historical campfire programs in summer.

Wineries

Visit **Woodward Canyon Winery,** 525-4129, about 10 miles W of town of Hwy. 12 in Lowden, for a taste of top-quality Chardonnay and Cabernet. These wines are higher priced than some of the mass-producers, but they're worth it. Open weekends May through New Year's.

ACCOMMODATIONS

Motels

For inexpensive lodging, try the **Tapadera Budget Inn,** 211 N. 2nd Ave., 529-2580 or (800) 722-8277, with 29 rooms from $24-28 s, $27-32 d, or the **Imperial Inn,** 305 N. 2nd Ave., 529-4410 or (800) 368-4400, with 35 rooms for $27 s, $30-34 d, plus a pool. Also inexpensive, the **Capri Motel,** 2003 Melrose, 525-1130, has 40 rooms and a heated pool; rates are $27-35 s, $30-40 d. One of Walla Walla's newer motels, the **Comfort Inn,** 520 N. 2nd, 525-2522 or (800) 228-5150, has a pool, sauna, and hot tub, plus rooms from $37-41 s, $41-47 d. The **TraveLodge,** 421 E. Main St., 529-4940 or (800) 255-3050, has 38 rooms for $39 s, $43-47 d, plus a pool and hot tub. The historic **Whitman Motor Inn,** 107 N. 2nd Ave., 525-2200, has a pool, one of the town's best restaurants, valet service, and some refrigerators, with 71 rooms starting at $43 s, $46-49 d. The **Best Western Pony Soldier,** 325 E. Main St., 529-4360 or (800) 528-1234, offers the best lodging in town. Freebies include continental breakfast, pool, hot tub, exercise room, laundry, and some refrigerators and balconies; the 85 rooms are well worth the $50-63 s, $52-66 d.

FOOD

The **Modern Restaurant,** 2200 Melrose Ave. at the Eastgate Plaza, 525-8662, specializes in Cantonese cuisine plus steak and sandwiches; open for lunch and dinner daily and Sunday brunch. The **Red Apple,** 57 E. Main, 525-5113, serves moderately priced steak and seafood in a casual atmosphere with a piano bar on weekends; open 24 hours daily. **The Whitman,** 107 N. 2nd, 529-6000, is a little fancier, serving steak, seafood, and chicken in the $7-13 range, although it looks like you're eating in the lobby; entertainment and dancing in the lounge. The **Homestead Restaurant,** 1528 Isaacs, 522-0345, serves 3 meals daily from a varied menu including steaks, seafood, sautés, and vegetarian selections, with dinners in the $7-14 range. The fast food chains are all centered around Wilber and Isaacs. For a pizza delivery, call **Pepe's Pizza,** 1533 Isaacs, 529-2550.

ENTERTAINMENT

Festivals

One of the events most popular with photographers is the **Hot Air Balloon Stampede,** held at Walla Walla High School in mid-May; after the balloons go up, enjoy the arts and crafts displays and demonstrations.

Labor Day weekend brings the **Southeastern Washington Fair** to the fairgrounds on Orchard Street, with horse racing, an evening rodeo, concerts, and educational exhibits.

The Arts

Little Theatre, 1130 E. Sumach, 529-3683, is a community theater founded in 1944 that produces 4 plays each season. **Harper Joy Theatre** at Whitman College, 345 Boyer, 527-5180, stages 10 productions each year. The **Walla Walla Symphony Orchestra,** 3 W. Alder, 529-8020, has been performing since 1907 (probably with some change in roster) with 80-100 amateur and professional musicians.

Art buffs will want to visit the **Clyde and Mary Harris Gallery** at Walla Walla College, off College Avenue. Other galleries include the **Sheehan Gallery** at Whitman College, 527-5111, **Carnegie Center,** 109 S. Palouse, 525-4270, and **Mill Creek Art Gallery,** upstairs at 39 E. Main, 525-7722.

Skiing

Ski Bluewood, 21½ miles SE of Dayton and 52 miles from Walla Walla, offers alpine skiing on 1,125 vertical feet in the Umatilla National Forest. Because Ski Bluewood is over 300 miles from the coast, conditions here are generally dryer than on most Washington ski slopes. In operation since 1979, the ski area has 2 chair lifts and one platterpull serving beginner through expert terrain. All day lift tickets are $15 adult, $12 kids; phone 529-9685 from Walla Walla or 545-6651 from Tri-Cities for conditions and more information.

Outdoor Activities

Enjoy the **bike path** from Cambridge Dr. to Rooks Park or from 9th and Dalles Military Rd. to Myra Road. **Veterans Memorial Golf Course,** off Hwy. 12, is an 18-hole course open to the public; 527-4507. For information on hiking and camping in the Blue Mountains of Umatilla National Forest (most of which is in Oregon), visit the **Walla Walla Ranger Station** on Rose St. W for detailed maps and information.

SHOPPING

Walla Walla and Umatilla counties are the world's only producers of genuine **Walla Walla sweet onions,** guaranteed not to bring tears to your eyes when you slice them! These onions are so mild you can bite into one like an apple, and so soft they have to be harvested by hand. Write or visit one of these packers to get a bag sent home: Bossini Packing, Rt. 1, Pranger Rd., 525-2122; Walla Walla Gardeners Assoc., 210 N. 11th, 529-7667; or Pacific Fruit and Produce, 1137 N. 13th, 525-9252. All addresses are in Walla Walla, zip 99362.

The **Blue Mountain Mall,** 1600 W. Rose St., hosts J.C. Penney, Sears, and Fred Meyer plus upwards of 40 other shops. For groceries and other supplies, shop at the **Albertson's** and **Payless Drug** at the corner of Wilbur and Isaacs.

SERVICES AND INFO

The Walla Walla area code is 509. For further information, contact the **Walla Walla Chamber of Commerce,** 29 E. Sumach, Walla Walla, WA 99362, 525-0850.

Dial 911 for fire, medical, and police emergencies in Walla Walla. In College Place, 911 won't work; phone 525-3242 for fire or medical help, 525-7773 for police. For other medical problems, phone **St. Mary Hospital,** 401 W. Poplar St., 525-3320, or **Walla Walla General Hospital,** 1025 S. 2nd Ave., 525-0480.

TRANSPORTATION

Walla Walla is about 260 miles from Seattle, 160 miles from Spokane. From Seattle, take I-90 eastbound to Ellensburg, then head S on I-82 to Tri-Cities; from there, take Hwy. 12 SW to Walla Walla. The highways aren't as wide coming from Spokane; the most direct route is to take Hwy. 195 S from Spokane to Colfax, then head W on Hwy. 26, S on Hwy. 127, then

S on Hwy. 12 to Walla Walla. There's a lot of nothing out here, so stock up on soft drinks before leaving Spokane.

Fly into Walla Walla Regional Airport, Airport Way, on **Horizon Air,** (800) 547-9308, from most major West coast cities.

Get around town on **Valley Transit,** 1401 W. Rose, 525-9140, with 5 routes serving the Walla Walla/College Place area Mon. through Sat. from 6 a.m.-7 p.m. Take **Greyhound,** 315 N. 2nd, 525-9313, for nationwide connections.

TRI-CITIES

Kennewick is—or was—the largest and fastest growing of the Tri-Cities, experiencing a 126 percent jump in population from 1970 to 1980, up to 34,000. Richland is the 2nd most populous with 33,000, while Pasco has 18,000. These 3 cities, together with smaller towns, comprise the 4th largest metropolitan area in the state—a fact that's sure to change with the recent shutting down of the Hanford Reactor. The Hanford Site was in business since 1944 employing thousands in the production of defense-related nuclear materials and diversifying into solar and geothermal energy research; the shutdown means a dismal economic future for the Tri-Cities area.

Besides the reactor, the Tri-Cities are famous for their hydroplane race—held annually in July—and their wineries, at the SE end of the fruitful Yakima Valley. The Tri-Cities area is also heavily involved in farming, with 1,800 farms covering 1,300,000 acres— 400,000 of them irrigated—in Benton and Franklin counties; potatoes, wheat, apples, grapes, alfalfa, field corn, and hops are the big money producers here.

The Tri-Cities suffer weather extremes that western Washingtonians never see. Plenty of below-zero days have been recorded here, as well as summer temperatures soaring over 100 bone-dry degrees; fortunately, a fairly constant breeze keeps the air clean and the heat almost tolerable. The area receives an average annual precipitation of just 6.25 inches, scattered between 225 sunny days; 44 percent of the total occurs from Nov. through Jan., generally in the form of snow, though accumulations of more than 6 inches are uncommon.

HISTORY

The Lewis and Clark expedition arrived at the confluence of the Columbia and Snake rivers in 1805. The first permanent settlers arrived in 1861 to raise cattle on these wide-open plains. Railroad workers established the town of Ainsworth, now Ainsworth Junction, in 1871 at the terminus of the Northern Pacific Railway. Ainsworth grew rapidly until the workers completed the Snake River railroad bridge; then the railroaders packed their bags, and Ainsworth faded into history.

Pasco had been growing quietly alongside Ainsworth, and in 1885 claimed the county seat. Incorporated in 1891, Pasco has always been the transportation hub of SE Washington: the first airport W of the Mississippi was built here in 1910; the first U.S. airmail service operated out of Tri-Cities Regional Airport by what would later become United Airlines; and Pasco is a significant upriver terminal for Columbia River barge traffic.

Franklin County irrigation projects began in the 1890s, when schemes were developed to pump water from the Snake River into the dry fields. Planners had little luck until the government got involved in the Columbia Basin Irrigation Project; now over 500,000 acres are irrigated by the Grand Coulee Dam and Columbia Basin Irrigation projects, with projections of up to 1,000,000 irrigated acres.

SIGHTS

Parks And Dams
Nine miles E of Pasco on the Snake River, **Ice Harbor Lock and Dam** is the first of 4

TRI-CITIES

Richland

1. Kadlec Medical Center
2. Tri-Cities Gallery of Fine Arts
3. Richland Chamber of Commerce
4. Greyhound
5. Allied Arts Gallery
6. Arts Council of the Mid-Columbia
7. Sha-Na-Pum Golf Course

Pasco

22. Apple Inn
23. Our Lady of Lourdes Hospital
24. Pasco Chamber of Commerce and Greyhound
25. Amtrak
26. Red Lion
27. Municipal Golf Course

Kennewick

8. Columbia Center Dunes
9. Tri-Cities Chamber of Commerce
10. vista field
11. Water Slide Park
12. Shaniko Inn and Clearwater Cinema
13. Flamingo Beach Club
14. Chapter 11
15. Columbia Park Golf course
16. Tapadera Inn
17. Beaux Art Gallery, Appleseed Gallery and Shops, C.D.'s Texas Barbecue, and Bruce's Steak & Lobster House
18. East Benton County Museum
19. Kennewick General Hospital
20. Benton-Franklin Fairgrounds and Racetrack
21. Clover Island Inn

© MOON PUBLICATIONS, INC.

dams on the Lower Snake, with one of the highest single-lift locks in the world, rising 103 feet. Take a self-guided tour, watch the fish climb the ladders, or stop by the visitor center, open daily April through October. The Ice Harbor dam creates **Lake Sacajawea,** accessible for fishing, waterskiing, or swimming via 4 developed parks: the dam itself, **Levey Park** on the Pasco-Kahlotus Rd. on the lake's W side, **Charbonneau Park** and **Fishhook Park** off Hwy. 124 on the E side. **Big Flat,** on the W side just NE of Levey Park, is a wildlife development area and open to foot traffic only; you can camp here April through Oct., 547-7781.

The Columbia River's **McNary Lock and Dam** 30 miles S of Pasco in Umatilla, Oregon, creates 61-mile-long Lake Wallula, which reaches up past the Tri-Cities to Ice Harbor Dam. The McNary Dam is open daily for self-guided tours, with guided tours given in summer; 922-3211. One of 12 parks on Lake Wallula is **Columbia Park,** 2 miles W of Kennewick on Hwy. 12. This 609-acre park has 4 boat ramps for fishing and waterskiing, an 18-hole golf course, tennis courts, picnic area, 6.2-mile paved bike path, nature trails, and standard camping and hookup sites ($6 for tent sites, $7-9 for hookups). Open year-round; 783-3711 or 783-3118. The **McNary National Wildlife Refuge,** next to McNary Dam, has a mile-long hiking trail popular with birdwatchers. Area species include hawks, golden and bald eagles, and prairie falcons.

Five miles E of Kennewick off Finley Rd., **Two Rivers Park** is open daily for boating, swimming, and picnicking.

Two miles E of Pasco off Hwy. 12, **Sacajawea State Park** sits at the junction of the Snake and Columbia rivers, at the site where Lewis and Clark camped in 1805. You can fish, waterski, or picnic here, or visit the interpretive center with displays of the famed expedition as well as local Indian history, open Wed. through Sun., mid-April to mid-September.

Horn Rapids Off-Road Vehicle Park, off Hwy. 240 in Richland, has 2 motocross tracks, 4x4 obstacle course, sand drag strip, and go-kart track, plus camping for $5 a night. Open all year; 967-5814.

Wineries

The bulk of the wineries in SE Washington are covered in "Yakima," p. 352. But the Tri-Cities area has a handful of its own, including **Preston Wine Cellars,** 545-1990, one of the area's biggest off Hwy. 395 in Pasco. Established in the early 1970s, Preston produces a full range of wines from Cabernet Sauvignon and Merlot to Rieslings and Fumé Blanc. The tasting room and gift shop are open daily, 10 a.m.-5:30 p.m.; take a self-guided tour or enjoy a picnic on the park-like grounds.

Bookwalter Winery, just N of Pasco near the junction of highways 395 and 12, opened in 1984 with a 1983 Chenin Blanc and Johannisberg Riesling, followed by a Chardonnay a year later and a Cabernet Sauvignon in 1987. The winery is open daily, 10 a.m.-5 p.m.; 547-8571.

Started in 1985, **Gordon Brothers Cellars,** overlooking the Snake River at 531 Levey Rd. in Pasco, has won medals in Northwest wine competitions for all of its first releases. Open weekends and holidays May through Sept., 10 a.m.-5 p.m.; 547-6224.

Quarry Lake Vintners has opened a temporary facility at 2505 Commercial Ave. C in Pasco, 547-7307, where you can taste their Johannisberg Riesling, Chenin Blanc, Semillon, Chardonnay, and Sauvignon Blanc. Open Mon. through Fri., noon to 5 p.m.

Caroway Vineyards, SW of Finley on Haney Rd., bottles 6 varieties including a Chardonnay, Dry Semillon, Merlot, and Lemberger. Open for tastings on weekend afternoons, March through Dec., or by appointment; 582-7041. Also in Kennewick, **Barnard Griffin Winery** plans to open visitor facilities soon; 586-6987. They've produced a White Reisling, Chardonnay, and Fumé Blanc.

Two other small wineries in the area are covered under "Walla Walla," p. 341. For wineries to the E, see "Vicinity of Yakima," p. 356.

Museums

Kennewick's **East Benton County Historical Museum,** 205 Keewaydin Dr., has exhibits from pioneer days in the Tri-Cities area; free, 582-7704. At 305 N. 4th St. in Pasco,

TRI-CITIES HOTELS AND MOTELS

Name	Address	Phone	Rates	Comments
RICHLAND				
Bali Hai Motel	1201 G. Washington	943-3101	24-35 s 30-45 d	pool
Columbia Center Dunes	1751 Fowler SE	783-8181	25 s 28-30 d	pool, sauna, laundry
Hanford House Thunderbird	802 G. Washington	946-7611	50-60 s 60-75 d	pool, poolside service, cafe, bar, dock
Holiday Inn	1515 G. Washington	946-4121	44-53 s 50-59 d	pool, sauna, hot tub, room and poolside service, cafe, bar, sun deck
Imperial Inn	515 G. Washington	946-6117	25 s 30-34 d	heated pool
Nendel's	615 Jadwin Ave.	943-4611	26 s 31 d	pool, shuttle
Shilo Inn Rivershore	50 Comstock	946-4661	42 s, 48 d	pool, cafe, bar, laundry, golf, boats, tennis
KENNEWICK				
Cavanaugh's	1101 N. Columbia Center Blvd.	783-0611	47-49 s 52-54 d	pool, hot tub, lounge, cafe
Clover Island Inn	Clover Island	586-0541	40-42 s 45-47 d	pool, hot tub, sauna, cafe, piano bar
Nendel's	2811 W. 2nd	735-9511	30-40 s 36-44 d	pool, some kitchenettes
Shaniko Inn	321 N. Johnson	735-6385	27 s 31-34 d	pool, laundry
Tapadera Inn	300 N. Ely	783-6191	24-34 s 27-37 d	pool, laundry
PASCO				
Hallmark Motel	720 W. Lewis St.	547-7766	22 s 26-31 d	pool
Motel 6	1520 N. Oregon St.	546-2010	21 s 27 d	pool
Red Lion	2525 N. 20th Ave.	547-0701	55-70 s 65-75 d	pool, poolside service, cafe, lounge, golf
Valu-Inn	1800 W. Lewis	547-0791	27-30 s 32-40 d	indoor pool, hot tub, sauna, laundry

the **Franklin County Historical Museum,** 547-3714, has exhibits depicting early Indian culture, railroad and aviation history, pioneer life, and agriculture. Open Wed. through Sun. afternoons; free.

ACCOMMODATIONS

See the chart on the facing page for hotel and motel accommodations.

Camping

At 611 Columbia Dr. SE in Richland, **Desert Gold Motel and Travel Trailer Park,** 627-1000, has RV hookup spaces for $9 per night or $63 per week; see chart above for motel rates and features. For camping in area parks, see "Parks And Dams" above.

FOOD

The newly opened **Blue Moon,** 21 W. Canal Dr., 582-6598, far outclasses the surrounding restaurants—OK, the entire city. Rather expensive for such an economically depressed area, the restaurant seems to be doing well nonetheless. The prix-fixe menu ($25) features seafood, pork, chicken, and more, and the wines are all local. Open weekends for dinner only.

Kennewick's **Chapter Eleven,** 3311 W. Clearwater, 783-7433, specializes in prime rib and seafood at moderate prices. Open weekdays for lunch, daily for dinner. At the Hanford House Thunderbird Motel at 802 George Washington Way, the **Hanford House** restaurant overlooks the Columbia River, specializing in moderately priced steak, veal, and seafood. Open for 3 meals daily, including Sunday brunch; 946-7611. **Baron's Beef 'N' Brew,** 1034 Lee Blvd. in Richland, has a good selection of Washington wines and microbrewery beers, plus what they claim is the largest bottled beer selection in the Northwest; 946-5500. The **Flamingo Beach Club,** next to the water park on W. Canal Dr., 735-3434, serves a moderately priced American menu, outdoors in summer. **Bruce's Steak and Lobster House,** 131 Vista Way in Kennewick, 783-

8213, serves lunch and dinner daily with entertainment in the lounge. For a gourmet burger, salad, or sandwich, visit the **Red Robin** at 924 George Washington Way in Richland. **Henry's,** next door to the Holiday Inn on George Washington Way, serves moderately priced steak and seafood. Try **C.D.'s Texas Style Barbecue,** 101 B Vista Way in Kennewick, 582-4269, for authentic pit-cooked barbecue. Clearwater and Kennewick avenues comprise fast-food city.

ENTERTAINMENT

Festivals And Events

Heat up the cold Pasco winter with a visit to the **Winter Wine Fair and Mardi Gras** in late February. Late May or early June means the start of Richland's **Sunfest,** a summer-long series of weekend events that feature international food, music, and dancing; one of these is **Jazzin' Up The Park,** a jazz festival with arts and crafts, held annually in June or July. Mid-July brings the **Tri-Cities Northwest Wine Festival** to Kennewick, featuring 180 wines represented by 60 wineries; betcha can't taste them all! Also in mid-July, Pasco hosts the **Tri-Cities Air Show** featuring high-flying acrobatics, and Richland sponsors **Free Day in the Country,** a picnic with country music. One of Tri-Cities' biggest events is the annual unlimited hydroplane races on the Columbia River, the highlight of the late-July **Tri-Cities Water Follies and Columbia Cup.** Also in late July is SE Washington's largest arts and crafts show, the **Allied Arts Sidewalk Show** in Richland. Kennewick hosts the **County Fair and Rodeo** every Aug., with top entertainers performing at the fairgrounds at 1500 S. Oak St., off 10th Avenue. Not to be outdone by the wine festival, 9 area micro-breweries come together for the late summer **Brew Ha-Ha** in Richland, featuring food, good beer, and entertainment. Summer winds down with the late Oct. **Rotary Chili Blast-Off** in Pasco, a chili cook-off with entertainment. Don't miss December's **Christmas Lights Boat Parade,** when boats adorned in festive holiday lights cruise down the Columbia.

Horse Racing

At Kennewick's Benton-Franklin Fairgrounds on E. 10th Ave., **Sun Downs Horse Racing Track** has quarter-horse racing in spring and fall; 586-9211.

Art Galleries And Shows

In the Tri-Cities area, Richland comes out way ahead in art galleries. Visit the **Allied Arts Gallery,** 89 Lee Blvd., 943-9815, and see paintings, pottery, and weavings by local artists. **The Arts Council of the Mid-Columbia,** 650 George Washington Way, sponsors the arts-and-crafts displays at the June International Folk Festival (above); 943-0524. The **Tri-Cities Gallery of Fine Arts,** 802 George Washington Way A, 943-ARTS, displays works by Southwest and Northwest artists in various media.

In Kennewick, **The Appleseed Gallery and Shops,** 108 Vista Way, 735-2874, has 11 shops filled with local arts and crafts, oil and watercolor paintings, toys, cards, and more. Across the street at 135 Vista Way, **Beaux Art Gallery,** 783-4549, has stained glass, pottery, paintings, and crafts.

The Arts

For those of classical taste, phone for scheduled events staged by the **Mid-Columbia Symphony Society,** Box 65, Richland, WA 99352, 735-7356, the **Mid-Columbia Regional Ballet,** 1405 Goethals, Richland, 946-1531, and the **Tri-City Repertory Theater,** 2212 Benton, Richland, 375-0673 or 627-3802.

Golf

Tri-Cities is a golfer's paradise—no umbrella required! Public courses include Pasco's **Municipal Golf Course,** 2335 N. 20th, 545-3440; Kennewick's **Columbia Park Golf Course** at Columbia Park, 586-4069, **Canyon Lakes,** 3700 Canyon Lakes Dr., 582-3736, and **Tri-Cities Country Club,** 314 N. Underwood, 783-6014 (non-members are allowed to play); Richland's **Sham-Na-Pum Golf Course,** 72 George Washington Way, 946-1914; and West Richland's **Tapteal**

Community Golf Course, 4000 Fallon Dr. 967-2165. These are all 18-hole courses open daily.

Work Out

The **Tri-City Court Club,** 1350 N. Gran St. in Kennewick, 783-5465, has facilities for racquetball, tennis, weightlifting, swimming, an indoor track, aerobics classes, and a sauna, and offers one-day passes for $7.

Water Slide

With all this heat and unrelenting sunshine you'll need a place to cool off. Take your suit to **Oasis Waterworks,** 6321 W. Canal Dr. in Kennewick, 735-8442, and try their 10 water slides, 5,000-square-foot swimming pool, shaded picnic area, astroturf sunbathing area, hot tub, basketball and volleyball courts, and more. All-day admission is $8.45.

Movies

Escape the heat *and* reality with a movie at Kennewick's **Clearwater Cinema,** 325 N. Johnson, 735-7511, Richland's **Uptown Cinema,** 1300 Jadwin, 943-6671, near the mall at **Columbia Center,** 900 Columbia Center Blvd., 783-1354, or **Metro 4 Cinemas,** 1390 Columbia Center Blvd., 735-0414. Save your quarters by phoning the **Theater Movie Line,** 582-5058, to see what's playing at all Tri-Cities and Walla Walla theaters.

SHOPPING

Columbia Center is the Tri-Cities' largest shopping mall, with 70 stores including The Bon and J.C. Penney; take the Columbia Center Blvd. exit off Hwy. 12. There are smaller shopping centers across the street. For the Tri-Cities' best selection of Northwest and imported wines, stop by **Le Cave du Vin Wine Merchants,** 1341B George Washington Way, Richland, 946-8300. For a different shopping experience, visit the **Pasco Farmers Market,** 4th and Lewis streets, for local produce, arts, and crafts, from early May through November; 545-0738.

SERVICES AND INFO

The Tri-Cities area code is 509. You can get all the current maps and information you need from the **Tri-Cities Visitor and Convention Bureau,** housed in the Vista Airport building at the end of Grandridge Blvd. in Kennewick, 735-8486 or (800) 835-0248. Or, more specifically, try the **Richland Chamber of Commerce,** 700 George Washington Way, Richland, WA 99352, 946-1651, or the **Pasco Chamber of Commerce,** 129 N. 3rd, Pasco, WA 99301, 547-9755.

Dial 911 in the Tri-Cities area for all emergencies. For medical attention, contact **Our Lady of Lourdes Hospital,** 520 N. 4th, Pasco, 547-0009; **Kadlec Medical Center,** open 24 hours at 888 Swift Blvd. in Richland, 946-4611; or **Kennewick General,** W. 10th Ave. and Dayton, 586-6111.

TRANSPORTATION

By Car
The Tri-Cities are an easy 200-mile drive from Seattle on I-90 to Ellensburg, then S on I-82 to Yakima and E on Hwy. 12.

By Train
The Tri-Cities are served by **Amtrak's** *Empire Builder,* providing daily service between Chicago and Seattle/Portland. The station is at W. Clark and N. Tacoma in Pasco, 545-1554 or (800) 872-7245.

By Bus
Greyhound serves the Tri-Cities from stations at 1325 Lee Blvd. in Richland, 946-4504, and 115 N. 2nd in Pasco, 547-3151. Hop aboard **Ben Franklin Transit,** 735-5100, to get around town, cheap: $.30 adults, 159 kids, with free transfers, with service to Tri-Cities Airport, downtown Kennewick, Richland, and Pasco, and out to West Richland.

By Air
Departing from the Tri-Cities Airport in Pasco, **Horizon Air,** (800) 547-9308, connects the Tri-Cities with Seattle, Spokane, Boise, Portland, and San Francisco. Other airlines serving the area are **Alaska,** 547-4200, and **USAir,** 545-1204.

By Balloon
Get an entirely different perspective on the Tri-Cities and the Columbia River—from sagebrush level to 3,000 feet up—by taking a hot-air balloon ride with **Over Land Ballooning,** Game Farm Rd., Kennewick, 586-9265. Flights last 1-2 hours, departing from a number of Tri-Cities locations, and cost $100 per person with a 4-person maximum, including a Champagne celebration upon landing.

YAKIMA

Yakima, a far cry weatherwise from its neighbors to the W, averages 300 sunny days per year with just 8 inches of precipitation. The "wet" season—Nov. to Jan.—accounts for almost half of the annual rain- or snowfall. Summer temperatures on the dry side of the mountains generally run 10 or more degrees higher than in Puget Sound cities, explaining why virtually every motel, no matter how cheap, has a pool. Despite the dry, brown hills surrounding the city, Yakima's suburbs are green, due to the constant *chit-chit-chit* of lawn sprinklers.

The Yakima Valley's volcanic soil is twice as productive as ordinary land—teamed with irrigation and a 200-day growing season, its hard to beat. The county ranks first in the country in apples, fruit trees, hops, and mint, and fourth in all fruits, with pears, grapes, cherries, peaches, and apricots as major crops. Though among the largest cities in eastern Washington and the commercial hub of the valley, Yakima's population is just under 50,000.

HISTORY

Yakima area Indians defended their ground, preventing any permanent white settlement here until the end of the 1855-57 Indian War. With the Indian's acceptance of the Yakima Reservation in 1858, pioneer cattlemen settled in the valley—farmers weren't interested in this arid region. In 1861, Fielding M. Thorpe and his wife Margaret became Yakima's first homesteaders. Dry soil was the area's biggest drawback, so in the 1860s, Sebastian Lauber and Joseph and Charles Schamo built an irrigation ditch to shift some of the Yakima River's water into town, paving the way for agriculture. In 1870, John W. Beck planted 50 apple trees and 50 peach trees in the region's first orchards, marking the end of the cattle era and the start of a major fruit industry. With a population of 400, "Yakima City" was incorporated in 1883. The Northern Pacific Railroad had a problem acquiring land from some of the property owners, so they

built their Yakima Valley station 4 miles N of town. Since the railroad couldn't come to the city, the townspeople put their houses on skids and rollers and moved the city to the railroad—in time to meet the first train pulling into town on Dec. 14, 1884.

SIGHTS

Wine Tour
Don't leave Yakima without visiting at least one of the valley's wineries! Because they're all strung along the Yakima River SE of Yakima proper, the wineries are listed under "Vicinity of Yakima," p. 360.

If you're a wine lover who can't get to the wineries, visit **The Wine Cellar,** 5 N. Front St., for a good selection of Yakima Valley and other wines; staffed by a friendly, knowledgeable staff, the shop always has a few bottles open for you to taste.

Brewery
In a region known for its wineries, it's easy for beer drinkers to feel left out—but there's a place here for you too! The **Yakima Brewing and Malting Co.,** 25 N. Front St., became the Northwest's first microbrewery when investors got a taste of Bert Grant's home brew in 1981. Grant's Scottish Ale launched the brewery, which now also produces Grant's Imperial Stout, India Pale Ale, and others from locally grown Cascade hops. You can tour the brewery daily at 2 and 3 p.m., or visit **The Brewery Pub** in the same building, where you'll find at least 5 different brews on tap at all times, plus Cornish pasties, sausage rolls, pub pies, and Scotch eggs in British-pub fashion. Smoking is not allowed.

Dinner Train
Take a ride through the Yakima River Valley aboard the **Spirit of Washington Dinner Train.** Enjoy the scenery from 1 of 5 stainless-steel cars, including a vista dome (with a bar). Three-hour RT brunch ($30) or dinner ($45) rides run Fri. night between Kennewick and Prosser, Sat. night and Sun. morning

between Yakima and Ellensburg. Reservations and meal selections must be made in advance; phone 452-2336 or (800) 876-RAIL or write 1 E. Yakima Ave., Yakima, WA 98901, for more information.

Parks

About a mile E of town off I-82, **Yakima Sportsman State Park** has a stocked pond for kids to fish—adults can try their luck in the Yakima—plus 28 standard and 36 hookup campsites along the greenbelt; a great spot to escape the summer heat. The **Yakima River Greenway,** currently being developed, will encompass 3,600 acres E of the city, connecting existing parks along a 10-mile paved bike path. Already completed is the riverside trail at the **Yakima Area Arboretum,** I-90 and Nob Hill Blvd., a partially developed, 70-acre park with Japanese garden and bird sanctuary. At **Eschbach Park,** 5 miles past the fish hatchery on the Old Naches Hwy., rent a tube ($1) and take a lazy float down the Yakima River. The day-use, 175-acre county park offers boating, swimming, picnicking, and play areas. **Randall Park,** S of Nob Hill Blvd. on S. 48th Ave., has a picnic area, trails, duck pond, and creek on 40 grassy acres. **Franklin Park,** behind the museum at Tieton Dr. and 20th Ave., has

tennis courts and grassy hills for romping or winter sledding. Seventeen miles E of Yakima on Hwy. 24, the 244-acre **ORV Park** has motorcycle, jeep, and 3-wheeler race tracks, and trap-shooting station. Open Sat. through Wed. till 6 p.m.

Across the Yakima River from Union Gap, **Moxee Bog,** a spring-fed preserve, is home to a rare breed of Monarch butterfly that feeds on the violets that grow here. Birders will want to visit the **Boise Cascade Bird Sanctuary** in the Wenas Valley, 5 miles W of Selah on Wean Road. The corporation donated 40 acres for the campground and sanctuary where over 100 species of birds have been sighted.

Bridges And Scenic Drives

Driving on I-82 between Ellensburg and Yakima, you'll realize that eastern Washington isn't the flat desert wasteland that it's sometimes made out to be—a desert wasteland, maybe, but not flat. As the road snakes up treeless ridges over 2,000 feet high, the brown hills in the distance look as if they're covered with velvet; up close, sagebrush dots the brown grass (in an imitation of a scruffy 3-day beard). Pull in at the "VIEW POINT" sign for broad vistas of green valley farmland below and the snowcapped Stuart Range to the north. Along the way, you'll cross the

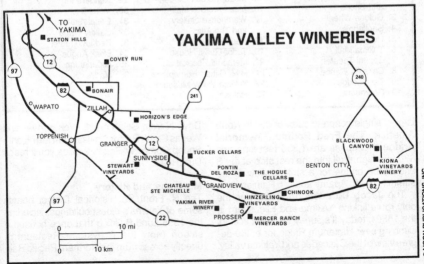

© MOON PUBLICATIONS, INC.

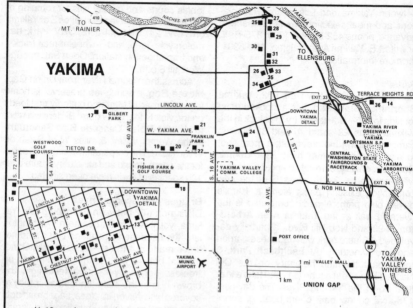

YAKIMA

(1-13 see insert map)
1. Yakima Brewing and Malting Co., Wine Cellar, and Greystone Restaurant
2. Track 29 Dining Co. and Shops
3. Golden Wheel
4. Santiago's
5. House of Art
6. Yakima Mall
7. Capitol Theater
8. Casa de Blanca
9. TraveLodge
10. Greyhound
11. Towne Plaza
12. visitor center
13. chamber of commerce
14. Best Western Rio Mirada
15. Meadowbrook Garden
16. Meadowbrook Mall
17. Warehouse Gallery and The Attic
18. Red Robin
19. Tudor Guest House
20. Memorial Hospital
21. H.M. Gilbert Homeplace
22. Yakima Valley Museum
23. Ichiban
24. St. Elizabeth Hospital
25. Comfort Inn
26. Bali Hai Motel
27. Red Lion Inn
28. Colonial Motor Inn
29. Nendel's Inn
30. Motel 6
31. Gasparetti's
32. Gallery Gage
33. Red Lion Motel
34. Black Angus
35. Imperial Inn
36. Marti's

largest single concrete span bridge in North America. The **Fred Redmon Memorial Bridge** twin spans are 1,336 feet long and 330 feet high. Pull into the rest stop at the S end of the bridge for a striking view of the summits of Mt. Adams and Mt. Rainier.

The **Jacob Durr Wagon Road** was the only route linking Yakima and Ellensburg in the 1880s; today it's surely the most scenic, climbing over Umtanum Ridge for a 360-degree view of the Cascades and Yakima valley.

Drive N from Selah on N. Wenas Ave. and Wenas Creek Rd. for 6 miles, then turn R onto Sheep Company Rd.; in 2 miles you'll reach Durr Road.

Museums And History

The N. Front St. Historical District boasts some of Yakima's oldest buildings, including the 1898 Lund Building that once housed a saloon (now the Greystone Restaurant) directly across from the Northern Pacific Railroad depot. Be sure to visit **The Wine Cellar** and **Brewery Pub** (mentioned above), also in the district.

Visit the **Yakima Valley Museum,** 2105 Tieton Dr., 248-0747, at the edge of Franklin Park to see Yakima Indian clothing, beadwork, and artifacts, a replica of Chief Justice William O. Douglas' office, and the most comprehensive collection of horse-drawn vehicles W of the Mississippi. Open Wed. through Sun. till 5 p.m., year-round; admission is $2.50 adults, $1.25 students and seniors.

Union Gap's **Central Washington Agricultural Museum** displays tractors, pea pickers, and other early Yakima Valley farm equipment on 15 acres in Fulbright Park.

The **H.M. Gilbert Homeplace,** 2109 W. Yakima Ave., was built in 1898 amidst 20 acres of sagebrush by Horace M. Gilbert, a farmer, land developer, and one of the pioneers in the irrigation of the Yakima Valley. You can tour this early Yakima Valley farm home on Fri., March through Dec., from 10 a.m.- 3 p.m., for $2.50; 248-0747.

Three miles NW of Yakima on Hwy. 12 you'll find the mysterious **Indian Painted Rocks,** a State Historical Site. Although the pictographs were partially destroyed by an early irrigation project, some remain at Naches Hwy. and Powerhouse Road.

The **Ahtanum Mission,** E of Yakima along Ahtanum Creek, was built in 1852 by Oblate priests. Though it burned down in the Indian War, the church was rebuilt in 1869 and is still used. You can visit the mission and surrounding park for a small fee.

Planetarium
Every Mon. at 7 p.m. the planetarium at Yakima Valley Community College puts on a stellar performance; S. 16th Ave. and W. Nob Hill, 575-2356 or 575-2209; free.

ACCOMMODATIONS

Bed And Breakfast
At 3111 Tieton Dr., the stately **Tudor Guest House,** 452-8112 or 452-6015, is an elegant bargain. Constructed in 1932, this English Tudor mansion is surrounded by park-like grounds and furnished in early 19th-century antiques (plus color TVs). All rooms are on the 2nd floor with shared baths and start at $40 d; breakfast is continental.

Eighteen miles E of Yakima on Hwy. 24, **The Desert Rose B&B,** 18170 Hwy. 24, 452-2237, is an English country manor surrounded by thousands of acres of rolling hills and views of the valley and Mt. Rainier. The greatest concentration of great horned owls in the state live nearby, and the night skies out here are dark and clear—great for stargazing. Peace and quiet are insured with just 2 guest rooms ($50 s, $60 d); families are welcome, and you can choose your breakfast when you make your reservation.

For more B&Bs, see "Vicinity of Yakima" below.

Hotels And Motels
Take the N. 1st St. exit off I-82 for "hotel row." See the charts on pp. 352-353 for a compre-

view from Umtanum Ridge, midway between Yakima and Ellensburg

Fred Redmon Memorial Bridge

hensive list of these and other hotels in and around Yakima.

FOOD

Yakima's finest is **Birchfield Manor Gourmet Restaurant,** 452-1960, a restored 1912 farmhouse 2 miles E of the city on Birchfield Road. Dinners are served Fri. through Sun., for $22.50, complemented by a vast selection of Yakima Valley wines; the owners ask that you leave the kids with a sitter. For Italian food from simple to fancy plus NW specialties, try **Gasperetti's,** 1013 N. 1st St., 248-0628; open for dinner only, Tues. through Saturday. **Marti's,** 1601 Terrace Heights Rd., serves everything from steak to seafood to pizza, and 3 meals daily, overlooking the Yakima River; 248-2062. In the historic district, **The Greystone Restaurant,** 5 N. Front St., 248-9801, has moderately priced Northwest cuisine, fresh seafood, and homemade pasta in an elegant atmosphere; open for dinner only, Tues. through Saturday. The **Track 29 Dining Co.,** Yakima Ave. and N. 1st St., serves moderately priced steak, chicken, pasta, and Mexican dishes for lunch and dinner daily in 2 restored 1920s' railroad cars; or, enjoy a beer and appetizers on their sunny patio. **Santiago's,** 111 E. Yakima Ave., 453-1644, is a popular Mexican restaurant open for

lunch and dinner daily; or, try **Casa de Blanca,** 402 E. Yakima Ave., 248-3501. For delicious Hawaiian and Polynesian fare, try **Haleaina,** 1406 N. 16th Ave., 248-1965, open daily for dinner, weekdays for lunch, plus Sunday brunch. For Cantonese and American cuisine, try the **Golden Wheel,** 9 S. 1st St., 457-8400. Get authentic Japanese food with a sushi bar at **Ichiban,** 1107 Tieton Dr., 248-2585. Enjoy good-old American steak and seafood, priced $7-17, at **Black Angus,** 501 N. Front St., 248-4540. **Red Robin,** 2706 W. Nob Hill Rd., features gourmet hamburgers, sandwiches, and light meals; open for lunch and dinner daily. For a great little English-style pub, see "Brewery" above.

The lounge at **Meadowbrook Garden** at the Meadowbrook Mall, 72nd and Nob Hill, has live music Wed. through Sat., with free dance lessons every Wed. at 7:30 p.m.; 965-0384.

ENTERTAINMENT

Festivals
Held in mid-June at the Central Washington State Fairgrounds on Fair Ave., the **Washington State Open Horse Show** is one of the largest in the country. The most popular fairgrounds event (aside from the horse racing, below) is the **Central Washington State Fair and Rodeo,** held in late September.

Horse Racing
For quarter horse and thoroughbred racing, check out **Yakima Meadows Racetrack** at the fairgrounds on Fair Avenue. The horses usually run Fri., Sat., and Sun., March through May and Sept. through Nov., with a scanty summer schedule; 248-3920.

Auto Racing
The **Yakima Speedway,** 1600 Pacific Ave., has NASCAR racing every Sat. night; 248-0647.

Golf
Yakima has 3 public golf courses: **Sun Tides,** 2215 Pence, 966-9065, has 18 holes, 8 miles W of town on Hwy. 12; **Fisher Golf Course,**

DOWNTOWN YAKIMA ACCOMMODATIONS

Name	Address	Phone	Rates	Comments
Bali Hai Motel	710 N. 1st St.	452-7178	19-25 s 24-32 d	pool
Best Western Rio Mirada Motor Inn	1603 Terrace Heights Dr.	457-4444	39-49 s 44-54 d	on the river, jacuzzi, pool, exercise facilities, adjacent restaurant; all rooms have river views
Colonial Motor Inn	1405 N. 1st St.	453-8981	29-32 s 36-50 d	heated pool, 2 hot tubs
Comfort Inn	1700 N. 1st St.	248-5650	41 s 45-48 d	pool, sauna, airport and bus shuttle
Imperial Inn	510 N. 1st St.	457-6155	28 s 32-36 d	pool
Motel 6	1104 N. 1st St.	454-0080	23 s 29 d	pool
Nendel's Inn	1300 N. 1st St.	248-6666	37 s 42-44 d	pool, playground, lounge, restaurant
Red Lion Motel	818 N. 1st St.	453-0391	40-41 s 50-55 d	pool, airport and bus shuttle
TraveLodge	110 S. Naches Ave.	453-7151	37 s 43-48 d	pool
Towne Plaza	N. 7th and E. Yakima	248-5900	46-56 s 56-66 d	2 pools, poolside service, lounge, cafe, airport and bus shuttle
Red Lion Inn	1507 N. 1st St.	248-7850	50-65 s 60-75 d	2 pools, poolside service, airport and bus shuttle, cafe, lounge

S. 40th Ave. and W. Arlington, 575-6075, and **Westwood Golf Course,** 6408 Tieton Dr., 966-0890, are 9-hole courses.

Theater
The historic **Capitol Theater** at 19 S. 3rd St. first opened its doors in 1920, featuring vaudeville and feature films. Today the theater hosts a full schedule of theatrical productions nearly year-round; 575-6267.

Movies
Yakima is one of few cities where you can still find drive-ins; in fact, they have 2: **Country**

MOTELS AND HOTELS —VICINITY OF YAKIMA

Name	Address	Phone	Rates	Comments
UNION GAP				
Best Western Tapadera Motor Inn	12 Valley Mall Blvd. Yakima	248-6924	36-48 s 40-52 d	next to mall, restaurant
Super 8	2605 Rudkin Rd.	248-8800	31-34 s 35-41 d	indoor pool, laundry, pets OK with notice
Yakima Motor Inn	2408 Rudkin Rd.	248-9700	30-34 s 34-44 d	pool, cafe, room service, airport and bus shuttle
SUNNYSIDE				
Nendel's Motor Inn	408 Yakima Valley Hwy.	837-7878	34-36 s 37-41 d	pool
Red Apple Motel	412 Hwy. 12	839-2100	26 s 29-32 d	kitchen $3 extra
Town House	509 Hwy. 12	837-5500	22-24 s 27-30 d	playground, pets OK
GRANDVIEW				
Apple Valley Motel	Hwy. 12	882-3003	22 s 24-28 d	pool
Grandview	522 E. Main St.	882-1323	18-22 s 23-30 d	pool

Drive-In, 4309 W. Nob Hill, 966-5340, and **Fruitvale Triple Drive-In,** 1819 Fruitvale, 248-3650. Indoor theaters include **Uptown Plaza** at 202 E. Chestnut, 248-0245, **Mercy 6-Plex** at the Valley Mall, 248-0242, and **Cinema West,** 2706 W. Nob Hill, 248-0243.

SHOPPING

Usually the giant covered shopping malls are found in suburbia; but Yakima's biggest shopping center is in the heart of downtown: the **Yakima Mall** has over 75 shops including The Bon, Nordstrom, J.C. Penney, and Mervyn's, plus 1,200 covered parking spaces to keep your car cool. At Yakima Ave. and N. 1st, 2 1920s railroad cars house **The Track 29 Dining Co.** (see "food" above) and serve as a backdrop for numerous gift shops and eateries. Just over the line into Union Gap, **Valley Mall** on S. 1st St. has 44 stores including Sears, Lamonts, and Payless Drugstore.

Art galleries abound in Yakima. Visit **Gallery Gage,** 1007 N. 1st St., **Warehouse Gallery** and **The Attic** at 5000 W. Lincoln, and **House of Art,** 106 N. 5th Ave.

Grocery stores are all over town, but the biggest and easiest to find are **Fred Meyer** and **Safeway,** both on S. 1st Street.

SERVICES AND INFO

The area code from Chinook Pass to the E border is 509. For maps, brochures, and current festival information, contact the **Yakima Valley Visitors and Convention Bureau,** 10 N. 8th St., Yakima, WA 98907, 575-1300, or the **Greater Yakima Chamber of Commerce,** 10 N. 9th St., 248-2021. For information on the surrounding towns, contact the **Toppenish Chamber of Commerce,** 219 S. Toppenish Ave., 865-3262; the **Sunnyside Chamber of Commerce,** 340 S. 6th Ave., 837-5939; the **Zillah Chamber of Commerce,** 111 7th St., 829-6994; or the **Prosser Chamber of Commerce,** 611 6th St., 786- 2626.

No 911 service here; in an emergency, phone 248-1010 for police or 248-2100 for fire. For medical emergencies, phone **Yakima Valley Memorial Hospital,** 2811 Tieton Dr., 575-8000; **St. Elizabeth Hospital,** 110 S. 9th Ave., 575-5060; or **Yakima Ambulance Medic 1,** 248-3610.

Post offices are located at 205 W. Washington and 112 S. 3rd Ave.

TRANSPORTATION

By Car
Coming from Seattle, the fastest and best winter or bad-weather route to Yakima is on I-90 over Snoqualmie Pass, turning S onto I-82 in Ellensburg. If you have time to spare, the routes through or near Mt. Rainier National Park are certainly more scenic. In the best weather, pick up Hwy. 410 in Enumclaw, following it through the park and over 2 mountain passes; or continue S from Cayuse Pass onto Hwy. 123, then go E on Hwy. 12 over White Pass. (See "Vicinity of Mount Rainier," p. 97). Before you try these routes in winter, phone 1-976-7623 for pass conditions from Nov. to March.

Getting oriented after you've arrived in Yakima can be difficult, until you figure out the system. North Front St., along the railroad tracks, divides the downtown area; from here, street numbers ascend, starting with "1," in both directions, leading to a confusing situation in which 6th St. and 6th Ave. are 12 blocks apart. Here's the key: "streets" are on the E side, "avenues" are on the west. East Yakima Ave. runs perpendicular to N. Front St. and divides the numbered streets into N and S sections, i.e. S. 2nd St. Simple?

By Air
The **Yakima Municipal Airport** off Washington Ave. is the largest in the area (which isn't saying much), served by **Horizon Airlines,** (800) 547-9308.

By Trolley
Ride the **Yakima Trolley Line's** restored 1906 trolley cars through orchards, over the Naches River, and past Congdon's Castle. Trains depart hourly on weekends from 44th Ave. and Nob Hill Blvd., late April through Labor Day, for a 45-minute ride; fares are $3 adults, $1.50 for kids, or $9 for the whole brood; phone 575-1700 for recorded information.

By Bus
Yakima Transit, 575-6175, has 9 routes serving the Yakima area, including the Municipal Airport. Fares are $.35 adults, $.20 kids. To get out of town or across the country, hop aboard **Greyhound** from their station at 602 E. Yakima Ave., 457-5131. Other Yakima-area Greyhound stations are at 602 W. 1st in Toppenish, 865-3773, and at 13th St. and Hwy. 12 in Sunnyside, 837-5344.

Tours
Since no one wants to be the "designated driver" on a day-long winery tour, leave the driving to **Custom Tours,** Route 1, Box 1474, Zillah, WA 98953, 865-3353 or 575-6595. **PW Charter Service,** Box 2455, Yakima, WA 98907, 575-3655 or (800) 572-2877, also offers local sightseeing and winery tours.

VICINITY OF YAKIMA

TOPPENISH

Toppenish, about 25 miles SE of Yakima, is the home of the Yakima Indian Agency and the commercial center for the Yakima Indian Reservation.

Yakima Nation Cultural Center

About 23 miles SE of Yakima, the **Yakima Nation Cultural Center,** 865-2800, features a museum that tells the story of the Yakima Nation from its beginnings to the present; a library specializing in the American Indian; and a theater that presents first-run movies and stage productions. Open daily; admission is $2 adults, $1 kids, or $5 for the family.

As you're driving near the reservation, keep an eye out for UFOs! The Yakima Indian Reservation, believe it or not, made the *National Enquirer* in late 1986 because of their alleged high frequency of UFO sightings, reportedly "an everyday part" of their culture.

Park

About 30 miles W of Toppenish in the heart of the Yakima Indian Reservation, **Fort Simcoe State Park,** 874-2372, is a day-use park surrounding Fort Simcoe, erected by the Army in 1856 and named a National Historic Site in 1956. Two blockhouses and a barracks have been reconstructed, and 5 of the original buildings have been restored and furnished. Tour the buildings and interpretive center, then enjoy a picnic lunch on the landscaped grounds. The grounds are open Wed. through Sun., April through mid-Oct., weekends the rest of the year; the museum and interpretive center are open Wed. through Sun., April through October.

Festival

Held annually in June, the **Toppenish Western Wine Fest** is a day-long feast of Yakima Valley wines and beers, food, arts and crafts, and country and western music.

Food

A tiny joint on W. 1st St., **El Paso Cafe** serves inexpensive Mexican lunches and dinners. Closed Sun.; no alcohol. Enjoy a root beer float and chili dog at **A&W,** 433 S. Elm.

YAKIMA VALLEY

While Toppenish is virtually a world—or a nation—apart, the rest of the Yakima Valley blends together to form a single conceptual region, basing its reputation, if not its economy, on the wineries that line the Yakima River.

Museum

In Prosser City Park, the **Benton County Historical Museum** has a natural history display, 1900 homestead, 1913 schoolhouse, ladies' gowns from the 1840s to 1920s, and an 1867 Chickering Square grand piano you can play. Open daily except Mon. 10 a.m.-4 p.m., Sun. 1 p.m.-5 p.m.; admission is $1 adults, $.50 for kids.

Bed And Breakfast

In the heart of wine country, **Cottage Court Bed & Breakfast,** 1824 Meade Ave., 786-1430, offers continental or full breakfast with 3 guest rooms (shared bath) for $30 s, $35-40 d. No pets; smoking permitted in the lounge. The **Rinehold Cannery Homestead,** Route 1, Box 1117, on Gurley Rd. in Granger, 854-2508, provides lodging and continental breakfast in a country setting for $45 s, $55 d.

Wine Tour

The Yakima and Columbia valleys comprise the premier wine-growing regions in Washington, located along the same latitude as France's Burgundy and Bordeaux regions. The 13 wineries along the Yakima River provide more than a day's touring; all of these wineries have tasting rooms, and all but Hinzerling have picnic facilities. So pack a hefty lunch, make room in your trunk for a case of your favorite, and hit the road!

From Yakima, your first stop will be **Staton Hills,** 2290 Gangl Rd. in Wapato, 877-2112, open for tastings Tues. through Sun., 11 a.m.-5 p.m. Here you'll get a nice view of the Yakima Valley.

Next stop is **Covey Run,** formerly named Quail Run, at Route 2, Box 2287, in Zillah, 829-6235; this is one of the area's big-name wineries (meaning you can find their wine in most Northwest grocery stores). Quail Run was the first major Washington winery to use only Yakima Valley grapes. Eighty-five percent of their production is white wine, most of it Riesling. The mezzanine tasting room affords a nice vineyard view; open daily from 11 a.m.-4:30 p.m., Sun. from noon to 5 p.m.

A brand new addition to the Valley is **Bonair Winery,** off Highland Dr. in Zillah, 829-6027. Their first productions were a 1985 Riesling, Chardonnay, and Cabernet Sauvignon. Visitors are welcome Thurs. through Mon., April through Nov., 10 a.m.-5 p.m.

Also in Zillah, at Route 2, Box 2396, is **Horizon's Edge,** 829-6401. Another of the valley's newest wineries future releases will include Cabernet Sauvignon and Pinot Noir. (their Chardonnay and Riesling releases started in 1984). The tasting room is open daily from April 1 to Christmas, 11 a.m.-5 p.m.

Stewart Vineyards, 854-1882, is another new addition to the Yakima Valley family at Route 3, Box 3578, in Sunnyside. Their tasting room opened in Aug. 1984, and their production includes Rieslings, Chardonnay, Muscat Canelli, Gewürztraminer, and Cabernet Sauvignon; open daily at 10 a.m., Sun. at noon.

Also in Sunnyside, **Tucker Cellars,** Route 1, Box 1696, 837-8701, is a family winery established in 1981 and now produces 9 varieties and over 20,000 gallons annually. This is a good first or last visit: the tasting room is open daily 9 a.m.-6 p.m. in summer (10 a.m.-4 p.m. in winter).

Chateau Ste. Michelle, W. 5th and Ave. B in Grandview, 882-3928, is Washington's oldest winery. Established in the 1930s, it has come to represent the Washington wine industry across the country. Grandview is the site of all Ste. Michelle red wine fermentation; 2 other facilities are located in Woodinville and Paterson. Try their award-winning Cabernet Sauvignon and Merlot daily from 10 a.m.-5 p.m.

Pontin del Roza, Route 1, Box 1129, in Prosser, 786-4449, is a relative newcomer, established in 1984 and producing Chardonnay, White Riesling, and Chenin Blanc. Open daily 10 a.m.-5 p.m.

Also in Prosser at Route 1, Box 1657, **Yakima River Winery,** 786-2805, was started in 1978 by the John W. Rauner family and produces a wide variety of wines from dry and semi-dry whites and reds to dessert and ice

Rosalie Harry and Annie May of the Yakima Tribe

wines, including some that are available only at the winery. The tasting room is open daily 10 a.m.-5 p.m.

Your next Prosser winery is **Hinzerling Vineyards,** 1520 Sheridan, 786-2163. The vineyard here was planted in 1972, the winery founded in 1976; their specialties include estate-grown Cabernet. Tastings are usually held in the wine cellar, Mon. through Sat. 10 a.m.-4 p.m. (closed for the noon hour); in winter, Sun. noon to 4 p.m.

You probably won't find **Chinook Wines** in your grocery store, so stop by the winery at Meade and Wittkopf roads in Prosser for some Sparkling Riesling, Sauvignon Blanc, Chardonnay, or Merlot. Open Thurs. through Mon. noon to 5 p.m.

The Hogue Cellars, Route 2, Box 2898, 786-4557, is the big-name Prosser winery, with a range of products from Rieslings to Merlot along with a very nice, summery Cabernet Blush. Hogue Farms grows asparagus, concord grapes, hops, and scotch mint along with wine grapes on 1,200 acres. Their tasting room, gift shop, and art gallery are open daily 10 a.m.-5 p.m.

One of the newer Prosser wineries is **Mercer Ranch Vineyards,** in the Horse Heaven Hills on Alderdale Rd., 894-4741. Premium reds are the specialty here, including Cabernet Sauvignon and Limberger. Open Mon. through Sat. 9:30 a.m. to 5:30 p.m. in summer, Sun. by appointment; phone for off-season hours.

Your wine tour ends with 2 Benton City wineries. **Kiona Vineyards,** Route 2, Box 2169E, 588-6716, sits on Red Mountain with a nice tasting-room view of the vineyards. In business since 1980, Kiona produces a full range of varietal wines. Open daily noon to 5 p.m. You'll need an appointment to taste the wines at Benton City's **Blackwood Canyon,** Route 2, Box 2169H, 588-6249. It may be worth your while, since their Chardonnays, Cabernets, and late harvest wines are available only at the winery and select restaurants.

The **F.W. Langguth Winery,** 932-4943, out in Mattawa is open to group tours by appointment only; if you don't have a group or don't want to drive that far, you can easily find their Riesling and Chardonnay in area stores.

Get a brochure describing the Yakima Valley wineries by sending a long, self-addressed, stamped envelope to the Yakima Valley Wine Growers Assoc., Box 39, Grandview, WA 98930, or phone 837-8701.

Cheese

Cheese is a natural accompaniment to good wine; so it's no surprise to find the **Yakima Valley Cheese Co.,** Alexander Rd., producing 1,300 pounds of Gouda (they pronounce it "GOW-da") daily. No tours are available, but you can pick up a pound or two at the sales room Tues. through Sat. 9:30 a.m.-5:30 p.m.; 837-6005.

Food

For Mexican food, antiques, gifts, or tortillas to take home (made on the premises), try **El Ranchito,** just off the Zillah exit, 829-5880; sorry, no alcohol. Or, stop by **Doc's Pizza,** 505 1st Ave. in Zillah, 829-6259.

In Sunnyside, the **Tillicum Restaurant,** 410 Hwy. 12, serves only Yakima Valley wines with their steak and prime rib dinners; 837-7222. For Szechuan and Mandarin cooking, try China Grove, 325 Hwy. 12, 839-3663.

Barrel Tasting

During the April **Yakima Valley Spring Barrel Tasting,** all the valley wineries pour samples of their new releases straight from the barrel, and offer tours, hors d'oeuvres, and educational exhibits. All 15 wineries are open 10 a.m.-5 p.m. during the 3-day event.

News

Pick up a copy of *The Wine Almanac of the Pacific Northwest* from area wine shops or by mail ($10.50 a year) from NWA Subscriptions, Box 85595, Seattle, WA 98145-1595. The *Almanac* has winery news and a calendar of events for festivals and competitions.

ELLENSBURG

Ellensburg's biggest claim to fame is their popular Labor Day weekend rodeo, attracting thousands of spectators and top rodeo talent from across the country. The town isn't particularly Western in appearance; the Western clothing stores, tack shops, and country-western bars that you might expect in a rodeo town just aren't there. Instead you'll find an old, quiet town of less than 12,000 with progress squeezing in on a historic city center. Ellensburg is at the more-or-less geographic center of the state, serving as commercial center for the small mining towns and cattle ranches surrounding it. Besides the rodeo, Ellensburg has something found nowhere else in the world: the beautiful "Ellensburg Blue" agate, fashioned at local jewelry stores into earrings, necklaces, and rings. Bring a charge card or full wallet to take these beauties home: at one shop, the smallest earrings start at $75.

Driving toward Ellensburg from Puget Sound, the change in weather and geography is dramatic. From Seattle to Snoqualmie Pass, you'll pass forested hills and snow-covered peaks, often under a thick cloud cover. When you're about 20 miles W of Ellensburg, the clouds start to thin out, the temperature rises, and the landscape flattens to low, rolling hills dotted with bushes and an occasional tree. Out here the summers are sunnier and hotter—nearly every motel has a pool—but the winters are harsh, with snow and bitter cold that the Puget Sound region rarely sees.

HISTORY

From the beginning, the Kittitas Valley has been blessed with an abundance of fish and wildlife. From the earliest days, Indians from the otherwise hostile Nez Perce, Yakima, and Wenatchee tribes tolerated each others' presence as they hunted and fished the area peaceably. White settlers first arrived in the Ellensburg area in 1867. By 1870, Jack Splawn and Ben Burch had built the town's first store, "Robber's Roost," and the town took on the store's name until a few years later, when John Shoudy bought the store and platted the town, naming it for his wife, Mary Ellen. Ellensburg's population grew rapidly in the late 1880s, when the Northern Pacific Railroad finished its line through town to Puget Sound. Ellensburg was a contender for the state capital seat until a fire in July, 1889 destroyed its new commercial center and 200 homes; but the town fought back, rebuilding the community in brick before the year was out. One of the first colleges in the state, Central Washington University, was established here in 1891. Since then, the town hasn't seen a great deal of growth, but remains the hub of the central Washington cattle business and commercial center of the mining and agricultural region.

SIGHTS

Museum And Historic District

At E. 3rd and Pine streets, the **Kittitas County Historical Museum,** 925-3778, has Indian artifacts and displays of pioneer tools, photographs of early Ellensburg, and an impressive collection of petrified wood and gemstones, including a 6-pound Ellensburg Blue agate. The museum is housed in the 1889 Cadwell Building, a 2-story brick structure with horseshoe-shaped windows. Open afternoons Tues. through Saturday; donation.

Pick up a map at the museum or chamber of commerce for a self-guided tour of 18 Victorian-era buildings, most located within a 5-block area between 6th and 3rd avenues and Main and Pearl streets. The **Davidson Building** at 4th and Pearl is probably the first you'll notice; it's hard to miss with its proud tower and ornate windows. Next door, the 1889 **Stewart Building** now houses the Community Art Gallery. **Lynch Block,** at 5th and Pearl, is the only remaining structure that survived the 1889 fire; when it was built, its front windows were the largest in central

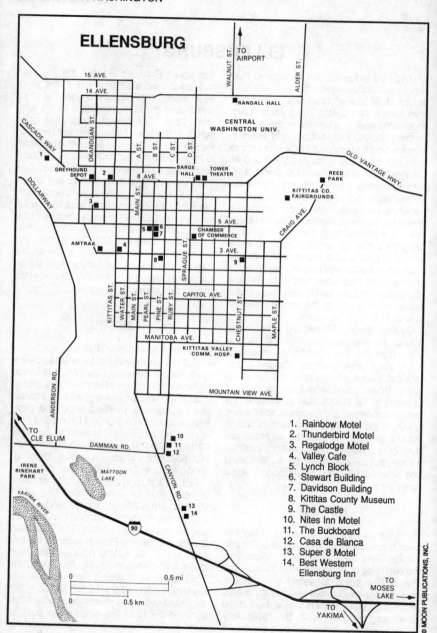

ELLENSBURG

1. Rainbow Motel
2. Thunderbird Motel
3. Regalodge Motel
4. Valley Cafe
5. Lynch Block
6. Stewart Building
7. Davidson Building
8. Kittitas County Museum
9. The Castle
10. Nites Inn Motel
11. The Buckboard
12. Casa de Blanca
13. Super 8 Motel
14. Best Western Ellensburg Inn

© MOON PUBLICATIONS, INC.

Washington. Travel down to 3rd and Chestnut to see **The Castle,** optimistically built in 1888 to be the Governor's Mansion when Ellensburg won the contest for state capital; it's lost much of its elegance since, and now houses apartments. Built in 1893-94, 4-story **Barge Hall,** 8th and D at CWU, is the oldest building on campus.

Parks

Four miles S of town off Kittitas Hwy., see one of the first Kittitas Valley farms at **Olmstead Place State Park.** The log cabin dates back to 1875; you can tour the 8 buildings, including a granary, dairy barn, and wagon shed, daily in summer, rest of year by appointment; 925-1943 or 856-2700. A ¾-mile trail leads from the red barn to the Seaton Cabin Schoolhouse, originally located farther away in a meadow; the kids didn't trudge miles through blizzards—they rode horseback.

In the city, **Irene Rinehart Park,** on the Yakima River off Damman Rd., is a welcome relief from the relentless summer sunshine. You can cool your toes in the swift green river, take a walk along shaded paths, or enjoy a riverside picnic. **Reed Park** at the end of Craig Ave. has a small shaded green for reading and relaxing, plus superb views of the county below and the snow-covered Stuart Range to the northwest.

Galleries

At 408½ N. Pearl, the **Ellensburg Community Art Gallery,** 925-2670, is open Tues. through Sat., with 7 display and sales rooms surrounding a central atrium in the 1889 G. R. Stewart Building. Central Washington University's **Sarah Spurgeon Art Gallery,** 963-2665, has regional artists' and students' work displayed in Randall Hall. Open Mon. through Friday.

ACCOMMODATIONS

For budget-minded travelers, the **Rainbow Motel,** 1025 Cascade Way, 925-3544, has a playground, laundry, and rooms from $27 s, $28-40 d. The **Regalodge Motel,** 300 W. 6th Ave., 925-3116, has rooms starting at $25 s,

$31-37 d, plus an indoor pool. At 1500 Canyon Rd., the **Super 8 Motel,** 962-6888, has an enclosed pool and spa, laundry, and RV hookups; rooms cost $31-34 s, $35-41 d. The **Nites Inn Motel,** 1200 S. Ruby, 962-9600, is one of the newer motels in town with laundry, RV parking, and rooms from $34 d. The **Thunderbird Motel,** 403 W. 8th, 962-9856, has a pool and live music Wed. through Sat. in the lounge; rooms are $38-40 d. Ellensburg's largest hotel is the **Best Western Ellensburg Inn,** 1700 Canyon Rd., 925-9801, home of the Western Art Show. The 105 guest rooms start at $34-44 s, $38-48 d, and include an indoor heated pool, putting green, restaurant, and lounge with nightly dancing.

FOOD

Downtown, **The Valley Cafe,** 103 W. 3rd, 925-3050, serves sandwiches and salads, Mexican and Italian dishes in '30s art deco surroundings. **Casa de Blanca,** Canyon and Ruby roads, 925-1693, has Mexican specialties plus moderately priced American-style steak and prime rib.

ENTERTAINMENT

Festivals And Events

Visit the **National Western Art Show and Auction,** 962-2934, in mid-May to add to your collection of Western paintings. The Western Art Association reserves the entire Best Western Ellensburg Inn for the event, renting out rooms to various artists to display their work. Three auctions give you a chance to purchase your favorites, but the highlight for many is the "Quick Draw," when about a dozen artists create a work of art in 45 minutes.

The **Whiskey Dick Triathlon,** held annually in July, consists of a 1-mile swim, 35-mile bicycle ride, and 8.1-mile run—not impossible, even though the swim is in the 60-degree Columbia River and the bike leg climbs 1,900 feet in the first 12 miles. At least the running leg is on level ground! Superb athletes can get an entry form by writing Whiskey Dick Triathlon, 436 N. Sprague, Ellensburg, WA 98926 ($40 for an individual entry); regular people can contact the chamber of commerce, 925-3137, for exact dates and places to set your lawn chair.

Labor Day weekend's **Ellensburg Rodeo** is one of the top rodeos in the nation, attracting high-priced cowboys from all over with a $100,000 purse. You can watch calf roping, Brahma bull riding, and wild cow milking during this 4-day event, held in conjunction with the carnival, exhibits, and entertainment of the **Kittitas County Fair** at the fairgrounds at the E end of 6th Avenue. Rodeo tickets include admission to the fair and cost $6-11; you can order in advance by writing the Ellensburg Rodeo Ticket Office, Box 777, Ellensburg, WA 98926, or phone 925-5381 or (800) 637-2444.

Held in Sept. at Olmstead Place State Park, the **Threshing Bee and Antique Equipment Show** gives city-slickers an opportunity to see blacksmithing, plowing, and steam and gas threshing; 925-3137.

River Trips

River Excursion Co. offers a 4-hour, 16-mile raft trip on the upper Yakima, where you can view striking canyon scenery and wildlife. Write Box 543, Ellensburg, WA 98926, or phone 925-9117.

CWU's **Tent-N-Tube/Outdoor Programs** offer Yakima River float trips as demand requires; 963-3537. If you'd rather do it yourself (and the Yakima is a good place to do that—it drops just 14 gentle feet per mile), their rental shop is the cheapest around (they claim they're not in it for the money). You can rent anything from inner tubes and canoes to cross-country skis and ice axes, as well as VCRs and instructional videos on golf, fishing, skiing, racquetball, and more. They also have a resource center with books, maps, and other outdoor information.

Rock Hounding

Kittitas County is the only place on Earth that you'll find the "Ellensburg Blue" agate. Most finds are made on private or leased land NW of Ellensburg (you'll need permission to hunt there), but you can check Dry Creek, on Hwy. 97, or Horse Canyon Road. Here are the rules: no digging—surface hunting only (respect property lines and fences), and don't bother the cows. If you come up empty-handed, Ellensburg stores sell the uncut stones as well as jewelry. For some nice handcrafted rings and necklaces visit **Art of Jewelry** on Pearl Street.

Theater

CWU's **Laughing Horse Summer Theatre** presents 4 professional productions, early July through mid-Aug., in Tower Theatre at 8th Ave. and Anderson Street. For schedule information, phone 963-3400 or write Box 1412, Ellensburg, WA 98926; you can purchase tickets at the box office at the Rotary Pavilion on Pearl St. or at Berry's department store at 5th and Ruby.

Nightlife

Aside from lounges at the Best Western Ellensburg and the Thunderbird Motel (see above), you can hear live music weekends at **The Buckboard,** 1302 S. Ruby, 925-9921.

SERVICES AND INFO

Ellenburg's area code is 509. The **Ellensburg Chamber of Commerce** is located at 436 N. Sprague; 925-3137. For emergencies, dial 911 or 925-5303 for the State Patrol. **Kittitas Valley Community Hospital** is located at 603 S. Chestnut; 962-9841.

TRANSPORTATION

Ellensburg sits at the junction of I-90 and I-82, an easy 107-mile, 65-mph drive on I-90 from Seattle. **Greyhound Bus Lines** can get you out of town from their 801 Okanogan depot; 925-1177. The nearest commercial airport is in Yakima, 36 miles to the south.

VICINITY OF ELLENSBURG

CLE ELUM

"Cle Elum," an Indian name meaning "swift water," was settled in 1870 by Thomas L. Gamble, but growth was slow until geologists working for the Northern Pacific Railroad discovered coal in 1884. A forest fire in the late 1880s wiped out a large part of the mining town, but coal veins discovered in 1889 gave Cle Elum 4 quite prosperous years. Today the town is a jumping-off point for hiking, fishing, and other recreational activities in the Wenatchee National Forest. Stop by the USFS Ranger Station at the W end of 2nd St. for maps ($2), detailed trail descriptions, and camping information.

Parks

East of Cle Elum off I-90, **Iron Horse State Park** is the start of the 25-mile-long John Wayne Pioneer Trail, extending to the Yakima-Teanaway River Canyon on property that once belonged to the Milwaukee Railroad. Open to hikers, skiers, mountain bikes, and horses (closed to motorized vehicles), the trail begins in a Douglas fir and pine forest and follows the Yakima River through canyons and farmland. No overnight camping. Day hikers can reach the trail at either Easton or S. Cle Elum. In Easton, take I-90 exit 71 and follow the signs; park at the trailhead gate; in S. Cle Elum, park at the end of 7th St. to reach the trailhead E of the old depot. There are no restrooms or facilities of any kind here yet, so plan ahead.

About 15 miles W of Cle Elum just off I-90, **Lake Easton State Park** encompasses almost 200 forested acres on the W and N sides of Lake Easton. The mile-long reservoir is good for swimming, boating, trout fishing, and waterskiing; hiking, cross-country skiing, and snowmobiling are popular dry-land sports. There are 100 tent sites and 45 trailer-hookup sites here, plus a Big-Toy playground, picnic tables, and bathhouse with hot showers.

Continue W from Cle Elem on I-90 to **Kachess Lake** (pronounced ka-CHEES), a National Forest campground and recreation area about 10 miles E of Snoqualmie Pass. The beautiful blue-green lake offers swimming, boating, picnicking, a nature trail through old-growth forest, and 183 campsites ($6-12).

Hiking

The Cle Elum Ranger District of the Wenatchee National Forest has a plethora of hiking trails; some are also open to motorized vehicles but, fortunately, a lot of them aren't. Take Hwy. 903 from Cle Elum NW to Cle Elem Lake; a number of forest roads leave it for wilderness hiking trails. From the N end of the lake, take forest roads 4308 and 4312 to the **Thorp Creek** trailhead for a 3.1-mile hike to Thorpe Lake and Kachess Ridge. Backpackers or sturdy day-hikers (with 2 cars) can

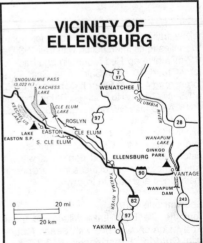

VICINITY OF ELLENSBURG

© MOON PUBLICATIONS, INC.

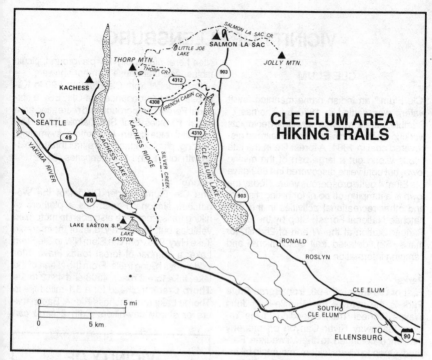

CLE ELUM AREA HIKING TRAILS

follow trail 1315 along the ridge for about 1½ miles to its intersection with trail 1330, a 6.7-mile hike up Red Mountain and back to forest road 46 near Salmon la Sac. Take forest road 4308 to **French Cabin** trail 1305, a 1.3-mile hike up to Kachess Ridge and trail 1315. A 6.2-mile OW hike on trail 1307 leaves Salmon la Sac and follows a ridge to an excellent view atop **Jolly Mountain.** Be sure to get a map at the Cle Elum Ranger Station before you set out, and don't hike without your compass; many of these trails are poorly maintained and hard to follow.

Snowmobile Tours

Tour the Cle Elum Lake wilderness (near Roslyn) on snowmobile with **Sasse Mountain Outdoor Experiences,** 649-2794 or 925-3334. Tours for 4 to 8 people include the "Deluxe Package," a 6-hour guided ride that includes the snowmobile and gasoline plus trail lunch and steak dinner with wine and dessert, for $125 pp. For tighter budgets, the standard night ride is a 4-hour guided trip with snowmobile and gasoline only for $60 pp.

Museum

The **Cle Elum Historical Telephone Museum** at 1st and Wright, 674-5702, exhibits the area's first phone system. Open daily except Mon. in summer, Tues. through Fri. mornings rest of year; donation.

Accommodations

Now a B&B on the National Historic Register, the **Moore House,** 674-5939 or (800) 572-2877, was built in 1909 by the Chicago, Milwaukee, Pacific, and St. Paul railroads to serve the men who worked on some of the most treacherous mountain tracks in the country. The 10 restored inn rooms are named after some of the railroad men who lived there; photographs and antique toy trains complete the decor. Covered wagon rides, mystery weekends, and sleigh rides are all part of the fun here. Rooms vary greatly in price, from $30 for a 2-bunk room (great for kids), $39 d with shared bath, $54 d with private bath, $89 for a honeymoon suite with private bath and 2-seat whirlpool, up to $75 (1-3 people; $85 for 4-5 people) for the caboose, with queen bed, private bath, TV, refrigerator, and deck. All rooms include a full breakfast and use of the outdoor hot tub. Kids welcome; smoking in the lobby only.

Hidden Valley Guest Ranch, off Hwy. 97, is the state's oldest dude ranch. Here you can indulge your cowboy fantasies while still enjoying heated cabins, hot showers, a heated pool, and someone else's cooking. Horseback rides leave twice daily, last 1½ hours, and cost $15; you don't have to be an overnight guest to join the rides. In winter, the ranch is generally open on Jan. and Feb. weekends for cross-country skiing; call ahead to check on conditions. Cabins cost $45-55 pp including ranch-style meals; families of up to 4 can stay in a housekeeping unit and cook their own meals for $110 per day. Babysitting is available with advance notice. Write Route 2, Box 111, Cle Elum, WA 98922, or phone 674-2422 for more information.

Food

For German food, beer, and wine try the Bavarian **Matterhorn Restaurant,** 212 W. Railroad St. (a block off the main street), 674-5863. Potato pancakes, homemade soups, Sauerbraten, and Wiener schnitzel highlight the menu; open Wed. through Mon. for lunch and dinner. **Cavallini's** on the main drag serves predictable food in a dressed-up diner; but at least it's cheap, with even their best steak dinners under $10. For a donut or cinnamon roll for the road, stop by the **Cle Elum Bakery,** 1st and Pennsylvania; closed Sun. of all days! Past Roslyn on Lake Cle Elum on Hwy. 903, the **Skookum Inn,** 649-3409, is a new (1983) restaurant catering to the area's hikers and snowmobilers. Dinners here include prime rib, steaks, seafood, and a handful of others, all under $11; sandwiches are under $5, and breakfast is a steal at less than $3.50. The lounge is a good spot for a post-hike brew.

VANTAGE

Vantage is a tiny town on the shores of Wanapum Lake, created in 1959 by the Wanapum Dam on the Columbia River. The dam was named for the Wanapum Indians, a peaceful and religious tribe that lived along the river from Pasco to Vantage. When Lewis and Clark passed through the area, the tribe numbered 2,500; now only 2 full-blooded Wanapums are left. Today, there's virtually nothing here, aside from the park, dam, a gas station, snack bar, rattlesnakes, and some breathtaking views of the river and surrounding brown hills. From Ellensburg, head W on I-90 for about 30 miles.

Parks

If you don't expect to see trees, you won't be as disappointed when you visit **Ginkgo Petrified Forest State Park.** Fifteen to 20 million years ago, this area was covered first by lakes and swamps and then by molten lava, which poured out of fissures in the Earth's crust. Submerged logs were preserved intact by the lava cover; water eventually leaked through to the logs, and the silica in the ground water replaced the natural structure of the wood. The tremendous erosion of the last Ice Age exposed 259 species of petrified wood, including the prehistoric ginkgo, that are now on display in outdoor "cages" or indoors at the interpretive center (open daily in summer), as are Indian petroglyphs. The real beauty of the park is evident when walking the ¾-mile interpretive trail or the 2½-mile hiking trail; the dry, windblown hills host an assortment of scrappy wildflowers, sagebrush, and broad views. Watch for bald eagles, hawks, deer, elk, coyote, and a variety of lizards and snakes, including the poisonous Northern Pacific rattlesnake. You can also fish or waterski on the Columbia, and camp in one of 50 sites.

Get a close-up look at a Columbia River dam at the **Wanapum Dam Tour Center,** 754-3541, 32 miles E of Ellensburg on Hwy. 243. The center is open April through Oct. for free self-guided tours, and also has a fish-viewing room and Indian and pioneer exhibits.

MOSES LAKE

The excess water draining from irrigated land in the northern part of the Columbia Basin Project collects in Potholes Reservoir, contained by the O'Sullivan Dam. Moses Lake is at the N end of the reservoir, held back by the smaller Moses Lake Dam. These 2 large bodies of water, in this hot and arid climate, would probably be surrounded by time-share condos and RV parks were they in a more populated part of the state; but in lonely central Washington, the lakes are often just a pit stop on the way to somewhere else (OK, except for fishermen, who come here for the trout and perch), and much of the area remains in its natural state. Like most of eastern Washington, Moses Lake gets little rainfall—about 8 inches a year—an average of 15 inches of snow, and some of the state's worst summer heat. Though eastern Washington is best known for its wheat production, the Columbia Basin leads the country in potato production per acre, with alfalfa and corn as other major crops.

SIGHTS

Parks And Lakes

The **O'Sullivan Dam,** on Hwy. 17 at the S end of Potholes Reservoir, is one of the largest earth-filled dams in the country. **Potholes State Park,** at the W end of O'Sullivan Dam, is a popular spot for launching a boat to catch the reservoir's numerous trout, walleye, and perch. Waterskiers, picnickers, and swimmers also enjoy the sunny east-of- the-mountains weather at this 2,500-acre park. Camp at one of 66 standard ($7) or 60 hook-up ($9.50) sites; 765-7271.

Eighteen-mile-long Moses Lake is the state's 2nd largest lake, just 2 miles W of town. **Moses Lake State Park** has swimming, fishing for trout, crappie, and catfish, a grassy picnic area, and a snack bar; open for day use only.

Cascade Park, on Valley Rd. and Cascade Valley on Moses Lake, also offers swimming, boating, waterskiing, and camping for $7.50,

$9 with hookups. Open daily from mid-April through mid-Oct.; 766-9240.

Sand Dunes/ORV Park

Hike, slide, or ride your ORV on the 3,000 acres of sand dunes S of town. Crab Creek, adjacent to the dunes, is good for paddling. Go S on Division St., which becomes Potato Hill Rd., to its end, then follow the signs—and 6 miles of gravel road—to the ORV park.

Museums

At 421 Balsam St. in the Civic Center, the **Adam East Museum** displays fossils from prehistoric animal and marine life and early man. Open Mon. through Fri. from mid-March through Oct., phone 766-9240 for hours; free.

At 408 W. Main in Ritzville, about 45 miles due E of Moses Lake on I-90, **Dr. Frank R. Burroughs Home** was built in 1890 and served for 37 years as the physician's office, containing records of house calls, births, and fees charged. The 1907 **Andrew Carnegie Library,** also in Ritzville at 302 W. Main, houses photos and artifacts from Ritzville's history, as well as the city's public library and a time capsule buried in its front lawn in 1981.

Wildlife Refuge

The **Columbia National Wildlife Refuge** on the S shore of the reservoir is in the famous Pacific Flyway; over 200 species of birds stop at the more than 50 seep lakes, making for good birdwatching throughout the area. Hunting for waterfowl, rabbit, and deer is permitted on about half of the refuge's 28,000 acres; stop by the refuge headquarters at 44 S. 8th St. in Othello for maps and other specifics.

Wineries

Three wineries are scattered around the Moses Lake area. In Othello, stop by **Hunter Hill Vineyards,** 2752 W. McManamon Rd., 346-2607. **Saddle Mountain/Langguth Winery** is at 2340 Winery Rd. in Mattawa, 932-4943. Enjoy a tour and sample the variety of wines produced at the **Champs de Brionne Winery,** 98 Rd. W NW in Quincy, 785-6685. The winery has a terraced amphitheater and hosts summer evening concerts with big-name stars like Rod Stewart, Bob Dylan and The Judds. Open daily 11 a.m.-5 p.m.

Gallery
Browse through the arts-and-crafts displays at **The Old Hotel,** a 1912 hotel-boarding house now dedicated to the arts, at 33 E. Larch St. in Othello, 488-5936. Open Tues. through Sat., 10:30 a.m.-4:30 p.m.

Petting Zoo
Sponsored by the Moses Lake/Grant County Humane Society, the Petting Zoo at the Grant County Airport on Randolph Rd. is home to a pony, sheep, goats, bunnies, chickens, and other livestock. Open Mon. through Fri. 10 a.m.-4 p.m., Sat. 1-4 p.m.; donations accepted.

ACCOMMODATIONS

Motels
The **Motel 6,** 2822 Wapato Dr., 766-0250, has budget lodging for $21 s, $27 d, plus a pool. **TraveLodge,** 316 S. Pioneer Way, 765-8631 or (800) 255-3050, has 39 rooms from $29 s, $36-39 d, with heated pool and hot tub. The **Imperial Inn,** 905 W. Broadway, 765-8626, has 29 rooms for $26-30 s, $30-36 d, plus a heated pool. The **Interstate Inn,** 2801 W. Broadway, 765-1777, has 30 rooms from $28 s, $33 d, an indoor pool, hot tub, and sauna. **Super 8,** 449 Melva Lane at I-90 exit 176, 765-8886, has 62 rooms from $31-34 s, $35-41 d, with indoor pool and guest laundry. The best in town, the **Best Western Hallmark Inn,** 3000 Marina Dr., 765-9211, has 132 rooms from $47-57 s, $51-61 d, plus swimming and wading pools, restaurant, lounge with dancing (nightly except Sun.), room service, and tennis courts.

Camping
At the W end of O'Sullivan Dam, **Mar Don Resort,** 346-2651, has 250 sites for RV and tent camping, plus a motel, restaurant,

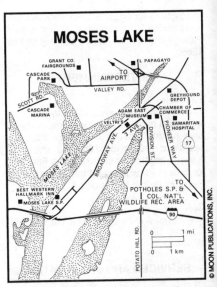

lounge, and more, for $13 per night; open year-round. **Willows RV Park,** 2½ miles S of I-90 exit 179 off Hwy. 17, 765-7531, has 64 trailer sites for $10 per night; open all year. See "Parks" above for more camping.

FOOD

One of Moses Lake's best family restaurants, **The Pantry,** 3001 W. Broadway Ave. just off I-90, 765-8385, looks like a highway chain from the outside, but inside boasts a pretty blue and pink interior and good food from a varied menu that includes burgers, chicken, steaks, pasta, and Mexican entrees for $10 and less; open 24 hours every day. A little more elegant with a lake view, **Cade's** at the Best Western Hallmark Inn, 3000 Marina Dr., 765-9211, serves 3 moderately priced meals daily from a varied American menu. Enjoy Japanese and American cuisine at the **Flight Deck Restaurant** at Grant County Airport's main terminal building, 762-2404; open for 3 meals weekdays, dinner only on Sat., closed Sunday. The **Porterhouse,** 217 N. Elder, 765-6041, is open for 3 meals daily, specializing in steak and seafood dinners in a casual atmosphere for under $7. For Mexican food and dancing Tues. through Sun. nights, try El Papagayo, Hwy. 17 and Stratford Rd., 765-1265.

ENTERTAINMENT

Festivals
The Memorial Day weekend **Spring Festival** features a carnival, arts and crafts, torchlight boat parade, antique cars, fireworks, ATV races and a 10-km run; 765-8248. The rodeo is the highlight of the **Grant County Fair,** held for 5 days in mid-Aug. at the Grant County Fairgrounds just N of town off Hwy. 17.

Golf
Play 18 holes in the sunshine at **Warden Golf Course,** 12 miles S of Moses Lake on Hwy. 17, 349-7794.

SERVICES AND INFORMATION

The area code in Moses Lake, Ephrata, and points E is 509. For more information on current festivals and events, contact the **Moses Lake Chamber of Commerce,** 324 S. Pioneer Way, 765-7888; open Mon. through Fri. during normal working hours.

Dial 911 for medical, fire, and police emergencies in Moses Lake, Ephata, Othello, and the surrounding area. **Samaritan Hospital,** 801 E. Wheeler Rd., 765-5606, has 24-hour emergency room service.

TRANSPORTATION

Moses Lake is 180 miles and an easy 3-hour drive from Seattle on I-90, all 65 mph after Issaquah.

The Moses Lake area is part of **Greyhound's** national network, served by bus stations at 630 E. Broadway in Moses Lake, 765-6441, 741 Basin NW in Ephrata, 754-3322, and 1176 S. Division in Ritzville, 659-1792.

Though there is no train station in Moses Lake, **Amtrak** serves nearby Ephrata at its 1st St. depot; (800) 872-7245.

Horizon Air, (800) 547-9308, has scheduled passenger service to Seattle, Portland, Spokane, and other major Northwest cities from Grant County Airport, N of town off Randolph Road. The airport is frequently used by Boeing to flight test new planes, and by major foreign and domestic airlines, including Japan Air Lines, to train pilots and crews (look out below!). Besides contributing to the local economy, JAL shows their community spirit by hosting 2 flights over the Columbia Basin each fall on their 747s for Moses Lake 6th graders and senior citizens.

Explore the islands in Potholes Reservoir on a motorboat rented from **Cascade Marina,** 2242 Scott Rd., 765-6718; open daily in summer.

VICINITY OF MOSES LAKE

EPHRATA AND SOAP LAKE

Ephrata is a small town of 5,000 set amidst a sprinkling of trees, surrounded by miles of dry, beige landscape. Though you'd never suspect it today, Soap Lake, about 5 miles NE of Ephrata on Hwy. 28, was once a bustling resort area surrounding the Soap Lake Sanitorium, a health retreat that capitalized on the lake's legendary medicinal qualities. The Smokiam Indians had sent their sick to soak in the Great Spirit's "smokiam" or "healing waters"; early white explorers called it Soap Lake because its 17 natural minerals and oils give the water a soapy feel and create a suds-like foam on windy days. In the early 1900s, great crowds of people from around the country came here to drink and bathe in the water to cure joint, skin, digestive, and circulatory ailments. Most of the visitors weren't *too* sick: they found time for drinking, dancing, and general hell-raising, leading the local newspaper to admonish them to "be more careful" about remembering their swimsuits! The drought and Depression of 1933 brought an end to the revelry, turning Soap Lake into a curiosity in the midst of a desolate region.

Parks

For a reprieve from the heat, head to aptly named **Oasis Park,** 5103 Hwy. 28, for a picnic and swim in a cool lake, enjoy the

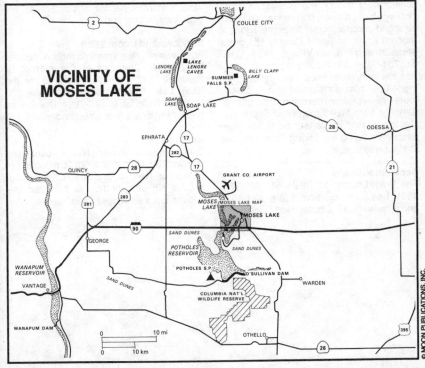

par-3, 9-hole golf course next door, or camp overnight for $7 (tents), $10 for full hookup; 754-5102.

Enjoy some healing or just a quick swim at **Soap Lake,** just off Hwy. 28 about 5 miles NE of Ephrata. Follow the signs for Notaras Lodge up 1st St. to East Beach, with play equipment, lake access, and rest rooms; the Soap Lake Chamber of Commerce is also here if you need maps or directions. **Smokiam Campground,** adjacent to the chamber of commerce, has waterfront camping for $8.50 for all sites.

Eight miles W of Quincy off Hwy. 28, **Crescent Bar Park** on the Wanapum Reservoir offers swimming, boating, waterskiing, picnicking, fishing, a playground, tennis courts, a 9-hole golf course, and camping; 787-1511.

Museum
The little town of Ephrata has an excellent collection of Indian and pioneer artifacts, clothing, tools, diaries, documents, and relics arranged chronologically from prehistoric to modern times, at **Grant County Historical Museum and Pioneer Village,** 742 N. Basin St., 754-3334. An 18-building pioneer village has a saloon, dress shop, barbershop, printing office, blacksmith, and more. Guided tours are available Thurs. through Tues. afternoons from May through mid-September. Demonstrations of pioneer crafts are given each year during the **Living Museum,** held the last weekend in June.

Accommodations
The **TraveLodge,** 31 Basin St. SW, 754-4651, has 28 rooms from $28 s, $34-40 d, and a heated pool. Cheaper still is the **Shar-lyn Motel,** 848 Basin St., 754-3575, with 19 no-frills rooms for $22 s, $30-35 d. In Soap Lake, the log **Notaras Lodge,** 231 Main St., 246-0462, features rooms from $32 up to $100; the more expensive units feature in-room whirlpools, bathroom phones, skylights, and balconies. See "Parks" above for camping options.

Food
Downtown Ephrata is no bustling commercial hub, but you can get a pizza at **Pizza Extravaganza** or Mexican food at **El Charro Cafe,** both on Basin St., the main drag. Up in Soap Lake, **Don's,** 14 Canna St. at the Notaras Lodge, 246-1217, specializes in steak, seafood, and Greek dishes; open daily for dinner.

Entertainment
The annual **Sage and Sun Festival,** held in June, features a parade, arts and crafts, antique cars, circus, and more.

Services And Information
For maps or other area information, contact the **Ephrata Chamber of Commerce,** 12 Basin St. SW, Ephrata, 754-4656, or the **Soap Lake Chamber of Commerce,** 300 Beach E, Soap Lake, 246-1821. Dial 911 for police, fire, or medical emergencies.

Getting There
Ephrata is about 20 miles NW of Moses Lake on Hwy. 282; Quincy is about 15 miles SW of Ephrata on Hwy. 28, and Soap Lake is about 5 miles NE of Ephrata. For train and bus information, see "Moses Lake," above.

COULEE DAM NATIONAL RECREATION AREA

The construction of Grand Coulee Dam, "the biggest thing built by the hand of man," employed thousands of workers during the Great Depression. Twice as high as Niagara Falls and nearly a mile long, the dam is the world's greatest producer of hydroelectric power, supplying energy to cities in several states and water to irrigate more than a half million acres of farmland. The enormous Franklin D. Roosevelt Lake, which stretches over 150 miles from the dam to beyond Kettle Falls, was designated the Coulee Dam National Recreation Area in 1946, and is immensely popular with boaters, waterskiers, swimmers, anglers, and campers. Banks Lake and the parks to the SW of the dam, in the coulee formed by the Columbia River during the Ice Age, are also scenic summer playgrounds. The dry, sunny climate is perfect for lake activities; summer temperatures range from the mid-70s to 100 degrees, with evenings cooling off to the 50s or 60s. The area is a popular winter recreation spot as well, with cross-country skiers, ice fishermen, and snowmobilers enjoying the off-season, along with the 200 bald eagles who winter here, heading N to British Columbia for the spring. Like many noteworthy sites in Eastern Washington, the NRA is barely developed—a plus for those seeking privacy and unspoiled settings, but a definite minus for people who enjoy plush hotels and fine dining.

SIGHTS

Grand Coulee Dam

Start your visit to the recreation area with a self-guided tour of the dam itself. A film is shown on the hour at the Visitor Arrival Center, 633-9265. A highlight of the dam tour is riding the glass incline elevator to the face of the 3rd powerplant for a spectacular view of the spillway from an outside balcony. An artifact room displays the Indian tools and arrowheads uncovered during the construction of the dam. In summer, the visitor center is open from 8:30 a.m.-10 p.m; guided tours of the 3rd powerplant are available from 9 a.m.-6

p.m. Water is released over the dam for about a half hour daily at 1:30 p.m. Be sure to come back for the evening laser light show, a first-class high-tech program that packs the house; held from 9:30 p.m.-10:20 p.m. Memorial Day through Labor Day. Winter visitors can take a self-guided tour and enjoy the free educational film from 9 a.m.-5 p.m. daily, with guided tours held 4 times a day.

Fort Spokane

From 1880-1898, the U.S. Army post at Fort Spokane served to keep the peace between the Indian tribes to the N and the white settlers to the south. These were peaceful years, in this area at least, so the soldiers practiced their drills and played a lot of baseball. Take a walking tour through the grounds to see 4 of the original buildings and a number of trailside displays relating the fort's history.

St. Paul's Mission

This small Catholic chapel in Kettle Falls, built in 1846, is one of the oldest churches in the state. Missionaries held services here for the Indians who often fished for salmon in these waters. The chapel was closed from 1858-62 due to Indian hostilities at other Northwest missions, but reopened for the summer salmon runs in the 1870s and '80s, after which it fell into disrepair. Restoration of the mission began in 1939, and in 1974 the site was turned over to the National Park Service.

Kettle Falls' falls are now submerged beneath Lake Roosevelt, but at one time they dropped 33 feet in less than a half mile. They were named *Les Chaudieres* ("The Kettles") by French-Canadian fur traders in reference to the bowl-shaped rocks carved by the water's force.

Banks Lake

Banks Lake lies outside the national recreation area, on the SW side of the dam, yet the 31-mile-long lake is a wide, clear-blue beauty surrounded by the deep sides of the coulee. In the early '50s, the coulee was dammed on both ends and filled with water from the Col-

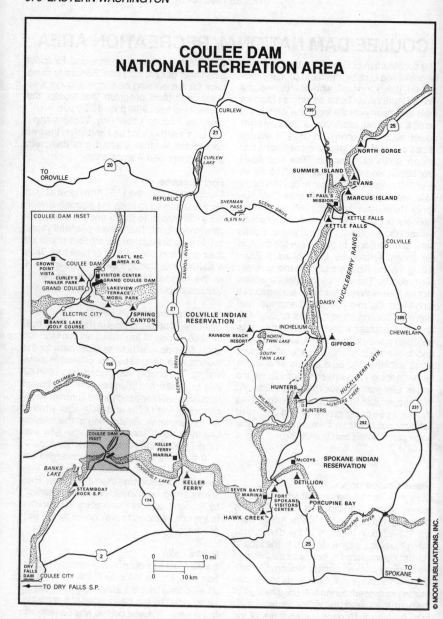

COULEE DAM
NATIONAL RECREATION AREA

CURLEW

CURLEW LAKE

TO OROVILLE

REPUBLIC

SHERMAN PASS
(5,575 ft.)

SCENIC DRIVE

NORTH GORGE

SUMMER ISLAND

EVANS

St. PAUL'S MISSION

MARCUS ISLAND

KETTLE FALLS

KETTLE FALLS

COLVILLE

HUCKLEBERRY RANGE

DAISY

COULEE DAM INSET

CROWN POINT VISTA

Curley's Trailer Park

GRAND COULEE

COULEE DAM

NAT'L. REC. AREA H.Q.

VISITOR CENTER GRAND COULEE DAM

LAKEVIEW TERRACE MOBIL PARK

ELECTRIC CITY

SPRING CANYON

Banks Lake Golf Course

SANPOIL RIVER

COLVILLE INDIAN RESERVATION

RAINBOW BEACH RESORT

NORTH TWIN LAKE

SOUTH TWIN LAKE

INCHELIUM

GIFFORD

CHEWELAH

ROOSEVELT LAKE

HUCKLEBERRY MTN.

COLUMBIA RIVER

SCENIC DRIVE

WILMONT CREEK

HUNTERS

HUNTERS

HUNTERS CREEK

STEAMBOAT ROCK S.P.

BANKS LAKE

COULEE DAM INSET

KELLER FERRY MARINA

KELLER FERRY

ROOSEVELT LAKE

SEVEN BAYS MARINA

FORT SPOKANE VISITORS CENTER

HAWK CREEK

McCOYS

DETILLION

PORCUPINE BAY

SPOKANE INDIAN RESERVATION

SPOKANE RIVER

DRY FALLS DAM

COULEE CITY

TO DRY FALLS S.P.

TO SPOKANE

0   10 mi
0   10 km

© MOON PUBLICATIONS, INC.

umbia. As well as being a popular recreational alternative to Lake Roosevelt for fishermen and waterskiers, water from Banks Lake irrigates over a half-million acres of farmland stretching as far S as the Oregon border.

State Parks

Eight miles S of Grand Coulee on Hwy. 155, **Steamboat Rock State Park** has 100 full-hookup campsites ($9.50), swimming, good fishing, play equipment, and an underwater park on Banks Lake. Steamboat Rock, an island in the Columbia River during the Ice Age, is now a scenic butte rising 1,000 feet above Banks Lake. You can hike to the top of the butte for a panoramic view, and then explore the 640 acres on the flat top. Bring repellent to combat the vicious mosquitos. Winter sports are also popular here, from ice fishing to snowmobiling and cross-country skiing.

Farther S, **Sun Lakes State Park,** 7 miles SW of Coulee City on Hwy. 17, is a large park famous for its "dry falls." When the Columbia ran through the coulee, Dry Falls were 400 feet high and 3½ miles wide. Look out over the "falls" from a lookout at the interpretive center on Hwy. 17. The main part of Sun Lakes park, just S of the dry falls interpretive center, boasts 3,300 acres with 175 standard campsites (18 with hookups), horse trails, boating, swimming, and trout fishing. Con-

cessions offer snacks, fishing supplies, horse rentals, and groceries.

Nine miles S of Coulee City on Pinto Ridge Rd., **Summer Falls State Park** is an appropriately named park, as the irrigation falls are operated only in summer. This is a cool spot for a picnic or fishing in Billy Clapp Lake.

South of Sun Lakes State Park and just N of Soap Lake, hike the short, uphill trail to **Lake Lenore Caves.** These caves, carved out of the coulee's walls by rushing meltwaters during the Ice Age, served as temporary shelters for prehistoric man's hunting trips.

Scenic Drives

After taking a dam tour, enjoy the scenery around Lake Roosevelt. Be sure to stock up on snacks, drinks, and gas in Coulee Dam or Electric City; there's nobody out here! One popular scenic drive starts at Keller Ferry, following Hwy. 21 and the Sanspoil River N toward Republic—a 3-gas-station, 2-saloon town—turning E on Hwy. 20 to cross Sherman Pass, the state's highest at 5,575 feet. And you thought all the passes were in the Cascades! You won't see dramatic snow-capped peaks, just thousands of acres of beautiful fir and deciduous trees covering rolling hills. The drive ends on the shores of Lake Roosevelt at Kettle Falls. Another scenic route starts at Fort Spokane, heading N

Steamboat Rock State Park

on Hwy. 25 along the lake's E shore through the Huckleberry Mountains. One of the best views of the dam and the evening spillway light show is from **Crown Point Vista,** 626 feet above the river, about 3 miles W of the Grand Coulee 4 corners on Hwy. 174.

Museum/Gift Shop

The **Colville Confederated Tribes Museum/Gift Shop,** Birch St., 633-0751, sells moccasins, beaded goods, turquoise jewelry, baskets, and has limited exhibits relating to the Colville Indians. Museum admission is $1; the gift shop is free.

ACCOMMODATIONS

Houseboat Rentals

The best way to explore the reaches of Lake Roosevelt, if you can afford it, is to rent a houseboat. Swimming and fishing are just outside your bedroom window; no noisy neighbors to contend with; and you'll see parts of the lake you just can't get to in a Winnebago. Each houseboat is at least 46 feet long and comes equipped with a kitchen, bath, sleeping areas for up to 13, swim slide and ladder, gas grill, and more. You can also rent 18-foot ski boats or 14-foot fishing boats to take along. Weekly rates range from $1200-1075 in the dead of winter to $1425-1600 mid-June through mid-September. Or, try a weekend: 3 days and 2 nights will run $645-720 in winter to $855-960 in the peak season. For more information phone (509) 633-1617, (800) 648-LAKE (in WA), or write Roosevelt Recreational Enterprises, Box 587, Grand Coulee, WA 99133.

Motels

All of the lodging is pretty "down home" out here; no Hiltons or even Super 8s have moved in yet. At the E end of the Columbia River Bridge on Hwy. 155, the **Coulee House,** 633-1101, overlooks the Grand Coulee Dam with 61 rooms from $32-47 s, $37-62 d, with heated pool and coin laundry. Every room has a view of the dam at the **Ponderosa Motel,** 10 Lincoln St. in Coulee Dam, 633-2100, and the rates are low, from $27 s, $32 d. The **Sky Deck Motel,** Hwy. 155 in Electric

City, sits on the shore of Banks Lake with a heated pool and waterfront rooms from $38-42 s or d, plus 5 kitchen units for $60-70.

Camping

Campers can stay at one of 579 campsites at 32 campgrounds that line both sides of Lake Roosevelt and the Spokane River arm. None of the campgrounds offer hookups; all of them have restrooms, and all but the most primitive have water. A $6 fee is charged at Evans, Fort Spokane, Gifford, Hunters, Keller Ferry, Kettle Falls, Porcupine Bay, and Spring Canyon; the rest are free. Summer evening programs are often offered at the fee campgrounds. Most campgrounds are open year-round; Porcupine Bay, Hunters, and Detillion are open May through October. There is a 14-day camping limit.

Private RV parks in the area charge $8-10 per night and are open year-round; these include **Lakeview Terrace Park,** 3½ miles E of Grand Coulee on Hwy. 174, 633-2169, and **Curley's Trailer Park,** ½ mile NW of Grand Coulee on Hwy. 174, 633-0750. Farther up-lake, **Rainbow Beach Resort** has 100 sites for $9, 10 miles W of Inchelium on Bridge Creek/Twin Lakes Rd.; open year-round, 722-5901.

FOOD

The Coulee Dam area is not for gourmands. If your French fries aren't *too* greasy, count your blessings; at least they're not over-priced. With expectations lowered, try Grand Coulee's **Sage Inn,** 415 Midway Ave., 633-0550, for sandwiches and meals in dark, diner-style surroundings. A block up the street, **The Wild Life Restaurant,** 113 Midway Ave., 633-1160, serves moderately priced steak and seafood and 3 meals daily. For Chinese, Thai, and American food, visit **Siam Palace,** open daily for lunch and dinner at 213 Main St., Grand Coulee; 633-2921 for orders to go. Up in Kettle Falls, **Barney's at the Junction** serves 3 meals daily, featuring moderately priced steak and seafood, on Hwy. 20; 738-6546. For a quick meal, there are snack bars at Spring Canyon, Porcupine Bay, Keller Ferry, and Kettle Falls.

ACTIVITIES

Swimming

Swim at beaches protected by lifeguards from July through Labor Day at Spring Canyon and Keller Ferry in lower Lake Roosevelt, at Fort Spokane and Porcupine Bay on the Spokane River arm, and at Kettle Falls and Evans on upper Lake Roosevelt. The water in the Spokane River arm tends to be 5-8 degrees warmer than the rest of the lake, which averages about 60 degrees in June, rising to the 70s in August. If you're swimming outside a protected area, keep an eye out for boats!

Boating And Fishing

Sixteen free public boat launches line Lake Roosevelt. From April through June only a few of them are usable, because the lake is lowered about 100 feet in late winter or early spring to accommodate the spring runoff; from late June through Oct., all boat launches are accessible. The lowest elevation launches are at Kettle Falls, Hunters, Keller Ferry, and Porcupine Bay, at 1,230-1,240 feet; the highest launches are at about 1,280 feet at Hawk Creek, Marcus Island, Evans, and North Gorge. Phone the reservoir hotline at (800) 824-4916 for an estimate of current and future water levels. Be sure to stay clear of protected swimming beaches and the waters near the dam.

A state fishing license is required to fish in the recreation area; you can pick one up, along with current fishing regulations, at most area hardware or sporting goods stores or marinas. The 30 species of fish inhabiting these waters include 1- to 4-pound walleye (more than 90 percent of the annual catch), 1- to 3-pound rainbow trout, and the enormous white sturgeon, averaging 100-300 pounds but growing up to 20 feet long and 1,800 pounds. Other residents include the kokanee salmon, yellow perch, bass, cutthroat trout, perch, and pike. The best months for fishing are Sept. through Nov. and May and June; in mid-summer, the fish retreat to cooler waters in streams or deep in the lake. Popular fishing spots are at the points where rivers and streams meet the lake—the Sanpoil River, Wilmont Creek, Hunters Creek, Kettle River, and others—or the waters near high shoreline cliffs, such as those near Keller Ferry.

Festivals

The 2nd weekend in May, the **Colorama Festival & WRA Rodeo** brings a rodeo, flea market, arts-and-crafts show, carnival, and cowboy breakfast to the Coulee Dam area; 633-3074. The annual **Memorial Day Festival** features arts and crafts, music, food, a fun run, and the grand opening of the laser light show followed by a fireworks display off the top of the dam; most events are held at the park below the visitor arrival center. See the **Junior Rodeo** at the Colorama Rodeo Grounds in Grand Coulee the last weekend in June. The Colville Confederated Tribes sponsor a July 4th **American Indian Pow Wow** with traditional dances, costumes, and Indian fry bread; 634-8212. Mid-August brings the nationally known **Golden Over the Dam Run,** with 5-km and 10-km races; contact the Grand Coulee Dam Chamber of Commerce for registration information.

Golf

About a mile S of Electric City on Grand Coulee Airport Rd., **Banks Lake Golf and Country Club** is a 9-hole public course, open from March until the first snow; 633-0163.

SERVICES AND INFORMATION

Services in the recreation area are generally open from June to September. There are small stores with groceries and supplies at Daisy and McCoys, and at Seven Bays, Keller Ferry, and Kettle Falls marinas.

The Coulee Dam area code is 509. For information on programs, park brochures, or books on the area's natural history, contact the Coulee Dam National Recreation Area Headquarters, 1008 Crest Dr., Box 37, Coulee Dam, WA 99116, 633-9441, or the ranger stations at Kettle Falls, 738-6266, and Fort Spokane, 725-2715. The Coulee Dam station is open weekdays year-round; the others are open in summer with varied winter hours. For information on events in the surrounding area, contact the Grand Coulee Dam Area Chamber of Commerce, Box 760, Grand Coulee, WA 99133, 633-3074.

TRANSPORTATION

By Car
Perhaps inaccessibility is one reason Coulee Dam NRA isn't the tourist trap it could be; there's just no quick and easy way to get here from the state's more populous cities. From Seattle, the quickest route is to take I-90 to George (between Ellensburg and Moses Lake), then go NE on highways 283, 28, 17, and 155 to the dam—about 220 miles. For a slower, more scenic route, try Hwy. 2 through Leavenworth to Coulee City, then head N on 155 to the dam. From Spokane, it's an easier drive: due W on Hwy. 2 to Wilbur, then NW on Hwy. 174 for a total of less than 150 miles.

Cross-lake Ferries
Two ferries cross Lake Roosevelt year-round: the **Keller Ferry** connects Hwy. 21 in the S part of the recreation area, and, farther N, the **Gifford Ferry** joins Hwy. 25 near Inchelium. Both ferries are free, carry passengers and vehicles, and take about 15 minutes for the crossing.

THE NORTHEAST CORNER

Washington's NE corner, N of Spokane and E of Roosevelt Lake, is dominated by Pend Oreille (pond-o-RAY) County, a "sportman's paradise" with good fishing in 55 lakes and 48 streams, all-season recreation from swimming to snow skiing, an abundance of wildlife, and very few people. The largest city in this not-quite-urban sprawl is Newport, pop. 1,700; the other 4 incorporated towns combined muster up another 1,300 bodies. This uninhabited forestland gives wildlife photographers plenty of opportunities: the Pend Oreille River hosts abundant osprey, ducks, cranes, and geese, and bighorn sheep, bear, cougar, elk, and a rare moose or grizzly may also be seen. For the most part, the area's beauty is understated and its resources must be sought out; it's easy to drive right by and miss trails, lakes, and wildlife. This corner of the state isn't on the way to *anywhere* (except Canada), so only a determination to escape civilization or a strong exploratory drive brings visitors out here.

RECREATION

Rivers And Lakes
Small lakes are scattered throughout Pend Oreille county. Many are circled by summer cabins, modest year-round homes, or low-budget resorts and RV parks. As is common in eastern Washington, the natural features here aren't played up or exploited to the degree they would be on the more crowded, beach-hungry E coast or other more populous areas of the country; yours is likely to be the only boat on the lake. With this serenity comes an appalling lack of services, so keep the car gassed up and your in-car ice chest filled. Off Hwy. 395, between Spokane and Chewelah, enjoy Loon, Deer, and Waitts lakes; on Hwy. 2, between Spokane and Newport, you'll find Diamond, Eloika, Trout, Sacheen, and Davis lakes. These and other lakes are generally clearly marked and easily accessible from the highway, though facilities are often limited to a boat ramp and porta-potty. The Pend Oreille River, popular for fishing and boating, follows highways 31 and 20 from the Canadian border to Newport and on into Idaho's Pend Oreille Lake.

Cave
Tour one of the largest limestone caves in the state, Gardner Cave, at **Crawford State Park,** 11 miles NW of Metaline Falls off Hwy. 31. Guided tours are held daily in summer; camping is limited to 10 primitive campsites.

Hiking
Contact any Colville National Forest ranger station for a map and detailed, printed descriptions of these and many other day hikes. This is bear country—even a few grizzlies

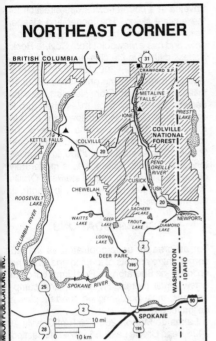

NORTHEAST CORNER

have been spotted—so make noise, keep your food in the trunk, and don't be too proud to choose another route if you encounter bears, bear tracks, or droppings.

In the Colville district, a popular 2½-mile-loop trail, **Springboard Trail #149,** begins at the E end of the E. Gillette campground, 26 miles E of Colville off Hwy. 20. This is a self-guided interpretive trail relating the history of an early homesteader and leading to a viewing platform at 3,600 feet.

Abercrombie Mountain Trail #117 is a 3.2-mile OW hike to a ridgetop with panoramic views of the Pend Oreille and Columbia River valleys from 7,300 feet. From Colville, take Aladdin Hwy. N for 23 miles to Deep Creek Rd.; turn N onto Deep Creek Rd. for 7 miles, then turn R on Silver Creek Rd. #4720 to the junction with Rd. #7078. Take #7078 N to Rd. #300, then follow #300 to the road's end. Most of the 3.2 miles is wooded, crossing several streams and huckleberry bushes

on the way to the ridge. This trail is also popular with hunters because of the abundance of deer—so look conspicuous!

Another hike with good views of the Pend Oreille and Columbia river valleys is the 3.6-mile OW **South Fork Silver Creek Trail #123.** Take Silver Creek Rd. #4720 E from Leadpoint to the junction with Rd. #070; follow #070 to the trailhead at the road's end. The trail parallels and sometimes crosses the S Fork of Silver Creek along an old jeep road on its way to the 5,400-foot ridge, at the saddle between Abercrombie and Sherlock mountains; the last mile is quite steep.

In the Sullivan lake district, **Nature Trail #509** is a 2½-mile interpretive loop through trees and lush vegetation. From County Rd. #9345, go E on Rd. #22 for ½ mile, then turn R onto Rd. #241 to the trailhead for Sullivan Lake Trail #504; the loop trail starts .1 mile in. **Sullivan Lake Trail #504** is a 4-mile OW hike along the eastern shore of Sullivan Lake through aspen and forested areas, ending at the Noisy Creek campground. The clear, blue lake is the main attraction, but keep your eyes peeled for bighorn sheep, black bear, and whitetail deer.

A short ½-mile loop trail beginning at Newport's Warren Ave. affords views of Ashenfelder Bay as it passes through forest and wildflowers, and is wheelchair accessible. To reach **Wolf Barrier Free Trail #305,** go N on Warren Ave. at the junction of Warren Ave. and Hwy. 20, continuing about a mile to the trailhead.

Backpacking

Two good overnight trips are in the Sullivan Lake district; other trails can be combined to form loops of virtually any length. Get a map from one of the ranger stations (see "Services" below) and ask for suggestions; the rangers have a wealth of printed material on hiking trails in the national forest.

Shedroof Divide Trail #512, begins off Rd. #22, which leaves Rd. #9345 just N of Sullivan Lake. Follow Rd. #22 for 6 miles, then turn R onto Pass Creek Pass Rd. #22 for ¼ mile to the trailhead. The first 15¾ miles go through timber stands and occasional clearings, with old, difficult lookout trails to the tops of Round Top, Thunder, Helmer, and Shedroof mountains. At the intersection of trail #535, the trail begins an 18-mile loop (Salmo Loop trails #535, 506, and 512) traversing the most scenic part of the area through numerous switchbacks. This loop can be reached from the 15¾-mile Shedroof Divide Trail, described above, or by road: go E about 6 miles on Rd. #22 from Sullivan Lake; at the junction with Pass Creek Pass Rd., the road number changes to #2220. Drive along #2220 for a ½ mile beyond the junction with Rd. #270. The trail passes through old-growth forest and along a ridge with views of Crowell Ridge, Gypsy Peak, the Sullivan Creek drainage, and part of Priest Lake. Much of the trail is at 6,000-feet elevation, so sea-level dwellers should expect to hike a little more slowly than usual.

Skiing

Nine miles E of Chewelah, **49 Degrees North** has day and night skiing on 1,900 vertical feet of slope from 4 chairlifts, about an hour N of Spokane off Hwy. 395. Sixteen runs offer beginner through expert skiing; terrain is set aside for powder skiing on weekends. Weekend lift tickets are $20 adults, $17 kids; lower midweek. Snowboarders and cross-country skiers are also welcome. Phone 924-5252 for ski conditions, 935-6649 for other information. Be sure to drive to the ski area from Hwy. 395 on the Chewelah (W) side; the road in from Hwy. 20 on the E is a narrow gravel logging road, impassable in winter and no fun the rest of the year.

Colville National Forest has miles of hiking trails that double as cross-country ski trails in winter. **Sherry Trail #147** is a set of 3 short loops that total 3.8 miles in length, beginning at the trailhead 23½ miles E of Colville on Hwy. 20 at the entrance to the national forest. The route passes through lodgepole pine and Douglas fir, with views of Lake Sherry and Little Pend Oreille River.

Frater Lake Trail #150 has 2 loops—one 3 miles long, the other 2—that start 29 miles E of Colville at Frater Lake. The shorter blue-blazed trail cuts through Douglas fir close to the lake on gentle terrain, and should be

traveled in a counter-clockwise direction for the easiest skiing. The longer and steeper yellow-blazed trail crosses a stream, meadow, and has a viewpoint from Coyote Rock; it's less difficult in the clockwise direction.

Three ski trails—#300, 301, and 302—provide 5.6 miles of skiing on 3 loops about 10 miles N of Newport. From Newport, take the Leclerc Creek Hwy. for 8 miles, then turn R onto Indian Creek Rd., following it for 1½ miles to the trailhead on the R side of the road. All 3 wind through Lodgepole pine and fir trees. The easiest loop, #300, is 2.1 miles long; the 2.6-mile loop, #301, is moderately difficult and affords a view of the Pend Oreille Valley; trail #302, nearly a mile in length, is the most difficult.

ACCOMMODATIONS

For an area as underpopulated as the NE corner, there are lots of lodging and camping options—no Sheratons or Red Lions, but quite a few small motels, RV parks, and campgrounds, most bordering on spartan, plus a delightful B&B.

Lakeside Manor, 25 miles E of Colville at 2425 Pend Oreille Lake, 684-8741, is nestled in the evergreens of Colville National Forest, on the shores of Lake Sherry. Enjoy a soak in the hot tub and huckleberry croissants at breakfast; the guest rooms ($50 s, $65 d) have king-sized waterbeds. No pets, kids, or smoking.

At the SW end of Deer Lake, off Hwy. 395 between Chewelah and Deer Park, **Styman's Resort,** W. Deer Lake Rd., 233-2233, has 5 cabins from $34-55 per night and RV parking with full hookups for $12.50 ($1 less for tents). Services include a boat launch, motorboat rentals for $30 a day, a swimming beach, playground, and grocery store. On the N side of Deer Lake, **Pearl-Ray Beach Resort,** 233-2166, rents 5 cabins for $150-200 per week, and also has boat rentals, groceries, and a swimming beach. **Sunrise Point Resort,** N. Deer Lake Rd., 233-2342, has 7 cabins renting for about $200 per week.

Up in Valley, 6 miles off Hwy. 395, **Silver Beach Resort** on Waitts Lake, 937-2811,

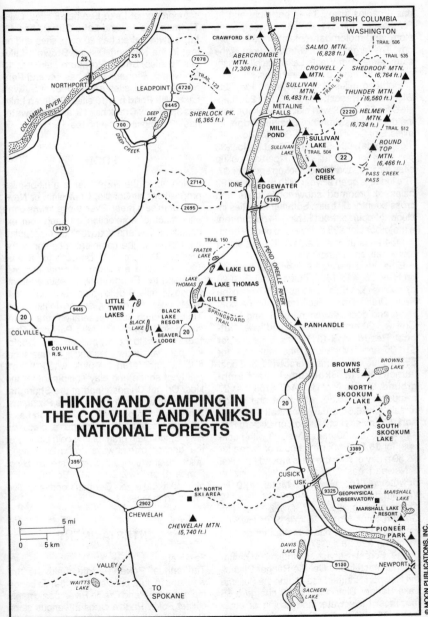

HIKING AND CAMPING IN
THE COLVILLE AND KANIKSU
NATIONAL FORESTS

has 6 cabins from $34-44 per night and 55 RV spaces for $11.50, plus a restaurant, store, and motorboat rentals for $34.50 per day. The largest rainbow trout caught in the state came from Waitts Lake; excellent fishing here for trout, perch, and bass.

Eighteen miles E of Colville off Hwy. 20, **Black Lake Resort,** 684-2093, has 20 campsites for $7.50 ($9 with electric hookup), fishing dock, and swimming. **Beaver Lodge,** 25 miles E of Colville on Lake Gillette (Box 196, Tiger Route), 684-5657, has 6 cabins for $30 per night for 4, 6 full- and 7 partial-hookup sites for $10, and 19 no-hookup spots for $7. The lodge is open all year, with access to 193 miles of groomed snowmobile trails and cross-country ski trails. Summer activities include, of course, trout fishing—you can rent a motorboat for $28 a day—and paddle boating ($4 an hour or $22 a day). There's also a store, deli, and laundromat.

Blueside Resort, 37 miles N of Newport on Hwy. 20, 445-1327, has a motel ($16-20 d), cabins ($24 d), and RV spots ($7-8) on the Pend Oreille River. Facilities include a boat ramp and dock, swimming pool, and store. On Hwy. 20 between Cusick and Ione, **Outpost Resort,** 445-1317, has 5 cabins for $16-35 and RV parking and tent sites for $8-10, plus a restaurant, groceries, and boat launch. **North Skookum Lake Campground,** 8 miles N of Usk, 447-4158, has 27 campsites for $5.50, with boat and canoe rentals for $6.50 a day. **Marshall Lake Resort,** 6½ miles N of Newport on Leclerc Rd., 447-4158, has 30 campsites (20 with hookups) for $6.50-7.50; rent a boat or canoe for $6.50 a day or hike the trails around the lake.

Newport has 2 budget motels close to downtown. The **Newport Motel,** 220 N. Washington (Hwy. 2), 447-3463, has 12 rooms starting at $23-27 s, $28-33 d. The **Golden Spur Motel,** ½ mile S of town on Hwy. 2, 447-3823, has a restaurant and 20 rooms for $25-28 s, $27-31 d.

The Forest Service maintains 4 campgrounds each in the Colville Ranger District, the Newport Ranger District, and the Sullivan Lake Ranger District. All but 3 charge a $5 fee; most have water and fishing or other water sports. In the Colville District, the campground at **Lake Leo** has 8 sites, **Lake Thomas** has 15, and **Lake Gillette** has 43; **Little Twin Lakes** has 20 campsites and no fee; in the Newport District, **Brown's Lake** has 10 sites, **South Skookum Lake** has 13 (no water), **Pioneer Park** has 14, and **Panhandle** has 11 sites and no fee; at Sullivan Lake, **Mill Pond** has 10 sites, **Sullivan Lake** has 35, **Noisy Creek** has 19, and **Edgewater** has 23 campsites and no fee.

FOOD

Eating out in the NE corner is a hit-or-miss proposition: hit Colville, Chewelah, or Newport, or miss a meal. Even these towns don't offer much of a selection, so keep your expectations low and you won't be disappointed. Colville is the commercial center of the region, with the only McDonald's for at least 100 miles and a handful of other choices, including the **Roadhouse,** a restored farmhouse ½ mile S of town on Hwy. 395, 684-3021, open for dinner, served family style, Thurs. through Sun.; reservations are appreciated. In Chewelah, try the **Parkside Restaurant,** next to the city park on Hwy. 395, for inexpensive sandwiches and light meals; get it to go and eat in the park, where there's plenty of shade and play equipment for the kids. Or, get Chinese food at the **Shanghai Inn** downtown, or try **Polanski's Pizza,** just S of downtown on Hwy. 395. Newport has a Chinese restaurant and a pizza place on Hwy. 2, the main drag, plus a coin laundry at the junction of highways 2 and 20; have a quick meal while your clothes are tumbling. Farther S on Hwy. 2, try **Al's Restaurant** S of Eloika Lake for German food and live music on the weekends.

ENTERTAINMENT

Festival

The annual **Poker Paddle,** held the 3rd weekend in July, consists of a 40-mile canoe trip down the Pend Oreille River; participants collect Poker Paddle cards at various stops along the 2-day route. Spectators can take the easy way out and join the fun on a paddle-wheeler, and a crowd congregates at the finish to greet the paddlers and enjoy food and game booths; phone 445-1212 for more information.

SERVICES AND INFORMATION

The area code in the NE corner is 509. For more information on events and activities in Pend Oreille County, contact **Pend Oreille Scenic,** Box 21-A, Usk, WA 99180, 445-1212. For more specific information on hiking, camping, and other recreational activities in the Colville National Forest, write or phone the **USDA Forest Service,** Colville National Forest, Colville Ranger District, 755 S. Main, Colville, WA 99114, 684-4557; at Sullivan Lake, contact the Forest Service at Sullivan Lake Ranger District, Metaline Falls, WA 99153, 446-2681; in Newport, write the Newport Ranger District, Box 770, Newport, WA 99156, 447-3129.

The Colville area has no 911 emergency service; phone 684-2211 for fire, 684-2525 for police, and 684-2555 for an ambulance. For the Stevens County Sheriff, phone 684-2555 or (800) 572-0947. Dial the Washington State Patrol (for emergencies only) at (800) 572-3222. To report a forest fire, phone (800) 562-6010.

TRANSPORTATION

To reach Pend Oreille County from Seattle, take I-90 to Spokane, then head N on Hwy. 2 to Newport or Hwy. 395 to Chewelah and Colville. You'll need your own car because no buses, trains, or planes service the area.

bighorn sheep

BOOKLIST

DESCRIPTION AND TRAVEL

Begoun, Paula. *Best Places To Kiss In The Northwest*. Seattle: Beginning Press, 1989. A silly title, sure, but a fun guide to romantic hideaways, intimate restaurants, viewpoints, gardens, and more in Oregon, Washington, and British Columbia.

Brewster, David. *Seattle Best Places*. Seattle: Sasquatch, 1988. The most complete guide on the market to restaurants, hotels, shopping, sights, and things to do in and around Seattle.

———. *Northwest Best Places*. Seattle: Sasquatch, 1989. A thorough guide to restaurants and lodging, with a smattering of things to do, in Washington, Oregon, and British Columbia.

Burke, Clifford. *Exploring Washington's Smaller Cities*. Seattle: Quartzite Books, 1984. Informative and readable guide to 11 of Washington's smaller cities along the lines of Pullman, Port Angeles, Yakima, and Vancouver.

Canniff, Kiki. *Washington Free*. Portland: Ki2 Enterprises, 1984. Listing of parks, dams, and other free attractions.

Green, Lewis. *Bed and Breakfast Washington*. Seattle: New Horizons Publishers, 1984. Photos, addresses, rates, and descriptions of B&Bs throughout the state.

Holden, Ronald, and Glenda Holden. *Touring the Wine Country of Washington*. Holden Pacific, Inc., 1983. Detailed information on Washington wineries.

Keith, Gordon. *The Ferryboat Islands: A Practical Guide To Washington State's San Juan Islands*. A detailed guide to beaches, sights, and points of interest by a 20-year island resident. Plenty of maps and photos.

Krenmayr, Janice. *Exploring Puget Sound by Car*. Seattle: The Writing Works, 1984. Tours, sights, parks, shops, and more around Puget Sound.

McFarlane, Marilyn. *Best Places To Stay In The Pacific Northwest*. Boston: The Harvard Common Press, 1988. There is more than one "best places" guide, and this one from the east coast does a fine job. Easy-to-use breakdowns by type of facility—destination resorts, island getaways, ski lodges—make vacation planning a breeze.

Meredith, Ted. *Northwest Wine*. Kirkland, WA: Nexus Press, 1983. Guide to wineries in Washington, Oregon, and Idaho.

Satterfield, Archie. *The Seattle Guidebook*. Seattle: Pacific Search Press, 1986. A guide to Seattle walking tours, sights, sports, parks, outdoor activities, and more.

Schmeltzer, Michael; photographs by Phil Schofield. *Spokane: The City and The People*. Helena, Montana: American Geographic Publishing, 1988. History, sights, lifestyle, economy, and people of Spokane highlighted by superb photography.

Shanks, Ralph and Lisa. *North American Indian Travel Guide*. Petaluma, California: Costano Books, 1987. A complete guide to North American Indian and Eskimo cultural centers, museums, pow-wows, reservations, historical sites, and more throughout the U.S. and

Canada, with ample photos, background material, and specific information for visitors.

Speidel, Bill. *The Wet Side of the Mountains.* Seattle: Nettle Creek Publishing Co., 1981. Tours and highlights of western Washington, peppered with little-known historical facts.

Sunset Washington Travel Guide. Menlo Park, CA: Lane Publishing Co., 1987. Washington's highlights, beautifully photographed.

Welke, Elton. *Places To Go With Children Around Puget Sound.* San Francisco: Chronicle Books, 1986. State parks, fish hatcheries, museums, and attractions that appeal to all ages.

HIKING AND CLIMBING

Adkison, Ron. *The Hiker's Guide To Washington.* Helena, Montana: Falcon Press Pubishing Co., 1988. Seventy-five of Washington's most popular hikes, from Hurricane Ridge to Mt. Spokane, along with lesser-known trails in wilderness areas; maps included.

Beckey, Fred. *Cascade Alpine Guide: Climbing And High Routes.* Seattle: The Mountaineers, 1987. Three volumes of very detailed Cascade climbing routes, plus historical information and photos.

Burton, Joan. *Best Hikes With Children In Western Washington & The Cascades.* Having kids doesn't have to mean the end of your days on the trail! Ninety hikes from 1.5 to 6.5 miles RT, all featuring lakes, waterfalls, views, or other points of interest that will motivate kids of all ages.

Darvill, Fred T. *Hiking the North Cascades.* San Francisco: Sierra Club Books, 1982. Pocket-size guide to North Cascade trails.

Landers, Rich, and Ida Rowe Dolphin. *100 Hikes in the Inland Northwest.* Seattle: The Mountaineers, 1987. Descriptions, photos, and maps of hikes in eastern Washington plus parts of Idaho, Montana, and Oregon.

Manning, Harvey. *Backpacking One Step At A Time.* New York: Vintage Books, 1980. A beginner's guide to backcountry travel covering equipment, route finding, winter camping, bugs, food, and more.

————. *Footsore 1, 2, 3, 4: Walks And Hikes Around Puget Sound.* Seattle: The Mountaineers. Descriptions and photos of hikes from Bellingham around the sound to the Olympic Peninsula.

————. *Guide to Trails of Cougar Mountain and Squak Mountain.* Issaquah, WA: Issaquah Alps Trail Club, 1982. Maps and trail descriptions.

Perreault, Norm and Diane. *Photographers Guide To Mt. Baker.* Glacier, WA: Norm and Diane Perreault. Excellent guide to Mt. Baker's charms for hikers, photographers, and sightseers, written in a friendly, conversant style and loaded with valuable tips and quality photos.

Peters, Ed. *Mountaineering: The Freedom of the Hills.* Seattle: The Mountaineers, 1982. The backcountry traveler's bible, filled with tips and techniques on snow travel, navigation, rock climbing, first aid, equipment, and alpine cuisine.

Spring, Ira, and Harvey Manning. *50 Hikes in Mount Rainier National Park.* Seattle: The Mountaineers, 1978. Maps, descriptions, and photos of 50 Mt. Rainier hikes.

————. *100 Hikes in the Alpine Lakes, South Cascades, and Olympics.* Seattle: The Mountaineers, 1978.

————. *100 Hikes in the Glacier Peak Region.* Seattle: The Mountaineers, 1988. Lesser-known areas of Glacier Peak Wilderness from Darrington to Wenatchee and Lake Chelan; maps, photos, trail descriptions.

———. 101 Hikes in the North Cascades. Seattle: The Mountaineers, 1979.

———. 100 Hikes in the South Cascades and Olympics. Seattle: The Mountaineers, 1985.

Sutliff, Mary. Teanaway County: A Hiking and Scrambling Guide to Washington's Central Cascades. Seattle: Signpost Books, 1980. Descriptions and photos of hikes from Lake Kachess to Blewett Pass.

Whitney, Stephen R. Nature Walks In & Around Seattle. Seattle: The Mountaineers, 1987. Short nature walks at 25 parks and natural areas between Redmond and Federal Way. Great for families, nature photographers, or a quick escape to the outdoors.

Wood, Robert L. Olympic Mountains Trail Guide. Seattle: The Mountaineers, 1984. Detailed trail descriptions, maps, and photos of national park and national forest trails on the Olympic Peninsula.

HISTORY

Bennett, Robert A. Walla Walla: Portrait of a Western Town 1804-1899. Walla Walla: Pioneer Press Books, 1980. Indians, treaties, trails, and Walla Walla's beginnings in Washington Territory days. The 3-book series features excellent historical photos and drawings and informative, interesting text.

———. Walla Walla: A Town Built To Be A City 1900-1919. Walla Walla: Pioneer Press Books, 1982. Early automobiles, aviation, Chinese community, street cars, and over 400 photos celebrating Walla Walla's turn-of-the-century growth spurt.

———. Walla Walla: A Nice Place to Raise a Family 1920-1949. Walla Walla: Pioneer Press Books, 1988. WWII, a new airport, the rise of the canning industry, and Walla Walla's emergence as a modern city.

Brewster, David, and David M. Buerge. Washingtonians: A Biographical Portrait of the State. Seattle: Sasquatch Books, 1988. This ambitious Centennial project presents Washington's history in a series of insightful biographies. Enjoyable reading.

Dodds, Gordon B. The American Northwest: A History of Oregon and Washington. Arlington Heights, Illinois: The Forum Press, Inc., 1986. A comprehensive history of the Northwest from 15,000 B.C. to the present, with emphasis on the people and their politics.

Dryden, Cecil. Dryden's History of Washington. Portland: Binfords and Mort, 1968. A very readable history of Washington.

Fiege, Bennye. The Story of Soap Lake. Soap Lake, WA: Soap Lake Chamber of Commerce, 1976. Photos and text describing Soap Lake's heyday.

Lambert, Dale A. The Pacific Northwest: Past, Present, and Future. Wenatchee, WA: Directed Media, Inc., 1986. A very readable, well-illustrated textbook on Pacific Northwest history.

Lampman, Ben Hur. Centralia: Tragedy and Trial. Seattle: reproduced by The Shorey Book Store, originally published by the American Legion, 1920. The American Legion's story of the Centralia Massacre.

LeWarne, Charles P. Washington State. Seattle: University of Washington Press, 1986. A detailed Washington history textbook covering pre-history through modern times.

McCoy, Keith. The Mount Adams Country: Forgotten Corner of the Columbia River Gorge. White Salmon, Washington: Pahto Publications, 1987. History of the Mt. Adams area from pre-Indians, Lewis and Clark, and early pioneers to modern-day climbers, the CCC, and Bigfoot. Interesting reading and numerous photographs, assembled by a lifetime Mt. Adams area resident.

Martinson, Arthur D. *Wilderness Above The Sound: The Story Of Mount Rainier National Park*. Flagstaff, Arizona: Northland Press, 1986. An enjoyable history covering the mountain's discovery, early ascents, and development of the national park, illustrated with lots of historical photos.

Olmsted, Gerald. *Fielding's Lewis & Clark Trail*. New York, New York: William Morrow & Co., Inc., 1986. A delightful blend of historical chronicle and travel guide. Relive Lewis and Clark's journey from Missouri to Oregon through excerpts from their journal while appreciating the sights, parks, and attractions of today.

Olson, Joan, and Gene Olson. *Washington Times and Trails*. Grants Pass, Oregon: Windyridge Press, 1970. A very enjoyable and readable history covering Washington's earliest explorers to modern times, illustrated with top-quality full-page photographs.

Ross, Alexander. *Adventures of the First Settlers on the Oregon or Columbia River, 1810-1813*. Lincoln: University of Nebraska Press, 1986. A reprint of Ross' original eyewitness account of John Jacob Astor's 1810 expedition from New York to the Columbia River aboard the Tonquin. Fascinating and lively, the book describes the fur trade existence as it happened, based on Ross' original journal entries.

Ruby, Robert H., and John A. Brown. *A Guide to the Indian Tribes of the Pacific Northwest*. Norman, Oklahoma: University of Oklahoma Press, 1986. History, location, numbers, culture, and contemporary life of over 150 Indian tribes of the Pacific Northwest. An excellent reference tool.

————. *The Chinook Indians: Traders of the Lower Columbia River*. Norman, Oklahoma: University of Oklahoma Press, 1976. Comprehensive history of the relationship between whites and the Indians of the lower Columbia Valley, from fur trading to modern-day legal battles.

Schwantes, Carlos, et al. *Washington: Images of a State's Heritage*. Spokane: Melior Publications, 1988. A comprehensive pictorial history of the state, covering early Native American life through the eruption of Mt. St. Helens and Bill Gates' Microsoft. Rarely seen photos and historic drawings highlight the easily digestible text.

Scofield, W.M. *Washington's Historical Markers*. Portland: The Touchstone Press, 1967. A handy reference book consisting of photographs of 49 roadside markers posted at notable historical sites throughout the state.

Shorey Book Store, The. *The Pacific Northwest: Oregon and Washington Territory*. Seattle: The Shorey Book Store, 1971. Reprint of an 1883 text describing the railroads, land, and settlement of Oregon State and Washington Territory.

Speidel, William C. *Sons of the Profits*. Seattle: Nettle Creek Publishing Co., 1967. Irreverent history of Seattle's growth between 1851-1901.

Spranger, Michael S. *The Columbia Gorge: A Unique American Treasure*. Pullman: Washington State University, 1985. History, geology, sights, development, maps, and photos of the Gorge. Interesting reading for visitors and researchers alike.

The Great Seattle Fire. Seattle: reproduced by The Shorey Book Store, 1965. A fascinating collection of original documents and news clippings describing the Seattle fire of 1889.

Wing, Robert C., with Gordon Newell. *Peter Puget*. Seattle: Gray Beard Publishers, 1979. Coffee-table-quality history of Peter Puget's meanderings around the Northwest.

NATURAL SCIENCES

Angell, Tony, and Kenneth C. Balcomb III. *Marine Birds and Mammals of Puget Sound*. Seattle: University of Washington Press,

1984. Habits and habitats of western Washington birds and marine mammals.

Grzimek's Animal Life Encyclopedia. New York: Van Nostrand Reinhold Company, 1974. Thirteen volumes of facts on everything from slugs to killer whales.

Hanners, Al. *Northwest Beginning Birding.* Bellingham, WA: North Cascades Audubon Society, 1984. Where to find which birds in western Washington.

Hora, Bayard. *The Oxford Encyclopedia of Trees of the World.* Oxford: The Oxford University Press, 1981.

Kirk, Ruth. *The Olympic Seashore.* Port Angeles, WA: The Olympic Natural History Association, 1962. Detailed information on where to go and what you'll find on Washington's most scenic coastline.

Smith, Lynwood. *Common Seashore Life of the Pacific Northwest.* Healdsburg, CA: Naturegraph Company, 1962. Everything you need to know about clams, starfish, crabs, and other sea creatures.

Sweeney, James B. *A Pictorial History of Sea Monsters and Other Dangerous Marine Life.* New York: Crown Publishers, 1972. What to look out for in the deep blue sea.

OUTDOOR RECREATION

Furrer, Werner. *Water Trails of Washington.* Edmonds, WA: Signpost Books, 1979. Maps and descriptions of Washington rivers for kayaks and canoes.

Kaysing, Bill. *Great Hot Springs Of The West.* Santa Barbara, California: Capra Press, 1984. A complete guide to well-known and obscure hot springs from Washington to Colorado, complete with maps, facilities, and clothing requirements; plenty of photos.

Kirkendall, Tom, and Vicky Spring. *Cross-Country Ski Trails of Washington's Cascades and Olympics.* Seattle: The Mountaineers, 1983. Descriptions and photos of more than 80 ski trails.

Mueller, Marge and Ted. *North Puget Sound: Afoot & Afloat.* Seattle: The Mountaineers, 1988. Painstakingly detailed guide to North Puget Sound, from Point Roberts to Whidbey Island and west to Neah Bay, helpful to both boaters and landlubbers. Boat launches, parks, points of interest, plus photos and maps.

————. *The San Juan Islands: Afoot & Afloat.* Seattle: The Mountaineers, 1988. Thorough guide to "the big four" and numerous lesser islands in the San Juan chain. Boating, biking, sightseeing, and more, with maps and photos.

Nelson, Sharlene P., and Joan LeMieux. *Cruising the Columbia and Snake Rivers.* Seattle: Pacific Search Press. Eleven cruises in the inland waterway.

North, Douglass A. *Washington Whitewater I.* Seattle: The Mountaineers, 1988. Seventeen white-water trips on the Cascades' most popular rivers for paddlers and rafters; every detail is covered, from put-ins and take-outs to camping, scenery, and special hazards.

————. *Washington Whitewater II.* Seattle: The Mountaineers, 1987. Seventeen lesser-known white-water trips from the Olympic Peninsula to Spokane and Washington's SE corner.

Perry, John, and Jane Greverus Perry. *The Sierra Club Guide to the National Areas of Oregon and Washington.* San Francisco:

Sierra Club Books, 1983. Features, activities, camping, boating, and more in national forests, parks, and beaches.

Schwartz, Susan. *Wildlife Areas of Washington.* Seattle: Superior Publishing Co., 1976. Flora and fauna (especially birds) of the national recreation areas, refuges, islands, and national parks.

Sheely, Terry W. *The Northwest Sportsman Almanac.* Edmonds: Alaska Northwest Books, 1988. A beautiful and thorough book, loaded with superb color photographs and artwork as well as exhaustive coverage of hunting, fishing, camp cooking, shellfishing, woodlore, and more in the northwest U.S. and Canada.

Sterling, E.M. *Trips And Trails 2.* Seattle: The Mountaineers, 1972. Short hikes, view roads, and family campgrounds in the South Cascades and Mt. Rainier.

Stienstra, Tom. *Pacific Northwest Camping.* San Francisco: Foghorn Press, 1988. No better guide to Washington's campgrounds! Over 1,400 campgrounds, from boat-in island sites to RV parks, state parks to wilderness areas.

Washburne, Randel. *Kayak Trips in Puget Sound and the San Juan Islands.* Seattle: Pacific Search Press, 1986. Destinations, routes, ratings, and launching info.

Williams, Chuck. *Mount St. Helens National Volcanic Monument.* Seattle: The Mountaineers, 1988. Great pocket guide for post-eruption hikers, sightseers, and skiers; photos, history, and detailed trail descriptions.

Woods, Erin, and Bill Woods. *Bicycling The Backroads.* Seattle: The Mountaineers.

Three volumes—*Around Puget Sound, Of Northwest Washington,* and *Of Southwest Washington*—provide in-depth information on bike routes, terrain, elevation gain, and points of interest, plus explicit directions and plenty of maps.

MISCELLANEOUS

Climates Of The States. Port Washington, New York: Water Information Center, Inc., 1974. Two volumes with more than you ever wanted to know about weather.

Herold, Stephen. *Tulipmania: The Skagit Valley Tulip Festival.* Berkeley, California: Celestial Arts, 1989. This official tulip festival guidebook features area history plus background on Skagit bulb growing and the festival itself, color photos, and listings of festival events and places to stay and eat.

Robbins, William G., et al. *Regionalism in the Pacific Northwest.* Corvallis, Oregon: University of Oregon Press, 1983. Ten essays examine the concept of regionalism and discuss the Pacific Northwest as a geographic, economic, political, and cultural entity.

Saling, Ann. *Our Superlative Pacific Northwest.* Edmonds, WA: Ansal Press, 1984. Pacific Northwest trivia and fun facts.

Scott, James W., and Ronald L. DeLorme. *Historical Atlas of Washington.* Norman, Oklahoma: University of Oklahoma Press, 1988. Very informative atlas depicting the many faces of Washington in map form, from the earliest explorers to the present day.

Washington's Almanac. Seattle: Evergreen Publishing, 1988. Unusual facts, recipes, and folklore from the editors of *Washington* magazine.

INDEX

Page numbers in **boldface** indicate the primary reference; numbers in *italics* indicate information in captions, illustrations, charts, or maps.

ABOUT THE AUTHOR

Dianne was born in Enfield, Connecticut, a growing suburb on the Massachusetts border. Her wanderlust took hold when her big sister bought Dianne her first airplane ticket at age 18. From then on, Dianne had a burning desire to see the world . . . or at least the country. She never passed on a chance to travel, joining her sister and others on trips to Colorado, Florida, Montreal, San Francisco, Washington, and up and down the East Coast. Not satisfied, she took off on her own at age 26 for a month-long cross-country car trip, spending most of her time photographing the West's national parks. Though traveling solo was not all she'd hoped for, she came back with a love for the breathtaking scenery of the Pacific Northwest.

An avid Boston Red Sox fan, her dad had hoped his youngest daughter's mean fastball and storytelling talents would evolve into a career in sportswriting. Sidetracked by a psychology major and a 4-year career in computer programming, Dianne's writing abilities lay dormant until she sold her first article, to a Hartford women's news magazine, in June 1984. The $28 payment she received didn't hold much promise, so she continued at her programming job and, shortly thereafter, married her boss. Bob and Dianne both loved Washington and shared a pioneering spirit; they traveled 3,000 miles from their roots to set up a home in northeast Tacoma. Dianne quit the computer business and devoted herself to trying to sell a book; Moon was the first publishing house to offer her a contract. The research for *Washington Handbook* was as easy as it could be, as Dianne explored her home state with a newcomer's enthusiasm and without preconceived notions. Dianne plans to continue her writing career while caring for her children, Scott and Kristina.

Moon Handbooks—The Ideal Traveling Companions

Open a Moon Handbook and you're opening your eyes and heart to the world. Thoughtful, sensitive, provocative, and highly informative, Moon Handbooks encourage an intimate understanding of a region, from its rich culture and history to essential practicalities. Fun to read and packed with valuable information on accommodations, dining, recreation, plus indispensable travel tips, detailed maps, charts, illustrations, photos, glossaries, indexes, Moon Handbooks are ideal traveling companions: informative, entertaining, and highly practical.

TO ORDER BY PHONE: (800) 345-5473 · Monday-Friday · 9 a.m.-5 p.m. PST

The Pacific/Asia Series

BALI HANDBOOK by Bill Dalton
Detailed travel information on the most famous island in the world. 12 color pages, 29 b/w photos, 68 illustrations, 42 maps, 7 charts, glossary, booklist, index. 428 pages. **$12.95**

INDONESIA HANDBOOK by Bill Dalton
This one-volume encyclopedia explores island by island the many facets of this sprawling, kaleidoscopic island nation. 30 b/w photos, 143 illustrations, 250 maps, 17 charts, booklist, extensive Indonesian vocabulary, index. 1,050 pages. **$17.95**

SOUTH KOREA HANDBOOK by Robert Nilsen
Whether you're visiting on business or searching for adventure, South Korea Handbook is an invaluable companion. 8 color pages, 78 b/w photos, 93 illustrations, 109 maps, 10 charts, Korean glossary with useful notes on speaking and reading the language, booklist, index. 548 pages. **$14.95**

SOUTHEAST ASIA HANDBOOK by Carl Parkes
Helps the enlightened traveler to travel with wide eyes and an open mind to discover the real Southeast Asia. 16 color pages, 75 b/w photos, 11 illustrations, 169 maps, 140 charts, vocabularies and suggested readings, index. 873 pages. **$16.95**

JAPAN HANDBOOK by J.D. Bisignani
An indispensable tool for understanding and enjoying one of the world's most complex and intriguing countries. 8 color pages, 200 b/w photos, 92 illustrations, 112 maps and town plans, 29 charts, appendix on the Japanese language, booklist, glossary, index. 504 pages. **$12.95**

HAWAII HANDBOOK by J.D. Bisignani
Winner of the 1989 Hawaii Visitors Bureau's Best Guide Book Award and Grand Award for Excellence in Travel Journalism, this guide takes you beyond the glitz and high-priced hype and leads you to a genuine Hawaiian experience. 12 color pages, 318 b/w photos, 132 illustrations, 74 maps, 43 graphs and charts, Hawaiian and pidgin glossaries, appendix, booklist, index. 788 pages. **$15.95**

KAUAI HANDBOOK by J.D. Bisignani
Kauai Handbook is the perfect antidote to the workaday world. 8 color pages, 36 b/w photos, 48 illustrations, 19 maps, 10 tables and charts, Hawaiian and pidgin glossaries, booklist, index. 236 pages. **$9.95**

MAUI HANDBOOK: Including Molokai and Lanai by J.D. Bisignani
"No fool-'round" advice on accommodations, eateries, and recreation, plus a comprehensive introduction to island ways, geography, and history. 8 color pages, 60 b/w photos, 72 illustrations, 34 maps, 19 charts, booklist, glossary, index. 350 pages. **$10.95**

SOUTH PACIFIC HANDBOOK by David Stanley
The original comprehensive guide to the 16 territories in the South Pacific. 20 color pages, 195 b/w photos, 121 illustrations, 35 charts, 138 maps, booklist, glossary, index. 740 pages. **$15.95**

MICRONESIA HANDBOOK:
Guide to the Caroline, Gilbert, Mariana, and Marshall Islands by David Stanley
Micronesia Handbook guides you on a real Pacific adventure all your own. 8 color pages, 77 b/w photos, 68 illustrations, 69 maps, 18 tables and charts, index. 287 pages. **$9.95**

FIJI ISLANDS HANDBOOK by David Stanley
The first and still the best source of information on travel around this 322-island archipelago. 8 color pages, 35 b/w photos, 78 illustrations, 26 maps, 3 charts, Fijian glossary, booklist, index. 198 pages. **$8.95**

TAHITI-POLYNESIA HANDBOOK by David Stanley
All five French-Polynesian archipelagoes are covered in this comprehensive guide by Oceania's best-known travel writer. 12 color pages, 45 b/w photos, 64 illustrations, 33 maps, 7 charts, booklist, glossary, index. 225 pages. **$9.95**

NEW ZEALAND HANDBOOK by Jane King
Introduces you to the people, places, history, and culture of this extraordinary land. 8 color pages, 99 b/w photos, 146 illustrations, 82 maps, booklist, index. 546 pages. **$14.95**

BLUEPRINT FOR PARADISE: How to Live on a Tropic Island by Ross Norgrove
This one-of-a-kind guide has everything you need to know about moving to and living comfortably on a tropical island. 8 color pages, 40 b/w photos, 3 maps, 14 charts, appendices, index. 212 pages. **$14.95**

The Americas Series

NORTHERN CALIFORNIA HANDBOOK by Kim Weir
An outstanding companion for imaginative travel in the territory north of the Tehachapis. Color and b/w photos, 69 maps, illustrations, booklist, index. Approximately 850 pages. **$16.95**

NEVADA HANDBOOK by Deke Castleman
Nevada Handbook puts the Silver State into perspective and makes it manageable and affordable. 34 b/w photos, 43 illustrations, 37 maps, 17 charts, booklist, index. 301 pages.
$10.95

NEW MEXICO HANDBOOK by Stephen Metzger
A close-up and complete look at every aspect of this wondrous state. 8 color pages, 85 b/w photos, 63 illustrations, 50 maps, 10 charts, booklist, index. 350 pages. **$11.95**

TEXAS HANDBOOK by Joe Cummings
Seasoned travel writer Joe Cummings brings an insider's perspective to his home state. 12 color pages, b/w photos, maps, illustrations, charts, booklist, index. Approximately 400 pages.
$11.95

ARIZONA TRAVELER'S HANDBOOK by Bill Weir
This meticulously researched guide contains everything necessary to make Arizona accessible and enjoyable. 8 color pages, 194 b/w photos, 74 illustrations, 53 maps, 6 charts, booklist, index. 505 pages. **$13.95**

UTAH HANDBOOK by Bill Weir
Weir gives you all the carefully researched facts and background to make your visit a success. 8 color pages, 102 b/w photos, 61 illustrations, 30 maps, 9 charts, booklist, index. 450 pages.
$11.95

ALASKA-YUKON HANDBOOK by Deke Castleman, Don Pitcher, and David Stanley
The inside story, with plenty of well-seasoned advice to help you cover more miles on less money. 8 color pages, 26 b/w photos, 92 illustrations, 90 maps, 6 charts, booklist, glossary, index. 384 pages. **$11.95**

WASHINGTON HANDBOOK by Dianne J. Boulerice Lyons
Covers sights, shopping, services, transportation, and outdoor recreation, and has complete listings for restaurants and accommodations. 8 color pages, 92 b/w photos, 24 illustrations, 81 maps, 8 charts, booklist, index. 400 pages. **$11.95**

BRITISH COLUMBIA HANDBOOK by Jane King
With an emphasis on outdoor adventures, this guide covers mainland British Columbia, Vancouver Island, the Queen Charlotte Islands, and the Canadian Rockies. 8 color pages, 56 b/w photos, 45 illustrations, 66 maps, 4 charts, booklist, index. 396 pages. **$11.95**

GUIDE TO CATALINA: and California's Channel Islands by Chicki Mallan
A complete guide to these remarkable islands, from the windy solitude of the Channel Islands National Marine Sanctuary to bustling Avalon. 8 color pages, 105 b/w photos, 65 illustrations, 40 maps, 32 charts, booklist, index. 262 pages. **$9.95**

GUIDE TO THE YUCATAN PENINSULA: Including Belize by Chicki Mallan
All the information you'll need to guide you into every corner of this exotic land. 8 color pages, 154 b/w photos, 55 illustrations, 57 maps, 70 charts, appendix, booklist, Mayan and Spanish glossaries, index. 391 pages. **$11.95**

CANCUN HANDBOOK: and Mexico's Caribbean Coast by Chicki Mallan
Covers the city's luxury scene as well as more modest attractions, plus many side trips to unspoiled beaches and Mayan ruins. Color and b/w photos, illustrations, over 30 maps, Spanish glossary, booklist, index. 257 pages. **$9.95**

The International Series

EGYPT HANDBOOK by Kathy Hansen
An invaluable resource for intelligent travel in Egypt. 8 color pages, 20 b/w photos, 150 illustrations, 80 detailed maps and plans to museums and archaeological sites, Arabic glossary, booklist, index. 510 pages. **$14.95**

PAKISTAN HANDBOOK by Isobel Shaw
For armchair travelers and trekkers alike, the most detailed and authoritative guide to Pakistan ever published. 28 color pages, 86 maps, appendices, Urdu glossary, booklist, index. 478 pages. **$15.95**

IMPORTANT ORDERING INFORMATION

TO ORDER BY PHONE: (800) 345-5473 · Monday-Friday · 9 a.m.-5 p.m. PST

PRICES: All prices are subject to change. We always ship the most current edition. We will let you know if there is a price increase on the book you ordered.

SHIPPING & HANDLING OPTIONS:
 1) Domestic UPS or USPS 1st class (allow 10 working days for delivery):
   $3.50 for the 1st item, 50 cents for each additional item.

Exceptions:
 · **Moonbelt** shipping is $1.50 for one, 50 cents for each additional belt.
 · Add $2.00 for same-day handling.
 2) UPS 2nd Day Air or Printed Airmail requires a special quote.
 3) International Surface Bookrate (8-12 weeks delivery):
   $3.00 for the 1st item, $1.00 for each additional item.

FOREIGN ORDERS: All orders which originate outside the U.S.A. must be paid for with either an International Money Order or a check in U.S. currency drawn on a major U.S. bank based in the U.S.A.

TELEPHONE ORDERS: We accept Visa or MasterCard payments. Minimum order is US$15.00. Call in your order: 1-(800) 345-5473. 9 a.m.-5 p.m. Pacific Standard Time.

MOONBELTS. A new concept in moneybelts. Made of heavy-duty Cordura nylon, the **Moonbelt** offers maximum protection for your money and important papers. This pouch, designed for all-weather comfort, slips under your shirt or waistband, rendering it virtually undetectable and inaccessible to pickpockets. Many thoughtful features: 1-inch-wide nylon webbing, heavy-duty zipper, and a 1-inch high-test quick-release buckle. No more fumbling around for the strap or repeated adjustments, this handy plastic buckle opens and closes with a touch, but won't come undone until you want it to. Accommodates travelers cheques, passport, cash, photos. Size 5 x 9 inches. Available in black only.   **$8.95**

ORDER FORM

FOR FASTER SERVICE ORDER BY PHONE: (800) 345-5473 · 9 a.m.-5 p.m. PST
(See important ordering information on preceding page)

Name:_____ Date:_____

Street:_____

City:_____

State or Country:_____ Zip Code:_____

Daytime Phone:_____

Quantity	Title	Price

Taxable Total	
Sales Tax (6.25%) for California Residents	
Shipping & Handling	
TOTAL	

Ship to: ☐ address above ☐ other_____

_____

_____

Make checks payable to:
Moon Publications, Inc., 722 Wall Street, Chico, California 95928, USA
We Accept Visa and MasterCard
To Order: Call in your Visa or MasterCard number, or send a written order with your Visa or
MasterCard number and expiration date clearly written.

Card Number: ☐ **Visa** ☐ **MasterCard**

☐☐☐☐ ☐☐☐☐ ☐☐☐☐ ☐☐☐☐

expiration date:_____

Exact Name on Card: ☐ same as above

☐ other_____

signature_____

WHERE TO BUY THIS BOOK

Bookstores and Libraries:
Moon Publications guides are sold worldwide. Please write Sales Manager Donna Galassi for a list of wholesalers and distributors in your area that stock our travel handbooks.

Travelers:
We would like to have Moon Publications guides available throughout the world. Please ask your bookstore to write or call us for ordering information. If your bookstore will not order our guides for you, please write or call for a free catalog.

MOON PUBLICATIONS, INC.
722 WALL STREET
CHICO, CA 95928 USA
tel: (800) 345-5473
fax: (916) 345-6751